Personality
Assessment

Personality Assessment

EDITED BY

Robert P. Archer

AND

Steven R. Smith

Routledge
Taylor & Francis Group
New York   London

Routledge
Taylor & Francis Group
711 Third Avenue
New York, NY 10017

Routledge
Taylor & Francis Group
2 Park Square
Milton Park, Abingdon
Oxon OX14 4RN

© 2008 by Taylor & Francis Group, LLC
Routledge is an imprint of Taylor & Francis Group, an Informa business

International Standard Book Number-13: 978-0-8058-6118-1 (Softcover) 978-0-8058-6117-4 (0)

Library of Congress Cataloging-in-Publication Data

Archer, Robert P.
  Personality assessment / Robert P. Archer and Steven R. Smith.
    p. cm.
  Includes bibliographical references.
  ISBN-13: 978-0-8058-6117-4
  ISBN-13: 978-0-8058-6118-1
  1. Personality assessment. I. Smith, Steven R. II. Title.

BF698.4.A74 2008
155.2'8--dc22   2007025586

Visit the Taylor & Francis Web site at
http://www.taylorandfrancis.com

and the Routledge Web site at
http://www.routledge.com

Dedication

For my daughter, Elizabeth M. Archer,
who is beginning her own career as a psychologist.
R.P.A.

For my wife, Dr. Suzanne Smith,
who helps remind me what's truly important.
S.R.S

Contents

Contributors

Steven J. Ackerman
Erik H. Erikson Institute of the
  Austen Riggs Center
Stockbridge, MA

Robert P. Archer
Eastern Virginia Medical School
Norfolk, VA

Yossef S. Ben-Porath
Kent State University
Kent, OH

Mark A. Blais
Massachusetts General Hospital
Boston, MA

A. Jill Clemence
Erik H. Erikson Institute of the
  Austen Riggs Center
Stockbridge, MA

Paul T. Costa, Jr.
Department of Health and Human
  Services
Washington, D.C.

Robert J. Craig
Roosevelt University
Chicago, IL

Stephen E. Finn
Center for Therapeutic Assessment
Austin, TX

Constance T. Fischer
Duquesne University
Pittsburgh, PA

J. Christopher Fowler
Erik H. Erikson Institute of the
  Austen Riggs Center
Stockbridge, MA

Jason E. Harlacher
University of Oregon
Eugene, OR

Christopher J. Hopwood
Texas A&M University
College Station, TX

Mark E. Maruish
Southcross Consulting
Burnsville, MN

Robert R. McCrae
Department of Health and Human
  Services
Washington, D.C.

Kenneth W. Merrell
University of Oregon
Eugene, OR

Gregory J. Meyer
University of Toledo
Toledo, OH

Leslie C. Morey
Texas A&M University
College Station, TX

Steven R. Smith
University of California
Santa Barbara, CA

Donald J. Viglione
Alliant International University
San Diego, CA

Preface

Personality assessment is a rapidly growing and expanding field. A major purpose of this edited text, *Personality Assessment*, is to provide an overview of the most popular self-report (objective) and performance-based (projective) personality assessment instruments. However, the overall objective of the text is not only to provide a summary of the status of the most important assessment instruments, but also to present impartial information in terms of methods of empirical evaluation of test instruments, a test feedback process that facilitates the personal growth of the patient or examinee, and methods of integrating test data from several sources in order to provide the optimal diagnostic and treatment planning information.

This book is primarily designed for clinical, counseling, and school psychology graduate students, whether these topics are covered in a single assessment class, or in separate graduate level courses in personality assessment. This text should also serve as a valuable reference for many clinicians and researchers because it was designed to provide coverage for the most popular assessment instruments used in the field today. Each test or assessment method is presented by expert authors who are readily identifiable because of their key roles in creating these important and influential instruments (e.g., Morey on the PAI; Costa and McCrae on the NEO, Ben-Porath on the MMPI-2) or in performing cutting edge work on a test or method (e.g., Meyer and Viglione on the Rorschach; Merrill and Harlacher on Behavior Rating Scales; Craig on the MCMI-III; Maruish on Semi-Structured Interview Procedures).

In addition to the generous and insightful work provided by our chapter authors, we would like to take the opportunity to acknowledge several individuals who made this work possible. First, we owe particular thanks to Steve Rutter, the book's first editor with Routledge (formerly with LEA). Steve was instrumental in conceiving and designing this text from its inception. His assistant, Nicole Buchmann was also a joy to work with as she shepherded us through the early stages of the process. As LEA transitioned into Routledge, we benefited the work of George Zimmar who saw the project to its completion. We wish the best for the continued integration of LEA and Routledge and hope that personality assessment titles will continue to flourish under the new publisher.

Next, we would like to acknowledge the work of Dr. David Elkins of the Eastern Virginia Medical School. David greatly aided in the editing and formatting of the chapters and provided substantial input on the finished product. Dr. Smith acknowledges the work of UCSB graduate students Aaron Estrada, MA, and Ilyssa Silverman, MA, for their invaluable help in helping their overworked advisor muddle through the details that he is ill-equipped to effectively handle. Last, both Drs. Archer and Smith thank the countless graduate students, interns, and post-docs we have taught and supervised over the years; without their feedback (some welcomed, some not!) on our course methods, materials, and content, this work would not be nearly as rich.

We hope that you will benefit and enjoy this text on how to select, use, and integrate personality assessment tests and test data, and we are deeply grateful to the outstanding contributors who have provided the information contained in these chapters from their unique and invaluable perspectives.

Robert P. Archer, PhD
Eastern Virginia Medical School
Steven R. Smith, PhD
University of California, Santa Barbara

CHAPTER 1

Introducing Personality Assessment

STEVEN R. SMITH
ROBERT P. ARCHER

Overview and Definition

"What is he like?" As social beings, we are continuously interested in the behavior and personality of those we meet. We are curious if someone is quiet, honest, proud, anxious, funny, indifferent, perceptive, or introspective. Those characteristics influence our experience of others and affect the quality of our relationships with them. When these characteristics tend to persist to varying degrees over time and across circumstances, we tend to think of them as *personality*. Certainly, we informally evaluate others' personality all the time, but the clinical assessment of personality using psychometrically robust tools is an important component of the professional practice of psychology.

When one speaks of personality assessment in psychology, activities include the diagnosis of mental illnesses, prediction of behavior, measurement of unconscious processes, and quantification of interpersonal styles and tendencies. Although all of these descriptions may be true for different clinicians working with various client groups, this listing may not accurately capture the full range of modern personality assessment. A general and encompassing definition is provided by Anastasi (1988): "A psychological test is essentially an objective and standardized measure of a sample of behavior" (p. 22). Some psychologists might find this definition too simplistic to capture the multitude of activities involved in assessment, and a broader definition has been proposed by Rorer (1990):

> I take the goal of personality assessment to be the description of people... It does not relate to physical appearance or physiological functioning, or behavior as such...; rather, it relates to a person's manner of behaving, his or her moods, and the situations and behaviors he or she chooses as opposed to the ones he or she avoids. (p. 693)

Therefore, Rorer (1990) sees assessment in general and personality assessment in particular not just as a discrete observation and sampling of behavior but a conceptualization of on-going dispositions. Stated differently, personality assessment attempts to find out not only what a person *does*, but what that person *is like*. As we'll see, an assessment of what a person does and what they are like is important in predicting their behavior and informing psychological treatment.

Psychological Assessment versus Psychological Testing

It is important to note the difference between psychological assessment and psychological testing. This distinction was made clear by Handler and Meyer (1998):

> Testing is a relatively straightforward process wherein a particular test is administered to obtain a specific score. Subsequently, a descriptive meaning can be applied to the score based on normative, nomothetic findings. For example, when conducting psychological testing, an IQ of 100 indicates a person possesses average intelligence...Psychological assessment, however, is a quite different enterprise. The focus here is not on obtaining a single score, or even a series of test scores. Rather, the focus is on taking a variety of test-derived pieces of information, obtained from multiple methods of assessment, and placing these data in the context of historical information, referral information, and behavioral observations in order to generate a cohesive and comprehensive understanding of the person being evaluated. These activities are far from simple; they require a high degree of skill and sophistication to be implemented properly. (pp. 4–5)

Thus, personality assessment is a complex clinical enterprise where the tools of assessment are used in concert with data from referring providers, clients, families, schools, courts, and other influential sources. Although tests form the cornerstone of the work, personality assessment is the comprehensive interpretation of a person given all relevant data. As Handler and Meyer (1998) point out, this is not an easy enterprise and relies on substantial clinical skill, knowledge, and experience. However, if done well, the results can be very fulfilling for both clinicians and clients alike.

Purposes of Personality Assessment

Although personality assessment is used in several different settings, there are five primary reasons to conduct personality assessment (Meyer et al., 2001).

1. Description of Psychopathology and Differential Diagnosis
   From the very first personality assessment tools devised in the early to mid-1900s, psychologists have hoped to use tests and measures to diagnose psychopathology in their clients. Compared to unstructured diagnostic interviews, psychological tests have the benefit of normative bases from which to begin interpretation. This characteristic, coupled with standardized administration procedures, yields diagnostic information that is often more predictive and robust than that obtained by interview alone.

2. Description and Prediction of Everyday Behavior
   As Rorer (1990) described, the goal of personality assessment is to describe what people are like. Although often used to examine issues of pathological behavior and mental illnesses, a comprehensive personality assessment should not focus solely on these aspects of functioning. The quality of a client's interactions, their expectations of relationships, their personal strengths and attributes, and their typical means of coping with stress are all components of everyday behavior that should be included in a comprehensive personality assessment.

3. Inform Psychological Treatment
   The interpersonal, intrapersonal, dispositional, and situational descriptors of a psychotherapy client yielded by personality assessment can be an immensely helpful and cost-effective way of planning mental health treatment (Miller, Spicer, Kraus, Heister, & Bilyeu, 1999). Given the diversity of psychological treatments available, including different modalities of psychotherapy and medication, personality assessment might offer some insights into which of these might be most effective. For example, if assessment indicates that a client is uncomfortable expressing emotion, they might be more appropriate for a cognitive form of psychotherapy. Furthermore, because of the impact of personality factors in treating Axis I disorders such as depression and anxiety, personality assessment might be particularly helpful in describing these important features that might call for a more complex treatment program. In addition to informing treatment, research indicates that personality assessment prior to psychotherapy can enhance alliance early in treatment (Ackerman, Hilsenroth, Baity, & Blagys, 2000; Hilsenroth, Peters, & Ackerman, 2004).

4. Monitoring of Treatment

   Personality assessment tests have shown to be sensitive to the changes that clients experience in psychotherapy (Abraham, Lepisto, Lewis, Schultz, & Finkelberg, 1994; Gronnerod, 2004). Some measures, such as the Beck Depression Inventory (BDI; Beck & Steer, 1987), were specifically designed to be used as adjuncts to treatment by measuring change. Personality assessment results can be used as baseline measures, with changes reflected in periodic retesting. Clinicians can use this information to modify or enhance their interventions based on test results.

5. Use of Personality Assessment as Treatment

   The Therapeutic Assessment model (TA; Finn & Tonsager, 1997) was developed to increase the utility of personality assessment and feedback by making assessment and feedback a therapeutic endeavor. Based on the principles of self and humanistic psychology, and the work of Fischer (1994, 2000), the Therapeutic Assessment model views assessment as a collaborative endeavor in which both the client and the assessor work together to arrive at a deeper understanding of the client's personality, interpersonal dynamics, and present difficulties. The client becomes an active collaborator in a mutual process to better understand the nature of his or her concerns and the assessor discusses (rather than delivers) test results in a manner that is comfortable and understandable to the client. This approach stands in contrast to the more typical information-gathering approach to assessment often used in neuropsychological and/or forensic psychology practice, where clients are less engaged in the process of assessment, and feedback may be provided in only a brief summary or written format.

There has been increased research attention on Therapeutic Assessment models in recent years. Finn and Tonsager (1992) conducted a study of students awaiting treatment in a college counseling center. Compared to "placebo attention," those students who took and received collaborative and therapeutic feedback on the MMPI-2 (Butcher, Dahlstrom, Graham, Tellegen, & Kaemmer, 1989) experienced decreased symptoms, increased feelings of hope, and increased self-esteem. These effects persisted over a period of several weeks (Finn & Tonsager, 1992). In addition, studies have shown that Therapeutic Assessment may improve the development of the working alliance in early psychotherapy (Ackerman et al., 2000; Hilsenroth et al., 2004). For example, Ackerman et al. (2000) found that clients receiving Therapeutic Assessment and feedback were less likely to terminate treatment prematurely than those who had received an information-gathering assessment. Hilsenroth et al. (2004) expanded these results, showing that clients who received a comprehensive assessment followed by therapeutic feedback were more likely to establish a positive alliance than were those who received little or no assessment. This effect lasted into the later stages of psychotherapy, indicating that Therapeutic Assessment is a powerful way to establish a lasting working alliance. Hilsenroth et al. (2004) posit that the process of working through the assessment procedure helps to form an important bond between the therapist and client that persists over time.

Types of Personality Assessment Tests

Given the myriad reasons that a client might be seen for personality assessment, it should not be surprising that there are a number of different forms of tests available. Traditionally, tests have fallen into one of two categories: *projective* and *objective* tests. However, there is a movement in the assessment field to replace these terms with the more accurate labels, *performance-based* and *self-report*, respectively. Furthermore, with increasing innovation and development in testing, this simple dichotomy is probably no longer sufficient because it cannot capture the important category of *behavioral* assessment.

Performance-based ("projective") tests generally have an unstructured response format, meaning that respondents are allowed to respond as much or as little as they like (within certain parameters) to a particular test stimulus. Traditionally, these tests were defined by the *projective hypothesis* articulated by Frank (1939):

> We may... induce the individual to reveal his way of organizing experience by giving him a field.... with relatively little structure and cultural patterning so that the personality can project upon that plastic field his way of seeing life, his meanings, significances, patterns, and especially his feelings. Thus we elicit a projection of the individual's *private world*. (p. 402–403)

Although many authors of modern performance-based measures might not fully agree on the projective nature of their tests, all seem to agree that the less structured nature of these measures is thought to allow for important individual characteristics to emerge in a manner that can be coded and interpreted by a clinician. This is why the term *performance-based measurement* may be more accurate; although test authors differ on the extent to which projection occurs during testing, all seem to agree that this form of test requires the client to respond (i.e., "perform") to a stimulus.

Although performance-based measures share the characteristic of having a relatively unstructured response format, it is inaccurate to group them together as a category. Some measures rely on a standardized administration procedure, response format, and scoring. When a measure is administered and scored according to such standardized procedures, we can rightly consider that measure a *test*. Conversely, if a measure does not necessarily have a standardized administration and scoring procedure, it is more accurate to think of that measure as a *technique*. For example, the Rorschach Inkblot Test (Exner, 2003), is a performance-based measure that is administered and scored in a highly standardized and reliable fashion; therefore, we can be comfortable referring to the Rorschach as a test. However, other popular performance-based measures are not as well standardized, or if such standardization exists, it is not widely used. For example, although a number of scoring systems are available for the Thematic Apperception Test (Cramer, 1996; Morgan & Murray, 1935; Murray, 1943; Westen, 1995; Westen, Lohr, Silk, Kerber, & Goodrich, 2002), none of these are used widely in the field. Furthermore, different clinicians might use different TAT cards in different sequences, leading to the collection of very different data samples. Although proponents of the TAT and similar measures suggest that this lack of standardization results in greater clinical flexibility, it is more accurate to refer to these instruments as techniques.

Self-report ("objective") measures simply ask a respondent to answer a series of questions about him or herself. There are a number of different types of response formats and question styles depending on the purposes of the test and the construct to be measured. For example, self-report measures can rely on paper-and-pencil questionnaires or structured interviews conducted by trained clinicians. Broadly, self-report measures fall into two categories: *omnibus* or *narrow-band*. Omnibus measures are those that assess multiple domains of personality, psychopathology, or functioning. For example, the Personality Assessment Inventory (PAI; Morey, 1991) is an omnibus or broad-band self-report measure because it assesses depression, anxiety, personality features, thought disorder, interpersonal expectations, and drug abuse, as well as many other constructs. Conversely, the Rosenberg Self-Esteem Scale (Rosenberg, 1965) is a narrow-band measure that purports only to measure facets of self-esteem. Although there are some exceptions, an omnibus measure will allow for the broad screening of individual characteristics and psychopathology, while a narrow-band self-report measure might be more suited to measure a few characteristics in depth. Both have utility in clinical settings.

Behavioral assessment is often considered separately from personality assessment because of its focus on overt behaviors as opposed to internal personality dispositions and tendencies. However, if we are to conduct a thorough personality assessment (as opposed to psychological testing) as espoused by Handler and Meyer (1998), then it is also vital to understand a client's overt behavior. This is particularly true for clients unable to report for themselves, particularly younger children and those with cognitive issues that might impair accurate self-representation (e.g., dementia). In such cases, the reports of others can be a vital source of information. Most behavioral measures rely on checklists that can be completed by someone who is able to observe the client in a number of different settings and situations. Like self-report measures, behavioral measures can be omnibus, covering a wide range of behavioral issues, or narrow-band, focusing on only a few (e.g., tantruming). See chapter 7 of this volume for more information on child behavior rating scales.

Introduction to the Field of Personality Assessment

A Brief History

For as long as there have been relationships, there have been attempts to quickly assess what people are like. From one perspective, *informal* personality assessment has been around forever. For example, ancient scholars such as Aristotle theorized that personality could be understood from a standpoint of physiognomy, the idea that physical traits could be informative about personality. Size of one's eyes, lips, and eyebrows were thought to convey information about criminality, virtue, and thoughtfulness. Indeed, Shakespeare's Julius Caesar distrusted Cassius because he "has a mean and hungry look." Further, as the perspective of the scientific method became more widespread in the 18th and 19th centuries, physicians and philosophers attempted to classify personalities based on these physical attributes.

Probably the best-known example of linking personality to physical characteristics is the phrenology movement. Spearheaded by Francis Gall, phrenology consisted of "reading" the contours in the skull in order to discern personality traits and attributes. By collecting data on research subjects with particular traits, Gall attempted to map these bumps and ridges into a system of measuring personality. As you might have guessed, none of these approaches worked particularly well and were often imbued with their developers' bigoted perspectives. But a more formal and scientific attempt to classify personalities is a much more recent phenomenon.

The origin of modern psychology is intimately connected with the development of psychological tests. Starting with Binet's work in the early 20th century developing tests to measure the cognitive abilities of children, psychology emerged as the science that best combined expertise in the measurement of human behavior and personality. However, it is a psychiatrist, Carl Jung, who is credited with creating the first "modern" personality test. His *association method* was a standardized list of words to which psychiatric patients were asked to free associate, or to say whatever came to mind. Jung provided interpretation guidelines by which responses could be judged and understood (Jung, 1910). What made this different from prior methods of assessing personality was its reliance on standardized administration and a data-based method of interpretation.

During World War I, noted psychologist Robert S. Woodworth was commissioned by the American Psychological Association to create a self-report measure that could be used to evaluate the personality of military recruits. The 116-item, true-false, self-report Personal Data Sheet (Woodworth, 1917) was created to measure neurotic symptoms that were described in the scientific literature of that time. Although it was finalized too late to be used with World War I military recruits, this measure was frequently used in early studies of psychopathology. Following the work of Woodworth, other personality measures were soon developed. Notable examples included Pressey and Pressey's (1919) Cross-Out Test and the Bernreuter Personality Inventory (Bernreuter, 1935).

In their development of the Minnesota Multiphasic Personality Inventory (MMPI), Hathaway and McKinley (1943) were quite aware of many of the problems that existed in the self-report personality inventories of that era, including the Personal Data Sheet and the Bernreuter Personality Inventory. These latter tests consisted of items logically or rationally selected by the test developers based on their clinical experience, judgment, and understanding of psychopathology. Over time, however, it became apparent that many items selected exclusively by this method were often not clinically useful or accurate. In some instances, for example, normal subjects actually answered items in the maladjusted direction more often than did subjects from various clinical samples. Further, because the content of these items was often quite obvious, test respondents were able to adjust their self-report to appear more or less maladjusted depending on their motivation and the purpose of testing. A central feature of Hathaway and McKinley's approach to the creation of the MMPI was the use of the *criterion keying* method, or contrasting group method. In this approach, the test constructor selects items based upon the observed or empirical relationship between item endorsement and membership in external criterion groups. Items are selected for scale membership that empirically demonstrates a significant difference in response frequency between normal individuals and patients in various clinical criterion groups manifesting well defined psychiatric disorders. Thus, for example, items selected for the MMPI Depression Scale consisted of those items endorsed more frequently by clinically-depressed patients (i.e., the criterion group for the depression scale) in contrast to individuals in the MMPI normative sample. The MMPI is usually cited as the outstanding example of empirical keying test construction as applied to personality assessment instruments (e.g., Anastasi, 1982), and the MMPI quickly became the most widely used self-report measure of personality and psychopathology over the past 50 years (Archer, 2005). Development of the MMPI-2 and MMPI-A (revisions of the MMPI for adults and adolescents, respectively) will be discussed in more detail in chapter 3.

Another important method of test development for self-report instruments is the factor-analytical approach. In this method of inventory construction, a large initial pool of items from a variety of content areas is assembled, and these items are administered to a large group of subjects. The responses of these subjects are then intercorrelated, and the resulting intercorrelations are factor analyzed in order to identify the underlying cluster of items that are related to each other, but relatively independent of other item groupings. Thus, in contrast to empirical keying methodology, the factor analytic approach does not typically employ an external criterion measure in scales developed based on the factor-analytic procedure. While a number of early inventories were developed using this approach, the most widely used test constructed according to the factor-analytic procedure is the Sixteen Personality Factor Questionnaire (16 PF) developed by Cattell in 1949. The 16 PF was developed starting with an initial pool of 4,000 adjectives believed to be descriptive of important personality characteristics. Using this initial pool, Cattell was able to derive a set of 171 adjectives eventually placed on 16 scales that Cattell felt represented the most relevant dimensions of personality. The 16 PF continues to be a widely used and important psychometric instrument. Most recently, the NEO Personality Inventory-Revised (NEO PI-R) developed by Costa and McCrae (1985) to measure five major domains of personality based on a factor analytically derived view of personality functioning referred to as the Big Five by Goldberg (1982). The Big Five refers to a set of underlying factor dimensions which have been widely replicated across various personality inventories and settings, and across national and cross cultural groups. The NEO PI-R is widely considered to be the best measure of these five dimensions of Neurotism (N), Extroversion (E), Openness to experience (O), Agreeableness (A), and Conscientiousness (C). The NEO PI-R also differentiates underlying facets of each dimension that might have particular relevance in various applications. Research on the NEO PI-R has been comprehensive and generally supportive, and this test instrument serves as a focus of chapter 6.

The most recent method of self-report inventory construction has been labeled the *sequential strategy* developed by Jackson (1970) based on a combination of content validation, internal consistency, and criterion keying. In this sequential strategy, the first step of inventory construction is usually to decide what theoretical construct is to be measured and to develop a precise and concise definition of the construct. A pool of items is then rationally and intuitively generated by the test developer based on the definition of the construct, and tentative scales are constructed to assess relevant domains of variables. These scales are then administered to subjects and refined by review of internal consistency results, typically removing items from scale membership if item removal results in higher internal consistency findings. Finally, in the sequential strategy, the resulting preliminary scales are validated by comparing scores on these scales through the use of appropriate external criterion measures. The sequential strategy was used by Jackson in developing the Personality Research Form (PRF) in 1974, and a more recent example of these sequential strategies can be found in the MMPI-2 content scales as reported by Butcher, Graham, Williams, and Ben-Porath (1990).

As psychologists continued to develop and refine self-report measures of personality and psychopathology, other psychologists and psychiatrists were enamored with projective techniques. Notable among these was Hermann Rorschach, a Swiss psychiatrist who developed a method of codifying his patients' free responses to a standard set of inkblots. Although the scoring systems for the Rorschach Inkblot Test have been considerably refined since the early 20th century, psychologists continue to use the same set of blots that Rorschach created so many years ago. Since the time of Rorschach, other personality assessments that rest on the projective hypothesis have been developed, including the Thematic Apperception Test (Murray, 1943).

Current Personality Assessment Test Use

Several recent surveys have examined the rates of usage of various personality assessment measures depending on setting and type of client (Archer & Newsom, 2000; Camara, Nathan, & Puente, 2000; Cashel, 2002; Clemence & Handler, 2001). Despite differences in client age, there appears to be a pattern of tests that are used most often in clinical practice. Although rates differ, surveys consistently indicate that the MMPI-2/MMPI-A (Butcher et al., 1989; Butcher et al., 1992) tends to be the most widely used measure, followed by the Rorschach Inkblot Test (Exner, 2003) and the Thematic Apperception Test (TAT; Morgan & Murray, 1935; Murray, 1943). Among child psychologists, sentence completion measures and behavior rating scales are also quite prominent (Archer & Newsom, 2000; Cashel, 2002) and gaining in popularity (Piotrowski, 1999).

But how often is personality assessment practiced by professional psychologists? Although the amount of time that psychologists spend conducting personality assessment has declined over the past decades due to the pressures of managed care and other factors (Piotrowski, 1999), it appears that assessment continues to be an important component of clinical practice. For example, Camara et al. (2000) found that 19% of practicing clinical psychologists conduct at least 5 hours of assessment per week, and more than one third of that time is spent conducting personality assessment. Thus, although the extensiveness of assessment batteries is changing, personality assessment continues to be important.

Of particular interest to graduate students in psychology, several studies have examined the expectations of predoctoral internship directors for new trainees (Clemence & Handler, 2001; Durand, Blanchard, & Mindell, 1988; Stedman, Hatch, & Schoenfeld, 2000, 2001, 2002; Watkins, 1991). What is it that internship directors will expect you to know? Part of the answer depends on the type of internship and clinical setting, with inpatient psychiatric hospitals, forensic settings, and child facilities requiring the most experience and university counseling centers requiring the least amount of assessment experience. However, the type of assessment practiced varies significantly across these settings (see Table 1.1). Results of surveys of internship directors consistently suggest that they see personality assessment skills as vital components to professional practice in psychology. However, surveys also suggest that internship directors find that many, if not most, of their trainees are inadequately trained in assessment. Particularly concerning to many survey respondents is a lack of experience with performance-based (projective) techniques, including the Rorschach and TAT (Stedman et al., 2000, 2001, 2002). There appears to be a discrepancy between the importance placed on assessment training in graduate programs and that by internships. Even as market demands continue to change, it is likely that personality assessment will continue to be an important aspect of clinical practice.

Note that there are several professional organizations that promote the use of personality assessment in professional psychology. All of these welcome the involvement of students in authoring conference presentations and through the provision of student research grants. The Society for Personality Assessment (www.personality.org) is the leading organization for personality assessment research, practice, and education. They offer a dissertation award for graduate students and provide travel funds for students to attend their annual conference. Section IX (Assessment) is the organization within Division 12 (Clinical Psychology) of the American Psychological Association that focuses on the advancement of psychological assessment (www.division-12section9.com). Membership is open to all graduate students regardless of APA or Division 12 membership. Last, the American Board of Assessment Psychology (ABAP) recognizes experts in the field of assessment psychology and designates these experts as "Diplomats" in assessment. These organizations will introduce you to the practice and science of personality assessment and provide you with exciting opportunities to network with other students and psychologists who recognize the value of this work.

Introduction to the Practice of Personality Assessment

These days, it seems that professional psychologists are inundated with catalogs, e-mails, and other mailings that advertise new tests or testing techniques.

Table 1.1 Personality Assessment Training Most Valued by Internship Training Directors (Clemence & Handler, 2001)

Test	University Counseling Centers	Community Mental Health Agencies	Inpatient and General Hospitals	Child Facilities	Veterans Affairs Hospitals	Correctional Facility
MMPI-2/MMPI-A	83%	95%	87%	52%	93%	100%
MCMI-III	44%	45%	45%	14%	52%	38%
PAI	17%	21%	25%	8%	34%	25%
Rorschach	35%	98%	81%	65%	64%	75%
TAT / CAT	TAT: 42%	TAT: 91% CAT: 29%	TAT: 72% CAT: 14%	TAT: 62% CAT: 54%	TAT: 43%	TAT: 50%
Sentence Completion	33%	67%	52%	59%	33%	38%
Behavior Rating Scales	41%	28%	19%	59%	13%	0%
Projective Drawings	17%	57%	40%	52%	21%	25%

We receive journals that publish studies of newly created measures of various psychological traits, conditions, and behaviors. All of these promise some new advancement or special utility that other measures do not have. For example, we are told that Measure X might be more sensitive to malingering than Measure Y, or that Measure A is better able to assess depression than Measure B. Yet, as we saw above, most psychologists use the same set of tests that psychologists have been using for the past 50 or so years (e.g., MMPI/MMPI-2, Rorschach, and TAT). The reasons for this are probably multifaceted and include issues of training, tradition, and the robustness of these particular measures. However, the question remains: how should a psychologist evaluate a test? What should be the criteria by which a test is chosen and what should psychologists look for in published studies?

How to Evaluate a Test

There are a number of resources available that will be helpful for students wishing to learn more about psychometrics, or the statistical characteristics of a test. For students particularly interested in assessment, a course or two in psychometrics and item response theory is highly recommended. However, what we present here are a series of questions (see Key Points to Remember) that psychologists should ask prior to adopting or using a test, as well as some guidelines about how to evaluate this information.

What Does this Test Measure?

Fundamentally, although we often use the word "test," "measure," and "assessment" interchangeably, what we are really concerned with is measurement of a construct. The construct that is measured by a test is often referred to as the *latent variable*. Although a test yields a score, that score is thought to be representative of the underlying latent variable identified by the test developer. Obviously, a measure of depression should measure depression and a measure of anxiety should measure anxiety. But it's often not that simple.

Key Points to Remember:	Questions to Ask When Evaluating a Test
Questions	Component Concepts
What does this test measure?	Theory
	Latent Variable
Is this test reliable?	Temporal Consistency
	Internal Consistency
	Rater Consistency
For what purposes is this test valid?	Translation Validity
	Criterion-Related Validity
	Clinical Utility Validity

For example, a psychodynamic psychologist might define depression using words like "anger" and "loss," whereas a cognitive-behavioral psychologist might use words like "negative beliefs" and "distorted cognitions." If both of these psychologists create measures of "depression," their different perspectives on the construct of depression will yield two potentially very different measures. Given that these measures would rest on different theories, the latent variable or underlying construct will also be different.

Therefore, inherent in all tests is a conceptualization of a construct, and research shows that although two measures might purport to assess the same construct, the results can be quite different depending on the theory. This is neither a good nor a bad thing, but before adopting a particular test, a psychologist should understand the theory of the construct being measured. In published tests, this information is usually easy to find in the test's manual or development manuscript.

Is This Test Reliable?

Simply put, the reliability of a test is an indication of its consistency. Test reliability is concerned with temporal consistency (consistency across time), internal consistency (the degree to which test items are consistent with one another), and inter-rater consistency (the degree to which two or more independent raters can use the same test and arrive at similar results). For example, if we were interested in measuring the latent variable of *time*, we might invent a tool such as a stopwatch to measure this variable. For various reasons, we would be quite concerned with issues of consistency when measuring time with this tool. So we might conduct a series of experiments on the ability of our measure to assess a one minute period of time. We would be concerned if, upon timing one minute at different points in time, some of those minutes took longer than others. That is, we would expect that the stopwatch would be consistent across time. Likewise, we would expect that each second indicated by our stopwatch would take the same amount of time as the one prior to it—that the "content" of the measuring tool would be consistent. Last, we would hope that two raters, who were trained in the proper use of the stopwatch, were able to measure lengths of time that were identical to one another.

Similarly, when a personality assessment measure is created, issues of consistency are vital to its utility; a measure of depression that was only accurate "sometimes" would be of little use. However, we must be a little careful here, because issues of consistency are often contingent upon the latent variable to be measured. For example, some latent variables are rapidly fluctuating "states" (e.g., mood, satiety, fatigue, etc.) whereas some will be more consistent "traits" (e.g., extroversion, coping resources, narcissism, etc.). Therefore, we would expect measures of states to be less consistent over longer periods of time than traits. Likewise, if our latent variable is broad (e.g., interpersonal functioning), then our test items may not be as consistent as those for a measure of a narrow variable such as "paranoia." So as we evaluate the reliability of a particular test, we need to keep in mind the nature of our latent variable and evaluate reliability statistics accordingly. These issues will be addressed further below.

There are a number of forms of reliability that will help psychologists evaluate a particular test. These can be broadly categorized as indicators of temporal consistency, internal consistency, and rater consistency.

Temporal Consistency

Temporal consistency is generally measured through *test-retest reliability*. Simply put, test-retest reliability involves administering the same test to the same group of individuals with a specified time delay in between these administrations. The assumption is that the latent variable will be consistent across the period of time and should be reflected in similar test scores. The correlation between the two test scores is seen as an indicator of the consistency of the test across time and testing situations. Although opinions vary depending on the purposes of the measure, one standard for evaluating the acceptability of test-retest reliability is that the test-retest correlation coefficient should be 0.80 or greater.

The length between the test and retest conditions should be clearly specified in the test manual or development manuscript. Test developers will often provide test-retest data for a number of different time periods depending on the type of test they have created. These lengths of time can range from a few days to several years. Most personality assessment measures will provide this information for 1- to 2-week intervals and beyond. As was hinted at above, one of the most important factors in interpreting test-retest reliability is the expected consistency of the latent variable over time. Thus if the test purports to measure a construct that changes relatively quickly, we could anticipate somewhat lower test-retest reliability than if the construct was more enduring and stable. This difference will usually be captured in the length of times that the test developer has chosen to evaluate in their test-retest analysis of the test.

An issue that should be remembered when evaluating test-retest reliability analyses is the issue of *practice effects*. Practice effects refer to the fact that when individuals are tested multiple times, their second performance will likely be an improvement on the first. This improvement may be due to simple practice with the test items or familiarity with the testing situation, examiner, and expectations for performance. This type of issue is likely to be most relevant to cognitive and neuropsychological assessments that rely on the performance of often complicated psychomotor tasks and problem-solving exercises. However, in personality assessment, test-retest reliability might be a difficult metric for some performance-based measures like the Rorschach where more time with the stimulus might result in a wider array of responses (however, test-retest studies with the Rorschach have generally been positive) (Gronnerod, 2003). Conversely, if the test-retest duration is too short, a respondent might be able to recall his or her responses to a particular test item and respond accordingly. In such situations, test-retest statistics will be spuriously high and will not be a true indication of the stability of the test.

To attenuate these issues, it is sometimes appropriate to conduct an *alternate-form reliability* analysis. This involves administering different forms of the same test to one group of individuals at two different points in time. It is assumed that the two forms of the test will both measure the same latent variable with the same degree of accuracy. Alternate-form reliability analyses limit problems with practice effects and do not suffer from spurious correlations due to item response recall by participants. However, this form of reliability analysis has its own practical limitations. Test development can be costly and expensive, so it is often impractical to create two forms of the same test. Likewise, if the two forms of a test measure the latent variable in slightly different ways, the researcher may not know if the lack of correspondence is a reliability issue or a difference in the measures' content. For these reasons, it is rare to find examples of alternate-form reliability analysis in personality assessment literature.

Internal Consistency

The internal consistency of a test is an indication of the extent to which the test items or scores consistently measure the same construct. For example, we would expect that on a measure of aggression, all of the items will be related to the same latent variable of aggression. Internal consistency is generally assessed by two related means: *split-half reliability* and *Cronbach's coefficient alpha*.

Unlike test-retest and alternative-form analyses, split-half reliability involves the administration of only one form of a test. Two scores are obtained from this administration by dividing the test into two relatively equal length forms and correlating the results. There are a number of ways to divide a test into equal forms. The simplest way is to divide the odd and even test items into two scores. A random grouping of items (based on a random number generator or computer selection) is another possibility. However, there are times when the structure of a test may not lend itself to such random selection. This is particularly true for tests that are quite short or that measure a construct encompassing a wide array of domains. In such cases, researchers are advised to be somewhat selective in dividing the test, making sure that both halves have equal numbers of items related to a particular construct.

Although a Pearson's correlation coefficient is adequate for most reliability analyses, it is usually not the statistic of choice for split-half reliability analyses. Imagine that a researcher has a personality assessment measure with 50 items. This researcher administers her test to a group of participants and then divides the 50 items into two equal length 25-item tests. Were she to use a typical correlation, she would lose some of the statistical power that might come from having a full 50-item test. Spearman-Brown "corrects" the Pearson's correlation by adjusting for the number of times that the test has been shortened, usually resulting in greater values for r. For this reason, the Spearman-Brown formula is usually calculated in studies of split-half reliability and is easily generated by most common statistics programs, including SPSS and SAS.

When a researcher conducts a split-half reliability, he or she must divide the test into "halves" based on either random or rational assignment of test items. Imagine, however, if the researcher could calculate split-half reliability coefficients based on *all* possible combinations of items. This method would remove all potential issues with item selection because all possible item groups would be included. Mathematically, this is the information provided by Cronbach's coefficient *alpha*. Although *alpha* is not calculated in such a way, it provides an average estimate of all possible split-half reliabilities for a given group of items. Although there are no strict guidelines for interpreting alpha, values above 0.70 are typically considered to be adequate, with values above 0.80 as good. Most modern self-report measure developers will provide alpha values for their tests. A variant on Cronbach's alpha is the Kuder-Richardson 20 (*KR20*) coefficient. *KR20* is appropriate for those measures that have "right or wrong" scoring, like those on an intelligence test. However, because most self-report personality assessment measures do not use this type of scoring method, you will be much more likely to see alpha reported as the internal consistency measure.

Rater Consistency

The final form of measure consistency or reliability applies to those situations where there are multiple raters charged with making observations, coding, or scoring a test. For our purposes in personality assessment, we are most likely to see calculations of rater consistency in analyses of performance-based personality assessments such as the Rorschach. In these cases, and in the case of some cognitive assessments, where scoring relies on some degree of judgment on the part of raters, it is important to demonstrate that trained raters will generate the same scores as one another. Generally, this typically involves having at least two trained raters score the same group of test responses without knowledge (blind) to the other's scores.

For data that is continuous, some form of correlation can be calculated to demonstrate the degree of their consistency with one another. Shrout & Fleiss' (1979) intraclass correlation coefficients (ICC) are a series of six correlations that can be computed based on certain rater and test characteristics. The formulas are based on three models that vary in their assumption of rater independence. Simply put, a *one-way random effects model* assumes that the raters are a random selection of all possible raters who rate all of the targets of interest. A *two-way random effects model* assumes a random selection of raters and targets. Last, a *two-way mixed model* assumes that all possible judges rate a random selection of targets. For all three ICC models, researchers can calculate two forms of agreement: exact agreement or general consistency. These are sometimes differentiated in the literature by number, where the first number corresponds to the model and the second number corresponds to the level of agreement (e.g., ICC (3,2), ICC (2,1) etc.). ICCs are interpreted based on the same guidelines as Pearson's *r*, with higher values reflecting better agreement. Typically, 0.74 or above reflects good agreement.

Although ICCs can be used when data is dimensional, the appropriate statistic for dichotomous interrater reliability is Cohen's *kappa*. Kappa is an estimate of agreement between two raters accounting for chance agreement. Most appropriate for those measures where raters must decide that score or behavior is either present or not present, kappa is generally acceptable when above 0.70.

For What Purposes Is this Test Valid?

A psychological test is the translation of a latent variable into a form that can be measured. Validity refers to the quality of that translation from a theoretical latent variable to test format. In other words, the validity of a test refers to the extent that it accurately measures the latent variable that it was designed to measure. Also important are the circumstances under which it is more or less likely to be accurate. It is not enough to say that a test is valid; research must examine the purposes for which a test is valid. In the assessment of psychological disorders, for instance, this distinction is an important one. A hypothetical measure of depression might be valid for identifying depression among college students, but it may not be valid for identifying depression among psychiatric inpatients. For this reason, assessment research must be an ongoing process to discover not *if* a measure is valid, but *for what*.

The literature is often unclear and somewhat inconsistent regarding the definition of validity types and how they relate to one another. If we assume that a psychological test is the translation of a latent variable into an operationalized form (Trochim, 2000), then, globally speaking, we are concerned about the quality of that operationalization. Does our test measure the construct we would like it to measure? Because the fundamental question

Just the Facts: Types of Validity
Construct Validity
    Translation Validity
        Content Validity
        Face Validity
    Criterion-Related Validity
        Concurrent Validity
        Predictive Validity
        Convergent Validity
        Discriminant Validity
    Clinical Utility Validity
        Incremental Validity
        Diagnostic Efficiency

of test validity relates to the quality of the translation of the construct into test form, we can refer to *all* validity related to testing as *construct validity*. Construct validity refers to the extent to which the test measures an underlying latent variable. There are several ways to measure different facets of construct validity (see Just the Facts).

Translation Validity

The term *translation validity* is likely to be unfamiliar because it is not one that is generally seen in the literature. Trochim (2000) coined the term to refer to the class of validity analyses that seek to examine the quality of the basic translation of a latent variable into a test format. There are two types of translation validity: content validity and face validity.

Content validity refers to completeness of the translation of the latent variable into the test format. Stated differently, this form of validity is a statement about the extent to which a test translates all facets of the latent variable into measurable form. For example, if a researcher wished to create a measure of anorexia, she would first need to create a list of all the different facets of anorexia including the behavioral components of diet restriction and excessive exercise. Furthermore, she might be interested in the experiential aspects of the disorder including perfectionism, anxiety, and need for control. In order to be sure that her final measure did, indeed, capture all of these facets of anorexia, content validity analyses would be needed.

Traditionally, content validity studies are carried out throughout the development of a test by having expert judges, for example, define the construct and rate the measure on representativeness. Focus groups of clients and patients can also be crucial in helping a researcher define and refine the content of a measure. A good example of this procedure can be seen in the development of the Schwartz Outcome Scale (Blais et al., 1999). In order to create this 10-item measure of well being that could be used as an outcome tool for inpatient settings, Blais et al. (1999) conducted interviews of psychologists, psychiatrists, social workers, and psychiatric patients. All respondents were asked to discuss what aspects of functioning change during a course of successful treatment. These responses were then distilled down into broad domain areas from which items were developed. This type of approach to test development helps to ensure that the content of the measure will sample broadly from the domain of interest.

Like content validity, *face validity* is another way to describe the translation of a latent variable into an operationalized test form. Face validity refers to the extent to which a test appears to the test taker to measure the construct of interest. A measure that is high in face validity will have item content that appears to be explicitly related to the latent variable of interest. A measure that is low in face validity will appear to be unrelated or only marginally related to the latent variable. Performance-based techniques that purport to measure defensiveness, interpersonal processing, and coping skills are probably among the least face valid measures because it is difficult for test takers to know what is being assessed. Some neuropsychological tests are also relatively low in face validity because of the difference in the appearance of the tasks to be solved and the information that the clinician derives from those tasks. In contrast, a self-report measure that asks about a client's mood, suicidal ideation, changes in energy, interests, and weight, and feelings of sadness will be a very face valid measure of depression.

The relevance of a test's face validity relates primarily to its intended purpose. For most purposes, a face valid measure is preferable. Face valid measures are easy to understand by clients and patients who will quickly appreciate the purposes of the evaluation and will be motivated to respond truthfully. Furthermore, face valid measures may be more likely to be adopted by clinicians. However, there are occasions when a face valid measure will not be preferable including those times that a respondent may be motivated to respond inaccurately. Forensic psychologists often face this challenge when their examinees wish to present themselves in a favorable light. Conversely, there are times when clients might be motivated to portray themselves as more impaired in order to receive services or other forms of compensation. Another consideration about whether to use a face valid measure is the *social desirability* of the latent variable. It is simple human nature to want to appear generally virtuous, honest, and upstanding, and to minimize our foibles and negative characteristics. For this reason, when researchers seek information about altruistic behaviors, for example, they often do so in ways that are not entirely face valid, including embedding these items in a longer list of questions in order to disguise the true nature of the test.

Criterion-Related Validity

Like translation validity, *criterion-related validity* relates to the quality of our operationalization of a latent construct into test format. This form of validity is primarily concerned with evaluating our test against an external marker or criterion. That is, if we have developed a good measure of creativity, for example, we would expect it to correlate with prior well-established measures of creativity as well as some other marker of our client's creativity (such as their ability to solve puzzles in an innovative fashion or their employment in a job that requires creativity).

One crucial consideration in criterion-related validity studies is the quality of the criterion chosen. If we are to validate a measure in comparison to an external criterion, the quality of that validation is only as good as the robustness of our criterion variable. For example, school performance might be a good external criterion for a measure of intelligence, but a weaker criterion measure of social adjustment. Likewise, a rigorously conducted diagnostic interview reviewed by multiple raters will be a stronger criterion for a measure of psychopathology than one clinician's diagnostic impressions.

According to Trochim (2000), there are four types of criterion-related validity: concurrent, predictive, convergent, and discriminant.

Concurrent validity is a form of criterion-related validity that involves comparing the results of a measure with some external measurement that was taken at nearly the same time. For example, if we wish to validate a new measure of sociability, we might conduct a concurrent validity study by administering our measure to a group of participants and then observing and rating their social behavior. The ratings of their social behavior serve as the external criterion against which we can compare the scores generated by our measure. As another example, if we were attempting to validate a measure of aggression in children, we might correlate our measure with incidents of classroom aggressive behavior collected around the same time. In personality assessment and the assessment of psychopathology, the presence or absence of a particular psychiatric diagnosis is often used as an external criterion in concurrent validity studies.

Predictive validity is somewhat similar to concurrent validity, but it involves the comparison of a test against an external measure that was taken at a date *later* than the test administration. We might explore the predictive validity of our childhood aggression measure by correlating results with the number of critical classroom aggressive incidents over the following year. Although it is an important part of measure validation, you are not likely to see many predictive validity studies in personality assessment. Traditionally, personality assessment has been more concerned with describing a client's "here and now" dispositions, symptoms, and behavior rather than predicting their future adjustment and behavior. An exception to this are studies of measures of life-threatening risk factors including suicidality and aggression. Although the predictive validity of such measures still tends to be relatively poor, there is a great deal of motivation to develop such measures due to their potential utility in clinical and forensic settings. Predictive validity studies are much more common in industrial-organizational psychology where measurement is used to predict job performance and the proper classification of personnel. For example, a researcher may wish to validate a measure of managerial ability that can be used to indicate which job candidates might be good leaders. A predictive validity study might correlate test scores with certain markers of managerial skill over the following year in order to examine the ability of the measure to predict such skills.

The final forms of criterion-related validity are *convergent* and *discriminant* validity (Campbell & Fiske, 1959). Convergent validity refers to examining the relationship between a test and another measure of the same construct. If both measures assess the same construct, we would expect that they would be related. Unlike concurrent validity that usually involves a nontest criterion, convergent validity of measurement often involves comparing a new measure with a previously established measure or measures. Returning to our example of a childhood measure of aggression, we would expect that this measure should be related to other measures of aggression, behavioral disinhibition, or poor school conduct. Generally speaking, researchers like these correlations to be relatively moderate in size. Very high correlations between a new and an old measure might call into question the rationale for using the new measure over the older, more established one, because the two tests would appear equivalent.

Discriminant validity (also sometimes known as divergent validity) is the counterpart to convergent validity and involves comparing a new measure to previously established measures of constructs to which the new measure is unlikely to be related. If our test is an adequate operationalization of a construct, we would expect it to be different from measures of unrelated constructs. Therefore, we might compare our childhood aggression measure to a test of anxiety, depression, or even intelligence.

Full interpretation of convergent and discriminant validity must take place simultaneously (Campbell & Fiske, 1959). Thus in order to fully demonstrate construct validity, a measure should correlate with conceptually similar measures and not correlate with conceptually dissimilar measures. Campbell and Fiske (1959) suggested that validity researchers create a *multitrait-multimethod matrix* that demonstrates both convergent and discriminant validity. They suggest that researchers make use of at least two measures of two different constructs so that the relationship between measurement types (method) can be examined in relationship to their ability to measure the dif-

Table 1.2 Simple Convergent and Divergent Validity Analysis of a Hypothetical Measure of Childhood Aggression

New Aggression Scale	
Old Aggression Scale	.85
Oppositionality Scale	**.75**
Classroom Disruption Scale	**.70**
Intelligence Scale	−.05
Depression Scale	.35
Anxiety Scale	.15

Note: Correlations shown in bold represent *convergent validity*. Other correlations represent *discriminant validity*.

ferent constructs (traits). A simplified example of this is shown in Table 1.2. To make this clearer, only our new measure of aggression is included. You can see that the correlations shown in bold represent evidence of convergent validity and the nonbolded correlations represent discriminant validity. Because the convergent correlations are higher than the discriminant validity correlations, we can safely conclude that this test measures the construct that we hoped it would. Now imagine that we achieved the results in Table 1.3 for this measure. As you can see, the results are a lot less clear in this case. The measure seems to moderately correlate with all of the criterion measures we have chosen, including the ones to which it is not conceptually related. In this case, we will be unable to conclude that our measure is an adequate operationalization of our latent variable. We would have to conduct further studies to determine why this measure is not performing as hoped, but it appears that either this measure is a poor translation of the latent variable or the latent variable is, in fact, conceptually related to factors such as depression, anxiety, and intelligence.

Table 1.3 Simple Convergent and Divergent Validity Analysis of a Hypothetical Measure of Childhood Aggression

New Aggression Scale	
Old Aggression Scale	**.65**
Oppositionality Scale	**.40**
Classroom Disruption Scale	**.40**
Intelligence Scale	.50
Depression Scale	.60
Anxiety Scale	.60

Note: Correlations shown in bold represent *convergent validity*. Other correlations represent *discriminant validity*.

Clinical Utility Validity

In recent years, there has been increasing focus on the utility of psychological tests for clinical practice. When a test is developed for clinical use, it is obviously important that the test is useful in clinical settings. Although a great deal of time and money can be spent on demonstrating the psychometric properties of a measure, the final utility of the measure in clinical practice is crucial. From the perspective of mere pragmatics, the clinical utility of a measure lies in its ease of use, time investment, and acceptability of the construct to be measured. It is difficult to measure these things directly, but instead, researchers can rely on common sense in developing measures that are either efficient or provide a wealth of information that cannot be easily obtained through other means.

However, there are some empirical methods of demonstrating that a measure has clinical utility. This form of validity is somewhat different than the more traditional definition of validity that we have discussed. Not necessarily an indication of the quality of our translation of a latent variable, this form of validity relates to the usefulness of our measure in clinical practice.

The primary form of clinical utility validity is *incremental validity*. Incremental validity refers to the ability of a measure to add a new form of information or improve classification accuracy *over and above* another established measure of the same construct. In clinical practice where reimbursement rates for assessment are reducing the number of measures that clinicians can reasonably administer (Cashel, 2002; Groth-Marnat, 1999; Piotrowski, 1999), it is important that each measure in an assessment battery provides some additional and non-redundant information. The cost effectiveness of measures must be demonstrated as a function of the information they provide in comparison to other measures. For example, if an older measure of anxiety correctly classifies those with and without anxiety with 90% accuracy, the addition of a second measure that classifies anxiety with 93% accuracy may not be worth the expense. However, if two measures of anxiety both have more limited classification ability, then the combination of these measures may result in an acceptable degree of classification.

Typically, studies of incremental validity have been conducted using different test methods such as a self-report measure and a performance-based test (Archer & Krishnamurthy, 1997; Blais, Hilsenroth, Castlebury, Fowler, & Baity, 2001; Hunsley & Meyer, 2003; Smith, Blais, Vangala, & Masek, 2005). For example, in a study of psychiatrically referred adolescents, Archer and Krishnamurthy (1997) found that Rorschach indices of depression and conduct problems did not significantly improve the classification accuracy, respectively, for depression and conduct disorder diagnoses of the MMPI-A. Conversely, Blais et al. (2001) found that Rorschach data improved the classification accuracy of the MMPI-2 in the identification of clients with personality disorders. Other studies have explored the incremental validity of psychological tests in relation to interviews and patient self-prediction (Garb, 1998, 2003).

A validity concept that is a form of criterion-related validity is a measure's *diagnostic efficiency*. We have included it here because it has the most implications for the clinical utility of a measure. Simply put, diagnostic efficiency relates to the ability of a diagnostic test to correctly classify a group of individuals into diagnostic groups. Validity information may inform a clinician about the extent to which a measure actually measures the construct it was designed to assess. Yet this does little to inform the clinician about the likelihood of the presence of a disorder given a particular test or assessment score. Therefore, in a clinical setting, an evaluation of a measure's accuracy in correctly classifying individuals with or without a particular disorder becomes paramount. This information is obtained through the calculation of diagnostic efficiency statistics including sensitivity, specificity, positive predictive power, negative predictive power, overall correct classification, and kappa (Kessel & Zimmerman, 1993).

Sensitivity and Specificity   Sensitivity refers to the probability that a person known to have a particular disorder will test positive for that disorder on the measure in question (Kessel & Zimmerman, 1993). If a measure is low in sensitivity, there is a greater likelihood of underidentification of a disorder (Type II error). Specificity is the probability that an individual without a psychiatric disorder will test negative for that disorder (Kessel & Zimmerman, 1993). If a measure is low in specificity, there is a greater likelihood of overidentification of a disorder (Type I error).

There are a number of characteristics of sensitivity and specificity that make them useful in test design and evaluation. Because they are both calculated using different samples of individuals, sensitivity and specificity can vary independently of one another. This gives a more accurate index of the test's ability to differentiate different diagnostic groups. Furthermore, both are somewhat independent of sample size and population base rates which make them more robust in relation to small clinical sample sizes.

Positive and Negative Predictive Power   Sensitivity and specificity are useful tests of a measure's accuracy when applied to groups with known characteristics such as the presence or absence of a particular disorder. Yet, this is not representative of the clinical assessment process when the presence or absence of a particular disorder is unknown. More important for clinicians is knowing the probability that a positive or negative test result is accurate. Calculations of positive and negative predictive power are used to address the question of clinical prediction. Positive predictive power (PPP) is defined as the percentage of individuals that test positive who truly have the disorder.

Stated differently, PPP is the ratio of true-positive results to all positive results. Conversely, negative predictive power (NPP) is the percentage of individuals testing negative who truly do not have the disorder. NPP is the ratio of true-negative results to all negative results.

Although PPP and NPP are more useful indices of clinical utility than sensitivity and specificity, consideration of population base rates is essential in their calculation and interpretation (Elwood, 1993). When the population base rate of a disorder is low, the predictive power of a negative test result (NPP) will be more than that of a positive test result (PPP). When a disorder is rare, a positive test result will most likely be incorrect. Therefore a loss in PPP results in a gain in NPP (Elwood, 1993). Because many tests are validated with normative samples and an equally sized clinical group (prevalence = 50%), the PPP and NPP calculated in these studies will be incorrect when applied to settings with a lower prevalence rate. Thus it is important to calculate PPP and NPP with samples reflecting rates as they are found in the population in question.

Overall Correct Classification   The *overall correct classification* rate (OCC), also known as the "hit rate," "overall level of agreement," or "overall diagnostic power," is the proportion of individuals with the disorder and individuals without the disorder correctly classified by the test (Kessel & Zimmerman, 1993). The OCC ratio can often be misleadingly high, especially when applied to low base rate disorders. When the base rate of a disorder is low, the high rate of true negatives grossly outweighs the low rate of true positives. In these situations, the loss of PPP is masked by the increase in NPP (Elwood, 1993).

Diagnostic efficiency statistics such as PPP, NPP, and OCC are often used by test developers to establish cut-off scores for determining group membership. For example, a test researcher may find that a measure of depression with a cut-off *T*-score of 70 may result in an OCC of .79 (that is 79% of patients will be correctly classified at this score), but that a *T*-score of 75 might increase the OCC to .90. Studies of diagnostic efficiency statistics can help researchers and clinicians determine which cut-off scores might be most efficient in their particular clinical setting (inpatients versus outpatients, etc.). Even though PPP and NPP are more relevant to clinical decision-making, you are likely to see sensitivity and specificity indices reported in the literature for many common tests.

A Note on the Relationship between Reliability and Validity

It is important to understand the relationship between the reliability and validity of a measure. Simply put, reliability is generally a prerequisite for validity. If a measure is useful and valid representation of an underlying latent variable, then first it must be consistent. Let's return to the example of the stopwatch discussed earlier. If the stopwatch is inconsistent (in terms of temporal consistency, rater consistency, or internal consistency), then it cannot be a valid translation of the underlying variable of time, which is a very consistent construct (although it may not seem this way when you're sitting in a boring class!).

There is at least one situation in which *decreasing* reliability might improve validity, however. Imagine that a test developer sought to create a measure of depression and she wrote the following five test items:

1. I feel very sad.
2. I am unhappy.
3. My mood is quite depressed.
4. I can't imagine being happy again.
5. I have been very down recently.

We can see that these items are likely to be very reliable, particularly when it relates to internal consistency. All of these items relate to the experience of a depressed mood and they are likely to correlate very highly (demonstrating high internal consistency). However, they are not a valid or complete translation of the latent trait (depression), which reduces the content validity of the measure. Therefore, in order to increase the validity of this measure, she would need to write items that tapped all facets of depression (including changes in sleep and appetite, social withdrawal, guilt, and lack of pleasure in activities). When she adds these additional items, her internal consistency statistics are likely to suffer somewhat because the content of the measure will be more broad. However, adding additional items will improve the validity of the measure overall.

Although reliability is a prerequisite for validity, validity is the most crucial element in evaluating the quality and utility of a measure. Without a demonstration of its validity, a measure has little clinical or research utility. Moreover, in clinical settings, a measure used for purposes for which it is not validated can have detrimental effects by falsely identifying or not identifying an important clinical phenomenon. Last, it is the validity of a measure that gives it its meaning. That is, we cannot be fully certain what a measure is *for* until it has been empirically explored. For example, although we may have wished to create a measure of simple phobias, empirical investigation may reveal that our measure is better for assessing generalized anxiety disorder. Thus, it is the process of examining the validity of the measure in which a test developer is able to discover the potential meaning and utility (if any) of their measure.

Ethical Test Use

Guidelines for ethical test use have been published by the American Psychological Association (APA, 2002) and by a joint committee from the American Educational Research Association, APA, and the National Council on Measurement in Education (American Educational Research Association, 1999). The 2002 APA *Ethical Principles of Psychologists and Code of Conduct* outlines 11 points of consideration for ethical test use. These include informed consent, empirical bases for interpretation, the sharing of test data, and the interpretation of assessments (See Quick Reference). Note that the information provided in the Quick Reference box is merely an overview and all students should carefully read and review the Ethical Principles (www. apa.org/ethics/code2002.html) prior to engaging in any assessment practice. Given these ethical guidelines, there are a few points that bear particular discussion.

Competence

The *Ethics Code* is clear that psychologists should not engage in any professional activity in which they are not competent to practice (Principles 2.01–2.06). This is particularly true for the use of psychological assessment. Competence in a particular test or technique can be gained through supervision, coursework, and continuing education experiences. Even the most experienced assessment psychologist will obtain consultation and supervision from colleagues. Competence extends not only to the use of particular tests, but also particular reasons for referral and client characteristics including cultural differences. All clinicians should take steps to make sure that they are versed in the issues relevant to each case that they see. If adequate supervision or consultation is not available, psychologists should work to refer a case to another provider, if possible.

Science and Practice

One component of competent assessment practice relates to the relationship between the clinical practice of assessment and the scientific literature of assessment research. For psychologists who choose to use personality assessments, it is vital that test users continually review, evaluate, and update their knowledge of the empirical bases for these tests. Although reliability and validity information must be presented in a test's manual or development manuscript, there is often published research that is more recent and might be particularly important. Furthermore, published research often suggests limits to the validity of a test or differential interpretations depending on certain referral reasons, client backgrounds, and setting or contextual factors. For example, the Depression Index (DEPI) from the Rorschach (Exner, 2003), is purported to measure the presence of clinically significant depressive features.

**Quick Reference: Ethical Principles of Assessment
(American Psychological Association, 2002)**

Domain	Ethical Principle
Bases for Assessments	Psychologists should base opinions on all relevant data. If sufficient data is not available, this should be made clear.
Use of Assessments	Psychologists should use reliable and valid measures for purposes that are appropriate given current research and evidence. Psychologists should attempt to use assessments in the language of the client.
Informed Consent in Assessments	Psychologists obtain informed consent for assessments except under very narrow exceptions (including legal mandate or when assessment is used to evaluate decision-making capacity).
Release of Test Data	If the client has provided consent, psychologists release test data to clients or the client's representative unless the psychologist feels that doing so would endanger the client or others.
Test Construction	Psychologists use appropriate psychometric procedures to design and evaluate tests.
Interpreting Assessment Results	Psychologists consider all relevant factors (including cultural and linguistic differences) in their interpretation of tests. They must note any limitations to their interpretations.
Assessment by Unqualified Persons	Unless it is for training purposes, psychologists do not promote test use by individuals who are unqualified.
Obsolete Tests and Outdated Test Results	Psychologists do not use tests that are outdated or obsolete for the current purpose.
Test Scoring and Interpretation Services	Psychologists retain final responsibility for test interpretation even when tests are initially interpreted by a computer or other interpretation service.
Explaining Assessment Results	Psychologists take steps to ensure that test results are explained to clients or the client's representative or guardian.
Maintaining Test Security	Psychologists protect the security of test manuals, protocols, and questions.

However, there is research that suggests that this might not be the case, at least for certain populations (Archer & Krishnamurthy, 1997; Ilonen et al., 1999; Jorgensen, Anderson, & Dam, 2000; Krishnamurthy, Archer, & House, 1996). Therefore, an ethical psychologist should attenuate her interpretation of this test score if other supporting circumstances are not present.

Cultural Differences

In all psychological practices, it is important to recognize the importance of culture. In personality assessment it may be particularly relevant because the very notion and definition of *personality* rests on cultural norms and values. We must be careful that our measures are content valid for all groups with whom we use them. For example, the concepts of *introversion* and *extroversion* might have a non-traditional meaning for members of collectivistic cultural groups. Therefore, a measure of these constructs would not be valid for such an individual. Issues of language, metrics of responding, and assessor bias are all important sources of test misinterpretation with cultural minorities (Dana, 1993; Dana, Aguilar-Kitibutr, Diaz-Vivar, & Vetter, 2002). Furthermore, research has indicated that many commonly-used personality assessment measures should be interpreted and/or used differently with minority groups (Dana, 1993; Dana et al., 2002; Leong, Levy, Gee, & Johnson, 2007). Competent assessors should be aware of these issues and integrate them into their assessments accordingly.

Dana (1993) provides a decision-making flowchart for competent and ethical multicultural assessment. He suggests that psychologists make a brief assessment of a client's cultural orientation prior to testing. This assessment should take into account acculturation and enculturation factors as well as the domains to be assessed. If the client has a worldview that is nontraditional according to their ethnic background (i.e., they share a worldview that is consistent with the dominant European worldview), then testing can proceed using measures developed with and normed on the dominant culture. If, however, the client has a bicultural or traditional cultural worldview, then that individual is best assessed using culture-specific measures, if possible. In many cases, however, there are no culture-specific assessments available. At this point, an assessor must make a decision about whether or not to proceed with a test-based assessment. In all cases, however, the limits of the interpretation must be discussed and any caveats must be indicated clearly.

Protection of Test Materials and Release of Test Data

The Ethics Code indicates that we should take steps to protect the security and integrity of test materials including test items, manuals, and protocols. The content of these materials represents a trade secret and their release to the general public could have very serious implications. Imagine that the items and scoring of self-report personality tests were generally available to the public. This means that anyone could study the items and respond in a way that allowed them to produce their desired test results. Similarly, if the Rorschach stimuli were easily available along with a list of "good" responses, clients could study these and respond in a very socially desirable fashion (unfortunately, it *is* the case that "cheat sheets" for some psychological tests are available online, primarily for the use of individuals attempting to avoid legal consequences or judgments; although this is a violation of the tests' copyrights, it is virtually impossible to "police" the entirety of the Internet). Therefore, it is important to treat test materials with the same care that you would treat confidential client information.

The *Health Information Portability and Protection Act of 1996* (HIPPA) is a federal law (PL104-191) that is designed to provide increased protection for specific forms of health care information, including psychological assessment. Although HIPPA rules only apply to organizations that use electronic billing or who have voluntarily opted to be subject to HIPPA guidelines, *all* providers of mental health services should be familiar with these rules and guidelines. Both the Ethics Code and HIPPA indicate that clients (or a representative such as a lawyer) should be provided a copy of test materials if the client has provided a release. However, HIPPA notes that information that is protected by trade secret or copyright law does not need to be released. Therefore, information such as test questions, manuals, scoring templates, or charts should not typically be released. Computer-generated reports are also not to be released. However, psychologists must provide all raw materials that the client generated including bubble sheets or other raw data. HIPPA regulations and state laws also allow for psychologists to provide written summaries of test data if the client agrees to this arrangement. Requests for information can be denied if the psychologist reasonably believes that releasing information might endanger the life of the client or others.

The full array of legal and ethical guidelines related to test information is far too broad a subject to be adequately addressed here and these issues become particularly complex as encountered within the context of forensic psychological assessments. The American Psychological Association has provided some guidelines on how to interpret test protection laws and most test publishers have issued statements that are very clear regarding which test data can and cannot be released. All clinicians who practice assessment should continually seek education and consultation regarding these matters.

Introduction to the Text

This text is designed to be used by graduate students in counseling and clinical psychology programs in courses on projective and objective personality assessment. To date, there is no single text that addresses this important niche of student education, and we hoped to create one that is informative, readable, and is both clinically useful and empirically grounded. Remembering that good personality assessment lies at the intersection of a test and a clinician, we assume that users of this text are working diligently to improve and enhance their clinical skills and understanding of personality theory so that test information can be seamlessly integrated into their clinical practice.

Organization and Selection of Chapter Topics

In organizing and developing the text, we struggled with which tests to include and which to leave out. Certainly there are seemingly endless personality tests, but we decided to pick the most commonly used and taught measures for inclusion in the text. By reviewing the literature on the most commonly used psychological measures (Camara et al., 2000; Cashel, 2002; Archer, 2005) with both child and adult populations, we managed to create a short list of the most common tests and techniques. We created a list of four broad assessment types (self-report, interview, performance-based, and behavioral) covering both normative and pathological personality assessment. Furthermore, because personality assessment is more than mere test interpretation, we included two chapters related to clinical practice issues including test integration, interpretation, report writing, and therapeutic feedback practices. We believe that you will find a good balance between the hard science of assessment research and the complexity of assessment practice.

After we identified chapter topics, we created a list of ideal authors for those chapters. In some cases, we identified the author(s) of the measure; in other cases, we identified leading experts and researchers on a particular test or technique. Our final list of authors reads like a "Who's Who" of personality assessment research and practice. These authors are all leaders in personality assessment with both clinical and scientific expertise in their particular areas. We hope that reading this text will be a real treat for you—the opportunity to learn from such experienced clinical researchers is an exciting one.

Chapter Format

You'll find that each test-based chapter in the text has a similar outline. We created an outline that we believe maximizes the information that students need to know about a particular test or technique. From the underlying latent variable through the test development and psychometrics to its use and limitations, you'll find that each chapter follows this format. Furthermore, because no test is without some degree of controversy, each chapter provides a balanced view of the criticisms of the included tests. Last, to provide some practice with test interpretation, each chapter will challenge you with some form of clinical dilemma. The standardization of presentations serves to clarify the most salient issues in a clear and concise way so that the most important information will be right at your fingertips. Our hope is that this text will be a great classroom resource for you and will continue to serve as a reference for your assessment work after you finish your formal education.

Acknowledgment

Thanks to Aaron Estrada, M.A. for his help in the preparation of this chapter.

References

Abraham, P. P., Lepisto, B. L., Lewis, M. G., Schultz, L., & Finkelberg, S. (1994). An outcome study: Changes in Rorschach variables of adolescents in residential treatment. *Journal of Personality Assessment, 62*, 505–514.

Ackerman, S. J., Hilsenroth, M. J., Baity, M. R., & Blagys, M. D. (2000). Interaction of therapeutic process and alliance during psychological assessment. *Journal of Personality Assessment, 75*(1), 82–109.

American Educational Research Association, American Psychological Association, & National Council on Measurement in Education. (1999). *Standards for educational and psychological testing.* Washington, DC: American Educational Research Association.

American Psychological Association (2002). *Ethical principals of psychologists and code of conduct.* Washington, DC: Author.

Anastasi, A. (1982). *Psychological testing* (5th ed.). New York: MacMillan.

Anastasi, A. (1988). *Psychological testing* (6th ed.). New York: MacMillan.

Archer, R. P. (2005). *MMPI-A: Assessing Adolescent Psychopathology* (3rd ed.). Mahwah, NJ: Erlbaum.

Archer, R. P., & Krishnamurthy, R. (1997). MMPI-A and Rorschach indices related to depression and conduct disorder: An evaluation of the incremental validity hypothesis. *Journal of Personality Assessment, 69*, 517–533.

Archer, R. P., & Newsom, C. R. (2000). Psychological test usage with adolescent clients: Survey update. *Assessment, 7*, 227–235.

Beck, A.T., & Steer, R. A. (1987). *Beck Depression Inventory manual.* San Antonio: The Psychological Corporation.

Bernreuter, R. G. (1935). *Manual for the Personality Inventory.* Oxford: Stanford University Press.

Blais, M. A., Hilsenroth, M. J., Castlebury, F., Fowler, J. C., & Baity, M. R. (2001). Predicting DSM-IV cluster B personality disorder criteria from MMPI-2 and Rorschach data: A test of incremental validity. *Journal of Personality Assessment, 76*, 150–168.

Blais, M. A., Lenderking, W. R., Baer, L., deLorell, A., Peets, K., Leahy, L., et al. (1999). Development and initial validation of a brief mental heath outcome measure. *Journal of Personality Assessment, 73*(3), 359–373.

Butcher, J. N., Dahlstrom, W., Graham, J. R., Tellegen, A., & Kaemmer, B. (1989). *Minnesota Multiphasic Personality Inventory (MMPI-2): Manual for administration and scoring.* Minneapolis: University of Minnesota Press.

Butcher, J. N., Graham, J. R., Williams, C. L., & Ben-Porath, Y. S. (1990). *Development and use of the MMPI-2 Content Scales.* Minneapolis: University of Minnesota Press.

Butcher, J. N., Williams, C. L., Graham, J. R., Archer, R. P., Tellegen, A., Ben-Porath, Y. S., et al. (1992). *Minnesota Multiphasic Personality Inventory — Adolescent (MMPI-A): Manual for administration, scoring, and interpretation.* Minneapolis: University of Minnesota Press.

Camara, W. J., Nathan, J. S., & Puente, A. E. (2000). Psychological test usage: Implications in professional psychology. *Professional Psychology: Research and Practice, 31*, 141–154.

Campbell, D. T., & Fiske, D. W. (1959). Convergent and discriminant validation by the multitrait-multimethod matrix. *Psychological Bulletin, 56*, 81–105.

Cashel, M. L. (2002). Child and adolescent psychological assessment: Current clinical practice and the impact of managed care. *Professional Psychology: Research and Practice, 33,* 446–453.

Cattell, R. (1949). *Handbook for the Sixteen Personality Factor Questionnaire.* Champaign, IL: Institute for Personality and Ability Testing.

Clemence, A. J., & Handler, L. (2001). Psychological assessment on internship: A survey of training directors and their expectations for students. *Journal of Personality Assessment, 76,* 18–47.

Costa, P. T., Jr., & McCrae, R. R. (1985). *The NEO Personality Inventory manual.* Odessa, FL: Psychological Assessment Resources.

Cramer, P. (1996). *Storytelling, narrative, and the Thematic Apperception Test.* New York: Guilford.

Dana, R. H. (1993). *Multicultural assessment perspectives for professional psychology.* Boston, MA: Allyn and Bacon.

Dana, R. H., Aguilar-Kitibutr, A., Diaz-Vivar, N., & Vetter, H. (2002). A teaching method for multicultural assessment: Psychological report contents and cultural competence. *Journal of Personality Assessment, 79,* 207–215.

Durand, V. M., Blanchard, E. B., & Mindell, J. A. (1988). Training in projective testing: Survey of clinical training directors and internship directors. *Professional Psychology: Research and Practice, 19,* 236–238.

Elwood, R. W. (1993). Psychological tests and clinical discriminations: Beginning to address the base rate problem. *Clinical Psychology Review, 13,* 409–419.

Exner, J. E. (2003). *The Rorschach: A comprehensive system* (4th ed.). New York: Wiley.

Finn, S. E., & Tonsager, M. E. (1992). Therapeutic effects of providing MMPI-2 test feedback to college students awaiting therapy. *Psychological Assessment, 4,* 278–287.

Finn, S. E., & Tonsager, M. E. (1997). Information-gathering and therapeutic models of assessment: Complementary paradigms. *Psychological Assessment, 9,* 374–385.

Fischer, C. T. (1994). *Individualizing psychological assessment.* Hillsdale, NJ: Erlbaum.

Fischer, C. T. (2000). Collaborative, individualized assessment. *Journal of Personality Assessment, 74,* 2–14.

Frank, L. K. (1939). Projective methods for the study of personality. *Journal of Psychology, 8,* 389–413.

Garb, H. N. (1998). *Studying the clinician.* Washington, DC: American Psychological Association.

Garb, H. N. (2003). Incremental validity and the assessment of psychopathology in adults. *Psychological Assessment, 15,* 508–520.

Goldberg, L.R. (1982). From ace to zombie: Some exploration in the language of personality. In C. D. Spielberger & J. N. Butcher (Eds.), *Advances in Personality Assessment* (Vol. 1, pp. 203–234). Hillsdale, NJ: Erlbaum.

Gronnerod, C. (2003). Temporal stability in the Rorschach method: A meta-analytic review. *Journal of Personality Assessment, 80,* 272–293.

Gronnerod, C. (2004). Rorschach assessment of changes following psychotherapy: A meta-analytic review. *Journal of Personality Assessment, 83,* 256–276.

Groth-Marnat, G. (1999). Financial efficacy of clinical assessment: Rational guidelines and issues for future research. *Journal of Clinical Psychology, 55,* 813–824.

Handler, L., & Meyer, G. J. (1998). The importance of teaching and learning personality assessment. In L. Handler & M. J. Hilsenroth (Eds.), *Teaching and learning personality assessment* (pp. 3–30). Mahwah, NJ: Erlbaum.

Hathaway, S. R., & McKinley, J. C. (1943). *Minnesota Multiphasic Personality Inventory.* Minneapolis: University of Minnesota.

Hilsenroth, M. J., Peters, E. J., & Ackerman, S. J. (2004). The development of therapeutic alliance during psychological assessment: Patient and therapist perspectives across treatment. *Journal of Personality Assessment, 83,* 331–344.

Hunsley, J., & Meyer, G. J. (2003). The incremental validity of psychological testing and assessment: Conceptual, methodological, and statistical issues. *Psychological Assessment, 15(4),* 446–455.

Ilonen, T., Taiminen, T., Karlsson, H., Lauerma, H., Leinonen, K.-M., Wallenius, E., et al. (1999). Diagnostic efficiency of the Rorschach schizophrenia and depression indices in identifying first-episode schizophrenia and severe depression. *Psychiatry Research, 87,* 183–192.

Jackson, D. N. (1970). A sequential system for personality scale development. In C.D. Spielberger (Ed.), *Current topics in clinical and community psychology* (Vol. 2, pp. 62–97). New York: Academic Press.

Jackson, D. N. (1974). Personality research form manual. Goshen, NY: Research Psychologists Press.

Jorgensen, K., Anderson, T. J., & Dam, H. (2000). The diagnostic efficiency of the Rorschach depression index and schizophrenia index: A review. *Assessment, 7,* 259–280.

Jung, C. G. (1910). The association method. *American Journal of Psychology, 21,* 219–269.

Kessel, J. B., & Zimmerman, M. (1993). Reporting errors in studies of the diagnostic performance of self-administered questionnaires: Extent of the problem, recommendations for standardized presentation of results, and implications for the peer review process. *Psychological Assessment, 5,* 395–399.

Krishnamurthy, R., Archer, R. P., & House, J. J. (1996). The MMPI-A and Rorschach: A failure to establish convergent validity. *Assessment, 3,* 179–191.

Leong, F. T. L., Levy, J. J., Gee, C. B., & Johnson, J. (2007). Clinical assessment of ethnic minority children and adolescents. In S. R. Smith & L. Handler (Eds.), *The clinical assessment of children and adolescents: A practitioner's handbook* (pp. 545–574). Mahwah, NJ: Erlbaum.

Meyer, G. J., Finn, S. E., Eyde, L. D., Kay, G. G., Moreland, K. L., Dies, R. R., et al. (2001). Psychological testing and psychological assessment: A review of evidence and issues. *American Psychologist, 56,* 128–165.

Miller, T. W., Spicer, K., Kraus, R. F., Heister, T., & Bilyeu, J. (1999). Cost effective assessment models in providing patient-matched psychotherapy. *Journal of Contemporary Psychotherapy, 29,* 143–154.

Morey, L. C. (1991). *The Personality Assessment Inventory professional manual.* Odessa, FL: Psychological Assessment Resources.

Morgan, C. D., & Murray, H. A. (1935). A method for investigating fantasies: The Thematic Apperception Test. *Archives of Neurology and Psychiatry, 34,* 289–306.

Murray, H. A. (1943). *Thematic Apperception Test manual.* Cambridge, MA: Harvard University Press.

Piotrowski, C. (1999). Assessment practices in the era of managed care: Current status and future directions. *Journal of Clinical Psychology, 55,* 787–796.

Pressey, S.L., & Pressey, L.W. (1919). Cross-Out Test, with suggestions as to a group scale of the emotions. *Journal of Applied Psychology, 3,* 138–150.

Rorer, L. G. (1990). Personality assessment: A conceptual survey. In L. A. Pervin (Ed.), *Handbook of personality: Theory and research* (pp. 693–720). New York: Guilford.

Rosenberg, M. (1965). *Society and the adolescent self-image.* Princeton, NJ: Princeton University Press.

Shrout, P. E., & Fleiss, J. L. (1979). Intraclass correlations: Uses in assessing rater reliability. *Psychological Bulletin, 86,* 420–428.

Smith, S. R., Blais, M. A., Vangala, M., & Masek, B. J. (2005). Exploring the hand test with medically ill children and adolescents. *Journal of Personality Assessment, 85,* 82–91.

Stedman, J. M., Hatch, J. P., & Schoenfeld, L. S. (2000). Pre-internship preparation in psychological testing and psychotherapy: What internship directors say they expect. *Professional Psychology: Research and Practice, 31,* 321–326.

Stedman, J. M., Hatch, J. P., & Schoenfeld, L. S. (2001). Internship directors' valuation of pre-internship preparation in test-based assessment and psychotherapy. *Professional Psychology: Research and Practice, 32,* 421–424.

Stedman, J. M., Hatch, J. P., & Schoenfeld, L. S. (2002). Pre-internship preparation of clinical and counseling students in psychological testing, psychotherapy, and supervision: Their readiness for medical school and nonmedical school internships. *Journal of Clinical Psychology in Medical Settings, 9,* 267–271.

Trochim, W. (2000). *The research methods knowledge base* (2nd ed.). Cincinnati, OH: Atomic Dog Publishing.

Watkins, C. E. (1991). What have surveys taught us about the teaching and practice of psychological assessment? *Journal of Personality Assessment, 56,* 426–437.

Westen, D. (1995). *Social Cognition and Object Relations Scale: Q-Sort for projective stories (SCORS-Q).* Unpublished manuscript: Cambridge Hospital and Harvard Medical School, Cambridge, MA.

Westen, D., Lohr, N., Silk, K., Kerber, K., & Goodrich, S. (2002). *Measuring object relations and social cognition using the TAT: Scoring manual:* Department of Psychology, University of Michigan.

Woodworth, R.S. (1917). *Personal Data Sheet.* Chicago: Stoelting.

CHAPTER 2

The Clinical Interview

MARK E. MARUISH

The core of any psychological assessment should be the clinical interview. Findings from psychological testing, review of medical and other pertinent records of historical value (e.g., school records, court records), collateral contacts (e.g., family, teachers, work supervisors), and other sources of information about the patient are important and can help to understand patients and their problems. However, there is nothing that can substitute for the type of information that can be obtained only through face-to-face contact with the patient. As Groth-Marnat (2003) stated,

> Probably the single most important means of data collection during psychological evaluation is the assessment interview. *Without interview data, most psychological tests are meaningless* [emphasis added]. The interview also provides potentially valuable information that may be otherwise unattainable, such as behavioral observations, idiosyncratic features of the client, and the person's reaction to his or her current life situation. In addition, interviews are the primary means of developing rapport and can serve as a check against the meaning and validity of test results. (p. 69)

The purpose of this chapter is to provide a broad overview of the three general types of clinical interview, followed by a detailed discussion of the process and content of a specific semistructured clinical interview. This will be followed by an overview of three of the more commonly used structured interviews in clinical practice and research. The goal of this chapter is to answer the following questions:

- Generally, what approaches can be taken in conducting a clinical interview and how do they differ from each other?
- What type of client information should be obtained during the clinical interview?
- What are some examples of structured clinical interviews?

The Clinical Interview: General Considerations

As suggested earlier, any number of approaches can be taken in conducting the clinical interview. Notwithstanding, there are several factors that should be taken into consideration with regard to the interview. Doing so will help ensure that the limited time typically allotted for direct assessment of the patient will yield the most valid, useful, and comprehensive information.

The Clinical Interview within the Context of the Assessment

Although the clinical interview is at the core of the assessment, in most cases it is only one component of the process. Other sources of information about the patient (e.g., collateral interviews, psychological testing, and medical records) may be available and these should be capitalized on as appropriate. Referral to another behavioral health professional for pertinent information should also be considered when necessary. For example, the presence of concomitant seizures, blackouts, severe memory lapses, or other signs or symptoms of pathognomonic disorders of the central nervous system should lead to a referral for a neurological or neuropsychological evaluation to help rule out a neurological basis for the presenting problem.

The primacy of the clinical interview over other means used to gather assessment information cannot be stressed enough. Information from other sources is important, but it often is indirect, second-hand information that has either been colored by others' perceptions of the patient, inferred from other information, or lacks the degree of detail or specificity that the clinician would have pursued if the clinician were the one who personally gathered the information. Other sources of information cannot provide the same sense of the patient and his or her circumstances that comes from the clinical interview. Furthermore, as Mohr and Beutler (2003) point out,

> The interview is usually the first assessment procedure administered because, (1) it is the method in which most clinicians place the most faith in…, (2)…it is the easiest method of facilitating the patient's cooperation, and (3) it is readily adapted to providing a context in which other instruments can be selected and interpreted. (pp. 93–94)

In addition, the clinical interview helps to establish a relationship with the patient and sets the tone and expectations for the remainder of the assessment process.

Objectives of the Clinical Interview

What one hopes to accomplish during the clinical interview will vary from clinician to clinician. Some may view it as only a formality required by the patient's insurance carrier that will make little difference in the patient's treatment. Others may view it as a means of gathering necessary, but not in itself sufficient, information for the assessment of the patient. Still others may view it as being the only legitimate source of information. Viewed properly, a clinical interview conducted as part of a psychological assessment provides information that supports data and hypotheses generated from psychological testing or other sources of information, and/or generates information or hypotheses to be explored or tested by using data obtained from those sources.

In turn, information from the clinical interview facilitates meeting the objectives of psychological assessment. According to Beutler, Groth-Marnat, and Rosner (2003), "The objectives of psychological assessment conducted in a clinical setting can include answering questions as they pertain to one or more of the following: the individual's disorder or diagnosis, the etiology of the problematic behavior, the degree of functional impairment caused by the behavior, the likely course or progression of the disorder, the types of treatments that positively affect course, and the strengths and abilities available to the individual that can facilitate treatment."

Structured, Unstructured, and Semistructured Clinical Interviews

Generally speaking, a clinician can take one of three approaches in conducting the clinical interview. The first is what is referred to as the *unstructured interview*. The approach taken here is just as the term implies, it is one that follows no rigid sequence or direction of inquiry; rather, it is tailored more to the individual's problems and relies heavily on the clinician's skills and creativity (Mohr & Beutler, 2003). The reliance on individual clinician skills makes the unstructured interview the least reliable and possibly the least valid of the assessment procedures. In addition, the unstructured interview allows for the introduction of interviewer bias, (e.g., halo effect, primacy effect) from both perceptual and interactional processes (Groth-Marnat, 2003).

At the other end of the continuum is the *structured interview*. As defined by Mohr and Beutler (2003), the structured interview format is one in which the patient is asked a standard set of questions covering specific topics or content, including a finite list of signs and symptoms. Beutler (1995) previously identified two types of structured interview. The first is the one in which decision trees are used to determine which among a pool of potential questions the patient should be asked. In essence, the responses to previous questions guide the clinician in selecting which questions to ask next. Two examples are the Diagnostic Interview Schedule, Version IV (Robins, Cottler, Bucholz, & Compton, 1995) and the Structured Clinical Interview for DSM-IV Axis I Disorders (SCID-I)-Clinician Version (First, Spitzer, Gibbon, & Williams, 1997). The second type of structured interview is focused more on assessing a broad or narrow array of symptomatology and its severity rather than being tied closely to a diagnostic system. Examples include the structured versions of the broad-based Mental Status Examination (Amchin, 1991) and the narrowly focused Hamilton Rating Scale for Depression (HRSD; Hamilton, 1967).

While the structured interview provides the best means of obtaining valid and reliable information about the patient, there are drawbacks to its use. As Mohr and Beutler (2003) point out, structured interviews generally tend to be viewed as rather lengthy, constraining, and relying too much on patient self-report. It is perhaps for these reasons that structured clinical interviews are more often used in research settings where standardization in data gathering and empirical demonstration of data validity and reliability are critical (Beutler, 1995).

Viewed from another perspective, Meyer et al., (2001) see the problem of structured versus unstructured interviews as follows,

> When interviews are unstructured, clinicians may overlook certain areas of functioning and focus more exclusively on presenting complaints. When interviews are highly structured, clinicians can lose the forest for the trees and make precise but errant judgments.... Such mistakes may occur when the clinician focuses on responses to specific interview questions (e.g., diagnostic criteria) without fully considering the salience of these responses in the patient's broader life context or without adequately recognizing how the individual responses fit together into a symptomatically coherent pattern.... (p. 144)

What is the best way to deal with the dilemma posed by structured and unstructured interviews? The solution is a compromise between the two, that is, the *semistructured interview.* Employing a semistructured interview provides clinicians with a means of ensuring that all important areas of investigation are addressed while allowing them the flexibility to focus more or less attention to specific areas, depending on their relevance to the patient's problems. In essence, the clinician conducts each interview according to a general structure addressing common areas of biopsychosocial functioning. At the same time, the clinician is free to explore in greater detail the more salient aspects of patient's presentation and history as they are revealed.

Moreover, the semistructured approach allows for the insertion of therapeutic interventions if such opportunities arise during the course of the interview. For these reasons, the semistructured approach is the one that is advocated by this author and therefore serves as the recommended method for gathering the interview information discussed later in this chapter. Note that one may find the term "semistructured interview," as described and used herein, may be different from how it is used by others (e.g., see Summerfeldt & Antony, 2002).

Some Keys to Good Clinical Interviewing

Conducting a good, useful clinical interview requires more that just knowing what areas in which to query the patient. It requires skills that are usually taught in graduate-level practicum and internship experiences and later honed through down-in-the-trenches experience. It is beyond the scope of this chapter to go into depth on the art of interviewing, even at the very basic level. However, there are some general tips that should maximize the amount of useful information that can be obtained during the clinical interview.

Mohr and Beutler (2003) provide several recommendations pertaining to conducting the clinical interview, regardless of the setting or circumstances in which it is conducted. First, there are recommendations pertaining to setting the stage for the interview and the interview environment itself. Included here is a discussion of such things as the purpose of the clinical interview and (assuming the interview is the first procedure in the assessment process) the assessment in general; the questions that will be addressed during the course of the assessment; the patient's impressions of the purpose of the assessment and how the results will be used; potential consequences of the findings; matters pertaining to the patient's right to confidentiality and right to refuse to participate in the evaluation or treatment; and any questions the patient may have as a result of this preliminary discussion. Questions regarding the administrative matters (e.g., completion of standard intake forms, insurance information) can also be addressed. In all, this preliminary discussion serves to instill in the patient a sense of reassurance and freedom regarding the assessment process.

As for the interview itself, Mohr and Beutler (2003) recommend the following:

- Avoid a mechanical approach to covering the desired interview content areas. Maintain a conversational approach to asking questions and eliciting information, modifying the inquiry (as necessary) to ensure a smooth flow or transition from one topic to another.
- Begin exploration of content areas with open-ended inquiries and proceed to closed-ended questions as more specificity and detail are required.

- Consistent with the previous recommendations, move from general topic areas to the more specific ones.
- At the end of the interview, invite the individual to add other information that he or she feels is important for the clinician to know. Also, invite questions and comments about anything related to the interview or the assessment process.
- Provide at least preliminary feedback to the individual based on the information presented during the interview. Arrange for another feedback session after all assessment procedures (e.g., testing, record reviews) have been completed in order to review the final results, conclusions, and recommendations of the assessment.

Similar recommendations are provided by Groth-Marnat (2003).

Key Points to Remember: Keys to Good Clinical Interviewing

- Avoid a mechanical approach to questioning.
- Move from open-ended inquiries to closed-ended inquiries.
- Move from general topics to specific topics.
- Invite the patient to add information and ask questions.
- Provide feedback to the patient.

Note. From Mohr & Beutler (2003).

Clinical Interview Content Areas

This section presents a discussion of the content areas that ideally would be addressed during the course of every assessment. These areas are outlined in the Quick Reference on the next page. However, the content areas or patient factors addressed in a given assessment will vary, depending on a number of factors. Among these are the patient's willingness to be involved in the assessment, the nature and severity of the patient's problems, the clinician's training and experience, the setting in or for which the assessment is being conducted, and time and reimbursement considerations. Consistent with a semistructured approach to clinical interviewing, flexibility and clinical judgment are called for. In some cases, one will want to ensure that certain content areas are thoroughly explored, while in other cases efforts should be directed to obtaining information about other content areas.

The methods for gathering the assessment information also will vary according to the patient, the clinician, and other factors. Some clinicians feel confident in their ability to elicit all necessary assessment information through the clinical interview. (Indeed, some types of assessment information, such as that pertaining to the patient's affect and continuity of thought, are only accessible through the clinical interview.) Others may find it useful or critical to employ adjuncts to the interview process. For example,

Quick Reference: Outline for a Recommended Semistructured Clinical Interview

1. Identifying information
2. Presenting problem/chief complaint
3. History of the problem
4. Family/social history
5. Educational history
6. Employment history
7. Mental health and substance abuse history
8. Medical history
9. Important patient characteristics
   a. Functional impairment
   b. Subjective distress
   c. Problem complexity
   d. Readiness to change
   e. Potential to resist therapeutic influence
   f. Social support
   g. Coping style
   h. Attachment style
10. Patient strengths
11. Mental status
12. Risk of harm to self and others
13. Motivation to change
14. Treatment goals

some psychologists may administer a MMPI-2 to every patient they assess, regardless of the patient or his or her presenting problems. Similarly, some clinicians may request neuropsychological evaluation for anyone suspected of being neurologically impaired. Thus, in the discussion that follows, no single means of gathering specific information for a given content area is required. However, certain methods or sources of information are recommended because they have been found to be useful or otherwise important for obtaining information about specific content areas.

Identifying Information

Much of the information that is typically labeled as identifying in psychological assessment reports is available on standard referral forms or intake questionnaires that the clinician will have in front of him or her at the beginning of the interview. This information typically includes basic demographic data such as name, gender, race, age, marital status, education level, and employment status. Although much of this type of information will come to light during the course of the interview, it is helpful to have as much of this type of information when the interview begins in that it may be used to guide the interview as it progresses.

Presenting Problem/Chief Complaint

One of the first pieces of information that the clinician will want to obtain is the chief problem or complaint that led the patient to seek treatment. This is usually elicited by fairly standard questions such as, "What brings you here today?" or "Why do you think you were referred to a psychologist [or other behavioral health professional]?" Responses to questions such as these can be quite telling and thus should be recorded verbatim. Besides providing immediate insight into what the patient considers the most pressing problems, the patient's response can provide clues as to how distressing these problems are, whether the patient is being seen voluntarily, how motivated the patient may be to work in therapy, and if required, what the patient's expectations for treatment are. Moreover, the contrast between the patient's report, that of the referring professional (if any), and the interviewer's observations can provide additional verification of the degree to which the patient is likely to engage in a therapeutic endeavor (Mohr & Beutler, 2003). In addition, the verbatim response can serve as a kind of baseline against which to measure the gains made from treatment.

History of the Problem

Groth-Marnat (2003) indicated that the main focus of the interview is to define the problem and its causes. This knowledge should include when the patient began experiencing the problem, the patient's perception of the cause of the problem, significant events that occurred at or around that time, its severity, antecedents/precipitants of the problem, what has maintained its presence, and its course over time. Also important is the effect that the problem has had on the patient's ability to function, what the patient has done to try to deal with the problem, and what has and has not been helpful in ameliorating it. Thorough knowledge and understanding of the problem's history can greatly facilitate its treatment.

Mohr and Beutler (2003) recommend that historical information obtained from the patient be cross-validated through other sources of information. This might necessitate interviewing family members or other significant collaterals, reviewing records of past treatment attempts, or reviewing school or employment records. Again, knowing the perceptions of the problem from multiple perspectives permits a more comprehensive understanding of its nature and course.

Family/Social History

Many would argue that an understanding of the patient's problems requires an understanding of the patient within a social context. How did the person who is being evaluated get to this point? What experiences have shaped the patient's ability to interact with others and cope with the demands of daily living? Knowing where the individual came from and where he or she is now vis-à-vis the patient's relationship with the world is critical when developing a plan to improve or at least come to terms with that relationship.

Important aspects of the family history include the occupation and education of parents; number of siblings and birth order; quality of the patient's relationship to parents, siblings, and significant extended family members; parental approach to child rearing (e.g., punitive, demeaning or abusive vs. loving, supportive and rewarding); and parental expectations for the patient's educational, occupational, and social accomplishments. Also important is the physical environment (e.g., type of housing, neighborhood) in which the child was reared, and whether the family was settled or subjected to uprooting or frequent moves (e.g., military families).

The patient's interaction with and experiences in the social environment outside the protection of the home provide clues to the patient's perception of the world, ability to derive comfort and support from others, and ability to cope with the daily, inescapable demands that accompany living and working with others. Information about the general number (a lot vs. a few) and types (close vs. casual) friendships, participation in team sports, involvement in clubs or other social activities, being a leader versus a follower, involvement in religious or political activities, and other opportunities requiring interpersonal interaction can all be insightful. Pointing to the work of Luborsky and Crits-Christoph (1990), Mohr and Beutler (2003) recommend that key relationships—parents or parental figures, siblings, significant relatives, and major love interests—should be explored, in that

> To the degree that similar needs, expectations, and levels of dissatisfaction are found to be working across different relationships, periods of time, and types of relationships, the clinician can infer that the pattern observed is pervasive, chronic/complex, rigid, and ritualistic. That is, the patient's relationships are more dominated by his or her fixed needs than by the nature of the person to whom the patient is relating or the emergence of any particular crisis. Alternatively, if different needs and expectations are found to be expressed in different relationships, it may be inferred that the patient has the ability to be discriminating, flexible, and realistic in social interactions. (Mohr & Beutler, p. 109)

In addition, as relevant, the patient's legal history and experiences stemming from being a member of a racial or ethnic minority should be explored as both can have a significant bearing on the current problems and coping styles. They also may provide information related to the patient's ability to relate well with and take direction from perceived authority figures (such as clinicians).

Educational History

The patient's educational history generally provides limited yet potentially important information. When not readily obvious, the attained level of education can yield a rough estimate of the patient's level of intelligence, an important factor in considering certain types of therapeutic intervention. It also speaks to the patient's aspirations and goals, ability to gain from learning experiences, willingness to make a commitment and persevere, and ability to delay gratification. Participation in both academic and school-related extracurricular activities (e.g., debate or theater clubs, school paper, yearbook staff, and varsity sports) is also worth noting in this regard.

Employment History

A patient's employment history can provide a wealth of information that can be useful in understanding the patient and developing an effective treatment plan. Interactions with supervisors and peers provide insights into the patient's ability to get along with others and take direction. Also, the type of position the patient holds relative to past educational or training experiences or level of intelligence can be enlightening in terms of the patient being a success versus a failure, an overachiever versus an underachiever, motivated to succeed versus just doing the minimum, being an initiator versus needing to be told what to do and when to do it, or being internally versus externally motivated. In addition, the patient's ability to assume the role and meet the expectations of a hired employee (e.g., being at work on time, giving a full day's work, adhering to company policies, respecting company property) may have implications for assuming the role of a patient and complying with treatment recommendations.

Mental Health and Substance Abuse History

It is important to know if the individual has a history of behavioral health problems and treatment. This would include any episodes of care for mental health or substance abuse problems, regardless of the level of care (e.g., inpatient, outpatient, residential) at which treatment for these problems was provided. Records pertaining to previous treatment, including psychological test results, are important in this regard and therefore should always be requested. Obtaining a thorough mental health and substance abuse history can shed light on whether the current problem is part of a single or recurrent episode, or a progression of behavioral health problems over a period of time; what treatment approaches or modalities have worked or not worked in the past; and the patient's willingness to engage in therapeutic interventions.

The cooccurrence of both mental health and substance abuse disorders is not uncommon. A 2005 survey conducted by the Substance Abuse and Mental Health Services Administration (SAMHSA) found that 5.2 million adults, or approximately 2.4% of all adults in the U.S., had both nonspecific psychological distress and a substance use disorder (SAMHSA, 2006). However, patients seeking services for mental health problems might not always know that they have an accompanying substance abuse problem, or they simply may not feel that it is worth mentioning since that is not what they are seeking help for. For these reasons, history taking should always include an inquiry about the patient's use of alcohol and other substances. A detailed exploration is called for when either current or past substance use suggests it is or has been problematic for the patient. Dual diagnosis patients often present unique challenges and warrant special considerations. It is therefore important to identify these individuals early on and ensure that they receive the specialized treatment that is warranted.

Medical History

Obtaining a medical history is always necessary, regardless of the problems that the patient presents. At the minimum, one should inquire about any significant illnesses or hospitalizations, past and current physical illnesses or conditions (e.g., breast cancer), chronic conditions (e.g., diabetes, asthma, migraine headaches), and injuries or disorders affecting the central nervous system (e.g., head injury, stroke), as well as any functional limitations they may impose on the patient. Not only may this provide clues to the presenting symptomatology and functioning (for a discussion of co-morbid psychiatric and medical disorders, see Derogatis & Culpepper, 2004; Derogatis & Fitzpatrick, 2004; Maruish, 2000), it may also suggest the need for referral to a psychiatrist or other medical professional (e.g., neurologist, endocrinologist) for evaluation, treatment, or management. It is also important to identify any current prescribed and over-the-counter medications that the patient is taking, as well as any medications to which the patient is allergic.

In addition, at least a cursory family history for significant medical problems is recommended. Information about blood relatives can reveal a history of genetically transmitted disorders that the patient may be unaware of. This could have a bearing on patient's current problems, or it may suggest a predisposition to develop medical problems in the future that could have negative consequences for the patient's mental health. A family history of illness might also provide insight into the environment in which the patient was raised and the impact of the demands of that environment.

Important Patient Characteristics

From the foregoing discussion, it should be obvious that assessment for the purpose of treatment planning should go beyond the identification and description of the patient's symptoms or problems. The individual's family/ social, psychiatric/medical, educational, and employment histories provide a wealth of information for understanding his or her personality and the origin, development, and maintenance of behavioral health problems. At the same time, other types of information can be quite useful for treatment planning purposes.

For nearly two decades, Beutler and his colleagues (Beutler & Clarkin, 1990; Beutler, Malik, Talebi, Fleming, & Moleiro, 2004; Fisher, Beutler, & Williams, 1999; Harwood & Williams, 2003; Mohr & Beutler, 2003) have worked to develop and promote the use of a system of patient characteristics considered important for treatment planning. According to Beutler et al. (2004),

> To bring some order to the diverse hypotheses associated with the several models of differential treatment assignment and to place them in the perspective of empirical research, Beutler and Clarkin (1990) grouped patient characteristics presented by the different theories into a series of superordinate and subordinate categories. This classification included seven specific classes of patient variables, distinguished both by their susceptibility to measurement using established psychological tests and by their ability to predict differential responses to psychosocial treatment.....To these, we add....an eighth category based on the results of a task force organized by Division 29 [Psychotherapy] of the American Psychological Association....(p. 115)

For this reason, the eight patient predisposing dimensions or variables that power Beutler's *Systematic Treatment Selection (STS)* model merit investigation by the clinician.

Functional Impairment   The degree to which behavioral health patients are impaired in their social, environmental, and interpersonal functioning has been identified as one of the most important factors to consider during an assessment, particularly for the purposes of treatment outcomes programs (Maruish, 2002b, 2004). Much of the information needed for this portion of the assessment can be obtained during the investigation of the patient's family, social, employment, and educational history. However, more in-depth questioning may be required. Not only is social functioning information important for treatment planning and outcomes assessment purposes, it also is critical for arriving at the Global Assessment of Functioning (GAF) rating for Axis V of the Diagnostic and Statistical Manual of Mental Disorders: DSM-IV-TR (4th ed.) Text Revision (American Psychiatric Association, 2000). Clinical indicators of functional impairment that may be observed or reported during the interview include being easily distracted or having difficulty in concentrating on the interview tasks, having difficulty functioning and interacting with the interviewer owing to problem severity, and reporting impaired performance in more than one areas of daily life (Gaw & Beutler, 1995).

Subjective Distress   Subjective distress "is a cross-cutting, cross-diagnostic index of well-being.... [that] is poorly correlated with external measures of impairment.... [It] is a transitory or changeable symptom state..." (Beutler et al., 2004, p. 118). It might be considered a measure of internal functioning separate from the external or objective measure just described, with its importance lying in its relationship with the patient's level of motivation to engage in and benefit from the therapeutic process (Beutler et al., 2004; Gaw & Beutler, 1995). Observable indicators of high distress include motor agitation, hypervigilance, excited affect, and hyperventilation, whereas reduced motor activity, slow or unmodulated verbalizations, blunted affect, low emotional arousal, and low energy level are indicative of low distress (Gaw & Beutler, 1995).

Problem Complexity   According to Beutler et al. (2004), the complexity of a problem can be increased by the presence of any of several factors, including the chronicity of the problem, comorbid diagnoses, the presence of more than one personality disorder, and recurring, pervasive patterns of conflict and other forms of negative interpersonal behavior. Important considerations here are the degree of social disruption and the number and type of life roles that are affected by these problems (Beutler et al., 2003). Whether the patient's presenting problems are high or low with respect to complexity can have an important bearing on treatment planning and prognosis. Ascertaining the level of problem complexity can be facilitated by historical information about other aspects of the patient's life (e.g., mental health, substance abuse history, family and interpersonal history, and employment history).

Readiness to Change   The importance of the patient's readiness to change in the therapeutic process comes from the work of Prochaska and his colleagues (Brogan, Prochaska, & Prochaska, 1999; DiClemente & Prochaska, 1998; Prochaska & Norcross, 2002a, 2002b; Prochaska & Prochaska, 2004; Velicer et al., 2000). They identified six stages which people go through when changing various aspects of their life. These stages apply not only to change that is sought through mental health or substance abuse treatment, but also in nontherapeutic contexts. These stages, in their order of progression, are labeled precontemplation, contemplation, preparation, action, maintenance, and termination. The distinguishing features of each stage are described in the Quick Reference on the next page. The further along in the progression of these stages the individual is, the greater the effort that individual is likely to exert to affect the desired change. The stage at which the patient is at any

Quick Reference: Transtheoretical Model Stages of Change

Stage	Distinguishing Features
Precontemplation	Little or no awareness of problems; little or no serious consideration or intent to change in the foreseeable future; often presents for treatment at the request of or under pressure from another party; change may be exhibited when pressured but reverts to previous behavior when pressure is removed. *Resistance to recognizing or changing the problem* is the hallmark of the precontemplation stage.
Contemplation	Awareness of problem and serious thoughts about working on it, but no commitment to begin to work on it immediately; weighs pros and cons of the problem and its solution. *Serious consideration of problem resolution* is the hallmark of the contemplation stage.
Preparation	Intention to take serious, effective action in the near future (e.g., within a month) and has already taken some action during the past year. *Decision making* is the hallmark of this stage.
Action	Overt modification of behavior, experiences, or environment within the past 6 months in an effort to overcome the problem. *Modification of problem behavior to an acceptable criterion* and *serious efforts to change* are the hallmarks of this stage.
Maintenance	Continuation of change to prevent relapse and consolidate the gains made during the action stage. *Stabilizing behavior change* and *avoiding relapse* are the hallmarks of this stage.
Termination	No temptation to engage in previously problematic behavior and 100% self-efficacy.

Note: From Prochaska, DiClemente, & Norcross (1992) and Prochaska & Prochaska (2004).

point in treatment can have an important bearing on the selection of the most appropriate psychotherapeutic approach.

Potential to Resist Therapeutic Influence Two different types of resistance are subsumed under this characteristic. One is *resistance*, which might be considered a state-like quality in which patients fail to comply with external recommendations or directions (Fisher et al., 1999). In some cases, this may be an indicator of their motivation to engage in treatment. The other is *reactance*, which reflects a more extreme, trait-like form of resistance that stems from patients feeling that their freedom or sense of control is being challenged by external forces. It is manifested in their active opposition (i.e., doing the opposite of what they are requested or directed to do) rather than through a passive, do nothing response during times of perceived threats to personal control. Indicators of reactance can include a history of interpersonal or social conflict, history of a poor response to previous treatment, and resistance to the interviewer's directions and/or interpretations (Gaw & Beutler, 1995).

Social Support   Beutler et al. (2004) discussed the importance of assessing the patient's social support system from both objective and subjective perspectives. *Objective social support* can be assessed from external evidence of resources that are available to the patient. This would include such things as marriage, physical proximity to relatives, a network of identified friends, membership in social organizations, and involvement in religious activities. *Subjective social support* refers to the self-report of such things as the *quality* of the patient's social relationships. In essence, it has to do with the patient's perception of potential sources of psychological and physical support that the patient can draw upon during the episode of care and thereafter. Beutler et al., also suggest that the individual's level of *social investment,* or effort to maintain his or her involvement with others, also may be an important predictor of treatment outcome.

Coping Style   Few would disagree with Beutler and his colleagues' identification of the patient's coping style as an important consideration for treatment planning. Here, coping styles is defined as "a characteristic way of responding to distress.... [that] embody both conscious and unconscious behaviors that endure across situations and times" (Beutler et al., 2004, p. 127). It is conceived as a mechanism falling along a continuum of *internalizing* and *externalizing* behaviors that are employed during times of psychological distress. Generally speaking, internalizers deal with problems by turning their attention inward and thinking or not thinking about problems, whereas externalizers are outward directed and tend to act on or against problems in order to resolve them. Defense mechanisms indicative of internalizers include undoing, intellectualization, denial, reaction formation, repression and somatization, whereas projection and conversion involving secondary gain are more characteristic of externalizers (Gaw & Beutler, 1995).

Attachment Style   The most recently incorporated treatment-relevant patient dimension in the STS model is attachment style. Here, attachment is construed as "the mental representation of one's capacity to form close bonds, to be alone, to achieve balance between autonomy and separation, and to enjoy intimacy" (Beutler et al., 2004, p. 129). Attachment styles can be classified into one of four types (secure, preoccupied, fearful, and dismissive) based on the dimensions of avoidance and anxiety. They can affect the individual's ability to form a relationship with a therapist and, consequently, can impact the outcome of treatment, although Beutler et al. point out that the American Psychological Association Division 29 Task Force on Empirically Supported Therapy Relations indicated that more evidence is required to conclude that treatment outcomes would be improved by tailoring the therapeutic relationship to the patient's attachment style.

Patient Strengths

Recall that Beutler et al. (2003) indicated that the identification of an individual's strengths and resources is one common question that accompanies requests for psychological assessment. Often, however, questions accompanying referrals for assessments are typically focused on uncovering the negative aspects of the patient, often to the neglect of the patient's more positive aspects (Snyder, Ritschel, Rand, & Berg, 2006). Groth-Marnat and Horvath (2006) note that by taking such a problem-oriented approach, the clinician runs the risk of overpathologizing the individual. Thus, for treatment planning and other purposes, it is just as important to focus on identifying the patient's strengths as it is the patient's deficits. Many clinicians may find this difficult to do since, as Lehnhoff (1991) indicated in speaking about *strength-focused assessment,* clinicians typically are not trained in uncovering patient successes. As he noted,

> Clinicians traditionally ask themselves, What causes the worst moments and how can we reduce them. They might then go on to scrutinize the pathology and the past. But one could also ask, What causes the patient's best moments and how can we increase them? Or similarly, Why is the patient not having more bad moments, how does the patient regain control after losing it, and why doesn't he lose control more often? Clearly, the strength-focused view of a patient seeks, for one thing, to uncover the reasons the pathology is not worse. The view assumes that almost any clinical condition varies in its intensity over time ..... (p. 12)

At the same time, Lehnhoff (1991) noted how the inclusion of the highest-level-of-functioning rating provided on Axis V into the multi axial schema of the *DSM-IV-TR* is evidence of the behavioral healthcare field's recognition of the importance of patient coping strengths. He provides a number of examples of questions that can be used to help both the clinician and the patient identify strengths that might not otherwise come to light. Some of these questions are presented in the Quick Reference on the next page.

In assessing strengths, Mohr and Beutler (2003) encourage the clinician to consider not only the individual's adaptive capacities, skills and past ac-

Quick Reference: Questions That Help Assess Patient Strengths

- I've been hearing mostly about how bad things are for you, but I'd like to balance the view I have of you. What kinds of things do you do well?
- Now that we've discussed some things about your symptoms and stresses, I'd like to learn more about some of your satisfactions and successes. What are some good things you have enjoyed doing well?
- To get a more complete picture of your situation, I now need to know more about when the problem does not happen.
- What have you noticed you do that has helped in the past?
- Which of your jobs lasted the longest? What did you do to help this happen?
- Right now, some things are keeping you from doing worse than you are. What are they?
- Which of your good points do you most often forget?

Note: From Lehnhoff (1991, pp. 13–14).

complishments but also the presence of his or her family members, reference organizations, and future hopes. Together, these assets can help identify the individual's ability to deal with stressors and motivate change. However, the benefits of assessing patient strengths go beyond this. The act of forcing patients to consider their psychological assets can have therapeutic value in itself (Lehnhoff, 1991). Essentially, strength-focused assessment can serve as an intervention before formal treatment actually begins. Consequently, it can help build self-esteem and self-confidence, reinforce patients' efforts to seek help, and increase their motivation to return to engage in the work of treatment.

Mental Status Examination

Any clinical assessment should include a mental status examination (MSE). Completion of the MSE usually takes place at the end of the clinical interview. For the most part, however, the information needed for an MSE comes from the clinician's observations of and impressions formed about the patient during the course of the clinical interview and as a result of other assessment procedures (e.g., psychological testing). However, some aspects of the MSE usually require specific questioning that typically would not be included during the other parts of the assessment.

The MSE generally addresses a number of general categories or aspects of the patient's functioning, including the following: description of the patient's appearance and behavior, mood and affect, perception, thought processes, orientation, memory, judgment, and insight (see Quick Reference on page 54). Trzepacz and Baker (1993) provide an excellent, detailed description of each of these general categories. Also, a general overview of the mental

Quick Reference: Areas Addressed in the Mental Status Examination

1. *Appearance* (level of arousal, attentiveness, age, position, posture, attire, grooming, eye contact, physical characteristics, facial expression)
2. *Activity* (movement, tremor, choreoathetoid movements, dystonias, automatic movements, tics, mannerisms, compulsions, other motor abnormalities or expressions)
3. *Attitude toward the clinician*
4. *Mood* (euthymic, angry, euphoric, apathetic, dysphoric, apprehensive)
5. *Affect* (appropriateness, intensity, mobility, range, reactivity)
6. *Speech and language* (fluency, repetition, comprehension, naming, writing, reading, prosody, quality of speech)
7. *Thought process* (circumstantiality, flight of ideas, loose associations, tangentiality, word salad, clang associations, ecolalia, neologisms, perseveration, thought blocking)
8. *Thought content* (delusion, homicidal/suicidal ideation, magical thinking, obsession, rumination, preoccupation, overvalued idea, paranoia, phobia, poverty of speech, suspiciousness)
9. *Perception* (autoscopy, déjà vu, depersonalization, hallucination, illusion, jamais vu)
10. *Cognition* (orientation, attention, concentration, immediate recall, short-term memory, long-term memory, constructional ability, abstraction, conceptualization)
11. *Insight* (awareness of problems and feelings, appreciation of consequences of actions)
12. *Judgment* (history of poor decision making, acting out)
13. *Defense mechanisms* (altruism, humor, sublimation, suppression, repression, displacement, dissociation, reaction formation, intellectualization, splitting, externalization, projection, acting out, denial, distortion)

Note: From Trzepacz & Baker (1993).

status examination is provided by Groth-Marnat (2003). As Ginsberg (1985) has indicated, the manner in which the MSE is conducted will depend on the individual clinician, who may decide to forego certain portions of the examination because of the circumstances of the particular patient. At the same time, he recommended that the MSE be conducted in detail, and that the patient's own words be recorded whenever possible.

Risk of Harm to Self and Others

Suicidal or homicidal ideation and potential should always be assessed, even if it consists of nothing more than asking the question, "Have you been having thoughts of harming yourself or others?" If the answer is "yes," further probing about how long the patient has been having these thoughts, how frequently they occur, previous and current plans or attempts, and opportunities to act on the thoughts (e.g., owning a gun) is warranted. Even when the individual denies any such thoughts, one may wish to carefully pursue this line of questioning with those who have a greater likelihood of suicidal or homicidal acting out. For example, individuals with major depression, especially when there is a clear element of hopelessness to the clinical picture, and paranoid individuals who perceive potential harm to themselves or have a history of violent acts, both would justify further exploration for signs of potential suicidal or homicidal tendencies.

Suicide risk factors have been identified in numerous publications. Bryan and Rudd (2006) provide an excellent discussion of areas to be covered during a suicide risk assessment interview (as summarized in the Quick Reference below). This discussion provides general recommendations regarding how to conduct the interview as well as specific probes for assessing some of these areas. The American Psychiatric Association (2003) also offers guidance with regard to the assessment of suicidality. Note that the presence of any given risk factor should always be considered in light of *all* available information about the individual.

Motivation to Change

An important factor to assess for treatment planning purposes is the patient's motivation to change. Arriving at a good estimate of the level of motivation can be derived from several pieces of information. One, of course, is whether

---

Quick Reference: Suicide Risk Assessment Considerations

- *Predisposition to suicide* (e.g., previous history of suicidal behavior or psychiatric diagnosis)
- *Precipitants or stressors* (e.g., health problems, significant loss)
- *Symptomatic presentation* (e.g., major mood disorder or schizophrenia, borderline or antisocial personality disorder)
- *Presence of hopelessness* (severity and duration)
- *Nature of suicidal thinking* (e.g., intensity, specific plans, availability of means)
- *Previous suicidal behavior* (e.g., frequency, context, means of previous attempts)
- *Impulsivity and self-control* (e.g., engagement in impulsive behaviors, use of alcohol or drugs)
- *Protective factors* (e.g., access to family or friends for support, reasons for living)

Note: From Bryan & Rudd (2006).

Caution

- Cross-validate historical information reported by patients for accuracy.
- Mental health patients might not always know when a co-morbid substance abuse problem exists.
- Don't overlook the patient's strengths.
- Always assess for suicidal and homicidal ideation.

seeking treatment stems from the patient's desire for help or the request (or demand) of another party. Another obvious clue is the patient's stated willingness to be actively involved in treatment, regardless of whether the treatment is voluntarily sought or not. Answers to questions such as "What are you willing to do to solve your problems?" can be quite revealing.

There are also other types of information that can assist in the assessment of patient motivation to change. Among them are the patient's subjective distress and reactance as well as the patient's readiness for, or stage of change, both of which were discussed earlier. In discussing the issue, Morey (2004) pointed to seven factors identified by Sifneos (1987) that should be considered in the evaluation of motivation to engage in treatment. Morey summarized them as follows:

1. A willingness to participate in the diagnostic evaluation.
2. Honesty in reporting about oneself and one's difficulties.
3. Ability to recognize that the symptoms experienced are psychological in nature.
4. Introspectiveness and curiosity about one's own behavior and motives.
5. Openness to new ideas, with a willingness to consider different attitudes.
6. Realistic expectations for the results of treatment.
7. Willingness to make a reasonable sacrifice in order to achieve a successful outcome (p. 1098).

Some of these factors may not be able to be fully assessed until treatment has actually begun. However, the clinician should be able to form at least a tentative opinion about the patient on each of them based on the interactions that take place during the assessment.

Treatment Goals

No clinical interview conducted in a treatment setting would be complete without the identification of treatment goals. In most cases, the goals for treatment are obvious. For example, for patients who complain of anxiety or depression, cannot touch a door knob without subsequently washing their hands, hear voices or feel that their spouses are trying to kill them, it goes without saying that the amelioration of the unwanted behaviors or other symptomatology that led them to seek treatment becomes a goal. But this may not be the only goal, nor may it be the primary goal from their standpoint. A quick, efficient way to obtain at least a preliminary indication of the individual's goals for treatment is to ask him or her directly. One managed care company (United Behavioral Systems, 1994, p. 8) recommends using three simple questions:

- What do you see as your biggest problem?
- What do you want to be different about your life at the end of your treatment?
- Does this goal involve changing things about you?

The inclusion of the last question can serve two purposes. First, it forces individuals to think through their problems and realize the extent to which they have control over their thoughts, feelings, and behavior. In short, it can provide a means for individuals to gain insight into their problems—a

Important References

Beutler, L. E., Malik, M., Talebi, H., Fleming, J., & Moleiro, C. (2004). Use of psychological tests/instruments for treatment planning. In M. E. Maruish (Ed.), *The use of psychological testing for treatment planning and outcomes* assessment: *Volume 1. General considerations* (3rd ed., pp. 111–145). Mahwah, NJ: Erlbaum. This chapter discusses how psychological test results may be predictive of differential response to an outcome of treatment. The discussion is organized around the predisposing patient factors or dimensions that were originally introduced by Beutler and Clarkin and later expanded upon by others.

Groth-Marnat, G. (2003). *Handbook of psychological assessment* (4th ed.). Hoboken, NJ: Wiley. This handbook includes a detailed chapter on the clinical interview as part of the psychological assessment process. Included are a history of development of interviews during the past century, recommended interview topics, considerations related to interpreting interview data, and an overview of some of the more commonly used structured interviews.

Maruish, M. E. (2002a). *Essentials of treatment planning.* New York: Wiley. This book provides a guide to gathering and integrating clinical interview and psychological testing information for the purpose of developing treatment plans. Monitoring patient progress after initiation of the plan and when to modify the treatment plan is also addressed.

Mohr, D., & Beutler, L. E. (2003). The integrative clinical interview. In L. E. Beutler, & G. Groth-Marnat (Eds.), *Integrative assessment of adult personality* (2nd ed., pp. 82–122). New York: Guilford. This chapter provides a general overview of structured, unstructured, and semistructured clinical interviews. A detailed outline and guide to conducting an integrated, semistructured interview are then presented.

Trzepacz, P. T., & Baker, R. W. (1993). *The psychiatric mental status examination.* New York: Oxford University Press. This book provides a detailed guide to conducting the mental status examinations. The inclusion of a glossary of terms within each chapter as well as case vignettes facilitates the learning how to conduct mental status exams in clinical practice.

therapeutic goal in and of itself. In addition, it elicits information about their motivation to become active participants in the therapeutic endeavor.

Structured Clinical Interviews

Summerfeldt and Antony (2002) noted that interest in the use of structured interviews has greatly increased since the 1970s, stemming from the recognition of and dissatisfaction with the unreliability of diagnoses that come from unstructured interviews. The standardization of the format, content, question order, and diagnostic algorithms afforded by structured interviews provided a solution to variation that resulted in unreliable diagnoses that are derived from unstructured interviews. Thus, although the focus of this chapter has been on the semistructured clinical interview, consideration of some commonly used structured clinical interviews is warranted.

Note that what is considered a *structured* interview by some may be considered a *semistructured* interview by others. Two of instruments that are discussed in this section—the Primary Care Evaluation of Mental Disorders (PRIME-MD) and the Structured Clinical Interview for DSM-IV Axis I Disorders (SCID-I)—have been identified as semistructured interviews by Rogers (2001) and Summerfeldt and Antony (2002). This appears to be based on the fact that some degree of probing in follow-up to some responses is permitted, and/or encouraged, in order to obtain accurate information. Regardless, the specific questions that must be asked as part of the interview, the branching rules that are used to guide the clinical inquiry, and the degree to which the interviewer is constrained in his or her questioning all lead this author to consider these interviews as being structured.

As each of these instruments is discussed, one common element will become apparent: the purpose of each is to be able to assign, with at least a minimally acceptable degree of accuracy, a diagnosis according to criteria. In these cases, the diagnostic system to which each is tied is the *DSM-IV*. The focus is on the presence, etiology, severity, and/or length of time one has been experiencing symptoms of diagnostic importance. Other symptoms and aspects of the individual's life are not inquired about except when necessary to determine whether the individual meets relevant diagnostic criteria. Therein lies the major limitation of this type of clinical interview to the assessment process.

Primary Care Evaluation of Mental Disorders (PRIME-MD)

Probably the best known of the structured interviews designed specifically for use in primary care settings is the Primary Care Evaluation of Mental Disorders, or PRIME-MD (Hahn, Sydney, Kroenke, Williams, & Spitzer, 2004; Spitzer et al., 1994). The PRIME-MD consists of two instruments that are used for two-staged screening and diagnosis. The first instrument administered, the Patient Questionnaire (PQ), is a patient self -report screener consisting of 26 items that assess for symptoms of mental disorders or problems that are commonly seen in primary care settings. The general areas screened for include: *somatization, depression, anxiety, alcoholism, eating disorder,* and *health status.*

The PQ essentially is a case-finding tool. Upon completion of the PQ, the physician scans the answer sheet to determine if the individual's responses suggest that he or she may have a specific *DSM-IV* diagnosis in one of the five targeted areas. If so, the physician administers relevant modules from the second part of the PRIME-MD, the Clinical Evaluation Guide (CEG), to the individual during the visit. For example, if the patient responds to either of the two depression screening questions from the PQ in a manner suggestive of the possible presence of a depressive disorder, the physician would administer the mood module from the CEG to the individual while in the examining room. The mood module, like the other four disorder-specific modules, is a structured interview consisting of yes/no branching questions that assess for the presence of each of the criteria for major depressive disorder, partial remission of major depressive disorder, dysthymia, and minor depressive disorder, with rule-outs for bipolar disorder and depressive disorder due to physical disorder, medication, or other drug. If other responses to the questions on the PQ suggest the possibility of the presence of *DSM-IV* diagnoses in any of the other four broad diagnostic areas, the modules related to the areas in questioned are also administered by the physician.

The major findings from the published research support the use of the PRIME-MD in primary care settings. Among them are the following:

- The overall rate of agreement between PRIME-MD diagnoses made by PCPs and diagnoses made within 48 hours of the PRIME-MD visit by mental health professionals using semistructured, blinded telephone interviews was relatively good for any psychiatric diagnosis in general (kappa = .71), as well as any mood, anxiety, alcohol, and eating disorder (kappa = .55–.73; Spitzer et al., 1994). Kappa coefficients for specific disorders ranged from .15 to .71. The diagnoses made by mental health professionals are considered the standard against which physician-determined PRIME-MD diagnoses are assessed. Because of the lack of medical training on the part of the mental health professionals, somatoform disorders were not considered in these or similar analyses.
- For specific diagnoses, sensitivities ranged from .22 for minor depressive disorder to .81 for probable alcohol abuse/dependence (Spitzer et al., 1994). Specificities ranged from .91 for anxiety disorder NOS to .98

for major depressive disorder and probable alcohol abuse/dependence. The high specificities obtained across the CEG modules indicate that physicians using the PRIME-MD rarely make false positive diagnoses. Positive predictive values ranged from .19 for minor depressive disorder to .80 for major depressive disorder.

- The prevalence of threshold mental disorders diagnosed by the PRIME-MD were quite similar to those obtained from the mental health professionals' telephone interviews (Spitzer et al., 1994).
- Using diagnoses made by mental health providers as the criteria, the PQ was found to have sensitivities ranging from 69% for the mood module to 94% for the anxiety module; positive predictive values (PPVs) ranging from 27% for the alcohol module to 62% for the mood module; and overall accuracy rates ranging from 60% for the anxiety module to 91% for the alcohol module (Spitzer et al., 1994).
- The sensitivity and specificity for the PQ two-item depression screen to major depression was essentially identical to that of the Zung Self-Rating Depression Scale, which was also administered to the same sample (Spitzer et al., 1994).
- Using the Short Form General Health Survey (SF-20; Stewart, Hays, & Ware, 1988), Spitzer et al. (1994) and Spitzer et al. (1995) also found that health-related quality of life (HRQOL) was related to severity of PRIME-MD-identified psychopathology. Thus, individuals with threshold disorders had significantly more HRQOL-related impairment than those who were symptom-screen negative, those who had symptoms but no diagnosis, and those with subthreshold diagnoses.
- Johnson et al.'s (1995) findings supported those of Spitzer et al. (1994) and Spitzer et al. (1995). Johnson et al. found that patients from the same PRIME-MD 1000 Study with CEG-diagnosed alcohol abuse and dependence (AAD) with a comorbid psychiatric disorder reported worse HRQOL impairment than those with ADD and no co-occurring psychiatric diagnosis on five of the six SF-20 scales. When compared to patients with no ADD or psychiatric diagnosis, their reported HRQL was worse on all six SF-20 scales.

The reader is referred to Hahn et al. (2004) for an excellent detailed overview of the major PRIME-MD development and validation research that has been conducted to this point. As a summary of these and other research findings, Hahn et al. indicated that

When the PRIME-MD is administered to an unselected group of primary care patients, 80% will trigger at least one module of the CEG. In half of those evaluations, the physician will be rewarded by the confirmation of a mental disorder. Two thirds of these disorders will meet criteria for a *DSM-IV* diagnosis, and the remaining third will have a minor, or "subthreshold," disorder. If the physician is familiar with the patient, the yield of new diagnoses will still double the number of patients whose psychopathology is detected. Finally, there is strong evidence that even previously detected disorders will be more specifically and precisely identified. (p. 268)

There may be other uses of the PRIME-MD that have not yet been empirically investigated but which should also benefit other types of medical patients. This might include those being seen by medical specialists or being followed in disease management programs. Also, one might consider administering only portions of the instrument. For example, the PQ might be used as a routine screener, to be followed by an unstructured or semistructured clinical interview regardless of the results. Similarly, a practice interested in increasing its providers' detection of mood disorders may wish to forgo the administration of the PQ and administer the CEG mood module to all patients.

Overall, research on the PRIME-MD to date supports its utility as a means for busy physicians to greatly improve their ability to screen/case-find, and diagnose patients with behavioral health disorders that commonly present themselves in primary care settings. With the exception of diagnosing somatoform disorders, this same instrument can be used by behavioral health-care professionals seeing patients in this type of setting. Case-finding and diagnosing somatoform disorders according to PRIME-MD results, require medical knowledge that non-physician behavioral healthcare professionals typically do not have.

Structured Clinical Interview for DSM-IV Axis I Disorders (SCID)

According to Summerfeldt and Antony (2002), the Structured Clinical Interview for *DSM-IV* Axis I Disorders (SCID) was, like its predecessors, designed to be consistent with the Axis I diagnostic criteria of the current version of the American Psychiatric Association's *Diagnostic and Statistical Manual,* beginning with the *DSM-III.* There are two versions of the *DSM-IV* instrument: the SCID-CV (clinician version; First, Spitzer, Gibbon, & Williams, 1997) and the SCID-I (research version; First, Spitzer, Gibbon, & Williams, 1996). The SCID-I itself comes in three versions: SCID-I/P for subjects known to be psychiatric patients; SCID-I/P with Psychotic Screen, a shortened version of the SCID-I/P; and the SCID-I/NP for use in studies where the subjects are not assumed to be psychiatric patients (i.e., community surveys). The SCID-CV addresses the criteria for only the most commonly seen disorders in clinical settings. The SCID can be supplemented with the

SCID-II (First, Gibbon, Spitzer, Williams, & Benjamin, 1997) for assessing for *DSM-IV* Axis II personality disorders.

The SCID-CV is appropriate for use with psychiatric and general medical patients as well as non-patients from the community (First, Gibbon, Spitzer, Williams, & MHS Staff, 1998). Clinicians may administer all nine diagnostic modules—Mood Episodes, Psychotic Symptoms, Psychotic Disorders Differential, Mood Disorders Differential, Substance Use Disorders, Anxiety Disorders, Somatoform Disorder, Eating Disorders, and Adjustment Disorders—or just the modules that are relevant to the individual (Summerfeldt & Antony, 2002). In addition, the SCID-CV has an Overview Section which is used to gather other types of information (e.g., demographic information, work history, current problems, treatment history).

Each module is hierarchically organized with decision-tree rules to guide the questioning and for discontinuing the administration (Rogers, 2001). Inquiries include standard questions, branched questions (based on known information), optional probes (for clarification of ratings of criteria), and as necessary, unstructured questions for clarification purposes. Symptoms are scored as either absent/false, subthreshold (criterion not fully being met), or threshold/true (criterion met). Note that not all *DSM-IV* Axis I diagnostic criteria (e.g., sleep and sexual disorders, dissociative disorders) are covered by the questioning.

In Rogers' (2001) summary of reliabilities found in his review of 11 studies in the published literature, he found interrater reliability kappa coefficients for current diagnosis ranging from .67 to .94, 2-week test-retest reliabilities of .68 and .51 for lifetime diagnosis, and 1-week test-retest reliability of .87 for symptoms. Although most of the studies reviewed were based on the *DSM-III-R* version of the SCID, both Rogers and Summerfeldt and Antony (2002) believe that the changes incorporated in the *DSM-IV* version were minimal enough that the findings would be comparable. From their review of the literature, Summerfeldt and Antony indicated that "In general, acceptable joint reliabilities (kappa > .70) have been reported in most studies for disorders commonly seen in clinical settings, such as major depressive disorder and the anxiety disorders, including generalized anxiety disorder and panic disorder and its subtypes. Patient characteristics may also have an impact on SCID reliabilities" (p. 28).

Both Rogers (2001) and Summerfeldt and Antony (2002) have noted that little attention has been paid to the concurrent validity of the SCID because of the close correspondence of its content with the DSM diagnostic criteria. However, in concurrent validity studies reported by Rogers, he noted findings such as:

- A kappa coefficient of .83 for diagnoses from the SCID and those assigned by senior psychiatrists (Maziade et al., 1992).
- The ability of the SCID to accurately identify 85% of bipolar disorders and 77% of schizophrenic disorders in a sample of 48 outpatients (Duncan, 1987), outperforming the Diagnostic Interview Schedule (DIS; see below) but agreeing only modestly with results from systematic clinical record reviews.
- Median kappas of .56 for commonly occurring substance abuse disorders and .22 for anxiety and mood disorders as well as an overall diagnostic agreement rate of 83.9% in a study involving the SCID and the Computerized DIS (C-DIS; Ross, Swinson, Larkin, & Doumani, 1994). In a similar study involving the Mini International Neuropsychiatric Interview (MINI), Sheehan et al. (1997) found kappas of .67 for 15 current disorders and .73 for 7 life-time disorders.

In reviewing some of the studies offering evidence of convergent validity, Rogers (2001) cited supportive evidence in those involving PTSD (e.g., Constans, Lenhoff, & McCarthy, 1997), panic disorders (e.g., Maier, Buller, Sonntag, & Heuser, 1986), depression (e.g., Stuckenberg, Dura, & Kiecolt-Glaser, 1990), and substance abuse (Kranzler, Kadden, Babor, Tennen, & Rounsaville, 1996).

Rogers (2001) also found that the utility of the SCID over traditional interviews was investigated in studies such as those conducted by Zimmerman and Mattia (1999) and Schwenk, Coyne, and Fechner-Bates (1996). Zimmerman and Mattia's comparison of 500 traditional interviews to 500 SCID interviews conducted on patients (with similar demographics and symptom scores) in a general adult psychiatric practice found that while more than one third of the SCID group were assigned three or more Axis I diagnoses, only 10% of the traditionally interviewed patients were assigned three or more diagnoses. Schwenk et al. found that primary care physicians failed to diagnose SCID-identified major depression in patients who screened positive for mild (81.6%), moderate (62.1%), or severe (26.7%) depression using the Center for Epidemiologic Studies–Depression (CES-D) scale.

In summarizing the SCID, both Rogers (2001) and Summerfeldt and Antony (2001) note that it has the widest coverage of any such instruments that is consistent with the *DSM-IV* inclusion criteria. At the same time, it does not cover all *DSM-IV* diagnoses. Also, it evaluates only for the criteria necessary to arrive at these diagnoses at the expense of ignoring important symptoms or subthreshold conditions that may be present. It also may be susceptible to response styles and faking. Rogers described the SCID as a "well-validated Axis I interview.... [that] should be given strong consideration in settings in which the emphasis is on current diagnosis rather than symptomatology" (p. 116).

Diagnostic Interview Schedule-IV (DIS-IV)

Another commonly used structured interview is the Diagnostic Interview Schedule-IV (DIS-IV; Robins et al., 1995). Although similar to the SCID in terms of its focus on *DSM-IV* Axis I symptoms and diagnostic criteria (with earlier versions being consistent with earlier versions of the *DSM*), Summerfeldt and Antony (2002) note important differences between the two interviews. Unlike the SCID, the DIS-IV was designed to be administered by either professional or lay interviewers in large-scale epidemiology studies. Rogers (2001) notes that it differs from other diagnostic interviews in its attempt to identify organic etiologies, formal assessment of cognitive impairment, and retention of other diagnostic criteria (e.g., Research Diagnostic Criteria [RDC]). Its 19 modules cover 30 *DSM-IV* Axis I and Axis II diagnoses. Each queried symptom is assigned a score of 1 through 5: did not occur (1); lacking clinical significance (2); significant symptom due to medication, drug, or alcohol use (3); significant symptom due to physical illness or injury (4); and significant symptom likely due to psychiatric disorder (5). The interviewer also asks about the onset, frequency, and recency of any clinically significant symptom likely due to a psychiatric disorder. Originally intended as a research instrument, it is now used for both clinician and lay interviewers in clinical and research settings.

Rogers' (2001) review of the DIS reported on only one reliability study for the DIS-IV while summarizing several other studies which investigated the reliability of earlier versions of the instrument. First, Horton, Compton, and Cottler (1998) investigated the reliability of the DIS-IV with 140 substance abusers using 10-day retest interval. They obtained a median kappa of .47 for symptoms or symptom constellations and a median kappa of .61 for lifetime diagnoses related to four substance abuse diagnoses. Earlier studies employing earlier versions of the DIS related to *DSM-III* and *DSM-III-R* with several different types of populations seen in several types of settings revealed test-retest kappas for agreement between lay and professional interviewers ranging from .57 to .69 for current diagnoses and .49 for lifetime diagnoses. Test-retest correlations using lay interviewers ranged from .46 to .53 for current diagnoses and .43 for lifetime diagnoses; for professional interviewers, these correlations were found to be .82 and .50, respectively. Interrater reliabilities among lay interviewers were high for both current diagnoses (.89) and lifetime diagnoses (.95).

Rogers' (2001) review of research on the concurrent validity of earlier English language versions (versions II and III) of the DIS revealed that kappa correlations for overall agreement between DIS diagnoses and psychiatrist-assigned diagnoses ranged from .07 to .38, which is lower than the .40 to .50 range often found in these types of studies. Kappas for major diagnostic categories in these same studies showed variation, ranging from .06 to .69 for substance use diagnoses, .15 to .53 for psychotic disorders, .05 to .38 for anxiety disorders, and .17 to .37 for mood disorders.

As for convergent validity, Rogers (2001) cites some of the key studies related to major diagnostic groups. Zimmerman and Coryell (1988) reported a kappa of .80 in a large study ($N = 613$) investigating the concordance of DIS-assigned major depression and depression indicated by the Inventory to Diagnose Depression. Even after a 2-week interval, Whisman et al. (1989) achieved a kappa of .89 for convergence of depression symptoms indicated by the DIS and an interview version of the Hamilton Depression Rating Scale. For assigned alcohol abuse/dependence disorders, the DIS correlated with the Michigan Alcoholism Screening Test and Alcohol Dependence Scale at .65 and .58 , respectively (Ross, Gavin, & Skinner, 1990); for substance abuse disorders, the DIS correlated with the Drug Abuse Screening tests at .75 (Gavin, Ross, & Skinner, 1989). For psychotic disorders, median kappas were achieved for the DIS with the Inpatient Multidimensional Psychiatric Scale (.47) and the Assessment and Documentation of Psychopathology (.31) based on interviews with 291 inpatients (Spengler & Wittchen, 1988).

Both Rogers (2001) and Summerfeldt and Antony (2002) point out the discrepancy between the DIS's sensitivity and specificity. As Rogers noted, "In general, practitioners can have greater confidence in establishing the absence [specificity] than the presence [sensitivity] of a DIS diagnosis" (p. 70). Note that the validity and reliability findings reported by these authors are based on findings using earlier versions of the instrument. Studies utilizing the current version may reveal more positive findings. Rogers and Summerfeldt and Antony also agree that like the SCID-I, the DIS-IV is vulnerable to response styles due to the face validity of its items, and it focuses on diagnoses rather than symptomatology. Because of this and the time required for administration (90-120 minutes), the DIS is felt to be of limited usefulness in clinical settings.

The PRIME-MD, SCID, and DIS are just a few of several structured interviews that are available. Some interviews, such as the Diagnostic Interview Schedule for Children (DISC; Columbia DISC Development Group, 1999) and the Diagnostic Interview for Children and Adolescents (DICA; Reich, Welner, Herjanic, & MHS Staff, 1997), were developed for use with children. Others, such as the International Personality Disorder Examination (IPDE; Loranger, 1999) and Structured Interview for DSM-IV Personality Disorders SCID-II; First, Gibbon, et al., 1997), were developed for the purpose of differential diagnosis of DSM Axis II personality disorders.

Integrating Interview Findings with Findings from Other Sources

Can one rely solely on the clinical interview for the information needed to conduct a thorough personality assessment? The answer is clearly *no*. Derogatis and Savitz (1999) have noted that

> before an effective treatment plan can be developed, a clinician must know as much as possible about the nature and magnitude of the patient's presenting condition. Diagnostic interviews, medical records, psychological testing, and interviews with relatives all represent sources of information that facilitate the development of an effective treatment plan. Rarely is information from a single modality (e.g., psychological testing) definitive. Ideally, each source provides an increment of unique information that, taken collectively with data from other sources, contributes to an ultimate understanding of the case at hand. (pp. 690–691)

Whether or not the individual is being evaluated for treatment planning purposes, Derogatis and Savitz's comments are relevant in all instances in which the goal of assessment is an ultimate understanding of the case at hand.

As evidenced in other chapters of this book, psychological testing can serve as an important source of clinical information. The standardized manner in which test data is gathered, along with the validity, reliability and normative data that support the conclusions drawn from test administration, provides a value-added dimension to clinical assessment. With information obtained during the clinical interview and from other sources, test-based information can assist in understanding the individual, his or her personality and problems, and the treatment planning process, including problem identification and clarification, identification of important patient characteristics that can facilitate or hinder treatment, and monitoring treatment progress.

Essentially, data from the clinical interview, psychological testing, and other sources of information complement each other. In addition to the unique contribution alluded to above, test data may serve as a source of hypotheses about the patient while data from other sources can be used to support or reject those hypotheses. Similarly, test data can be used to validate information obtained from other sources. Moreover, as Meyer et al. (2001) have observed, a growing body of findings support the value of combining data from more than one type of assessment method, even when these methods disagree within or across individuals" (p. 153).

Just as it is important to remember that psychological test data should not be used in isolation from other data, it is also important to remember that there are times when psychological testing may not be called for in the assessment of a mental health or substance abuse patient. As Meyer et al. (2001) indicate, "the key that determines when [psychological testing] is appropriate is the rationale for using specific instruments with a particular patient under a unique set of circumstances to address a distinctive set of referral questions" (p. 129).

Diagnosis and Related Considerations

Assignment of diagnoses to mental health and substance abuse patients has long been an objectionable activity for many behavioral healthcare professionals. Some feel that it demeans patients to label them as belonging to a specific group to which general, often negative, characterizations and expectations have been assigned. This problem is exacerbated by the fact that labels (and the implications thereof) may accompany patients throughout their lives. Others feel that by labeling patients, their individuality is ignored. Still other clinicians feel that diagnoses have no bearing on the treatment that patients receive (Beutler et al., 2004; Jongsma & Peterson, 1999). At the same time, there have been efforts by the American Psychological Association to identify efficacious treatments that are tied to specific diagnostic groups (see Chambless et al., 1996, 1998; Task Force on Promotion and Dissemination of Psychological Procedures, 1995), suggesting that at least in some instances, an accurate diagnosis can have important implications in the development of an effective course of treatment.

Regardless, the fact is that third-party payers and many other stakeholders who are influential in the treatment of patients (e.g., accreditation bodies, regulatory agencies) require that they be assigned a diagnosis. Currently, the use of the diagnostic classification system presented in the *DSM-IV-TR* (American Psychiatric Association, 2000) is usually required in the United States and several other countries. Its multiaxial system permits a more descriptive, individualized presentation of the patients than may be found in other diagnostic systems. Consequently, the use of the *DSM-IV-TR*'s five axes to report diagnosis-related information about the patient can provide a means addressing some of the limitations and objections raised by critics of diagnostic systems.

The requirement for a diagnosis will not disappear any time in the foreseeable future—nor should it. Diagnoses based on a common system of classification criteria continue to be important, efficient tools for communicating among professionals and organizations, a fact that has tremendous implications for those involved in the clinical, research, or administrative aspects of behavioral healthcare provision. Information obtained from the semistructured clinical interview model described in this chapter, supported by information from psychological testing or other sources, should enable the clinician to form at least a working diagnostic impression that can help guide him or her in the initial therapeutic efforts.

Case Vignette

Following are the findings from a clinical interview with a hypothetical mental health patient, Mary Smith. They are organized in a manner that is consistent with the recommended outline presented in the Quick Reference on page 43. This can serve as a generic model for developing a written report of information obtained from a semistructured clinical interview. Modifications to this model (e.g., elimination of MMPI-2 scale names and T scores) may be necessary depending on the purpose of and intended audience for the report.

Identifying Information

Mary Smith is a 28-year-old white, married female who is a student at the Acme University School of Law. She was referred to this clinic by the university's student counseling center after it was determined that Ms. Smith is experiencing problems that the counseling center would not be able to effectively treat.

Presenting Problem

When asked what prompted her to seek psychological treatment, Ms. Smith indicated, "I can't get these thoughts out of my head. I can't concentrate. It's getting worse and it's affecting my ability to study. I don't know what I'll do if I flunk out of school."

History of the Problem

Ms. Smith described a history of obsessive thinking and accompanying compulsive behavior dating back to the beginning of puberty in early adolescence. Messages about sex that were conveyed by her religious parents and her parochial school teachers made her feel guilty and anxious about the normal thoughts, feelings, and desires related to the burgeoning sexuality that accompanies adolescence. Thoughts about boys and sex took on a taboo quality, and she attempted to control them by turning her attention to other things or by distracting herself (e.g., repetitively counting to 25). Ms. Smith also began having thoughts about unintentionally harming others in various ways. For example, she worried about people getting sick from handling utensils and cooking implements after she had touched them with her so-called dirty hands; or as she got older, she became fearful that she would accidentally run over a pedestrian while driving her car. She soon learned that she could better control these thoughts through ritualistic behaviors; such as excessive hand washing, touching certain objects (e.g., her watch), moving parts of her body (e.g., tapping her foot to a specific rhythm), or saying silent prayers, asking God for forgiveness for these perceived sins.

Ms. Smith found that these problematic behaviors could also be used to control the anxiety and nervousness she felt when she did not live up to the expectations that come with being a "good Catholic girl," or when her academic work fell short of her parents' goals for her. In addition, these behaviors began to be employed when her parents began to delegate increasing responsibility for the care of her younger siblings. Taking on child care and other household responsibilities began when she about 15 years old when her mother was diagnosed with ovarian cancer. Initially, she expressed protest and resentment for having to do these chores, "instead of being with my friends and having fun." However, this rebellious behavior soon dissipated as her parents made her feel guilty about her anger and resentment by continually reminding her of her obligations as the oldest child and how they had sacrificed for her. Ms. Smith assumed full woman-of-the-house responsibilities when her mother died 3 years later. Since then, obsessive-compulsive behavior in one form or another began to appear in other aspects of life in which she felt she had not done her best, or had not done the right thing.

Her approaches to coping have not provided any relief or been without a personal cost. The past few years have been quite wearing for Ms. Smith, as she tries to meet the expectations she perceives from her husband as well as those she sets for herself. She reports feeling tired much of the time, has lost interest in formerly pleasurable activities (e.g., sex, playing the piano), and has experienced difficulties in sleeping and concentrating. During the past six months, concentration has become even more difficult. It was at about this time that her husband started expressing a desire to have a child as soon as possible. At the same time, more demands were placed on her: to care for her ailing father. This has included taking time away from her busy class and study schedule to make daily visits to her father's home. Because of these increased difficulties, her obsessive-compulsive symptoms have become more frequent and intense. Ms. Smith has also had problems concentrating on class lectures and completing reading assignments. Moreover, she has become forgetful in other aspects of her life, which has led to conflicts with her husband, father, and her younger siblings.

Mr. Smith accompanied his wife to this assessment and was able to provide additional information. He reported that for the past several months his wife has been spending more time studying because "she can't keep her mind focused on her books." "She has also seemed to be more irritable, tense and withdrawn, and less interested in having sexual relations," he stated. This latter problem appears to be of greater concern to Mr. Smith than it is to Ms. Smith, especially because he is eager to have a child. He attributes the more frequent occurrence of arguments to the disruption in their sexual relationship as well as to the amount of time she devotes to attending to the demands of law school and her family. Mr. Smith also noted that his wife is not sleeping well and that she seems to be skipping meals more frequently than usual.

Family/Social History

Ms. Smith was born, raised, and lives locally in Plainville. Her father is a 59-year-old retired sheet metal worker who is receiving disability benefits for emphysema and cardiac problems. Her mother, a former administrative assistant at Acme University, died of ovarian cancer 10 years ago. Neither parent attended college. She grew up in a household with deeply religious, Catholic parents who expected strict adherence to church teachings and instilled a strong sense of commitment to family and achievement in the world. She describes her parents as having been strict but loving as she was growing up. She now sees her father as being very dependent on her.

She is the oldest of her parents' three children. Her brother, age 20, is a sophomore at Acme University and her sister is a senior at the local high school. Both live with their father at the family home located a few miles from the house she shares with her husband. As indicted earlier, Ms. Smith assumed increasing responsibility for the care and raising of her siblings after her mother's death and continues to do so. She provides her sister and brother with emotional support and help with academic assignments when they request it. In addition, she makes sure that all of her father's bills are paid, his house is clean, and that he receives the required medical care.

Ms. Smith met and began dating her 29-year-old husband John in college while she was a junior and he was a senior at Acme. After receiving his bachelor's degree in business administration, he continued for two more years at the Acme Business School until he received his MBA. Upon graduation, he began working for a local bank and he and Ms. Smith were married. He is now a senior loan officer and is said to be on the fast track to move up in the ranks of bank management. Ms. Smith describes her husband as, "a loving husband who is intent on making sure that their financial needs are provided for both now and in the future." Mr. Smith is also described as, "a gregarious, ambitious person who is very focused on achieving his professional goals." They have been married for almost five years and have no children.

Ms. Smith says that she has a few friends, most are either married to people who work with her husband, work with her, or otherwise know her husband. For the most part, her time is occupied by attending and studying for law classes and keeping up two households (her own and her father's). When she does have free time and can concentrate, she prefers to spend it alone reading; otherwise, she watches TV or goes for a long walk in order to relax.

Educational History

Ms. Smith was a member of the National Honor Society and graduated in the top 2% of her high school class. Because of her responsibilities at home, she was not able to participate in any extracurricular activities during high school. Her grades and test scores were good enough to earn her a full undergraduate scholarship at Acme University, where she majored in art history. She graduated with a bachelor's degree six years ago. Her GPA for the four years at Acme was 3.92. Three years ago, she was admitted to Acme's School of Law. She is currently a second-year law student with a GPA of 3.75.

Employment History

Ms. Smith is attending law school full-time and is currently unemployed. She has had only one paying job outside of the home. Upon graduating with a bachelor's degree, she went to work for the Gotham County Art Museum as an assistant to the curator. Her primary responsibilities included assisting the curator in his daily duties and leading one or two tour groups each day. Ms. Smith enjoyed this work, reporting that "When I was at work, I was surrounded by all of those beautiful works of art. I could forget about meeting everyone else's needs and focus on what pleases me. I hardly ever had any of those crazy thoughts or did those crazy things when I was there." She said that she hated to leave that job two years ago to go to law school. When asked why she did so, she indicated that she did it at her husband's encouragement. She reported, "He kept telling me that I was too smart for that type of work, that I could make a lot more money if only I lived up to my potential, that lawyers can make a whole lot of money doing a lot of important and different things. He said that he would be so proud of me if I would just make something of myself."

Mental Health and Substance Use History

Ms. Smith sought help for her problems twice during her undergraduate years; once during her sophomore year, and then again during her junior year. These were described as the most academically demanding of her undergraduate years. In both instances, she experienced an exacerbation of her "usual" concentration difficulties and obsessive-compulsive behaviors. Both times, treatment consisted of time-limited, goal-focused psychotherapy provided by the school's student counseling center. According to Ms. Smith, each of these episodes of care was effective enough to, "get me back on the right track." She denied any experimentation or regular use of illegal drugs but did report that she has a couple of glasses of wine every week.

Medical History

Ms. Smith's medical history is unremarkable. Generally, she attained developmental milestones at the appropriate ages, had the usual childhood illnesses, and reports no hospitalizations or treatment for any chronic illnesses. There is a family history of cardiac disease on her father's side of the family, as well as a family history of cancer on her mother's side. Because of this, she reports that during each of the past four years she has had a routine physical examination. Ms. Smith also tries to exercise regularly but says that it is now hard to do because of the demands of school, her husband, and her family.

Important Characteristics

The information presented by Ms. Smith and her husband is indicative of an individual who has been experiencing distress to varying degrees for many years. Her problems are complex and as she tries to meet the needs and expectations of others, she uses methods to control her anger and resentment. Her coping style has been to internalize her anxieties. With few exceptions, this approach allowed her to successfully adapt to their presence in that the accompanying distress generally has not significantly interfered with her functioning as wife, student, and caregiver. However, the recent additional stress appears to have pushed her to the point whereby she is now beginning to experience difficulties. In her favor is the fact that she appears to be ready to make changes in her life and likely to show little resistance to therapeutic efforts. On the other hand, the amount of support for her efforts that she will receive from her husband and others is likely to be minimal, given that those closest to her are, in one way or another, a source of her problems. A preoccupied attachment style is suggested.

Strengths

Ms. Smith is a very bright woman who displays an awareness of her problems and how they interfere with multiple aspects of her functioning. Her ability to successfully meet the rigors and demands of law school and her family while coping with intrusive thoughts and behaviors attests to her perseverance and determination to not allow her psychological problems to interfere with goals that she has set for herself. This level of ego strength bodes well for positive treatment outcomes.

Mental Status

Ms. Smith is an attractive young woman of medium build who looks her stated age of 28. She came to this assessment session after attending a law class, neatly dressed in jeans, a sweater, and sandals. Initially, she sat rigidly in her chair, appeared nervous and made only occasional eye contact, but she began to relax and became more engaged with me as the assessment session progressed. Rapport with Ms. Smith was established in a relatively short amount of time. Her mood was dysphoric but her affect was appropriate to the topics of discussion. She exhibited no unusual speech patterns or language deficits, nor were there any observations or reports of perceptual distortions or impairments in her thought processes. Ms. Smith did report long-standing problems with obsessive thinking and compulsive behavior that appear to worsen during conflictual or other stressful events. These are often accompanied by magical thinking. Cognitively, she was attentive and oriented to time, place, and person. There were no apparent deficits in her abstraction, conceptualization or constructional abilities, and her immediate, short-term, and long-term memory all seemed to be intact. Although she was able to successfully perform serial seven subtraction from 100 within average time limits, difficulties in concentrating were occasionally noted throughout the interview. Ms. Smith displayed adequate judgment and insight into her problems. Intellectualization, repression, suppression, and undoing are frequently employed defense mechanisms.

Risk of Harm to Self and Others

There are no indications that Ms. Smith is currently at risk of harming herself or anyone else.

Diagnostic Impression

Based on information obtained during this assessment, Ms. Smith meets the *DSM-IV-TR* criteria for Axis I diagnoses of obsessive-compulsive disorder (300.3) and dysthymic disorder (300.4). There are also traits of Axis II obsessive-compulsive personality disorder (301.4) but it is not clear at this time as to whether she meets all criteria for this diagnosis.

Motivation to Change

Ms. Smith has actively sought help for her problems and appears willing to work on making changes in her life. She is likely to become an active participant in her treatment and thus appears to be an excellent candidate for psychotherapy.

Psychological Test Results

In order to further clarify the nature and severity of her problems, Ms. Smith was administered the MMPI-2 immediately after the interview. The results of the testing are as shown in the box on the following page.

The MMPI-2 results are generally quite consistent with the impressions formed from the assessment interview information. This is not surprising, given that the MMPI-2 is a self-report instrument that asks for many of the same types of information that are obtained through clinical interviews. Examination of the MMPI-2 validity scales indicates that Ms. Smith was

MMPI-2 Clinical & Supplemental Scales		MMPI-2 Content Scales	
Scale	T Score	Scale	T Score
L	52	ANX	66
F	72	FRS	59
K	54	OBS	87
Hs	59	DEP	67
D	77	HEA	57
Hy	63	BIZ	52
Pd	58	ANG	50
Mf	45	CYN	46
Pa	59	ASP	49
Pt	86	TPA	64
Sc	63	LSE	70
Ma	53	SOD	57
Si	66	FAM	68
A	71	WRK	67
R	65	TRT	46
Es	66		

open and honest in responding to the items of the inventory. The pattern of scores for the basic clinical scales reveals clinically significant elevations on Depression (D) and Psychasthenia (Pt). The prototypical 2-7 codetype is indicative of anxious depression and is characterized by anxiety, depression, guilt, self-devaluation, tension, and proneness to worry (Friedman, Lewak, Nichols, & Webb, 2001). Ruminations are present and are frequently accompanied by insomnia, feelings of inadequacy, and a reduction in work inefficiency. Individuals with this profile tend to overreact to minor stress with anxious preoccupations and somatic concerns. Also, they may become meticulous, compulsive, and perfectionistic. They have a strong sense of right and wrong, and they tend to focus on their deficiencies, even though they have experienced many personal achievements in their lives. Often these achievements are attained out of a sense of responsibility and accomplished in a compulsive manner.

The MMPI-2 results also are indicative of people who tend to be dependent and lack assertiveness, resulting in their taking on increased responsibilities. This can lead to their becoming overwhelmed and, consequently, more anxious and depressed. When things go wrong, they tend to see themselves as being responsible. For people with this profile, suicide ideation is common, with actual attempts being a realistic possibility. Historical information and direct questioning, however, indicate that Ms. Smith is not a suicidal risk.

Ms. Smith's responses to the MMPI-2 also revealed a pattern of clinically significant elevations on several MMPI-2 content scales—Anxiety (ANX), Obsessiveness (OBS), Depression (DEP), Low Self-esteem (LSE), Family Problems (FAM), and Work Interference (WRK)—that is consistent with her history and presentation. Indicated again are anxiety, depression, worry, obsessive ruminations, concentration problems, difficulty completing tasks, low self-esteem, giving in to the needs of others, family discord, and not being able to work as well as she used to (Greene & Clopton, 2004). Moreover, the scores on the Anxiety and Repression factor scales suggest the presence of general distress and maladjustment. This, along with the elevated score on the Ego Strength (ES) scale and the low score on the Negative Treatment Indicators (TRT) Content scale, are positive indications that Ms. Smith is likely to become easily engaged and to remain in treatment.

Treatment Goals

Ms. Smith's stated goals for treatment include:

1. Amelioration or alleviation of obsessions, compulsions, depressed mood, and concentration problems.
2. Increased ability to say "no" to others and meet her own needs.
3. Improvement in her marital relationship.

Important to the achievement of each of these goals is Ms. Smith's ability to learn to recognize and express anger and resentment in appropriate, effective ways.

Summary

The manner in which personality assessment is conducted will vary from one clinician to another, depending on any number of factors related to the patient, the clinician, and the situation. But in all cases, the clinical interview should serve as the core of the information gathering process. A semistructured format is recommended as the best means of gathering the information from the patient. This approach ensures that all interview information that is generally helpful or needed in formulating a clinical picture of the patient is obtained; at the same time, it allows the clinician flexibility in the manner in which information is gathered. The focal areas or content of the interview include the patient's presenting problem and its history, as well as other historical information important to understanding the problem's development, maintenance, and effects on the patient's current functioning. Included here is the patient's medical and behavioral health history.

Key Points to Remember

- The clinical interview is probably the single most important means of data collection that can be used while conducting a psychological assessment.
- The clinical interview provides information that can generate hypotheses about the individual and/or support hypotheses generated by psychological testing or other sources of information.
- The unstructured clinical interview follows no rigid sequence or direction of inquiry; instead, it is tailored to the individual's problems and relies on the clinician's skills and judgment.
- The structured clinical interview is one in which the individual is asked a standard set of questions in a specific order, allowing little or no variation from the interview content or format.
- The semistructured interview provides clinicians with a means of ensuring that all important areas of investigation are addressed while allowing the flexibility to focus more or less attention to specific areas, depending on their relevance to the patient's problems.
- Information obtained from a semistructured interview should include identifying information; the presenting problem and its history; the individual's background history (family/social, educational, employment); medical, mental health, and substance abuse history; information pertaining to important patient characteristics identified by Beutler and his colleagues; assessment of the individual's mental status and risk of harm to self and others; the individual's strengths and motivation to change; and the self-reported goals for treatment.
- Together with information obtained from psychological testing and other sources, information from the clinical interview can assist in various aspects of the treatment planning process, including problem identification and clarification, identification of important patient characteristics that can facilitate or hinder treatment, and monitoring treatment progress.
- Although frequently decried, diagnoses based on a common system of classification criteria continue to be important, efficient tools for communicating among professional and organizations, a fact that has tremendous implications for those involved in the clinical, research, or administrative aspects of behavioral healthcare provision.
- No clinical interview conducted in a treatment setting would be complete without the identification of treatment goals. A quick, efficient way to obtain at least a preliminary indication of the individual's goals for treatment is to ask him or her directly.
- Examples of some commonly used structured interviews include the Primary Care Evaluation of Mental Disorders (PRIME-MD), the Structured Clinical Interview for DSM-IV Axis I Disorders (SCID), and the Diagnostic Interview Schedule (DIS).

Information regarding other patient characteristics is also pertinent due to its importance in treatment planning. Some of those characteristics were identified by Beutler (1995) as part of his systematic treatment selection model for treatment planning. Others include the patient's strengths or assets that can be mobilized in the service of effecting change, and the motivation to engage in a therapeutic relationship and work to affect change in one's life. Information obtained from a mental status examination and assessment of the patient's risk of harm to self or others can assist in determining various aspects of care, including the level of care that is most appropriate for the patient at the time. The mental status examination can also facilitate the assignment of a diagnosis. Although of limited value for treatment planning, diagnoses are a necessary evil that enable communication among professionals and meet third-party requirements for reimbursement.

Finally, no assessment would be complete without knowing the desired goals of treatment. Except in some cases of involuntary treatment, patients will be able to state one or more goals. At the same time, other parties (e.g., relatives, insurers, employers) may have additional goals in mind and these are also important to know.

Note

1. Portions of this chapter were adapted from the following works with permission of the publisher: M. E. Maruish, Essentials of treatment planning. Copyright © 2002 John Wiley & Sons. Adapted with permission of John Wiley & Sons, Inc. M. E. Maruish, Psychological testing in the age of managed behavioral health care. Copyright © 2002 Lawrence Erlbaum Associates. Adapted with permission of Taylor and Francis.

References

Amchin, J. (1991). *Psychiatric diagnosis: A biopsychosocial approach using DSM-III-R*. Washington, DC: American Psychiatric Press.

American Psychiatric Association. (2000). *Diagnostic and statistical manual of mental disorders: DSM-IV-TR* (4th ed.). Washington, DC: Author.

American Psychiatric Association. (2003). Practice guidelines for the assessment and treatment of patients with suicidal behaviors. *Official Journal of the American Psychiatric Association, 160* (Suppl.11), (pp.1–60).

Beutler, L. E. (1995). The clinical interview. In L. E. Beutler & M. R. Berren (Eds.), *Integrative assessment of adult personality* (pp. 94–120). New York: Guilford.

Beutler, L. E., & Clarkin, J. F. (1990). *Systematic treatment selection: Toward targeted therapeutic interventions*. New York: Brunner/Mazel, Inc.

Beutler, L. E., Groth-Marnat, G., & Rosner, R. (2003). Introduction to integrative assessment of adult personality. In L. E. Beutler & G. Groth-Marnat (Eds.), *Integrative assessment of adult personality* (2nd ed., pp. 1–36). New York: Guilford.

Beutler, L. E., Malik, M., Talebi, H., Fleming, J., & Moleiro, C. (2004). Use of psychological tests/instruments for treatment planning. In M. E. Maruish (Ed.), *The use of psychological testing for treatment planning and outcomes assessment: Volume 1. General considerations* (3rd ed., pp. 111–145). Mahwah, NJ: Erlbaum.

Brogan, M. M., Prochaska, J. O., & Prochaska, J. M. (1999). Predicting termination and continuation status in psychotherapy using the transtheoretical model. *Psychotherapy, 36,* 105–113.

Bryan, C. J., & Rudd, M. D. (2006). Advances in the assessment of suicide risk. *Journal of Clinical Psychology, 62,* 185–200.

Chambless, D. L., Baker, M. J., Baucom, D. H., Beutler, L. E., Calhoun, K. S., Crits-Christoph, P., et al. (1998). Update on empirically validated therapies, II. *The Clinical Psychologist, 51*(1), 3–16. Manuscript submitted for publication. [Online] Available: http://www.apa.org/divisions/div12/est/97REPORT.SS.htm.

Chambless, D. L., Sanderson, W. C., Shoham, V., Johnson, S. B., Pope, K. S., Crits-Christoph, P., et al. (1996). An update on empirically validated therapies. *The Clinical Psychologist, 49,*.5–18.

Columbia DISC Development Group (1999). *National Institute of Mental Health Diagnostic Interview for Children (NIMH-DISC).* Unpublished report, Columbia University/New York State Psychiatric Institute.

Constans, J. I., Lenhoff, K., & McCarthy, M. (1997). Depression subtyping in PTSD patients. *Annals of Clinical Psychology, 9,* (pp. 235–240).

Derogatis, L. R., & Culpepper, W. J. (2004). Screening for psychiatric disorders. In M. E. Maruish (Ed.), *The use of psychological testing for treatment planning and outcomes assessment: Volume 1. General considerations* (3rd ed., pp. 65–109). Mahwah, NJ: Lawrence Erlbaum Associates.

Derogatis, L. R., & Fitzpatrick, M. (2004). The SCL-90-R, the Brief Symptom Inventory (BSI), and the BSI-18. In M. E. Maruish (Ed.), *The use of psychological testing for treatment planning and outcomes assessment: Volume 3. Instruments for adults* (3rd ed., pp. 1–41). Mahwah, NJ: Erlbaum.

Derogatis, L.R., & Savitz, K. L. (1999). The SCL-90-R, Brief Symptom Inventory, and matching clinical rating scales. In M .E. Maruish (Ed.), *The use of psychological testing for treatment planning and outcomes assessment* (2nd ed., pp. 679–724). Mahwah, NJ: Erlbaum.

DiClemente, C. C., & Prochaska, J. O. (1998). Toward a comprehensive, transtheoretical model of change. In W. R. Miller & N. Healther (Eds.), *Treating addictive behaviors* (pp. 3–24). New York: Plenum Press.

Duncan, D. K. (1987). A comparison of two structured diagnostic interviews (Doctoral dissertation, York University, 1987). *Dissertation Abstracts International, 48,* 3109B.

First, M. B., Gibbon, M., Spitzer, R. L., Williams, J. B., & Benjamin, L. (1997). *The Structured Clinical Interview for DSM-IV Axis II Personality Disorders (SCID-II).* Washington, DC: American Psychiatric Press.

First, M. B., Gibbon, M., Spitzer, R. L., Williams, J. B., & MHS Staff (1998). *Computer-assisted SCID-Clinician Version (CAS-CV) Windows version software manual.* Toronto: Multi-Health Systems and American Psychiatric Press.

First, M. B., Spitzer, R. L., Gibbon, M., & Williams, J. B. (1996). *Structured Clinical Interview for DSM-IV Axis I Disorders Research Version–Patient Edition (SCID-I/P, ver. 2.0).* New York: New York State Psychiatric Institute, Biometrics Research Department.

First, M. B., Spitzer, R. L., Gibbon, M., & Williams, J. B. (1997). *Structured Clinical Interview for DSM-IV Axis I Disorders (SCID-I)–Clinician Version.* Washington, DC: American Psychiatric Association.

Fisher, D., Beutler, L. E., & Williams, O. B. (1999). Making assessment relevant to treatment planning: The STS Clinician Rating Form. *Journal of Clinical Psychology, 55,* 825–842.

Friedman, A. F., Lewak, R., Nichols, D. S., & Webb, J. T. (2001). *Psychological assessment with the MMPI-2.* Mahwah, NJ: Erlbaum.

Gavin, D. R., Ross, H. E., & Skinner, H. A. (1989). Diagnostic validity of the Drug Abuse Screening Test in the assessment of DSM-III drug disorders. *British Journal of Addictions, 84,* 301–307.

Gaw, K. F., & Beutler, L. E. (1995). Integrating treatment recommendations. The clinical interview. In L. E. Beutler & M. R. Berren (Eds.), *Integrative assessment of adult personality* (pp. 94–120). New York: Guilford.

Ginsberg, G. L. (1985). Psychiatric history and mental status examination. In H. I. Kaplan & B. J. Sadock (Eds.), *Comprehensive textbook of psychiatry/IV* (4th ed., pp. 487–495). Baltimore: Williams & Wilkins.

Greene, R. L., & Clopton, J. R. (2004). Minnesota Multiphasic Personality Inventory -2 (MMPI-2). In M. E. Maruish (Ed.), *The use of psychological testing for treatment planning and outcomes assessment: Volume 3. Instruments for adults* (3rd ed., pp. 449–477). Mahwah, NJ: Erlbaum.

Groth-Marnat, G. (2003). *Handbook of psychological assessment* (4th ed.). Hoboken, NJ: Wiley.

Groth-Marnat, G., & Horvath, L. S. (2006). The psychological report: A review of current controversies. *Journal of Clinical Psychology, 62,* 73–81.

Hahn, R., Sydney, E., Kroenke, K., Williams, J. B., & Spitzer, R. L. (2004). Evaluation of mental disorders with the Primary Care Evaluation of Mental Disorders and Patient Health Questionnaire. In M. E. Maruish (Ed.), *The use of psychological testing for treatment planning and outcomes assessment: Volume 3. Instruments for adults* (3rd ed., pp. 235–291). Mahwah, NJ: Erlbaum.

Hamilton, M. (1967). Development of a rating scale for primary depressive illness. *British Journal of Social and Clinical Psychology, 6,* 278–296.

Harwood, T. M., & Williams, O. B. (2003). Identifying treatment-relevant assessment. Systematic Treatment Selection. In L. E. Beutler & G. Groth-Marnat (Eds.), *Integrative assessment of adult personality* (2nd ed., pp. 65–81). New York: Guilford.

Horton, J., Compton, W. M., & Cottler, L. (1998). *Assessing psychiatric disorders among drug users: Reliability of the DSI-IV.* Unpublished manuscript. St. Louis, MO: Washington University School of Medicine.

Johnson, J. G., Spitzer, R. L., Williams, J. B., Kroenke, K., Linzer, M., Brody, D., et al. (1995). Psychiatric comorbidity, health status, and functional impairment associated with alcohol abuse and dependence in primary care patients: Findings of the PRIME-MD 1000 study. *Journal of Consulting and Clinical Psychology, 63,* 133–140.

Jongsma, A. E., & Peterson, L. M. (1999). *The complete adult psychotherapy treatment planner* (2nd ed.). New York: Wiley.

Kranzler, H. R., Kadden, R. M., Babor, T. F., Tennen, H., & Rounsaville, B. J. (1996). Validity of the SCID in substance abuse patients. *Addiction, 91,* 859–868.

Lehnhoff, J. (1991). Assessment and utilization of patient strengths in acute care treatment planning. *The Psychiatric Hospital, 22,* 11–15.

Loranger, A. W. (1999). *International Personality Disorder Examination (IPDE) manual.* Odessa, FL: Psychological Assessment Resources.

Luborsky, L., & Crits-Christoph, P. (Eds.). (1990). *The core conflictual relationship theme.* New York: Basic Books.

Maier, W., Buller R., Sonntag, A., & Heuser, I. (1986). Subtypes of panic attacks and ICD-9 classification. *European Archives of Psychiatry and Neurological Sciences, 235,* 361–366.

Maruish, M. E. (2000). Introduction. In M.E. Maruish (Ed.), *Handbook of psychological assessment in primary care settings* (pp. 3–41). Mahwah, NJ: Erlbaum.

Maruish, M. E. (2002a). *Essentials of treatment planning.* New York: Wiley.

Maruish, M. E. (2002b). *Psychological testing in the age of managed behavioral health care.* Mahwah, NJ: Erlbaum.

Maruish, M. E. (2004). Introduction. In M. E. Maruish (Ed.), *The use of psychological testing for treatment planning and outcomes assessment: Volume 1. General considerations* (3rd ed., pp. 1–64). Mahwah, NJ: Erlbaum.

Maziade, M., Roy, A. A., Fournier, J. P., Cliché, D., Merette, C., Caron, C., et al. (1992). Reliability of best-estimate in genetic linkage studies of major psychoses. *American Journal of Psychiatry, 149,* 1674–1686.

Meyer, G. J., Finn, S. E., Eyde, L. D., Kay, G. G., Moreland, K. L., Dies, R. R., et al. (2001). Psychological testing and psychological assessment: A review of evidence and issues. *American Psychologist, 56,* 128–165.

Mohr, D., & Beutler, L. E. (2003). The integrative clinical interview. In L. E. Beutler & G. Groth-Marnat (Eds.), *Integrative assessment of adult personality* (2nd ed., pp. 82–122). New York: Guilford.

Morey, L. C. (2004). The Personality Assessment Inventory (PAI). In M. E. Maruish (Ed.), *The use of psychological testing for treatment planning and outcomes assessment: Volume 3. Instruments for adults* (3rd ed., pp. 509–551). Mahwah, NJ: Erlbaum.

Prochaska, J. O., DiClemente, C. C., & Norcross, J. C. (1992). In search of how people change: Applications to addictive behaviors. *American Psychologist, 47,* 1102–1114.

Prochaska, J. O., & Norcross, J. C. (2002a). *Systems of psychotherapy: A transtheoretical analysis* (5th ed.). Pacific Grove, CA: Brooks/Cole.

Prochaska, J. O., & Norcross, J. C. (2002b). Stages of change. In J. C. Norcross (Ed.), *Psychotherapy relationships that work.* New York: Oxford University Press.

Prochaska, J. O., & Prochaska, J. M. (2004). Assessment as intervention within the transtheoretical model. In M. E. Maruish (Ed.), *The use of psychological testing for treatment planning and outcomes assessment: Volume 1. General considerations* (3rd ed., pp. 147–170). Mahwah, NJ: Erlbaum.

Reich, W., Welner, Z., Herjanic, B., & MHS Staff. (1997). *Diagnostic Interview for Children and Adolescents-IV (DICA-IV) Windows version. User's manual for the child/adolescent and parent versions.* Toronto: Multi-Health Systems.

Robins, L. N., Cottler, L., Bucholz, K., & Compton, W. (1995). *The Diagnostic Interview Schedule Version IV.* St. Louis, MO: Washington University Medical School.

Rogers, R. (2001). *Handbook of diagnostic and structured interviewing.* New York: Guilford.

Ross, H. E., Gavin, D. R., & Skinner, H. A. (1990). Diagnostic validity of the MAST and the Alcohol Dependence Scale in the assessment of DSM-III alcohol disorders. *Journal of Studies on Alcohol, 51,* 506–513.

Ross, H. E., Swinson, R., Larkin, E. J., & Doumani, S. (1994). Diagnosing comorbidity in substance abusers. *Journal of Nervous and Mental Disease, 182,* 556–563.

Schwenk, T. L., Coyne, J. C., & Fechner-Bates, S. (1996). Differences between detected and undetected patients in primary care and depressed psychiatric inpatients. *General Hospital Psychiatry, 18,* 407–415.

Sheehan, D. V., Lecrubier, Y., Sheehan, K. H., Amorim, P., Janavs, J., Weiller, E., et al. (1997). The validity of the Mini International Neuropsychiatric Interview (MINI) according to the SCID-P and its reliability. *European Psychiatry, 12,* 232–241.

Sifneos, P. E. (1987). *Short-term dynamic psychotherapy: Evaluation and technique* (2nd ed.). New York: Plenum.

Snyder, C. R., Ritschel, L. A., Rand, K. L., & Berg, C. J. (2006). Balancing psychological assessments: Including strengths and hope in client reports. *Journal of Clinical Psychology, 62,* 33–46.

Spengler, P. A., & Wittchen, H. U. (1988). Procedural validity of standardized symptom questions for the assessment of psychotic symptoms: A comparison of the DIS with two clinical methods. *Comprehensive Psychiatry, 29,* 309–322.

Spitzer, R. L., Kroenke, K., Linzer, M., Hahn, S. R., Williams, J. B., deGruy, F. V., et al. (1995). Health-related quality of life in primary care patients with mental disorders: Results from the PRIME-MD 1000 study. *Journal of the American Medical Association, 274,* 1511–1517.

Spitzer, R. L., Williams, J. B., Kroenke, K., Linzer, M., deGruy, F. V., Hahn, S. R., et al. (1994). Utility of a new procedure for diagnosing mental disorders in primary care: The PRIME-MD 1000 study. *Journal of the American Medical Association, 272,* 1749–1756.

Stewart, A. S., Hays, R. D., & Ware, J. E. (1988). The MOS short-form General Health Survey: Reliability and validity in a patient population. *Medical Care, 26,* 724–732.

Stuckenberg, K. W., Dura, J. R., & Kiecolt-Glaser, J. K. (1990). Depression screening scales validation in an elderly, community-dwelling population. *Psychological Assessment: A Journal of Clinical and Consulting Psychology, 2,* 134–138.

Substance Abuse and Mental Health Services Administration. (2006). *Results from the 2005 National Survey on Drug Use and Health: National findings* (Office of Applied Studies, NSDUH Series H-30, DHHS Publication No. SMA 064194). Rockville, MD: Author.

Summerfeldt, L. J., & Antony, M. M. (2002). Structured and semistructured diagnostic interviews. In M. M. Antony & D. H. Barlow (Eds.), *Handbook of assessment and treatment planning for psychological disorders* (pp 3–37). New York: Guilford.

Task Force on Promotion and Dissemination of Psychological Procedures. (1995). Training in and dissemination of empirically-validated psychological treatments. *The Clinical Psychologist, 48,* 3–23.

Trzepacz, P. T., & Baker, R. W. (1993). *The psychiatric mental status examination.* New York: Oxford University Press.

United Behavioral Systems. (1994). *Writing effective treatment plans.* Unpublished training manual.

Velicer, W. F., Prochaska, J. O., Fava, J. L., Rossi, J. S., Redding, C. A., Laforge, R. G., et al. (2000). Using the transtheoretical model for population-based approaches to health promotion and disease prevention. *Homeostasis in Health and Disease, 40,* 74–19.

Whisman, M. A., Strosahl, K., Fruzzetti, A. E., Schmaling, K. B., Jacobson, N. S., & Miller, D. M. (1989). A structured interview version of the Hamilton Rating Scale for Depression: Reliability and validity. *Psychological Assessment, 1,* 238–241.

Zimmerman, M., & Coryell, W. (1988). The validity of a self-report questionnaire for diagnosing major depressive disorder. *Archives of General Psychiatry, 45,* 738–740.

Zimmerman, M., & Mattia, J. I. (1999). Psychiatric diagnosis in clinical practice: Is comorbidity being missed? *Comprehensive Psychiatry, 40,* 182–191.

CHAPTER 3

The MMPI-2 and MMPI-A

YOSSEF S. BEN-PORATH
ROBERT P. ARCHER

Introduction

The Minnesota Multiphasic Personality Inventory – Second edition (MMPI-2) (Butcher et al., 2001), is a 567-item true-false personality questionnaire. It is the most widely used self-report measure of personality and psychopathology in a variety of settings including traditional mental health (Camara, Nathan, & Puente, 2000), criminal and civil forensic assessments (Archer, Buffington-Vollum, Stredny, & Handel, 2006; Boccaccini & Brodsky, 1999; Borum & Grisso, 1995), and neuropsychological evaluations (Lees-Haley, Smith, Williams, & Dunn, 1996), among others. It is also the most widely researched psychological test (Butcher & Rouse, 1996).

The MMPI-2 is used to identify and quantify dysfunction in three broad domains encompassing emotion, thought, and behavior. It consists of validity scales, used to assess various threats to the validity of a given test protocol, and numerous substantive scales grouped under the headings Clinical, Restructured Clinical, Content, Supplementary, and Personality-Psychopathology Five (*PSY-5*). The Clinical and Content scales also have subscales designed to assist in their interpretation.

The Minnesota Multiphasic Personality Inventory – Adolescent (MMPI-A), by Butcher et al. (1992), is a 478-item true-false objective personality assessment instrument designed for use with adolescents. It provides an array of validity and clinical scales, and interpretation is based on a substantial research literature. The MMPI-A is an adaptation of the Minnesota Multiphasic Personality Inventory (MMPI) and closely related in structure and psychometric characteristics to the MMPI-2. It is the most widely used objective self-report measure of psychopathology with adolescents (Archer & Newsom, 2000), and Forbey (2003) has observed that the research literature on the MMPI-A exceeds that of any other self-report measure used with adolescents. Further, Archer (2005) has noted that the research on adolescents done with the original version of the MMPI appears largely generalizable to the MMPI-A. While the MMPI-A is closely related to both the original version of the MMPI and the MMPI-2, it also contains features that are unique to this version for adolescents, including several content scales and supplementary scales not found on other MMPI forms. These unique features will be discussed later in this chapter.

The chapter will address three primary questions about the MMPI-2 and MMPI-A:

1. What are the empirical foundations of the two versions of the test?
2. What are their recommended uses?
3. What is the current status of, and future directions for, the MMPI-2 and MMPI-A?

Theory and Development

We begin this section by describing the methods used to develop the original MMPI and their theoretical underpinnings. Next, we turn to the three major efforts to update the test, which yielded first the revised adult version of the instrument, MMPI-2 (Butcher et al., 1989), then the adolescent-specific version of the test, MMPI-A (Butcher et al., 1992), and most recently a modern, shorter version of the inventory, the MMPI-2 Restructured Form (MMPI-2-RF).

The MMPI

Early History

The MMPI-2 is an empirically grounded instrument. The original Clinical Scales of the test were developed empirically, using the method of contrasted groups. This involved administering a large pool of items to members of eight different diagnostic groups and contrasting the responses of members of each group with a sample of non-patients. Items answered differently by the members of a given group than the "normal" sample were assigned to a scale designed to detect membership in that diagnostic group. The eight target diagnoses correspond to the labels of the eight original Clinical Scales: Hypochondriasis, Depression, Hysteria, Psychopathic Deviance, Paranoia, Psychasthenia, Schizophrenia, and Hypomania.

The original intent of Hathaway and McKinley (1942), developers of the MMPI, was to devise a psychometric instrument that could generate differential diagnoses. It is a mistake to attribute a nontheoretical approach to the construction of the original MMPI Clinical Scales. Hathaway and McKinley's efforts, and particularly the collection of items they used to develop the MMPI, were informed by the then prevailing descriptive Kraepelinian nosology, other existing surveys of psychiatric symptoms, and their own clinical experience. Thus, the item pool used to derive the MMPI was informed by, and reflected the prevailing understanding of, the symptoms, beliefs, and behaviors associated with commonly occurring forms of psychopathology. On the other hand, the assignment of items to the eight original Clinical Scales was strictly empirical, with no consideration given to item content.

Soon after the MMPI was put into clinical use it became evident that the instrument was not performing as had been intended. Rather than yield distinctive indications of specific diagnoses to the exclusion of others, Clinical Scale profiles were frequently characterized by multiple, and sometimes seemingly contradictory, patterns of elevation. However, users of the test soon noticed that certain patterns (i.e., combinations of scores) tended to reoccur, and were associated with common features among the patients who produced them. This sparked empirical research designed to identify commonly occurring patterns and the features associated with producing such results on the MMPI.

Because of the shift away from diagnosis, and in order to facilitate identification of score patterns on the test, the Clinical Scales were assigned numeric codes corresponding to the order of their appearance on the profile. By this time, the eight original Clinical Scales had been augmented by two additional scales, Masculinity-Femininity and Social Introversion. Table 3.1 lists the labels, abbreviations (also used to avoid diagnostic terminology), and numeric codes of the 10 MMPI Clinical Scales. As mentioned, the numeric codes were used to describe patterns of scores on the MMPI Clinical Scale profile and were therefore called Code Types. For example, a profile where

Table 3.1 Labels, Abbreviations, and Numeric Codes of the MMPI Clinical Scales

Label	Abbreviation	Numeric Code
Hypochondriasis	Hs	Scale 1
Depression	D	Scale 2
Hysteria	Hy	Scale 3
Psychopathic Deviance	Pd	Scale 4
Masculinity-Femininity	Mf	Scale 5
Paranoia	Pa	Scale 6
Psychasthenia	Pt	Scale 7
Schizophrenia	Sc	Scale 8
Hypomania	Ma	Scale 9
Social Introversion	Si	Scale 0

the first two scales (Hypochondriasis and Depression) had the highest scores would be designated a 12/21 code type.

Code Types

Code types have played a pivotal role in MMPI interpretation. As just mentioned, Hathaway and McKinley's initial goal to develop scales that would lead directly to psycho-diagnosis was not realized. Early MMPI code type research still focused on attempts to predict diagnoses, now based on patterns of scores across the MMPI profiles (e.g., Gough, 1946; Meehl, 1946: Schmidt, 1945). Soon thereafter, investigators began to expand their search to identify nondiagnostic correlates of MMPI code types. Hathaway and Meehl (1951) developed an adjective checklist that was modified by Black (1953) in his study of the empirical correlates of MMPI code types.

With the shift from single scale scores to code types, the theoretical foundations and interpretation of the MMPI had changed dramatically. The rather restricted goal of developing a differential diagnostic test was replaced by a broader, far more ambitious objective, to develop a scheme for classifying patients into meaningful types and detecting the empirical correlates of membership in these classes. Meehl (1954) articulated this goal, and marshaled compelling evidence that actuarial interpretation of tests such as the MMPI—that is, interpreting test results on the basis of their known empirical correlates—consistently yielded more accurate information than clinical interpretation based on the user's own experiences with the test and impressions of the patient. He later issued his well-known call for a "good cookbook" (Meehl, 1956), designed to yield the information needed for actuarial, code-type-based MMPI interpretation.

Following Meehl's (1956) call, a number of large scale investigations were conducted to yield a broad empirical foundation for MMPI code-type interpretation (e.g., Gilberstadt & Duker, 1965; Gynther, Altman, & Sletten, 1973a, b; Marks & Seeman, 1963). The empirical correlates identified in these investigations continue to form the foundation for current practices in MMPI-2 interpretation. However, at the same time that some MMPI authors were implementing Meehl's scheme for actuarial interpretation based on empirical correlates, others were beginning to enter what heretofore had been largely forbidden territory, capitalizing on item content in MMPI scale construction and interpretation.

Content-Based Scale Construction

As just reviewed, the early history of MMPI scale construction and interpretation was characterized by a strong emphasis on strictly empirical approaches, and an eschewing of any consideration of item content in either of these tasks. Some early exceptions to this trend involved the development of content-based subscales for the Clinical Scales first by Wiener and Harmon (1946) and later by Harris and Lingoes (1955). However, Wiggins (1966) was the first to launch a successful, full-fledged effort to develop content-based scales for the MMPI. In justifying this shift, Wiggins (1966) noted:

> The viewpoint that a personality test protocol represents a communication between the subject and the tester (or institution which he represents) has much to commend it, not the least of which is the likelihood that this is the frame of reference adopted by the subject himself. (p. 2)

Wiggins (1966) began his content-based scale construction effort by examining the internal consistency of 26 content-based item groupings of the MMPI item pool described originally by Hathaway and McKinley (1940). He then set about revising the content categories based on a rational analysis followed by additional empirical analyses that yielded a set of 15 content dimensions that were promising enough to warrant further analyses. Empirical analyses involving the entire item pool of the MMPI yielded eventually a set of 13 internally consistent and relatively independent content scales.

The significance of Wiggins's (1966) efforts cannot be overstated. His methods served as the prototype for all subsequent content-based scale development for the MMPI and later, other instruments. The psychometric success of his endeavor provided much needed empirical support for the still fledgling content-based approach to MMPI scale construction and interpretation.

Use of the Original MMPI with Adolescents

While many people think of the MMPI as an evaluation instrument designed for use with adults, the application of the original MMPI with adolescents began around the time of the original publication of the test instrument. Dora Capwell undertook the first research investigation of the MMPI with adolescents in the early 1940s and demonstrated the ability of the MMPI to accurately discriminate between groups of delinquent and non-delinquent girls based on *Pd* Scale elevations (Capwell, 1945a). Capwell's further investigation demonstrated that these *Pd* scale differences were maintained in follow-up studies conducted from 4 to 15 months following the initial administration of the MMPI (Capwell, 1945b). Then in the largest MMPI data set ever collected with adolescents, Hathaway and Monachesi (1953, 1963) conducted a large-scale longitudinal study of the relationship between MMPI test scores and delinquent behavior. Their sample of approximately 15,000 Minnesota adolescents was based on data collections conducted in the late 1940s and early 1950s. This study provided invaluable information on the MMPI correlates of delinquency, including their findings that elevations on the MMPI scales *Pd, Sc,* and *Ma* (labeled by Hathaway and Monachesi as the excitatory scales) were associated with higher delinquency rates, whereas elevations on MMPI scales D, Mf, and Si (the inhibitory scales) were related to a reduced risk of antisocial or delinquent behaviors.

The most frequently used adolescent norms available for the original form of the MMPI were developed by Marks and Briggs in the late 1960s, and subsequently published in a variety of MMPI guides and textbooks. These adolescent norms developed by Marks and Briggs (1972) were based on the responses of 1,766 normal adolescents grouped by ages 17, 16, 15, and a category of 14 and below, with norms presented separately for boys and girls. Marks, Seeman, and Haller (1974), reported the first actuarially based personality descriptors for a series of 29 MMPI code types based on the responses of approximately 1,250 adolescents who had undergone a minimum of 10 hours of psychotherapy between 1965 and 1973. The Marks et al. (1974) study was crucial in providing clinicians with the first clinical correlate information necessary to interpret adolescent code-type patterns. In 1987, Archer produced a comprehensive guide to using the MMPI with adolescents that summarized the available research literature and presented several sets of adolescent norms for the MMPI. Archer noted that there had been roughly 100 studies reported on the original version of the MMPI in adolescent samples from its release in 1943 until the mid 1980s.

We turn now to the next major development in the history of the test, the MMPI Restandardization Project, which yielded the two current versions of the instrument—the MMPI-2 and MMPI-A.

The MMPI Restandardization Project

A need to update and revise the MMPI had been recognized and expressed for some time prior to the launching of the Restandardization Project (c.f. Butcher, 1972). However, for a variety of reasons, it was not until the early 1980s that the test publisher, the University of Minnesota Press, launched an effort to examine the feasibility of, and eventually fund, a major revision of what by then had become the most widely used self report measure of personality (Lubin, Larsen, & Matarazzo, 1984).

As implied by the project's moniker, its primary focus was to update the test's original norms, which were based on a sample of Minnesotans tested in the late 1930s. As the project evolved, several additional goals emerged: to explore the feasibility of developing a separate, adolescent specific version of the test; to replace nonworking original MMPI items (i.e., ones that were not scored on the basic scales of the instrument) with new ones designed to assess then contemporary issues not covered adequately by the original item pool (e.g., suicidal ideation); to rewrite awkwardly phrased or otherwise problematic basic scale items; and to develop a new method for deriving standard scores for the scales of the instrument. The project was launched in 1982 and culminated in the publication of the revised adult version of the test, the MMPI-2 (Butcher et al., 1989) and an adolescent specific version, the MMPI-A (Butcher et al., 1992).

The MMPI-2

The MMPI-2 consists of 567 items. The new norms, collected throughout the United States during the mid 1980s, were based on a sample of 1,462 women and 1,138 men. Compared with the original normative sample of the test, the new sample was more representative of the U.S. population in terms of geographic residence and basic demographic features (e.g., race, age, and education). However, the new normative sample was considerably higher in Social Economic Status (SES) as indexed by education level in comparison with the U.S. population. This resulted in some early concerns that the new norms may be skewed as a result of the over representation of individuals with higher education levels. Schinka and LaLone (1997) recalculated the MMPI-2 norms based on a reduced sample designed to match national SES distributions and concluded that the resulting norms were not meaningfully different from the MMPI-2 norms. Thus, the relatively high SES standing of the MMPI-2 normative sample did not affect the utility of the revised norms.

At the outset of the Restandardization Project, the committee overseeing its execution decided that the original Clinical Scale would be left essentially intact. This was done in order to ensure continuity between the original and restandardized versions of the test. Consequently, only a very small number of objectionable items (e.g., ones dealing with religious practices and beliefs, sexual orientation, and bowel and bladder movements) were deleted. Other items were slightly modified in order to correct grammatical errors, improve awkwardly phrased statements, or remove sexist language. Studies by Ben-Porath and Butcher (1989a, 1989b) established that scores on the slightly modified Clinical Scales were essentially interchangeable with the original versions of these scales.

An important apparent exception to this finding involved the Clinical Scale code types. Even if the Clinical Scales had been left entirely intact, it was possible for patterns of scores on the scales to change if the new norms changed differentially across scales. Indeed, shortly after the MMPI-2 was released some authors questioned whether the new norms might impede code-type interpretation, based on observations that when code-types were derived, the new norms yielded seemingly discrepant results. Initial data suggesting this possibility were provided in the 1989 MMPI-2 manual, where it was reported that the same two-point code type is found in only two-thirds of cases where the same responses are plotted on MMPI and MMPI-2 norms. Dahlstrom (1992) reported similar results.

Concerns regarding code-type congruence or comparability across the two sets of norms were not trivial. At issue was the applicability of nearly 50 years of research and clinical experience with the MMPI, to MMPI-2 interpretation, which, as described earlier, is heavily influenced by code-type classification. If, in fact, in roughly one third of the cases the two sets of norms yielded different code types, which set of empirical correlates should be used in interpreting the profile? As it turned out, this concern was based on misleading data analyses including those reported in the 1989 MMPI-2 manual.

The method used to define code types in the analyses reported in the 1989 MMPI-2 manual and by Dahlstrom (1992) yields highly unstable and thus unreliable code types. A change of one T-score point on two scales can lead to an entirely different code type designation. Because neither MMPI nor MMPI-2 scales are perfectly reliable, meaningful code-type classification schemes cannot be sensitive to such minuscule changes. Rather, a minimal degree of differentiation between the scales in the code type and the remaining scales on the profile must be present for the code type to be stable.

Analyses conducted by Graham, Timbrook, Ben-Porath, and Butcher (1991) indicated that scales in a code type need to be at least five points higher than the remaining scales in a profile for the code type to be sufficiently stable. Such well-defined code types are also quite stable across the MMPI and MMPI-2 norms. Graham et al. (1991) reported congruence in 80% to 95% of clinical and nonclinical profiles when well-defined code types are evaluated. In nearly all of the relatively small proportion of cases where the same code type does not emerge, at least one scale appeared in both code types. McNulty, Ben-Porath, and Graham (1998) demonstrated subsequently that as expected, well defined code types produce more valid empirical correlates than nondefined ones.

Another potential source of change at the T-score level was the development of Uniform T-scores for the MMPI-2 (Tellegen & Ben-Porath, 1992). Briefly, uniform T-scores were developed to correct a long-recognized problem with MMPI T-scores. Because the raw score distributions for the clinical scales are differentially skewed, when using linear T-scores, the same value does not correspond to the same percentile across different scales. The lack of percentile equivalence across scales makes direct comparisons of T-scores on different clinical scales potentially misleading. The solution adopted for the MMPI-2 and MMPI-A was to compute the average distribution of non-K-corrected raw scores for men and women in the normative sample and correct each scale's distribution slightly to correspond to this composite. This is accomplished in the transformation of raw scores to T-scores. This approach yields percentile-equivalent T-scores while retaining the skewed nature of the clinical scales' distributions. By comparing profiles based on uniform versus traditional linear T-scores (both derived from the new normative sample), Graham et al. (1991) demonstrated that the uniform T-scores do not alter substantially the nature and characteristics of the MMPI-2 profile.

Thus, the Restandardization Committee's primary goal for the project, maintaining continuity of the Clinical Scale in the revised version of the test, was accomplished. As already mentioned, a secondary goal was to modernize the test by replacing nonworking items with new ones that would introduce new item content. These items were incorporated in a new set of scales introduced with the publication of the revised inventory, the MMPI-2 Content Scales (Butcher, Graham, Williams, & Ben-Porath, 1990).

The MMPI-2 Content Scales

The MMPI-2 Content Scales were developed through a series of rational-conceptual and empirical analyses fashioned after the ones used by Wiggins (1966) in developing the original content scales for the MMPI. Items were assigned first to potential scales based on a consensus among judges who conducted a rational examination of their content. Then, a series of statistical analyses was carried out to eliminate items that did not contribute to the internal consistency of a scale and to identify potential items for inclusion that were missed in the first round of rational analyses. The latter were then inspected rationally and added to a scale if they were found by consensus to be related to the domain that they were designed to measure. Final statistical analyses were conducted to eliminate items that created excessive intercorrelation among the content scales. This process yielded a set of 15 content scales. As might be expected, some of these scales are similar in composition to the ones developed by Wiggins (1966). Nearly all the scales have new items on them; some (e.g., Type A Behaviors and Negative Treatment Indicators) are composed predominantly of new items.

Although item analyses designed to maximize their internal consistency ensured that the MMPI-2 Content Scales would be considerably more homogeneous than the Clinical Scales, it remains possible to parse some of them even further into relatively independent item clusters. The MMPI-2 Content Component Scales were constructed by Ben-Porath and Sherwood (1993) to serve as subscales designed to clarify Content Scale interpretation much like the Harris Lingoes subscales are used with the Clinical Scales. The Content Component Scales were derived through a series of principal component and item analyses of each of the Content Scales separately, resulting in a total of 28 subscales for 12 of the 15 Content Scales (Anxiety, Obsessiveness, and Work Interference did not produce sufficiently independent subscales). Most Content Scales yielded only two component subscales.

During the decade following publication of the MMPI-2, research focused initially on comparing Clinical Scale scores based on the MMPI versus MMPI-2 norms. Surveys of practitioners (e.g., Webb, Levitt & Rojdev, 1993) indicated that most were quick to adopt the revised instrument. Consequently, the focus of MMPI-2 research soon shifted to validating the new scales and exploring further scale development based in part on the new items added to the inventory. To incorporate the wealth of information just mentioned, in 2001 a revised edition of the MMPI-2 manual was published (Butcher et al., 2001). The 2001 manual was designed to update interpretive guidelines for some scales of the MMPI-2 included in the 1989 manual, to formalize the discontinuation of others, and to provide guidelines for interpreting several new scales developed during the decade following the revision. The revised manual did not introduce any changes in the norms or item composition of the MMPI-2 scales included in the 1989 manual. Of the newer scales included in the 2001 manual, the Personality Psychopathology Five (PSY-5), introduced first by Harkness, McNulty, and Ben-Porath (1995) have been the most influential.

The PSY-5 Scales. The PSY-5 Scales are based on a personality model developed and described in detail by Harkness and McNulty (1994). The PSY-5 constructs originated from research conducted by Harkness (1992) using the clinical criteria for diagnosing personality disorders. Harkness, McNulty, and Ben-Porath (1995) used the MMPI-2 item pool to construct scales corresponding to these five constructs: Aggressiveness (AGGR), a measure of offensive, instrumental aggression designed to achieve a desired goal (as opposed to being reactive); Psychoticism (PSYC), a disconnection from reality reflected in unshared beliefs or unusual sensory and perceptual experiences; Disconstraint (DISC), a propensity toward risk taking, impulsivity, and the absence of moral restraint; Negative Emotionality Neuroticism (NEGE), a disposition to experience negative emotions; and Introversion/ Low Positive Emotions (INTR), a measure of low hedonic capacity and interpersonal isolation.

As already discussed, a primary goal of the committee responsible for developing the MMPI-2 was to maintain continuity with the original version of the test. This was accomplished by leaving the original Clinical Scales essentially intact. However, even their developer was keenly aware of the limitations of some of these scales:

> Our most optimistic expectation was that the methodology of the new test would be so clearly effective that there would soon be better devices with refinements of scales and general validity. We rather hoped that we ourselves might, with five years experience, greatly increase its validity and clinical usefulness, and perhaps even

develop more solidly based constructs or theoretical variables for a new inventory. (Hathaway, 1960)

Nevertheless, no successful effort to revise and modernize the basic source of information on the MMPI was launched for several additional decades following Hathaway's comments. This long-standing need was addressed with the introduction of the MMPI-2 Restructured Clinical (RC) Scales (Tellegen et al., 2003).

The MMPI-2 RC Scales. Soon after the revision process was completed, one MMPI-2 Restandardization Committee member, Auke Tellegen, began work on a major research project designed to explore the feasibility of improving the Clinical Scales. A decade later, this work culminated in the publication of the MMPI-2 RC. Tellegen et al. (2003) describe in detail the rationale, methods, and results of Tellegen's efforts. In the following, we briefly summarize this work.

Why Restructure the Clinical Scales? The Clinical Scales' primary limitation involves their discriminant validity. Because of unexpectedly high correlations (based on what is known about the constructs they assess) between them, amplified by considerable item overlap, the Clinical Scales individually have limited discriminant abilities. This shortcoming is in part a product of how the empirical keying technique was applied in assigning items to the Clinical Scales, based primarily on their ability to discriminate between a patient group and a common normal comparison sample. Because (essentially) the same normal reference group was used in constructing them, each of the eight scales wound up with items that either characterizes the patient group or the difference between being a patient and not being one. Their heterogeneous makeup is another limitation of the Clinical Scales that diminishes their convergent validity. Finally, the near-total absence of theory to help guide their interpretation restricts the ability MMPI users to rely on construct validity in Clinical Scale interpretation.

Goals and Method of Developing the RC Scales Tellegen's goal in developing the RC Scales was to explore the feasibility of restructuring the Clinical Scales in a manner that would address directly the limitations just noted; yielding a parsimonious set of scales\ with improved discriminant and/or convergent validity that may be linked to contemporary theories and models of personality and psychopathology. Tellegen et al. (2003) describe the methods used in developing the RC Scales in detail; they will be summarized briefly here. Scale development proceeded in four steps. The first involved devising a marker of the MMPI common factor, which is overrepresented in the Clinical Scales as a result of how they were constructed. Tellegen et al. (2003) labeled this factor Demoralization. Step 2 was designed to identify the major distinctive core component of each Clinical Scale, and it was hypothesized that this would consist of something other than Demoralization. Factor analyses were conducted separately with the items of each Clinical Scale combined with the Demoralization markers identified in Step 1. The first factor that emerged in each case included the Demoralization markers as well as Clinical Scale items that are primarily correlated with this construct. The second (and in some cases third) factor included items representing a core component of the Clinical Scale that was distinct from Demoralization. In Step 3, these core markers were refined further to yield a maximally distinct set of Seed (S) scales. This step included the removal of all item overlap and retention for the S scales of core items that correlated maximally with a given potential S scale and minimally the remaining candidate S scales. Step 4 involved analyses of the entire MMPI-2 item pool. An item was added to a given S scale and included on the final Restructured Scale if it correlated more highly with that S scale than any other, the correlation exceeded a certain specified value, and it did not correlate beyond a specified level with any other seed scale. The specific criteria varied across scales as specified by Tellegen et al. (2003).

The result of this four step process was a set of nine nonoverlapping scales representing Demoralization and the distinct core component of each of the eight original Clinical Scales. Restructured Scales were not developed for Clinical Scales 5 or 0 because the focus of the RC Scales was on measuring psychopathology. Further, ongoing scale development efforts described later include some of the core components of these two scales. The nine RC Scales are made up of 192 MMPI-2 items and described briefly in Table 3.2.

We turn next to the adolescent-specific version of the MMPI, the MMPI-A (Butcher et al., 1992).

MMPI-A

In July 1989, an advisory committee was appointed by the University of Minnesota Press to develop an adolescent form of the MMPI. A main goal was to maintain substantial continuity with the original MMPI, including the preservation of the basic validity and clinical scale. An additional goal of the project involved the collection of a normative sample representative of a contemporary and diverse adolescent population.

The MMPI-A is designed to be used with adolescents ages 14 through 18, and should never be given to an individual older than 18 (Butcher et al., 1992). At the other end of the age continuum, the MMPI-A can be used selectively with 12- and 13-year-old adolescents if they are developmentally advanced and have the necessary cognitive and reading skills (i.e., 6th- to 7th-grade reading ability) to successfully respond to test items (Butcher et al., 1992; Archer, 2005).

While the MMPI-A consists of 478 items, an abbreviated administration

Table 3.2 MMPI-2 Restructured Clinical (RC) Scales

Scale Label	Abbreviation	Brief Description
Demoralization	RCd	General dissatisfaction, unhappiness, inefficacy
Somatic Complaints	RC1	Self-reported pain related, gastrointestinal, and neurological complaints
Low Positive Emotions	RC2	Lack of, or incapacity to, experience positive emotions; anhedonia
Cynicism	RC3	Non-self-referential belief in human badness, misanthropia
Antisocial Behavior	RC4	Juvenile misconduct, family problems, substance mis-use
Ideas of Persecution	RC6	Self-referential persecutory ideation
Dysfunctional Negative Emotions	RC7	Anxiety, irritability, anger, over-sensitivity, vulnerability
Aberrant Experiences	RC8	Unusual perceptual and thought processes
Hypomanic Activation	RC9	Impulsivity, grandiosity, aggression, and generalized activation

may be conducted using the first 350 items which permits the scoring of all ten basic clinical scales and most validity scales. The MMPI-A basic scales were adapted from the original MMPI form with the deletion of a total of 58 basic scale items. Similar to the MMPI-2, items eliminated from the original form in the creation of the MMPI-A typically related to religious attitudes and practices, sexual preferences, and bowel and bladder functioning, but also included some additional items that were deemed inappropriate in the evaluation of adolescents (e.g., voting in elections). The resulting MMPI-A included the original ten clinical scales and the three basic validity scales of *L*, *F*, and *K*. Four additional validity scales were added to the MMPI-A, which were the *F1* and *F2* 33-item subscales of the 66-item *F* scale, the True Response Inconsistency (TRIN) Scale, and the Variable Response Inconsistency (VRIN) Scale. Table 3.3 provides an overview of the scale structure of the MMPI-A.

In addition to the Basic and Validity scales, the MMPI-A contains 15 Content Scales which have a considerable degree of overlap with the 15 Content Scales found on the MMPI-2. The Content Scales uniquely found on the MMPI-A are Alienation (*A-aln*), Low Aspiration (*A-las*), School Problems (*A-sch*), and Conduct Problems (*A-con*). The prefix A is used to differentiate MMPI-A Content Scales from their MMPI-2 counterparts. A comprehensive discussion of the development of the MMPI-A Content Scales is provided in

Table 3.3 Overview of the MMPI-A Scale Structure

Basic Profile Scales (17 scales)

Standard Scales (13)
  L (Lie)
  F (Infrequency)
  K (Defensiveness)
  Clinical Scales Hs (Hypochondriasis) through Si (Social Introversion)
Additional Validity Scales (4)
  F_1/F_2 (Subscales of F Scale)
  VRIN (Variable Response Inconsistency)
  TRIN (True Response Inconsistency)
Content Scales (15)
  A-anx (Anxiety)
  A-obs (Obsessiveness)
  A-dep (Depression)
  A-hea (Health Concerns)
  A-aln (Alienation)
  A-bix (Bizarre Mentation)
  A-ang (Anger)
  A-cyn (Cynicism)
  A-con (Conduct Problems)
  A-lse (Low Self-esteem)
  A-las (Low Aspirations)
  A-sod (Social Discomfort)
  A-fam (Family Problems)
  A-sch (School Problems)
  A-trt (Negative Treatment Indicators)
Supplementary Scales (11)
  MAC-R (MacAndrew Alcoholism-Revised)
  ACK (Alcohol/Drug Problem Acknowledgment)
  PRO (Alcohol/Drug Problem Proneness)
  IMM (Immaturity)
  A (Anxiety)
  R (Repression)
PSY-5 Scales
  Aggressiveness (AGGR)
  Psychoticism (PSYC)
  Disconstraint (DISC)
  Negative Emotionality/Neuroticism (NEGE)
  Introversion/Positive Emotionality (INTR)
Additional Subscales
  Harris-Lingoes and Si Subscales (31 subscales)
  Content Component Subscales (31 subscales)

Williams, Butcher, Ben-Porath, and Graham (1992). After the identification of MMPI-2 Content Scale items that were appropriate for adaptation for adolescents, the MMPI-A Content Scales were refined by deleting or adding items based on their relative contribution to the overall reliability of each of the Content Scales. A rational review of scale-item content was then completed to ensure that items appeared appropriate for measuring the underlying scale constructs. Finally, items correlating more strongly with scales other than the content scale to which they were originally assigned were deleted from the item content of that scale. The developmental process utilized in developing the MMPI-A and MMPI-2 Content Scales produced scales which contained a high degree of face validity and are, therefore, easily influenced by response style factors such as an individual's tendency to underreport or overreport their actual level of symptomatology. Further, although the MMPI-A Content Scales have relatively high alpha coefficient values given the methodology used to develop these measures, most of these scales have also been found to possess two or more discrete subcomponents. Sherwood, Ben-Porath, and Williams (1997) have recently developed a set of content component scales for 13 of the 15 MMPI-A Content Scales to facilitate the evaluation of specific areas of content endorsement. The description of these content component scales\, as well as other newer features of the MMPI-A, can be found in the MMPI-A Manual Supplement by Ben-Porath, Graham, Archer, Tellegen, and Kaemmer (2006).

The supplementary scales of the MMPI-A include three scales developed for the original MMPI which are the Anxiety (A), Repression (R), and the MacAndrew Alcoholism Scale Revised (MAC-*R*). Additional supplemental scales include the Immaturity (*IMM*) Scale which was developed by Archer, Pancoast, and Gordon (1994), the Alcohol/Drug Problem (PRO) Scale, and the Alcohol/Drug Acknowledgement (ACK) Scale developed by Weed, Butcher, and Williams (1994). The relatively low number of item deletions made to the MMPI-A Clinical Scales rendered it possible to retain the Harris-Lingoes (1955) Content Scales and to extend their application to the MMPI-A. Additionally, the Si subscales developed for the MMPI-2 by Ben-Porath, Hostetler, Butcher, and Graham (1989) are also included on the MMPI-A Subscale Profile Sheet. Most recently, the MMPI-A Personality Psychopathology-5 (PSY-5) scales developed by McNulty, Harkness, Ben-Porath, and Williams (1997) have been incorporated into the supplementary scales of the MMPI-A. The 115 item MMPI-A version of the PSY-5 scales shares 87 items with the MMPI-2 PSY-5 scales, and psychometrically focuses on the same underlying constructs related to Aggressiveness (AGGR), Psychoticism (PSYC), Disconstraint (DISC), Negative Emotionality/Neuroticism (NEGE), and Introversion/Positive Emotionality (INTR). Thus, a review of the MMPI-A scale and subscale features reveal numerous similarities between the MMPI-A and both the original MMPI and the MMPI-2.

In addition to the MMPI-A scale and subscale structure, an MMPI-A critical item list has been developed by Forbey and Ben-Porath (1998) using a combination of empirical and rational methods. The 82 items identified in the MMPI-A critical item list were nominated by doctoral-level clinicians familiar with the MMPI-A or adolescent development, and were endorsed by 30% or less of the adolescents in the normative sample. The final set of critical items included 15 critical item content categories including, Aggression, Conduct Problems, and Depression/Suicidal Ideation.

Approaches to MMPI-2 and MMPI-A Interpretation

As just reviewed, MMPI scales were first developed following strictly empirical procedures, but content-based approaches were eventually incorporated as well. Ben-Porath (2003) reviewed the extensive literature on the relative merits of empirical versus content-based approaches to self report inventory scale construction. A consensus has emerged in this research that content-based approaches, provided that they are augmented by empirical refinement of the initial content-based selection of items, can yield scales of at least comparable (to empirically constructed ones) validity. Ben-Porath (2003) also noted that empirically developed scales can be interpreted on the basis of their content, and measures constructed initially based on item content considerations can be interpreted on the basis of their empirical correlates.

Such was the case with the original MMPI. Harris and Lingoes (1955) developed a set of subscales for most of the original Clinical Scales by rationally assigning their items to content categories. The *Harris-Lingoes (H-L) subscales* are still used routinely in MMPI-2 and MMPI-A interpretation. Because their content is very heterogeneous, it is possible for very different sets of responses to yield comparable scores on the Clinical Scales. The H-L subscales assist the interpreter by indicating which set(s) of items contributed to an elevated score on a given Clinical Scale. Thus, content considerations are incorporated in the interpretation of the empirically-constructed Clinical Scales.

Conversely, interpretation of content-based scales, such as those constructed by Wiggins (1966), and Butcher et al. (1990) for the MMPI-2, and Williams et al. (1992) for the MMPI-A need not be limited to attributing the item content of an elevated scale to the test taker (e.g., describing someone who produced an elevated score on a content-based measure of depression as "reporting symptoms of depression"). Rather, empirical research can establish the correlates of elevated scores on Content Scales, and thus allow their interpretation to be based both on content and empirical considerations.

The two foundations for MMPI scale interpretation just described are based on considerations of criterion (for empirical correlates) and content (for content-based interpretation) validity. A third source for generating valid interpretation of scores on self report inventories is construct validity. Cronbach and Meehl (1955) described construct validation as an ongoing process of learning (through empirical research) about the nature of psychological constructs that underlie scale scores and using this knowledge to guide and refine their interpretation. They defined the seemingly paradoxical "bootstraps" effect whereby a test may be constructed based on a fallible criterion and, through the process of construct validation, that same test winds up having greater validity than the criterion used in its construction. As an example, they cited the MMPI *Pd* scale, which was developed using an external scale construction approach with the intent that it be used to identify individuals with a psychopathic personality. Cronbach and Meehl (1955) noted that the scale turned out to have a limited degree of criterion validity for this task. However, as its empirical correlates became elucidated through subsequent research, a construct underlying Pd scores emerged that allowed MMPI interpreters to describe individuals who score high on this scale based on both a broad range of empirical correlates and a conceptual understanding of the Pd construct. The latter allowed for further predictions about likely Pd correlates to be made and tested empirically. These tests, in turn, broadened or sharpened (depending on the research outcome) the scope of the Pd construct and its empirical correlates.

Regrettably, although early experiences with the MMPI inspired some of Cronbach and Meehl's (1955) formulation of construct validity, this particular approach has played a rather minimal role in MMPI, MMPI-2, and MMPI-A interpretation. Current interpretive guides to the tests (e.g., Archer, 2005; Graham, 2006; Greene, 2000) focus primarily on the empirical correlates of MMPI-2 and MMPI-A scales and code types. Until recently, construct validity played a rather limited role in MMPI interpretation. With the introduction of the PSY-5 Scales for the MMPI-2 and MMPI-A, and, most recently, the RC Scales for the MMPI-2 construct validity has taken on an increased role in the interpretation of these tests.

We turn next to a vital aspect of MMPI-2 and MMPI-A interpretation, the use of validity scale to assess a number of threats to the interpretability of a test-taker's protocol. We begin by describing the threats, and then the MMPI-2 and MMPI-A Validity Scales used to assess these threats.

Assessing Protocol Validity with the MMPI-2 and MMPI-A

Ben-Porath (2006) identified two general classes of threats to the validity of a self-report test protocol. *Noncontent based threats* involve any response pattern that is not based on an accurate reading, comprehension, and consideration of the instrument's items. *Content-based threats* are the product of misleading responses to properly read, comprehended, and considered test items.

The MMPI-2 and MMPI-A Validity Scales target three types of non-content based threats. *Nonresponding* occurs when a test taker fails to answer an item or answers it both true and false. *Random responding* occurs when the test taker responds to the items in a nonsystematic manner without accurately considering their content. Random responding may be intentional, as in the case of an individual who marks her or his answers without attempting to read the items. It may also be unintentional if the individuals lacks the requisite reading or language comprehension skills to be able to read and comprehend the test's items or is confused and disorganized and responds, therefore, based on an inaccurate consideration of their content. The VRIN Scale (on both the MMPI-2 and MMPI-A) assists in identifying random responding, but not in distinguishing between its intentional or unintentional origins. The third type of noncontent-based responding is *fixed responding*, which involves a fixed pattern of responding without consideration of an item's content. The MMPI-2 and MMPI-A TRIN scale provides information on the extent and direction of fixed responding. Unlike random responding, fixed responding, although rare, is almost always volitional. It too threatens the validity of all MMPI-2 scales including measures of content-based invalid responding.

The MMPI-2 Validity Scales assess for two types of content-based invalid responding. Over reporting involves any response pattern where the individual describes herself or himself as being worse off psychologically than an objective assessment would indicate. Three MMPI-2 *Infrequency Scales* F, F_B, and Fp are used to gauge over reporting. They have recently been augmented by a fourth Validity Scale, the *Fake Bad Scale* (FBS; Lees-Haley, English, & Glenn, 1991). Recent research, summarized effectively by Greiffenstein Fox, and Lees-Haley (In Press), indicates that elevated scores on this scale are helpful in detecting noncredible reports of cognitive and somatic problems, particularly in neuropsychological evaluations.

The MMPI-A also has three infrequency scales which are F, $F1$, and $F2$. The F Scale underwent a major revision in its transition from the original MMPI to the MMPI-A, leading to the creation of a 66-item F Scale determined by selecting items endorsed in the deviant direction by no more that 20% of the 1,620 boys and girls in the MMPI-A normative sample. The first 33 of these items, which extends roughly to the midpoint of the test booklet, form the $F1$ subscale. The last 33 items to appear in the F Scales comprise the $F2$ subscale, which appears in the second half of the test booklet. Similar to the MMPI-2, elevations on the MMPI-A F or its subscales indicate that adolescents are endorsing a high number of unusual or infrequently endorsed symptoms, and are often related to adolescents who are randomly responding to the test booklet or who are over-reporting their actual degree of symptomatology.

The second content based threat to protocol validity is *Under Reporting*. Here, a comparison between the individual's self-report and an objective assessment would reveal that the test taker has failed to report the nature and/or extent of her/his psychological difficulties. The original MMPI scales *L* and *K* are used to detect and quantify the presence, nature and extent of under-reporting with both the MMPI-2 and MMPI-A. Butcher and Han (1995) developed another MMPI-2 underreporting measure, the *Superlative Self-Presentation (S) Scale* by contrasting the responses of individuals highly motivated to under report with those of MMPI-2 normative sample members. Preliminary studies (e.g., Baer & Miller, 2002; Baer, Wetter, Nichols, & Greene, 1995) have indicated that this scale may add to *L* and *K* in detecting under reporting with the MMPI-2. Further research is needed to clarify how it might best be used to augment *L* and *K* interpretation in this task.

Basic Psychometrics

Reliability

MMPI-2

The MMPI-2 manual (Butcher et al., 2001), the PSY-5 test report (Harkness, McNulty, Ben-Porath, & Graham, 2002), and the RC Scale monograph (Tellegen et al., 2003) provide detailed information concerning the reliability of the various MMPI-2 scales. A concise summary is provided here.

The Clinical Scales are the least internally consistent of the MMPI-2 substantive scales, which is expected as they were not designed to be homogeneous. The Content, PSY-5, and RC Scales were all constructed with an emphasis on internal consistency. In the MMPI-2 normative sample, internal consistencies for the Clinical Scales range from .34 to .85 for men and from .37 to .87 for women, the RC Scales from .63 to .87 for men and 62 to .89 for women, and the Content Scales from .72 to .86 for men and from .68 to .86 for women. The Supplementary Scales' internal consistencies range from .34 to .89 for men and .24 to .90 for women, whereas the PSY-5 Scales range from .65 to .84 for both men and women.

In the normative sample, test-retest correlations for the Clinical Scales range from .67 to .93 for men and from .54 to .92 for women. For the RC Scales, they range from .62 to .88 for the combined sample, and the Content Scales from .77 to .91 for men and .78 to .91 for women. The Supplementary Scales have test-retest correlations that range from .63 to .91 for men and from .69 to .91 for women. Harkness et al. (2002) reported PSY-5 Scale test-retest coefficients for the overall sample, which range from .78 to .88.

Overall scores on the substantive scales of the MMPI-2 are sufficiently reliable. The test manual and RC Scale monograph provide data on the standard errors of measurement associated with these scales based on the test-retest reliability data just cited.

MMPI-A

The MMPI-A Manual (Butcher et al., 1992) provides information concerning the internal consistency and reliability of the MMPI-A Basic Scales, Content Scales, and Supplementary Scales. The test-retest correlations of the MMPI-A Basic Scales range from .49 to .84. In general, MMPI-A values are quite similar to test-retest correlations reported for the MMPI-2 Basic Scales. Stein, McClinton, and Graham (1998) evaluated the long-term (1-year) test-retest reliability for the MMPI-A scales and these authors reported Basic Scale values ranging from .51 to .75. Test-retest correlations for the Content Scales, in contrast, ranged from .40 to .73.

The standard error of measurement for MMPI-A Basic Scales has been estimated to be in the range of two to three raw score points, generally corresponding to about 5 T-score points (Butcher et al., 1992). This standard error of measurement is quite important when attempting to evaluate changes shown on repeated administrations of the MMPI-A in terms of separating significant clinical changes representing real changes in psychological functioning from changes that might be attributable to measurement error. In general, changes shown on the MMPI-A that occur within a range of five T-score points or less are more likely to reflect measurement error than reliable changes in psychological functioning.

The internal consistency of the MMPI-A Basic Scale, as represented by coefficient alpha values, range from relatively low values on such scales as *Mf* and *Pa* (.40 to .60) to substantially higher values for other basic scales such as *Hs* (.78) and *Sc* (.89). The coefficient alpha statistic is a measure of the extent to which items within a scale tend to intercorrelate, a desirable feature of scales measuring a homogeneous or unitary construct. In contrast to the basic scale, internal consistency scores tend to be higher for other MMPI-A scales, such as content scale s, because alpha coefficient results were utilized in the construction of these more recent MMPI-A scales. The MMPI-A Manual Supplement (Ben-Porath et al., 2006) provides information concerning the reliability characteristics of the MMPI-A content component scales and the MMPI-A PSY-5 Scales.

In addition to the test-retest and internal consistency measures of reliability, the MMPI-A Manual (Butcher et al., 1992) also provides information concerning the item endorsement frequencies and reading levels required by each of the MMPI-A items. The manual also presents findings from a Principal Component Analyses (PCA) of the MMPI-A Basic Scales using a

Varimax rotation procedure. As reported in the manual, the large first factor identified in this PCA was labeled General Maladjustment, the second factor was identified as Over Control, and the third and fourth factors appear to reflect the nonclinical dimensions related to MMPI-A Basic Scales *Si* and *Mf*, respectively.

Validity

MMPI-2

A vast literature exists on the validity of the MMPI-2, and it is by far the most widely studied measure of psychopathology and personality (Butcher & Rouse, 1996). Dahlstrom, Welsh, and Dahlstrom (1975) referenced more than 6,000 research studies conducted with the original MMPI. Many of these studies followed Meehl's (1956) call for a "good cookbook" where he urged researchers to identify empirical correlates for the test's scales and code types. Numerous studies were conducted with psychiatric inpatients (e.g., Marks & Seeman, 1963; Gilberstadt & Duker, 1965), medical patients (Guthrie, 1949), adolescents (Archer, Gordon, Giannetti, & Singles, 1988; Hathaway & Monachesi, 1963), and normal college students (e.g., Black, 1953).

This trend has continued with the MMPI-2. Graham (2006) indicated that more than 2,800 journal articles, book chapters, and textbooks about the test have been published since the release of the MMPI-2 in 1989. Although it is well beyond the scope of this chapter to summarize these studies, we provide some overall conclusions regarding the validity of the various MMPI-2 scales.

Many research studies have supported the use of the MMPI-2 Validity Scales as measures of protocol validity. Rogers, Sewell, Martin, and Vitacco (2003) conducted a meta-analysis on the MMPI-2 over reporting scales and found that the infrequency scales (F, F_B, and F_p) were effective in detecting malingering. They also noted that F_p consistently had the largest effect size in differentiating individuals asked to malinger from those who took the test under standard instructions. Arbisi and Ben-Porath (1998) found that F_p added incrementally to F in differentiating psychiatric inpatients asked to over report from those who took the test honestly. Another meta-analysis by Baer and Miller (2002) indicated that the L scale was consistently the best predictor of under reporting, but noted effectiveness for K as well. A recent addition to the standard set of MMPI-2 Validity Scales, the Fake Bad Scale (FBS, Lees-Haley, English, & Glenn, 1991) has also been the subject of substantial research that has established its validity as an indicator of noncredible symptom reporting, particularly in neuropsychological and personal injury evaluations. This literature was recently meta-analyzed by Nelson, Sweet, and Demakis (2006), who found good empirical support for the FBS.

The convergent validity of the Clinical, Content, Supplementary, and

PSY-5 Scales and Code Types has been established in outpatient (Graham, Ben-Porath, & McNulty, 1999; Harkness et al., 2002), inpatient (Arbisi, Ben-Porath, & McNulty, 2003; Archer, Griffin, & Aiduk, 1995; Archer, Aiduk, Griffin, & Elkins, 1996), forensic (Petroskey, Ben-Porath, & Stafford, 2003), college student (Ben-Porath, McCully, & Almagor, 1993), and private practice samples (Sellbom, Graham, & Schenk, 2005). These correlates have been remarkably similar across studies and also congruent with those of the original MMPI (Graham, 2006), indicating that the correlates of the MMPI-2 generalize well across settings.

However, the discriminant validity for several MMPI-2 scales has been problematic, stemming in large part (but not exclusively) from the influence of Demoralization as described earlier in the development of the RC Scales. Item overlap within the Clinical and Content Scales has also restricted their discriminant validity. In their monograph on the RC Scales, Tellegen et al. (2003) demonstrate with large datasets of individuals receiving inpatient and outpatient mental health services that the RC Scales have substantially improved discriminant validity when compared with the original Clinical Scales. These findings have subsequently been replicated in a variety of settings including outpatient mental health clients (Simms, Casillas, Clark, Watson, & Doebbeling; 2005; Wallace, & Liljequist, 2005), private practice clients (Sellbom, Graham, & Schenk, 2006), college counseling clients (Sellbom, Ben-Porath, & Graham, 2006), substance abuse treatment receivers (Forbey & Ben-Porath, 2007a), and others. Sellbom & Ben-Porath (2005) provided evidence of the improved construct validity of the RC Scales, findings that support increased reliance on construct validity in the interpretation of these scales.

MMPI-A

The MMPI produced a considerable literature base with adolescents, and much of this can be extended to the MMPI-A because of the substantial similarities between the original test instrument and the revised form (Archer, 2005). Archer (1987) noted that there are roughly 100 studies using the original form of the MMPI in adolescent populations that were published between 1943 and the mid-1980s. More recently Forbey (2003) reviewed the literature on the MMPI-A and identified approximately 112 books, chapters, and research articles published in the initial decade following the release of the MMPI-A. In his review of this literature, Forbey observed that the content of research studies addressing the MMPI-A may be grouped into several broad categories. One category focused on general methodological issues including articles describing the development and performance of validity scales, particularly research findings evaluating the usefulness of detecting various forms of invalid responding through the use of the MMPI-A Validity Scales. A second general content area included the use of the MMPI-A with specific diagnostic groups (e.g., eating disorders, conduct disorders, or depressed adolescents). A third major MMPI-A grouping consisted of articles related to ethnical and cultural issue translations of the MMPI-A. Finally, Forbey identified several books and book chapters as those that serve as instructional guides for the use of the MMPI-A. Archer and Krishnamurthy (2002), for example, have provided a detailed guide for the appropriate administration, scoring, and interpretation of the MMPI-A and Pope, Butcher, and Seelen (2006) have provided guidance regarding the use of the MMPI-A (and MMPI-2) in courtroom settings. Overall, it would appear that research with the MMPI-A is progressing at an accelerated rate in contrast to the adolescent research investigations reported through the original form of the MMPI and much of this literature is relevant to the validity of this instrument in various settings or applications.

Information concerning the correlates of the original MMPI-A Basic Scales for adolescents have been reported by several researchers, including Hathaway and Monachesi (1963) and by Archer (1987). In addition, the MMPI-A Manual (Butcher et al., 1992) provides substantial MMPI-A Basic Scale correlate information based on analyses conducted with the adolescents from the MMPI-A normative sample as well as adolescents in treatment settings. Furthermore, basic clinical scale correlate information has been provided in Archer (2005) for samples of adolescents receiving psychiatric inpatient treatment. In general, the clinical correlates found for the MMPI-A Basic Scale show a high degree of consistency with correlate patterns produced for the MMPI-2 corresponding basic scaless. Empirically derived MMPI-A Content Scale descriptors have also been reported by Williams, Butcher, Ben-Porath, and Graham (1992), and by Archer and Gordon (1991).

The MMPI-A also has an extensive literature on the validity of this test instrument when applied to a variety of special populations. The identification and assessment of juvenile delinquents with the MMPI and MMPI-A, for example, has an extensive history beginning with the landmark studies of Dora Capwell (1945a, 1945b). Capwell demonstrated the usefulness of the *Pd* Scale in identifying delinquent adolescents. Hathaway and Monachesi (e.g., 1963) conducted longitudinal investigations that showed that elevations on three of the MMPI Basic Scales (i.e., *Pd*, *Sc*, and *Ma*) were related to an increased risk of juvenile delinquency. More recent investigations such as those by Hicks, Rogers, and Cashel (2000) have shown that elevations on MMPI-A individual Basic Scales, such as scale *Pa*, were important in predicting violent infractions for incarcerated adolescents.

A converging body of literature also shows the effectiveness of the MMPI-A substance abuse scales in identifying adolescents with drug and alcohol problems. Weed, Butcher, and Williams (1994), for example, have demonstrated the ability of the *ACK* and *PRO* supplementary scales in differentiating adolescents with substance abuse histories from nonabusers. Their findings were based on an initial evaluation of these scales using 1,620 adolescents from the MMPI-A normative sample, 462 adolescents in alcohol treatment units, and 251 adolescents receiving psychiatric treatment. The literature has also produced substantial support for the use of the *MAC* Scales (and the revised form of this scale developed for the MMPI-A, i.e., *MAC-R*) in identifying adolescents with a wide array of substance abuse problems. Findings by Gantner, Graham, and Archer (1992), for example, indicated the effectiveness of the *MAC* in accurately discriminating substance abusers from psychiatric inpatients and from normal high school students.

As noted by Archer and Krishnamurthy (2002), the MMPI-A has also received research attention in the evaluation of adolescents with eating disorders and with sexually abused adolescents. These research findings demonstrate that eating disorder adolescents are likely to show signs of emotional distress and psychopathology, but attempts to diagnosis specific forms of eating disorders from MMPI-A profile results are not recommended. These authors also noted that the MMPI and MMPI-A profiles of sexually-abused teenagers are also likely to show clinical scale elevations reflective of emotional distress including depression and anxiety, but cautioned that no single MMPI-A profile pattern can be used to identify sexually abused adolescents.

Administration and Scoring

The MMPI-2 should only be administered to those who are 18 years of age or older. The MMPI-A has been normalized for adolescents 14 through 18 years of age. An 18- year-old can be administered either version of the test, depending upon the circumstances of the assessment. Certain conditions may preclude an individual from taking the MMPI-2 or MMPI-A. The MMPI-2 manual authors (Butcher et al., 2001) recommend that individuals who have less than a 6th-grade reading level not be administered the test in the standard format; however, some persons with limited reading ability can complete the test if it is presented using a standard audio version of the test available on cassette or CD. Audio versions of both the MMPI-2 and MMPI-A are available. In addition, both versions of the test can be administered by computer using software distributed by Pearson Assessments. Computerized test administration is discussed further later in this chapter. Other conditions that might preclude an MMPI-2 or MMPI-A administration include altered cognitive states or confusion stemming from brain impairment, significant physical disability, or severe psychopathology.

According to the test manuals, the MMPI-2 and MMPI-A should be administered in a quiet and comfortable place for the test taker. The test booklets include standard instructions to the test taker that should not be altered. It takes about 60 to 75 minutes to complete the MMPI-2 and up to 75 minutes to complete the MMPI-A. Computerized administration speeds up the process considerably. Complicating factors such as disabling psychopathology, low reading level, or lower intellectual functioning may result in a longer test taking time.

The MMPI-2 and MMPI-A can be scored by hand, using standard scoring templates and profile sheets available from Pearson Assessments, or by computer. Hand scoring the tests is a laborious process that is laden with potential for error. Moreover, because it is time consuming, hand scorers often do not score all of the standard scales of these instruments. Automated scoring, using approved, quality-controlled scoring software is faster and more reliable, and recommended whenever possible. Automated scoring can be accomplished by use of scannable answer sheets or manual entry of the test-taker's responses as recorded on an answer sheet. The former is recommended for increased speed and reliability.

Administration and scoring of the MMPI-2 and MMPI-A can be assigned to psychometric assistants provided that they are trained and supervised by a qualified user of the test. The Cautions box provides some reminders and cautions for personnel assigned to administration and scoring responsibilities for these tests.

Cautions: Administration and Scoring Cautions

- Establish rapport with the adolescent or adult before testing.
- Never administer the MMPI-2 to someone under 18 years of age or the MMPI-A to someone over 18 years of age.
- Don't forget to determine the test taker's reading capacity.
- Don't send the test booklet home with an adolescent or adult to complete on their own.
- Always provide an appropriate, quiet, supervised testing environment.
- Audiotape/CD versions of the MMPI-2 and MMPI-A are available for test takers with reading problems or visual limitations.
- If hand scoring, use gender-appropriate scoring templates for all scales and the appropriate profile sheets for K-corrected versus non-K-Corrected scores on the Clincial Scales.
- If computer scoring by manual entry of responses, be sure that the correct response is key-entered for each item.
- Computer-generated test interpretations can be helpful, but the user is responsible for taking all of the circumstances of the evaluation into account in generating her/his own interpretation of the results.

Computerization

As just mentioned, the MMPI-2 and MMPI-A can be administered and scored by computer. It is important that only officially sanctioned and quality controlled software be used for these purposes. Computerized administration of the MMPI-2 and MMPI-A is designed to mimic, as closely as possible, booklet administration of the instruments, the modality used to collect normative data for these tests. Thus, the 567 or 478 items of the MMPI-2 and MMPI-A respectively are administered in their standard booklet order.

An alternative approach to computerized administration of the MMPI-2 and MMPI-A, which has been under investigation for some time, is Computerized *Adaptive* (CA) administration. Forbey and Ben-Porath (2007b) review the literature on *CA* administration of the MMPI instruments. They define *CA* testing as involving discontinuation of administration of a test's or scale's items once the assessment question has been answered. A series of studies have focused on the feasibility and utility of CA administration of the MMPI-2 (Ben-Porath, Slutske, & Butcher, 1989; Forbey and Ben-Porath, 2007b; Handel, Ben-Porath, & Watt, 1999; and Roper, Ben-Porath, & Butcher, 1991, 1995). These studies have established that it is possible to reduce substantially the number of MMPI-2 items administered while producing comparable scale scores and validities. Early research with a CA version of the MMPI-A (Forbey, Handel, & Ben-Porath, 2000) has also been promising. However, CA versions of the MMPI-2 and MMPI-A are still in research and development, and are not presently available for applied assessments.

Computer technology has also been used extensively in MMPI-2 and MMPI-A interpretation. Unlike administration and scoring software, which is quality controlled by the test distributor, computer-based test interpretation (CBTI) systems are unregulated or controlled. Early CBTIs provided bulleted lists of features attributed to the test taker based on the test results. More recent systems have provided narrative interpretations designed to mimic a psychological report. Williams and Weed (2004a) provide a review of the primary features of the major MMPI-2 CBTIs. In an empirical study, these authors (Williams & Weed, 2004b) collected rating data from potential users on features of the various MMPI-2 interpretive programs. Some programs were found to be more consistent and comprehensive than others, and there were also differences between the programs in the degree to which they produced seemingly contradictory interpretations. No single program stood out as the best in all respects among the reports included in that study.

CBTI users are often admonished by statements included in their output indicating that generating a CBTI does not relieve the test user of the obligation to interpret the resulting test scores on their own. Automated interpretations may be a source of assistance in the interpretation process, but they should not take the place of the responsible clinician. These programs produce very reliable output; that is, the same set of scores generated in the same setting will always yield the same interpretation. However, this is both an advantage (reliability) and disadvantage (inflexibility) of these systems. Another challenge for CBTI users is that these products rarely provide a detailed account of the source of the interpretive statements they generate (i.e., what score(s) are responsible for a given interpretive statement). This lack of transparency may create difficulties for users, especially in cases where they may need to testify about their findings in court.

Applications and Limitations

MMPI-2

The MMPI-2 is used broadly across a wide range of settings and for a variety of assessments (cited earlier). The most common application for the test is in traditional mental health settings (e.g., outpatient, inpatient) where the MMPI-2 is used frequently in diagnostic assessments, treatment planning, and as a general measure of psychopathology and personality. Although it has been long established that the MMPI, and later the MMPI-2, is not able to predict specific psychiatric diagnoses with sufficient accuracy to derive diagnoses on the basis of test scores alone, scores on the test are associated with symptoms of psychopathology and can serve as the basis for identifying potential diagnoses that require follow up by the clinician to determine whether the individual satisfies criteria for a given diagnosis. Current interpretive guides (e.g., Graham, 2006; Greene, 2000) list the empirical correlates of scores on the MMPI-2 and the possible diagnoses they suggest. Nichols and Crowhurst (2006) and Greene (2006) offer up-to-date reviews of the use of the MMPI-2 in inpatient and outpatient mental health settings respectively. Young and Weed (2006) review the literature on using the MMPI-2 in assessing individuals in treatment for substance abuse.

The MMPI-2 is frequently used in treatment planning. Administration of the test at the outset of therapy can assist in identifying specific treatment needs and suggesting the advisability (or lack thereof) of certain modes of intervention (e.g., behavioral, pharmacological, etc.). Perry, Miller, and Klump (2006) offer a recent review of the literature on using the MMPI-2 in treatment planning. A unique and particularly promising application of the test in the treatment process involves therapeutic assessment; a method developed by Finn (1996) that allows the practitioner to work collaboratively with the test-taker in identifying questions to be answered in the assessment and provide test-based responses to these questions. Finn and Kamphuis (2006) summarize the literature on therapeutic assessment with the MMPI-2, which documents impressive therapeutic effects for this procedure.

The MMPI-2 is also used frequently in general medical settings, where test scores can be helpful in screening medical patients for comorbid psychopathology, identifying psychological consequences of medical diseases, and assisting medical providers in making decisions about treatment options that involve a behavioral component (e.g., smoking cessation). Arbisi and Seime (2006) review the literature on use of the MMPI-2 in medical settings, and observe that the instrument's broad use is not surprising since it was developed originally for application in a general medical hospital. Some specific applications they describe include use of the MMPI-2 in identifying psychological aspects of chronic pain in general, and headache in particular, as well as chronic fatigue. The MMPI-2 is also used frequently in presurgical assessments of potential organ donations or bariatric surgery patients, to identify potential obstacles to successful compliance with the rigorous postsurgical requirements for behavioral change.

A related application of the MMPI-2 is in neuropsychological assessments, where the instrument is often included as part of a battery of tests administered to individuals suspected of experiencing neurological dysfunction. Gass (2006) reviews the current literature on use of the MMPI-2 in neuropsychological assessments, and notes that assessment of the patient's emotional functioning is an integral component of the neuropsychological evaluation. MMPI-2 data can be of particular utility in identifying emotional and behavioral manifestations of neurological disease or dysfunction as well as psychological consequences of a variety of brain-related disorders.

The MMPI-2 is also used broadly in a variety of nonclinical settings. Sellbom and Ben-Porath (2006) review uses of the test in a variety of forensic assessments including criminal court related evaluations (e.g., competence to stand trial and criminal responsibility), and civil court proceedings (e.g., child custody and personal injury evaluations). These authors observe that use of the MMPI-2, as well as any other clinical instrument, in forensic settings requires an adjustment on the practitioner to the more adversarial (than in traditional mental health and medical settings) nature of the legal system. Arbisi (2006) reviewed the literature on use of the MMPI-2 in personal injury and disability evaluations and noted that the test is frequently used to gauge the credibility of claims and the nature of psychological dysfunction in such assessments.

A related application of the MMPI-2 is in correctional settings, where the test is sometimes administered at intake as a general screener for psychological problems that need to be addressed over the course of the inmate's incarceration, and in other settings it is used primarily when an inmate is referred for mental health services as part of the treatment need identification and planning process. Megargee (2006) provides a current summary of the literature on using the MMPI-2 in correctional settings.

A final setting where the MMPI-2 is used widely is in personnel screening for individuals being considered for positions involving the public's safety such as law enforcement officers and fire fighters. Use of the MMPI-2 in such evaluations is restricted by federal laws, rules, and regulations that prohibit discrimination in employment against individuals with both physical and mental disabilities. Such prohibitions do not preclude the use of the MMPI-2 in such assessments, but they do require that the psychological assessment be conducted only after a potential employee has passed all other hurdles, and been tendered a conditional offer of employment. At that point, the MMPI-2 is frequently used as part of an assessment battery that may include measures of cognitive functioning and an interview to identify personality characteristics and behavioral proclivities (e.g., antisocial tendencies, emotional instability) that may preclude the candidates from effectively fulfilling the obligations of a position and, as a result, place the public at risk. Substantial literature exists to guide MMPI-2 users in such assessments. Most recently, Sellbom, Fischler, and Ben-Porath (In Press) reported the results of a prospective study of the prediction of negative behavioral outcomes in police officer applicants based on their pre-employment scores on the MMPI-2. They found that the MMPI-2 RC Scales were particularly effective in this task.

Limitations

As just reviewed, the MMPI-2 is used in a very broad array of settings and types of evaluations. As long as its application is limited to areas for which the test has been well validated and studied, the MMPI-2 provides very useful information about the individual's self presentation (as measured by the validity scales) and psychological findings. However, there are limits to what type of information any one psychological test can provide. For example, in forensic assessments the MMPI-2 rarely, if ever, will provide direct answers to psycho-legal questions such as: "Is this person competent to stand trial?" or, "What is the optimal child custody arrangement?" It is important that users of the test recognize these limitations, and restrict MMPI-2 interpretation to those aspects of behavior and psychological functioning for which there is an ample empirical foundation.

A related limitation is a tendency for some authors of interpretive guides or computer interpretative programs to blur the distinction between empirically grounded interpretation of the MMPI-2 and statements that are based on clinical lore. As discussed throughout this chapter, there is an abundance of empirical research to guide MMPI-2 interpretation. However, several interpretive guides and computer-based test interpretive systems fail to distinguish adequately, if at all, between statements that can be tied to existing empirical data and those that are based on clinical lore. MMPI-2 users should attend carefully to information about the empirical foundations of the sources they rely upon for interpretation of test results.

MMPI-A

While the MMPI-A is typically viewed as a psychodiagnostic instrument for the evaluation of adolescents in outpatient, residential, and inpatient clinical treatment settings, it has also been applied in evaluating adolescents in a variety of other specialized settings. For example, the MMPI-A has been used widely in the assessment of adolescents with substance abuse and addiction problems, eating disorders, and adolescents who have been victims of sexual abuse (Archer & Krishnamurthy, 2002). In addition, the MMPI-A is extensively used in the evaluation of adolescents in medical settings, including those adolescents assessed within the context of neuropsychological evaluations.

A recent survey by Archer, Buffington-Vollum, Stredny, and Handel (2006) also found that the MMPI-A was the most widely used self-report instrument in evaluating adolescent psychological functioning in forensic settings. Pope, Butcher, and Seelen (2006) recently provided an overview of the MMPI-2 and MMPI-A in forensic applications. In addition, forensic uses of the MMPI-A have also been the subject of several recent book chapters including those by Archer and Baker (2005), Archer, Zoby, and Stredny (2006), and Butcher and Pope (2006). Pennuto and Archer (2006) have noted that the popularity of the MMPI-A in forensic applications may be related to the well- validated validity scales on the test instrument capable of detecting various response sets of particular interest or relevancy in forensic issues including adolescents' tendencies to underreport or overreport symptomatology. Further, these authors observed that the MMPI-A may also be widely used in forensic settings because test findings are relatively easy to communicate to nonpsychologists. Pope et al. (2006) commented that the MMPI-A is likely to meet the standards for admissibility in most courtroom settings.

As noted by Archer and Krishnamurthy (2002), the MMPI-A is typically administered as part of an intake assessment procedure to obtain information relevant to treatment planning. In this application, the MMPI-A is particularly useful in evaluating initial resistances or barriers to treatment, assessing the adolescent's degree of emotional distress, and identifying the most appropriate type of treatment intervention including the possible need for a substance abuse evaluation and treatment. The MMPI-A is also frequently used, however, as a means of monitoring treatment progress and evaluating treatment outcomes when administered at multiple points during the treatment process. The examination of changes made across time is possible with the MMPI-A because this test has reasonably good temporal stability, as revealed in psychometric evaluations of test-retest reliability over relatively short periods of time. Therefore, changes seen in adolescents' MMPI-A profile features at retesting can typically be used to infer actual changes in the adolescents' functioning rather than measurement error.

Some of the common limitations of the MMPI-A may be related to test users relative unfamiliarity with the test and/or insufficient knowledge concerning appropriate uses. For example, while the MMPI-A can be quite useful in diagnostic assessments, test scales that do not directly correspond to *DSM-IV* diagnoses and the MMPI-A should not be used in isolation to form a diagnosis for adolescents in treatment settings. Further, since the MMPI is primarily a measure of psychopathology and not normal range personality functioning, this test instrument is quite limited in its ability to offer information concerning adaptive functioning or normal range personality characteristics. It should also be noted that the MMPI-A is not intended to be used in the evaluation of an adolescent's cognitive capacities or neurological status. Although several MMPI-A scales may be associated with cognitive deficits, the descriptors associated with elevations on these scales should be seen within the context of psychological impairment rather than as diagnostic tools for identifying cognitive or neurological deficits.

While the MMPI-A is considerably shorter than the original form of the test, it remains a lengthy self report questionnaire. In terms of administration time requirements, the 60 to 75 minutes required for the typical administration of the MMPI-A is substantially longer than the administration requirements for several other self-report questionnaires developed for, or adapted for, adolescents. Therefore, the use of the MMPI-A with adolescents involves a trade off in which the extensiveness and usefulness of the information derived from this test instrument is balanced against the increased test administration demands associated with the overall test length. Further, related to test limitation, are the issues of reading comprehension and cognitive maturation that are required for successful MMPI-A administration. The reading difficulty level of the MMPI-A test items varies considerably from the 1st-grade level for the easiest items, up to college level reading requirements for a few of the most difficult items. On average, however, the reading level required for the MMPI-A is typically estimated to be at the 6th-grade level. Dahlstrom, Archer, Hopkins, Jackson, and Dahlstrom (1994), for example, evaluated the reading difficulty of the MMPI-A in comparison with the original form of the MMPI and the MMPI-2. These researchers reported that the MMPI-A test booklet, instructions, and items were slightly easier to read compared with the MMPI and MMPI-2, but these differences were relatively small in magnitude. The average difficulty for all forms of the MMPI reported by Dahlstrom and his colleagues was 6th grade. These researchers also found, however, that approximately 6% of the MMPI-A items requires at least a

Just the Facts

	MMIP-2	MMPI-A
Manual Authors	Butcher, J. N., Graham, J. R, Ben-Porath, Y. S., Tellegen, A., Dahlstrom, W. G., & Kaemmer, B.	Butcher, J. N., Williams, C. L., Graham, J.R., Archer, R. P., Tellegen, A., Ben-Porath, Y. S, & Kaemmer, B.
Publication Date	1989/2001	1992
Normative Sample	1,462 women, 1,138 men	815 girls, 805 boys
Age Range	18 and older	14–18 years old, inclusive
Reading Level	6th grade	6th grade
Items	567	478
Administration Time	60 to 90 minutes	60 to 75 minutes
Abbreviated Administration	Items 1 thru 370	Items 1 thru 350
Validity Scales	L, F, Fb, Fp, FBS, K, S, VRIN, and TRIN	L, F, F_1, F_2, K, VRIN, and TRIN
Basic Clinical Scales	10 standard (Hs thru Si)	10 standard (Hs thru Si)
Content Scales	15	15

10th-grade reading level for adequate comprehension. The Just the Facts box below summarizes the comparison of the major features of the MMPI-2 and MMPI-A along a number of relevant dimensions.

Research Findings

The Important References box provides an annotated list of some important references related to the use of the MMPI-2 and MMPI-A.

The research literature relevant to the reliability and validity of the MMPI-2 encompasses thousands of publications and the comparable literature for the MMPI-A involves several hundred studies. While it is beyond the scope of this chapter to provide a detailed review of this literature, several useful summaries can be provided for the reader. In terms of the MMPI-2, for example, useful summaries may be found in Graham (2006) and Greene (2000). Summaries of the early research on the MMPI can be found in Dahlstrom, Welsh, and Dahlstrom (1972) and Dahlstrom and Dahlstrom (1980).

Comprehensive summaries of the research literature on the MMPI-A have been provided by Archer (2005) and by Butcher and Williams (2000). Both of these guides offer a general overview of the MMPI-A test instrument while also providing specific references to several hundred studies supporting the reliability and validity of this instrument. Additionally, recent chapters providing information on the construct validity of various scales and subscales of the MMPI-A can be found in chapters by Archer (2004) and in Archer, Krishnamurthy, and Stredny (2006).

Important References

MMPI-2:

Butcher, J. N., Graham, J. R., Ben-Porath, Y. S., Tellegen, A., Dahlstrom, W. G., & Kaemmer, B. (2001). *MMPI-2 (Minnesota Multiphasic Personality Inventory-2): Manual for administration, scoring, and interpretation (rev. ed.)*. Minneapolis: University of Minnesota Press.
This is the must have revised manual for the MMPI-2, including a variety of new scales developed since the original release of the MMPI-2 in 1989.

Dahlstrom, W. G., Archer, R. P., Hopkins, D. G., Jackson, E., & Dahlstrom, L. E. (1994). *Assessing the readability of the Minnesota Multiphasic Personality Inventory Instruments — the MMPI, MMPI-2, MMPI-A*. Minneapolis: University of Minnesota Press.
Comprehensive information on the reading requirements of all MMPI forms. The average difficulty level across forms was approximately the 6th grade. The authors noted that approximately 6% of the MMPI-A items required at least a 10th grade-reading level.

Tellegen, A., Ben-Porath, Y. S., McNulty, J. L., Arbisi, P. A., Graham, J. R., & Kaemmer, B. (2003). *The MMPI-2 Restructured Clinical (RC) Scales: Development, validation, and interpretation*. Minneapolis: University of Minnesota Press.
The presentation of basic reliability and validity data for the *RC Scales* by the research group responsible for their development.

MMPI-A:

Archer, R. P. (2005). *MMPI-A: Assessing adolescent psychopathology* (3rd ed.). Mahwah, NJ: Erlbaum.
This book provides practical information regarding the use of the MMPI-A, while also providing a comprehensive and contemporary review of the research literature on this instrument. The text illustrates interpretation principles through several clinical case examples and includes a chapter on test use in forensic settings.

Ben-Porath, Y. S., Graham, J. R., Archer, R. P., Tellegen, A., & Kaemmer, B. (2006). *Supplement to the MMPI-A Manual for administration, scoring, and interpretation*. Minneapolis: University of Minnesota Press.
A guide to the MMPI-A *PSY-5* Scales, content component scales, and the Forbey and Ben-Porath MMPI-A critical items.

Butcher, J. N., & Williams, C. L. (2000). *Essentials of MMPI-2 and MMPI-A interpretation* (2nd. ed.). Minneapolis: University of Minnesota Press.
This text provides extensive information on interpretive strategies for both the MMPI-A and MMPI-2, including details on the rationale for the development of both instruments.

Butcher, J. N., Williams, C. L., Graham, J. R., Archer, R. P., Tellegen, A., Ben-Porath, Y. S., & Kaemmer, B. (1992). *MMPI-A (Minnesota Multiphasic Personality Inventory - Adolescent): Manual for administration, scoring, and interpretation*. Minneapolis: University of Minnesota Press.
This test manual provides extensive information on the reliability and validity of the MMPI-A with concise clinical use recommendations. Appendices provide comprehensive scale membership and normative information, and correlates are provided for MMPI-A basic scales based on normative and clinical adolescent samples.

Williams, C. L., Butcher, J. N., Ben-Porath, Y. S., & Graham, J. R. (1992). *MMPI-A content scales: Assessing psychopathology in adolescents*. Minneapolis: University of Minnesota Press.
This text is a comprehensive review of the development and use of the MMPI-A Content Scales by the individuals involved in the creation of this set of scales.

Cross Cultural Considerations

MMPI-2

The utility of the MMPI-2 has been studied extensively across racial and ethnic groups, cultures, nationalities, and languages. The test has been translated into dozens of languages and adapted for use across very different cultures throughout the world (c.f., Butcher, 1996 for an edited volume on international applications of the MMPI-2). The test's publisher, the University of Minnesota Press, has established formal procedures for translating the test and adapting it for use in other countries, and provides information on the availability of current, approved translations of the MMPI-2 at http://www.upress.umn.edu/tests/translations.html. Current approved translations exist for the following languages: Chinese, Croatian, Czech, Dutch/Flemish, French, French-Canadian, German, Greek, Hebrew, Hmong, Italian, Korean, Norwegian, Spanish for Mexico, Spanish for Spain, South America, and Central America, Spanish for the U.S., and Swedish. Projects to translate the MMPI-2 and adapt it for use are ongoing in Arabic, Danish, Ethiopian, Farsi, Icelandic, Indonesian, Japanese, Latvian, Polish, Romanian Russian, Thai, Turkish, and Vietnamese.

Research conducted in the broad array of cultures represented by these translations, summarized most recently by Butcher, Mosch, Tsai, and Nezami (2006), indicates that the MMPI-2 is remarkably robust to cross cultural adaptation. In many countries it has been necessary to develop local norms that account for cultural and translational effects on responses to the test. However, in others the U.S. norms have held well. The procedures for translation and adaptation developed by the University of Minnesota Press include the collection of both normative and clinical data to assess the need for local norms and the utility of the translated instrument.

Within the United States a great deal of research has been conducted on the utility of the MMPI-2 across racial and ethnic groups. Until recently, most of this research has focused on comparisons of African Americans and Caucasians. Studies in this area have typically identified significant differences in mean scores across the two groups, some of which can be accounted for by social economic factors. However, group mean differences alone (or lack thereof) are not sufficient to warrant (or alleviate) concerns about potential test bias. This requires comparisons of the predictive validity of the MMPI-2 across racial groups. The few studies that have focused on such analyses (e.g., Arbisi, Ben-Porath, & McNulty, 2002; McNulty, Graham, Ben-Porath, & Stein, 1997) have not yielded any evidence of bias in the predictive validity of the MMPI-2 when comparing African Americans and Caucasians.

With the growth in the size of the Hispanic/Latino population in the United States, greater attention has been paid in the literature to the use of the Spanish language translation of the MMPI-2. Garrido and Velasquez (2006) summarize and review the literature in this area and offer specific recommendations for culturally competent use and interpretation of the MMPI-2 with Hispanics/Latinos assessed in the United States. Of particular interest have been observations that it may not be possible to use only one of the several existing Spanish language translations of the MMPI-2 with Spanish speakers residing in the U.S. Linguistic and cultural differences may justify use of the Spanish translation created in Mexico by Lucio and colleagues with U.S. residents of Mexican dissent, and the Spanish for U.S. version developed by Garcia and Azan-Chaviano (1993) with individuals of Caribbean origin.

Overall, ample empirical evidence indicates that the MMPI-2 can be used effectively across a wide range of nationalities, languages, cultures, and racial/ethnic groups. The test is unparalleled in the extent to which it has been adapted for use and studied empirically across cultures.

MMPI-A

The applicability of the MMPI and MMPI-A for evaluating adolescents from varying ethnic minority groups has been an extensive issue of investigation for several decades. Archer and Krishnamurthy (2002) reviewed the literature on the MMPI-A responses of American ethnic minorities, and concluded that the MMPI-A may be used in evaluations of adolescents from various ethnic minority groups using the standard adolescent norms provided for this instrument. These authors also noted that given the relatively limited literature in this area, however, clinicians should exercise a substantial caution in interpreting the MMPI-A profiles of ethnic minorities. This caution should include an awareness that the majority of MMPI and MMPI-A research studies involving ethnicity have been heavily based on comparisons of profiles produced by Black and White groups of adolescents, with less known about other minority group adolescents. A number of studies have been conducted, however, on the MMPI-A profiles of Hispanic adolescents. Corrales et al. (1998), for example, reviewed all research studies conducted with the MMPI-2 and MMPI-A using Latino samples in the United States, including samples consisting of people from Puerto Rico. This bibliography included a total of 52 studies completed since 1989. Gumbiner (2000) provided a critique of the limitations found in research studies on ethnicity with the MMPI-A, noting that most researchers have restricted their investigations to simple comparisons of mean values produced by two or more ethnic groups. Gumbiner recommended that future research be focused on the external correlates found for MMPI-A scales among various ethnic groups, and that data analysis also presents separate findings for male and female adolescents. Negy, Leal-Puente, Trainor, and Carlson (1997) investigated the MMPI responses of 120 Mexican American adolescents based on their observation that Hispanic adolescents are substantially under represented in the MMPI-A normative sample. These authors reported that the MMPI-A responses of Mexican-American adolescents showed minimal differences from those reported for the overall MMPI-A normative group, and that the response patterns of Mexican-American adolescents were influenced by their level of culturization and socioeconomic status.

Current Controversies

The history of the MMPI-2 is marked by a number of controversies related to efforts to modernize the test. As described by Wiggins (1966), initial suggestions that item content be considered in MMPI scale construction and interpretation were met with skepticism, if not outright hostility, from purists. The restandardization of the MMPI and publication of the MMPI-2 were similarly greeted with denigration by traditionalists, who predicted that the revised inventory would share the fate of the "New Coke," and quickly be replaced by the original version of the test, the MMPI Classic (Adler, 1990).

We characterize these transitional phases as marked by controversies, because although a small but vocal cohort of traditionalists responded negatively, the vast majority of users and researchers quickly adopted these improvements to the test. The first comprehensive effort to modernize the basic source of information on the MMPI-2, the Clinical Scales, has also been greeted by some traditionalists with skepticism and scorn, creating the appearance of a controversy. In a recent issue of the *Journal of Personality Assessment* devoted to the RC Scales, three traditionalists (Butcher, Hamilton, et al., 2006; Caldwell, 2006; and Nichols, 2006) express their misgivings about the RC Scales. Tellegen et al. (2006) offer responses to the main points of criticism and several other commentators offer their views of the scales. Space limitations preclude a review of the specific points made by the contributors. The very appearance of such a special issue may lend credence to the argument that the RC Scales are controversial. However, we encourage readers to avoid simplistic characterizations and delve into the substance of these articles in order to decide for themselves whether, as was the case during prior periods of transition, the controversy exists mainly in the eyes of traditionalists who have achieved a level of comfort with the test and are reluctant to embrace any change, no matter how badly it is needed.

Clinical Dilemma

A common dilemma in MMPI-2 use is how to interpret protocols marked by multiple elevations on the original Clinical Scales of the test. Such protocols are quite common in clinical settings in general and ones where clients have severe psychological problems in particular (e.g., inpatient facilities). A number of strategies for interpreting such profiles have been devised over the years. As described earlier, they include code type interpretation (a focus on the two to three highest scales on the profile), reliance on subscales in order to hone in more precisely on sources of elevation on the Clinical Scales, and reliance on a broad array of additional scales including the Content Scales, Content Component Scales, PSY-5 Scales and other supplementary measures.

When they were first introduced, the authors of the RC Scales recommended that they be used as another source of information for clarifying scores on the Clinical Scales. Tellegen et al. (2003) included in the monograph introducing the RC Scales nine case studies designed to illustrate how the RC Scales can serve this function. For this more limited initial purpose, Tellegen et al. (2003) reported only scores on the Clinical and RC Scales for the nine case studies in the monograph.

Experienced users of the RC Scales are increasingly turning to them as a focal point for MMPI-2 interpretation, with the restructured scales providing a blue print for the overall interpretation once scores on the validity scales have been reviewed and considered. To illustrate this approach to resolving the dilemma posed by MMPI-2 protocols marked by elevation on many Clinical Scales, we revisit one of the case studies from the Tellegen et al. (2003) monograph, and illustrate a strategy where the RC Scales are the focus of the interpretation. We begin with some of the case background reported by Tellegen et al. (2003).

Case Description

"Ms. A." is a 49-year-old, married woman tested at intake for inpatient treatment with a primary presenting complaint of depression. During intake, Ms. A. attributed her problems to concerns that she had acquired HIV in a manner that she refused to specify. She presented with loss of interest, anhedonia, decreased energy, difficulties in attention and concentration, and a variety of vague somatic complaints, which she attributed to the HIV infection. There were no indications of persecutory ideation or Hypomanic symptoms. Ms. A. had a prior history of inpatient and outpatient treatment for depression, including psychotropic medication. She was treated for 11 days and discharged to the community for follow up care with a diagnosis of major depressive disorder and a prescription for antidepressant and antipsychotic medication. HIV testing was negative.

MMPI-2 Interpretation

Figures 3.1 through Figure 3.6 provide output from the current version of the MMPI-2 Extended Score Report, which includes all of the standard scales of the instrument. As with any MMPI-2 interpretation, the first step is consideration of the Validity Scales, reported in Figure 3.1. With a noteworthy exception (Ms. A.'s score on FBS), scores on the Validity Scales are well within the expected range for an individual tested at intake to an inpatient facility. At a raw score of 39 (T-score = 111), the FBS indicates that Ms. A. presented with a very noncredible admixture of somatic and cognitive complaints. It should be noted that this score, in itself, does indicate an intentional effort at malingering. An alternative explanation, particularly in cases where there is

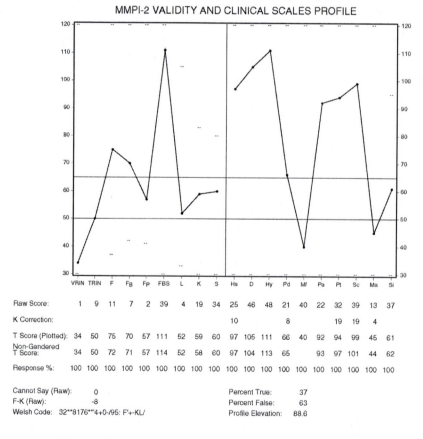

MMPI-2 VALIDITY AND CLINICAL SCALES PROFILE

	VRIN	TRIN	F	F_B	Fp	FBS	L	K	S	Hs	D	Hy	Pd	Mf	Pa	Pt	Sc	Ma	Si
Raw Score:	1	9	11	7	2	39	4	19	34	25	46	48	21	40	22	32	39	13	37
K Correction:										10		8			19	19	4		
T Score (Plotted):	34	50	75	70	57	111	52	59	60	97	105	111	66	40	92	94	99	45	61
Non-Gendered T Score:	34	50	72	71	57	114	52	58	60	97	104	113	65		93	97	101	44	62
Response %:	100	100	100	100	100	100	100	100	100	100	100	100	100	100	100	100	100	100	100

Cannot Say (Raw):	0	Percent True:	37
F-K (Raw):	-8	Percent False:	63
Welsh Code:	32**8176*"'4+0-/95: F'+-KL/	Profile Elevation:	88.6

The highest and lowest T scores possible on each scale are indicated by a "--".

For information on FBS, see Ben-Porath, Y. S., & Tellegen, A. (2006). The Fake Bad Scale (FBS): Current Status, a report on the Pearson Assessments web site (www.pearsonassessments.com/tests/mmpi_2.htm).

Figure 3.1

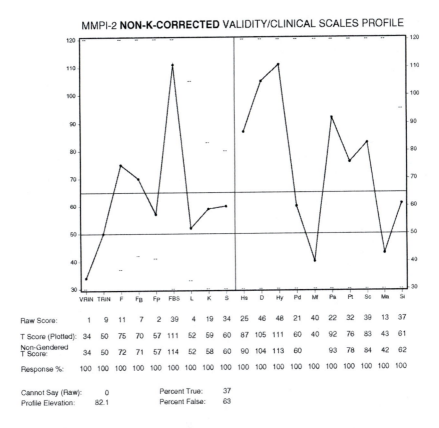

MMPI-2 **NON-K-CORRECTED** VALIDITY/CLINICAL SCALES PROFILE

	VRIN	TRIN	F	F$_B$	Fp	FBS	L	K	S	Hs	D	Hy	Pd	Mf	Pa	Pt	Sc	Ma	Si
Raw Score:	1	9	11	7	2	39	4	19	34	25	46	48	21	40	22	32	39	13	37
T Score (Plotted):	34	50	75	70	57	111	52	59	60	87	105	111	60	40	92	76	83	43	61
Non-Gendered T Score:	34	50	72	71	57	114	52	58	60	90	104	113	60		93	78	84	42	62
Response %:	100	100	100	100	100	100	100	100	100	100	100	100	100	100	100	100	100	100	100

Cannot Say (Raw):	0	Percent True:	37
Profile Elevation:	82.1	Percent False:	63

The highest and lowest T scores possible on each scale are indicated by a "--".

Non-K-corrected T scores allow interpreters to examine the relative contributions of the Clinical Scale raw score and the K correction to K-corrected Clinical Scale T scores. Because all other MMPI-2 scores that aid in the interpretation of the Clinical Scales (the Harris-Lingoes subscales, Restructured Clinical Scales, Content and Content Component Scales, PSY-5 Scales, and Supplementary Scales) are not K-corrected, they can be compared most directly with non-K-corrected T scores.

For information on FBS, see Ben-Porath, Y. S., & Tellegen, A. (2006). The Fake Bad Scale (FBS): Current Status, a report on the Pearson Assessments web site (www.pearsonassessments.com/tests/mmpi_2.htm).

Figure 3.2

no apparent incentive for fabrication of symptoms, is that they are the product of a somatoform disorder or somatic delusions. Differentiating between these possibilities requires consideration of extra-test data and scores on the substantive scales of the test.

Ms. A's Clinical Scale profile (Figure 3.1) is marked by the type of multiple elevations just mentioned, with clinically significant high score on Scales 1, 2, 3, 4, 6, 7, and 8. Removal of the K correction (Figure 3.2) leaves all but one (Scale 4) of these scales elevated, with all but Scale 7 (T = 76) falling more than three standard deviations above the normative mean. Examination of scores on the RC Scales (Figure 3.3) provides a much more specific

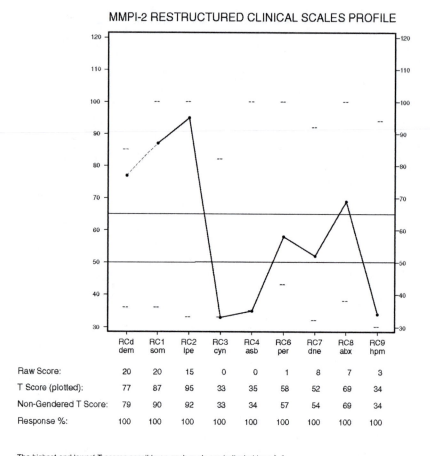

MMPI-2 RESTRUCTURED CLINICAL SCALES PROFILE

	RCd dem	RC1 som	RC2 lpe	RC3 cyn	RC4 asb	RC6 per	RC7 dne	RC8 abx	RC9 hpm
Raw Score:	20	20	15	0	0	1	8	7	3
T Score (plotted):	77	87	95	33	35	58	52	69	34
Non-Gendered T Score:	79	90	92	33	34	57	54	69	34
Response %:	100	100	100	100	100	100	100	100	100

The highest and lowest T scores possible on each scale are indicated by a "--".

LEGEND

dem= Demoralization   **cyn** = Cynicism   **dne** = Dysfunctional Negative Emotions
som= Somatic Complaints   **asb** = Antisocial Behavior   **abx** = Aberrant Experiences
lpe = Low Positive Emotions   **per** = Ideas of Persecution   **hpm**= Hypomanic Activation

For information on the RC scales, see Tellegen, A., Ben-Porath, Y.S., McNulty, J.L., Arbisi, P.A., Graham, J.R., & Kaemmer, B. 2003. The MMPI-2 Restructured Clinical (RC) Scales: Development, Validation, and Interpretation. Minneapolis: University of Minnesota Press.

Figure 3.3

indication of the problems likely presented by Ms. A. Her elevated score on RCd (Demoralization) indicates that Ms. A is likely feeling very distressed and overwhelmed. She is unhappy and dissatisfied with her life, and reports feeling depressed and anxious. She feels incapable of dealing effectively with her current life circumstances. Her elevated score on RCd likely explains the diffuse pattern of multiple, very high elevations on the Clinical Scales, and the RC Scales are likely to provide a more specific indication of her current problems.

Ms. A's highly elevated score on RC2 indicates that she reports a profound absence of positive emotional experiences in her life, feels incapable of joy or pleasure, and is extremely anhedonic. This score indicates that she is at very substantial risk for a major depressive disorder. Ms. A also produced a very high score on RC1 coupled with a very low score on RC3, indicating that she presents with a combination of significant somatic complaints of a vague and nonfocused nature, coupled with a naïve disavowal of cynicism sometimes found in individuals with conversion disorders. This combination

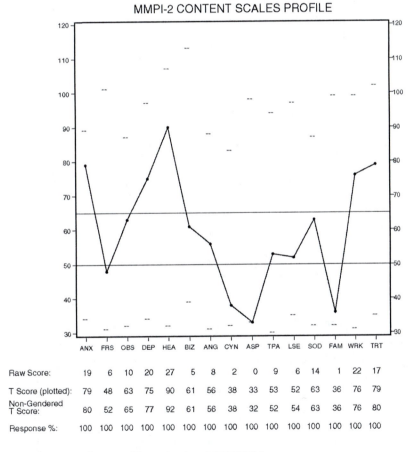

MMPI-2 CONTENT SCALES PROFILE

	ANX	FRS	OBS	DEP	HEA	BIZ	ANG	CYN	ASP	TPA	LSE	SOD	FAM	WRK	TRT
Raw Score:	19	6	10	20	27	5	8	2	0	9	6	14	1	22	17
T Score (plotted):	79	48	63	75	90	61	56	38	33	53	52	63	36	76	79
Non-Gendered T Score:	80	52	65	77	92	61	56	38	32	52	54	63	36	76	80
Response %:	100	100	100	100	100	100	100	100	100	100	100	100	100	100	100

The highest and lowest T scores possible on each scale are indicated by a "--".

Figure 3.4

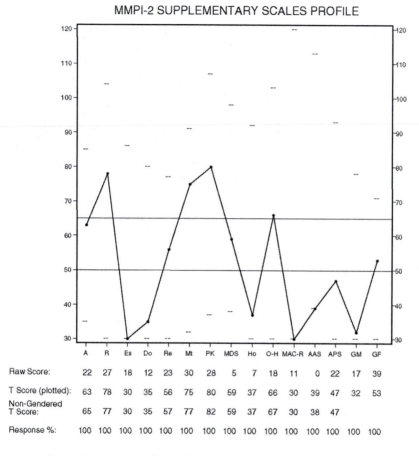

MMPI-2 SUPPLEMENTARY SCALES PROFILE

	A	R	Es	Do	Re	Mt	PK	MDS	Ho	O-H	MAC-R	AAS	APS	GM	GF
Raw Score:	22	27	18	12	23	30	28	5	7	18	11	0	22	17	39
T Score (plotted):	63	78	30	35	56	75	80	59	37	66	30	39	47	32	53
Non-Gendered T Score:	65	77	30	35	57	77	82	59	37	67	30	38	47		
Response %:	100	100	100	100	100	100	100	100	100	100	100	100	100	100	100

The highest and lowest T scores possible on each scale are indicated by a "--".

Figure 3.5

of extreme scores accounts for the highly elevated score on Clinical Scale 3. Finally, Ms. A.'s moderately elevated score on RC8 indicates that she presents with some unusual thoughts and perceptions of a nonpersecutory nature (given the lack of elevation on RC6). Although there is no indication of psychotic symptoms in her history, it is noteworthy, in this context, that Ms. A. was prescribed antipsychotic medication (in addition to an antidepressant) during the course of her hospitalization. Also of note is that treatment staff perceived her vague somatic complaints as related to what turned out to be her false belief that she was HIV positive.

In light of her *RC* Scale scores, Ms. A.'s diffuse pattern of elevation on the Clinical Scales is best understood as reflecting her very elevated state of demoralization. In particular, her elevations on Clinical Scales 6 and 7, which are not matched by elevations on the corresponding restructured scales, are likely an artifact of demoralization (and in the case of Scale 6, the "naiveté" items included in that scale). Ms. A's scores on the MMPI-2 Content Scales (Figure 3.4) can also be best understood in the context of the RC Scales. The elevation on Health Concerns (HEA) is consistent with RC1 (and Clinical Scale 1) in identifying a diffuse pattern of pervasive somatic complaints, and the elevation on Depression (DEP), a scale heavily saturated with demoralization, reflects the combined findings of elevation on RCd and RC2. The Work Interference (WRK) and Negative Treatment Indicators (TRT) Scales

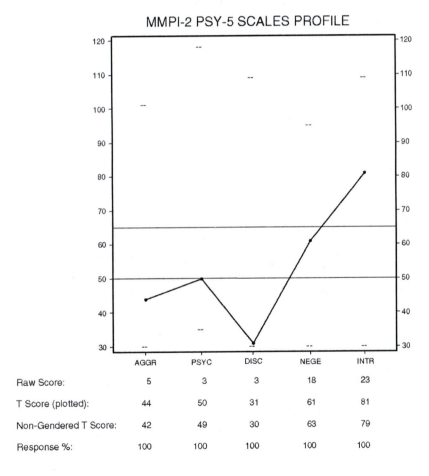

The highest and lowest T scores possible on each scale are indicated by a "--".

Figure 3.6

are both heavily saturated with demoralization and therefore cannot be interpreted in a protocol marked by a very high score on RCd. The elevation on Anxiety (ANX), in the context of a nonelevated score on RC7, indicates that the former, rather than reflecting symptoms of an anxiety disorder indicates that Ms. A.'s demoralization is in part manifested in complaints of anxiety. The absence of elevation on Bizarre Mentation (BIZ), in contrast with RC8, reflects the former's more heterogeneous item content, which includes elements of both RC6 and RC8.

Ms. A.'s scores on the Supplementary Scales of the MMPI-2 (Figure 3.5) reflect partly the impact of demoralization (particularly on scales Mt and PK, both heavily saturated with demoralization variance). The high score on R is consistent with Ms. A.'s very low scores on RC4 and RC9 in indicating a very constrained personality with little or no proclivities toward externalization behavior. The nonclinically elevated score on A (T = 63) belies assertions by some (e.g., Nichols, 2006) that this scale is essentially interchangeable with RCd (T = 77). Finally, on the PSY-5 Scales (Figure 3.6) Ms. A.'s elevated score on INTR is best understood in the context of RC2 (and the nonelevated score on Si) as indicating the absence of positive emotional experiences in her life, and the very low score on DISC, like Welsh's R, is consistent with the absence of elevation on RC4 and RC9. Like the BIZ Content Scale, the absence of elevation on PSYC reflects the combination of elements of RC6 and RC8 in this PSY-5 Scale.

Overall, Ms. A.'s MMPI-2 results indicate that she is experiencing significant emotional turmoil and distress, she is at very substantial risk for a major depressive disorder, and she presents with a diffuse and vague set of noncredible somatic complaints. Given her background and the information provided by the intake staff, it is most likely that Ms. A.'s somatic preoccupation has a delusional basis, and the possibility of a psychotic disorder, or psychotic manifestations of a mood disorder should be considered. This case illustrates both how the RC Scales can serve as an organizing framework for interpreting the MMPI-2, and the contribution of the recently added FBS in identifying noncredible somatic complaints that, in this case, are not the product of intentional fabrication, but rather are delusional in nature.

Chapter Summary

Readers of this chapter will have observed that the original MMPI and its progeny, the MMPI-2 and MMPI-A, are a product of a long tradition of research and development efforts designed to maintain and enhance the empirical foundations of the instrument. Although at various points throughout the history of test some traditionalists have opposed these efforts, users of the MMPI-2 and MMPI-A are able to rely on an unparal-

Key Points to Remember

- Revised forms of the MMPI specifically developed for evaluations of adults and adolescents.
- Automated administration, scoring, and interpretation programs available for both instruments.
- Most widely used self report measures of psychopathology across varied settings including clinical, neuropsychological, and forensic.
- Contains multiple validity scales which are extensively evaluated and capable of effectively detecting important test-taking response sets, including random responding and underreporting and ove reporting of symptoms.
- The most widely studied measures of psychopathology among adults and adolescents, respectively, and also used widely in cross-cultural applications and translated into many languages.
- In addition to use in clinical treatment planning and outcome evaluation, also widely used in medical settings, substance abuse treatment, and correctional and forensic settings.

leled body of empirical research to guide their interpretation of individuals' test results. The two versions of the test have been adapted for use across a broad range of cultures throughout the world, and have proven effective with individuals of various cultural backgrounds within the United States. The instruments are used widely in both traditional mental health applications and in forensic, correctional, pre-employment screening, and medical settings. Available automated administration, scoring, and administration procedures can streamline these processes considerably, however users of automated interpretive software should attend closely to the extent to which a particular system they are considering is empirically grounded versus others that are primarily based on clinical lore and the developer's own experience with the instrument.

References

Adler, R. (April, 1990). Does the "new" MMPI beat the "classic?" *APA Monitor*, 18–19.

Arbisi, P. A. (2006). Use of the MMPI-2 in Personal Injury and Disability Evaluations. In J. N. Butcher (Ed.), *The MMPI-2: A practitioner's guide* (pp. 407–442). Washington, DC: American Psychological Association.

Arbisi, P. A., & Ben-Porath, Y. S. (1998). The ability of Minnesota Multiphasic Personality Inventory-2 validity scale to detect fake-bad responses in psychiatric inpatients. *Psychological Assessment, 10,* 221–228.

Arbisi, P. A., Ben-Porath, Y. S., & McNulty, J. (2002). A comparison of MMPI-2 validity in African American and Caucasian psychiatric inpatients. *Psychological Assessment, 14,* 3–15.

Arbisi, P. A., & Seime, R. J. (2006). Use of the MMPI-2 in medical settings. In J. N. Butcher (Ed.), *The MMPI-2 :A practitioner's guide* (pp. 273–300). Washington, DC: American Psychological Association.

Archer, R. P. (1987). *Using the MMPI with adolescents.* Hillsdale: Erlbaum.

Archer, R. P. (2004). Overview and update on the Minnesota Multiphasic Personality Inventory – Adolescent (MMPI-A). In M. Maruish (Ed.), *The use of psychological testing for treatment planning and outcomes assessment* (2nd ed., pp. 341–380). Mahwah, NJ: Erlbaum.

Archer, R. P. (2005). *MMPI-A: Assessing adolescent psychopathology* (3rd ed.). Mahwah, NJ: Erlbaum.

Archer, R. P., Aiduk, R., Griffin, R., & Elkins, D. E. (1996). Incremental validity of the MMPI-2 content scales in a psychiatric sample. *Assessment, 3,* 79–90.

Archer, R. P., & Baker, E. M. (2005). Use of the Minnesota Multiphasic Personality Inventory – Adolescent (MMPI-A) in juvenile justice settings. In D. Seagraves & T. Grisso (Eds.), *Handbook of screening and assessment tools for juvenile justice.* New York: Guilford.

Archer, R. P., Buffington-Vollum, J. K., Stredny, R. V., & Handel, R. W. (2006). A survey of psychological test use patterns among forensic psychologists. *Journal of Personality Assessment, 87,* 84–94.

Archer, R. P., & Gordon, R. A. (1991, August). Use of content scales with adolescents: Past and future practices. In R. C. Colligan (Chair), *MMPI and MMPI-2 supplementary scales and profile interpretation — Content scales revisited.* Symposium conducted at the annual convention of the American Psychological Association, San Francisco, CA.

Archer, R. P., Gordon, R. A., Giannetti, R. A., & Singles, J. M. (1988). MMPI scale clinical correlates for adolescent inpatients. *Journal of Personality Assessment, 52,* 707–721.

Archer, R. P., Griffin, R., & Aiduk, R. (1995). MMPI—2 clinical correlates for ten common codes. *Journal of Personality Assessment, 65,* 391–407.

Archer, R. P., & Krishnamurthy, R. (2002). *Essentials of MMPI-A assessment.* Hoboken, NJ: Wiley.

Archer, R. P., Krishnamurthy, R., & Stredny, R. V. (2006). Guidelines for the MMPI-A. In S. R. Smith & L. Handler (Eds.), *The clinical assessment of children and adolescents: A practitioner's guide* (pp. 233–262). Mahwah, NJ: Erlbaum.

Archer, R. P., & Newsom, C. R. (2000). Psychological test usage with adolescent clients: Survey update. *Assessment, 7,* 227–235.

Archer, R. P., Pancoast, D. L., & Gordon, R. A. (1994). The development of the MMPI-A Immaturity Scale: Findings for normal and clinical samples. *Journal of Personality Assessment, 62,* 145–156.

Archer, R. P., Zoby, M., & Stredny, R. V. (2006). The Minnesota Multiphasic Personality Inventory – Adolescent. In R. P. Archer, *Forensic uses of clinical assessment instruments* (pp 57–87). Mahwah, NJ: Erlbaum.

Baer, R. A., & Miller, J. (2002). Underreporting of psychopathology on the MMPI-2: A meta-analytic review. *Psychological Assessment, 14,* 16–26.

Baer, R. A., Wetter, M. W., Nichols, D. S., & Greene, R. (1995). Sensitivity of MMPI-2 validity scales to underreporting of symptoms. *Psychological Assessment, 7,* 419–423.

Ben-Porath, Y. S. (2003). Self-report inventories: Assessing personality and psychopathology. In J. R. Graham & J. Naglieri (Eds.). Vol X: *Handbook of assessment psychology.* New York: Wiley.

Ben-Porath, Y. S. (2006). Differentiating normal from abnormal personality with the MMPI. In S. Strack (Ed.) Differentiating normal from abnormal personality (2nd ed.), pp. 337–381. New York: Springer.

Ben-Porath, Y. S., & Butcher, J. N. (1989a). Psychometric stability of rewritten MMPI items. *Journal of Personality Assessment, 53,* 645–653.

Ben-Porath, Y. S., & Butcher, J. N. (1989b). The comparability of MMPI and MMPI-2 scales and profiles. *Psychological Assessment, 1,* 345–347.

Ben-Porath, Y. S., Graham, J. R., Archer, R. P., Tellegen, A., & Kaemmer, B. (2006). *Supplement to the MMPI-A Manual for Administration, Scoring and Administration.* Minneapolis: University of Minnesota Press.

Ben-Porath, Y. S., Hostetler, K., Butcher, J. N., & Graham, J. R. (1989). New subscales for the MMPI-2 Social Introversion (Si) scale. *Psychological Assessment, 1,* 169–174.

Ben-Porath, Y. S., McCully, E., & Almagor, M. (1993). Incremental validity of the MMPI-2 Content Scales in the assessment of personality and psychopathology by self report. *Journal of Personality Assessment, 61,* 557–575.

Ben-Porath, Y. S., & Sherwood, N. E. (1993). *The MMPI-2 Content Component Scales: Development, psychometric characteristics, and clinical application.* Minneapolis: University of Minnesota Press.

Ben-Porath, Y. S., Slutske, W. S., & Butcher, J. N. (1989). A real-data simulation of computerized adaptive administration of the MMPI. *Psychological Assessment 1*, 18–22.

Black, J. D. (1953). The interpretation of MMPI profiles of college women. *Dissertation Abstracts, 13*, 870–871.

Boccaccini, M. T., & Brodsky, S. L. (1999). Diagnostic test usage by forensic psychologists in emotional injury cases. *Professional Psychology: Research and Practice, 30,* 253–259.

Borum, R., & Grisso, T. (1995). Psychological test use in criminal forensic evaluations. *Professional Psychology: Research and Practice, 26,* 465–473.

Butcher, J. N. (Ed.) (1972). *Objective personality assessment: Changing perspectives.* Oxford: Academic Press.

Butcher, J. N. (1996). *International adaptations of the MMPI-2: Research and clinical applications.* Minneapolis: University of Minnesota Press.

Butcher, J. N., Dahlstrom, W. G., Graham, J. R., Tellegen, A., & Kaemmer, B. (1989). *Minnesota Multiphasic Personality Inventory-2 (MMPI-2): Manual for administration, scoring and interpretation.* Minneapolis: University of Minnesota Press.

Butcher, J. N., Graham, J. R., Ben-Porath, Y. S., Tellegen, A., Dahlstrom, W. G., & Kaemmer, B. (2001). *Minnesota Multiphasic Personality Inventory-2 (MMPI-2): Manual for administration, scoring and interpretation* (rev. ed.). Minneapolis: University of Minnesota Press.

Butcher, J. N., Graham, J. R., Williams, C. L., & Ben-Porath, Y. S. (1990). *Development and use of the MMPI-2 Content Scales.* Minneapolis: University of Minnesota Press.

Butcher, J. N., Hamilton, C. K., Rouse, S. V., & Cumella, E. J. (2006). The deconstruction of the Hy Scale of MMPI-2: Failure of RC3 in measuring somatic symptom expression. *Journal of Personality Assessment, 87,* 186–192.

Butcher, J. N., & Han, K. (1995). *Development of an MMPI-2 scale to assess the presentation of self in a superlative manner: The S Scale.* Hillsdale, NJ: Erlbaum.

Butcher, J. N., Mosch, S. C., Tsai, J., & Nezami, E. (2006). *Cross-Cultural applications of the MMPI-2.* Washington, DC: American Psychological Association.

Butcher, J. N., & Pope, K. S. (2006). The MMPI-A in forensic assessment. In S. Sparta & G. P. Koocher (Eds.), *Forensic mental health assessment of children and adolescents* (pp. 401–411). New York: Oxford University Press.

Butcher, J. N., & Rouse, S. V. (1996). Personality: Individual differences and clinical assessment. *Annual Review of Psychology, 47,* 87–111.

Butcher, J. N., & Williams, C. L. (2000). *Essentials of MMPI-2 and MMPI-A interpretation* (2nd ed.). Minneapolis: University of Minnesota Press.

Butcher, J .N., Williams, C. L., Graham, J. R., Archer, R. P., Tellegen, A., Ben-Porath, Y. S., & Kaemmer, B. (1992). *Minnesota Multiphasic Personality Inventory (MMPI-A): Manual for administration, scoring and interpretation.* Minneapolis: University of Minnesota Press.

Caldwell, A. B. (2006). Maximal measurement or meaningful measurement: The interpretive challenges of the MMPI-2 Restructured Clinical (RC) Scales. *Journal of Personality Assessment, 87,* 193–201.

Camara, W. J., Nathan, J. S., & Puente, A. E. (2000). Psychological test usage: Implications in professional psychology. *Professional Psychology: Research and Practice, 31,* 141–154.

Capwell, D. F. (1945a). Personality patterns of adolescent girls: I. Girls who show improvement in IQ. *Journal of Applied Psychology, 29,* 212–228.

Capwell, D. F. (1945b). Personality patterns of adolescent girls: II. Delinquents and nondelinquents. *Journal of Applied Psychology, 29,* 289–297.

Corrales, M. L., Cabiya, J. J., Gomes, F., Ayala, G. X., Mendoza, S., & Velasquez, R. J. (1998). MMPI-2 and MMPI-A research with U.S. Latinos: A bibliography. *Psychological Reports, 83,* 1027–1033.

Cronbach, L. J., & Meehl, P. E. (1955). Construct validity in psychological tests. *Psychological Bulletin, 52,* 281–302.

Dahlstrom, W. G. (1992). Comparability of two-point high-point code patterns from original MMPI norms to MMPI-2 norms for the restandardization sample. *Journal of Personality Assessment, 59,* 153–164.

Dahlstrom, W. G., Archer, R. P., Hopkins, D. G., Jackson, E., & Dahlstrom, L. E. (1994). *Assessing the readability of the Minnesota Multiphasic Personality Inventory Instruments – the MMPI, MMPI-2, MMPI-A.* Minneapolis: University of Minnesota Press.

Dahlstrom, W. G., & Dahlstrom, L. E. (Eds.). (1980). *Basic readings on the MMPI: A new selection on personality measurement.* Minneapolis: University of Minnesota Press.

Dahlstrom, W. G., Welsh, G. S., & Dahlstrom, L. E. (1972). *An MMPI handbook: I. Clinical interpretation* (rev. ed.). Oxford, England: University of Minnesota Press.

Dahlstrom, W. G., Welsh, G. S., & Dahlstrom, L. E. (1975). *An MMPI handbook, Volume II: Research Applications.* Minneapolis: University of Minnesota Press.

Finn, S. E. (1996). *Manual for using the MMPI-2 as a therapeutic intervention.* Minneapolis: University of Minnesota Press.

Finn, S. E., & Kamphuis, J. H. (2006). Therapeutic Assessment with the MMPI-2. In J. N. Butcher (Ed.), *The MMPI-2: A practitioner's guide* (pp. 165–191). Washington, DC: American Psychological Association.

Forbey, J. D. (June 2003). A review of the MMPI-A research literature. Paper presented at the 38th Annual Symposium on Recent Developments in the use of the MMPI-2 and MMPI-A. Minneapolis.

Forbey, J. D., & Ben-Porath, Y. S. (1998). *A critical item set for the MMPI-A.* (MMPI-2/MMPI-A Test Reports No. 4). Minneapolis: University of Minnesota Press.

Forbey, J. D., & Ben-Porath, Y. S. (2007a). A comparison of the MMPI-2 Restructured Clinical (RC) and Clinical Scale in a substance abuse treatment sample. *Psychological Services, 4(1),* 46–58.

Forbey, J. D., & Ben-Porath, Y. S. (2007b). Computerized adaptive personality testing: A review and illustration with the MMPI-2 Computerized Adaptive Version. *Psychological Assessment, 19(1),* 14–24.

Forbey, J. D., Handel, R. W., & Ben-Porath, Y. S. (2000). A real-data simulation of computerized adaptive administration of the MMPI-A. *Computers in Human Behavior, 16,* 83–96.

Gantner, A. B., Graham, J. R., & Archer, R. A. (1992). Usefulness of the MAC scale in differentiating adolescents in normal, psychiatric, and substance abuse settings. *Psychological Assessment, 4,* 133–137.

Garcia, R. E., & Azan-Chaviano, A. A. (1993). *Inventorio Multifasico de la Personalidad Minnesota-2: Version Hispana* [Minnesota Multiphasic Personality Inventory-2: Spanish Version]. Minneapolis: University of Minnesota Press.

Garrido, M., & Velasquez, R. (2006). Interpretation of Latino/Latina MMPI-2 Profiles: Review and Application of Empirical Findings and Cultural- Linguistic Considerations. In J. N. Butcher (Ed.), *The MMPI-2-: A practitioner's guide* (pp. 477–504). Washington, DC: American Psychological Association.

Gass, C. S. (2006). *Use of the MMPI-2 in Neuropsychological Evaluations.* Washington, DC: American Psychological Association.

Gilberstadt, H., & Duker, J. (1965). *A handbook for clinical and actuarial MMPI interpretation.* Oxford: W. B. Saunders.

Gough, H. G. (1946). Diagnostic patterns on the Minnesota Multiphasic Personality Inventory. *Journal of Clinical Psychology, 2,* 23–37.

Graham, J. R. (2006). *MMPI-2: Assessing personality and psychopathology* (4th ed.). New York: Oxford University Press.

Graham, J. R., Ben-Porath, Y. S., & McNulty, J. L. (1999). *MMPI-2 correlates for outpatient community mental health settings.* Minneapolis: University of Minnesota Press.

Graham, J. R., Timbrook, R. E., Ben-Porath, Y. S., & Butcher, J. N. (1991). Code-type congruence between MMPI and MMPI-2: Separating fact from artifact. *Journal of Personality Assessment, 57,* 205–215.

Greene, R. L. (2000). *The MMPI-2: An interpretive manual* (2nd ed.). Needham Heights, MA: Allyn & Bacon.

Greene, R. L. (2006). Use of the MMPI-2 in mental health settings. In J.N. Butcher (Ed.), *The MMPI-2: A practitioner's guide* (pp. 253–272). Washington, DC: American Psychological Association.

Greiffenstein, M. F., Fox, D., & Lees-Haley, P. R. (in press). The MMPI-2 Fake Bad Scale in Detection of Noncredible Brain Injury Claims. In K. Boone (Ed), *Detection of Noncredible Cognitive Performance.* New York: Guilford.

Gumbiner, J. (2000). Limitations in ethnic research on the MMPI-A. *Psychological Reports, 87,* 1229–1230.

Guthrie, G. M. (1949). *A study of the personality characteristics associated with the disorders encountered by an internist.* Unpublished doctoral dissertation, University of Minnesota.

Gynther, M. D., Altman, H., & Sletten, I. W. (1973). Replicated correlates of MMPI two-point code types: The Missouri actuarial system. *Journal of Clinical Psychology, 29,* 263–289.

Gynther, M. D., Altman, H., & Sletten, I. W. (1973). Development of an empirical interpretive system for the MMPI: Some after-the-fact observations. *Journal of Clinical Psychology, Vol. 29,* 232–234.

Handel, R. W., Ben-Porath, Y. S., & Watt, M. (1999). Computerized adaptive assessment with the MMPI-2 in a clinical setting. *Psychological Assessment, 11,* 369–380.

Harkness, A. R. (1992). Fundamental topics in the personality disorders: Candidate trait dimensions from lower regions of the hierarchy. *Psychological Assessment, 4,* 251–259.

Harkness, A. R., & McNulty, J. L. (1994). The Personality Psychopathology Five (PSY-5): Issues from the pages of a diagnostic manual instead of a dictionary. In *Differentiating normal and abnormal personality* (pp. 291–315). New York: Springer Publishing Co.

Harkness, A. R., McNulty, J. L., & Ben-Porath, Y. S. (1995). The Personality Psychopathology Five (PSY-5): Constructs and MMPI-2 scales. *Psychological Assessment, 7,* 104–114.

Harkness, A. R., McNulty, J. L., Ben-Porath, Y. S., & Graham, J. R. (2002). *MMPI-2 Personality-Psychopathology Five (PSY-5) Scales: Gaining an overview for case conceptualization and treatment planning.* Minneapolis: University of Minnesota Press.

Harris, R. E., & Lingoes, J. C. (1955). *Subscales for the MMPI: An aid to profile interpretation.* Department of Psychiatry, University of California School of Medicine and the Langley Porter Clinic, mimeographed materials.

Hathaway, S. R. (1960). Forward. In W. G. Dahlstrom, & G. S. Welsh (Eds.), *An MMPI handbook: A guide to use in clinical practice and research.* Minneapolis: University of Minnesota Press.

Hathaway, S. R., & McKinley, J. C. (1940). A multiphasic personality schedule (Minnesota): I. Construction of the schedule. *Journal of Psychology: Interdisciplinary and Applied, 10,* 249–254.

Hathaway, S. R., & McKinley, J. C. (1942). *The Minnesota Multiphasic Personality Schedule.* Minneapolis: University of Minnesota Press.

Hathaway, S. R., & Meehl, P. E. (1951). *An atlas for the clinical use of the MMPI.* Oxford: University of Minnesota Press.

Hathaway, S. R., & Monachesi, E. D. (1953). *Analyzing and predicting juvenile delinquency with the MMPI.* Minneapolis: University of Minnesota Press.

Hathaway, S. R., & Monachesi, E. D. (1963). *Adolescent personality and behavior: MMPI patterns of normal, delinquent, dropout, and other outcomes.* Minneapolis: University of Minnesota Press.

Hicks, M. M., Rogers, R., & Cashel, M. (2000). Predictions of violent and total infractions among institutionalized male juvenile offenders. *Journal of the American Academy of Psychiatry and the Law, 28,* 183–190.

Lees-Haley P. R., English L. T., & Glenn W. J. (1991). A Fake Bad Scale on the MMPI-2 for personal injury claimants. *Psychological Reports, 68,* 203–210.

Lees-Haley, P. R., Smith, H. H., Williams, C. W., & Dunn, J. T. (1996). Forensic neuropsychological test usage: An empirical survey. *Archives of Clinical Neuropsychology, 11,* 45–51.

Lubin, B., Larsen, R. M., & Matarazzo, J. D. (1984). Patterns of psychological test usage in the United States: 1935–1982. *American Psychologist, 39,* 451–454.

Marks, P. A., & Briggs, P. F. (1972). Adolescent norm tables for the MMPI. In W. G. Dahlstrom, G. S. Welsh, & L. E. Dahlstrom (Eds.), *An MMPI handbook: Vol. 1. Clinical interpretation* (rev. ed., pp. 388–399). Minneapolis: University of Minnesota Press.

Marks, P. A., & Seeman, W. (1963). *The actuarial description of abnormal personality: An atlas for use with the MMPI-2.* Baltimore: Williams & Wilkins.

Marks, P. A., Seeman, W., & Haller, D. L. (1974). *The actuarial use of the MMPI with adolescents and adults.* Baltimore: Williams & Wilkins.

McNulty, J. L., Ben-Porath, Y. S., & Graham, J. R. (1998). An empirical examination of the correlates of well-defined and not defined MMPI-2 code types. *Journal of Personality Assessment, 71,* 393–410.

McNulty, J. L., Graham, J. R., Ben-Porath, Y. S., & Stein, L. A. R. (1997). Comparative validity of MMPI-2 scores of African American and Caucasian mental health center clients. *Psychological Assessment, 9,* 464–470.

McNulty, J. L., Harkness, A. R., Ben-Porath, Y. S., & Williams, C. L. (1997). Assessing the Personality Psychopathology Five (PSY-5) in adolescents: New MMPI-A Scales. *Psychological Assessment, 9*, 250–259.

Meehl, P. E. (1946). Profile analysis of the Minnesota Multiphasic Personality Inventory in differential diagnosis. *Journal of Applied Psychology, 30*, 517–524.

Meehl, P. E. (1954). *Clinical vs. statistical prediction: a theoretical analysis and a review of the evidence.* Minneapolis: University of Minnesota Press.

Meehl, P. E. (1956). Wanted—a good cook-book. *American Psychologist, 11*, 263–272.

Megargee, E. I. (2006). *Use of the MMPI-2 in Correctional Settings.* Washington, DC: American Psychological Association.

Negy, C., Leal-Puente, L., Trainor, D. J., & Carlson, R. (1997). Mexican American adolescents' performance on the MMPI-A. *Journal of Personality Assessment, 69*, 205–214.

Nelson, N. W., Sweet, J. J., & Demakis, G. J. (2006). Meta-analysis of the MMPI-2 Fake Bad Scale: Utility in forensic practice. *Clinical Neuropsychologist, 20*, 39–58.

Nichols, D. S. (2006). The trials of separating bath water from baby: A review and critique of the MMPI-2 Restructured Clinical Scales. *Journal of Personality Assessment, 87*, 121–138.

Nichols, D. S., & Crowhurst, B. (2006). Use of the MMPI-2 in Inpatient Mental Health Settings. In J.N. Butcher (Ed.) *The MMPI-2: A practitioner's guide* (pp. 195–252). Washington, DC: American Psychological Association.

Pennuto, T., & Archer, R. P. (2006). MMPI-A forensic case studies: Uses in documented court decisions. Manuscript submitted for publication.

Perry, J. N., Miller, K. B., & Klump, K. (2006). Treatment Planning With the MMPI-2. In J. N. Butcher (Ed.), *The MMPI-2-: A practitioners guide* (pp. 143–164). Washington, DC: American Psychological Association.

Petroskey, L. J., Ben-Porath, Y. S., & Stafford, K. P. (2003). Correlates of the Minnesota Multiphasic Personality Inventory—2 (MMPI-2) Personality Psychopathology Five (PSY-5) scales in a forensic assessment setting. *Assessment, 10*, 393–399.

Pope, K. S., Butcher, J. N., & Seelen, J. (2006). *The MMPI, MMPI-2, & MMPI-A in court: A practical guide for expert witnesses and attorneys* (3rd ed.). Washington, DC: American Psychological Association.

Rogers, R., Sewell, K. W., Martin, M. A., & Vitacco, M. J. (2003). Detection of feigned mental disorders: A meta-analysis of the MMPI-2 and malingering. *Assessment, 10*, 160–177.

Roper, B. L., Ben-Porath, Y. S., & Butcher, J. N. (1991). Comparability of computerized adaptive and conventional testing with the MMPI-2. *Journal of Personality Assessment, 57*, 278–290.

Roper, B. L., Ben-Porath, Y. S., & Butcher, J. N. (1995). Comparability and validity of computerized adaptive testing with the MMPI-2. *Journal of Personality Assessment, 65*, 358–371.

Schinka, J. A., & LaLone, L. (1997). MMPI-2 norms: Comparisons with a census-matched subsample. *Psychological Assessment, 9*, 307–311.

Schmidt, H. O. (1945). Test profiles as a diagnostic aid: the Minnesota Multiphasic Inventory. *Journal of Applied Psychology, 29*, 115–131.

Sellbom, M., & Ben-Porath, Y. S. (2005). Mapping the MMPI-2 restructured clinical scales onto normal personality traits: Evidence of construct validity. *Journal of Personality Assessment, 85*, 179–187.

Sellbom, M., & Ben-Porath, Y. S. (2006). *The Minnesota Multiphasic Personality Inventory-2.* Mahwah, NJ: Erlbaum.

Sellbom, M., Ben-Porath, Y. S., & Graham, J. R. (2006). Correlates of the MMPI-2 restructured clinical (RC) scales in a college counseling setting. *Journal of Personality Assessment, 86*, 89–99.

Sellbom, M., Fischler, G. L., & Ben-Porath, Y.S. (in press). Identifying MMPI-2 predictors of police officer integrity and misconduct. *Criminal Justice and Behavior.*

Sellbom, M., Graham, J. R., & Schenk, P. W. (2005). Symptom correlates of MMPI-2 Scales and code types in a private practice setting. *Journal of Personality Assessment, 84*, 163–171.

Sellbom, M., Graham, J. R., & Schenk, P. W. (2006). Incremental validity of the MMPI-2 restructured clinical (RC) scales in a private practice sample. *Journal of Personality Assessment, 86*, 196–205.

Sherwood, N. E., Ben-Porath, Y. S., & Williams, C. L. (1997). The MMPI-A content component scales. (MMPI-2/MMPI-A Test Reports No. 3). Minneapolis: University of Minnesota Press.

Simms, L. J., Casillas, A., Clark, L. A., Watson, D., & Doebbeling, B. N. (2005). Psychometric evaluation of the restructured clinical scales of the MMPI-2. *Psychological Assessment, 17*, 345–358.

Stein, L. A. R., McClinton, B. K., & Graham, J. R. (1998). Long-term stability of MMPI-A scales. *Journal of Personality Assessment, 70,* 103–108.

Tellegen, A., & Ben-Porath, Y. S. (1992). The new uniform T scores for the MMPI-2: Rationale, derivation, and appraisal. *Psychological Assessment, 4,* 145–155.

Tellegen, A., Ben-Porath, Y. S., McNulty, J. L., Arbisi, P. A., Graham, J. R., & Kaemmer, B. (2003). *The MMPI-2 Restructured Clinical Scales: Development, validation, and interpretation.* Minneapolis: University of Minnesota Press.

Tellegen, A., Ben-Porath, Y. S., Sellbom, M., Arbisi, P. A., McNulty, J. L., & Graham, J. R. (2006). Further evidence on the validity of the MMPI-2 Restructured Clinical (RC) Scales: Addressing questions raised by Rogers et al. and Nichols. *Journal of Personality Assessment, 87,* 148–171.

Wallace, A., & Liljequist, L. (2005). A comparison of the correlational structures and elevation patterns of the MMPI-2 Restructured Clinical (RC) and Clinical Scales. *Assessment, 12,* 290–294.

Webb, J. T., Levitt, E. E., & Rojdev, R. (March, 1993). After three years: A comparison of the clinical use of the MMPI and MMPI-2. Paper presented at the 53rd Annual Meeting of the Society for Personality Assessment, San Francisco, CA.

Weed, N. C., Butcher, J. N., & Williams, C. L. (1994). Development of MMPI-A alcohol/drug problem scales. *Journal of Studies on Alcohol, 55,* 296–302.

Wiener, D. N., & Harmon, L. R. (1946). Subtle and obvious keys for the MMPI: Their development. *Advertisement Bulletin, No. 16.* Minneapolis, MN: Regional Veterans Administrative Office.

Wiggins, J. S. (1966). Substantive Dimensions of Self-Report in the MMPI Item Pool. *Psychological Monographs: General & Applied, 80,* 1–42.

Williams, C. L., Butcher, J. N., Ben-Porath, Y. S., & Graham, J. R. (1992). *MMPI-A content scales: Assessing psychopathology in adolescents.* Minneapolis: University of Minnesota Press.

Williams, J. E. & Weed, N. C. (2004a). Review of computer-based test interpretation software for the MMPI-2. *Journal of Personality Assessment, 83,* 78–83.

Williams, J. E. & Weed, N. C. (2004b). Relative User Ratings of MMPI-2 Computer-Based Test Interpretations. *Assessment, 11,* 316–329.

Young., K. R., & Weed, N. C. (2006). Assessing alcohol and drug abusing clients with the MMPI-2. In J. N. Butcher (Ed.) *The MMPI-2-: A practitioners guide* (pp. 361–380). Washington, DC: American Psychological Association.

CHAPTER 4

Millon Clinical Multiaxial Inventory-III

ROBERT J. CRAIG

Introduction

In a recent survey on contemporary test usage, researchers found that clinical psychologists were using test instruments that were used 20 to 40 years ago (Watkins, Campbell, Nieberding, & Hallmark, 1995). Test practices have changed very little over the past few decades. The one exception was the Millon Clinical Multiaxial Inventory[1] (MCMI-III) (Millon, 1983, 1987, 1994, 1997), which is now frequently used in clinical settings., In a survey of tests used by forensic psychologists for child custody evaluations, the MCMI was used by 34% of forensic psychologists (Ackerman & Ackerman, 1997); in a similar survey 10 years before the test was not used at all for this purpose (Keilen & Bloom, 1986). The MCMI is now the second most frequently used personality test in civil (Boccaccini & Brodsky, 1999) and criminal cases (Borum & Grisso, 1995), and it continues to be used in child custody evaluations (Quinnell & Bow, 2001). Nine books have been published on this test (Choca, 2004; Craig, 1993a,b, 1999a, 2005a,b; Jankowski, 2002; McCann & Dyer, 1996; and Retzlaff, 1995), and 12 reviews have been written, in mostly peer-reviewed journals (Choca, 2001; Craig, 1999b; Dana & Cantrell, 1988; Fleishaur, 1987; Greer, 1984; Haladyna, 1992; Hess, 1985, 1990; Lanyon, 1984; McCabe, 1984; Reynolds, 1992; and Wetzler, 1990). The test is now routinely covered in edited books on major psychological tests (Bohlian, Meagher, & Millon, 2005; Craig 1997, 2001, 2006a; Davis, Meagher, Gonclaves, Woodward, & Millon, 1999; Davis & Millon, 1993, 1997; Gonclaves, Woodward & Millon, 1994; Groth-Marnatt, 1997; Hall & Phung, 2001; Lehne, 1994, 2002;

Millon, 1984; Millon & Davis, 1996, 1998; Millon & Meagher, 2003), and, of course, in texts which deal with the various Millon inventories (Craig, 1997, 2002). What accounts for this growth?

The MCMI–III is a 175-questionnaire-based self-report inventory designed to diagnose personality disorders (PD) and major psychiatric syndromes in adult patients who are being evaluated for or receiving mental health services. There is a plethora of other personality tests, and there are many tests of personality disorders. So why has the MCMI become so popular? This chapter attempts to address three major questions:

1. Does the MCMI meet psychometric standards for reliability and validity?[2]
2. Do the strengths of this test justify its use, given its limitations?
3. Does it have a compendia of research base that justifies its use in the clinical context?

First, we look at how theory was used to develop this test, how this test was standardized, and how it is under continuous revision.

Theory and Development

Millon employed a three-stage validation process for all versions of the test. At step 1, referred to as the phase of *theoretical-substantive validity*, Millon wrote initial items largely from his theoretical model of personality. Ultimately, 1,100 items were generated and then divided into two equivalent form lists. These items were administered to two clinical samples. The items were retained if they correlated well with the total scale and if the inter-item correlations were within reasonable boundaries (ie., >.15 and <.85). In step 2, called the phase of *internal-structural validation*, Millon reviewed the items and patient responses to ensure the items were working as planned. The items were sent out to clinicians who were familiar with Millon's theory. The clinicians then judged the degree of fit of those items to his theoretical model of the disorder. The remaining 289 items were sent out to 167 clinicians who gave the test to their patients and who also completed a diagnostic form.

In the final phase of *external-criterion validation*, or sometimes called convergent and discriminant validity, the test was validated against similar instruments. The test was continuously revised as items were added. The initial test construction, was then repeated. Revisions were made until the final item pool reached 175.

For the MCMI-II, Millon developed a provisional form with 368 items and added two other scales (Sadistic and Self-Defeating). He repeated the validation steps for these items and then added an item-weighting system,in which he assigned higher scores to prototype items—items that strongly relate to the disorder. Finally he added the modifying indices of Disclosure, Desirability, and Debasement.

For the MCMI-III, Millon added two additional PD scales (Depressive and PTSD), added unscored but "noteworthy" items dealing with child abuse and eating disorders, changed the item-weighting scoring system, changed 95 of the 175 items, and substantially reduced the number of items for each scale. Again, he submitted these items to the three-stage validation process described above.

Some researchers have lamented that the MCMI is being revised too frequently to allow them time to adequately study it (Choca et al., 1992). However, just as Freud altered his theory and method of psychoanalysis, Millon has changed his instruments to account for new developments in his theory, as well as changes in the *DSM*. For example, the MCMI-I Major Depression scale lacked vegetative items which are the hallmark of the disorder. Research demonstrated that this scale was showing poor convergent validity with similar measures. This problem was corrected with the MCMI-II Major Depression Scale, which did contain vegetative items of depression. Most recently, Millon has added facet subscales to his PD scales, which allow for more interpretive refinement. These refinements occurred 8 years after the publication of the MCMI-III. Millon has added a fourth dimension to his theory called "Abstraction." Although he has not yet developed a typology of styles and disorders associated with this polarity, this could be another example of how theory would predate taxonomy and instrumentation.

Theory guided Millon's development of the scales as well as the choice of items in the scale. He argued that there are five basic styles of reinforcement (dependent, independent, ambivalent, discordant and detached), and two ways of seeking reinforcement (active and passive). This leads to a five X two matrix of normal personality styles and their extensions into the personality disorders. For example, the active dependent style is called "sociable" at the normal level and "Histrionic" (PD) at the disordered level. Similarly, the passive dependent style at the normal level is called "cooperative" but labeled "Dependent" (PD) at the level of a disorder. Thus, each normal personality style and personality disorder can be indexed into one of the five styles and one of two ways of seeking reinforcement, according to his theory (2).

Millon believes that theory predates taxonomy and measurement follows taxonomy. Thus he developed his theory of personality first, then developed his taxonomy of classifying personality styles and disorders and ultimately developed instrumentation to measure it. Millon is not tied to the questionnaire method as a measurement tool. Instead, he has tried a list of diagnostic statements that the clinician would answer. Craig (2004) has developed a measure of personality disorders using adjectives which assess both *DSM* disorders as well as Millon's typology.

A preliminary working version of the test was initially called the Millon Illinois Self Report Inventory. The name was changed to the Millon Multiaxial Clinical Inventory and then initially published as the Millon Clinical Multiaxial Inventory (MCMI) (Millon, 1983), which coincided with the revision of *DSM-II*. It was revised in 1987 (Millon, 1987), which coincided with the publication of *DSM-III-R*. The inventory was again revised in 1994 (Millon, 1994) which coincided with the publication of *DSM-IV*. The MCMI-III manual was revised in 1997 (Millon, 1997) to address problems with the validity study.

Basic Psychometrics

The current iteration contains three modifying indices (i.e., validity scales), 11 clinical personality patterns (i.e., personality disorders), three severe personality pathology disorders, 7 clinical syndromes (i.e., Axis I disorders) and three severe clinical syndromes. Thus, there are 27 scales with which to assess reliability and validity, not counting the 42 Grossman facet scales. The ability to provide an overview of all the research that pertains to this psychometric data for all 27 scales is beyond the scope of this chapter. Instead this section will highlight the reliability and validity of selected basic PD and clinical scales.

Reliability

There are two types of reliability statistics; internal consistency and test-retest. Few MCMI researchers have been concerned with the former Most of the research has concentrated on the latter. The MCMI test manuals provide data on the internal consistency of the scales. These data demonstrate that the scales meet *alpha* level requirements and are internally consistent. This brings us to the issue of test-retest reliability. This matter is complicated because the test has been revised twice (Millon, 1987, 1994) from its original appearance (Millon, 1983). Items have been changed upon each revision and Millon has exerted great effort to maintain conceptual consistency with each revision of the test. Nevertheless, many view these as different tests. Information is presented below on the MCMI scale reliabilities according to each test version (see Table 4.1).

One would expect the reliability to be higher for personality disorder scales, than for the clinical symptom scales. This is because PDs are considered to be ingrained ego-syntonic personality traits which are relatively impervious to treatment, whereas clinical symptoms are seen as ego alien and tend to be more responsive to treatment. The evidence in Table 4.1 verifies this hypothesis. Across all versions of the test the retest reliabilities are generally higher for the personality disorder scales than they are for the clinical symptom scales.

Table 4.1 Test-Retest Median Reliability Estimates of Three Versions of the Millon Clinical Multiaxial Inventory[3]

Scale	MCLI I		MCMI-II		MCMI-III	
	# *	r'	#*	r'	#*	r'
Personality Pattern						
Schizoid	8	.71	5	.70	2	.52
Avoidant	9	.70	3	.71	3	.78
Depressive	NA	NA	NA	NA	3	.65
Dependent	8	.63	5	.68	3	.83
Histrionic	8	.82	4	.73	3	.81
Narcissistic	8	.71	3	.79	3	.79
Antisocial	8	.82	4	.73	3	.76
Aggressive/Sadistic	NA	NA	3	.70	3	.72
Compulsive	8	.70	4	.69	3	.92
Negativistic	8	.61	4	.62	3	.73
Masochistic	NA	NA	3	.72	3	.76
Schizotypal	8	.74	4	.64	3	.74
Borderline	8	.54	4	.53	3	.69
Paranoid	8	.65	4	.67	3	.80
Clinical Syndromes						
Anxiety	7	.65	4	.55	3	.80
Somatoform	7	.45	4	.43	3	.50
Bipolar: Manic	7	.66	3	.66	2	.84
Dysthymia	7	.57	3	.43	3	.61
Alcohol	7	.55	3	.76	3	.68
Drug	8	.70	3	.72	3	.76
Post-Traumatic Stress	NA	NA	NA	NA	3	.71
Thought Disorder	7	.68	3	.65	3	.92
Major Depression	7	.61	3	.50	3	.50
Delusional Disorder	7	.66	3	.70	3	.70

#* = Number of studies on which these data are based.
r' = median test-retest reliability estimate.

Validity

Convergent Validity For diagnostic tests, there are two basic ways to judge its validity. First, we correlate it against similar tests, thereby establishing its convergent validity. Second, we resort to diagnostic power statistics to determine its diagnostic accuracy. Recall that this would have to be done for all 27 scales on the MCMI, ignoring for the moment the convergent validity of the recently published Grossman facet scales (Grossman & del Rio, 2006).

Space limitations preclude an exhaustive presentation of the MCMI-III convergent validity studies. These data have been presented elsewhere for the Antisocial PD scale, for Major Depression (Craig, 2006a), for the Narcissistic and Compulsive PD scales (Craig, 1997), and for the Alcohol and Drug abuse scales (Craig, 2005b). We add to this literature by reporting data on the convergent validity of the Dependent and Borderline PD scales. These scales were selected for presentation because of their central role in many psychopathological conditions. Tables 4.2 and 4.3 present these data.

Evidence has been presented that suggests method variance affects validity coefficient scores when assessing PDs. That is, tests within a method (i.e., comparing two self-report inventories or two structured clinical interviews) tend to yield higher convergent validity estimates than tests which cross methods (i.e., comparing a self-report inventory to a structured clinical interview) (Craig, 2003a). In order to review the data presented here against this general finding, both tables have been organized by method. Self-report inventories appear first, followed by structured clinical interviews, and then miscellaneous criterion measures. Inspection of Table 4.2 for scale Dependent shows higher correlations when this scale is compared to similar self-report inventories. The scale shows more modest correlations when it is compared to structured clinical interviews. Comparison for Table 4.3 suggests that scale Borderline generally correlates in the .50s or .60s with MMPI/MMPI-2 PD Borderline in 12 data sets, with the correlations ranging from .37 to .88. Collapsing all comparisons of scale Dysthymia with similar self-report inventories reveals a median correlation of .59. Similarly, comparing scale Dependent with all structured PD clinical interviews yields a median correlation of .48. Since there is no gold standard with which to determine the presence or absence of a PD, the criterion becomes quite relevant.

Much of the PD literature suggests that (a) structured personality evaluations, either via self-report or via structured clinical interviews, yielded more PD diagnoses than are commonly diagnosed by an individual clinician who may be interviewing that same patient, and (b) there is low agreement between PD measures at the level of individual diagnosis. That is, giving two separate measures to the same patient often does not result in the same PD diagnosis (Craig, 2003a). This fact should be kept in mind as we turn to the next way of evaluating the accuracy of a diagnostic test, termed "diagnostic power statistics."

Diagnostic Power Statistics   Sometimes referred to as the operating characteristics of a diagnostic test (Gibertini, Brandenberg, & Retzlaff, 1986), there are five such statistics of importance. A test's *sensitivity* tells whether the patient has the disorder if the test is positive for the disorder. *Specificity* tells whether the patient does not have the disorder if the test is negative for the disorder. *Positive predictive power* tells us whether the test is positive if the patient is known to have the disorder, while *negative predictive power* tells us

Table 4.2 Correspondence of Scale Dependent with Similar Measures

Author(s)	Instrument	MCMI	r'
Morey & Levine (1988)	MMPI PD	I	.89
Dubro & Wetzler (1989)	MMPI PD	I	.68
McCann (1989)	MMPI PD	I	.50
Zarella et al. (1990)	MMPI PD	I	.60
Zarella et al. (1990)	MMPI PD	I	.59
Schuler et al. (1994)	MMPI PD	I	.67
Wise (1994a)	MMPI PD	I	.53
Klein et al. (1993)	Wisc PD Invent	I	.77
Hogg et al. (1990)	SIDP	I	.21
Torgersen & Alnaes (1990)	SIDP	I	.38
Overholser (1991)	SIDP	I	.37
Widiger & Sanderson (1987)	PDI	I	.68
Morey (1985)	ICL Dependent	I	.52
Chick et al. (1993)	*DSM-III-R* Cklt	I	.05
Wise (1994b)	MBHI Cooperative	I	.46
Blackbrun (1998)	CIRCLE Compliant	I	.33
McCann (1991)	MMPI PD	II	.56
Wise (1996)	MMPI-2 PD	II	.63
Wise (2001)	MMPI-2 PD	II	.31
Jones (2005)	MMPI-2 PD (Morey)	II	.49
	MMP1-2 PD(S&B)	II	.50s
Coolidge & Merwin (1992)	Coolidge	II	.38
Silberman et al. (1997)	Coolidge	II	.20
Renneberg et al. (1992)	SCID	II	.35
Hart, Dutton, et al. (1993)	PDE sym. count	II	.15
Soldz et al. (1993)	PDE	II	.38
Kennedy et al. (1995)	SCID-II	II	.20
Marlowe et al. (1997)	SCID-II	II	.20
Wierzbicki & Gorman (1995)	PDQ-R	II	.26
Hicklin & Widiger (2000)	MMPI PD	III	.75
Lindsay et al. (2000)	MMPI-2 PD	III	.75
Hicklin & Widiger (2000)	MMPI-2 PD	III	.80
Lindsay et al. (2000)	PDQ-4	III	.77
Clark et al. (1998)	Personal Concerns Dependent scale	III	.49

Note: MMPI = Minnesota Multiphasic Personality Inventory; MMPI-2 = Minnesota Multiphasic Personality Inventory -2; SIDP = Structured Interview for DSM Personality Disorders; Wisc. PD Invent = Wisconsin Personality Disorder; PDI = Personality Disorder Interview; Coolidge = Coolidge Axis II Inventory; SCID = Structured Clinical Interview for DSM Personality Disorders; PDE = Personality Disorder Examination; MBHI = Millon Behavioral Health Inventory; PDQ-R= Personality Disorder Questionnaire – Revised; (all correlated with corresponding Dependent PD scale from these instruments).

Table 4.3 Correspondence of Scale Borderline with Similar Measures

Author(s)	Instrument	MCMI	r'
Morey & Levine (1988)	MMPIPD	I	.70
McCann (1989)	MMPI PD	I	.42
Zarella et al. (1990)	MMPI PD	I	.49
Schuler et al. (1994)	MMPI PD	I	.37
Wise (1994)	MMPI PD	I	.46
Klein et al. (1993)	Wisc PD	I	.66
Hogg et al. (1990)	SIDP	I	.33
Torgersen & Alnaes (1990)	SIDP	I	.32
Patrick (1993)	SIDP	I	.54
Renneberg et al. (1992)	SCID	I	.25
Lewis & Harder (1991)	DSM-III-R	I	.37
	Kernberg Intv	I	.77
	BSI	I	.77
	DIB	I	.43
Sansone et al. (1992)	DIB	I	.62
	Bord.Syn Index	I	.87
Chick et al. (1993)	DSM-III-R Cklt	I	.13
McCann (1991)	MMPI PD	II	.68
Wise (1996)	MMPI-2 PD	II	.68
Wise (2001)	MMPI-2 PD	II	.41
Jones (2005)	MMPI-2 PD (Morey)	II	.70
	MMP1-2 PD(S&B)	II	.88
Coolidge & Merwin (1992)	Coolidge	II	.46
Silberman et al. (1997)	Coolidge	II	.88
Kennedy et al. (1995)	SCID-II	II	−.09
Marlowe et al. (1997)	SCID-II	II	.40
Hart, Dutton, et al. (1993)	PDE	II	.39
	PDE sym count	II	.43
Soldz et al. (1993a)	PDE	II	.60
Dutton (1994)	Bord.Per.Org.	II	.71
Wierzbicki & Gorman (1995)	PDQ-R	II	.57
Bayon et al. (1996)	TCI Harm Avoid	II	.46
Hicklin & Widiger (2000)	MMPI PD	III	.57
	MMPI-2 PD	III	.82
Clark et al. (1998)	Personal Concerns Borderline scale	III	.59

Note: MMPI = Minnesota Multiphasic Personality Inventory; Minnesota Multiphasic Personality Inventory -2; SIDP = Structured Interview for DSM Personality Disorders; BSI = Borderline Symptom Interview; DIB = Diagnostic Interview for Borderlines; Bord. Syn. Index = Borderline Syndrome Index; SCID = Structured Clinical Interview for DSM Personality Disorders; Coolidge = Coolidge Axis II Inventory; Wisc. PD = Wisconsin Personality Disorder; PDE = Personality Disorder Examination; PDQ-R= Personality Disorder Questionnaire – Revised; TCI Harm Avoid = Temperament Character Inventory Harm Avoidance (all tests correlated with corresponding Borderline Personality Disorder scale from these listed tests).

whether the test is negative if the patient is known to not have the disorder. Overall *diagnostic power* collapses all of these statistics into one figure which captures the overall diagnostic power of the test. Again, keep in mind that for a 27-scale test, we would need each of these five statistics for each scale, for a total of 135 power statistics. Obviously, the validity of a diagnostic test, especially a multi-scale test, would depend on its diagnostic power for the scale most relevant to the diagnostic issue.

Again, space constraints preclude a total exposition of the MCMI's diagnostic power statistics for each scale. These data have previously been published for the Borderline Personality Disorder scale (Craig, 2006a) and for the Alcohol and Drug scales (Craig, 2005b). Here we present diagnostic power statistics for the Antisocial Personality Disorder scale and for the Dysthymia scale. These were chosen due to their association (i.e., co-morbidity) with many disorders. These data are presented in Table 4.4 and Table 4.5.

Table 4.4 Diagnostic Power of MCMI Antisocial Personality Disorder

Classification	MCMI	Prev	Sens	Spec	PPP	NPP	DxP
1) BR > 74	I	.13	.62	.94	.61	.94	.90
BR > 84		.08	.42	.97	.55	.95	.93
2) BR > 74	I	.26	.40	.82	.57	.69	X
BR >84		.13	.25	.94	.71	.67	X
3) BR > 75	I	X	.75	.75	.75	.75	X
BR > 85	X	.85	.85	.85	.85	X	X
4) Clin. Dx	I	X	.52	.95	X	X	X
5) Not Provided	I	.05	.63	.94	.34	.98	.63
6) BR > 74	I	.08	.50	.65	.11	.94	.73
BR > 84		.08	.25	.77	.09	.92	.96
7) 2 Highest Scales	II	.09	.71	.98	.80	.97	.97
Highest in Code		.05	.60	.99	.68	.98	.92
8) PCL BR > 74	II	X	.53	.92	.24	.23	X
BR > 84	II	X	.88	.38	.26	.92	X
DSM III Dx BR > 74	II	.53	.91	.34	.61	.76	X
BR > 84	II	X	.78	.45	.61	.64	.91
9) SCID Dx	II	.13	1.00	.90	.29	1.00	.74
10) SCID-II	II	XX	.69	.76	.43	.90	.80
11) BR > 74	III	.17	.39	.88	.16	X	.89
BR > 84	III	.07	.04	.96	.04	X	X
12) Clin Dx	III	XX	.50	X	.61	X	

Note: Prev = prevalence; Sens = sensitivity; Spec = specificity; PPP = positive predictive power; NPP = negative predictive power; DxP = diagnostic power; PCL = Psychopathy Checklist. 1) Gibertini, Brandenberg, & Retzlaff, 1986; 2) Widiger & Sanderson, 1987: *N* = 53 inpt psych.; 3) Torgeson & Alnaes, 1990 (* Norwegian sample); 4) Streiner & Miller, 1991; *N* = 237 ; 5) Miller et al., 1992 ; 6) Chick et al., 1993; *N* = 107 misc. psych pts.; 7) Millon, 1987; 8) Hart, Forth, & Hare, 1991; 9) Guthrie & Mobley, 1994 (*N* = 55 opts); 10) Hills, 1995 (*N* = 125) ; 11) Millon, 1994 (*N* = 398) ; 12) Millon, 1997.

Table 4.5 Diagnostic Power of Scale Dysthymia

Classification	MCMI	Prev	Sens	Spec	PPP	NPP	DxP
1) BR > 74	I	.41	.91	.88	.84	.93	.89
BR > 84		.26	.73	.92	.76	.91	.87
2) Clinical Dx	I	.41	.71	.70	.63	.77	.69
3) Clin Dx	I	XX	.67	1.00	XX	XX	XX
4) BR > 74	II	.46	.81	.83	.80	.84	.82
BR > 84		.29	.76	.88	.72	.90	.84
5) Clinical Dx	II	.77	.86	.32	.81	.40	.73
6) BR > 74	I	XX	.89	.53	.65	.83	.71
BR > 84		XX	.74	.73	.73	.74	.74
BR > 74	II	XX	.16	.87	.55	.52	.52
BR > 84		XX	.08	.93	.55	.51	.51
7) Highest/2nd high ratings	III	.36	.37	.59	.39	X	.51
8) BR >74	III	.38	.85	X	.61	X	X
BR > 84		X	.55	X	.88	X	X

Note: Prev = prevalence; Sens = sensitivity; Spec = specificity; PPP = positive predictive power; NPP = negative predictive power; DxP = diagnostic power. 1) Gibertini, Brandenberg, & Retzlaff, 1986 ; 2) Wetzler et al., 19893; 3) Streiner & Miller, 199 ; 4) Millon, 1987 ; 5) Piersma 1991 ; 6) Wetzler & Marlowe, 1993 ; 7) Millon, 1994 ; 8) Millon, 1997.

Diagnostic power statistics are affected by the prevalence rate of the disorder in the sample studied by the researcher. Also, *positive predictive power* is of great importance to a clinical diagnostician because if the patient has a disorder we want to be able to uncover it. Finally, for a scale or test to have incremental validity, its positive predictive power should be greater than the prevalence rate of the disorder. Perfect congruence would be expressed as a value of 1.00, whereas values less than perfect are expressed as a percentage. Inspection of Table 4.4 suggests that researchers have resorted to a variety of criteria to diagnose antisocial PD. Of the 12 reported studies which included information from the MCMI test manuals, several used the test manual guidelines of BR>84 or BR>74, while clinical diagnosis and diagnosis based on SCID-II findings have also been used as a standard. It is interesting to note that as the Psychopathy Check List (PCL) has become the gold standard to diagnose antisocial PD, at least, in a criminal sample (Craig, 2005c), only one study has compared the diagnostic efficiency of the MCMI to the PCL. Median values for scales averaged across all studies were: sensitivity (.60), specificity (.84), positive predictive power (.56), negative predictive power (.92), and overall diagnostic power (.89). This scale is quite effective at ruling out the disorder, and it is able to correctly diagnose the disorder more than half the time. (The notion of a Base Rate (BR) score is explained in the section on Administration and Scoring).

Does this mean that the scale is only about as good as flipping a coin? No! Flipping a coin would result in a diagnosis of antisocial at a rate of 50%. However, the rate of the disorder in the general population is 3%, and in some clinical settings as high as 30% depending on the population studied (*DSM-IV*, 1994). Therefore, a coin flip would be substantially wrong in the majority of cases, whereas the accuracy of the MCMI Antisocial PD scale is substantially higher than the prevalence rate of the disorder. As is true with most diagnostic tests in psychology, we do a better job at ruling out a disorder than ruling it in. Furthermore, the overall diagnostic power of this scale appears excellent, but is largely due to its ability to rule out the disorder, which approaches a 90% accuracy rate. The bulk of this information is based on the MCMI-I and MCMI-II. To date, we only have diagnostic power statistics from the test manual for the MCMI-III ASPD scale.

For scale Dysthymia, there have been eight reports in the literature, but three of them are from the test manual. All have used BR scores as the diagnostic criteria. This is somewhat unusual since there are several tests that assess depression. Median diagnostic power statistics for the Dysthymia scale are as follows: sensitivity (.74), specificity (.85), positive predictive power (.73), negative predictive power (.80), and overall diagnostic power (.73). These values are quite noteworthy and suggests that the scale does what it was designed to do, which is to indicate validity.

MCMI Modifying Indices   I want to say a few words about the MCMI validity scales, referred to as "modifying indices". These are the MCMI validity scales but are termed "modifying indices" because they modify (i.e., raise or lower) scores on other scales, based on the magnitude of their values. Compared to the MMPI validity scales, there has been little research interest in the validity of the MCMI validity scales. While it is feasible that a respondent might take one test-taking approach on one test and quite another approach on a different test, researchers assume that there would be some expected correlation between validity scales of the two tests (Grossman & Craig, 1995). Bagby and Marshall (2005) have recently reviewed the extant research on the MCMI validity scales. They concluded that although analogue research suggests that the "modifying indices are somewhat effective in detecting underreporting, over-reporting, and inconsistent response bias" (p. 244), there was insufficient evidence to warrant their use in real-world clinical situations.

Finally, although the MCMI-III has been available for more than a decade, there has been little validity data published on any of its scales. More distressing is the apparent fact that published research with the MCMI appears to be decreasing over time (Craig & Olson, 2005), despite the increased popularity of this test among clinicians.

Administration and Scoring

The MCMI was designed to be used with adults 18 years and older who are currently being evaluated or treated in mental health settings and who have only a 5th grade reading level. Use of this test with patients who do not meet these criteria will result in inaccurate assessments and personality description. The test should not be used for people in non-clinical (i.e., industrial, personnel) settings. Also, one needs a firm grounding in understanding personality theory, psychopathology, and in tests and measurement, in order to render a professional, competent interpretation of this test.

The test is generally administered in a single sitting. No group administrations of this test have been reported. It may be hand scored or computer scored. Hand scoring is time-consuming, burdensome, and leads to scoring errors due to the multiple adjustments required of this test. The adjustments are based on (a) whether the test setting is inpatient or outpatient, (b) denial versus a complaint adjustments (these are based on validity scale scores), and (c) whether the Anxiety and Depression scales are elevated. Most clinicians prefer mail-in computer scoring, though that adds to the cost of the test.

Raw scores are converted to a transformed score called a "Base Rate" (BR) score. Because personality disorders are not normally distributed in the general population, it is inappropriate to use a transformed score, which assumes an underlying normal distribution. Instead, Millon discovered that point in the distribution of raw scores which matched the prevalence rate of the disorder and assigned that point a value of BR 85. A BR score of 60 represents the average score of all psychiatric patients and a raw score of 30 represents the average score of non-clinical respondents in the standardization sample. He then interpolated the remaining values.

A BR score of 85 or 115 means exactly the same thing. The patient has all of the traits of the disorder at the diagnostic level. BR scores between 75 and 84 indicate that the patient has some but not all of the traits to warrant a diagnosis.

Which traits might a patient have at a BR score of 77 and does a patient with a BR score of 107 really have all of the defining traits? *DSM-IV* (1994) requires that four of possible seven criteria must be met for a diagnosis of Schizoid PD. Similarly, a Borderline PD diagnosis requires five of nine criteria, and an Antisocial PD diagnosis requires three of seven to be met. It is possible and even probable that two patients with the same PD diagnosis will manifest different personality behavior patterns. Can the MCMI make these kinds of distinctions?

All three versions of the test were not able to determine which of several traits a given patient had in order to reach the diagnostic level. Both Millon and Craig developed computer narrative interpretive reports based on a prototype behavior of a "typical" patient. With the recent advances of the Grossman subscales (Grossman & del Rio, 2006), we are now able to refine our personality description of the basic diagnostic style.

Millon has described each PD prototype in terms of its structural and functional properties. These are *behavioral domains* (expressive acts and interpersonal conduct), phenomenological domains (cognitive style, object representations, self image), *intrapsychic domains* (regulatory mechanisms, morphological organization), and *biophysical domains* (mood and temperament). The Grossman facet subscales were derived from items that represent the three most salient domains of each PD. For example, Millon argues that the Avoidant PD would be most troubled in the domains of social interaction (behavioral domain), with self esteem issues, and with their perceptions of others (phenomenological domain). Hence the Grossman facet scales for the Avoidant PD are "interpersonally aversive," "alienated self image," and "expressively passive."

To demonstrate this, below is a computer-derived description of the antisocial personality disorder from Craig's (2006b) MCMI-III interpretive report, based on generic patients who have this disorder:

> These patients are essentially fearless, aggressive, impulsive, irresponsible, dominating, and narcissistic. At less severe levels they appear self-reliant, tough and competitive, At their more severe manifestations, they are ruthless, intimidating, pugnacious, victimizing and brutal, vindictive, and vengeful. They harbor grudges and resentments over people that disapprove of their behavior. They seem to be excessively touchy and jealous and brood over perceived slights. They provoke fear in those around them through their intimidating social demeanor. They seem to be chronically dissatisfied and often display an angry and hostile affect. They feel most comfortable when they have power and control over others, who are viewed as weak and who desire to control them. Thus they maintain a fiercely independent stance and act in a self-reliant manner. They often ascribe their own malicious motives onto others. They are continuously on guard against anticipated ridicule and act out in a socially intimidating manner in order to provoke fear and control other people. They are driven by power, by malevolent projections and by an anticipation of suffering from others, so they react to maintain their autonomy and independence. They believe that other people are malicious and devious, justifying to themselves a forceful counteraction. They are prone towards substance abuse, relationship difficulties, vocational deficits, and legal problems. Some are able to sublimate these traits into various businesses whereby

these traits have instrumental value. Most, however, have a myriad of problems with societal institutions.

Grossman has developed three subscales for the Antisocial scale. These are Expressively Impulsive, Acting-Out Mechanism, and Interpersonally Irresponsible. If these are all elevated, then the basic personality description above could still be used. But let us assume, however improbable and for purposes of illustration, that only the facet subscale of Acting-Out Mechanism is clinically elevated, and the other two facet subscales are within normal values. Then the personality description would place emphasis on that aspect of behavior and minimize aspects of interpersonal irresponsibility. It would also attenuate any description of impulsive expression. Similarly, by consulting other elevated Grossman subscales associated with the parent scales, one can move beyond a prototype description to a more refined and individualistic description.

Now let us add another wrinkle to the diagnosis. Millon has further theorized that there are anywhere from three to six possible personality disorder subtypes. While each of the disorders would maintain the essential features of the main disorder, they would primarily show distinctive features of that subtype. For example, he has argued that the Antisocial Disorder is composed of five subtypes: Covetous (6A), Nomadic (6A-1/2A), Risk-Taking (6A-4), Reputation-Defending (6A-5), and Malevolent (6A-6B/P). The number in parentheses represents the MCMI-III scale numbers corresponding to these diagnoses. Descriptions for these subtypes can be found in Davis and Patterson (2005).

The addition of the Grossman scales and the development of ways to use the MCMI-III to diagnose personality disorder subtypes are perhaps the most useful refinements of the test since its publication.

Computerization

The MCMI can be hand scored or computer scored. The latter requires mail-in service through Pearson Assessments, the test's publisher. Hand scoring takes almost 30 minutes and can result in scoring and transformation errors

Cautions

- Do not give this test to non-clinical populations.
- The test cannot be computer-scored if gender is not provided, if the patient is under age 18, or more than 12 items have been left unanswered.
- Before proceeding with scoring, check the Validity Index Items to ensure proper responding.

due to the many adjustments that affect scale scores. Most clinicians prefer computer scoring, though this adds to the cost.

There are two computer narrative interpretive reports. Pearson Assessments publishes an interpretive report, while Psychological Assessment Resources (Craig, 2006b) publishes a computer narrative report but not a scoring report. The Pearson MCMI-III Interpretive Report requires a pay-as-you-use approach, whereas the PAR MCMI-III Interpretive Report allows unlimited uses after purchase of the disc. Both programs are written as a professional consultation to the clinician and are written in such a way as to discourage direct downloads into a clinical report. To date, there has been no interest in computer-adapted assessment using the MCMI, but this could be feasible in the future.

Applications and Limitations

The MCMI was designed as a measure to be used with adults who are receiving mental health services. Use of this instrument with other populations is inappropriate and will lead to inaccurate assessments. The MCMI has been used in both inpatient and outpatient psychiatric hospitals and clinics. It has been frequently used with substance abusers (alcohol and drug), spouse abusers, patients with PTSD and, patients with anxiety and depressive disorders. It has also been used in correctional settings and in forensic applications. Other commonly used psychological tests (e.g., MMPI-2, Rorschach) do not provide the same degree of diagnostic accuracy for Axis I and II disorders that is available with the MCMI. On the other hand, it was not meant to provide an assessment of patient strengths and ego resources; other tools are necessary to determine those important aspects of personality functioning.

Research Findings

Treatment Planning and Intervention   Millon (1999) has published his ideas of treatment intervention using his theoretical model of polarities. Other clinicians have provided examples of how the MCMI can be used for treatment planning. Retzlaff's (1995) book is rich with clinical examples of how the MCMI-III can be used in treatment planning and intervention, using the tactical approach side of Millon's theoretical notions on treatment. Magnavita (2005a) suggested that the MCMI-III can be used to help make decisions as to the type of therapy, modality of treatment, and format of treatment based on diagnostic considerations. He argues that the test can help with complex diagnostic issues and treatment-planning strategizing. He then offers an illustrative case example . An increasing number of publications have recently appeared which use Millon's theoretical approach for purposes of

Just the Facts

Date published	1994
Publisher	Pearson Assessments
Ages	18 and above
Strengths	Anchored to Millon's Theory of Personality
	Relatively Brief in Length
	Well-validated through a 3-stage validation process
	Uses Base rate Scores
Limitations	Little diagnostic efficiency with non-clinical populations and with the severely disturbed psychiatrically impaired client
	Tends to produce multiple personal disorder diagnoses compared to structured clinical interviews
	Complicated hand scoring tends to results in scoring errors
Administration Time	30 minutes
Scoring time	30 minutes by hand

treatment (Bockian, 2006; Farmer & Nelson-Gray, 2005; Magnavita, 2005b; and Rasmussen, 2005).

Few researchers have studied Millon's (1999) ideas of treatment for this aspect of his theory. Since personality disorders are theorized to be relatively entrenched and impervious to treatment, studies on scale changes following treatment have focused on the MCMI clinical syndrome scales. In a recent study, 125 recently detoxified opiate addicts were placed in a 12-week randomized outpatient treatment of naltrexone, a narcotic antagonist, in conjunction with relapse prevention counseling. Additionally, groups were randomly selected to be placed in no-incentive vouchers groups, incentive vouchers alone, or incentive vouchers plus counseling on relationships. The MCMI-III was used to subtype the personality styles or disorders. In the patient X treatment analysis, some subgroups had better outcomes with certain treatments. The study is an excellent example of how the MCMI-III can be used in treatment planning (Ball, Nich, Rounsaville, Eagan, & Carroll, 2004).

Other studies have reported on whether or not particular MCMI scales change as a result of treatment. Patients with Major Depression ($N = 98$) significantly reduced their scores on MCMI-II Scale D after inpatient treatment (Piersma, 1989). Libb, Stankovic, Sokol, Houck, and Switzer (1990) found that, after 3 months of treatment for major depression, scores on Scale D went from BR 99 to BR 72. The criteria was as follows: that a patient move from the dysfunctional to functional range during inpatient treatment, and that the change in D scores between pre-test and post-test was statistically reliable. Piersma and Smith (1991) found that 39/109 (36%) met these criteria. Inpatient psychiatric patients ($N = 97$) showed significant decreases on MCMI-III Scale D after seven to ten days of treatment (Piersma & Boes, 1997).

In one study, patients with PTSD ($N = 50$) showed no significant changes on Scale D after 35 days of inpatient treatment, which suggests that depression associated with PTSD does not respond to short-term treatment (Hyer, Woods, Bruno, & Boudewyns, 1989). In another study, patients ($N = 36$) with PTSD significantly reduced their scores on D after 140 days of inpatient treatment (Funari, Piekarski, & Sherwood, 1991).

Alcoholic patients ($N = 28$) with lingering depression had elevated MCMI-I scale D scores 6 weeks into treatment, whereas alcoholics ($N = 31$) with transient depression had an initial BR score of 92 on D and 6 weeks later scored <75, indicating their depression had abated (McMahon & Davidson, 1986). Alcoholics ($N = 14$) showed significant decreases in MCMI-I Scale D scores following 20, 40-minute sessions of alpha-theta brainwave neurofeedback training (Saxby & Peniston, 1995).

Cocaine patients from three separate treatment programs, ranging in sample size from 38 to 109, showed no significant differences after treatment. The range in duration spanned from an average of 30 days to an average of 4 months for MCMI-II Scale D. However, their scores remained within the same non-clinically significant range post-treatment (McMahon & Richards, 1996).

Scores on MCMI-I scale D decreased after 18 months of treatment among 89 male and female patients on methadone maintenance, whose drug use was rated as light, but the scores showed no changes among addicts whose drug use was rated as heavy ($N = 141$) (Calsyn, Wells, Fleming, & Saxon, 2000).

Clinically significant improvement occurred on MCMI-II Scale D scores among a group of 35 patients with Dissociative Identity Disorder following a 2-year post-inpatient treatment program (Ellason & Ross, 1996). Bulimics with good treatment outcome ($N = 17$) after 18 weeks of individual therapy, scored lower on Scale D at the end of treatment compared to those with poor treatment outcome ($N = 19$) (Garner, Olmsted, Davis, & Rocket, 1990).

Patients ($N = 16$) who underwent gastric stapling for morbid obesity, significantly reduced there scores on Scale D post-surgically (Chandarana, Conlon, Holliday, Deslippe, & Field, 1990). Among a group of neck sprain patients, ($N = 88$) there were no significant changes after 6 months of treatment in one subgroup. However, two subgroups significantly decreased their scores on MCMI-I Scale D (Borchgrevink, Stiles, Borchgrevink, & Lereim, 1997).

Important References

Ball, S. A., Nich, C., Rounsaville, B. J., Eagan, D., & Carroll, K. M. (2004). Millon Clinical Multiaxial Inventory-III subtypes of opioid dependence: Validity and matching to behavioral therapist. *Journal of Consulting and Clinical Psychology, 72,* 698–711.

> The authors studied the concurrent and predictive validity of two different methods of MCMI-III subtyping in 125 recently detoxified opiate addicts who were receiving a 12-week randomized clinical trial with three different interventions. This study is an example of how the MCMI-III can be used for treatment planning and intervention.

Craig, R. J. (1999). Overview and current status of the Millon Clinical Multiaxial Inventory. *Journal of Personality Assessment, 72,* 390–406.

> The author presents an historical overview of the test and summarizes its current status in the research literature. It also discusses Millon's suggestions for linking MCMI code types to theory-derived methods of interventions.

Craig, R. J. (Ed.). (2005). *New directions in interpreting the Millon Clinical Multiaxial Inventory-III.* New York: Wiley.

> The author presents the latest information on the MCMI-III, including the Grossman facet subscales, diagnosing Millon's theorized personality disorder subtypes using the MCMI-III, alternative interpretations to some MCMI-III scales, forensic and international applications, as well as ways to use the measure for treatment planning and intervention.

Hsu, L. M. (2002). Diagnostic validity statistics and the MCMI-III. *Psychological Assessment, 14,* 410–422.

> The author discusses five diagnostic validity statistics (incremental validities of positive and negative test diagnosis, kappa, effect size, and areas under receiver operating characteristics (ROC) curves, and he applies them to the 24 MCMI-III scales.

McCann, J. T. (2002). Guidelines for forensic application of the MCMI-III. *Journal of Forensic Psychology Practice, 2,* 55–69.

> McCann gives an overview of issues regarding the use of the MCMI-III in forensic evaluations. He addresses the issue of admissibility of MCMI-III as evidence, advantages and disadvantages of using the test in forensic cases, and discusses what aspects of this test may be questioned in court testimony.

In summary, research with all three versions of the MCMI and from a variety of clinical and medical populations suggests that scores on the Dysthymia (D) scale do reflect responses to treatment effects or the lack thereof. Scores on D are lower in patients judged improved or unchanged, and higher in patients judged unimproved after treatment.

Cross-Cultural Considerations

The MCMI has been successfully used with minorities and the publisher offers a Spanish-language version. The test has been researched and/or is in clinical use in such countries as Belgium (Sloore & Derksen, 1997), Korea (Gunsalus & Kelly, 2001), the Netherlands (Luteijn, 1991) and Scandanavia (Mortensen & Simonsen, 1991; Ravndal & Vaglum, 1991), as well as in more Westernized countries (Jackson, Gazis, & Edwards, 1991; Nazikian, Edwards, & Jackson, 1990; O'Callaghan, Bates, Jackson, & Edwards, 1990). No MCMI research has explored the question of possible changes in interpretation based on cultural considerations. However, a major issue with a test like the MCMI is that BR scores take into account the prevalence rate of the disorder. To use the MCMI-III with scores unaltered is to assume that the prevalence rate of personality disorders in the country of use is identical to the rate of personality disorders in the MCMI-III standardization sample. Recently, Rossi and Sloore (2005) reported that scores in a Belgium sample change based on the preference for higher sensitivity or higher specificity. These researchers found that Receiver Operator Curve (ROC) statistics were more sensitive than BR scores.

Can the MCMI be used with minorities in American? There has been little research comparing MCMI scores by race and none by ethnicity. The only comparisons in the empirical literature compare Caucasians with African Americans. This research has been summarized by Craig (2006a). He reported that Blacks scored higher on Narcissistic, Paranoid, Drug, and Delusional Disorder, while Whites scored higher on Dysthymia. Two cautions are noteworthy: (1) This research was based on only a few studies and emanated from the MCMI-I and MCMI-II. No data on race have been reported for the MCMI-III. (2) These studies do not demonstrate racial bias in the previous versions of the MCMI. First, an alternative explanation is that the test is detecting true differences on these scales between these populations. Second, although there may be a difference in magnitude between Blacks and Whites in these scales, it does not imply a difference in diagnosis. If one group scores a BR of 65 on these scales and another group scores a BR of 32, then there would be a statistically significant difference between these groups, but neither group would be diagnosed as having the disorder. The few published studies only reported scale magnitude differences but did not address the fundamental question. This remains to be explored.

Current Controversies

Three issues continue to dominate the MCMI research literature. The first is the extent to which the MCMI attains the same personality disorder diagnosis as other similar tests at the level of the individual patient. A secondary issue is the extent to which the MCMI over-pathologizes and arrives at more personality disorder diagnoses than similar instruments. An additional concern is the degree to which the MCMI can be used in forensic applications.

Diagnostic Agreement

Regarding the first issue, the preponderance of data suggests that there is low agreement between MCMI PD scales and those based on structured clinical interviews, and that the MCMI does produce more PD diagnoses than comparable instruments. There are very few exceptions to this research finding.

In a literature review, Ronningstam (1996) concluded that there is poor diagnostic agreement between the MCMI-I and Axis I disorders and low agreement between the MCMI-I and the Structured Interview for DSM Personality Disorders (SIDP). The MCMI-I diagnosed more patients as narcissistic in several samples. Still, she concluded that the MCMI-I PD scales had high specificity and good sensitivity. A typical example is the study by Inch and Crossley (1993). They found that both the MCMI-I and MCMI-II over-diagnosed PDs compared to clinician-generated diagnoses.

This general conclusion appears to be equally valid for the MCMI-II. For patients with agoraphobia, there was little diagnostic agreement between the SCID-II and the MCMI-II. Kappas ranged from –.06 (Histrionic) to .47 (Passive-Aggressive) (Renneberg, Chambless, Dowdell, Fauerbach, & Gracely, 1992). There was low agreement between the SIDP and MCMI-II with the latter test yielding more multiple diagnoses (Turley, Bates, Edwards, & Jackson, 1992). The diagnostic agreement between the Personality Disorder Examination (PDE), a semi-structured clinical interview for DSM PDs, and the MCMI-II was compared as to the presence of a PD, the number of PD diagnoses assigned to a patient, specific diagnosis assigned, and assignment of PD clusters. Diagnostic agreement was low, except for Borderline and Avoidant. Agreement was positive in predicting the absence of a PD (Soldz, Budman, Demby, & Merry, 1993). There was low correspondence between the Personality Diagnostic Questionnaire, a structured clinical interview, and the MCMI-II (Wierzbicki & Gorman, 1995). Using the SCID as the criterion, the MCMI produced a high rate of false positives but accurate negative predictive power. This general finding also held true for the PDQ-R (Guthrie & Mobley, 1994). Also, the MCMI tends to diagnose more PDs compared to the MMPI-PD scales (Wise, 1995).

Using the SCID-II as the diagnostic criterion, there was low to moderate agreement between the MCMI-II and the SCID-II. The MCMI-II was more sensitive while the MMPI-PDs were more specific. There was good convergence between these two instruments, but not between these self-report measures and the SCID-II (Hills, 1995). Diagnostic agreement between the SCID-II and the MCMI-II was deemed inadequate for most PDs. Positive predictive power was poor, based on SCID-II diagnosis, while negative predictive power was generally excellent (Marlowe, Husband, Bonieskie, Kirby, & Platt, 1997).

In one study of 275 patients, there was low agreement in diagnosing antisocial personality disorder between the MCMI-II and the Structured Clinical Interview for Diagnosing DSM Personality Disorders (SCID-II) (Messina, Wish, Hoffman, & Nemes, 2001).

On the other hand, relatively accurate hit rates were reported for the diagnoses of affective disorders and substance abuse with hit rates ranging from

68% to 79% for these Axis II disorders (Libb, Murray, Thurstin, & Alarcon (1992). Also, the MCMI diagnosed Borderline Personality Disorder at better-than-chance levels (Lewis & Harder, 1991).

However, some studies find that the MCMI-II produced prevalence rates of personality disorders that were similar to those produced by the Coolidge Axis II Inventory and the personality disorder subscales of the MMPI (Sinha & Watson, 2001). Furthermore, Wise (2001) produced evidence that both the MCMI-II and the MMPI-2 are measuring comparable (personality disorder) constructs in a forensic population. Finally, Craig (2003c) found that Antisocial PD had the highest prevalence rates among samples of cocaine and heroin addicts. This finding generalized across all assessment instruments, though the MCMI-I/MCMI-II had the highest prevalence rates for these samples.

Gibeau and Choca (2005) looked at the diagnostic efficiency of the MCMI-III clinical scales for detecting Axis I disorders. Their work had "ecological validity" because they used clinical diagnoses established by a single clinician. They reported generally acceptable diagnostic power for most of the MCMI-III clinical scales, with a few exceptions. We can hopefully look forward to more of this kind of research.

How can we explain these overall findings? The discrepancy may be due to the fact that structured clinical interviews have criteria sets that emphasize observable behavior whereas the MCMI items emphasize personality traits. Item derivation for the MCMI scales was based on Millon's theory as well as on diagnostic nomenclature. For example, Millon believes that the motivation of someone with an antisocial PD is to avoid being controlled at all costs. These people feel that others are out to control and dominate them so they (the sublects) have to act precipitously and dominate others before they themselves are controlled. They are motivated to fiercely maintain this independence. So there are items on the Antisocial PD scale which tap into this dimension of maintaining independence (e.g., "At no time do I let myself be tricked by people who say they need help"). This idea of fierce independence is not a part of *DSM-IV*. Hence we would not expect large agreements between instruments that are concordant with the *DSM* and an instrument that partially strays from it conceptually.

Forensic Application

Regarding the second issue, the concern is that the MCMI-III normative sample may not be appropriate for forensic cases.

Otto and Butcher (1995) argued that the MCMI should not be used in child custody evaluations because many of the litigants would not be expected to have personality disorders. Meanwhile, normative base rates of MCMI-III scores have been published for parents who are undergoing child custody evaluations (Halon, 2001; Lampel, 1999; McCann, Flens, Campagna, Coll-man, Lazarro, & Connor, 2001).

Lally (2003) surveyed diplomats in forensic psychology to ascertain their opinion as to which tests should be used in common areas of forensic practice in order to determine the admissibility of their testimony. The MCMI was considered unacceptable for violence risk assessments, sexual violence examinations, competency to stand trial, competency to waive Miranda rights evaluations, and assessment of malingering.

It has been argued that the MCMI-III scales lack sufficient construct validity to be used in forensic applications because most scales show negligible relationships to diagnoses, generating errors in diagnosis in 80% of the cases (Rogers, Salekin, & Sewell, 1999). They concluded that only the Avoidant, Schizotypal, and Borderline PD scales had acceptable construct validity to meet the *daubert* (1983) standard for admissibility of evidence in expert testimony.

Dyer and McCann (2000) refuted these arguments suggesting that the content validity of the MCMI-III was superior to that of other instruments, that case law has allowed testimony based on MCMI findings, and that the MCMI-III is an improvement on the MCMI-II. They also criticized the procedures used by Rogers et al. to reach what they considered to be inaccurate conclusions.

One study concluded that the concordance rates of personality disorders for two self-report measures (MCMI-II and Coolidge Axis II Inventory) were comparable to concordance rates between two structured clinical interviews (the SCID and PDE) (Silberman, Roth, Segal, & Burns, 1997).

Both Craig (1999c) and McCann (2002) have provided suggestions for using the MCMI-III in forensic applications and address many of the allegations made by those opposed to the use of the MCMI for these purposes. Schutte (2001) argued that the MCMI-III is excellent in ruling out a personality disorder and that diagnostic efficiency statistics are quite good for several MCMI-III scales. He argued that the MCMI-III is appropriate for competency evaluations, criminal responsibility, and sentencing evaluations. Even so, there are some areas within forensic practice where the MCMI-III would not be the instrument of choice (competency to stand trail, insanity pleas).

There is substantial evidence on the use of the MCMI in substance abuse (Craig & Weinberg,1992a,b; Flynn, McCann, & Fairbank, 1995), PTSD (Craig, & Olson, 1997; Hyer, Brandsma, & Boyd, 1997), and domestic violence (Craig, 2003b), such that the MCMI-III should be used as part of a forensic evaluation involving these problems.

Clinical Dilemma

Here we present data on a 38-year-old, divorced, White male in outpatient psychotherapy for problems related to post-divorce adjustment. He was a police officer in a medium size village, who also had worked part time as a security officer in order to save money for a house. Meanwhile, his wife became lonely and began an affair with his best friend, who was an alcoholic. She eventually married this man and was awarded custody of her three children in the divorce decree. Stewing over feelings of rejection and unresolved anger towards her and his former best friend, he began to park his car a short distance away and then follow them when they would leave the house. He also began having nightmares of killing her new husband. He then sought counseling to deal with these matters.

At issue were the following questions:

1. Does his behavior meet the legal standards of stalking?
2. What is his underlying personality style that may contribute to his reactions?
3. Is his verbal reports in psychotherapy of wanting to kill his former best friend simply catharsis or is he at risk of acting on his impulses, and how can we use the MCMI-III to make this distinction?

His MCMI-III test scores appear in Table 4.6.

First, does his behavior meet the legal standards of stalking? Although the legal definition of stalking varies from state to state, there are generally three elements contained in most stalking laws: (1) unwanted behavioral intrusion, (2) an implicit or explicit threat that is part of the behavioral intrusion, and (3) the threatened person experiences reasonable fear. While the MCMI does not directly address stalking behaviors, this patient's behavior currently would not meet these standards, since his wife does not know that he is following her and since he never had threatened her. However, if she became aware of his behavior, then two of the three elements (unwanted and fear) would be met.

Does his personality style contribute to his current problems? The patient's validity scales are within acceptable norms and do not suggest undo faking good nor undo exaggeration. His Debasement score is within the range of distressed patients. His elevated score on the Depressive PD scale is interpreted as a result of item redundancy associated with the other two depression-related scales. Hence he does not have a depressive PD, but rather is elevated because his depression-related scales are also elevated. This patient is clearly in much psychic distress. While he is able to maintain his day to day functions (Maj. Dep), he, nevertheless, is experiencing a substantial

Table 4.6 MCMI-III Scores for Case Study: 38-Year-Old White Male

Scales	BR Score	Scales	BR Score
Disclosure	66		
Desirability	62		
Debasement	80		
Schizoid	63	Anxiety	99
Avoidant	64	Somatoform	77
Depressive	95	Bipolar: Manic	60
Histrionic	80	Dysthymia	111
Narcissistic	70	Alcohol Dependence	73
Antisocial	68	Drug Dependence	62
Aggressive	70	PTSD	60
Compulsive	46	Thought Disorder	60
Negativistic	66	Major Depression	71
Self-Defeating	74	Delusional Disorder	60
Schizotypal	48		
Borderline	75		
Paranoid	55		

amount of depression (Dysthymia) consistent with his known stressors and verbal reports in therapy.

We can now answer the second question. The patient has a histrionic style but not a histrionic personality disorder. He would have such traits as tendencies towards exaggeration, a certain kind of boisterousness, some impulsivity, over-emotional behavior, and a perceptual style that tends to be more global in nature. People with this style are at risk for somatoform disorders and marital problems. Thus his style is consistent with his presenting complaint.

How can we use the MCMI-III to determine if his fantasies of murdering his wife's current husband are mere catharsis and part of his personality style or whether he will act upon these impulses? First, we refer to MCMI-derived research to help us with this question.

There is a substantial body of research that has explored the personality styles of men who abuse their partner. This domestic violence research is only tangentially related to the question at hand but it can serve as one guide post to help us in our determination. This research has clearly shown that perpetrators of domestic violence have personality styles of either antisocial, aggressive-sadistic, or passive-aggressive (negativistic). Histrionic personality styles are infrequently mentioned in the MCMI research literature (Craig, 2003b). However, the histrionic style is commonly encountered in patients in martial therapy (Craig & Olson, 1995).

So far we have determined that the patient's present behavior probably does not meet the major elements of most stalking laws, and that he has a histrionic style which is infrequently associated with partner abuse in the MCMI research literature. Next, we must use clinical judgment as a final guide to our assessment.

The patient does not show tendencies towards substance abuse (Alc, Drug). Hence it is unlikely, based on test findings, that he might get high or drunk, experience reduced defenses and act on impulse. Furthermore, he does not have antisocial traits nor does he have aggressive-sadistic traits of clinical significance. His borderline score of BR 75 probably is related to his emotional tendencies, which might become erratic.

The overall conclusion is that his verbal reports of wanting to kill this man are probably catharsis and related to some histrionic traits. However, he is a policeman and must carry his weapon even when off duty. Having a gun with him while he is following his wife could result in disturbed behavior, despite our best conclusions. Therefore, it was absolutely imperative to get this patient to stop following his wife and then begin to deal with his feelings about his divorce (which was accomplished).

Chapter Summary

We have seen that the MCMI meets psychometric standards for reliability and validity. In fact, development and use of the BR score has raised measurement to a more defining level compared to other tests. Its research base is now over 700 articles . Therefore, we know how the test operates with a substantial number of clinical populations. Despite some limitations, test usage surveys indicate that the strength of this measurement tool has made it a commonly used instrument for a variety of contexts and purposes. The bottom line is that the MCMI would not be in common clinical use if it did not have clinical utility at the level of the individual patient.

Summary

- The MCMI-III is a test designed to diagnose personality disorders and major clinical syndromes for adults being evaluated and/or treated in mental health settings.
- The test shows adequate reliability.
- Research has shown that the MCMI shows low agreement with structured clinical interviews that assess for personality disorders. Items on the MCMI were theory-derived, as well as written to conform to the *DSM* criteria sets. This may account for the low agreement.
- A substantial amount of research suggests that previous versions of

Key Points to Remember

- The MCMI is the most researched self-report inventory that assesses personality disorders.
- Millon has advanced measurement theory and diagnostic efficiency statistics with the introduction of the Base Rate score.
- The MCMI-III has been refined and now is able to score of salient domains associated with each disorder as well as assess theorized personality disorder subtypes.
- Psychologists can prudently use the MCMI-III to screen for personality disorders and major clinical syndromes in mental health patients if they remain cognizant of the strengths and limitations of the instrument.

the MCMI may over-pathologize patients who tend to obtain multiple personality disorders on this test.

- The test also boasts a substantial research base with patients who are addicted to alcohol or drugs, PTSD, spouse abusers, and patients with anxiety and depression.
- Research suggests that the clinical syndrome scales do reflect treatment effects.
- MCMI-based testimony has been allowed for a variety of cases before the court. This has been true despite some researchers' arguing to the contrary.
- Millon has suggested ways that his personality-guided theory can be used for treatment planning and measuring treatment progress. Clinicians have offered several examples of the utility of the MCMI-III in this process.
- There is little research published on the MCMI-III. This is true after over 10 years of its availability to researchers. There is some data that suggests that MCMI-derived published research is declining year by year. Thus we continue to lack information on many basic issues discussed here.

Closing Comment

Is it easier to criticize than to create. Millon has created a useful instrument that many clinical psychologists appreciate. Despite some limitations, the MCMI-III will remain an essential clinical instrument for use in a variety of clinical and forensic applications.

Notes

1. The designation MCMI is used when referring to the test qua test. A numeric suffix is included with the MCMI (i.e., MCMC-I, MCMI-II, MCMI-III) when referring to that specific version of the test.

2. Millon's theoretical model is far more elegant, elaborate, and sophisticated than presented here. The interested reader should consult Millon (1990) for more in-depth presentation of this theory.
3. Researchers interested in obtaining the actual study references on which these data are based are invited to contact the author at rjcraig41@comcast.net.

References

Ackerman, M. J., & Ackerman, M. C. (1997). Custody evaluation practices: A survey of experienced professionals revisited. *Professional Psychologist: Research and Practice, 28,* 137–145.

Bagby, R. M., & Marshall, M. B. (2005). Assessing response bias with the MCMI modifying indices. In R. J. Craig (Ed.), *New directions in interpreting the Millon Clinical Multiaxial Inventory* (pp. 227–247). New York: Wiley.

Ball, S. A., Nich, C., Rounsaville, B. J., Eagan, D., & Carroll, K. M. (2004). Millon Clinical Multiaxial Inventory-III subtypes of opioid dependence: validity and matching to behavioral therapies. *Journal of Consulting and Clinical Psychology, 72,* 698–711.

Bayon, C., Hill, K., Svrakic, D. M., Przybeck, T. R., & Cloninger, C. R. (1996). Dimensional assessment of personality in an outpatient sample: Relations of the systems of Millon and Cloninger. *Journal of Psychiatric Research, 30,* 341–352.

Blackburn, R. (1998). Relationship of personality disorders to observer ratings of interpersonal style in forensic psychiatric patients. *Journal of Personality Disorders, 12,* 77–85.

Boccaccini, M. T., & Brodsky, S. L. (1999). Diagnostic test usage by forensic psychologists in emotional injury cases. *Professional Psychologist: Research and Practice, 30,* 253–259.

Bockian, N. R. (2006). *Personality-guided therapy for depression.* Washington, DC: American Psychological Association.

Bohlian, N., Meagher, S., & Millon, T. (2005). Assessing personality with the Millon Behavioral Health Inventory, the Millon Medicine Diagnostic, and the Millon Clinical Multiaxial Inventory. In R. Gatchel, J. N. Weiberg, & N. James (Eds.), *Personality characteristics of patients with pain* (pp. 61–88). Washington, DC: American Psychological Association.

Borchgrevink, G. E., Stiles, T. C., Borchgrevink, P. C., & Lereim, I. (1997). Personality profile among symptomatic and recovered patients with neck sprain injury, measured by MCMI-I acutely and 6 months after car accidents. *Journal of Psychosomatic Research, 42,* 357–367.

Borum, R., & Grisso, T. (1995). Psychological test use in criminal forensic evaluations. *Professional Psychologist: Research and Practice, 26,* 465–473.

Calsyn, D. A., Wells, E. A., Fleming, C., & Saxon, A. J. (2000). Changes in Millon Clinical Multiaxial Inventory scores among opiate addicts as a function of retention in methadone maintenance treatment and recent drug use. *American Journal of Drug and Alcohol Abuse, 26,* 297–309.

Chandarana, P. C., Conlon, P., Holliday, M. D., Deslippe, T., & Field, V. A. (1990). A prospective study of psychosocial aspects of gastric stapling surgery. *Psychiatric Journal of the University of Ottawa, 15,* 32–35.

Chick, D., Sheaffer, C. I., & Goggin, W. C. (1993). The relationship between MCMI personality scales and clinician-generated DSM-III-R personality disorder diagnoses. *Journal of Personality Assessment, 61,* 264–276.

Choca, J. (2001). Review of the Millon Clinical Multiaxial Inventory – III (Manual second edition). In J. C. Impara & B. S. Plake (Eds.), *Fourteenth mental measurements yearbook* (pp. 765–767. Lincoln, NB: Buros Institute of Mental Measurements.

Choca, J. P. (2004*). Interpretive guide to the Millon Clinical Multiaxial Inventory,* (3rd ed.). Washington, DC: American Psychological Association.

Choca, J. P., Shanley, L. A., VanDenburg, E., Agresti, A., Mouton, A., & Vidger, L. (1992). Personality disorder or personality style: That is the question. *Journal of Counseling and Development, 70,* 429–431.

Clark, J. W., Schneider, H. G., & Cox, R. L. (1998). Initial evidence for reliability and validity of a brief screening inventory for personality traits. *Psychological Reports, 82,* 1115–1120.

Coolidge, F. L., & Merwin, M. M. (1992). Reliability and validity of the Coolidge Axis II Inventory: A new inventory for the assessment of personality disorders. *Journal of Personality Assessment, 59,* 233–238.

Craig, R., J. (Ed.). (1993a). *The Millon Clinical Multiaxial Inventory: A clinical and research informa- tion synthesis.* Hillsdale, NJ: Erlbaum.

Craig, R. J. (1993b) *Psychological assessment with the Millon Clinical Multiaxial Inventory (II): An interpretive guide.* Odessa, FL. Psychological Assessment Resources.

Craig, R. J. (1997). A selected review of the MCMI empirical literature. In T. Millon (Ed.), *The Millon inventories: Clinical and personality assessment* (pp. 303–326). New York: Guilford.

Craig, R. J. (1999a). Millon Clinical Multiaxial Inventory-III. (Ch. 2). *Interpreting personality tests: A clinical manual for the MMPI-2, MCMI-III, CPI-R, and 16 PF* (pp. 101–192).New York: Wiley.

Craig, R. J. (1999b). Overview and current status of the Millon Clinical Multiaxial Inventory. *Journal of Personality Assessment, 72,* 390–406.

Craig, R. J. (1999c). Testimony based on the Millon Clinical Multiaxial Inventory: Review, com- mentary, and guidelines. *Journal of Personality Assessment, 73,* 290–316.

Craig, R. J. (2001). MCMI-III. In W. Dorfman & M. Hersen (Eds), *Understanding psychological as- sessment: A manual for counselors and clinicians* (pp. 173–186). New York: Plenum.

Craig, R. J. (2002). Essentials of MCMI-III interpretation. In S. Strack (Ed.), *Essentials of Millon inventories assessment* (2nd ed., pp. 1–51). New York: Wiley.

Craig, R. J. (2003a). Assessing personality and psychopathology with interviews. In J. R. Graham & J. A. Neglieri (Eds.), *Assessment psychology* (Vol. 10, pp. 487–508). In I. B. Weiner (Editor- in-Chief, *Handbook of psychology.* New York: Wiley.

Craig, R. J. (2003b). Use of the Millon Clinical Multiaxial Inventory in the psychological assessment of domestic violence: A review. *Aggression and Violent Behavior, 8,* 235–243.

Craig, R. J. (2003c). Prevalence of personality disorders among cocaine and heroin addicts. *Directions in Addiction Treatment and Prevention, 7,* 33–42.

Craig, R. J. (2004). *The Personality Disorder Adjective Check List.* Unpublished test manual. Chicago.

Craig, R. J. (Ed.). (2005a). *New directions in interpreting the Millon Clinical Multiaxial Inventory.* New York: Wiley.

Craig, R. J. (2005b). *Assessing substance abusers with the Millon Clinical Multiaxial Inventory (MCMI- III).* Springfield, IL: Charles C. Thomas.

Craig, R. J. (2005c). *Personality-guided forensic psychology.* Washington, DC: American Psychologi- cal Association.

Craig, R. J. (2006a). Millon Clinical Multiaxial Inventory – III. In R. P. Archer (Ed). *Forensic uses of clinical assessment instruments* (pp. 121–145). Mahwah, NJ: Erlbaum.

Craig, R. J. (2006b) *Millon Clinical Multiaxial Inventory interpretive report for MCMI-II/III* (2nd ed). Odessa, FL: Psychological Assessment Resources.

Craig, R. J., & Olson, R. E. (1995). MCMI-II profiles and typologies for patients seen in marital therapy. *Psychological Reports, 76,* 163–170.

Craig, R. J., & Olson, R. (1997). Assessing PTSD with the Millon Clinical Multiaxial Inventory – III. *Journal of Clinical Psychology, 53,* 943–952.

Craig, R. J., & Olson, R. E. (2005). On the decline in MCMI-based research. In R. J. Craig, (Ed.), *New directions in interpreting the Millon Clinical Multiaxial Inventory* (pp. 284–289). New York: Wiley.

Craig, R. J., & Weinberg, D. (1992a). Assessing drug abusers with the Millon Clinical Multiaxial Inventory: A review. *Journal of Substance Abuse Treatment, 9,* 249–255.

Craig, R. J., & Weinberg, D. (1992b) Assessing alcoholics with the Millon Clinical Multiaxial Inven- tory: A review. *Psychology of Addictive Behaviors, 6,* 200–208.

Dana, R., & Cantrell, J. (1988). An update on the Millon Clinical Multiaxial Inventory (MCMI). *Journal of Clinical Psychology, 44,* 760–763.

Daubert v. Merrel Dow Pharmaceuticals, 113, S. Ct. 27893 (1983).

Davis, R. D., Meagher, S. E., Gonclaves, M., Woodward, M., & Millon, T. (1999). Treatment plan- ning and outcome in adults: The Millon Clinical Multiaxial Inventory-III. In M. E. Maruish (Ed.), *The use of psychological testing for treatment planning and outcomes assessment.* (2nd. ed.). Mahwah, NJ: Erlbaum.

Davis, R. D., & Millon, T. (1993). Putting Humpty Dumpty back together again: The MCMI in personality assessment. In L. Beutler (Ed.), *Integrative personality assessment* (pp. 240–279). New York: Guilford.

Davis, R. D., & Millon, T. (1997). Teaching and learning assessment with the Millon clinical mul- tiaxial inventory (MCMI-III). In L. Handler & M. Hilsenroth (Eds.), *Teaching and learning personality assessment.* Hillsdale, NJ: Erlbaum.

Davis, R. D., & Patterson, M. J. (2005). Diagnosing personality disorder subtypes with the MCMI-III. In R. J. Craig (Ed.), *New directions in interpreting the Millon Clinical Multiaxial Inventory-III (MCMI-III)* (pp. 32–70).New York: Wiley.

Diagnostic and Statistical Manual of Mental Disorders 4th ed. (1994). Washington, DC: American Psychiatric Association.

Dubro, A. F., & Wetzler, S. (1989). An external validity study of the MMPI personality disorder scales. *Journal of Clinical Psychology, 45,* 570–575.

Dutton, D. G. (1994). The origin and structure of the abusive personality. *Journal of Personality Disorders, 8,* 181–191.

Dyer, F. J., & McCann, J. T. (2000). The Millon clinical inventories, research critical of their application, and *Daubert* criteria. *Law and Human Behavior, 24,* 487–497.

Ellason, J. W., & Ross, C. A. (1996). Millon Clinical Multiaxial Inventory-II: Follow-up of patients with dissociative identity disorder. *Psychological Reports, 78,* 707–716.

Farmer, R. F., & Nelson-Gray, R. O. (2005). *Personality-guided behavior therapy.* Washington, DC: American Psychological Association.

Fleishauer, A. (1987). The MCMI-II: A reflection of current knowledge. *Journal of Psychopathology and Behavioral Assessment, 7,* 185–189.

Flynn, P. M., McCann, J. T., & Fairbank, J. A. (1995). Issues in the assessment of personality disorder and substance abuse using the Millon Clinical Multiaxial Inventory (MCMI-II). *Journal of Clinical Psychology, 51,* 415–421.

Funari, D. J., Piekarski, A. M., & Sherwood, R. J. (1991). Treatment outcomes of Vietnam veterans with post-traumatic stress disorder. *Psychological Reports, 68,* 571–578.

Garner, D. M., Olmsted, M. R., Davis, R., Rockert, W., Goldbloom, D., & Eagle, M. (1990). The association between bulimic symptoms and reported psychopathology. *International Journal of Eating Disorders, 9,* 1–15.

Gibeau, P., & Choca, J. (2005). The diagnostic efficiency of the MCMI-III in the detection of Axis I disorders. In R. J. Craig (Ed.), *New directions in interpreting the Millon Clinical Multiaxial Inventory* (pp. 272–283). New York: Wiley.

Gibertini, M., Brandenberg, N., & Retzlaff, P. (1986). The operating characteristics of the Millon Clinical Multiaxial Inventory. *Journal of Personality Assessment, 50,* 554–567.

Gonclaves, A. A., Woodward, M. J., & Millon, T. (1994). Millon Clinical Multiaxial Inventory-II. In M. E. Maruish (Ed.), *The use of psychological testing for treatment planning and outcome assessment* (pp. 161–184). Hillsdale, NJ: Erlbaum.

Greer, S. (1984). Testing the test: A review of the Millon Multiaxial Inventory. *Journal of Counseling and Development, 63,* 262–263.

Grossman, L., & Craig, R. J. (1995). Comparison of MCMI-II and 16PF validity scales. *Journal of Personality Assessment, 64,* 384–389.

Grossman, S. D., & del Rio, C. (2006). The MCMI-III facet subscales. In R. J. Craig (Ed.), *New directions in interpreting the Millon Clinical Multiaxial Inventory-III (MCMI-III)* (pp. 3–31). New York: Wiley.

Groth-Marnatt, G. (1997). Millon Clinical Multiaxial Inventory. *Handbook of psychological assessment* (pp. 301–342).New York: Wiley.

Gunsalus, A. J., & Kelly, K. R. (2001). Korean cultural influences on the Millon Clinical Multiaxial Inventory III. *Journal of Mental Health Counseling, 23,* 151–161.

Guthrie, P. C., & Mobley, B. D. (1994). A comparison of the differential diagnostic efficiency of three personality disorder inventories. *Journal of Clinical Psychology, 50,*656–665.

Haladyna, T. M. (1992). Review of the Millon Clinical Multiaxial Inventory-II. In J. J. Kramer & J. C. Conoley (Eds), *Eleventh mental measurement yearbook* (pp. 532–533). Lincoln: University of Nebraska Press.

Hall, G. C., & Phung, A. H. (2001). The Minnesota Multiphasic Personality Inventory and Millon Clinical Multiaxial Inventory. In L. A. Suzuki, & J. G. Pontero (Eds.), *Handbook of multicultural assessment: Clinical, psychological, and educational applications* (2nd ed., pp. 307–330). San Francisco, CA: Jossey-Bass.

Halon, R. L. (2001). The Millon Clinical Multiaxial Inventory-III: The normal quartet in child custody cases. *American Journal of Forensic Psychology, 19,* 57–75.

Hart, S. D., Dutton, D. G., & Newlove, T. (1993). The prevalence of personality disorder among wife assaulters. *Journal of Personality Disorders, 7,* 329–341.

Hart, S. D., Forth, A. E., & Hare, R. D. (1991). The MCMI-II and psychopathy. *Journal of Personality Disorders, 5*, 318–327.

Hess, A. K. (1985). Review of Millon Clinical Multiaxial Inventory. In J. Mitchell Jr. (Ed.), *Ninth mental measurements yearbook, Vol. 1* (pp. 984–986). Lincoln: University of Nebraska Press.

Hess, A. K. (1990). Review of the Millon Clinical Multiaxial Inventory-III. *Mental Measurements Yearbook.* Lincoln: University of Nebraska Press.

Hicklin, J., & Widiger, T. A. (2000). Convergent validity of alternative MMPI-2 personality disorder scale. *Journal of Personality Assessment, 75*, 502–518.

Hills, H. A. (1995). Diagnosing personality disorders: An examination of the MMPI-2 and MCMI-II. *Journal of Personality Assessment, 65*, 21–34.

Hogg, B., Jackson, H. J., Rudd, R. P., & Edwards, J. (1990). Diagnosing personality disorders in recent-onset schizophrenia. *Journal of Nervous and Mental Disease, 179*, 194–199.

Hsu, L. M. (2002). Diagnostic validity statistics and the MCMI-III. *Psychological Assessment, 14*, 410–422.

Hyer, L., Brandsma, J., & Boyd, S. (1997). The MCMIs and Posttraumatic stress disorder. In T. Millon (Ed.), *The Millon inventories: Clinical and personality assessment* (pp. 191–216). New York: Guilford.

Hyer, L., Woods, M. G., Bruno, R., & Boudewyns, P. (1989). Treatment outcomes of Vietnam veterans with PTSD and consistency of the MCMI. *Journal of Clinical Psychology, 45*, 547–552.

Inch, R., & Crossley, M. (1993). Diagnostic utility of the MCMI-I and MCMI-II with psychiatric outpatients. *Journal of Clinical Psychology, 49*, 358–366.

Jackson, H. J., R., Gazis, J., & Edwards, J. (1991). Using the MCMI to diagnose personality disorders in inpatients: Axis I/axis II associations and sex differences. *Australian Psychologist, 26*, 37–4l.

Jankowski, D. (2002). *A beginner's guide to the MCMI-III.* Washington, DC: American Psychological Assn.

Jones, A. (2005). An examination of three sets of MMPI-2 personality disorder scales. *Journal of Personality Disorders, 19*, 370–385.

Keilen, W. J., & Bloom, L. J. (1986). Child custody evaluation practices: A survey of experienced professionals. *Professional Psychologist: Research and Practice, 17*, 338–346.

Kennedy, S. H., Katz, R., Rockert, W., Mendlowitz, S., Ralevski, E., & Clewes, C. J. (1995). Assessment of personality disorders in anorexia nervosa and bulimia nervosa: A comparison of self-report and structured interview methods. *Journal of Nervous and Mental Disease, 183*, 358–364.

Klein, M. H., Benjamin, L. S., Rosenfeld, R., Treece, C., Husted, J., & Greist, J. H. (1993). The Wisconsin Personality Disorders Inventory: Development, reliability, and validity. *Journal of Personality Disorders, 7*, 285–303.

Lally, S. J. (2003). What tests are acceptable for use in forensic evaluations? A survey of experts. *Professional Psychology: Research and Practice, 34*, 491–498.

Lampel, A. K. (1999). Use of the Millon Clinical Multiaxial Inventory-III in evaluating child custody litigants. *American Journal of Forensic Psychology, 17*, 19–31.

Lanyon, R. (1984). Personality Assessment. *Annual Review of Psychology, 35*, 667–701.

Lehne, G. K. (1994). The NEO-PI and the MCMI in the forensic evaluation of sex offenders. In P. T. Costa & T. A. Widiger (Eds.), *Personality disorders and the five-factor model of personality* (pp. 175–188). Washington, D C: American Psychological Association.

Lehne, G. K. (2002). The NEO Personality Inventory and the Millon Clinical Multiaxial Inventory in the forensic evaluation of sex offenders. In P. T. Costa & T. A. Widiger (Eds.), *Personality disorders and the five-factor model of personality* (2nd ed., pp. 269–282). Washington, D C: American Psychological Association.

Lewis, S. J., & Harder, D. W. (1991). A comparison of four measures to diagnose DSM-III-R borderline personality disorder in outpatients. *Journal of Nervous and Mental Disease, 179*, 320–337.

Libb, J. W., Murray, J., Thurstin, H., & Alarcon, R. D. (1992). Concordance of the MCMI-II, the MMPI, and Axis I discharge diagnosis in psychiatric inpatients. *Journal of Personality Assessment, 58*, 580–590.

Libb, J. W., Stankovic, S., Sokol, A., Houck, C., & Switzer, P. (1990). Stability of the MCMI among depressed psychiatric outpatients. *Journal of Personality Assessment, 55*, 209–2l8.

Lindsay, K. A., Sankis, L. M., & Widiger, T. A. (2000). Gender bias in self-report personality disorder inventories. *Journal of Personality Disorders, 14*, 218–232.

Luteijn, F. (1991). The MCMI in the Netherlands: First Findings. *Journal of Personality Disorders, 4*, 297–303.

Magnavita, J. J. (2005a). Using the MCMI-III for treatment planning and to enhance clinical efficacy. In R. J. Craig (Ed.), *New directions in interpreting the Millon Clinical Multiaxial Inventory* (pp. 164–184). New York: Wiley.

Magnavita, J. J. (2005b). *Personality-guided cognitive behavior therapy.* Washington, DC: American Psychological Association.

Marlowe, D. B., Husband, S. D., Bonieskie, L. M., Kirby, K. C., & Platt, J. J. (1997).Structured interview versus self-report test vantages for the assessment of personality pathology in cocaine dependence. *Journal of Personality Disorders, 11,* 177–190.

McCabe, S. (1984). Millon Clinical Multiaxial Inventory. In D. Keyser & R. Sweetland (Eds.), *Test critiques (Vol. 1)* (pp. 455–456). Kansas City, KS: Westport.

McCann, J. T. (1989). MMPI personality disorder scales and the MCMI: Concurrent validity. *Journal of Clinical Psychology, 45,* 365–369.

McCann, J. T. (1991). Convergent and discriminant validity of the MCMI-II and MMPI personality disorder scales. *Psychological Assessment: A Journal of Consulting and Clinical Psychology, 3,* 9–18.

McCann, J. T. (2002). Guidelines for forensic application of the MCMI-III. *Journal of Forensic Psychology Practice, 2,* 55–69.

McCann, J., & Dyer, F. J. (1996). *Forensic assessment with the Millon inventories.* New York: Guilford.

McCann, J. T., Flens, J. R., Campagna, V., Collman, P., Lazarro, T., & Connor, E. (2001). The MCMI-III in child custody evaluations: A normative study. *Journal of Forensic Psychology Practice, 1,* 27–44.

McMahon, R. C., & Davidson, R. S. (1986). An examination of depressed and non-depressed alcoholics in inpatient treatment. *Journal of Clinical Psychology, 42,* 177–184.

McMahon, R. C., & Richards, S. K. (1996). Profile patterns, consistency, and change in the Millon Clinical Multiaxial Inventory-II in cocaine abusers. *Journal of Clinical Psychology, 52,* 75–79.

Messina, N., Wish, E., Hoffman, J., & Nemes, S. (2001). Diagnosing antisocial personality disorder among substance abusers: the SCID versus the MCMI-II. *American Journal of Drug and Alcohol Abuse, 27,* 699–717.

Miller, H. R., Streiner, D. L., & Parkinson, A. (1992). Maximum likelihood estimates of the ability of the MMPI and MCMI personality disorder scales and the SIDP to identify personality disorders. *Journal of Personality Assessment, 59,* 1–13.

Millon, T. (1983). *Millon Clinical Multiaxial Inventory Manual* (3rd ed.). New York: Holt, Rinehart & Winston.

Millon, T. (1984). Interpretive guide to the Millon Clinical Multiaxial Inventory. In P. McReynolds & G. J. Chelune (Eds.), *Advances in personality assessment* (Vol. 6, pp. 1–41). San Francisco: Jossey-Bass.

Millon, T. (1987). *Millon Clinical Multiaxial Inventory-II: Manual for the MCMI-II.* Minneapolis, MN: Pearson Assessments.

Millon, T. (1990). *Toward a new personology.* New York: Wiley.

Millon, T. (1994). *Millon Clinical Multiaxial Inventory-III: Manual.* Minneapolis, MN: Pearson Assessments.

Millon, T. (1997). *Millon Clinical Multiaxial Inventory-III: Manual* (2nd ed.). Minneapolis, MN: Pearson Assessments.

Millon, T. (with contributions by S. Grossman, S. Meagher, C. Millon, & G. Everly) (1999). *Personality-guided therapy.* New York: Wiley.

Millon, T., & Davis, R. (1996). The Millon Clinical Multiaxial Inventory-III (MCMI-III). In C. Newmark (Ed.), *Major psychological assessment instruments* (2nd ed., pp. 108–147). Boston: Allyn & Bacon.

Millon, T., & Davis, R. D. (1998). Millon Clinical Multiaxial Inventory (MCMI-III). In G. Koocher, J. Norcross, & S. Hill (Eds.), *Psychologists' desk reference* (pp. 142–148). New York: Oxford University Press.

Millon, T., & Meagher, S. E. (2003). The Millon Clinical Multiaxial Inventory (MCMI-III). In D. L. Segal & M. J. Hilsenroth (Eds.), *Personality assessment* (Vol. 2, pp. 108–121). In M. Hersen Editor-in-Chief, *Comprehensive handbook of psychological assessment.* New York: Wiley.

Morey, L. C. (1985). An empirical approach of interpersonal and DSM-III approaches to classification of personality disorders. *Psychiatry, 48,* 358–364.

Morey, L. C., & Levine, D. J. (1988). A multitrait-multimethod examination of Minnesota Multiphasic Personality Inventory (MMPI) and Millon Clinical Multiaxial Inventory (MCMI). *Journal of Psychopathology and Behavioral Assessment, 10,* 333–344.

Mortensen, E. L., & Simonsen, E. (1991). Psychometric properties of the Danish MCMI-I translation. *Scandinavian Journal of Psychology,* 1(31), 149–153.

Nazikian, H., Rudd, R. P., Edwards, J., & Jackson, H. J. (1990). Personality disorder assessment for psychiatric inpatients. *Australian & New Zealand Journal of Psychiatry, 24,* 37–46.

O'Callaghan, T., Bates, G. W., Jackson, H. J., R. P., & Edwards, J. (1990). The clinical utility of the Millon Clinical Multiaxial depression subscales. *Australian Psychologist, 25,* 45–61.

Otto, R. K., & Butcher, J. N. (1995). Computer-assisted psychological assessment in child custody evaluations. *Family Law Quarterly, 29,* 79–96.

Overholser, J. C. (1991). Categorical assessment of the dependent personality disorder in depressed inpatients. *Journal of Personality Disorders, 5,* 243–255.

Patrick, J. (1993). Validation of the MCMI-1 borderline personality disorder scale with a well-defined criterion sample. *Journal of Clinical Psychology, 49,* 29–32.

Piersma, H. L. (1989). The MCMI-II as a treatment outcome measure for psychiatric inpatients. *Journal of Clinical Psychology, 45,* 87–93.

Piersma, H. L. (1991). The MCMI-II depression scales: Do they assist in the differential prediction of depressive disorders? *Journal of Personality Assessment, 56,* 478–486.

Piersma, H. L., & Boes, J. L. (1997). The relationship between length of stay to MCMI-II and MCMI-III change scores. *Journal of Clinical Psychology, 53,* 535–542.

Piersma, H. L., & Smith, A. Y. (1991). Individual variability in self-reported improvement for depressed psychiatric inpatients on the MCMI-II. *Journal of Clinical Psychology, 47,* 227–232.

Quinnell, F. A., & Bow, J. N. (2001). Psychological tests used in child custody evaluations. *Behavioral Science and the Law, 19,* 491–501.

Rasmussen, P. R. (2005). Magnavita, J. J. (2005b). *Personality-guided relational psychotherapy.* Washington, DC: American Psychological Association.

Ravndal, E., & Vaglum, P. (1991). Psychopathology and substance abuse as predictors of program completion in a therapeutic community for drug abusers: A prospective study. *Acta Psychiatrics Scandinavia, 83,* 217–222.

Renneberg, B., Chambless, D. L., Dowdall, D. J., Fauerbach, J. A., & Gracely, E. J. (1992). The Structured Clinical Interview for DSM-IIIR, AXIS-II and the Millon Clinical Multiaxial Inventory: A concurrent validity study of personality disorders among anxious patients. *Journal of Personality Disorders, 6,* 117–124.

Retzlaff, P. D. (Ed.). (1995). Tactical psychotherapy of the personality disorders: An MCMI-III-based approach. Needham Heights, MA: Allyn & Bacon.

Reynolds, C. R. (1992). Review of the Millon Clinical Multi-axial Inventory-II. In J. J. Kramer & J. C. Conoley (Eds.), *Eleventh mental measurement yearbook* (pp. 533–535). Lincoln: University of Nebraska Press.

Rogers, R., Salekin, R. T., & Sewel, K. W. (1999). Validation of the Millon Mulaxial Inventory for Axis II disorders. Does it meet the Daubert standard? *Law and Human Behavior, 23,* 425–443.

Ronningstam, E. (1996). Pathological narcissism and narcissistic personality disorder in Axis I disorders. *Harvard Review of Psychiatry, 3,* 326–340.

Rossi, G., & Sloore, H. (2005). *International uses of the MCMI: Does interpretation?* In R. J. Craig (Ed.), *New directions in interpreting the Millon Clinical Multiaxial Inventory-III (MCMI-III)* (pp. 144–164). New York: Wiley.

Sansone, R. A., & Fine, M. A. (1992). Borderline personality disorder as a predictor of outcome in women with eating disorders. *Journal of Personality Disorders, 6,* 176–186.

Saxby, E., & Peniston, E. G. (1995). Alpha-theta brainwave neurofeedback training: An effective treatment for male and female alcoholics with depressive symptoms. *Journal of Clinical Psychology, 51,* 685–693.

Schuler, C. E., Snibbe, J. R., & Buckwalter, J. G., (1994). Validity of the MMPI personality disorder scales (MMPI-Pd). *Journal of Clinical Psychology, 50,* 220–227.

Schutte, J. W. (2001). Using the MCMI-III in forensic evaluations. *American Journal of Forensic Psychology, 19,* 5–20.

Silberman, C. S., Roth, L., Segal, D. L., & Burns, W. J. (1997). Relationship between the Millon Clinical Multiaxial Inventory-II and Coolidge Axis II Inventory in chronically mentally ill older adults: A pilot study. *Journal of Clinical Psychology 53,* 559–566.

Sinha, B. K., & Watson, D. C. (2001). Personality disorder in university students: A multitrait-multilethod matrix study. *Journal of Personality Disorders, 15*, 235–244.

Sloore, H., & Derksen, J. (1997). Issues and procedures in MCMI translations. In T. Millon (Ed.), *The Millon inventories: Clinical and personality assessment*. New York: Guilford.

Soldz, S., Budman, S., Demby, A., & Merry, J. (1993). Diagnostic agreement between the Personality Disorder Examination and the MCMI-II. *Journal of Personality Assessment, 60*, 486–499.

Streiner, D. L., & Miller, H. R. (1991). Maximum likelihood estimates of the accuracy of four diagnostic techniques. *Educational and Psychological Measurement, 50*, 653–662.

Torgersen, S., & Alnaes, R. (1990). The relationship between the MCMI personality scales and DSM-III, Axis II. *Journal of Personality Assessment, 55*, 698–707.

Turley, B., Bates, G. W., Edwards, J., & Jackson, H. J. (1992). MCMI-II personality disorders in recent-onset bipolar disorders. *Journal of Clinical Psychology, 48*, 320–329.

Watkins, C., Campbell, V., Nieberding, R., & Hallmark, R. (1995). Contemporary practice of psychological assessment by clinical psychologists. *Professional Psychologist: Research and Practice, 26*, 54–60.

Wetzler, S. (1990). The Millon Clinical Multiaxial Inventory: A review. *Journal of Personality Assessment, 55*, 445–464.

Wetzler, S., Kahn, R. S., Strauman, T. J., & Dubro, A. (1989). Diagnosis of major depression by self-report. *Journal of Personality Assessment, 53*, 22–30.

Wetzler, S., & Marlowe, D. B. (1993). The diagnosis and assessment of depression, mania, and psychosis by self-report. *Journal of Personality Assessment, 60*, 1–31.

Widiger, T. A. (2001). Review of the Millon Clinical Multiaxial Inventory. In J. Mitchell Jr. (Ed.), *Ninth mental measurements yearbook. Vol. I* (pp. 986–988). Lincoln: University of Nebraska Press.

Widiger, T., & Sanderson, C. (1987). The convergent and discriminant validity of the MCMI as a measure of the DSM III personality disorders. *Journal of Personality Assessment, 51*, 228–242.

Wierzbicki, M., & Gorman, J. L. (1995). Correspondence between students' scores on the Millon Clinical Multiaxial Inventory-II and Personality Diagnostic Questionnaire-Revised. *Psychological Reports, 77*, 1079–1082.

Wise, E. A. (1994a). Managed care and the psychometric validity of the MMPI and MCMI personality disorder scales. *Psychotherapy in Private Practice, 13*, 81–97.

Wise, E. A. (1994b). Personality style codetype concordance between the MCMI and MBHI. *Journal of Clinical Psychology, 50*, 367–380.

Wise, E. A. (1995). Personality disorder correspondence between the MMPI, MBHI, and MCMI. *Journal of Clinical Psychology, 51*, 367–380.

Wise, E. A. (1996). Comparative validity of MMPI-2 and MCMI-II personality disorder classifications. *Journal of Personality Assessment, 66*, 569–582.

Wise, E. A. (2001). The comparative validity of MCMI-II and MMPI-2 personality disorder scales with forensic examinees. *Journal of Personality Disorders, 15*, 275–279.

Zarella, K. L., Schuerger, J. M., & Ritz, G. H. (1990). Estimation of MCMI DSM-III Axis II constructs from MMPI scales and subscales. *Journal of Personality Assessment, 55*, 195–201.

CHAPTER 5

The Personality Assessment Inventory

LESLIE C. MOREY
CHRISTOPHER J. HOPWOOD

Introduction

The *Personality Assessment Inventory* (PAI; Morey, 1991) is a self-report inventory intended to provide clinically useful information about a host of important client variables in professional and research settings. It contains 344 items that are answered on a four-alternative scale, with the options of *totally false, slightly true, mainly true,* and *very true.* The 344 items comprise 22 nonoverlapping full scales: 4 validity, 11 clinical, 5 treatment consideration, and 2 interpersonal. Ten of the full scales include subscales that facilitate the assessment of the breadth of measured constructs. Several additional indicators are also available to augment PAI interpretation (see Tables 5.1 and 5.2 for PAI scales and indexes). This chapter provides a brief overview of the theory and procedures employed in developing the PAI and highlights relevant research and practical applications of the PAI in a variety of assessment contexts. More detailed discussion is available in primary sources (Morey, 1996, 2003, 2007; Morey & Hopwood, 2007).

Although many aspects of PAI development, research, and interpretation will be covered, a goal of the chapter is to provide specific answers to the following questions: (a) What considerations guided the development of the PAI, (b) what differentiates the PAI from other multiscale self-report instruments, (c) how are PAI validity scales used, and (d) how can the PAI be used for treatment planning?

Table 5.1 PAI Scales and Subscales

	Scale	Interpretation of High Scores
	Validity Scales	
ICN	Inconsistency	Poor concentration or inattention
INF	Infrequency	Idiosyncratic or random response set
NIM	Negative Impression Management	Negative response set due to pessimistic worldview and/or intentional dissimulation
PIM	Positive Impression Management	Positive response set due to naïveté or intentional dissimulation
	Clinical Scales	
SOM	Somatic Complaints	Focus on physical health related issues
SOM-C	Conversion	Rare sensorimotor symptoms associated with conversion disorders or certain medical conditions
SOM-S	Somatization	The occurrence of common physical symptoms or vague complaints of ill health or fatigue
SOM-H	Health Concerns	Preoccupation with physical functioning and symptoms
ANX	Anxiety	Experience of generalized anxiety across different response modalities
ANX-C	Cognitive	Ruminative worry and impaired concentration and attention
ANX-A	Affective	Experience of tension, difficulty relaxing, nervousness, and fatigue
ANX-P	Physiological	Overt signs of anxiety, including sweating, trembling, shortness of breath, and irregular heartbeat
ARD	Anxiety Related Disorders	Symptoms and behaviors related to specific anxiety disorders
ARD-O	Obsessive-Compulsive	Intrusive thoughts, compulsive behaviors, rigidity, indecision, perfectionism, and affective constriction
ARD-P	Phobias	Common fears, including social situations, heights, and public or enclosed places; low scores suggest fearlessness
ARD-T	Traumatic Stress	Experience of trauma that continues to cause distress
DEP	Depression	Experience of depression across different response modalities
DEP-C	Cognitive	Worthlessness, hopelessness, indecisiveness, and difficulty concentrating; low scores indicate personal confidence

	Scale	Interpretation of High Scores
DEP-A	Affective	Feelings of sadness, diminished interest, and anhedonia
DEP-P	Physiological	Level of physical functioning, activity, and sleep and diet patterns
MAN	Mania	Experience of behavioral, affective, and cognitive symptoms of mania and hypomania
MAN-A	Activity Level	Disorganized overinvolvement in activities, accelerated thought processes and behavior
MAN-G	Grandiosity	Inflated self-esteem and expansiveness; low scores indicate low self-esteem
MAN-I	Irritability	Frustration intolerance, impatience, and resulting strained relationships
PAR	Paranoia	Experience of paranoid symptoms and traits
PAR-H	Hypervigilance	Suspiciousness and tendency to closely monitor environment; low scores suggest interpersonal trust
PAR-P	Persecution	Belief that others have intentionally constructed obstacles to one's achievement
PAR-R	Resentment	Bitterness and cynicism in relationships, tendency to hold grudges, and externalization of blame
SCZ	Schizophrenia	Symptoms relevant to the broad spectrum of schizophrenic disorders
SCZ-P	Psychotic Experiences	Unusual perceptions and sensations, magical thinking, and unusual ideas
SXZ-S	Social Detachment	Social isolation, discomfort, and awkwardness
SCZ-T	Thought Disorder	Confusion, concentration difficulties, and disorganization
BOR	Borderline Features	Attributes indicative of borderline levels of personality functioning
BOR-A	Affective Instability	Emotional responsiveness, rapid mood change, poor modulation
BOR-I	Identity Problems	Uncertainty about major life issues and feelings of emptiness or lack of fulfillment or purpose
BOR-N	Negative Relationships	History of intense, ambivalent relationships and feelings of exploitation or betrayal
BOR-S	Self-Harm	Impulsivity in areas likely to be dangerous
ANT	Antisocial Features	Focuses on behavioral and personological features of antisocial personality
ANT-A	Antisocial Behaviors	History of antisocial and illegal behavior
ANT-E	Egocentricity	Lack of empathy or remorse, exploitive approach to relationships

(continued)

Table 5.1 Continued

	Scale	Interpretation of High Scores
ANT-S	Stimulus Seeking	Cravings for excitement, low boredom tolerance, recklessness
ALC	Alcohol Problems	Use of and problems with alcohol
DRG	Drug Problems	Use of and problems with drugs
	Treatment Consideration Scales	
AGG	Aggression	Characteristics and attitudes related to anger, assertiveness, and hostility
AGG-A	Aggressive Attitude	Hostility, poor control over anger and belief in instrumental utility of violence
AGG-V	Verbal Aggression	Assertiveness, abusiveness, and readiness to express anger to others
AGG-P	Physical Aggression	Tendency to be involved in physical aggression
SUI	Suicidal Ideation	Frequency and intensity of thoughts of self-harm or fantasies about suicide
STR	Stress	Perception of an uncertain or difficult environment
NON	Nonsupport	Perception that others are not available or willing to provide support
RXR	Treatment Rejection	Attitudes that represent obstacles or indicate low motivation for treatment
	Interpersonal Scales	
DOM	Dominance	Desire and tendency for control in relationships; low scores suggest meekness and submissiveness
WRM	Warmth	Interest and comfort with close relationships; low scores suggest hostility, anger, and mistrust

Theory and Development

The development of the PAI was based on a construct validation framework that places a strong emphasis on both a theoretically informed approach to the development and selection of items and the assessment of their psychometric properties. Constructs were initially chosen to be included on the PAI for their (a) demonstration of stable historical representation in the research literature and clinical practice and (b) contemporary importance among practicing clinical evaluators. The theoretical and empirical literature related to each construct was then closely examined because this articulation had to serve as a guide to the content of information sampled and to the subse-

Table 5.2 Supplementary PAI Indexes

	Index	Development	Interpretation of High Scores
		Validity Indexes	
MAL	Malingering Index	Eight configural features observed with relatively high frequency in malingering samples	Negative response set, malingering
RDF	Rogers Discriminant Function	Function found to discriminate patients from naive and coached malingerers	Malingering
DEF	Defensiveness Index	Eight configural features observed with relatively high frequency in positive dissimulation samples	Self and/or other deception in the positive direction
CDF	Cashel Discriminant Function	Function found to discriminate real from fake good inmates and college students	Intentional concealment of specific problems
ALCe	ALC Estimated Score	ALC estimated by other elements of the profile	ALCe > ALC suggests deception regarding alcohol use
DRGe	DRG Estimated Score	DRG estimated by other elements of the profile	DRG > DRGe suggests deception regarding drug use
ACS*	Addictive Characteristics Scale	Algorithm used to predict addictive potential	Deception regarding substance use (with low ALC, DRG)
BRR	Back Random Responding	Differences > 5T on front and back halves of ALC and SUI scales	Random responding on back half of PAI
INF-F*	Infrequency-Front	First four INF items	Random responding on first half of PAI
INF-B*	Infrequency-Back	Last four INF items	Random responding on second half of PAI
ICN-C*	Inconsistency-Corrections	Inconsistent responses to two similar items regarding illegal behavior	Inattention

(continued)

Table 5.2 Continued

	Index	Development	Interpretation of High Scores
		Predictive Indices	
TPI	Treatment Process Index	Twelve configural features of the PAI associated with treatment amenability	Difficult treatment process, high probability of reversals
VPI	Violence Potential Index	Twenty configural features of the PAI associated with dangerousness to others	Increased likelihood of violence to others
SPI	Suicide Potential Index	Twenty configural features of the PAI associated with suicide	Increased likelihood of suicide

*Developed for use in correctional settings (Edens & Ruiz, 2005).

quent assessment of content validity. After items were selected, the test went through four iterations of development in a sequential construct validation strategy similar to that described by Loevinger (1957) and Jackson (1970) and including the consideration of a number of item parameters that were not described by those authors. Of paramount importance at each point of the development process was the assumption that *no single quantitative item parameter should be used as the sole criterion for item selection*. An overreliance on a single parameter in item selection typically leads to a scale with one desirable psychometric property and numerous undesirable ones.

The PAI scales were developed to provide a balanced sampling of the most important elements of the constructs being measured. This content coverage was designed to include both a consideration of breadth as well as depth of the construct. The breadth of content coverage refers to the diversity of elements subsumed within a construct. For example, in measuring anxiety it is important to inquire about physiological (sweaty palms, racing heart) and cognitive (rumination, worry) symptoms and features. Anxiety scales that focus exclusively on one of these elements have limited breadth of coverage and compromised content validity. The PAI is designed to insure breadth of content coverage through the use of subscales representing the major elements of the measured constructs, as indicated by the theoretical and empirical literature.

The depth of content coverage refers to the need to sample across the full range of construct severity. To assure adequate depth of coverage, the scales were designed to include items reflecting both milder and most severe difficulties. The use of four-alternative scaling provides each item with the capacity to capture differences in the severity of the manifestation of a feature of a particular disorder, and is further justified psychometrically in that it allows a scale to capture truer variance per item, meaning that even scales of modest length can achieve satisfactory reliability. This item type may also be preferred by clinicians interested in a more detailed analysis of particular issues as represented by particular item responses (e.g., critical risk indicators) or clients themselves, who often express dissatisfaction with forced choice alternatives because they feel that the truth is between the two extremes presented. In addition to differences in depth of severity reflected in response options, the items themselves were constructed to tap different levels of severity. For example, cognitive elements of anxiety can vary from mild rumination to severe feelings of panic and despair. Item characteristic curves were used to select items that provide information across the full range of construct severity. The nature of the severity continuum varies across the constructs. For example, severity on the SUI scale involves the imminence of the suicidal threat. Thus, items on this scale vary from vague and ill articulated thoughts about suicide to immediate plans for self-harm.

Quick Reference

- The PAI can provide important information about adult respondents in clinical, forensic, and personnel selection settings and for psychological research.
- The PAI requires a fourth-grade reading level.
- Basic knowledge of personality and psychopathology are required for the interpretation of most features of the PAI profile.

The use of item response theory parameters during scale development to ensure that items measure a range of severity for each construct is a unique strength of the PAI.

Psychometrics

Reliability

The reliability of the PAI scales and subscales has been examined in a number of different studies that have evaluated the internal consistency (Alterman et al., 1995; Boyle & Lennon, 1994; Karlin et al., 2005; Morey, 1991; Rogers, Flores, Ustad & Sewell, 1995; Schinka, 1995), test-retest reliability (Boyle & Lennon, 1994; Morey, 1991; Rogers et al., 1995) and configural stability (Morey, 1991) of the instrument. Internal consistency alphas for the full scales are generally found to be in the 0.80s, whereas the subscales yield alphas in the 0.70s. For the standardization studies, median test-retest reliability values, over a 4-week interval, for the 11 full clinical scales was 0.86 (Morey, 1991), leading to standard error of measurement (SEM) estimates for these scales on the order of three to four *T*-score points, with 95% confidence intervals of +/- 6 to 8 *T*-score points. Absolute *T*-score change values over time were quite small across scales, on the order of 2 to 3 *T*-score points for most of the full scales (Morey, 1991). Boyle and Lennon (1994) reported a median test-retest reliability of 0.73 in their nonclinical sample over 28 days.

Because multiscale inventories are often interpreted configurally (i.e., in terms of the relations between scale elevations within the same profile), additional questions should be asked concerning the stability of configurations on the 11 PAI clinical scales. One such analysis involved determining the inverse (or Q-type) correlation between each subject's profile at Time 1 and the profile at Time 2. Correlations were obtained for each of the 155 subjects in the full retest sample, and a distribution of the within subject profile correlations was obtained. Conducted in this manner, the median correlation of the clinical scale configuration was 0.83, indicating a substantial degree of stability in profile configurations over time (Morey, 1991).

Validity

In the examination of test validity presented in the manual (Morey, 1991, 2007), a number of the best available clinical indicators were administered concurrently to various samples to determine their convergence with corresponding PAI scales. Diagnostic and other clinical judgments have also been examined to determine if their PAI correlates were consistent with hypothesized relations. Finally, a number of simulation studies have been performed to determine the efficacy of the PAI validity scales in identifying response sets. A comprehensive presentation of available validity evidence for the various scales is beyond the scope of this chapter; the PAI manual alone contains information about correlations of individual scales with more than 50 concurrent indexes of psychopathology (Morey, 1991), and hundreds of subsequent studies provide further evidence of validity against varied criteria. A number of these independent research findings are discussed later in this chapter; the following paragraphs discuss some of the more noteworthy findings from the initial PAI validation studies with respect to individual scales, divided into the four broad classes of PAI scales: validity scales, clinical scales, treatment consideration scales, and interpersonal scales.

Validity Scales

The PAI validity scales were developed to provide an assessment of the potential influence of certain response tendencies on PAI test performance, including both random and systematic influences upon test responding. The PAI has two scales for the assessment of random response tendencies (Infrequency [INF] and Inconsistency [ICN]) and one scale for the assessment of systematic negative (Negative Impression Management [NIM]) and positive (Positive Impression Management [PIM]) response styles, as well as several other validity indicators that will be discussed below. To model the performance of individuals completing the PAI in a random fashion, various studies have created profiles by generating random responses to individual PAI items and then scoring all scales according to their normal scoring algorithms (Morey, 1991; Clark, Gironda, & Young, 2003). Generally, when the entire PAI protocol is answered randomly, the ICN or INF scales will identify these profiles at very high sensitivity rates. However, these scales are less sensitive to distortion arising from a response set where only part of the protocol has been answered randomly (Clark et al., 2003). To assist in the identification of such protocols, Morey and Hopwood (2004) developed an indicator of back random responding involving short form/full scale score discrepancies $\geq 5T$ on the alcohol (ALC) and suicide (SUI) scales. This index demonstrated satisfactory positive and negative predictive power across levels and base rates of back random responding, a finding that has been validated in an independent patient sample (Seifert, Baity, Blais, & Chriki, 2006).

Responses may also be systematically distorted in the negative and/or positive direction, and the nature of distortion can be intentional (i.e., faking) or implicit (e.g., defensiveness, negative exaggeration). Thus, several PAI indicators have been developed to assess intentional dissimulation and exaggeration in the positive and negative directions. The PIM scale comprises items that allow the respondent to represent an unreasonably favorable impression, but which are rarely endorsed. Validation studies have consistently demonstrated that those scoring above $57T$ on PIM are much more likely to be in a positive dissimulation sample than a community sample (Morey, 1991; Cashel, Rogers, Sewell, & Martin-Cannici, 1995; Fals-Stewart, 1996; Morey & Lanier, 1998 Peebles & Moore, 1998), although this rate may vary, and in particular may increase among individuals with motivation to present themselves favorably (e.g., personnel selection, child custody evaluation).

The Defensiveness Index (DEF; Morey, 1996) is a composite of configural features designed to augment PIM in the detection of positive dissimulation (i.e., systematic positive distortion). Hit rates in detecting "fake good" profiles in simulation studies tend to range in the high 0.70s to mid 0.80s (Baer & Wetter, 1997; Peebles & Moore, 1998), although there is some evidence suggesting that these hit rates decrease when respondents are coached on how to escape detection (Baer & Wetter, 1997). Along similar lines, the Cashel Discriminant Function (CDF; Cashel et al., 1995) is an empirically derived function designed to maximize differences between honest responders and individuals instructed to fake good in both college student and forensic populations. Follow up studies (Morey, 1996; Morey & Lanier, 1998) indicated that the CDF demonstrated substantial cross validation when applied to new, independent samples. The CDF appears to measure positive dissimulation unassociated with psychopathological factors that may minimize problems (e.g., naïveté, lack of insight), an inference supported by its relatively modest association with validity scales from the PAI (Morey & Lanier, 1998) and other instruments (Rosner, 2004) and PAI clinical scales (Morey, 1996).

With respect to markers of negative response distortion, the initial studies reported by Morey (1991) indicated that normal individuals feigning severe clinical disorders produced marked elevations on the NIM scale relative to bona fide clinical patients. Numerous subsequent studies (e.g. Rogers, Ornduff, & Sewell, 1993; Wang et al., 1997; Blanchard et al., 2003) have generally supported the ability of this scale to distinguish simulators from actual protocols across a variety of response set conditions that can potentially moderate the effectiveness of NIM, such as population (e.g., clinical, forensic, college student), coaching, and sophistication of respondents (e.g., undergraduate and graduate students). Hit rates tend to range from 0.50 to 0.80; research suggests that NIM sensitivity is negatively affected by coaching and is positively related to the severity of feigned disorders (Rogers et al., 1995).

The Malingering Index (MAL; Morey, 1996) is a composite of several configural indicators that was designed to measure malingering more directly than NIM, which is often affected by response styles consequent to psychopathology (e.g., exaggeration associated with depression) as well as overt attempts at negative dissimulation. To further assist the interpretation of negative distortion, Rogers, Sewell, Morey, and Ustad (1996) developed the Rogers Discriminant Function (RDF). Like the CDF, the RDF is unassociated with psychopathology, and thus provides a potentially important differential indicator of exaggeration associated with clinical disorders versus intentional feigning (Morey, 1996). Simulation studies of these two indexes have been generally indicated that they can successfully distinguish feigned from genuine psychopathology (Morey & Lanier, 1998; Bagby, Nicholson, Bacchiochi, Ryder, & Bury, 2002; Blanchard et al., 2003; Edens et al., 2007).

Clinical Scales

A number of instruments were used to provide initial information on the convergent and discriminant validity of the PAI clinical scales (Morey, 1991), and there has been substantial subsequent research on these scales, which will be described later in this chapter. The initial convergence correlations (as reported in Morey, 1991) tended to follow hypothesized patterns; for example, strong associations were found between neurotic spectrum scales such as Somatic Complaints (SOM), Anxiety (ANX), Anxiety Related Disorder (ARD), and Depression (DEP) and the personality trait Neuroticism (Costa & McCrae, 1992; Montag & Levin, 1994; Morey, 1991), and these scales achieved their largest correlations with various widely used indicators of similar constructs. For example, SOM exhibited a strong association with the Wahler Physical Symptoms Inventory (Wahler, 1983; .72) and MMPI Wiggins content scales (Wiggins, 1966) health concerns (.80) and organic problems (.82) scales and moderate correlations with measures of depression and anxiety. ANX correlated strongly with the anxiety facet of the NEO-PI-R (Costa & McCrae, 1992; .76) and the State-Trait Anxiety Inventory (Spielberger, 1983) trait anxiety (.73) and moderately with measures of physical symptoms and depression. The pattern of correlations of external indicators with ARD indicated the more specific diagnostic content of that scale, in contrast with the content relative to more diffuse anxiety as represented on ANX. For example, ARD demonstrated its largest correlations with the Fear Survey Schedule (Wolpe & Lang, 1964; .66) and Mississippi PTSD scale (Keane, Caddell, & Taylor, 1988; .81), and was more modestly correlated with NEO-PI-R anxiety (.57) than ANX. DEP demonstrated strong correlations with the Beck Depression Inventory (Beck & Steer, 1987a; range across samples = .70 –.81) and the Depression facet of the NEO-PI-R (.70) and moderate correlations were observed between DEP and external measures of anxiety and somatic difficulties.

The three PAI scales from the psychotic spectrum, Mania (MAN), Paranoia (PAR), and Schizophrenia (SCZ), were correlated with a variety of other indicators of severe psychopathology during the validation studies (Morey,

1991). Consistent with expectations, MAN demonstrated strong correlations with MMPI-2 Scale 9 (.53), and MMPI Wiggins content scale Hypomania (.63) and moderate correlations with indicators of psychosis. PAR achieved its strongest associations with MMPI Paranoid Personality Disorder (Morey, Waugh, & Blashfield, 1985 .70) and NEO-PI-R Agreeableness (−.54), whereas SCZ correlated most strongly with MMPI Wiggins Content Scale Psychoticism (.76).

Two scales on the PAI directly target character pathology, the Borderline Features (BOR) scale and the Antisocial Features (ANT) scale. These disorders were chosen because they are better developed, empirically and theoretically, than other personality disorders in the research and clinical literature. BOR achieved the largest correlations with NEO-PI-R Neuroticism (.67) and the MMPI Borderline Personality Disorder Scale (.77), and ANT demonstrated its largest correlations with the MMPI Antisocial Personality Disorder Scale (range = .60–.77) and the Self-Report Psychopathy test (Hare, 1985; range = .54–80). The PAI contains two scales, Alcohol Problems (ALC) and Drug Problems (DRG) that inquire directly about behaviors and consequences related to alcohol and drug use, abuse, and dependence. Correlations from the validation studies with the Michigan Alcohol Screening Test (Selzer, 1971; ALC: .89, DRG: −.25) and Drug Abuse Screening Test (Skinner, 1982; ALC: −.31, DRG: .69) attested to the convergent and discriminant validity of these scales.

Treatment Consideration Scales

Correlations between the PAI treatment consideration scales and a variety of validation measures provide support for their construct validity (Costa & McCrae, 1992; Morey, 1991). Substantial correlations have been identified between the Aggression (AGG) scale and NEO-PI Hostility (.83) and State-Trait Anger Expression Inventory (STAXI; Spielberger, 1988) Trait Anger scales (.75). The Suicidal Ideation (SUI) scale was most positively correlated with the Beck (Beck & Steer, 1987b Hopelessness (.64) and Depression (.61) scales and the Suicidal Ideation (.56) and Total Score (.40) of the Suicide Probability Scale (SPS; Cull & Gill, 1982). As expected, the Nonsupport (NON) scale was found to be highly and inversely correlated with the Perceived Social Support scales (PSS; Procidano & Heller, 1983); −.67 with PSS-Family and −.63 with PSS-Friends. The Stress (STR) scale displayed its largest correlations with the Schedule of Recent Events (SRE; .50), a unit-scoring adaptation of the widely used Holmes and Rahe (1967) checklist of recent stressors. Finally, the Treatment Rejection (RXR) scale was negatively associated with Wiggins MMPI scale Poor Morale (−.78) and the NEO-PI Vulnerability (−.54) scales, consistent with the assumption that distress can serve as a motivator for treatment.

Interpersonal Scales

The interpersonal scales of the PAI were designed to provide an assessment of the respondent's interpersonal style along two dimensions: (a) a warmly affiliative versus a cold rejecting axis, and (b) a dominating, controlling versus a meekly submissive axis. These axes can be useful in guiding the nature of the therapeutic process (Kiesler, 1996; Tracey, 1993) and conceptualizing variation in normal personality and mental disorder (Kiesler, 1996; Pincus, 2005). The PAI manual describes a number of studies indicating that diagnostic groups differ on these dimensions; for example, spouse abusers are relatively high on the Dominance (DOM) scale, whereas patients with schizophrenia are low on the Warmth (WRM) scale (Morey, 1991). The correlations with the Interpersonal Adjective scales (Wiggins, 1979) vector scores are consistent with expectations, with PAI DOM associated with the dominance vector (.61) and PAI WRM associated with the love vector (.65). The NEO-PI Extroversion scale roughly bisects the high DOM/high WRM quadrant, because it is moderately positively correlated with both scales; this finding is consistent with previous research using other interpersonal measures (Trapnell & Wiggins, 1990). The WRM scale was also correlated with the NEO-PI Gregariousness facet (.46), whereas DOM was associated with the NEO-PI Assertiveness facet (.71).

Administration and Scoring

The PAI was developed and standardized for use in the clinical assessment of individuals in the age range of 18 through adulthood. PAI scale and subscale raw scores are transformed to T-scores (mean of 50, standard deviation of 10) to provide interpretation relative to a standardization sample of 1,000 community dwelling adults. This sample was carefully selected to match 1995 U.S. census projections on the basis of gender, race and age; the educational level of the standardization sample (mean of 13.3 years) was representative of a community group with the required fourth-grade reading level. For each scale and subscale, the T-scores were linearly transformed from the means and standard deviations derived from the census-matched standardization sample.

Unlike similar instruments, the PAI does not calculate T-scores differently for men and women; instead, combined norms are used for both genders. Separate norms are only necessary when the scale contains some systematic bias that alters the interpretation of a score based on the respondent's gender. To use separate norms in the absence of such bias would only distort the natural epidemiological differences between genders. For example, women are less likely than men to receive the diagnosis of antisocial personality disorder, and this is reflected in the lower mean scores for women on the Antisocial Features (ANT) scale. A separate normative procedure for men and women would result in similar numbers of each gender scoring in the clinically significant range, a result that does not reflect the established gender ratio for this disorder. The PAI included several procedures to eliminate items that might be biased due to demographic features, and items that displayed any signs of being interpreted differently as a function of these features were eliminated in the course of selecting final items for the test. With relatively few exceptions, differences as a function of demography were negligible in the community sample. The most noteworthy effects involve the tendency for younger adults to score higher on the BOR and ANT scales, and the tendency for men to score higher on the ANT and ALC relative to women.

Because T-scores are derived from a community sample, they provide a useful means for determining if certain problems are clinically significant, because relatively few normal adults will obtain markedly elevated scores. However, other comparisons are often of equal importance in clinical decision making. For example, nearly all patients report depression at their initial evaluation; the question confronting the clinician considering a diagnosis of Major Depressive Disorder is one of relative severity. Knowing the individual's score on the PAI Depression scale is elevated in comparison to the standardization sample is of value, but a comparison of the elevation relative to a clinical sample may be more critical in forming diagnostic hypotheses.

To facilitate these comparisons, the PAI profile form also indicates the T-scores that correspond to marked elevations when referenced against a representative clinical sample. This profile skyline indicates the score for each scale and subscale that represents the raw score that is two standard deviations above the mean for a clinical sample of 1,246 patients selected from a wide variety of different professional settings. The configuration of this skyline serves as a guide to base rate expectations of elevations when the setting shifts from a community to a clinical frame of reference. Thus, interpretation of the PAI profiles can be accomplished in comparison to both normal and clinical samples.

Training Requirements for Administration and Interpretation

Psychological Assessment Resources, the publisher of the PAI, requires that individuals provide their educational and license credentials before they will fulfill requests for the PAI, or related scoring software packages. Like all psychological tests, sound understanding of personality, psychometrics, diagnosis, ethics, and other issues related to the assessment context (e.g., law, psychotherapy, and neuropsychology) is necessary for adequate PAI interpretation. Also like all other multivariate inventories, the adequacy of interpretation is presumed to be correlated with exposure to didactic training, information on uses and test properties, and direct experience. Training, research, and experience would be particularly useful for understanding special features of the PAI profile, such as validity scale configurations, operating characteristics of certain scales, and diagnostic algorithms.

Computerization

Three computer software packages have been developed for using the PAI in the assessment of clinical, correctional (i.e., assessment of inmates), and correctional personnel selection (i.e., assessment of individuals applying to work in correctional settings) contexts that can be used for computerized administration and scoring, and provide narrative feedback regarding the respondent's results. The PAI Software Portfolio (Morey, 2000) provides scoring of PAI scales and transformation to T-scores based on comparison with both community and clinical normative samples. This software also provides a narrative report, diagnostic hypotheses, and critical items relevant for clinical assessment. Several additional indexes are computed that would be difficult or impossible to compute by hand, such as coefficients of configural profile fit with known diagnostic groups sampled in the standardization studies, profiles that take statistical account of dissimulation indicated by the validity scales that assist the clinician in interpretation in light of distortion, and various supplemental indices, such as the Rogers and Cashel Discriminant Functions and the Malingering and Defensiveness Indexes.

The PAI Law Enforcement, Corrections, and Public Safety Selection Report Module (Roberts, Thompson, & Johnson, 2000) provides scoring of PAI scales and T-transformation based on data from a normative sample of approximately 18,000 public safety applicants. This package also provides a comparison of the applicant's scores to a sample of individuals who have successfully completed a post-hiring probation period to further facilitate assessment predictions. In addition to scores and narrative reports, several features uniquely relevant to correctional personnel selection are provided. For example, a probability estimate of the likelihood that a given applicant would be judged acceptable, based on all available PAI data, is provided, as are estimates that applicants would be found unacceptable for several specific reasons, such as potential integrity problems or substance use.

The PAI Correctional Software (Edens & Ruiz, 2005) scores the PAI and transforms raw scores based on normative data gathered from multiple correctional settings. The correctional normative sample consisted of inmates in a prerelease treatment facility in New Jersey ($N = 542$), a treatment program for convicted sex offenders in Texas ($N = 98$), state prison inmates in Washington ($N = 515$), and forensic inpatients in New Hampshire ($N = 57$). In addition to scoring the PAI and providing a narrative report, several indexes relevant to correctional populations are provided, including front and back infrequency scales, an inconsistency scale that focuses on criminal behavior,

Just the Facts

Ages: 18 and older
Purpose: Comprehensive clinical and personality assessment
Strengths: Brevity, clarity, and content and discriminant validity
Limitations: Lack of representation of some important constructs (e.g., eating
  disorders)
Time to Administer: 45–60 minutes
Time to Score: 10 minutes with computer software, 60 minutes by hand

and an addictive characteristics scale designed to assist the clinician in the
assessment of substance use denial.

Applications and Limitations

Settings and Purposes

The PAI is commonly and increasingly used in clinical training and assessment (Belter & Piotrowski, 2001; Piotrowski, 2000), for correctional and
risk assessments, custody, personnel, and other forensic assessments (Lally,
2003; Stredny, Archer, Buffington-Vollum, & Handel, 2006), and research,
and can also be informative in health (e.g., Bruce & Dean, 2002; Karlin et
al., 2005; Wagner et al., 2005) and neuropsychological (e.g., Kurtz, Shealy,
& Putnam, 2007) evaluations.

Why use this test versus others in clinical settings?

Several strengths of multiscale, self-report instruments in general and
the PAI in particular make it desirable for use in clinical settings. Self-report measures such as the PAI provide a unique opportunity to capture the
phenomenology of the person being assessed and to yield information that
is unfiltered by clinical inference and directly linked to standardization data
for the purpose of normative comparison. Generating data from the client's
perspective on a variety of indicators potentially relevant to presenting issues and goals provides the opportunity to consider multiple explanations
for clinical phenomena and protects the evaluator from confirmation bias
by generating competing hypotheses and disconfirming data.

Some advantages of the PAI relative to other multiscale, self-report instruments involve practical characteristics of the test that were designed to
ease administrative and interpretive strain. For example, commonly used
personality and diagnostic constructs are assessed directly on the PAI, and
the scales are named according to common usage. The theoretical neutrality
of the PAI scales facilitates its use in a relatively wide variety of contexts by a
relatively wide range of evaluators. As discussed above, relative brevity despite
nonoverlapping scales, four-alternative response scales, and relatively easily
read items represent other practical advantages of the PAI.

The main psychometric strengths of the PAI relative to other multiscale, self-report inventories relate to *content* and *discriminant validity* (White, 1996). To ensure content validity, constructs were chosen for their likely importance to clinicians in a variety of assessment settings, broad pools of items were generated to represent those constructs, and a variety of procedures were employed to select the best indicators of each construct as discussed above. One implication of a careful consideration of content validity in the construction of a test is that it is assumed that item content is critical in determining an item's ability to capture the phenomenology of various disorders and traits, hence its relevance for the assessment of the construct. Empirically derived tests may include items that have no apparent relation to the construct in question. However, research (e.g., Holden, 1989; Holden & Fekken, 1990; Peterson, Clark, & Bennett, 1989) has consistently indicated that such items add little or no validity to self-report tests. The available empirical evidence is entirely consistent with the assumption that the content of a self-report item is critical in determining its utility in measurement. This assumption does not preclude the potential utility of items that are truly subtle in the sense that a lay audience cannot readily identify the relationship of the item to mental health status. However, the assumption does suggest that the implications of such items for mental health status should be apparent to the expert diagnosticians for the item to be useful.

Although discriminant validity has been long recognized as an important facet of construct validity, it traditionally has not played a major role in the construction of psychological tests, and it continues to represent one of the most difficult challenges in the measurement of psychological constructs. There are a variety of threats to validity where construct discrimination plays a vital role. One such area of involves test bias. A test that is intended to measure a psychological construct should not be measuring a demographic variable, such as gender, age, or sex. This does not mean that psychological tests should never be correlated with demographic variables, but that the magnitude of any such correlations should not exceed the theoretical overlap of the demographic feature with the construct. For example and as discussed above, nearly every indicator of antisocial behavior suggests that it is more common in men than in women; thus, it would be expected that an assessment of antisocial behavior would yield average scores for men that are higher than that for women. However, the instrument should demonstrate a considerably greater correlation with other indicators of antisocial behavior than it does with gender; otherwise, it may be measuring gender rather than measuring the construct it was designed to assess.

The issue of test bias is particularly salient in light of past abuses of testing and current legislation designed to prevent such abuses. However, such bias is just one form of potential problems with discriminant validity. It is particularly common in the field of clinical assessment to find that a scale designed to measure one construct is in fact highly related to many constructs. It is this tendency that makes many instruments quite difficult to interpret. How does the clinician evaluate an elevated score on a scale measuring schizophrenia if that scale also measures alienation, indecisiveness, family problems, and depression? At each stage of the development of the PAI, items were selected that had maximal associations with indicators of the pertinent construct and minimal associations with the other constructs. The initial decision to construct nonoverlapping scales represented the first important effort to enhance discriminant validity. Overlapping scales confound test structure and the natural relationships between measured constructs and make differential diagnosis—an already challenging endeavor—even more difficult. Several subsequent steps in test development further enhanced the discriminant validity of the PAI. During item selection, psychopathology experts sorted items into diagnostic categories to ensure they were not incidentally measuring different but related constructs. During beta testing, differential item functioning was used to investigate differential relations between test items and criteria across demographic groups to address the potential for demographic bias. Finally, correlations of scales with more than 50 commonly used instruments during the validation studies provided a multitrait, multimethod matrix (Campbell & Fiske, 1959) in which convergent and discriminant validity could be assessed directly. Relative to instruments which did not undergo such efforts to maximize discriminant validity, the PAI is likely to be less susceptible to test bias and more capable of differential diagnosis.

Major Nonclinical Uses

As discussed above, normative transformations and scoring software are available for corrections and correctional personnel selection assessments. The PAI has been shown to provide reliable information in other forensic contexts as well, such as parenting capacity evaluations (Loving & Lee, 2006), and meets contemporary legal standards for court admissibility for a variety of purposes (Morey, Warner, & Hopwood, 2006; Lally, 2003). It is also often used in health settings. For example, it has been observed that the PAI reliability coefficients and factor structure in a chronic pain sample are consistent with those reported in the PAI manual (Karlin et al., 2005). As anticipated, individuals in that sample tended to achieve higher scores than individuals in the community normative sample on several neurotic scales, particularly SOM and DEP. The PAI is informative with individuals with traumatic brain injury and epilepsy. For example, Keiski, Shore, and Hamilton (2003) demonstrated that the PAI DEP of individuals with brain injuries affected scores on a memory task after controlling for global cognitive impairment, while Wagner et al. (2005) noted that SOM was capable of distinguishing epileptic from nonepileptic (conversion) seizures. Finally, research suggests the utility of the PAI in the assessment of individuals with constructs not directly represented by the PAI. For example, Tasca, Wood, Demidenko, and Bissada (2002) observed that individuals with eating disorders tend to achieve elevations relative to community norms on several clinical scales, most notably ANX, DEP, and BOR.

Limitations

The PAI shares the limitations common to all self-report assessment methods, and it is often useful to supplement self-reports with performance based, interview, physiological, collateral, and behavioral assessments. In addition, the respondent must have the physical and educational capacity to understand test content and respond coherently. The PAI is inappropriate for individuals with significant difficulties related to seeing, reading, or comprehending. Two additional limitations result from efforts to balance the breadth of content coverage and the brevity and efficiency of the instrument. On one hand, a variety of potentially important constructs are not measured directly (e.g., dependency, gender identity, openness to experience). In cases where these constructs are important for a given assessment question, the PAI should be supplemented or replaced by other assessment methods. On the other hand, there are some instances in which clinicians may feel a PAI administration and interpretation would be too time consuming, particularly in a large-scale screening setting where the base rate of psycholopathology might be low. The Personality Assessment Screener (PAS; Morey, 1997) was developed to assist clinicians in this situation. The PAS is a 22-item measure that yields element scores that provide an estimate of the likelihood that significant elevations would occur were the PAI given.

Depending on the theoretical orientation and training of the evaluator, there may also be conceptual limitations of the PAI relative to other multi-scale, self-report instruments. Other measures have been designed to provide information more directly related to particular theories of personality and psychopathology that may be preferable to the more theory-neutral PAI. Another consideration involves breadth of relevant research. Although the PAI tends to compare favorably to other methods in validity studies, there may be some test uses for which previous research has not been conducted with the PAI. In such cases, it may be preferable to use a method that has received consistent research support in well conducted studies investigating that assessment purpose.

Assessing Strengths

The assessment of strengths is important in any psychological evaluation where predictions are made about future behavior. A lack of distress or dysfunction in a nondefensive profile suggests overall psychological strengths and adaptive coping. Particular scale configurations also suggest specific strengths. In the PAI Structural Summary (Morey, 1996), these configurations are organized around three sets of specific psychological issues: self-concept, interpersonal style, and perception of one's environment.

It is important to assess self-concept because the view that people have of themselves can play a critical role in determining their behavior. Three PAI subscales correspond to specific elements of self-concept that are often discussed in the literature: *self-esteem, self-efficacy,* and *identity stability.* The most direct measure of self-esteem on the PAI is the grandiosity subscale (MAN-G), with moderate scores suggesting healthy levels of self esteem, low scores suggesting limited self-esteem, and high scores suggesting potentially maladaptive grandiosity. The cognitive depression subscale (DEP-C) assesses self-efficacy, with low scorers feeling generally competent and high scorers feeling hopeless and helpless. Some individuals may have rapidly shifting views of their own worth or competence, whereas the self evaluations of others might be quite stable. The identity problems subscale (BOR-I) assesses *identity stability,* with high scorers having more variable self concepts which would thus also be more vulnerable to situational influences such as personal failure or disappointment.

Unlike most clinical assessment instruments, the PAI includes two interpersonal scales with psychometric properties consistent with normative traits (Morey & Glutting, 1994; Morey & Hopwood, 2006). The interpersonal scales provide a depiction of the respondent's interpersonal strategies and implied strengths and weaknesses. For example, a warm person is likely to be adept at forming and maintaining relationships, whereas a dominant person is likely to be effective at work, particularly if placed in a managerial role. These scales can also be used in combination to ascertain general interpersonal strategies and likely correlates. For example, a cold submissive person is more likely than individuals with other styles to present with depression or anxiety, and it is likely that they will view the clinician as responsible for therapeutic change (submissive) and approach therapy with some degree of mistrust (cold). Factors such as these alert the clinician to strengths and weaknesses and have direct treatment implications. For example, a clinician would be wise to appear to the cold and submissive person described above as competent, optimistic, and relatively concrete (i.e., complement the client's submissiveness with dominance), and to pay special attention to the pace of interventions so as to avoid pushing the client to expose their vulnerability too quickly (i.e., respect the client's caution in warming up) and thereby compromise the therapeutic alliance.

External factors, such as the respondent's perception of his or her environment, often play a very important role in behavior. Thus, the PAI includes two scales specifically designed to assess the respondent's perception of their environment. The STR scale provides an evaluation of life stressors that the respondent is currently or has recently experienced, such as those involving family, financial, or occupational difficulties. To the extent that individuals feel as though they have fewer psychological resources than are necessary to keep up with their rapidly changing environment, they will endorse items on the STR scale. The NON scale includes items that ask if the respondent's social environment is adequate to meet their personal needs. Low scores suggest individuals with available and supportive families and friends, whereas high scores suggest individuals who feel that those around them would be unavailable if needed. The combination of high STR and NON scores are particularly problematic, as this suggests a person with inadequate personal and social resources to meet the needs of their environment.

Other PAI scales may suggest specific strengths. For example, balanced validity scale indicators suggest a realistic perception of the respondent's internal and external environment. Mild to moderate elevations on the obsessive-compulsive subscale (ARD-O) scale indicates organizational capacity and conscientiousness. On some scales (e.g., psychotic experiences, SCZ-P), low scores are not interpretable apart from their not being high, whereas for others low scores may represent specific strengths. For example, low scores on MAN-I may indicate better than average frustration tolerance, low scores on the egocentricity subscale (ANT-E) scale suggest capacity for empathy, and low scores on the Sensation-Seeking subscale (ANT-S) suggest boredom tolerance. Low scores on the BOR scale suggests overall ego strength, and low scores on the self-harm and affective instability subscales (BOR-S, BOR-A) suggest capacity for impulse and affect regulation, respectively. Finally, moderately low scores on the RXR scale suggest a person who is open and committed to personal change, a positive sign for treatment.

Diagnostic Decision Making

Diagnostic decision making involves a complex array of clinical judgments and typically uses data from a variety of sources. Two sets of diagnostic decisions, the estimation of the degree of distortion in an individual's presentation and the derivation of psychiatric diagnoses, will be discussed in turn in the context of relevant PAI indicators.

Profile Validity

Research using simulation samples suggests varying validity scale cut scores across different settings and demand characteristics, and it is inappropriate to interpret validity scale scores without attending to the assessment context. However, research has also consistently revealed cut-score suggestions that are useful in most clinical assessments. Scores above $64T$ on ICN and/or $71T$ on INF indicate probable distortion that may have resulted from factors such as confusion, inattention, or reading difficulties, and suggest a cautious interpretation of other aspects of the profile. Scores at or above $73T$ for ICN and/or $75T$ for INF suggest marked nonsystematic distortion that would counterindicate interpretation.

Scores at or above $57T$ on PIM indicate prominent defensiveness or naïveté (Cashel et al., 1995; Morey & Lanier, 1998; Peebles & Moore, 1998), with marked distortion suggestive of invalidity at $68T$. Research suggests appropriate cut scores on the DEF of 5 ($64T$; Morey, & Lanier, 1998), and of CDF at 148 ($57T$; Morey & Lanier, 1998) in most samples. The combination of three positive dissimulation scales that vary in their relationship to psychopathology assists the examiner in teasing apart the relative effects of clinical issues and intentional faking when interpreting test data (Morey, 1996, 2003; Morey & Hopwood, 2007). For example, a profile in which PIM is elevated, DEF is moderate, and CDF is within normal limits suggests a defensive or naïve respondent. Conversely, elevation on all three indicators suggests intentional denial of psychological issues.

Scores above $84T$ on NIM generally indicate significant distortion, and scores above $92T$ suggest invalid profiles. Scores at or above 3 ($84T$) on the MAL suggest interpretive caution, as do RDF scores at or above 0.57 ($65T$; Morey & Lanier, 1998). As with indicators of positive dissimulation, the combination of negative dissimulation scales that vary in their relation to psychopathology allow for an analysis of the both the extent and nature of distortion. A profile in which NIM is elevated, MAL is moderate, and RDF is within normal limits suggests prominent negative distortion associated with the respondent's true psychological issues, as might be the case in an individual with borderline personality. Conversely, elevations across negative distortion indicators suggest purposeful feigning.

Two additional strategies have been designed to further assist the clinician in understanding the effects of dissimulation. The first involves a regression based prediction of the PAI profile based on the observed elevation of PIM or NIM alone and the correlations of these indicators with the other PAI scales observed in standardization studies. For example, in an exaggerated profile (NIM elevated, RDF within normal limits), an observed score on the DEP scale that is no higher than would be anticipated based on the NIM elevation may be related to a general exaggeration factor rather than a prominent clinical issue. Conversely, if DEP is significantly higher than the NIM predicted score, it may be concluded that depression represents an important diagnostic issue over and above exaggeration. Hopwood, Morey, Rogers, and Sewell (2007) developed a method to identify, in the case where negative distortion markers are elevated and malingering is suspected, which specific disorder the respondent is attempting to malinger. For example, if the observed score on DEP is much higher than the NIM predicted score on a profile where malingering is already suspected because of an RDF elevation, the clinician would infer that depression, and not other clinical problems, is likely being malingered.

A second strategy involves the comparison of an observed profile to a sample of individuals from the standardization studies with similar PIM or NIM elevations. For example, if a moderate elevation is observed on PIM, the PIM-specific profile can be interpreted in order to highlight elevations on the observed profile relative to similarly defensive/naïve respondents, allowing the clinician to note significant clinical issues in light of the respondent's reticence to report problems.

Indicators of positive dissimulation have also been developed specifically for the substance abuse scales (Fals-Stewart, 1996; Morey, 1996) in light of the fact that items on these scales are mostly face valid and can be faked relatively easily if respondents are motivated to misrepresent their substance use, a common concern among clinicians working with substance using populations. The ALC and DRG estimated scores involve regression-based predictions of substance use scales based on other scales commonly associated with this behavior. These scores can be compared to observed ALC and DRG scores on the PAI to estimate the degree of dissimulation regarding substance use.

Psychiatric Diagnosis

Several methods are available for deriving psychiatric diagnoses from the configuration of PAI scales. Because clinical scales typically correspond to specific diagnostic or symptomatic constructs, the most profound clinical scale elevation generally represents the most likely diagnosis or symptom. However, other methods using data from several aspects of the profile are also useful in suggesting, confirming, and disconfirming diagnostic hypotheses. Two diagnostic methods are available through the PAI scoring software. First, a coefficient of fit that represents the overall similarity of the observed profile to a mean profile for groups with a variety of common diagnoses and clinical issues in the standardization sample is provided. A second approach involves a logistic function based method in which the probability of a certain diagnosis is derived, based upon scores of individuals with that diagnosis in the standardization sample, and diagnostic hypotheses generated by these probabilities are provided in the automated report.

A final method for generating and ruling out diagnostic hypotheses involves the structural summary approach to PAI profile interpretation (Morey & Hopwood, 2007). In this approach, features of the PAI that map conceptually onto psychiatric (i.e., *DSM*) diagnoses are checked for relative elevations and suppressions on the profile. For example, Major Depressive Disorder is indicated by relative elevations on all three Depression subscales

(DEP-C, depressive cognitions; DEP-A, subjective sadness; and DEP-P, physical symptoms), the thought disorder (SCZ-T; concentration difficulties) and social withdrawal (SCZ-S; lack of interest) scales, and SUI, and relative suppressions on grandiosity (MAN-G; worthlessness) and activity (MAN-A; lethargy). Configural algorithms such as this have been provided for most common psychiatric diagnoses (Morey, 1996).

Treatment Planning and Progress

A variety of PAI indicators are useful for treatment planning in addition to diagnosis. For example, the assessment of risk to self can be one of the most important pieces of information emanating from a psychiatric evaluation. The SUI scale provides an indication of the degree to which the respondent is thinking about suicide, but the risk for self-harm is heightened by a variety of factors in addition to suicidal ideation. The PAI Suicide Potential Index (SPI) was developed to account for such factors as indicated by aspects of the profile in addition to SUI. The SPI comprises 20 PAI indicators that correspond to factors identified in the theoretical and empirical literature as related to risk for self-harm, such as mood fluctuations as represented by the BOR-A. The SPI scores of individuals who have been put on suicide precautions or had made a suicide or selfmutilating gesture tend to be above 9, whereas individuals in the community sample tend to have scores that are lower than 6 (Morey, 1996).

Another important issue in clinical evaluations involves the likelihood of risk to others. As with suicidality, risk for other harm is related to many factors in addition to aggressive ideation and behavior, which is measured most directly by the AGG scale. Thus, the Violence Potential Index (VPI) was developed in a manner similar to the SPI, again using 20 indicators from the PAI profile that correspond to risk factors identified in the literature, such as substance use (ALC, DRG). Standardization studies demonstrated that individuals from the community standardization sample tend to achieve VPI scores that are lower than 4, whereas individuals with violent histories score above 6 (Morey, 1996).

Two PAI indicators were developed to help the clinician predict the course of therapy. The first is the RXR scale. High scorers on RXR are likely to be resistant to the idea of personal change because they see their lives going basically as they would like, or, to the extent that this is not the case, they do not view themselves as responsible for their misfortune. A second indicator, the Treatment Process Index (TPI) is composed of several indicators from the PAI profile suggestive of a difficult therapy course, such as AGG. The higher the TPI score, the more likely therapy threatening issues such as noncompliance are likely to surface (Hopwood, Ambwani, & Morey, in press; Hopwood, Creech, Clark, Meagher, & Morey, in press). In addition to indicators of therapy process, a variety of recommendations are made in the PAI Interpretive Guide (Morey, 1996) regarding treatment length, type, and format.

Because the PAI provides a reliable assessment of a variety of diagnoses, it can be used to indicate change over the course of treatment. Given the reliability coefficients in the manual, T-score differences of 3-4 points or greater generally represent reliable change. The PAI has demonstrated sensitivity as an outcome measure in several research projects that are discussed below.

Research Findings

Diagnostic Utility

Research regarding the PAI validity scales has been discussed in some detail above, as have the properties and correlates of other scales observed in the initial validation studies. The purpose of the current section is to discuss postvalidation research that has been conducted on the clinical, treatment consideration, and interpersonal scales, and supplemental indices of the PAI.

A great deal of research has been conducted on the utility of PAI scales to predict neurotic level diagnoses and related phenomena, as assessed by the SOM, ANX, ARD, and DEP scales. SOM tends to be the highest average PAI elevation in medical samples (Osborne, 1994; Karlin et al., 2005 Keeley et al., 2000), and are likely to be particularly high among individuals seeking workers compensation (Ambroz, 2005. Keeley et al. (2000) reported that SOM was significantly higher among individuals who did not adhere to antidepressant treatment due to side effects (80.8T, SD = 7.1) than those who did (65.2T, SD = 12.4) in a family medical center sample, suggesting the potential utility of SOM in decisions regarding the use of psychotropic medication. Research also suggests that SOM elevations may indicate an exaggerated representation of physical difficulties, particularly if those elevations are observed on the Conversion (SOM-C) subscale. For example, Rogers, Flores, Ustad, and Sewell (1995) observed that this SOM-C significantly distinguished individuals instructed to simulate factitious and malingering profiles related to medical disabilities from controls (Cohen's d = 1.31 for dependent factitious group, 1.76 for demanding factitious group, and 1.98 for malingering group). Wagner et al. (2005) observed that SOM-C effectively distinguished individuals with epileptic (mean = 65.5T) vs. nonepileptic (i.e., conversion; mean = 77.3T) seizure disorders, an effect also obtained by Mason, Doss, & Gates (2000). The Wagner et al. (2005) study reported that a simple rule, where SOM-C > SOM-H was suggestive of nonepileptic seizures, demonstrated an 84% sensitivity and 73.3% specificity for the identification of nonepileptic seizures.

Research findings regarding the ANX scale reflect the broad range of clinical phenomena associated with anxiety. For example, as was observed in the validation studies, ANX is among the strongest PAI correlates of Neuroticism (Costa & McCrae, 1992; $r = .63$). This scale has also been found to relate significantly to indices of anxiety sensitivity (Plehn, Peterson, & Williams, 1998), acculturative stress (Hovey & Magana, 2002), dissociation (Briere, Weathers, & Runtz, 2005), and sexual dysfunction (Bartoi, Kinder, & Tomianovic, 2000. Woods, Wetterneck, and Flessner (2006) reported that individuals with trichotillomania treated with 10 sessions of Acceptance and Commitment Therapy experienced an 8% decrease in ANX scores (from 63.8T to 58.3T) that remained at 3-month follow up (57.2T), whereas there was an average increase in ANX scores for a wait-list control group, suggesting the utility of ANX as an outcome measure. The configuration of ANX subscales may also be helpful in the selection of treatments for individuals with anxiety symptoms. For example, scores on the physiological (ANX-P) subscale is associated with greater levels of medication compliance among individuals taking anti-anxiety medications (Oswald, Roache, & Rhoades, 1999).

The ARD scale has been studied for a variety of applications, with much of this research focusing on the traumatic distress (ARD-T) subscale. As anticipated, ARD-T tends to elevate among individuals both diagnosed with and instructed to malinger posttraumatic stress disorder (PTSD). Liljequist, Kinder, and Schinka (1998) found the average PTSD group score on ARD-T was 77T in an inpatient setting (diagnoses were assigned according to DSM criteria based on all information at intake and confirmed at discharge). Similar results were obtained by McDevitt-Murphy, Weathers, Adkins, and Daniels (2005) in a sample of adult women from the community. ARD-T has been found to differentiate women psychiatric patients who were victims of childhood abuse from other women patients who did not experience such abuse (Cherepon & Prinzhorn, 1994; abused mean = 77T, nonabused mean = 65T) and PTSD (mean = 62.2T) from ASD (50.8T) among individuals traumatized in motor vehicle accidents (Holmes, Williams, & Haines, 2001).

The DEP scale has been shown to be strongly related to other depression measures in postvalidation studies (e.g., Mascaro, Rosen, & Morey, 2004; Romain, 2000). Keeley et al. (2000) demonstrated its utility as an outcome measure: in their study DEP was sensitive to the effects of a 14-week course of antidepressant treatment, differing on average by 8.6T in adults sampled in a family medical center. Consistent with commonly observed relationships between depression and other difficulties, Keiski et al. (2003) showed that individuals with DEP elevations tend to do poorly on memory tasks, and Freeman (1998) found that DEP was related to sleep problems.

Several studies have investigated the diagnostic utility of the PAI in the assessment of psychotic disorders. Douglas, Hart, and Kropp (2001) found that a model including the SCZ-S and MAN-G scales significantly differentiated psychotic from nonpsychotic men in a forensic sample. The MAN, PAR, and SCZ scales have been found to correlate well with diagnostic assessments of psychotic disorders made via structured clinical interview (Rogers, Ustad, & Salekin, 1998: MAN = .31 with interview diagnosed mania, PAR = .53 with paranoia, SCZ = .46 with schizophrenia). PAR scores are also related to a variety of psychotic behaviors. For example, Gay and Combs (2005) showed that individuals with persecutory delusions scored higher on the persecution scale (PAR-P; mean = 75T) than did individuals without such delusions (60T). Combs and Penn (2004) demonstrated individuals with relatively high PAR scores (mean = 62T) performed poorly on an emotion perception task, sat further away from the examiner, and took longer to read the research consent forms than individuals with low PAR scores (44T). The SCZ scale has been found to be related to the Rorschach Schizophrenia Index in an inpatient sample (Klonsky, 2004; r = .42). SCZ was also found capable of distinguishing schizophrenic patients from non-psychotic patient controls in that sample, with respective mean T-scores of 77 and 59.

Both the BOR and ANT scales have been found to relate to other measures of these constructs as well as to predict relevant behavioral outcomes (e.g., Jacobo, Blais, Baity, & Harley, 2007; Salekin, Rogers, Ustad, & Sewell, 1998; Stein, Pinsker-Aspen, & Hillsenroth, 2007; Trull, Useda, Conforti, & Doan, 1997). Salekin, Rogers, and Sewell (1997) found that BOR correlated .60 with an interview based diagnosis of borderline personality disorder, and the BOR scale in isolation has been found to distinguish borderline patients from unscreened controls with an 80% hit rate, and successfully identified 91% of these subjects as part of a discriminant function (Bell-Pringle, Pate, & Brown, 1997). Classifications based upon the BOR scale have been validated in a variety of domains related to borderline functioning, including depression, personality traits, coping, Axis I disorders, and interpersonal problems (Trull, 1995). These BOR scale classifications were found to be predictive of 2-year outcome on academic indexes in college students, even controlling for academic potential and diagnoses of substance abuse (Trull et al., 1997. Salekin et al. (1997) examined the relationship between ANT and psychopathic traits in a sample of female offenders and found that elevations on ANT among this population were primarily the result of endorsements on the antisocial behaviors (ANT-A) subscale. Also, support was found for the convergent validity of ANT with other measures including the revised Psychopathy Checklist (PCL-R, Hare, 1991), Total score (r = .53) and the Personality Disorder Examination (Loranger, 1988) Antisocial scale (r = .78). In a similar study, Edens, Hart, Johnson, Johnson, & Olver (2000) demonstrated moderately strong relationships of the ANT scale to the screening version of the Psychopathy Checklist (PCL:SV; Hart, Cox, & Hare, 1995; r = .54) and the PCL-R (r = .40).

The ALC scale has been found to differentiate patients in an alcohol rehabilitation clinic from patients with schizophrenia (Boyle & Lennon, 1994) as well as normal controls (Ruiz, Dickinson, & Pincus, 2002). In the latter sample, T-scores near 80 provided optimal cut scores for predicting diagnostically significant alcohol related problems. The DRG scale has also been found to effectively discriminate drug abusers (Kellogg et al., 2002; mean = 82T) and methadone maintenance patients (Alterman et al., 1995; mean = 84T) from general clinical and community samples. As discussed above, empirically derived procedures to assess the likelihood that a profile underrepresents the extent of alcohol or drug problems that exist to assist the examiner in interpreting these scales (Fals-Stewart, 1996; Morey, 1996).

Treatment Planning and Progress

Several issues related to treatment planning and progress have been investigated using the PAI, including risk for violence to self or others, treatment amenability, and treatment outcome. The SUI scale and SPI have demonstrated strong correlations with other indicators of suicidality (DeMaio, Holdwick, & Withers, 1998), and have demonstrated an association with suicidal behaviors in a correctional setting (Wang et al., 1997). More research has been conducted on aggressive behavior. For example, the WRM and PAR scales were found to be related to self-destructive behavior in a sample of inpatients diagnosed with borderline personality disorder (Yeomans, Hull, & Clarkin, 1994; r = -.41, .41, respectively). The ANT scale has also demonstrated validity in predicting violence in a sample of incarcerated mentally ill individuals (Wang & Diamond, 1999), and in predicting treatment course for women with borderline personality (Clarkin, Hull, Yeomans, Kakuma, & Cantor, 1994). As expected, the AGG scale has been found to be related to a variety of Rorschach indicators of aggression in a nonclinical sample (Mihura, Nathan-Montano, & Alperin, 2003). Salekin et al. (1998) investigated the ability of the ANT and AGG scales of the PAI to predict recidivism among women inmates over a 14-month follow-up interval. Findings indicated that both were significantly related to recidivism (r = .27, .29, respectively). Caperton, Edens, & Johnson (2004) demonstrated that ANT and AGG significantly predicted both aggressive and nonaggressive infractions among incarcerated men, and that the VPI predicted aggressive infractions. In the same study, the RXR scale was modestly effective at predicting treatment noncompliance. Recent research in outpatient psychotherapy (Hopwood et al., in press) and chronic pain (Hopwood et al., in press) samples suggests that the TPI, a supplemental index developed using a strategy similar to that of SPI and VPI, is a reliable predictor of treatment non-compliance, but that this is the particularly the case when RXR suggests the client/patient is appropriately motivated for change.

Cross-Cultural Considerations

Cultural considerations can affect the interpretation of PAI scales among English speakers and readers from diverse ethnic backgrounds or among individuals who take a translated version of the test. With respect to the former, strategies to avoid retaining biased items were discussed above. Validation studies suggested that differences in PAI scores attributable to race are generally less than or equal to the standard error of measurement for a given scale. The PAR may represent one important exception, as African Americans tend to score roughly 7 T higher than Caucasians. It is important to remember that such a difference in isolation does not constitute bias. African Americans continue to experience prejudice, and it is therefore not surprising if, as a group, they tend to maintain a vigilant stance and to experience feelings of being treated unjustly, as would be indicated by a modest PAR elevation. Bias would be indicated by varying relations of PAI scales to criteria as a function of race, a finding that has not been demonstrated. As such, available data suggest that the English version PAI is appropriate for use for English speaking individuals regardless of cultural background, insofar as all individuals are anticipated to share the potential to experience any of the phenomena tapped by PAI scales. Nevertheless, there are occasions where it may be useful to make comparisons with reference to particular groups. Thus, the raw score means and standard deviations needed to convert raw scores to T-scores with reference to normative data from particular subsamples, including various ethnic groups, are provided in the manual for this purpose. However, for most clinical and research applications, the use of T-scores derived from the full normative data is recommended because of its representativeness and larger sample size.

The PAI has been translated into several languages, and studies generally indicate similar psychometric properties across translations. For example, Rogers et al. (1995) compared English and Spanish versions of the PAI among a group of bilingual outpatients, and concluded that the clinical scales have "moderate to good correspondence from English to Spanish versions, generally good stability for the Spanish version, and modest to good internal consistency. . ." (p. 346). These investigators also point out that, as with any translation, the utility of the PAI among non-English speakers is most directly assessed by examining correlates, and a number of studies provide such correlates for different translations (e.g., Fantoni-Salvador & Rogers, 1997; Groves & Engel, 2007; Gryzwacz et al., 2006; Hovey & Magana, 2002 Montag & Levin, 1994).

Current Controversies

The PAI has been subject to some controversy in its history, with particular debates regarding the invariance of PAI factor structure and the operating

Key Points to Remember

- The PAI has 344 items answered on a 4-point scale that load onto 22 nonoverlapping scales representing constructs related to profile validity, clinical diagnoses, treatment consideration issues, and interpersonal style.
- The PAI was developed based on a construct validation strategy that employs theory to guide the selection of representative constructs and items, and contemporary empirical methods to test the operating characteristics of items and scales.
- PAI scales are named for the constructs they represent, the test is relatively brief despite having nonoverlapping scales, and items are written at a fairly low reading level, all of which facilitate administration and interpretation.
- Of central concern throughout development was the consideration of multiple psychometric indicators. This concern avoided maximizing a single indicator at the expense of many others, and yielded an instrument with relatively strong content and discriminant validity, which are essential characteristics of any method used for psychological assessment.
- The configuration of PAI validity scales allows for an assessment of (a) type (nonsystematic, negative, positive), and (b) quality (intentional or unintentional) of distortion.
- Several methods have been developed for facilitating the interpretation of distorted profiles, including the NIM/PIM Predicted and Specific methods.
- Several methods have been developed for testing diagnostic hypotheses, including coefficients of fit with known clinical groups, logistic functions which estimate the probability of a given respondent having a certain disorder, and conceptual algorithms designed to map commonly observed diagnostic criteria.
- The PAI includes a variety of scales and supplemental indexes designed to facilitate treatment planning by assessing factors in addition to profile validity and diagnosis, such as risk to self or others, perception of environment, treatment amenability, and interpersonal style.
- Three software packages have been developed for the PAI to be used in clinical, correctional personnel selection, and forensic setting, and norms and translations are available for use with several other groups.

characteristics of validity scales across samples that vary in terms of prominent psychological issues.

PAI Factor Structure

Morey (1991) conducted an exploratory factor analysis with orthogonal factor rotation using the 11 clinical scales and the 22 full scales in both clinical and community standardization samples as part of the initial validation of the PAI. Results across these analyses generally converged in suggesting three factors. The first factor across all analyses involved subjective distress and affective disruption (e.g., large positive factor weights for DEP, ANX, ARD, BOR, SCZ); the second factor involved behavioral acting out, impulsivity, and poor judgment (e.g., ANT, ALC, DRG); and the third factor involved egocentricity and exploitativeness (e.g., MAN, ANT, DOM). A fourth factor emerged only in the analyses of 22 full scales, and appeared to differ across groups. For the clinical sample, this factor appeared to involve profile validity, with large weights for the ICN and INF scales. For the community sample, this factor appears to have captured variability in social detachment and interpersonal sensitivity, with large weights for NON, SCZ, PAR, and (–) WRM.

Boyle and Lennon (1994) published the results of an exploratory factor analysis with an oblique rotation from a sample composed of community controls and alcoholic and schizophrenic inpatients as well as the correlation matrices reported in the PAI manual, and noted a lack of convergence with the results from Morey (1991). As noted in Morey (1995), the Boyle and Lennon (1994) analysis utilized different extraction and rotation methods than had been used in Morey's original analysis, which undoubtedly contributed to differences in results. Morey (1995) also argued that the use of factor analysis to test the structural validity of the PAI is of limited theoretical relevance because, unlike other instruments (e.g., MCMI-III), the PAI scales do not represent an operationalization of an internally coherent theory of psychopathology. Rather, like the scales of the MMPI-2 or diagnoses of the *DSM-IV*, the PAI scales represent a set of constructs whose inclusion on the instrument was not based on interrelationships but on perceived clinical relevance. Validity from a construct validation framework is tested by an investigation of relationships between PAI scales and external indicators, not relationships among PAI scales (this criticism does not apply to the confirmatory factor analysis of items to test the theoretical structure of subscale–full scale relationships, see Morey, 1995).

Subsequent factor analyses of PAI scales in community (Deisinger, 1995) and clinical samples (Demakis et al., 2005; Karlin et al., 2005) have demonstrated results that are similar to those reported in the manual. Hoelzle, Farrer, Meyer, and Mihura (2006) reanalyzed data from several previous samples as well as their own clinical data, using extraction methods thought to provide more stable solutions than principal components or principal factor extraction (i.e., parallel analysis, minimum average partial), and concluded that: (a) Common retention criteria such as the screen test or Kaiser's rule lead to overextraction of unreliable factors (i.e., retention of factors that are unlikely to generalize to new samples); (b) contemporary extraction methods consistently yield three factors (they named these factors distress, energetic dominance, and aggressive impulsivity); and (c) a fourth factor is likely to emerge in certain samples that is specific to salient issues within that sample. Thus, it might be anticipated that a somatic factor would emerge in a pain sample, a confusion factor in a neuropsychiatric sample, or a sociability factor in a community sample.

Three important points can be gleaned from factor analytic investigations of PAI scales. First, based on the theory of test construction employed in developing the instrument, factor analysis cannot be considered a validation technique. Instead, it is best thought of as a method for understanding the relationship between variables relevant to psychopathology and personality, and how those relationships might change across samples. Second, the results of factor analytic work depend largely on extraction and rotation methods. To the extent that variability in methodological factors is anticipated to yield varying results, extracted factors should be interpreted with caution and in light of the methods by which they were generated. Third, with respect to the PAI, evidence from analyses of PAI scales across several samples suggests that three robust factors are obtained, as well as specific factors with meaning that is somewhat specific to the sample from which data were drawn.

The Efficiency of Negative Dissimulation Indicators in Forensic Samples

The PAI negative dissimulation indicators have generally fared well in comparative studies with other instruments (e.g., Blanchard et al., 2003; LePage & Mogge, 2001). As discussed above, the RDF has the unique characteristic among negative dissimulation indicators of not correlating with clinical scales. This implies the important possibility that the RDF could provide an estimate of malingering that is not influenced by negative response sets that are associated with psychopathology, and, thus, be more specific than such indicators. However, Rogers, Sewell et al. (1998) cautioned against use of the RDF in forensic samples because it performed poorly in discriminating between groups identified as malingering based on the Structured Interview of Reported Symptoms (SIRS; Rogers, Bagby, & Dickens, 1992). However, because the SIRS scales, like the PAI MAL, NIM scale, and most negative dissimulation indicators, may correlate with psychopathology, another possible interpretation of the data involves the validity of the SIRS-based classification in the Rogers et al. data.

Edens, Poythress, and Watkins-Clay (2007) tested the ability of the PAI validity indicators and the SIRS to distinguish (a) forensic inmates judged to be free of mental disorder and (b) prison inmates diagnosed with mental disorder from (c) individuals from a forensic setting instructed to malinger and (d) individuals suspected by forensic psychiatrists to be malingering. They observed that NIM, MAL, and SIRS correlated strongly with one another and with clinical scales of the PAI, whereas the RDF correlated modestly with these indicators and nonsignificantly with PAI clinical scales. This is consistent with the Rogers, Sewell, et al. (1998) demonstration of higher agreement between MAL, NIM and the SIRS than is observed between those

Important References

Edens, J. F., Poythress, N. G., & Watkins-Clay, M. M. (2007). Detection of malingering in psychiatric unit and general population prison inmates: A comparison of the PAI, SIMS, and SIRS. *Journal of Personality Assessment, 88*(1), 33–42.
This study demonstrated the unique ability of the Rogers Discriminant Function to detect malingering among individuals with relatively severe psychopathology.

Morey, L. C. (2003). *Essentials of PAI Assessment.* New York: John Wiley.
This book provides a thorough review of PAI development and detailed discussion of clinical applications of the instrument in a reader friendly format.

Peebles, J., & Moore, R. J. (1998). Detecting socially desirable responding with the Personality Assessment Inventory: The Positive Impression Management Scale and the Defensiveness Index. *Journal of Clinical Psychology, 54,* 621–628.
This study provided important information about the operating characteristics of PAI defensiveness indicators.

Rogers, R., Sewell, K. W., Morey, L. C., & Ustad, K. L. (1996). Detection of feigned mental disorders on the Personality Assessment Inventory: A discriminant analysis. *Journal of Personality Assessment, 67,* 629–640.
This article tested the capacity of PAI negative impression indicators to detect malingering, and developed and cross-validated the Rogers Discriminant Function to supplement existing validity indicators for that purpose.

Trull, T. J., Useda, J. D., Conforti, K., & Doan, B. T. (1997). Borderline personality disorder features in nonclinical young adults: 2. Two-year outcome. *Journal of Abnormal Psychology, 106,* 307–314.
This study demonstrated the predictive validity of the Borderline Features scale in the prediction of academic and psychosocial outcomes, even after controlling a host of other potentially important variables such as Axis I and II disorders and GPA.

indicators and RDF, and further suggests the possibility that the former indicators, due to their association with psychiatric disorders, may tend to misclassify individuals when attempting to discriminate patients from malingerers. To test this hypothesis, they compared the predictive accuracy of validity indicators when discriminations were between malingerers and clinical as well as nonclinical comparison groups, and found that rates were worse when the comparison group manifested clinical disorder for every indicator other than the RDF. Indeed, only the RDF and MAL (and not NIM or the SIRS) achieved statistically significant Areas Under the Curve (.64, .65, respectively) in discriminating staff-suspected malingerers from forensic clinical patients. Nevertheless, regression analyses suggested that the SIRS incremented the PAI indicators, including RDF, in making discriminations in the entire sample, suggesting that structured interview methods may increment the PAI in determining the validity of reported data.

Case Vignette

Andrea was a 30-year-old European American woman who worked as a massage therapist in a medium-sized Midwestern town in which she was raised with her older brother, 5 years her senior, by both of her parents. She noted that, although the family kept appearances as healthy and stable, life inside the household was characterized by hostile mistrust and manipulation. Her brother was often in trouble, at first at school and eventually in the legal system, and Andrea viewed her parents as somewhat naïve to their son's behavior, describing him to others as bright and talented and quickly forgiving him for bad behavior. When Andrea was in junior high school, she caught her brother, in high school at the time, stealing money from her. Later, her friend became very upset when Andrea's brother unsuccessfully attempted to force sexual behavior, and subsequently spread malicious rumors about Andrea at school. Andrea described her parents' response to these and others similar incidents as dismissive. Andrea was expected to forgive her brother for his various transgressions, and to be perpetually available to support him. She enacted this role throughout childhood and into adulthood. When her brother had a daughter for whom he could not care because he and the child's mother were addicted to methamphetamine, she adopted her. Several times Andrea invited her brother to live at her home during his efforts at rehabilitation, and had often loaned him money; he had never repaid her any debts, and several times he stole money from her or took advantage in other ways.

Andrea had married about 2 years before presenting for therapy to an unemployed man roughly her age. She reported that this relationship provided additional stress, because he spent a great deal of time and money at a local bar, even though she explicitly requested that he discontinue this behavior when they married. She reported that, when asked, her husband denied being at the bar, but made little effort to conceal his behavior, and became angry and dismissive when presented with tangible proof of his having lied. As a result, Andrea reported being increasingly mistrustful of him, and also reported that his drinking habit coupled with unemployment had become exceedingly expensive.

About two months before presenting for therapy, Andrea's brother again had requested to stay with her during a course of outpatient rehabilitation, and she suspected that when he used her credit cards to buy several expensive items without her consent he was under the influence of methamphetamine. When she threatened to call the police if he did not leave her home, her brother told her parents that Andrea had "abandoned" him, and they threatened to disown her if she did not take care of him. This experience appears to have consolidated a variety of patterns in her life, and was quite upsetting to her. She described herself as becoming very depressed, and "questioning everything." She said she felt like "running away, from my husband, my brother, and my family, and finding myself." However, she also reported some ambivalence, saying "If I can't make it work with my family, I'll never make anything work."

Andrea impressed her therapist as intelligent, attractive, empathic, and genuinely motivated for personal change. They conducted a collaborative therapeutic assessment (Finn & Tonsager, 1992), which involved using client generated questions for direct treatment effects and to facilitate the therapeutic alliance (see chapter 10). Andrea posed three questions for the PAI: (a) Why am I not a social person; (b) why or how am I so different than my brother; and (c) could my life have been different if I had set different standards for myself? The remainder of this vignette will address profile validity, suggest how PAI data (depicted in Figure 5.1 and Table 5.3) could assist the therapist in framing answers to Andrea's questions, and infer diagnostic hypotheses and treatment recommendations.

The validity scales suggested that Andrea attended to item content and responded in a coherent manner (ICN, INF). The NIM scale was moderately elevated, raising the possibility of negative distortion. MAL and RDF were within normal limits, suggesting that the NIM elevation reflected exaggeration associated with a generally negative and pessimistic outlook on life rather than intentional malingering. Given no other indications of positive dissimulation (PIM, DEF, ALC and DRG Estimated Scores, apparent lack of motivation), the moderate elevation and CDF could be treated as anomalous. As discussed above, the NIM Predicted Method (obtained through the PAI Interpretive Software or the Structural Summary Form) could be used to

Table 5.3 PAI Suplemental Indices and Coefficients of Profile Fit for Andrea at Intake and 3-month Follow Up.

Supplemental Indexes	Raw	T
Defensiveness Index (DEF)	1	38
Cashel Discriminant Function (CDF)	169.06	71
Malingering Index (MAL)	0	44
Rogers Discriminant Function (RDF)	−1.56	45
Suicide Potential Index (SPI)	10	71
Violence Potential Index (VPI)	5	66
Treatment Process Index (TPI)	3	60
ALC Estimated Score		48
DRG Estimated Score		44
Mean Clinical Elevation		59
Coefficients of Profile Fit	0.719	
Schizophrenia	0.673	
Paranoid Delusions	0.630	
Anxiety Disorder	0.610	
Major Depressive Disorder	0.609	
Posttraumatic Stress Disorder	0.609	
Borderline Personality Disorder		

enhance the interpretability of a profile in which some negative exaggeration is operating. This method estimated the scale scores on the profile based on the correlations of those scales to the NIM profile observed in the standardization sample, and facilitates an investigation of clinical issues in relation to these estimates. On Andrea's profile, several clinical issues appeared to be salient even after accounting for her NIM score, including rumination (ANX-C), orderliness (ARD-O), activity (MAN-A), self-regard (MAN-G), mistrust (PAR-H), feelings of persecution (PAR-P), social withdrawal (SCZ-S), cognitive disorganization (SCZ-T), affective liability (BOR-A), identity inconsistency (BOR-I), chaotic relationships (BOR-N), coldness (WRM), and submissiveness (DOM). Conversely, several scale elevations were attributable to her negative perceptual style, including depression (DEP), anxiety (ANX, ARD), suicidality (SUI), stress (STR), and inadequacy of her social environment (NON). The profile indicated no significant problems in the areas of health (SOM), antisocial practices or empathy (ANT), or substance use (ALC, DRG) and suggested appropriate motivation for treatment (RXR). These data were used to assist Andrea and her therapist to answer her questions about herself, as described below.

Why Am I Not a Social Person?

PAI data were consistent with Andrea's belief that she was not a social person (SCZ-S, WRM), and that this represented one of her most pressing problems. It does not appear that she was particularly fearful of or anxious about interactions with others (ARD-P), and given her loneliness and desire for companionship (NON), it may have been a little difficult for her to understand why she was not more socially active. One factor may have involved her difficulty trusting others (PAR-H), which was understandable given her history. Her skepticism of others' motivations may have gone so far as perceiving others as actively blocking personal opportunities to live a better life (PAR-P), as was the case with her brother recently. She valued herself (MAN-G), and had a strong capacity to be empathic with others (ANT-E), which suggested simultaneous counter-motivations to protect her own interests and to help her brother. The resulting conflict may have been compounded by her parents' chronic message that the latter choice would also win their approval, if only temporarily. Given her tendency to mistrust others, and to the extent that friendships with others who provided tangible evidence that they can be trusted may help her achieve her personal goals, developing such friendships would probably be an important treatment goal. These factors also alerted the therapist to the delicacy and importance of the therapeutic relationship.

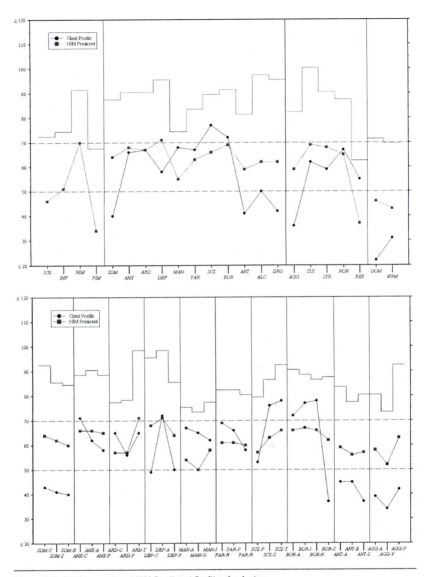

Figure 5.1 PAI Observed and NIM Predicted Profiles for Andrea.

Why or How Am I so Different Than My Brother?

Andrea described her brother as impulsive, angry, and manipulative, and noted his extensive history of drug use and criminal activity. Her data suggested that his cardinal characteristics do not apply to her (BOR-S, AGG,

ANT-E, ALC, DRG, and ANT-A, respectively). Perhaps one key to understanding differences between Andrea's brother and herself involved their respective roles in their family system. She reported that her parents viewed her brother as intelligent, and appeared to have invested a great deal of hope in his success, so it is understandable, although not necessarily defensible, that they would excuse his bad behavior and expect her to do the same. He apparently never had to answer for his indiscretions, which became more malicious over time. Andrea was rewarded for her passive (DOM) and supportive (ANT-E) role relative to her brother with her parents' approval, and in the end, she appeared to have compromised between her need for approval (NON, BOR-I) and distrust of others (PAR, BOR-N) with interpersonal distance (WRM, SCZ-S). The examiner could use such a description of her developmental role to help Andrea understand her parents' recent and hurtful reaction to her assertion of greater levels of independence and her similarly passive role with respect to her husband. Developing ways to be assertive that Andrea could be comfortable with would appear to have been an important treatment goal.

Could My Life Have Been Different if I Had Set Different Standards for Myself?

Andrea reported being fairly active (MAN-A) and organized (ARD-O); she successfully ran a business that supported her, her niece, her unemployed husband and his drinking habit, and, occasionally, her brother. She appeared to have been waiting for some time to stand up to her family, and had finally had enough. The stress in her life had reached a nearly debilitating level, and she was sad (DEP-A), disorganized (SCZ-T), and ruminative (ANX-C) most of the time. Data suggested that her distress had become so salient for her that she felt unable to control her emotions at times (BOR-A) and had a somewhat variable self-concept (BOR-I). Her developmental adaptation to her family system appeared to have involved being competent and supportive for others while at the same time protecting herself from the inevitable emotional insults inherent in that role. This question, which no doubt emanated from genuine curiosity about her role in her current problems, reflected her tendency to internalize and take responsibility for others' behavior. This tendency could be used therapeutically in that Andrea's capacity to accept responsibility for her own behavior would be anticipated and could be used to maintain the motivation necessary for her to make the difficult personal changes that psychotherapy required. More specifically, this question could be used to demonstrate to Andrea during feedback her willingness to take responsibility for the behaviors of others that is out of her control, to the detriment of her own well being.

Based on results from their collaborative assessment, Andrea and her therapist committed to a treatment aimed at increasing her assertiveness, establishing clear boundaries with family members, developing the capacity to differentiate those that could be trusted from those that could not, reducing her negative affect, and clarifying future goals. The PAI data alerted the therapist to Andrea's sensitivity and mistrust as well as her tendency to take a passive interpersonal stance and to internalize blame. Based on these observations, Andrea was referred for medication evaluation for mood symptoms, and the therapist began the treatment with manualized assertiveness training, a technique that was highly structured and which, initially, was directive, but which slowly required the client to take a more active role. In addition, the therapist noted special attention to regularly checking in with Andrea regarding their relationship, with the expectation that Andrea may involve therapist in a recapitulation of developmental patterns established with her abusive father, dismissive mother, or manipulative brother and husband.

The following questions have been designed to facilitate deeper thinking and understanding of this case: How did the clinician determine that this profile was valid, and that any distortion that was present was due to exaggeration and not intentional faking? What options other than the NIM Predicted method chosen by this evaluator might you use to disentangle the effects of subjective response style from objective clinical issues in this case? What do the scores on RXR and TPI as well as the configuration of her treatment consideration and interpersonal scales suggest about Andrea's approach to psychological treatment? Based on data from the PAI profile, do you agree with the treatment decisions made by Andrea and her therapist? Why or why not?

Chapter Summary

The Personality Assessment Inventory is a 344 item self-report instrument whose items are answered on a 4-point scale and comprise 22 nonoverlapping scales that measure constructs related to profile validity, psychiatric diagnoses, treatment related issues, and interpersonal style. The primary strengths of the PAI relative to similar instruments involve its ease of administration and interpretation due to the combined use of theory and contemporary empirical methods in constructing and evaluating its scales. In particular, the PAI is notable for its content and discriminant validity and its ability to capture both the depth and breadth of measured constructs despite being relatively brief and having no overlapping scales. Interpretation benefits from scales that were chosen and named to reflect the constructs psychological evaluators are typically interested in measuring in various contexts, such as clinical, correctional, and personnel selection settings. Validity indicators on the PAI augment the decision making processes of clinicians endeavoring to assess the degree of nonsystematic versus systematic, and negative versus positive, response distortion that is likely to affect other scales on the profile. Finally, several scales are provided in addition to those measuring response style and diagnosis which may be important for treatment planning, such as risk for aggression to self or others, interpersonal style, and the respondent's perception of his or her environment.

References

Alterman, A. I., Zaballero, A. R., Lin, M. M., Siddiqui, N., Brown, L. S., Rutherford, M. J., & McDermott, P. A. (1995). Personality Assessment Inventory (PAI) scores of lower-socioeconomic African American and Latino methadone maintenance patients. *Assessment, 2,* 91–100.

Ambroz, A. (2005). Psychiatric disorders in disabled chronic low back pain workers' Compensation compensation claimants. Utility of the Personality Assessment Inventory [abstract]. *Pain Medicine, 6,* 190.

Baer, R. A., & Wetter, M. W. (1997). Effects of information about validity scales on underreporting of symptoms on the Personality Assessment Inventory. *Journal of Personality Assessment, 68,* 402–413.

Bagby, R. M., Nicholson, R. A., Bacchiochi, J. R., Ryder, A. G., & Bury, A.S. (2002). The predictive capacity of the MMPI-2 and PAI validity scales and indexes to detect coached and uncoached feigning. *Journal of Personality Assessment, 78,* 69–86.

Bartoi, M. G., Kinder, B. N., & Tomianovic, D. (2000). Interaction effects of emotional status and sexual abuse on adult sexuality. *Journal of Sex and Marital Therapy, 26,* 1–23.

Beck, A. T., & Steer, R. A. (1987a). *Beck Depression Inventory Manual.* San Antonio, TX: The Psychological Corporation.

Beck, A. T., & Steer, R. A. (1987b). *Beck Hopelessness Scale Manual.* San Antonio, TX: The Psychological Corporation.

Bell-Pringle, V. J., Pate, J. L., & Brown, R. C. (1997). Assessment of borderline personality disorder using the MMPI-2 and the Personality Assessment Inventory. *Assessment, 4,* 131–139.

Belter, R. W., & Piotrowski, C. (2001). Current status of doctoral-level training in psychological testing. *Journal of Clinical Psychology, 57,* 717–726.

Blanchard, D. D., McGrath, R. E., Pogge, D. L., & Khadivi, A. (2003). A comparison of the PAI and MMPI-2 as predictors of faking bad in college students. *Journal of Personality Assessment, 80*(2), 197-205.

Boyle, G. J., & Lennon, T. (1994) Examination of the reliability and validity of the Personality Assessment Inventory. *Journal of Psychopathology & Behavioral. Assessment, 16,* 173–187.

Briere, J., Weathers, F. W., & Runtz, M. (2005). Is dissociation a multidimensional construct? Data from the Multiscale Dissociation Inventory. *Journal of Traumatic Stress, 18,* 221-231.

Bruce, D. R., & Dean, J. C. (2002). Predictive value of the Personality Assessment Inventory (Conversion subscale) for non-epileptic seizures vs. alcohol patch induction using closed circuit video-EEG [Abstract]. *Epilepsia, 43,* 158.

Campbell, D. T., & Fiske, D. W. (1959). Convergent and discriminant validation by the multitrait-multimethod matrix. *Psychological Bulletin, 56,* 81–105.

Caperton, J. D., Edens, J. F., & Johnson, J. K, (2004). Predicting sex offender institutional adjustment and treatment compliance using the Personality Assessment Inventory. *Psychological Assessment, 16,* 187–191.

Cashel, M. L., Rogers, R., Sewell, K., & Martin-Cannici, C. (1995). The Personality Assessment Inventory and the detection of defensiveness. *Assessment, 2,* 333–342.

Cherepon, J. A., & Prinzhorn, B. (1994). The Personality Assessment Inventory (PAI) profiles of adult female abuse survivors. *Assessment, 1,* 393–400.

Clark, M. E., Gironda, R. J., & Young, R. W. (2003). Detection of back random responding: Effectiveness of MMPI-2 and Personality Assessment Inventory validity indices. *Psychological Assessment, 15,* 223-234.

Clarkin, J. F., Hull, J., Yeomans, F., Kakuma, T., & Cantor, J. (1994). Antisocial traits as modifiers of treatment response in borderline patients. *Journal of Psychotherapy Practice and Research, 3,* 307–312.

Combs, D. R., & Penn, D. L. (2004). The role of subclinical paranoia on social perception and behavior. *Schizophrenia Research, 69*, 93–104.

Costa, P. T., & McCrae, R. R. (1992). Normal personality assessment in clinical practice: The NEO Personality Inventory. *Psychological Assessment, 4*, 5–13.

Cull, J. G., & Gill, W. S. (1982). *Suicide probability scale manual.* Los Angeles: Western Psychological Services.

Deisinger, J. A. (1995). Exploring the factor structure of the Personality Assessment Inventory. *Assessment, 2*, 173–179.

DeMaio, C. M., Holdwick, D. J., & Withers, L. (1998). Evaluation of the Beck Scale for Suicide Ideation (BSS), the Personality Assessment Inventory Suicide Ideation Scale (PAI-SUI), and the Suicide Probability Scale (SPS). Proceeding of the Annual Meeting of the American Association of Suicidology, Houston, TX.

Demakis, G., Cooper, D., Clement, P., Kennedy, J., Hammond, F., & Knotts, A. (2005). Factor structure of the Personality Assessment Inventory in traumatic brain injury. *Archives of Clinical Neuropsychology, 20*, 935.

Douglas, K. S., Hart, S. D., & Kropp, P. R. (2001). Validity of the Personality Assessment Inventory for forensic assessments. *International Journal of Offender Therapy & Comparative Criminology, 45*, 183–197.

Edens, J. F., & Ruiz, M. A. (2005). *PAI interpretive report for correctional settings* (PAI-CS). Odessa, FL: Psychological Assessment Resources.

Edens, J. F., Hart, S. D., Johnson, D. W., Johnson, J. K., & Olver, M. E. (2000). Use of the Personality Assessment Inventory to assess psychopathy in offender populations. *Psychological Assessment, 12*, 132–139.

Edens, J. F., Poythress, N. G., & Watkins-Clay, M. M. (2007). Detection of malingering in psychiatric unit and general population prison inmates: A comparison of the PAI, SIMS, and SIRS. *Journal of Personality Assessment, 88*(1), 33–42.

Fals-Stewart, W. (1996). The ability of individuals with psychoactive substance use disorders to escape detection by the Personality Assessment Inventory. *Psychological Assessment, 8*, 60–68.

Fantoni-Salvador P., & Rogers R. (1997). Spanish versions of the MMPI-2 and PAI: An investigation of concurrent validity with Hispanic patients. *Assessment, 4*, 29–39.

Finn, S. E., & Tonsager, M. E. (1992). Therapeutic effects of providing MMPI-2 test feedback to college students awaiting therapy. *Psychological Assessment, 4*, 278–287.

Freeman, J. (1998). The nature of depression in obstructive sleep apnea. (Doctoral Dissertation, New School for Social Research, New York, NY, 1998.) *Dissertation Abstracts International-B, 60/08*, 4221.

Gay, N. W., & Combs, D. R. (2005). Social behaviors in persons with and without persecutory delusions. *Schizophrenia Research, 80*, 361–362.

Groves, J. A., & Engel, R. R. (2007). The German adaptation and standardization of the Personality Assessment Inventory (PAI). *Journal of Personality Assessment, 88*(1), 49–56.

Grzywacz, J. G., Hovey, J. D., Seligman, L. D., Arcury, T. A., & Quandt, S. A. (2006). Evaluating short-form version of the CES-D for measuring depressive symptoms among immigrants from Mexico. *Hispanic Journal of Behavioral Sciences, 28*, 404–424.

Hare, R. D. (1985). Comparison of procedures for the assessment of psychopathy. *Journal of Consulting and Clinical Psychology, 53*, 7–16.

Hare, R. D. (1991). *Manual for the Hare psychopathy checklist* (Rev. ed.). Toronto, Ontario, Canada: Multi-Health Systems.

Hart, S. D., Cox, D. N., & Hare, R. D. (1995). *Manual for the psychopathy checklist – Screening version (PCL:SV).* Unpublished manuscript, University of British Columbia, Vancouver, Canada.

Hoelzle, J. B., Farrer, E. M., Meyer, G. J., & Mihura, J. L. (2006). *Understanding divergent findings in the factor structure of the Personality Assessment Inventory.* Paper presented at the meetings of the Society for Personality Assessment, San Diego, CA.

Holden, R. R. (1989). Disguise and the structured self-report assessment of psychopathology: II. A clinical replication. *Journal of Clinical Psychology, 45*, 583–586.

Holden, R. R., & Fekken, G. C. (1990). Structured psychopathological test item chracteristics and validity. *Psychological Assessment: A Journal of Consulting and Clinical Psychology, 2*, 35–40.

Holmes, G. E., Willams, C. L., & Haines, J. (2001). Motor vehicle accident trauma exposure: Personality profiles associated with posttraumatic diagnoses. *Anxiety, Stress, and Coping, 14*, 301–313.

Holmes, T. H., & Rahe, R. H. (1967). The social readjustment rating scale. *Journal of Psychosomatic Research, 11*, 213–218.

Hopwood, C. J., Ambwani, S., & Morey, L. C. (in press). Predicting nonmutual therapy termination with the Personality Assessment Inventory. *Psychotherapy Research.*

Hopwood, C. J., Creech, S., Clark, T. S., Meagher, M. W., & Morey, L.C. (in press-a). The convergence and predictive validity of the Multidimensional Pain Inventory and the Personality Assessment Inventory in a chronic pain sample. *Rehabilitation Psychology.*

Hopwood, C. J., Creech, S., Clark, T. S., Meagher, M. W., & Morey, L. C. (in press-b). Predicting the completion of an integrative and intensive outpatient chronic pain treatment. *Journal of Personality Assessment.*

Hopwood, C. J., Morey, L. C., Rogers, R., and Sewell, K. W. (2007). Malingering on the PAI: The detection of feigned disorders. *Journal of Personality Assessment, 88*(1), 43–48.

Hovey, J. D., & Magana, C. G. (2002). Psychosocial predictors of anxiety among immigrant Mexican migrant farmworkers: Implications for prevention and treatment. *Cultural Diversity and Ethnic Minority Psychology, 8,* 274–289.

Jackson, D. N. (1970). A sequential system for personality scale development. In C. D. Spielberger (Ed.), *Current topics in clinical and community psychology* (Vol. 2, pp. 62–97). New York: Academic Press.

Jacobo, M. C., Blais, M. A., Baity, M. R., & Harley, R. (2007). Concurrent validity of the Personality Assessment Inventory Borderline Scale in patients seeking dialectical Behavior Therapy. *Journal of Personality Assessment, 88*(1), 74–80.

Karlin, B. E., Creech, S. K., Grimes, J. S., Clark, T. S., Meagher, M.W., & Morey, L. C. (2005). The Personality Assessment Inventory with chronic pain patients: psychometric properties and clinical utility. *Journal of Clinical Psychology, 61,* 1571–1585.

Keane, T. M., Caddell, J. M., & Taylor, K. L. (1988). Mississippi scale for combat-related posttraumatic stress disorder: Three studies in reliability and validity. *Journal of Consulting and Clinical Psychology, 56,* 85–90.

Keeley, R., Smith, M., & Miller, J. (2000). Somatoform symptoms and treatment nonadherence in depressed family medicine outpatients. *Archives of Family Medicine, 9,* 46-54.

Keiski, M. A., Shore, D. L., & Hamilton, J. M. (2003). CVLT-II performance in depressed versus nondepressed TBI subjects. *The Clinical Neuropsychologist, 17,* 107.

Kellogg, S. H., Ho, A., Bell, K., Schluger, R. P., McHugh, P. F., McClary, K. A., & Kreek, M. J. (2002). The Personality Assessment Inventory drug problems scale: A validity analysis. *Journal of Personality Assessment, 79,* 73–84.

Kiesler, D. (1996). *Contemporary interpersonal theory and research: Personality, psychopathology, and psychotherapy.* New York: Wiley.

Klonsky, E. D. (2004). Performance of Personality Assessment Inventory and Rorschach indices of schizophrenia in a public psychiatric hospital. *Psychological Services, 1,* 107–110.

Kurtz, J. E., Shealy, S. E., & Putnam, S. H. (2007). Another look at paradoxical severity effects in head injury with the Personality Assessment Inventory. *Journal of Personality Assessment, 88*(1), 66–73.

Lally, S. J. (2003). What tests are acceptable for use in forensic evaluations? A survey of experts. *Professional Psychology: Research and Practice, 34,* 491–498.

LePage, J. P., & Mogge, N. L. (2001). Validity rates of the MMPI-2 and PAI in a rural inpatient psychiatric facility. *Assessment, 8,* 67–74.

Liljequist, L., Kinder, B. N., & Schinka, J. A. (1998) An investigation of malingering posttraumatic stress disorder on the Personality Assessment Inventory. *Journal of Personality Assessment, 71,* 322–336.

Loevinger, J. (1957). Objective tests as instruments of psychological theory. *Psychological Reports, 3,* 635–694.

Loranger, A. W. (1988). *The personality disorder examination professional manual.* Yonkers, NY: DV Communications.

Loving, J. L., & Lee, A. J. (2006). Use of the Personality Assessment Inventory in parenting capacity evaluations. Paper presented at the Society of Personality Assessment Annual Conference, San Diego, CA.

Mascaro, N., Rosen, D. H., & Morey, L. C. (2004). The development, construct validity, and clinical utility of the Spiritual Meaning Scale. *Personality and Individual Differences, 37,* 845–860.

Mason, S. M., Doss, R. C., & Gates, J. R. (2000). Clinical utility of the Personality Assessment Inventory in the diagnosis of psychogenic nonepileptic seizures (NES). *Epilepsia, 41(S7),* 156.

McDevitt-Murphy, M. E., Weathers, F. W., Adkins, J. W., & Daniels, J. B. (2005). Use of the Personality

Assessment Inventory in assessment of Posttraumatic Stress Disorder in women. *Journal of Psychopathology and Behavior Assessment, 27,* 57–65.

Mihura, J. L., Nathan-Montano, E., & Alperin, R. J. (2003). Rorschach measures of aggressive drive derivatives: A college student sample. *Journal of Personality Assessment, 80,* 41–49.

Montag, I., & Levin, J. (1994). The five factor model and psychopathology in nonclinical samples. *Personality and Individual Differences, 17,* 1–7.

Morey, L. C. (1991). *Personality Assessment Inventory professional manual.* Odessa, FL: Psychological Assessment Resources.

Morey, L. C. (1995). Critical issues in construct validation. *Journal of Psychopathology and Behavioral Assessment, 17,* 393–402.

Morey, L. C. (1996). *An interpretive guide to the Personality Assessment Inventory.* Odessa, FL: Psychological Assessment Resources.

Morey, L. C. (1997). *Personality Assessment Screener (PAS) technical manual.* Odessa, FL: Psychological Assessment Resources.

Morey, L. C. (2000). *PAI software portfolio manual.* Odessa, FL: Psychological Assessment Resources.

Morey, L. C. (2003). *Essentials of PAI assessment.* New York: Wiley.

Morey, L. C. (2007). *Personality Assessment Inventory professional manual* (2nd ed.). Lutz, FL: Psychological Assessment Resources.

Morey, L. C., & Glutting, J. H. (1994). The Personality Assessment Inventory: Correlates with normal and abnormal personality. In S. Strack, & M. Lorr (Eds.), *Differentiating normal and abnormal personality* (pp. 402–420). New York: Springer.

Morey, L. C., & Hopwood, C. J. (2004). Efficiency of a strategy for detecting back random responding on the Personality Assessment Inventory. *Psychological Assessment, 16,* 197–200.

Morey, L. C., & Hopwood, C. J. (2006). The Personality Assessment Inventory and the measurement of normal and abnormal personality constructs. In S. Strack (Ed.), *Differentiating normal and abnormal personality.* New York: Springer.

Morey, L. C., & Hopwood, C. J. (2007). *Casebook for the Personality Assessment Inventory: A structural summary approach.* Lutz, FL: Psychological Assessment Resources.

Morey, L. C., & Lanier, V. W. (1998). Operating characteristics for six response distortion indicators for the Personality Assessment Inventory. *Assessment, 5,* 203–214.

Morey, L. C., Warner, M. B., & Hopwood, C. J. (2006). The Personality Assessment Inventory and the Daubert Criteria. In A. Goldstein (Ed.). *Forensic psychology: Advanced topics for forensic mental experts and attorneys.* Hoboken, NJ: Wiley.

Morey, L. C., Waugh, M. H., & Blashfield, R. K. (1985). MMPI scales for *DSM-III* personality disorders: Their derivation and correlates. *Journal of Personality Assessment, 49,* 245–251.

Osborne, D. (1994). *Use of the Personality Assessment Inventory with a medical population.* Paper presented at the meetings of the Rocky Mountain Psychological Association, Denver, CO.

Oswald, L. M., Roache, J. D., & Rhoades, H. M. (1999). Predictors of individual differences in Alprazolam self medication. *Experimental and Clinical Psychopharmacology, 7,* 379–390.

Peebles, J., & Moore, R. J. (1998). Detecting socially desirable responding with the Personality Assessment Inventory: The positive impression nanagement scale and the defensiveness index. *Journal of Clinical Psychology, 54,* 621–628.

Peterson, G. W., Clark, D. A., & Bennett, B. (1989). The utility of MMPI subtle, obvious scales for detecting fake good and fake bad response sets. *Journal of Clinical Psychology, 45,* 575–583.

Pincus, A. L. (2005). A contemporary integrative theory of personality disorders. In M. F. Lenzenweger & J. F. Clarkin (Eds.), *Major theories of personality disorder* (pp. 282–331). New York: Guilford.

Piotrowski, C. (2000). How popular is the Personality Assessment Inventory in practice and training? *Psychological Reports, 86,* 65–66.

Piotrowski, C., & Belter, R. W. (1999). Internship training in psychological assessment: Has managed care had an impact? *Assessment, 6,* 381–389.

Plehn, K., Peterson, R. A., & Williams, D. A. (1998). Anxiety sensitivity: Its relationship to functional status in patients with chronic pain. *Journal of Occupational Rehabilitation, 8,* 213–222.

Procidano, M. E., & Heller, K. (1983). Measures of perceived social support from friends and from family: Three validation studies. *American Journal of Community Psychology, 11,* 1–24.

Roberts, M. D., Thompson, J. A., & Johnson, M. (2000). *PAI law enforcement, corrections, and public safety selection report module.* Odessa, FL: Psychological Assessment Resources.

Rogers, R., Bagby, R. M., & Dickens, S. E. (1992). *The structured interview of reported symptoms (SIRS) and professional manual.* Odessa, FL: Psychological Assessment Resources.

Rogers, R., Flores, J., Ustad, K., & Sewell, K. W. (1995). Initial validation of the Personality Assessment Inventory-Spanish version with clients from Mexican American communities. *Journal of Personality Assessment, 64,* 340–348.

Rogers, R., Jackson, R. L., & Kaminski, P. L. (2005). Factitious psychological disorders: The overlooked response style in forensic evaluations. *Journal of Forensic Psychology Practice, 5,* 21–41.

Rogers, R., Ornduff, S. R., & Sewell, K. (1993). Feigning specific disorders: A study of the Personality Assessment Inventory (PAI). *Journal of Personality Assessment, 60,* 554–560.

Rogers, R., Sewell, K. W., Cruise, K. R., Wang, E. W., & Ustad, K. L. (1998). The PAI and feigning: A cautionary note on its use in forensic correctional settings. *Assessment, 5,* 399–405.

Rogers, R., Sewell, K. W., Morey, L.C., & Ustad, K. L. (1996). Detection of feigned mental disorders on the Personality Assessment Inventory: A discriminant analysis. *Journal of Personality Assessment, 67,* 629–640.

Rogers, R., Ustad, K. L., & Salekin, R. T. (1998). Convergent validity of the Personality Assessment Inventory: A study of emergency referrals in a correctional setting. *Assessment, 5*(1), 3–12.

Romain, P. M. (2000). Use of the Personality Assessment Inventory with an ethnically diverse sample of psychiatric outpatients. (Doctoral Dissertation, Pepperdine University, CA, 2000.) *Dissertation Abstracts International-B, 61/11,* 6147.

Rosner, J. (2004). Concurrent validity of the Psychopathic Personality Inventory. (Doctoral Dissertation, Fairleigh Dickinson University, New Jersey, 2004.) *Dissertation Abstracts International-B, 65/06,* 3181.

Ruiz, M. A., Dickinson, K. A., & Pincus, A. L. (2002). Concurrent validity of the Personality Assessment Inventory Alcohol Problems (ALC) Scale in a college student sample. *Assessment, 9*(3), 261-270.

Salekin, R. T., Rogers, R., & Sewell, K. W. (1997). Construct validity of psychopathy in a female offender sample: A multitrait-multimethod evaluation. *Journal of Abnormal Psychology, 106,* 576–585.

Salekin, R. T., Rogers, R., Ustad, K. L., & Sewell, K. W. (1998). Psychopathy and recidivism among female inmates. *Law & Human Behavior, 22,* 109–128.

Schinka, J. A. (1995). Personality Assessment Inventory scale characteristics and factor structure in the assessment of alcohol dependency. *Journal of Personality Assessment, 64,* 101-111.

Schinka, J. A., & Borum, R. (1993). Readability of adult psychopathology measures. *Psychological Assessment, 5,* 384–386.

Seifert, C. J., Baity, M. R., Blais, M. A., & Chriki, (2006). The effects of back random responding on the PAI in a sample of psychiatric inpatients. Paper presented at the Society of Personality Assessment Annual Conference, San Diego, CA.

Selzer, M. L. (1971). The Michigan alcoholism screening test: The quest for a new diagnostic instrument. *American Journal of Psychiatry, 127,* 1653–1658.

Skinner, H. A. (1982). The drug abuse screening test. *Addictive Behaviors, 7,* 363–371.

Spielberger, C. D. (1983). *Manual for the state-trait anxiety inventory.* Palo Alto, CA: Consulting Psychologists Press.

Stein, M. B., Pinsker-Aspen, J. H., & Hilsenroth, M. J. (2007). Borderline pathology and the Personality Assessment Inventory (PAI): An evaluation of criterion and concurrent validity. *Journal of Personality Assessment, 88*(1), 81–89.

Stredny, R., Archer, R. P., Buffington-Vollum, J. K., & Handel, R. W. (2006). A survey of psychological test use patterns among forensic psychologists. Paper Presented at the Annual Meeting of the Society of Personality Assessment, San Diego, CA.

Tasca, G. A., Wood, J., Demidenko, N., & Bissada, H. (2002). Using the PAI with an eating disordered population: Scale characteristics, factor structure and differences among diagnostic groups. *Journal of Personality Assessment, 79,* 337–356.

Tracey, T. J. (1993). An interpersonal stage model of therapeutic process. *Journal of Counseling Psychology, 40,* 396–409.

Trapnell, P. D., & Wiggins, J. S. (1990). Extension of the interpersonal adjective scale to the big five dimensions personality. *Journal of Personality and Social Psychology, 59,* 781–790.

Trull, T. J. (1995). Borderline personality disorder features in nonclinical young adults: 1. Identification and validation. *Psychological Assessment, 7,* 33–41.

Trull, T. J., Useda, J. D., Conforti, K., & Doan, B. T. (1997). Borderline personality disorder features in nonclinical young adults: Two-year outcome. *Journal of Abnormal Psychology, 106,* 307–314.

Wagner, M. T., Wymer, J. H., Topping, K. B., & Pritchard, P. B. (2005). Use of the Personality Assessment Inventory as an efficacious and cost-effective diagnostic tool for nonepileptic seizures. *Epilepsy & Behavior, 7,* 301–304.

Wahler, H. J. (1983). *Wahler physical symptoms inventory* (1983 ed.). Los Angeles: Western Psychological Services.

Wang, E. W., & Diamond, P. M. (1999). Empirically identifying factors related to violence risk in corrections. *Behavioral Sciences & the Law, 17,* 377–389.

Wang, E. W., Rogers, R., Giles, C. L.,, Diamond, P. M., Herrington-Wang, L. E., & Taylor, E. R. (1997). A pilot study of the Personality Assessment Inventory (PAI) in corrections: Assessment of malingering, suicide risk, and aggression in male inmates. *Behavioral Sciences & The Law , 15,* 469–482.

White, L. J. (1996). Review of the Personality Assessment Inventory (PAI): A new psychological test for clinical and forensic assessment. *Australian Psychologist, 31,* 38–39.

Wiggins, J. S. (1966). Substantive dimensions of self-report in the MMPI item pool. *Psychological Bulletin, 59,* 224–242.

Wiggins, J. S. (1979). A psychological taxonomy of trait descriptive terms. *Psychological Monographs, 80,* 22 (whole no. 630).

Wolpe, J., & Lang, P. (1964). A fear survey schedule for use in behavior therapy. *Behaviour Research and Therapy, 2,* 27–30.

Woods, D. W., Wetterneck, C. T., & Flessner, C. A. (2006). A controlled evaluation of acceptance and commitment therapy plus habit reversal for trichotillomania. *Behaviour Research and Therapy, 44,* 639–656.

Yeomans, F. E., Hull, J. W., & Clarkin, J. C. (1994). Risk factors for self damaging acts in a borderline population. *Journal of Personality Disorders, 8,* 10–16.

CHAPTER 6

The NEO Inventories[1]

PAUL T. COSTA, JR.
ROBERT R. MCCRAE

Introduction

The Revised NEO Personality Inventory (NEO-PI-R; Costa & McCrae, 1992b) and its variations are questionnaire measures of a comprehensive model of general personality traits, the Five-Factor Model (FFM; Digman, 1990), or "Big Five." The NEO-PI-R and a slightly simplified NEO-PI-3 (McCrae, Costa, & Martin, 2005) consist of 240 items that assess 30 specific traits, which in turn define the five factors: Neuroticism (N), Extraversion (E), Openness to Experience (O), Agreeableness (A), and Conscientiousness (C). The NEO Five-Factor Inventory (NEO-FFI) and its revisions (McCrae & Costa, 2004) consist of selections of 60 of the items that assess only the five factors. Responses use a five-point Likert scale, from *strongly disagree* to *strongly agree*. Both self-report (Form S) and observer rating (Form R) versions have been validated and extensively used (Costa & McCrae, 1992b).

Although the NEO inventories are used around the world for basic research on personality structure and development, they are also intended for clinical use. Counselors, clinical psychologists, and psychiatrists can use the personality profiles provided by the NEO inventories to understand the strengths and weaknesses of the client, assist in diagnosis and the identification of problems in living, establish rapport, provide feedback and insight, anticipate the course of therapy, and select optimal forms of treatment. In this chapter we will provide an overview of the instruments, and address three basic questions:

1. What is the scientific basis of the inventories?
2. For what populations are the NEO inventories appropriate?
3. How can clinicians use the instrument most effectively?

Theory and Development

Throughout most of the 20th century, personality psychologists debated the question of personality structure: What are the enduring individual differences that allow us to describe the distinctive features of a person, and how are they organized? Some of this debate concerned the nature of the units—should we measure needs, or traits, or temperaments, or character—and some concerned the nature and breadth of the factors or dimensions that describe how the units are structured. Guilford had 10 factors; Cattell had 16 factors; Eysenck had 2 or 3 factors. After decades in which it seemed impossible to reconcile these alternative models, it began to become clear in the 1980s that five factors were necessary and more-or-less sufficient to encompass the trait descriptive terms in natural languages such as English and German, and that these same five factors were found, in whole or in part, in most measures of individual differences (Digman, 1990; McCrae & John, 1992; Tupes & Christal, 1992). It is now known that the FFM incorporates both normal and abnormal personality traits (Markon, Krueger, & Watson, 2005), and that it is a universal feature of the human species (McCrae et al., 2005a), grounded in the human genome (Yamagata et al., 2006). Although alternative models are still sometimes proposed (Ashton et al., 2004), it is fair to say that the FFM is "the most scientifically rigorous taxonomy that behavioral science has" (H. Reis, personal communication, April 24, 2006).

Since their inception in 1978, the NEO inventories have been designed to assess the most important general personality traits and the factors they define, and it has grown with our understanding of the FFM. No single theory of personality was used to guide development; instead, the selection of traits was based on our reviews of the personality literature as a whole (Costa & McCrae, 1980). At first we distinguished only three major personality factors, N, E, and O (hence the name); in the 1980s, work with the natural language of personality traits convinced us that five factors were needed to form a comprehensive model (McCrae & Costa, 1985, 1987). We related these factors to instruments based on Murray's needs (Costa & McCrae, 1988), Jung's types (McCrae & Costa, 1989), Gough's folk concepts (McCrae, Costa, & Piedmont, 1993) and many other conceptions of personality, and thus grounded the FFM in personality theory (McCrae & Costa, 1996).

To assess these traits, we developed scales using a combination of rational and factor analytic methods. Simple, straightforward items were written that were intended to tap into each trait, and trial items were then analyzed in large samples of adult volunteers. Targeted factor analyses were used to select items that showed the best convergent and discriminant validity with respect to the intended set of traits (Costa, McCrae, & Dye, 1991; McCrae & Costa, 1983). The use of transparent items assumes that respondents are willing and able to describe themselves accurately, and that premise has been supported by a wealth of data on the multimethod validation of NEO scales (e.g., McCrae et al., 2004). Many of these same studies support another assumption, namely, that third-person rephrasings of the self-report items would yield valid observer rating scales. Our choice of a five-point Likert response format (instead of true–false) resulted in scales that provide accurate assessments across the full range of the trait (Reise & Henson, 2000), and our decision to use balanced keying eliminated most of the problematic effects of acquiescent responding (McCrae, Herbst, & Costa, 2001).

When first published (Costa & McCrae, 1985), the NEO Personality Inventory consisted of 180 items, with six facet scales for each of the N, E, and O domains, and brief global scales to measure A and C. Four years later we introduced the short version, the NEO-FFI, as well as new norms appropriate for use with college age and adult respondents (Costa & McCrae, 1989). In 1992 the NEO-PI-R appeared, with new facet scales for A and C, and replacement of 10 of the original N, E, and O items. In 1994 a Spanish translation intended for use by Hispanics was published (Psychological Assessment Resources, 1994), and translations have by now been made into over 40 languages. Research showed that the inventory could be used by children as young as 10, but that some items were difficult for adolescents to understand; a more readable version, the NEO-PI-3, has been developed, along with a NEO-FFI-3. These instruments can be used by both adolescents and adults, and may be particularly useful in populations with limited literacy. We expect both to be published shortly. Computer administration, scoring, and interpretation has been available since 1985; a major update, with many features intended for the clinical use of the instrument, was released in 1994 (Costa, McCrae, & PAR Staff, 1994).

All the NEO inventories assess the five factors. Because these broad constructs summarize so much information, they are the logical starting place for personality assessment. They explain whether the client is chronically predisposed to emotionally distressed or emotionally stable (N); energetic and thrill seeking or sober and solitary (E); curious and unconventional or traditional and pragmatic (O); kind and trusting or competitive and arrogant (A); disciplined and fastidious or laid back and careless (C). The domain scales of the NEO-PI-R and NEO-FFI provide measures of all five factors; more precise estimates can be obtained as NEO-PI-R factor scores.

Much research on the FFM has employed global measures that assess only the five factors. But for clinical purposes, we recommend the full length inventories that provide detailed information on 30 distinct traits. This information can affect the interpretation of the overall factor. For example, a client who is very high on E3: Assertiveness, but average on E1: Warmth, may have the same high E score as one who is very high on Warmth but only average on Assertiveness—yet surely these two clients are likely to have rather different interpersonal styles: The former will be forceful and directive while the latter will be more friendly and invested in others. The constructs assessed by the NEO-PI-R facets are suggested by their labels, but prior to using the instrument, clinicians should study the descriptions of the individual facets given in the *Manual* (Costa & McCrae, 1992b).

Scores from the NEO inventories can also be interpreted by examining pairs of factors, called *styles*. For example, the Style of Impulse Control is based on scores for N and C: High N, high C is called Overcontrolled; high N, low C is Undercontrolled; low N, low C is Relaxed; and low N, high C is Directed. Style graphs describe each of these styles. For example, clients who have an Overcontrolled style "have perfectionistic strivings and will not allow themselves to fail even in the smallest detail . . . they are prone to guilt and self-recrimination. They may be susceptible to obsessive and compulsive behavior" (Costa, McCrae, & PAR Staff, 1994).

Basic Psychometrics

Internal consistencies of the 48-item domain scores are high. For example, in an adult sample ($N = 635$), coefficient alphas for N, E, O, A, and C domain scores from the NEO-PI-R were 0.92, 0.89, 0.88, 0.90, and 0.91, respectively, for Form S and 0.93, 0.90, 0.88, 0.93, and 0.93 for Form R (McCrae, Martin, & Costa, 2005). The corresponding values for 14- to 20-year-olds ranged from .87 to .94 (McCrae, Costa, et al., 2005). Coefficient alphas for the 8-item facet scales are understandably lower; in the adult sample they ranged from .51 to .86 (*Mdns* = .75 for Form S, .78 for Form R); in the adolescent sample they ranged from .44 to .84 (*Mdns* = .73 for Form S, .75 for Form R). Internal consistencies below .70 are sometimes considered problematic, but the few NEO-PI-R facet scales with values lower than .70 have nevertheless shown evidence of heritability, cross-observer agreement, and longitudinal stability (McCrae, Martin, et al., 2005). Internal consistencies for the five NEO-FFI 12-item domain scales ranged from .69 to .86 (McCrae & Costa, 2004).

Robins, Fraley, Roberts, and Trzesniewski (2001) reported 2-week retest reliabilities of .86 to .90 for the NEO-FFI scales. McCrae, Yik, Trapnell, Bond, and Paulhus (1998) reported two-year retest reliabilities for the full NEO-PI-R; coefficients for N, E, O, A, and C were .83, .91, .89, .87, and .88. Retest reliabilities for the 30 facet scales ranged from .64 to .86 (*Mdn* = .79). Terracciano, Costa, and McCrae (2006) reported 10-year stability coefficients for the NEO-PI-R. The median value was .70 for facets and .81 for factors.

As an operationalization of the FFM, the foremost test of the validity of the NEO-PI-R is the replicability of its factor structure, and that has been the topic of dozens of articles. The structure has been satisfactorily recovered in adults, college students, and children as young as 12, in men and women, in Black and White Americans (Costa et al., 1991). Recently, observer rating data were obtained from 50 cultures using translations of the NEO-PI-R into over 20 languages (McCrae et al., 2005a). Of 250 factor congruence coefficients, 236 (94.4%) were higher than .85, indicating factor replication (Haven & ten Berge, 1977), and all but one were significantly higher than chance. Deviations from the intended structure were found only in cultures where the quality of the data was low (e.g., where the respondents took the test in a second language).

Cross-observer agreement is key in evaluating the validity of any personality inventory. On the one hand, human judges who are well acquainted with the target can integrate a wealth of knowledge into an accurate assessment of personality; on the other hand, they do not share the artifacts that can inflate the correlation of one self-report with another. To the extent that a self-report and an observer rating agree, both are likely to be valid. Cross-observer validity for the NEO inventories has been repeatedly demonstrated, with correlations generally in the .40 to .60 range—far above the so-called ".3 barrier" that was once thought to represent the limit of validity for trait measures. In analyses of the NEO-PI-3, self/other correlations for N, E, O, A, and C factors ranged from .56 to .67 (McCrae, in press). Comparable correlations were reported by Bagby et al. (1998) in a sample of depressed outpatients. Using a Mandarin translation of the NEO-PI-R, Yang et al. (1999) reported agreement between Chinese psychiatric patients and their spouses ranging from .32 to .51 ($N = 160$, all $ps < .001$). Soldz, Budman, Demby, and Merry (1995) found modest agreement between group psychotherapy patients' NEO-PI scores and other group members' ratings on an adjective measure of the FFM.

Note, however, that these correlations seldom approach 1.0. Different observers have different opinions about an individual's personality, and the views of all informed observers are worth considering. Indeed, discrepancies in perceptions between members of a couple may be particularly informative (Singer, 2005).

The validity of NEO scales is attested by the results published in more than 2,000 articles, chapters, and books. NEO scales have been correlated in meaningful ways with scales from the Minnesota Multiphasic Personality Inventory (MMPI; Hathaway & McKinley, 1983; Siegler et al., 1990), the Millon Clinical Multiaxial Inventory (Lehne, 2002), the Personality Assessment Inventory (PAI; Morey, 1991) and the Basic Personality Inventory (Costa & McCrae, 1992a). They have proven useful in predicting vocational interests

(De Fruyt & Mervielde, 1997), ego development (Einstein & Lanning, 1998), attachment styles (Shaver & Brennan, 1992), and psychiatric diagnoses of personality disorders (McCrae, Yang, et al., 2001).

In the past 20 years, the FFM has become the dominant model in personality psychology (Funder, 2001; Markon et al., 2005), consolidating decades of research on personality structure. Of the many operationalizations of the FFM, the most widely used and extensively validated are the NEO inventories.

Administration and Scoring

Instructions for the administration and scoring of the NEO-PI-R are given in the Manual (Costa & McCrae, 1992b). The instrument can be administered to individuals or groups, and can be administered orally to those with limited literacy or visual problems. Both machine- and hand-scoring answer sheets are available; the test booklet is reusable.

The NEO-PI-R is intended for individuals age 18 and older, although it has been used successfully with high school students (McCrae, Costa, et al., 2002). It has a Flesch-Kincaid reading level of 5.7 overall. The NEO-PI-3, in which 37 NEO-PI-R items were replaced, has an overall Flesch-Kincaid level of 5.3, and has eliminated most of the items that were difficult for adolescents to understand. It can be used by adults or by children as young as 12. If respondents do not understand an item, the administrator can explain it; suggested language is provided for use with the NEO-PI-3 (Costa, McCrae, & Martin, 2006).

The publisher has classified the NEO inventories as Level B or S, meaning that they are available to individuals with a college degree in psychology or a related discipline, or in one of the health care professions, provided that they have appropriate training in the use and interpretation of psychological tests. We assume that users will familiarize themselves with the *Manual*

Perhaps the most important requirement is that the administrator makes every effort to engage the cooperation of the respondent. Providing a comfortable setting and ample time, giving assurances of privacy, explaining the purpose of testing, and perhaps offering feedback can minimize problems of careless or distorted responding.

Computerization

The NEO Software System (Costa et al., 1994) administers, scores, and interprets the NEO-PI-R or NEO-FFI. Interpretive statements reflect our understanding of ranges of scores. For example, an individual whose most extreme score is $T = 72$ on the O factor would receive a report that begins:

> The most distinctive feature of this individual's personality is his standing on the factor of Openness. Very high scorers like him have a strong

interest in experience for its own sake. They seek out novelty and variety, and have a marked preference for complexity. They have a heightened awareness of their own feelings and are perceptive in recognizing the emotions of others . . . Peers rate such people as imaginative, daring, independent, and creative.

The NEO-PI-R Interpretive Report provides a graphic profile, a discussion of protocol validity, descriptions at the level of factors and facets, and a summary of personality correlates based on published findings. A clinical module calculates profile agreement statistics that lead to hypotheses about possible Axis II diagnoses. Another module provides a description of personality suitable for use as client feedback. A special feature allows the clinician to input two different assessments (e.g., a self-report and a spouse rating); this generates a combined report based on the adjusted average of the two sets of scores, and calls attention to traits on which there is substantial disagreement, suggesting the need for additional inquiry.

Reise and Henson (2000) showed that the items of the NEO-PI-R could be used in a Computer Adaptive Testing system, but this is not currently available.

Applications and Limitations

Settings and Uses

As general personality trait measures, the NEO inventories can be used in a wide variety of settings. They have been widely used in clinical practice in both inpatient (Yang et al., 1999) and outpatient (Piedmont, 2001) settings. Health psychologists use them in medical settings (Christensen & Smith, 1995). The questionnaire can be mailed to respondents.

The NEO inventories are useful in a wide variety of contexts, from selecting police in New Zealand (Black, 2000) to documenting personality changes in Alzheimer's disease (Strauss & Pasupathi, 1994) to school counseling (Scepansky & Bjornsen, 2003). For the clinician, these measures are particularly valuable because they assess strengths as well as weaknesses. Measures of

---

Quick Reference

The NEO inventories are available from Psychological Assessment Resources, 16204 N. Florida Avenue, Lutz, FL 33549. Fax: 1-800-727-9329. Phone: 1-800-331-8378. Internet: http://www.parinc.com.

To request a license to adapt the instruments or use an authorized translation, contact Customer Support at custsup@parinc.com.

A bibliography of articles, chapters, and presentations using NEO inventories is available at http://www3.parinc.com/uploads/pdfs/NEO_bib.pdf

psychopathology are useful in identifying problems, but may give few clues about the client's creativity, organization, or generosity. Inventories like the MMPI that are supposed to assess both normal and abnormal aspects of the individual often lack the scope of the NEO-PI-R with respect to general personality traits. For example, the MMPI lacks items that measure C (Johnson, Butcher, Null, & Johnson, 1984). The full length NEO-PI-R and NEO-PI-3 assess 30 facet scales as well as the five factors, and these facet scales have incremental validity in predicting behaviors (Paunonen & Ashton, 2001) and personality disorder symptoms (Reynolds & Clark, 2001); thus, these instruments are preferable to the shorter NEO-FFI and other Big Five measures that provide only global scores.

A relatively novel feature of the NEO inventories is their emphasis on feedback. A brief, nonthreatening description of high, low, and average scores for the five factors is provided by *Your NEO Summary*; the administrator checks the appropriate level for each factor. This sheet has been widely used as an incentive for research volunteers and an educational tool for psychology students.

Traditionally, psychological assessments were not shared with clients, on the assumption that results might be misunderstood or cause distress. These concerns do not appear to be applicable to the NEO inventories because of the general nature of the traits they assess, and many clinicians discuss plotted NEO profiles with patients as part of the therapeutic process (e.g., Singer, 2005). Mutén noted that even high N scores are not problematic: "Most people who score very high on N facets are well aware of their depression, hostility, or impulsiveness and appear to welcome a candid discussion" (1991, p. 454). At the request of clinicians, the NEO Software System now includes a Client Report that gives a detailed explanation of factor and facet scores in lay language.

Limitations

The NEO inventories assess general personality traits. Although these cover a wide range of emotional, interpersonal, experiential, attitudinal, and motivational characteristics of the individual, they do not constitute a complete psychological assessment. They do not address cognitive abilities or distortions. Although they can be interpreted as a guide to likely problems in living or psychopathology, they do not assess these conditions directly. A client who scores very low on A is likely to have interpersonal problems, but the clinician must determine by interview or other assessment instruments exactly what those problems are, and whether they merit attention as a focus of treatment. Certain profiles can suggest Axis-II diagnoses, but one cannot determine from the NEO-PI-R alone that the client meets *DSM-IV* criteria for a personality disorder.

Use of the NEO inventories is not appropriate in all situations. Respondents must have a minimal level of intellectual competence and must not be demented, delirious, or floridly psychotic. However, illiterate clients can be administered the instrument orally, and clients with many kinds of severe mental disorder such as acute major depression, can nevertheless provide valid information through self-reports (Costa, Bagby, Herbst, & McCrae, 2005). For other patients, such as those with dementia or mental retardation, observer ratings from knowledgeable informants provide clinically useful data (Bagby et al., 1998).

Of particular concern are questions of motivated test distortion. Although there are some simple checks on protocol validity, the NEO inventories do not include validity scales intended to detect lying, defensiveness, or malingering. Such scales have been proposed (Schinka, Kinder, & Kremer, 1997), but we have not incorporated them into the scoring of the instrument because we are not convinced that such scales actually work (see, e.g., Morey, Quigley, et al., 2002; Piedmont, McCrae, Riemann, & Angleitner, 2000; Yang, Bagby, & Ryder, 2000). We discuss this issue in detail in Current Controversies. This precludes the use of the NEO inventories in a few contexts. For example, a study of child custody litigants (Langer, 2004) showed that ex-spouses described each other as almost three standard deviations lower than they described themselves on A and C. It is unclear that any questionnaire measure could provide valid assessments in such a situation.

Contributions to Psychotherapy Planning

Scales from the NEO inventories have been linked to a wide range of psychiatric diagnoses, and a clinician familiar with this literature would be guided towards many diagnoses. For example, individuals very low in A and C are prone to psychopathy (Miller, Lynam, Widiger, & Leukefeld, 2001) and substance abuse (Ball, Tennen, Poling, Kranzler, & Rounsaville, 1997); those scoring high on N and low on E are prone to depression (Bagby et al., 1998). The most intensive research, however, has been on the utility of NEO-PI-R scores as predictors of Axis II personality pathology.

Widiger and Costa (2002) reviewed a large body of research which shows that particular patterns of NEO-PI-R profiles are associated in theoretically meaningful ways with *DSM* personality disorders. For example, individuals diagnosed with Paranoid Personality Disorder generally score high on N2: Angry Hostility and low on A1: Trust, A2: Straightforwardness, and A4: Compliance (A4). The computer Interpretive Report for the NEO-PI-R includes a Clinical Hypotheses section, in which prototype profiles for the personality disorders are compared to client profiles. If profile agreement is substantially higher than that normally found in nonclinical populations, the clinician is alerted to the possibility that the client may have features of the disorder. We (Costa & McCrae, 2005) have proposed a simplified system for hand scoring NEO-PI-R personality disorder scales that can yield the same clinical hypotheses (see also Miller, Bagby, Pilkonis, Reynolds, & Lynam, 2005). Clinicians are cautioned that these hypotheses need to be confirmed by evaluation of the *DSM* diagnostic criteria.

However, the categorical personality disorders of *DSM-IV* have been widely criticized: They are arbitrary, show serious co-morbidity, are unstable over time, and generally lack empirical foundation (McCrae, Löckenhoff, & Costa, 2005). Instead of attempting to predict membership in one of these rather dubious categories, Widiger, Costa, and McCrae (2002) have proposed that clinicians assess the factors and facets of the FFM and then focus on problems or symptoms associated with high or low standing on each. For example, a client who scores high on C2: Order may be "preoccupied with order, rules, schedules, and organization . . . [T]asks remain uncompleted due to a rigid emphasis on proper order and organization; friends and colleagues are frustrated by this preoccupation" (Widiger et al., 2002, p. 442). Of course, not all clients who score high on C2 will have these problems, but the clinician should enquire about these issues, and may discover problems in living that should become a focus of treatment. If they are sufficiently severe, they may warrant a diagnosis. Under Widiger et al.'s proposal, this would be styled a *High Conscientiousness-related Personality Disorder*; under the existing Axis II it would be Personality Disorder Not Otherwise Specified.

Among the first clinicians to appreciate the value of the NEO-PI-R in treatment planning was T. Miller (1991). Drawing on his experience with a series of 119 clients, he reported that information from the NEO-PI was useful in understanding the client and in anticipating problems in therapy. He offered a list of key problems, treatment opportunities, and treatment pitfalls associated with each of the factors. For example, a client who is high in A is likely to form a therapeutic alliance easily, but may be so uncritical in accepting interpretations that the therapy misses the essential problems. Traits can also suggest the most promising forms of therapy: Clients high in O may enjoy and profit from imaginative role playing, whereas those low in O may prefer concrete therapies such as behavior modification.

More recently, implications of NEO scores for the treatment of personality disorders have been discussed by Stone (2002) and others in the Costa and Widiger (2002) volume. Harkness and McNulty (2002) go beyond the use of trait information in characterizing a patient; they draw out the implications for psychotherapy of the whole body of individual differences science. For example, evidence on the heritability and stability of personality traits suggests that it will be useful to adopt realistic expectations for what can and cannot be changed in therapy, and to focus therapeutic interventions on

Just the Facts

Ages: 12 to 99+

Purpose: Provides a comprehensive assessment of general personality traits.

Strengths: Assesses the best established model of personality structure using either self-report or observer rating methods; provides scales with demonstrated longitudinal stability and cross-cultural generality. Feedback can be provided.

Limitations: Susceptible to conscious distortion under some circumstances.

Time to Administer: 35–45 minutes.

Time to Score: 5 minutes.

the client's characteristic maladaptations rather than focus on the enduring underlying traits they express.

Singer (2005) integrated trait psychology into a program for treating the whole person, and found that the NEO-PI-R has great utility in the crucial first phase of beginning to understand the patient. Because the NEO-PI-R assesses both broad factors and specific facets, and because patterns and combinations of facets can be interpreted by the experienced clinician, it provides a wealth of data. As Singer illustrated in a case study of therapy for a couple, even richer characterizations can be obtained by examining both self-reports and ratings from a knowledgeable informant.

Research Findings

Psychiatrists and clinical psychologists trained in the use of the *DSM* are familiar with categorical models of psychopathology, in which patients either do or do not have a disorder. It is sometimes claimed that clinicians are so accustomed to categorical or typological thinking that they would not be able to use dimensional models of personality. Samuel and Widiger (2006) put this claim to the test. They provided descriptions of individuals with personality pathology and asked the clinicians to describe the individuals in terms of the FFM and the *DSM-IV* personality disorders. When asked to evaluate these two characterizations, the clinicians preferred the FFM for describing personality, communicating with the patient, covering the full range of problems, and formulating effective treatments. The FFM and the NEO inventories are clinician friendly.

The NEO-PI-R bibliography (http://www3.parinc.com/uploads/pdfs/ NEO_bib.pdf) lists more than 350 publications in its section on Counseling, Clinical Psychology, and Psychiatry. Many of these refer to studies concerning personality disorders collected in Costa and Widiger (2002), or published as part of the Collaborative Longitudinal Personality Disorders Study (e.g., Morey, Gunderson et al., 2002). In this section we review selected studies on other aspects of psychopathology and psychotherapy.

Diagnostic Utility

Katon et al. (1995) showed that patients who do not meet *DSM-III-R* criteria for panic disorder because their attacks are infrequent score just as high on NEO-PI-R N as patients who do, and much higher than controls. Further, despite the fact that they did not meet diagnostic criteria, patients with infrequent panic attacks showed as much disability as those who obtained the diagnosis. In this case, N was a better predictor of disability than diagnostic status was.

It is well known that N is associated with clinical depression—indeed, one of the NEO-PI-R facet scales is N3: Depression. But Wolfenstein and Trull (1997) showed that NEO-PI-R O, a factor rarely measured by clinical instruments, is also a predictor of depressive symptoms in a college sample. Although O is generally regarded as a desirable trait, the sensitivity it imparts also puts some individuals at risk for depressive episodes.

Nigg et al. (2002) used data from 1,620 respondents in six community and clinical samples to link symptoms of childhood or current attention deficit/hyperactivity disorder (ADHD) to self-reports and (in one sample) spouse ratings on the NEO-FFI. They found that the inattention-disorganization cluster of ADHD symptoms was strongly related to low C, whereas the hyperactivity and oppositional symptoms were associated with low A. Some of these correlations were strikingly large; for example, attention problems showed correlations ranging from −.42 to −.78 with C. Results from self-reports were replicated when spouse ratings were analyzed, suggesting that both forms are useful in clinical assessment.

Quirk, Christiansen, Wagner, and McNulty (2003) addressed the critical question of incremental validity: Do NEO-PI-R scores tell the clinician anything more than assessment with standard clinical instruments? To answer this question they administered the NEO-PI-R and the MMPI-2 to a sample of 1,342 inpatient substance abusers and predicted Axis I and Axis II diagnoses. They concluded that NEO-PI-R scales were substantially related to most diagnoses they examined, and that they explained variance above and beyond that accounted for by 28 MMPI-2 scales. They also showed that NEO-PI-R facet scales provide additional information over the five domain scales, and that facet scales from each of the five factors contributed incrementally to the prediction of diagnoses. For example, O1: Fantasy made a unique contribution to the diagnosis of bipolar disorder, and low E2: Gregariousness made a unique contribution to the diagnosis of posttraumatic stress disorder. Quirk et al. (2003) concluded that their results "support the use of FFM scales in an adjunct role in clinical assessment" (p. 323).

Treatment Planning

Several studies have shown that NEO inventories can be helpful in anticipating the course of therapy and predicting outcomes. Mattox (2004) assessed the personality of 53 undergraduates who participated in a mock interview with clinical psychology students; the interviewers, participants, and two observers rated the treatment alliance established in the single session. NEO-PI-R E was significantly related to all three assessments of alliance, probably because extraverts excel in initiating social contacts. (In the long term, A may be more important for the treatment alliance; see Miller, 1991.)

Ogrodniczuk, Piper, Joyce, McCallum, and Rosie (2003) assessed personality with the NEO-FFI before treatment by interpretive or supportive group therapy in a sample of 107 patients with complicated grief reactions. Those patients who were initially higher in E, O, and C, and lower in N, showed more favorable outcomes in both treatments, whereas patients high in A showed better outcomes only in the interpretive group.

Talbot, Duberstein, Butzel, Cox, and Giles (2003) examined the influence of personality on outcomes to two different therapies in a sample of 86 women with histories of childhood sexual abuse. A Women's Safety in Recovery (WSIR) group was a highly structured treatment that focused on problem solving skills for dealing with current problems. Comparison with a less structured treatment-as-usual group showed that women low in A and E benefited most in the WSIR group. These findings are consistent with other research showing that highly structured therapies are more effective for introverted patients (Bliwise, Friedman, Nekich, & Yesavage, 1995).

Lozano and Johnson (2001) examined manic and depressive symptoms in 39 bipolar patients. High N predicted increased depressive symptoms, whereas high C predicted increasing manic symptoms, consistent with the "increase in goal directed activity" noted by *DSM-IV* as a criterion for a manic episode.

Psychotherapy is only possible when the client is willing to accept treatment. Hill, Diemer, and Heaton (1997) asked which students were willing to participate in a therapeutic dream interpretation session. Of 336 students initially assessed on the NEO-FFI, 109 indicated an interest in participating, and 65 of these attended the session. Whether or not they actually participated, students who were interested in dream interpretation sessions scored nearly three-quarters of a standard deviation higher in O than those who were not. Dream interpretation is probably not a therapeutic option for closed patients.

Treatment Progress Evaluation

In nonclinical samples, the traits assessed by the NEO inventories are highly stable over time (Terracciano et al., 2006). Even in patients treated for psychiatric disorders, stability rather than plasticity is the rule (Costa et al., 2005). As a result, Harkness and McNulty (2002) have argued that substantial change in personality trait levels is not a realistic goal of psychotherapy, which should focus instead on how traits are manifested in concrete problems in living.

Nevertheless, true personality change is sometimes the result of psychotherapy, especially when the disorder, such as major depression, has a neurochemical basis. Two studies have shown that NEO trait levels are affected by pharmacological treatments for depression—but only among patients who responded to medication (Costa et al., 2005; Du, Baksih, Ravindran, & Hrdina, 2002). In both studies, N decreased and E increased as the result of successful treatment. Piedmont (2001) assessed personality change in 99 outpatient drug rehabilitation patients. At the end of a 6-week treatment program, there were significant decreases in N and increases in E, O, A, and C; the effects for N, A, and C were also seen in a subsample followed 15 months later.

The changes seen in all three studies were modest in magnitude. For example, in Piedmont's follow-up sample mean N T-scores declined from 63 to 58; among Costa et al.'s (2005) responders, N declined from 72 to 62. Compared to the normal average T-score of 50, both sets of effectively treated patients remained high in N. As Harkness and McNulty (2002) would have predicted, therapy did not radically alter basic personality traits. Nevertheless, the changes seen are statistically and clinically significant, and they

Important References

Costa, P. T., Jr., & McCrae, R. R. (1992). *Revised NEO Personality Inventory (NEO-PI-R) and NEO Five-Factor Inventory (NEO-FFI) professional manual.* Odessa, FL: Psychological Assessment Resources. This is the manual covering the basics of development and validity evidence as of 1992.

Costa, P. T., Jr., & Widiger, T. A. (Eds.). (2002). *Personality disorders and the Five-Factor Model of personality (2nd ed.).* Washington, DC: American Psychological Association. This volume reports research, theory, and practical applications of the FFM in the context of *DSM* Personality Disorders. Chapter 25 presents a radical proposal for dimensionalizing Axis II.

McCrae, R. R., & Costa, P. T., Jr. (2003). *Personality in adulthood: A Five-Factor Theory perspective (2nd. ed.).* New York: Guilford. This book focuses on adult personality development, but includes nontechnical introductions to the psychometric and theoretical bases of the NEO-PI-R.

Piedmont, R. L. (1998). *The Revised NEO Personality Inventory: Clinical and research applications.* New York: Plenum. A book-length guide to clinical use of the instrument.

Singer, J. A. (2005). *Personality and psychotherapy: Treating the whole person.* New York: Guilford. Reports an attempt to integrate therapy at the level of traits, characteristic adaptations, life narratives, and relational dynamics. Both individual and couple case studies illustrate use of the NEO-PI-R.

demonstrate that NEO inventories are capable of registering change when it occurs. That is also shown by a study of caregiver ratings of Alzheimer's disease patients (Strauss & Pasupathi, 1994): The personality changes that characterize that disease could be detected through observer ratings on the NEO-PI-R over a period as short as one year.

Cross-Cultural Considerations

With versions in over 40 languages, the NEO inventories are among the most widely used psychological tests in the world. Published versions, complete with manuals and local normative information, are available in Croatian, Czech/Slovak, Danish, Dutch, French, German, Hebrew, Japanese, Korean, Norwegian, Polish, Portuguese, Spanish, Turkish, and British English. Chinese, Russian, Arabic, Italian and many other versions are available from the publisher by license (usually without normative information).

When psychological measures are translated and used in a new cultural context, it cannot be assumed that their meaning has been retained. The characteristics assessed may not exist in the new culture, or the items may not validly assess them. Some evidence of construct validity must be offered for each new translation. In the case of the NEO-PI-R, the most straightforward criterion of construct validity is found in factor replicability. A valid measure of anxiety ought to load on the same general factor as measures of depression and vulnerability; recovery of the N factor is thus a form of evidence that meaning has been retained. Demonstrations of factor replicability for the NEO-PI-R have been published in dozens of languages, for both self-reports (McCrae & Allik, 2002) and observer ratings (McCrae et al., 2005a). In addition, cross-cultural evidence of construct validity has been demonstrated in meaningful patterns of correlates, including cross-observer agreement (McCrae et al., 2004). The quality of data varies across translations and cultures, and in some cases further adaptation and refinement is clearly needed, but the NEO inventories appear to be promising research and clinical tools everywhere.

Use of any validated NEO translation within a culture seems appropriate. Much more controversial is the comparison of scores across cultures (e.g., Poortinga, van de Vijver, & van Hemert, 2002). The effect of translation may be to make items easier or more difficult; different cultures may have different self-presentational styles; frames of reference may vary; acquiescence or extreme responding may introduce systematic cultural biases. All of these are threats to what is known as *scalar equivalence*, which is a prerequisite to meaningful cross-cultural comparisons. McCrae and colleagues (2005b) have argued that if cross-cultural comparisons yield meaningful results, the data must have shown at least rough scalar equivalence, and they have offered evidence of such meaningful results. For example, cultures scoring high in Power Distance (a cultural pattern in which people show authoritarian deference to those of higher status) have individuals who on average score low on NEO-PI-R O (McCrae et al., 2005b).

The merits and limitations of this argument are perhaps of little interest to clinicians, but they have an important practical application. If McCrae and colleagues are correct, then scalar equivalence for well constructed personality tests is the rule, not the exception; and if this is so, then raw scores from anywhere in the world are comparable. In particular, one could use American norms to interpret the NEO-PI-R profile of a client from Singapore or Zimbabwe, provided one recalls that the client is being compared to Americans. Because Americans (on average) are more extraverted than most people in the world, most people would appear as relatively introverted when judged by American norms, even though they might be more extraverted than their compatriots. Where local norms are available, they are preferable—so long, once again, as one recalls that the client is being compared to the local group.

An instrument that works in Sweden, Burkina Faso, and Indonesia is likely to work well in minority groups in North America. The NEO inventories have been used effectively to assess personality in Chinese Canadians (McCrae et al., 1998), African Americans (Terracciano, Merritt, Zonderman, & Evans, 2003), and Hispanics (Benet-Martínez & John, 1998). Simakhodskaya (2000) used a Russian translation to study acculturation in Russian emigrants to the United States; Moua (2006) studied the structure of personality in Hmong Americans.

Current Controversies

The most controversial issue in the clinical use of the NEO inventories has always been the role of validity scales (Ben-Porath & Waller, 1992). Psychometricians have known for decades that questionnaire measures are subject to a variety of biases that threaten their validity. Among these are response styles including acquiescence, nay-saying, and extreme responding; faking, including both positive and negative impression management; and random responding, either with a mixed pattern of answers, or with a single repeated response. Most clinical instruments, including the MMPI and the PAI, have extensive validity scales to detect and correct for these kinds of biases. The NEO inventories do not.

The NEO-PI-R does include some checks on protocol validity. At the bottom of the answer sheet a statement and two questions are presented: I have tried to answer all of these questions honestly and accurately; have you responded to all of the statements; and have you entered your responses in the correct areas? Respondents who strongly disagree or disagree with the first statement, and those who say *no* to the last are considered to have invalid data. Protocols are not scored if more than 40 items are missing. In the computer version, strings of repetitive responses are noted, and protocols with more than 6 consecutive *strongly disagrees*, 9 *disagrees*, 10 *neutrals*, 14 *agrees*, or 10 *strongly agrees* are considered invalid, because longer strings were never found in a large, cooperative sample. (When using the hand scored version, a visual sweep of the answer sheet can often spot suspicious response patterns.)

Carter et al. (2001) examined the stability of NEO-PI-R scores in a sample of 301 opioid-dependent outpatients. In this drug-abusing sample, a large number (71) of protocols were deemed invalid by these rules. The 4-month retest correlations for the valid protocols were .72, .68, .74, .72, and .71 for N, E, O, A, and C, respectively; the corresponding values for the invalid protocols were .48, .48, .46, .57, and .38. In a sample of 500 adolescents with valid protocols on the NEO-PI-3, coefficients alphas for the five domains ranged from .87 to .95; in a sample of 36 adolescents with invalid protocols, they ranged from .75 to .90 (McCraė, Costa, et al., 2005). Both these studies show that the validity rules successfully distinguish more from less valid protocols. But they also show that there is still valid information in invalid protocols. Clinicians should be reluctant to discard any assessment, although some should be interpreted with particular caution.

The computer scored version also counts the number of items to which the respondent has answered *agree* or *strongly agree*. Fewer than 1 in 100 cooperative volunteers agreed with more than 150 items; larger counts can be viewed as evidence of acquiescent responding. Counts lower than 50 are similarly viewed as evidence of nay saying. However, these counts are used only to caution the interpreter, not to invalidate the data, because NEO scales are balanced with roughly equal numbers of positively- and negatively-keyed items, and thus the net effect of acquiescent responding is limited.

Most conspicuously absent from the NEO inventories are validity scales that can assess social desirability, defensiveness, faking good, or malingering. There is no question that respondents can give false responses to the NEO items; faking studies clearly show that (Paulhus, Bruce, & Trapnell, 1995). In principle, high scores on a scale designed to measure good qualities might be a tip off to socially desirable responding, but it might also be an honest assessment from a person with desirable traits. Screening out such people would be counterproductive, and controlling for scores on such a scale might actually lower validity (McCrae et al., 1989).

In an effort to make the NEO-PI-R more consistent with common clinical practice, Schinka, Kinder, and Kremer (1997) selected NEO-PI-R items to create validity scales to assess positive presentation management (PPM), negative presentation management (NPM) and inconsistency (INC). These scales were related in the expected way to PAI validity scales (Schinka et al., 1997), and distinguished genuine patients from students instructed to fake (Berry et al., 2001). However, we found no evidence in support of their use in volunteer samples (Costa & McCrae, 1997; Piedmont et al., 2000). Yang et al. (2000) examined the correspondence of psychiatric patients' self-reports and their spouses' ratings of them and found that PPM moderated cross-observer validity for N, but not for any of the other factors; NPM showed no significant differences. Morey, Quigley, et al. (2002) used a multimethod design in a large clinical sample and concluded that "attempts to correct NEO-PI-R profiles through the use of scales like PPM or NPM are likely to decrease rather than increase validity" (p. 596). Scoring for the research validity scales is available from their first author, J. A. Schinka, and clinicians who wish to use them may do so. However, we do not recommend them.

In principle, no set of validity scales, however sophisticated, can guarantee the accuracy of results. Imagine that a client simply decides to fool the clinician by describing not himself or herself, but, say, John Phillip Sousa. If the client makes a conscientious attempt to describe Sousa's personality, there will be no evidence of malingering or positive presentation management or random responding—yet the resulting personality profile will be utterly invalid.

It is ironic that people who are skeptical of substantive scales are eager to believe that their accuracy can be detected by the use of another scale. The fact is that clinicians are often called upon to make life altering decisions based on fallible data, and it is not surprising that they would cling to methods that promise guidance. Unfortunately, the data in support of validity scales is weak.

What, then, should clinicians do? First, they can be aware that the data in support of substantive scales from well validated instruments like the NEO inventories is strong: Most of the time, assessments from psychotherapy clients will be reasonably accurate. Second, they can encourage honest and accurate responding by establishing rapport with the client, explaining the purpose and utility of the assessment, assuring confidentiality, and perhaps promising feedback. Third, they can take note of the unobtrusive validity indicators that the NEO-PI-R offers, such as the checks for random responding and acquiescence, and weigh their reliance on the data accordingly. Fourth, they can compare results from the NEO inventories with other information from life, medical, and legal histories, and from the behavior of the client in therapy. Fifth, they can take advantage of the knowledge of significant others, who may provide a more objective portrait of the client, using validated observer rating forms. Sixth, they can recognize that all assessments are tentative and subject to revision as more information is gathered over the course of therapy.

Clinical Case

Costa and Piedmont (2003) presented the case of Madeline G., a young Native American woman who, after a troubled childhood, emerged as a successful attorney noted for defending the rights of her people. At the time she volunteered to be a case study, she was living with a common-law husband who provided ratings on Form R of the NEO-PI-R. Soon afterwards, their relationship ended, and she entered a long period of depressed affect. She had not reestablished a relationship 3 years later.

Figure 6.1 shows her NEO-PI-R profile, based on her common-law husband's ratings of her and using combined-sex norms, i.e., comparing her to adult men and women. Because this profile was generated by the NEO Software System, the more precise factor scores are given instead of domain scores. There is considerable within-domain scatter, which complicates the interpretation of factor scores. For example, most extraverts are high in Warmth, and overall, Madeline G. is clearly an extravert. Yet her score on Warmth is very low. In such cases, the facet scores provide the more accurate description, and one should characterize her as an extravert who lacks interpersonal warmth.

This case was selected to illustrate the interpretation of a NEO-PI-R profile and to show the potential utility of an observer rating version of the

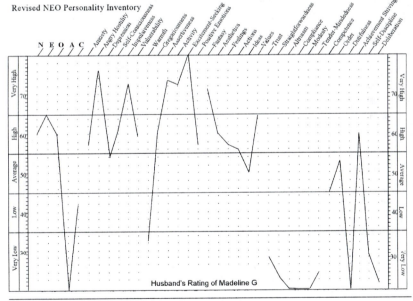

Figure 6.1 Personality profile of Madeline G as rated by her husband. T-scores (M = 50, SD = 10) comparing her to other adult men and women are plotted. The five-factors are given on the left; the 30 facets, grouped by factor, are given toward the right.

instrument for clinical assessment. Below are given excerpts from the NEO Software System Interpretive Report that describe the profile and some of its implications. The Clinical Hypotheses section is included, although normally it is only appropriate when the individual is a client in psychotherapy. For a more complete treatment of this case, see Costa and Piedmont (2003), who interpret a joint profile of Madeline's self-report and her common-law husband's rating of her. Note, however, that within-gender norms were used in that interpretation.

Global Description of Personality: The Five Factors

The most distinctive feature of this individual's personality is her standing on the factor of Agreeableness. People who score in this range are antagonistic and tend to be brusque or even rude in dealing with others. They are generally suspicious of other people and skeptical of others' ideas and opinions. They can be callous in their feelings. Their attitudes are tough minded in most situations. They prefer competition to cooperation, and express hostile feelings directly with little hesitation. People might describe them as relatively stubborn, critical, manipulative, or selfish. (Although antagonistic people are generally not well liked by others, they are often respected for their critical independence, and their emotional toughness and competitiveness can be assets in many social and business roles. Recall that Madeline G. is a lawyer, where antagonism may be an asset.)

This person is described as being high in Extraversion. Such people enjoy the company of others and the stimulation of social interaction. They like parties and may be group leaders. They have a fairly high level of energy and tend to be cheerful and optimistic. Those who know such people would describe them as active and sociable.

Next, consider the individual's level of Openness. High scorers like her are interested in experience for its own sake. They enjoy novelty and variety. They are sensitive to their own feelings and have a greater-than-average ability to recognize the emotions of others. They have a high appreciation of beauty in art and nature. They are willing to consider new ideas and values, and may be somewhat unconventional in their own views. Peers rate such people as original and curious.

This person is described as being high in Neuroticism. Individuals scoring in this range are likely to experience a moderately high level of negative emotion and occasional episodes of psychological distress. They are somewhat sensitive and moody, and are probably dissatisfied with several aspects of their lives. They are rather low in self-esteem and somewhat insecure. Friends and neighbors of such individuals might characterize them as worrying or overly emotional in comparison with the average person. (It is important to recall that Neuroticism is a dimension of normal personality, and high Neuroticism scores in themselves do not imply that the individual is suffering from any psychological disorder.)

Finally, the individual is rated in the low range in Conscientiousness. Women who score in this range have a fairly low need for achievement and tend not to organize their time well. They usually lack self-discipline and are disposed to put pleasure before business. They have a relaxed attitude toward their responsibilities and obligations. Raters describe such people as relatively unreliable and careless.

Detailed Interpretation: Facets of N, E, O, A, and C

Each of the five factors encompasses a number of more specific traits, or facets. The NEO-PI-R measures six facets in each of the five factors. An examination of the facet scores provides a more detailed picture of the distinctive way that these factors are seen in this person.

Neuroticism This individual is perceived as being anxious, generally apprehensive, and prone to worry. She often feels frustrated, irritable, and angry at others, but she has only the occasional periods of unhappiness that most people experience. Embarrassment or shyness when dealing with people, especially strangers, is often a problem for her. She is described as being poor at controlling her impulses and desires and she is unable to handle stress well.

Extraversion This person is rated as being somewhat formal and distant in her relationships with others, but she usually enjoys large and noisy crowds or parties. She is seen as being forceful and dominant, preferring to be a group leader rather than a follower. The individual is described as having a high level of energy and likes to keep active and busy. Excitement, stimulation, and thrills have great appeal to her, and she frequently experiences strong feelings of happiness and joy.

Openness In experiential style, this individual is described as being generally open. She has a vivid imagination and an active fantasy life. She is particularly responsive to beauty found in music, art, poetry, or nature, and her feelings and emotional reactions are varied and important to her. She enjoys new and different activities and has a high need for variety in her life. She has a moderate level of intellectual curiosity and she is generally liberal in her social, political, and moral beliefs [as shown in her defense of the rights of Native Americans].

Agreeableness According to the rater, this person tends to be cynical, skeptical, and suspicious, and has a low opinion of human nature. She is described as being willing at times to flatter or trick people into doing what she wants, and she tends to put her own needs and interests before others'. This individual can be very competitive and is ready to fight for her views if necessary. She is described as quite proud of herself and her accomplishments, and happy to take credit for them. Compared to other people, she is hard headed and tough minded, and her social and political attitudes reflect her pragmatic realism.

Conscientiousness   This individual is perceived as being reasonably efficient and generally sensible and rational in making decisions. She is described as moderately neat, punctual, and well organized, but she is sometimes less dependable and reliable and more likely to bend the rules than she should be. She has a high aspiration level and strives for excellence in whatever she does. She finds it difficult to make herself do what she should, and tends to quit when tasks become too difficult. She is occasionally hasty or impetuous and sometimes acts without considering all the consequences.

Personality Correlates: Some Possible Implications

Research has shown that the scales of the NEO-PI-R are related to a wide variety of psychosocial variables. These correlates suggest possible implications of the personality profile, because individuals who score high on a trait are also likely to score high on measures of the trait's correlates.

The following information is intended to give a sense of how this individual might function in a number of areas. It is not, however, a substitute for direct measurement. If, for example, there is a primary interest in medical complaints, an inventory of medical complaints should be administered in addition to the NEO-PI-R.

Coping and Defenses

In coping with the stresses of everyday life, this individual is described as being likely to react with ineffective responses, such as hostile reactions toward others, self-blame, or escapist fantasies. She is more likely than most adults to use humor and less likely to use faith in responding to threats, losses, and challenges. In addition, she is somewhat more likely to use positive thinking and direct action in dealing with problems. Her general defensive style can be characterized as maladaptive and self-defeating. She is more likely to present a defensive facade of superiority than to be self-sacrificing. She may use such defense mechanisms as acting out and projection.

Somatic Complaints   This individual may be somewhat oversensitive in monitoring and responding to physical problems and illnesses. She may sometimes exaggerate medical problems.

Psychological Well Being   Although her mood and satisfaction with various aspects of her life will vary with circumstances, in the long run this individual is likely to feel both joys and sorrows frequently, and be moderately happy overall. Because she is open to experience, her moods may be more intense and varied than those of the average woman.

Cognitive Processes   This individual is likely to be more complex and differentiated in her thoughts, values, and moral judgments than others of her level of intelligence and education. She would also probably score higher on measures of ego development. Because she is open to experience, this individual is likely to perform better than average on tests of divergent thinking ability; that is, she can generate fluent, flexible, and original solutions to many problems. She may be considered creative in her work or hobbies.

Interpersonal Characteristics   Many theories propose a circular arrangement of interpersonal traits around the axes of Love and Status. Within such systems, this person would likely be described as arrogant, calculating, gregarious, sociable, and especially dominant and assured. Her traits are associated with high standing on the interpersonal dimension of Status.

Needs and Motives   Research in personality has identified a widely used list of psychological needs. Individuals differ in the degree to which these needs characterize their motivational structure. This individual is likely to show high levels of the following needs: achievement, affiliation, aggression, change, dominance, exhibition (attention), play, sentience (enjoyment of sensuous and aesthetic experiences), succorance (support and sympathy), and understanding (intellectual stimulation). This individual is likely to show low levels of the following needs: abasement, cognitive structure, endurance (persistence), harm avoidance (avoiding danger), and nurturance.

Clinical Hypotheses: Axis II Disorders and Treatment Implications

The NEO-PI-R is a measure of personality traits, not psychopathology symptoms, but it is useful in clinical practice because personality profiles can suggest hypotheses about the disorders to which patients are prone and their responses to various kinds of therapy. This section of the NEO-PI-R Interpretive Report is intended for use in clinical populations only. The hypotheses it offers should be accepted only when they are supported by other corroborating evidence.

Psychiatric diagnoses occur in men and women with different frequencies, and diagnoses are given according to uniform criteria. For that reason, information in this section of the interpretive report is based on combined sex norms.

Axis II disorders

Personality traits are most directly relevant to the assessment of personality disorders coded on Axis II of the *DSM-IV*. A patient may have a personality disorder in addition to an Axis I disorder, and may meet criteria for more than one personality disorder. Certain diagnoses are more common among individuals with particular personality profiles; this section calls attention to diagnoses that are likely (or unlikely) to apply.

Borderline Personality Disorder   The most common personality disorder in clinical practice is Borderline, and the mean NEO-PI-R profile of a group of patients diagnosed as having Borderline Personality Disorder provides a basis for evaluating the patient. Profile agreement between the patient and this mean profile is higher than 90% of the subjects in the normative sample, suggesting that the patient may have Borderline features or a Borderline Personality Disorder.

Other Personality Disorders   Personality disorders can be conceptually characterized by a prototypic profile of NEO-PI-R facets that are consistent with the definition of the disorder and its associated features. The coefficient of profile agreement can be used to assess the overall similarity of the patient's personality to other DSM-IV personality disorder prototypes.

The patient's scores on Anxiety, Angry Hostility, Warmth, Gregariousness, Positive Emotions, Aesthetics, Feelings, Trust, Straightforwardness, Compliance, Modesty), Tender Mindedness, and Competence suggest the possibility of a Paranoid Personality Disorder. Paranoid Personality Disorder is rare in clinical practice; the patient's coefficient of profile agreement is higher than 99% of the subjects' in the normative sample.

The patient's score on Anxiety (N1), Depression (N3), Self-Consciousness (N4), Vulnerability (N6), Warmth (E1), Gregariousness (E2), Fantasy (O1), Feelings (O3), Ideas (O5), Values (O6), and Trust (A1), suggest the possibility of a Schizotypal Personality Disorder. The patient's coefficient of profile agreement is higher than 95% of subjects' in the normative sample.

The patient's scores on Anxiety, Angry Hostility, Depression, Impulsiven ess,Warmth,Excitement Seeking, Straightforwardness, Altruism, Compliance, Tender-Mindedness, Dutifulness, Self-Discipline, and Deliberation suggest the possibility of an Antisocial Personality Disorder. The patient's coefficient of profile agreement is higher than 95% of subjects' in the normative sample.

The patient's scores on Angry Hostility, Self-Consciousness, Vulnerability, Warmth, Gregariousness, Activity, Excitement Seeking, Positive Emotions, Fantasy, Feelings, Actions, Ideas, Trust, Straightforwardness, Altruism, Competence, and Self-Discipline suggest the possibility of a Histrionic Personality

Disorder. Histrionic Personality Disorder is relatively common in clinical practice; the patient's coefficient of profile agreement is higher than 90% of subjects' in the normative sample.

The patient's scores on Angry Hostility, Depression, Self-Consciousness, Fantasy, Straightforwardness, Compliance, Modesty, and Tender Mindedness suggest the possibility of a Narcissistic Personality Disorder. Narcissistic Personality Disorder is relatively common in clinical practice; the patient's coefficient of profile agreement is higher than 90% of the subjects' in the normative sample.

It is unlikely that the patient has Schizoid Personality Disorder, Avoidant Personality Disorder, or Dependent Personality Disorder because the patient's coefficients of profile agreement are lower than 50% of the subjects' in the normative sample.

Treatment Implications

Like most individuals in psychotherapy, this patient is high in Neuroticism. She is likely to experience a variety of negative emotions and to be distressed by many problems, and mood regulation may be an important treatment focus. Very high Neuroticism scores are associated with a poor prognosis and treatment goals should be appropriately modest.

Because she is extraverted, this patient finds it easy to talk about her problems, and enjoys interacting with others. She is likely to respond well to forms of psychotherapy that emphasize verbal and social interactions, such as psychoanalysis and group therapy.

This patient is open to experience, probably including the novel experience of psychotherapy. She tends to be introspective and psychologically minded, and will probably be willing to try a variety of psychotherapeutic techniques. Free association, dream interpretation, and imaging techniques are likely to be congenial. Focusing on concrete solutions to problems may be more difficult for extremely open individuals.

The patient scores low on Agreeableness. She is therefore likely to be skeptical and antagonistic in psychotherapy, and reluctant to establish a treatment alliance until the therapist has demonstrated his or her skill and knowledge. Individuals with extremely low levels of Agreeableness are unlikely to seek treatment voluntarily, and may terminate treatment early.

Because the patient is low in Conscientiousness, she may lack the determination to work on the task of psychotherapy. She may be late for appointments and may have excuses for not having completed homework assignments. Some evidence suggests that individuals low in Conscientiousness have poorer treatment outcomes, and the therapist may need to make extra efforts to motivate the patient and structure the process of psychotherapy.

Stability of the Profile

Research suggests that the individual's personality profile is likely to be stable throughout adulthood. Barring catastrophic stress, major illness, or therapeutic intervention, this description will probably serve as a fair guide even in old age.

Questions to Ponder

How much confidence would you place in this informant rating as a basis for understanding the client and her problems? If a self-report was not available, what steps would you take to increase your confidence? The low A and C scores of this client suggest that there will be resistance to therapy. What are the client's strengths, and how could you use them to engage the client in psychotherapy? What kinds of psychotherapy would you select for Madeline G; what would you avoid?

Chapter Summary

The NEO inventories were originally developed at a time when "normal" and "abnormal" were thought to represent categorically distinct forms of psychological functioning. As a result, the use of the NEO inventories in clinical practice was initially a matter of some controversy (Ben-Porath

---

Key Points to Remember

The NEO inventories operationalize the scientifically rigorous Five-Factor Model.

- The NEO-PI-R provides detailed information on 30 facets; the brief NEO-FFI gives an overview of the five factors; both are suitable for ages 18 and up.
- Both self-report and observer rating versions are available, and studies show convergence as well as different perspectives.
- The NEO-PI-3 is more readable, and suitable for ages 12 and older.
- The NEO Software System administers, scores, and interprets NEO inventories.
- NEO-PI-R facet scales predict *DSM* Personality Disorders and can alert clinicians to likely problems in living.
- NEO inventories are used around the world in more than 40 authorized translations; they are appropriate for minority and ethnic groups in North America.
- Unlike most clinical scales, the NEO inventories avoid the use of validity scales because their utility is suspect.
- Personality feedback can be offered in a brief summary or in a more extended computer report.
- NEO inventories facilitate the use of informant reports as substitutes for or supplements to self-reports in clinical practice.
- Assessment with the NEO-PI-R can help clinicians develop empathy, identify strengths and weaknesses, anticipate the course of therapy, and select optimal treatment methods.

& Waller, 1992). Now, in large part because of research on the FFM, it is widely recognized that personality traits characterize all people and that the general traits assessed by the NEO inventories are not only relevant to but essential for an understanding of psychological functioning in clinical populations. The NEO-PI-R, in particular, has become a standard part of clinical assessment. Informant ratings on Form R of the instrument are so far underutilized by clinicians, but have great promise as a new tool for routine assessment (Singer, 2005).

Note

1. Paul T. Costa, Jr. and Robert R. McCrae receive royalties from the NEO inventories. This research was supported by the Intramural Research Program of the NIH, National Institutes on Aging. NEO-PI-R profile forms and NEO Software System Interpretive Report reproduced by special permission of the publisher, Psychological Assessment Resources, 16204 North Florida Avenue, Lutz, Florida 33549, from the Revised NEO Personality Inventory by Paul T. Costa, Jr., and Robert R. McCrae. Copyright 1978, 1985, 1989, 1991, 1992 by Psychological Assessment Resources. (PAR). Further reproduction is prohibited without permission of PAR.

References

Ashton, M. C., Lee, K., Perugini, M., Szarota, P., De Vries, R. E., Di Blass, L., et al. (2004). A six-factor structure of personality descriptive adjectives: Solutions from psycholexical studies in seven languages. *Journal of Personality and Social Psychology, 86*, 356–366.

Bagby, R. M., Rector, N. A., Bindseil, K., Dickens, S. E., Levitan, R. D., & Kennedy, S. H. (1998). Self-report ratings and informant ratings of personalities of depressed outpatients. *American Journal of Psychiatry, 155*, 437–438.

Ball, S. A., Tennen, H., Poling, J. C., Kranzler, H. R., & Rounsaville, B. J. (1997). Personality, temperament, and character dimensions and the *DSM-IV* personality disorders in substance abusers. *Journal of Abnormal Psychology, 4*, 545–553.

Ben-Porath, Y. S., & Waller, N. G. (1992). Five big issues in clinical personality assessment: A rejoinder to Costa and McCrae. *Psychological Assessment, 4*, 23–25.

Benet-Martínez, V., & John, O. P. (1998). Los cinco Grandes across cultures and ethnic groups: Multitrait multimethod analyses of the Big Five in Spanish and English. *Journal of Personality and Social Psychology, 75*, 729–750.

Berry, D. T. R., Bagby, R. M., Smerz, J., Rinaldo, J. C., Cadlwell-Andrews, A., & Baer, R. A. (2001). Effectiveness of NEO-PI-R research validity scales for discriminating analog malingering and genuine psychopathology. *Journal of Personality Assessment, 76*, 496–516.

Black, J. (2000). Personality testing and police selection: Utility of the Big Five. *New Zealand Journal of Psychology, 29*, 2–9.

Bliwise, D. L., Friedman, L., Nekich, J. C., & Yesavage, J. A. (1995). Prediction of outcome in behaviorally based insomnia treatments. *Journal of Behavior Therapy and Experimental Psychiatry, 26*, 17–23.

Carter, J. A., Herbst, J. H., Stoller, K. B., King, V. L., Kidorf, M. S., Costa, P. T., Jr., et al. (2001). Short-term stability of NEO-PI-R personality trait scores in opioid-dependent outpatients. *Psychology of Addictive Behaviors, 15*, 255–260.

Christensen, A. J., & Smith, T. W. (1995). Personality and patient adherence: Correlates of the Five-Factor Model in renal dialysis. *Journal of Behavioral Medicine, 18*, 305–312.

Costa, P. T., Jr., Bagby, R. M., Herbst, J. H., & McCrae, R. R. (2005). Personality self-reports are concurrently reliable and valid during acute depressive episodes. *Journal of Affective Disorders, 89*, 45–55.

Costa, P. T., Jr., & McCrae, R. R. (1980). Still stable after all these years: Personality as a key to some issues in adulthood and old age. In P. B. Baltes & O. G. Brim, Jr. (Eds.), *Life span development and behavior* (Vol. 3, pp. 65–102). New York: Academic Press.

Costa, P. T., Jr., & McCrae, R. R. (1985). *The NEO Personality Inventory manual.* Odessa, FL: Psychological Assessment Resources.

Costa, P. T., Jr., & McCrae, R. R. (1988). From catalog to classification: Murray's needs and the Five-Factor Model. *Journal of Personality and Social Psychology, 55,* 258–265.

Costa, P. T., Jr., & McCrae, R. R. (1989). *The NEO-PI/NEO-FFI manual supplement.* Odessa, FL: Psychological Assessment Resources.

Costa, P. T., Jr., & McCrae, R. R. (1992a). Normal personality assessment in clinical practice: The NEO Personality Inventory. *Psychological Assessment, 4,* 5–13, 20–22.

Costa, P. T., Jr., & McCrae, R. R. (1992b). *Revised NEO Personality Inventory (NEO-PI-R) and NEO Five-Factor Inventory (NEO-FFI) professional manual.* Odessa, FL: Psychological Assessment Resources.

Costa, P. T., Jr., & McCrae, R. R. (1997). Stability and change in personality assessment: The Revised NEO Personality Inventory in the year 2000. *Journal of Personality Assessment, 68,* 86–94.

Costa, P. T., Jr., & McCrae, R. R. (2005). A Five-Factor Model perspective on personality disorders. In S. Strack (Ed.), *Handbook of personology and psychopathology* (pp. 257–270). Hoboken, NJ: John Wiley & Sons.

Costa, P. T., Jr., McCrae, R. R., & Dye, D. A. (1991). Facet scales for agreeableness and conscientiousness: A revision of the NEO Personality Inventory. *Personality and Individual Differences, 12,* 887–898.

Costa, P. T., Jr., McCrae, R. R., & Martin, T. A. (2006). Incipient adult personality: The NEO-PI-3 in middle school-aged children. Manuscript submitted for publication.

Costa, P. T., Jr., McCrae, R. R., & PAR Staff. (1994). NEO Software System [Computer software]. Odessa, FL: Psychological Assessment Resources.

Costa, P. T., Jr., & Piedmont, R. L. (2003). Multivariate assessment: NEO-PI-R profiles of Madeline G. In J. S. Wiggins (Ed.), *Paradigms of personality assessment* (pp. 262–280). New York: Guilford.

Costa, P. T., Jr., & Widiger, T. A. (Eds.). (2002). *Personality disorders and the Five-Factor Model of personality* (2nd ed.). Washington, DC: American Psychological Association.

De Fruyt, F., & Mervielde, I. (1997). The Five-Factor Model of personality and Holland's RIASEC interest types. *Personality and Individual Differences, 23,* 87–103.

Digman, J. M. (1990). Personality structure: Emergence of the Five-Factor Model. *Annual Review of Psychology, 41,* 417–440.

Du, L., Baksih, D., Ravindran, A. V., & Hrdina, P. D. (2002). Does fluoxetine influence major depression by modifying five-factor personality traits? *Journal of Affective Disorders, 71,* 235–241.

Einstein, D., & Lanning, K. (1998). Shame, guilt, ego development and the Five-Factor Model of personality. *Journal of Personality, 66,* 555–582.

Funder, D. (2001). Personality. *Annual Review of Psychology, 52,* 197–221.

Harkness, A. R., & McNulty, J. L. (2002). Implications of personality individual differences science for clinical work on personality disorders. In P. T. Costa, Jr., & T. A. Widiger (Eds.), *Personality disorders and the Five-Factor Model of personality* (2nd ed., pp. 391–403). Washington, DC: American Psychological Association.

Hathaway, S. R., & McKinley, J. C. (1983). *The Minnesota Multiphasic Personality Inventory manual.* New York: Psychological Corporation.

Haven, S., & ten Berge, J. M. F. (1977). *Tucker's coefficient of congruence as a measure of factorial invariance: An empirical study.* Heymans Bulletin No. 290 EX: University of Groningen.

Hill, C. E., Diemer, R. A., & Heaton, K. J. (1997). Dream interpretation sessions: Who volunteers, who benefits, and what volunteer clients view as most and least helpful. *Journal of Counseling Psychology, 44,* 53–62.

Johnson, J. H., Butcher, J. N., Null, C., & Johnson, K. N. (1984). Replicated item level factor analysis of the full MMPI. *Journal of Personality and Social Psychology, 47,* 105–114.

Katon, W., Hollifield, M., Chapman, T., Mannuzza, S., Ballenger, J., & Fyer, A. (1995). Infrequent panic attacks: Psychiatric comorbidity, personality characteristics, and functional disability. *Journal of Psychiatric Research, 29,* 121–131.

Langer, F. (2004). Pairs, reflections, and the EgoI: Exploration of a perceptual hypothesis. *Journal of Personality Assessment, 82,* 114–126.

Lehne, G. K. (2002). The NEO-PI and MCMI in the forensic evaluation of sex offenders. In P. T. Costa, Jr. & T. A. Widiger (Eds.), *Personality disorders and the Five-Factor Model of personality* (pp. 269–282). Washington, DC: American Psychological Association.

Lozano, B. E., & Johnson, S. L. (2001). Can personality traits predict increases in manic and depressive symptoms? *Journal of Affective Disorders, 63*, 103–111.

Markon, K. E., Krueger, R. F., & Watson, D. (2005). Delineating the structure of normal and abnormal personality: An integrative hierarchical approach. *Journal of Personality and Social Psychology, 88*, 139–157.

Mattox, L. M. (2004). The relationship between preexisting client personality and initial perceptions of the treatment alliance. *Dissertation Abstracts International, Section B: The Sciences and Engineering, 64*, 5225.

McCrae, R. R. (in press). A note on some measures of profile agreement. *Journal of Personality Assessment.*

McCrae, R. R., & Allik, J. (Eds.). (2002). *The Five-Factor Model of personality across cultures.* New York: Kluwer Academic/Plenum Publishers.

McCrae, R. R., & Costa, P. T., Jr. (1983). Joint factors in self-reports and ratings: Neuroticism, Extraversion, and Openness to Experience. *Personality and Individual Differences, 4*, 245–255.

McCrae, R. R., & Costa, P. T., Jr. (1985). Updating Norman's "adequate taxonomy": Intelligence and personality dimensions in natural language and in questionnaires. *Journal of Personality and Social Psychology, 49*, 710–721.

McCrae, R. R., & Costa, P. T., Jr. (1987). Validation of the Five-Factor Model of personality across instruments and observers. *Journal of Personality and Social Psychology, 52*, 81–90.

McCrae, R. R., & Costa, P. T., Jr. (1989). Reinterpreting the Myers-Briggs Type Indicator from the perspective of the Five-Factor Model of personality. *Journal of Personality, 57*, 17–40.

McCrae, R. R., & Costa, P. T., Jr. (1996). Toward a new generation of personality theories: Theoretical contexts for the Five-Factor Model. In J. S. Wiggins (Ed.), *The Five-Factor Model of personality: Theoretical perspectives* (pp. 51–87). New York: Guilford.

McCrae, R. R., & Costa, P. T., Jr. (2004). A contemplated revision of the NEO Five-Factor Inventory. *Personality and Individual Differences, 36*, 587–596.

McCrae, R. R., Costa, P. T., Jr., Dahlstrom, W. G., Barefoot, J. C., Siegler, I. C., & Williams, R. B., Jr. (1989). A caution on the use of the MMPI *K*-correction in research on psychosomatic medicine. *Psychosomatic Medicine, 51*, 58–65.

McCrae, R. R., Costa, P. T., Jr., & Martin, T. A. (2005). The NEO-PI-3: A more readable Revised NEO Personality Inventory. *Journal of Personality Assessment, 84*, 261–270.

McCrae, R. R., Costa, P. T., Jr., Martin, T. A., Oryol, V. E., Rukavishnikov, A. A., Senin, I. G., et al. (2004). Consensual validation of personality traits across cultures. *Journal of Research in Personality, 38*, 179–201.

McCrae, R. R., Costa, P. T., Jr., & Piedmont, R. L. (1993). Folk concepts, natural language, and psychological constructs: The California Psychological Inventory and the Five-Factor Model. *Journal of Personality, 61*, 1–26.

McCrae, R. R., Costa, P. T., Jr., Terracciano, A., Parker, W. D., Mills, C. J., De Fruyt, F., et al. (2002). Personality trait development from 12 to 18: Longitudinal, cross-sectional, and cross-cultural analyses. *Journal of Personality and Social Psychology, 83*, 1456–1468.

McCrae, R. R., Herbst, J. H., & Costa, P. T., Jr. (2001). Effects of acquiescence on personality factor structures. In R. Riemann, F. Ostendorf, & F. Spinath (Eds.), *Personality and temperament: Genetics, evolution, and structure* (pp. 217–231). Berlin: Pabst Science Publishers.

McCrae, R. R., & John, O. P. (1992). An introduction to the Five-Factor Model and its applications. *Journal of Personality, 60*, 175–215.

McCrae, R. R., Löckenhoff, C. E., & Costa, P. T., Jr. (2005). A step towards DSM-V: Cataloging personality-related problems in living. *European Journal of Personality, 19*, 269–270.

McCrae, R. R., Martin, T. A., & Costa, P. T., Jr. (2005). Age trends and age norms for the NEO Personality Inventory-3 in adolescents and adults. *Assessment, 12*, 363–373.

McCrae, R. R., Terracciano, A., & 78 Members of the Personality Profiles of Cultures Project. (2005a). Universal features of personality traits from the observer's perspective: Data from 50 cultures. *Journal of Personality and Social Psychology, 88*, 547–561.

McCrae, R. R., Terracciano, A., & 79 Members of the Personality Profiles of Cultures Project. (2005b). Personality profiles of cultures: Aggregate personality traits. *Journal of Personality and Social Psychology, 89*, 407–425.

McCrae, R. R., Yang, J., Costa, P. T., Jr., Dai, X., Yao, S., Cai, T., et al. (2001). Personality profiles and the prediction of categorical personality disorders. *Journal of Personality, 69*, 121–145.

McCrae, R. R., Yik, M. S. M., Trapnell, P. D., Bond, M. H., & Paulhus, D. L. (1998). Interpreting personality profiles across cultures: Bilingual, acculturation, and peer rating studies of Chinese undergraduates. *Journal of Personality and Social Psychology, 74*, 1041–1055.

Miller, J. D., Bagby, R. M., Pilkonis, P. A., Reynolds, S. K., & Lynam, D. R. (2005). A simplified technique for scoring *DSM-IV* personality disorders with the Five-Factor Model. *Assessment, 12*, 404–415.

Miller, J. D., Lynam, D. R., Widiger, T. A., & Leukefeld, C. (2001). Personality disorders as extreme variants of common personality dimensions: Can the Five-Factor Model adequately represent psychopathy? *Journal of Personality, 69*(2), 253–276.

Miller, T. (1991). The psychotherapeutic utility of the Five-Factor Model of personality: A clinician's experience. *Journal of Personality Assessment, 57*, 415–433.

Morey, L. C. (1991). *Personality Assessment Inventory: Professional manual* Odessa, FL: Psychological Assessment Resources.

Morey, L. C., Gunderson, J., Quigley, B. D., Shea, M. T., Skodol, A. E., McGlashan, T. H., et al. (2002). The representation of Borderline, Avoidant, Obsessive-Compulsive, and Schizotypal personality disorders by the Five-Factor Model of personality. *Journal of Personality Disorders, 16*, 215–234.

Morey, L. C., Quigley, B. D., Sanislow, C. A., Skodol, A. E., McGlashan, T. H., Shea, M. T., et al. (2002). Substance or style? An investigation of the NEO-PI-R validity scales. *Journal of Personality Assessment, 79*, 583–599.

Moua, G. (2006, March). Trait structure and levels in Hmong Americans: A test of the Five-Factor Model of personality. Paper presented at the First International Conference on Hmong Studies, St. Paul, MN.

Mutén, E. (1991). Self-reports, spouse ratings, and psychophysiological assessment in a behavioral medicine program: An application of the Five-Factor Model. *Journal of Personality Assessment, 57*, 449–464.

Nigg, J. T., John, O. P., Blaskey, L. G., Huang-Pollock, C. L., Willcutt, E. G., Hinshaw, S. P., et al. (2002). Big Five dimensions and ADHD symptoms: Links between personality traits and clinical symptoms. *Journal of Personality and Social Psychology, 83*, 451–469.

Ogrodniczuk, J. S., Piper, W. E., Joyce, A. S., McCallum, M., & Rosie, J. S. (2003). NEO Five-Factor personality traits as predictors of response to two forms of group psychotherapy. *International Journal of Group Psychotherapy, 53*, 417–442.

Paulhus, D. L., Bruce, M. N., & Trapnell, P. D. (1995). Effects of self-presentation strategies on personality profiles and their structure. *Personality and Social Psychology Bulletin, 21*, 100–108.

Paunonen, S. V., & Ashton, M. C. (2001). Big Five factors and facets and the prediction of behavior. *Journal of Personality and Social Psychology, 81*, 524–539.

Piedmont, R. L. (2001). Cracking the plaster cast: Big Five personality change during intensive outpatient counseling. *Journal of Research in Personality, 35*, 500–520.

Piedmont, R. L., McCrae, R. R., Riemann, R., & Angleitner, A. (2000). On the invalidity of validity scales in volunteer samples: Evidence from self-reports and observer ratings in volunteer samples. *Journal of Personality and Social Psychology, 78*, 582–593.

Poortinga, Y. H., van de Vijver, F., & van Hemert, D. A. (2002). Cross-cultural equivalence of the Big Five: A tentative interpretation of the evidence. In R. R. McCrae & J. Allik (Eds.), *The Five-Factor Model of personality across cultures* (pp. 273–294). New York: Kluwer Academic/ Plenum Publishers.

Psychological Assessment Resources. (1994). *The Revised NEO Personality Inventory: Manual supplement for the Spanish edition.* Odessa, FL: Author.

Quirk, S. W., Christiansen, N. D., Wagner, S. H., & McNulty, J. L. (2003). On the usefulness of measures of normal personality for clinical assessment: Evidence of the incremental validity of the Revised NEO Personality Inventory. *Psychological Assessment, 15*, 311–325.

Reise, S. P., & Henson, J. M. (2000). Computerization and adaptive administration of the NEO-PI-R. *Assessment, 7*, 347–364.

Reynolds, S. K., & Clark, L. A. (2001). Predicting dimensions of personality disorder from domains and facets of the Five-Factor Model. *Journal of Personality, 69*, 199–222.

Robins, R. W., Fraley, R. C., Roberts, B. W., & Trzesniewski, K. H. (2001). A longitudinal study of personality change in young adulthood. *Journal of Personality, 69*, 617–640.

Samuel, D. B., & Widiger, T. A. (2006). Clinicians' judgments of clinical utility: A comparison of the *DSM-IV* and Five-Factor Models. *Journal of Abnormal Psychology, 115*, 298–308.

Scepansky, J. A., & Bjornsen, C. A. (2003). Educational orientation, NEO-PI-R personality traits, and plans for graduate school. *College Student Journal, 37*, 574–581.

Schinka, J., Kinder, B., & Kremer, T. (1997). Research validity scales for the NEO-PI-R: Development and initial validation. *Journal of Personality Assessment, 68*, 127–138.

Shaver, P. R., & Brennan, K. A. (1992). Attachment styles and the "Big Five" personality traits: Their connection with each other and with romantic relationship outcomes. *Personality and Social Psychology Bulletin, 18*, 536–545.

Siegler, I. C., Zonderman, A. B., Barefoot, J. C., Williams, R. B., Jr., Costa, P. T., Jr., & McCrae, R. R. (1990). Predicting personality in adulthood from college MMPI scores: Implications for follow-up studies in psychosomatic medicine. *Psychosomatic Medicine, 52*, 644–652.

Simakhodskaya, Z. (2000, August). Russian Revised NEO-PI-R: Concordant validity and relationship to acculturation. Paper presented at the 108th Convention of the American Psychological Association, Washington, DC.

Singer, J. A. (2005). *Personality and psychotherapy: Treating the whole person.* New York: Guilford Press.

Soldz, S., Budman, S., Demby, A., & Merry, J. (1995). Personality traits as seen by patients, therapists, and other group members: The Big Five in personality disorder groups. *Psychotherapy: Theory, Research, Practice, Training, 32*, 678–687.

Stone, M. H. (2002). Treatment of personality disorders from the perspective of the Five-Factor Model. In P. T. Costa, Jr., & T. A. Widiger (Eds.), *Personality disorders and the Five-Factor Model of personality* (2nd ed., pp. 405–430). Washington, DC: American Psychological Association.

Strauss, M. E., & Pasupathi, M. (1994). Primary caregivers' descriptions of Alzheimer patients' personality traits: Temporal stability and sensitivity to change. *Alzheimer Disease & Associated Disorders, 8*, 166–176.

Talbot, N. L., Duberstein, P. R., Butzel, J. S., Cox, C., & Giles, D. E. (2003). Personality traits and symptom reduction in a group treatment for women with histories of childhood sexual abuse. *Comprehensive Psychiatry, 44*, 448–453.

Terracciano, A., Costa, P. T., Jr., & McCrae, R. R. (2006). Personality plasticity after age 30. *Personality and Social Psychology Bulletin, 32*, 999–1009.

Terracciano, A., Merritt, M., Zonderman, A. B., & Evans, M. K. (2003). Personality traits and sex differences in emotion recognition among African Americans and Caucasians. *Annals of the New York Academy of Sciences, 1000*, 309–312.

Tupes, E. C., & Christal, R. E. (1961/1992). Recurrent personality factors based on trait ratings. *Journal of Personality, 60*, 225–251.

Widiger, T. A., & Costa, P. T., Jr. (2002). Five-Factor Model personality disorder research. In P. T. Costa, Jr., & T. A. Widiger (Eds.), *Personality disorders and the Five-Factor Model of personality* (2nd ed., pp. 59–87). Washington, DC: American Psychological Association.

Widiger, T. A., Costa, P. T., Jr., & McCrae, R. R. (2002). A proposal for Axis II: Diagnosing personality disorders using the Five-Factor Model. In P. T. Costa, Jr. & T. A. Widiger (Eds.), *Personality disorders and the Five-Factor Model of personality* (2nd ed., pp. 431–456). Washington, DC: American Psychological Association.

Wolfenstein, M., & Trull, T. J. (1997). Depression and Openness to Experience. *Journal of Personality Assessment, 69*, 614–632.

Yamagata, S., Suzuki, A., Ando, J., Ono, Y., Kijima, N., Yoshimura, K., et al. (2006). Is the genetic structure of human personality universal? A cross-cultural twin study from North America, Europe, and Asia. *Journal of Personality and Social Psychology, 90*, 987–998.

Yang, J., Bagby, R. M., & Ryder, A. G. (2000). Response style and the Revised NEO Personality Inventory: Validity scales and spousal ratings in a Chinese psychiatric sample. *Assessment, 7*, 389–402.

Yang, J., McCrae, R. R., Costa, P. T., Jr., Dai, X., Yao, S., Cai, T., et al. (1999). Cross-cultural personality assessment in psychiatric populations: The NEO-PI-R in the People's Republic of China. *Psychological Assessment, 11*, 359–368.

Appendix

Multiple Choice Questions

1. For which population is the self-report Form S of the NEO-PI-R unsuitable?
   A. Acutely depressed clients.
   B. Adolescents younger than 18.
   C. Hmong Americans.
   D. Demented patients.
2. Correlations between Form S and Form R of the NEO-PI-R show that
   A. Cross-observer agreement is substantial but not perfect.
   B. Agreement is found only in individualistic cultures, not collectivistic cultures like China.
   C. Self-reports are more flattering than observer ratings.
   D. Only observable traits, like Extraversion, show cross-observer agreement.
3. The NEO-PI-3 is a modification of the NEO-PI-R that
   A. Is shorter.
   B. Is more readable.
   C. Assesses only the 3 clinically relevant factors.
   D. Is for use only by adolescents.
4. Which of the following is *not* provided by the Computer Interpretive Report?
   A. A description of the client's personality traits.
   B. Clinical hypotheses about possible personality disorders.
   C. *DSM-IV* diagnoses.
   D. Indicators of protocol validity.
5. Cross-cultural studies show that
   A. The FFM structure of personality is universal.
   B. The NEO-PI-R must be administered in the client's native language.
   C. Americans are more introverted than Asians.
   D. Scalar equivalence is lost in translation.
6. The NEO-PI-R does not have social desirability scales because
   A. They were developed by Schinka et al.
   B. Their use threatens the treatment alliance.
   C. There is little evidence that they work as intended.
   D. The instrument is already too long.
7. The observer rating Form R is especially useful
   A. When the client is mentally incapacitated.
   B. As a supplement to Form S.
   C. When there is reason to believe self-reports would be deliberately distorted.
   D. All the above.
8. Feedback on personality scores
   A. Is appropriate only for normal volunteers.
   B. Must be at a very broad and superficial level.
   C. Can be an important part of therapy.
   D. Has no role in couples therapy.
9. Research on the clinical use of the NEO inventories shows that
   A. Personality traits are related to Axis II disorders, but not Axis I disorders.
   B. The NEO-PI-R adds nothing to standard clinical assessments.

C. Attention deficit/hyperactivity disorder is chiefly predicted by low Openness.

D. High Conscientiousness predicts increases in manic symptoms in bipolar disorder patients.

10. NEO-PI-R scores are helpful to the clinician in
    A. Identifying strengths as well as weaknesses.
    B. Developing empathy.
    C. Selecting the optimal form of treatment.
    D. All the above.

Essay Questions

1. Questionnaires like the NEO-PI-R are subject to conscious distortion and bias. What can the clinician do to optimize the accuracy of test results when using such instruments?

   [Response ought to include the following: (a) validity indicators should be considered, but not necessarily used to discard protocols; (b) self-reports can be supplemented by observer ratings from an informed and impartial observer; (c) the clinician should encourage the cooperation of the client by explaining the need for accurate assessments, ensuring confidentiality, and perhaps offering feedback; and (d) the accuracy of all assessments should be considered and reconsidered in light of interactions with the client and all other available information.]

2. At your first session with a new client, the NEO-PI-R suggests that her most distinctive traits are high O and low E. How do you anticipate that your interactions with the client will go, and what does this information suggest about the best approaches to therapy?

   [Response should include: (a) it may take a few sessions for the client to warm up to the therapist; (b) structured therapies may be preferred over open-ended talking; (c) novel and imaginative forms of therapy may intrigue the client; and (d) depending on the specific problems associated with low E, the client might benefit from assertiveness or other social skills training.]

CHAPTER 7

Behavior Rating Scales[1]

KENNETH W. MERRELL
JASON E. HARLACHER

The use of behavior rating scales for clinical assessment of behavioral, social, and emotional characteristics of children and adolescents has increased dramatically during the past two decades. This assessment method is now one of the most frequently used components of assessment batteries, and is a key means of obtaining information on a children or adolescents before making diagnostic and classification decisions, implementing interventions, and monitoring the effectiveness of interventions and programs. As behavior rating scales have become more widely used, there have been numerous advances in research on rating scale technology that have strengthened the desirability of using this form of assessment (Elliott, Busse, & Gresham, 1993; Merrell, 2000a, 2000b, 2007).

The purpose of this chapter is to provide a detailed introduction and overview to the use of behavior rating scales in assessing personality and behavioral characteristics of children and adolescents. First, the characteristics of behavior rating scales are discussed in depth, including the critical elements of this assessment method, its advantages, and its challenges. Second, as an example of the tools that are available for use by clinicians and researchers, an overview of three of the most popular cross-informant behavior ratings scale systems is provided. Third, cross-cultural issues in using behavior rating scales are evaluated, including many of the challenges and practices for which research evidence is not yet conclusive. Finally, some of the current questions and controversies regarding child behavior rating scales are discussed, setting the stage for future developments in this arena.

Characteristics of Behavior Rating Scales

Behavior rating scales provide a standardized format for making *summary judgments* regarding a child or adolescent's behavioral characteristics. These judgments are made by an informant who knows the child or adolescent well enough to make an informed rating. The informant is usually a parent or teacher, but other individuals who are familiar with the child or adolescent—work supervisors, classroom aides, temporary surrogate parents, and extended family members, for example—might legitimately be a source for behavior rating scale data.

Behavior rating scales measure *perceptions* of specified behaviors, but this method is empirically-based, has many psychometric strengths, and meet Martin's (1988) four criteria for being considered an objective measurement technique: (1) individual differences in responses to stimuli are measured, relatively consistent across times, items, and situations; (2) comparison of responses of one person to those of other persons can be made; (3) the use of norms for comparison purposes; and (4) responses are shown to be related to other stimuli in some meaningful way. Behavior rating scales, almost without exception, meet these four criteria of empirical objectivity.

Because of their empirical nature, rating scales have been found to yield behavioral assessment data that are more reliable than the data typically obtained through unstructured interviewing or performance-based techniques (Martin, Hooper, & Snow, 1986; Merrell, 2007). In addition, because systematic and direct observations of child behavior may require several observations over a period of time to yield reliable data, particularly when younger children are being observed (Doll & Elliott, 1994; Hintze, 2005; Hintze & Mathews, 2004), rating scale measures appear to offer several advantages for reliability over direct observation, even though the two methods tap somewhat differing constructs. Direct behavioral observation provides a measure of clearly specified behaviors that occur within a specific environmental context and within a given time constraint. Behavior rating scales, on the other hand, provide summative judgments of general types of behavioral characteristics that may have occurred in a variety of settings an over a long period of time. Both methods of behavioral assessment are important in the overall clinical analysis of behavior.

It is useful to differentiate *rating scale* from a related term, *checklist*. A checklist format for identifying behavioral problems or competencies lists a number of behavioral descriptors, and if the rater perceives the symptom to be present, he or she simply "checks" the item. After completing the checklist, the number of checked items is summed. Checklists are thus considered to be *additive* in nature, because the obtained score is a simple additive summation of all the checked items. Rating scales, like checklists, allow the rater to indicate whether a specific symptom is present or absent. However, rating scales also provide a means of estimating the degree to which a characteristic is present. A common 3-point rating system (there are many variations of this) allows the rater to score a specific behavior descriptor from 0 to 2, with 0 indicating the symptom is never present, 1 indicating the symptom is sometimes present, and 2 indicating the symptom is frequently present. Because rating scales allow the rater to weight the specified symptoms differentially, and each weighting corresponds with a specific symbolic numerical value and frequency or intensity description, rating scales are said to be *algebraic* in nature. Conners and Werry (1979) defined rating scales as an "... algebraic summation, over variable periods of time and numbers of social situations, of many discrete observations ..." (p. 341). This algebraic rating scale format is preferred to the additive format provided by checklists because it allows for more precise measurement and differentiation of behavioral frequency or intensity (Merrell, 2000a, 2000b, 2007). A wider range of possible scores and variance is possible using the algebraic rating scale format as opposed to the checklist format, which seems to have continually lost favor over time.

Advantages of Behavior Rating Scales

The popularity of behavior rating scales is not incidental—they offer many advantages for clinicians and researchers who conduct child and adolescent assessments. The main advantages of behavior rating scales may be summarized in the following six points:

1. In comparison with direct behavioral observation, behavior rating scales are less expensive in terms of professional time involved and amount of training required to use the assessment system.
2. Behavior rating scales may provide information on low frequency but important behaviors that might not be observed in a limited number of direct observation sessions, such as violent and assaultive behavior. In most cases, these types of low-frequency behaviors do not occur constantly or at a high response rate, so they might be missed when conducting one or two brief observations.
3. Behavior rating scales are an assessment method that provide behavioral data that are more reliable than what is yielded from some unstructured interviews or performance-based techniques.
4. Behavior rating scales may be used to assess children and adolescents who cannot easily provide information about themselves. Consider the difficulty in obtaining valid assessment data on an adolescent who is in a secure unit in a psychiatric hospital or juvenile detention center, and who is unavailable or unwilling to be assessed through interviews and self-reports.

5. Rating scales capitalize on observations over a period of time in a child or adolescent's "natural" environments (i.e., school or home settings).
6. Rating scales capitalize on the judgments and observations of persons who are very familiar with the child's or adolescent's behavior, such as parents or teachers, who are considered to be "expert" informants.

By considering these advantages of behavior rating scales, it is clear why they are so widely used—they tend to get at the "big picture" of the assessment problem very quickly, at a relatively low cost, and with a good deal of technical precision and practical utility.

Problems Associated with Using Behavior Rating Scales

Despite these advantages, there are some problems or disadvantages inherent in the use of behavior rating scales. The nature of rating scale technology contains several challenges that are important to consider. It is useful to remember that by their nature (i.e., assessing perceptions of problems), rating scales are capable of providing a portrait of a general idea or conception of behavior, but they do not provide actual observational data, even though their technical characteristics allow for actuarial prediction of behavior.

The first area of limitation or challenge for behavior rating scales is in the clinical or practice domain. It is important to consider, as has already been suggested, that rating scales measure informants' *perceptions* of behavior, rather than actual behaviors. This characteristic is not a limitation per se, if clinicians properly understand and use the obtained data. Rather, potential problems arise when the person responsible for interpreting the rating scale data considers these data as representing actual behavior, which they may or may not. Along with this caveat, it is critical for clinicians to always consider that the quality of the rating scale data are only as good as they quality of the informant rating, which can be impacted by many factors.

Thus, the second area of limitation or challenge for behavior rating scales relates to the technical or psychometric characteristics. More than 2 decades ago, Martin and colleagues (1986) categorized the measurement problems of behavior rating scales into two classes: *bias of response* and *error variance*. These classes still represent an excellent way to understand some of the measurement challenges associated with rating scales. Bias of response refers to the way that informants who complete the rating scales potentially may create additional error by the way they use the scales. There are three specific types of response bias, including (1) *halo effects* (rating a child in a positive or negative manner simply because they possess some other positive or negative characteristic not pertinent to the rated item), (2) *leniency or severity* (the tendency of some raters to have an overly generous or overly critical response set when rating all behaviors), and (3) *central tendency effects* (the proclivity of raters to select midpoint ratings and to avoid endpoints of the scale such as never and always). Error variance is related closely to and often overlaps with response bias as a form of rating scale measurement problems but provides a more general representation of some of the problems encountered with this form of assessment. Four types of variance that may create error in the obtained results of a rating scale assessment are outlined in Table 7.1. These types of variance are summarized as follows.

Source variance refers to the subjectivity of the rater and any of the idiosyncratic ways in which they complete the rating scales. *Setting variance* occurs as a result of the situational specificity of behavior (Kazdin, 1979), given that we tend to behave differently in different environments because of the unique eliciting and reinforcing properties present. *Temporal variance* refers to the tendency of behavior ratings to be only moderately consistent over time—partly as a result of changes in the observed behavior over time and partly as a result of changes in the rater's approach to the rating task over time. Finally, *instrument variance* refers to the fact that different rating scales measure often related but slightly differing hypothetical constructs (e.g., aggressive behavior versus delinquent behavior), and a severe problem behavior score on one scale may be compared with only a moderate problem behavior score on a differing rating scale for the same person.

Another problem that creates instrument variance is the fact that each rating scale uses different normative populations with which to make score comparisons, and if the norm populations are not stratified and selected in the same general manner, similar score levels on two different rating scales may not mean the same thing.

Table 7.1 Types of Error Variance Found with Behavior Rating Scales

Type of Error Variance	Examples
Source Variance	Various types of response bias; different raters may have different ways of responding to the rating format
Setting Variance	Related to situational specificity of behavior; eliciting and reinforcing variables present in one environment (e.g., classroom 1) may not be present in a closely related environment (e.g., classroom 2)
Temporal Variance	Behavior is likely to change over time, and an informant's approach to the rating scale task may change over time
Instrument Variance	Different rating scales may be measuring different hypothetical constructs; there is a continuum of continuity (ranging from close to disparate) between constructs measured by different scales

Although there are several potential problems in using behavior rating scales, there are also effective ways of minimizing those problems. One such approach is the *multimethod, multisource, multisetting assessment*. This approach involves using multiple methods of assessment (e.g., direct observation, interviews, rating scales, records review), multiple sources (e.g., parents, teachers, peer group, clinicians), and multiple settings (e.g., home, school, clinic) in order to reduce the amount of error variance and gather a comprehensive representation of the child's behavioral, social, and emotional functioning. For behavior rating scales, this assessment method requires several informants from different settings completing measures on the youth. For example, a teacher and parent may complete similar rating measures on a student, thus providing a more detailed picture of the youth's functioning. Although it may be difficult to obtain diverse informants and settings, the crucial goal is to obtain an aggregated picture of the youth's behavioral, social, and emotional functioning. Such an assessment design is considered to be best practice (see Merrell, 2007).

Overview of Three Rating Scale Systems

Having discussed some of the general characteristics and background of behavior rating scales, this section focuses on providing an overview of three of the most widely used behavior rating scale systems: The Behavior Assessment System for Children—Second Edition (BASC-2), the child and adolescent rating forms of the Achenbach System of Empirically Based Assessment (ASEBA), and the Conners' Rating Scales, Revised. These instruments are referred to as *rating scale systems* because they provide cross-informant rating forms that may be completed by multiple ratings across multiple settings. These three rating systems, which are exemplary in many respects, are not the only technically adequate and widely used rating scale systems available. On the contrary, there are a number of high quality behavior rating scales available for use by clinicians and researchers. These three rating scale systems have been selected for inclusion in this chapter as exemplars for this genre of assessment method, and because they are in wide use. Each of the three rating systems is considered in turn, providing a description of the scales and their administration and scoring procedures. In addition, the psychometric properties and empirical support for each scale is summarized, along with information on the applications and uses of the scale. This discussion of three comprehensive rating scale systems is certainly not meant to be exclusive. In addition to these, there are other popular and comprehensive rating scale systems that have components available to allow ratings across settings, such as the Clinical Assessment of Behavior (Bracken & Keith, 2004), the Social Behavior Scales (Merrell, 2002; Merrell & Caldarella, 2002). There is also a large number of behavior rating scales designed for very specific purposes, settings, and populations, well beyond the scope of this chapter. For more detailed descriptions of these additional rating scale systems and tools, readers are referred to more comprehensive treatments of the topic by the first author (Merrell, 2000a, 2000b, 2007).

Behavior Assessment Scale for Children—Second Edition (BASC-2)

The Behavior Assessment System for Children, Second Edition (BASC-2; Reynolds & Kamphaus, 2004) is a comprehensive system for assessing child and adolescent behavior, and is designed to assess a variety of problem behaviors, school problems, and adaptive skills. The system was designed to be used in facilitating differential diagnosis and educational classification of behavior and learning problems, and to assist in developing intervention plans. Included in the BASC-2 are parent and teacher rating scales for preschool age children (2 to 5 years old), children (6 to 11 years old), and adolescents (12 to 21 years old). These behavior rating scales are separately normed and are unique across age range and informant versions but still share a common

---

Quick Reference: Three Rating Scale Systems
To Order or for Additional Information
Behavioral Assessment System for Children, 2nd edition (BASC-2)
    Pearson Assessments
    Phone: 1-800-627-7271
    Fax: 1-800-632-9711
    E-mail: pearsonassessments@pearson.com
    Web: www.pearsonassessments.com
Achenbach System of Empirically-Based Assessment (ASEBA)
    Research Center for Children, Youth, and Families
    1 South Prospect Street
    Burlington, VT 05401-3456
    Phone: 802-264-6432
    Fax: 802-264-6433
    E-mail: mail@ASEBA.org
    Web: www.ASEBA.org
Conners' Rating Scales, Revised (CRS-R)
    Multi-Health Systems
    P.O. Box 950
    North Tonawanda, NY 14120-0950
    Phone: 1-800-456-3003
    Fax: 1-888-540-4484
    E-Mail: customerservice@mhs.com
    Web: www.mhs.com

conceptual and practical framework and have many items in common across versions. Also included in the overall BASC-2 are comprehensive self-report forms for children (ages 6 to 7 and 8 to 11), adolescents (ages 12 to 21), and college age young adults (ages 18 to 25), a structured developmental history form, and a student observation system.

Administration and Scoring The parent and teacher rating forms for school age children and adolescents include the PRS–C (parent rating scale for ages 6 to 11), PRS–A (parent rating scale for ages 12 to 21), TRS–C (teacher rating scale for ages 6 to 11), and TRS–A (teacher rating scale for ages 12 to 21). These instruments are somewhat long in terms of number of items (ranging from 139 to 160 items), compared with most other published rating scales. The primary components of the BASC-2 are available in both English and Spanish versions. The items are rated by circling adjacent letters indicating how frequently each behavior is perceived to occur, based on N (never), S (sometimes), O (often), and A (almost always). The basic hand scored form is self-scoring and easy to use. After the rating is completed, the examiner tears off the top perforated edge and separates the forms, which reveals an item scoring page and a summary page with score profiles. Norm tables in the test manual are consulted for appropriate raw score conversions by rating form and age and gender of the child.

Raw scores on BASC-2 scales are converted to *T*-scores (based on a mean score of 50 and standard deviation of 10). Examiners may use any of several possible normative groups, including general, sex specific, combined sex clinical, ADHD, and learning disabilities. *T*-scores for clinical scales are converted to five possible classification levels, ranging from very low (T-scores of ≤ 30) to clinically significant (*T*-scores of ≥ 70). Other classification levels include low, average, and at risk. In addition to the clinical and adaptive scales, the BASC-2 rating scales contain several validity indexes, which are designed to detect unusable, excessively negative, or excessively positive responses made by a teacher or parent.

The empirically derived scale structure of the BASC-2 rating scales is relatively complex, consisting of composite and scale scores. The composites and scales primarily focus on emotional and behavior problems, but also include adaptive skills and competencies. The scale structure of the TRS and PRS are mostly similar. The primary difference in this regard is found in competency areas that are more specific to the school or home setting. The TRF includes three scales not found on the PRS, including School Problems, Learning Problems, and Study Skills, whereas the PRS includes an Activities of Daily Living scale that is not found on the TRS, and covers item content related to the parent's rating of their child's daily activities and routine. The composite scores of the BASC-2 are divided into four main areas of content and scale coverage, include Adaptive Skills, the Behavioral Symptoms Index (a sort of a composite problem total score that includes critical emotional and behavioral problem symptom scales), Externalizing Problems, and Internalizing Problems. The School Problems composite is found only on the TRF version of the system.

Computer Scoring   A comprehensive computer-assisted scoring program is also available, which requires input of individual item responses and basic information about the respondent and child/adolescent, and which provides not only T-score and percentile rank conversions of raw scores, but detailed information regarding score profile patterns, clinical significance of scores, and other useful interpretive information. A scannable response form for mail-in scoring is also available.

Development and Standardization   Extensive development procedures for the BASC-2 rating scales are described in the test manual. An initial item pool for the original BASC was constructed using literature reviews, existing rating scale items, and the clinical expertise of the authors as a basis for selection. Two separate item tryout studies were conducted that resulted in extensive deletion and revision of items. Final item selection was determined empirically through basic factorial analysis and covariance structure analysis to determine appropriate item fit within their intended domain. Readability analyses and bias analyses also were conducted during the item development phase of the original BASC, which resulted in the deletion of some items. The BASC-2 includes item content that is mostly similar to the original BASC, with a few slight changes.

The various components of the BASC-2 system include extensive and well-stratified norm samples that are models of painstaking detail. The norming samples for the BASC-2 were gathered from August 2002 to May 2004, from a total of 375 testing sites. Over 12,000 participants were used in norming the entire system, an extremely large number by almost any assessment any standard, and particularly so in the behavioral/social-assessment realm. The TRS norms are based on a sample of 4,650 at all levels, whereas the PRS norms are based on an across-age sample of 4,800. The norming samples were matched to the March 2001 U.S. Census data, and were controlled for sex, race-ethnicity, geographic region, socioeconomic status, and inclusion of special populations. Although the number of participants in the norming samples vary somewhat by age and version (TRS or PRS), they are high and acceptably stratified by nearly any standard, and are among the very best of any child assessment instrument.

Psychometric Properties   The BASC-2 includes a detailed and comprehensive description of evidence of the psychometric properties of the various parts of the system. Given that the BASC-2 is a revision of the original BASC, and that the two versions are mostly similar, much of the accumulated evidence regarding psychometric properties of the first edition should also be considered in evaluating the BASC-2. The parent and teacher versions of the child and adolescent forms are probably the most widely researched components of the BASC-2. Median internal consistency reliability (coefficient alpha) estimates for the PRS–C, PRS–A, TRS–C, and TRS–A are impressive, ranging from .93 to .97 for the composites, and from .83 to .88 for the scale scores. In some cases, reliability coefficients for scale scores are somewhat lower than the medians—as low as .70—but only in cases where the number of items in the scale is relatively few. Short-term and moderate-term test-retest coefficients were calculated for the TRS and PRS forms. The resulting temporal stability indexes are adequate to good, with median values ranging from .78 to .93 for the composites, and .65 to .90 for scale scores. In general, longer retest intervals produced lower coefficients, which is typical for behavior rating scales and other social-emotional assessment tools.

Several interrater reliability studies of the BASC and BASC-2 have been conducted. Cross-informant reliability of these rating scales varies considerably, depending on specific rater and setting pairs that were analyzed. This variation is not necessarily a problem, given that variability of behavior rating scale scores across raters and settings is a known phenomenon, and is attributable to not only source and setting variance, but actual behavior differences across contexts. Median interrater reliability coefficients reported in the BASC-2 manual range from .53 to .61 for the TRS, and from .69 to .78 for the PRS, with some individual scale coefficients showing considerably lower cross-informant stability, and some producing higher coefficients. These values are generally consistent with the expected ranges for cross-informant comparisons reported by Achenbach, McConaughy, and Howell (1987) in their highly influential review. A review of the first edition of the BASC by Merenda (1996), although generally positive, was critical of the test-retest and interrater reliability of the measures within the system. It is my opinion, however, that Merenda's review did not adequately take into account the overall evidence regarding source and setting variance and expected reliability performance with behavior rating scales. Both of these areas of reliability for the BASC and BASC-2 child and adolescent forms are in the expected range or higher compared with other widely researched behavior rating scales and taking into account the yield of evidence regarding cross-informant and cross-setting reliability of third-party ratings.

Validity evidence from a variety of studies are presented in the BASC-2 manual, which bolsters the evidence that was first presented in the original BASC manual, and the external published research evidence that has accrued on the BASC since it was first published. The complex factorial structure for the scales was based on strong empirical evidence derived from extensive covariance structure analyses, and the empirically derived scale structure appears to be quite robust. Studies reported in the BASC-2 test manual showing correlations between the TRS and PRS with several other behavior rating scales (including the original BASC, scales from the ASEBA system, and scales from the Conners' Rating Scale system) provide evidence of convergent and discriminant construct validity, as do studies regarding intercorrelation of scales and composites of the various TRS and PRS forms. BASC-2 profiles of various clinical groups (e.g., ADHD, learning disabilities, etc.), when compared with the normative mean scores, provide strong evidence of the construct validity of the TRS and PRS through demonstrating sensitivity and discriminating power to theory-based group differences. Again, the validity evidence presented in the BASC-2 manual should be considered as building upon the basic foundation of evidence that had accrued for the original BASC (which included several externally published studies), as the two versions are more similar than different.

Applications and Limitations   Although some other components of the BASC-2 system are not as strong as the TRS–C, TRS–A, PRS–C, and PRS–A rating scales, overall, the system is impressive, and there is very little room for significant criticism. The BASC-2 rating scales may be used in a variety of settings, including inpatient, outpatient, and school settings. Because it provides separate forms based on a youth's age and can be completed by virtually any informant familiar with the youth, its applications are diverse.

These instruments were developed with the latest and most state-of-the-art standards and technology, have an impressive empirical research base, and are practical, if not easy, to use. They represent the best of the newer generation of behavior rating scales. The original BASC was positively reviewed in the professional literature (e.g., Flanagan, 1995; Sandoval & Echandia, 1994), and it is reasonable to anticipate that the BASC-2 will receive similar accolades. One of the few drawbacks of the BASC-2 rating scales may be that their extensive length (as many as 160 items) may make these instruments difficult to use for routine screening work and a poor choice for frequent progress monitoring, which requires a much briefer measure. Routine screening and progress monitoring may require the use of shorter measures. For a thorough and comprehensive system of behavior rating scales, however, the BASC-2 is representative of the best of what is currently available. From the mid 1990s to the publication of the BASC-2 in 2004, the original BASC had become extremely popular for use in schools, through a combination of design quality, user-friendly features, and aggressive marketing by the publisher. There is no doubt that the BASC-2 will continue and perhaps increase the widespread popularity of the system.

Just the Facts: BASC-2

Ages:	2 to 21
Purpose:	assess variety of behavior and school problems and adaptive skills facilitate differential diagnosis and educational classification of behavior and learning problems assist in developing intervention plans
Strengths:	Extensive, stratified norms Strong psychometrics Diverse application Empirically derived scale structure
Limitations:	Lengthy measure Not recommended for progress monitoring or routine screening
Time to Administer:	30 to 60 minutes (139 to 160 items)
Time to Score:	10 to 20 minutes by computer 30 to 60 minutes by hand

Achenbach System of Empirically Based Assessment (ASEBA)

Among the most well researched, widely used, and technically sound general purpose problem behavior rating scales are those included in the Achenbach System of Empirically Based Assessment (ASEBA). This collection of instruments incorporates several rating scales, self-report forms, interview schedules, and observation forms for children, adolescents, and adults. Several of these instruments—particularly those for use with school age children and youth—use a common cross-informant system of similar subscales and items. Two of the instruments in this system, the Child Behavior Checklist for ages 6 to 18 (CBCL/6-18; Achenbach, 2001a), and the Teacher's Report Form for ages 6 to 18 (TRF/6-18; Achenbach, 2001b), are conceptually similar, and provide the heart of the ASEBA assessment system for school age children and adolescents. These two rating scales are reviewed herein, and some general comments about the ASEBA system are also provided.

Administration and Scoring   The CBCL/6-18 and TRF/6-18 both include 120 problem items: 118 items that reflect specific behavioral and emotional problems, and two items that are used for open-ended description of rater's concerns regarding the child or adolescent's behavior. These items are rated on a 3-point scale: 0 (not true, 1 (somewhat or sometimes true), or 2 (very true or often true). The 120 items on the two checklists have a high degree of continuity, with 93 items the same across the scales, and the remainder of the items more specific to the home or school settings. Downward extensions of both of these measures have been developed for use with younger children. In addition to the problem behavior rating scales on the CBCL/6-18 and TRF/6-18, both instruments contain sections wherein the informant provides information on the adaptive behavioral competencies of the subject. On the CBCL/6-18, this section includes 20 items where the parents provide information on their child's activities, social relations, and school performance. On the TRF/6-18, the competency items include sections for academic performance and adaptive functioning.

Raw scores for the CBCL/6-18 and TRF/6-18 are converted to broad-band and narrow-band scores that are based on a T-score system (with a mean of 50 and standard deviation of 10). These normative scores are grouped according to gender and age level (6 to 11, 12 to 18). For both instruments, three different broad-band problem behavior scores are obtained. The first two are referred to as *Internalizing* and *Externalizing* and are based on a dimensional breakdown of overcontrolled and undercontrolled behavior, with the former dimension relative to the internalizing domain, and the latter dimension relative to the externalizing domain. The third broad-band score is a total problems score, which is based on a raw score to T-score conversion of the total ratings of the 120 problem behavior items. The total problems score is not obtained by merely combining the Internalizing and Externalizing scores because there are several rating items on each instrument that do not fit into either of two broad-band categories but are included in the total score. The CBCL/6-18 and TRF/6-18 scoring systems also provide T-score conversions of the data from the competence portions of the instruments, which were discussed previously.

In terms of narrow-band or subscale scores, the CBCL/6-18 and TRF/6-18 score profiles both provide a score breakdown into eight common subscale or syndrome scores that are empirically derived configurations of items. These eight "cross-informant syndromes" include the internalizing area scales of Anxious/Depressed, Withdrawn/Depressed, and Somatic Problems; the externalizing area scales Rule-Breaking Behavior and Aggressive Behavior; and three scales which are considered "other" problems (not specifically internalizing or externalizing): Social Problems, Thought Problems, and Attention Problems. This broad-band and narrow-band configuration is consistent across the school-age measures of the ASEBA. 2001 versions of the CBCL and TRF behavior profiles are, like the 1991 version, based on different norms for boys and girls and by age group. The names of the narrow-band syndromes are constant, however, and the general item content within these syndrome scores is similar. For the narrow-band and broad-band scale scores of these measures, clinical cutoff points have been established, based on empirically validated criteria. In addition to the basic narrow-band and broad-band scales, the 2001 versions of both instruments include six optional

DSM (*Diagnostic and Statistical Manual of Mental Disorders*)-oriented scales: Affective Problems; Anxiety Problems; Somatic Problems; Attention Deficit/Hyperactivity Problems; Oppositional Defiant Problems; and Conduct Problems. These *DSM*-oriented scales were added to the 2001 versions to enhance consistency with the *DSM* diagnostic criteria, and to aid in initial decision making regarding possible classifications to consider.

Computer Scoring   Both rating scales can be hand scored using the test manual and appropriate versions of the hand scoring profiles that include scoring keys for the internalizing-externalizing total scores, plus the various subscales scores, and a graph to plot the scores. The hand scoring process is somewhat tedious, taking at least 15 minutes for an experienced scorer and longer for a scorer who is not familiar with the system. Available hand scoring templates make this job quicker and easier, however, and a computerized scoring program (ADM Windows software) or Web-based scoring system on the publisher's website are available for additional cost. These latter two scoring methods provide convenient and easy-to-read printouts of score profiles. For ASEBA users who use the CBCL/6-18 and TRF/6-18 on more than an occasional basis, it is well worth purchasing the ADM computerized scoring programs.

Development and Standardization   The 2001 edition of the CBCL/6-18 includes a large nationwide normative sample of 1,753 nonreferred child and adolescent cases, with 4,994 additional clinically referred cases used for construction of the narrow-band and DSM-oriented subscales, and establishment of clinical cutoff criteria. The test developers report that normative standardization sample is representative of the 48 contiguous U.S. states for socioeconomic status, ethnicity, geographic region, and urban-suburban-rural residence patterns. The 2001 TRF/6-18 norming sample is based on of ratings of 2,319 nonreferred students, with 4,437 additional cases of referred students used for establishing the subscale structure and developing clinical cutoff criteria. The CBCL/6-18, the TRF/6-18 norming sample is based on a broad sample that is generally representative of the larger U.S. population in several respects.

Psychometric Properties   The psychometric properties of the two ASEBA child behavior rating forms are reported in the test manual and in hundreds of externally published research reports. The number of externally published studies on the ASEBA system is staggering, with refereed journal articles numbering in the thousands. Given that the 2001 revisions of these instruments are relatively slight in terms of item content and that the rating format remains the same as previous versions, the huge body of accumulated evidence from previous versions of the scales should be counted as supporting the reliability and validity of the current measures. In general, the psychometric properties of the current versions of the CBCL and TRF, as well as previous versions, ranges from adequate to excellent. In terms of test-retest reliability, most of the obtained reliabilities for the CBCL/6-18, taken at 1-week intervals, are in the .80 to mid-.90 range and are still quite good at 3-, 6-, and 18-month intervals (mean reliabilities ranging from the .40s to .70s at 18 months). On the TRF/6-18, the median test-retest reliability at has been reported at .90 for 7-day intervals, and at .84 for 15-day intervals. The median TRF test-retest correlation at 2 months has been reported as .74 and at 4 months, 68. These data suggest that ratings from the both the CBCL and TRF rating scales can be quite stable over short to moderately long periods.

Interrater reliabilities (between fathers and mothers) on previous versions of the CBCL and TRF have been reported in many studies, and were in part the topic of a highly influential article by Achenbach et al. (1987) on cross-informant reliability of scores within the ASEBA system. Median correlations across scales of the two forms have been reported at .66. On previous versions of the TRF, interrater reliabilities between teachers and teacher aides on combined age samples have ranged from .42 to .72. Although lower than the test-retest reliabilities, the interrater agreement is still adequate. On a related note, Achenbach et al.'s (1987) meta-analytic study examined cross-informant correlations in ratings of child-adolescent behavioral and emotional problems and discussed in detail the problem of situational specificity in interpreting rating scale data. Based on the data from this study, average cross-informant correlations across all forms of the ASEBA were found to be closer to the .30 range.

Various forms of test validity on the CBCL/6-18 and TRF/6-18 and previous versions of these scales have been inferred through years of extensive research, and are catalogued in the staggering array of published studies. Through demonstration of sensitivity to theoretically based group differences, strong construct validity has been inferred for each instrument. The scales have been shown to distinguish accurately among clinical and normal samples and among various clinical subgroups. The convergent construct validity for both scales has been demonstrated through significant correlations between the scales and other widely used behavior rating scales. The factor analytic evidence regarding the validity of the eight-subscale cross-informant syndrome structure is presented in impressive detail in the test manual, and has been replicated externally with independent samples for the CBCL (Dedrick, 1997) and the TRF (deGroot, Koot, & Verhulst, 1996).

Applications and Limitations The CBCL/6-18 and TRF/6-18 have a great deal of clinical utility, given that they provide general and specific information on the nature and extent of a subject's rated behavioral, social, and emotional problems. When used in tandem by both parents and teachers, these rating scales have been shown to be powerful predictors of present and future emotional and behavioral disorders of children and adolescents (Verhulst, Koot, & Van-der-Ende, 1994). It has been the opinion of several reviewers (e.g., Christenson, 1990; Elliott & Busse, 1990; Myers & Winters, 2002) that the ASEBA system is a highly useful clinical tool for assessing child psychopathology.

Despite their enormous popularity and unparalleled research base, The CBCL/6-18 and TRF/6-18 are more useful for some types of assessment purposes and problems than others, and are not necessarily the best choice for routine assessment situations. Many of the behavioral symptoms on the checklists are psychiatric or clinical in nature (e.g., hearing voices, bowel and bladder problems, handling one's own sex parts in public) and certainly have a great deal of relevance in assessing childhood psychopathology. However, many of these more severe low-rate behavioral descriptions on the scales are not seen on a day-to-day basis in most children who have behavioral or emotional concerns, and some teachers and parents tend to find certain ASEBA items irrelevant, if not offensive, for the children they are rating. In addition to limited sensitivity of these instruments to identify less serious problems, other weaknesses of the ASEBA cross-informant system for school-age children and youths have been pointed out, including limited

Just the Facts: ASEBA

Ages:	6 to 18
Purpose:	Assess presence of behavioral & emotional problems
	Provide information on child's social activities & functioning and academic performance
Strengths:	Useful for assessing child psychopathology
	Provides measure of *DSM-IV* diagnoses
	Extensive norm sampling
	Excellent research base and psychometrics
	Provide general and specific information on a child's behavioral, social, and emotional problems
Limitations:	Not recommend for routine assessment
	Some items may be irrelevant for certain assessments
	Possible limited assessment of social competence
Time to Administer:	30 to 45 minutes (120 items)
Time to Score:	10 to 20 minutes by computer
	30 to 60 minutes by hand

(and perhaps misleading) assessment of social competence, possible bias in interpreting data regarding physical symptoms, and difficulties raised by combining data across informants (Drotar, Stein, & Perrin, 1995). Although Achenbach's empirically based assessment and classification system is without question the most widely researched child rating scale currently available for assessing substantial childhood psychopathology, and has become in essence a gold standard in this regard, and despite the fact that it has much to commend it, as a rating scale for social skills and routine behavioral problems in home and school settings, it may not always be the best choice. Despite some limitations, for assessing significant psychopathology or severe behavioral and emotional problems of children and youth from a cross-informant perspective, the school age tools of the ASEBA system are without peer.

Conners' Rating Scale, Revised

The Conners' Rating Scales, Revised (Conners, 1997) are referred to as a system because they form a set of several behavior rating scales for use by parents and teachers that share many common items and are conceptually similar. Several versions of these scales have been in use since the 1960s (Conners, 1969) and were originally developed by Keith Conners as a means of providing standardized behavioral assessment data for children with hyperactivity, attention problems, and related behavioral concerns. Although a broad range of behavioral, social, and emotional problem descriptions are included in the scales, they have been touted primarily as a measure for assessing attentional problems and hyperactivity, and historically they have been among the most widely used scales for that purpose (Conners, 1997, p. 5).

In 1997, a revised, expanded, and completely restandardized version of Conners' Ratings Scales was published. This most recent revision—available for the past decade—is considered to be a comprehensive behavior assessment system because it contains six main scales and five brief auxiliary scales, including numerous parent and teacher rating scales and an adolescent self-report scale. The revised Conners' scales were designed ultimately to replace the original Conners' scales and to provide ratings scales useful for identification of Attention-Deficit/Hyperactivity Disorder (ADHD) and other behavioral problems in youths (e.g., opposition, anxiety). In addition, Knoff (2001) reported that the three goals of the revision of the original CRS were to align the CRS-R with the *DSM-IV* criteria for ADHD, update the norms using a large, representative sample, and to add an adolescent self-report form.

Administration and Scoring   In terms of general problem behavior rating scales, this discussion focuses on long and short forms of the Conners' Parent Rating Scale, Revised (CPRS–R:L, 80 items, and CPRS–R:S, 27 items) and long and short forms of the Conners' Teacher Rating Scale, Revised

(CTRS–R:L, 59 items, and CTRS–R:S, 28 items). These instruments all are designed for assessment of children and adolescents ages 3 to 17 and use a common 4-point rating scale: 0 (not at all), 1 (just a little), 2 (pretty much), and 3 (very much).

The revised Conners' scales are similar in many respects to their predecessors (the CTRS–39, CTRS–28, CPRS–48, and CPRS–93). With the exception of the Psychosomatic scales, the long forms of the teacher and parent measures have the same scales. Both the teacher and parent short forms include the same scales (Oppositional, Cognitive Problems/Inattention, Hyperactivity, ADHD Index). Even though there is much similarity in item overlap between the original and revised rating scales, some items were added or deleted to make the revised scales specifically compatible with the *Diagnostic and Statistical Manual of Mental Disorders*, fourth edition (*DSM-IV*) diagnostic criteria for ADHD. The rationally derived subscale structure of the revised Conners' scales also differs somewhat from that of the predecessor instruments. Specifically, in addition to the general subscales, the long form scales contain the 10-item Conners' Global Index (formerly referred to as the Hyperactivity Index), a 12-item ADHD index, and an 18-item *DSM-IV* Symptom Scale for ADHD. The Global Index is now specifically touted as a brief measure of psychopathology that is useful for screening or progress monitoring. These 10 items are embedded into the long form rating scales and are available on a separate short scale for screening use. The ADHD index includes critical items that are considered to be important in determining the existence of ADHD. The *DSM-IV* Symptoms subscales, however, are used specifically in determining whether ADHD characteristics fall into the Inattentive or Hyperactive-Impulsive subtypes from *DSM-IV*. The CRS-R scales are available in English, Spanish, and French Canadian. Scoring of these instruments is accomplished by using the Quick Score hand-scoring forms provided on the forms.

Computer Scoring   Computer assisted administration and scoring programs and an online administration and scoring system for the Conners' scales are available from the publisher. The computer programs provide not only administration and scoring possibilities, but also the generation of brief interpretive summary paragraphs related to individual score configurations and levels.

Development and Standardization   The standardization sample for the CRS–R system is very large, with more than 8,000 normative cases in aggregate and about 2,000 to 4,000 for the specific rating scales reviewed in this section. The normative sample is well stratified, including extensive samples from the United States and Canada. Extensive data are provided in the technical manual regarding gender and racial/ethnic breakdowns of the various samples and the effects of gender and ethnicity on CRS–R scores. The norm samples are largely Caucasian, comprising 83% for the parent scales and 78%–81% for the teacher scales. Additionally, the percentage of Caucasians for the adolescent scales drops to 62%, leading to some concern interpreting across forms (see Knoff, 2001).

Psychometric Properties   Internal consistency reliability for all CRS–R scales is adequate to excellent. For example, the internal consistency coefficients for the CPRS-R:L subscales range from .73 to .94. The scales with lower reliability coefficients tend to be the scales with fewer items. Test-retest reliability at 6- to 8-week intervals for the CPRS-R:L and CTRS–R:L has been shown to range from .47 to .88 for the various subscales. Extensive factorial validity evidence (including confirmatory factor analyses) for the CRS-R scales is presented in the technical manual. Additional validity evidence for the CRS-R scales is presented in the form of extensive convergent and divergent validity coefficients among various scales within the system and correlations with scores from the Children's Depression Inventory.

The original Conners' rating scales have extensive validity and reliability evidence (see Merrell, 1999. for a review). Given that the CRS-R is based heavily on the already extensively researched original Conners' rating scales, it is assumed that the developers did not consider it as essential to gather as extensive validity evidence as would be needed with a totally new system of instrumentation. Although it probably can be assumed that much of the existing validity evidence for the original Conners' scales may translate reasonably well to the revised scales, there is still a need to continue to conduct a full range of reliability and validity studies with the CRS-R.

Applications and Limitations   The instruments in the Conners' rating system have enjoyed a rich history of use and popularity. The CRS-R, the most recent version of these tools, has many improvements, such as the alignment with DSM-IV criteria for ADHD, and having long and short forms with norms that are stratified between gender and age groups. Professionals can use these tools with diverse informants (e.g., teachers, parents, guardians) and for various purposes (e.g., screening, progress monitoring, treatment planning, assessing).

Although the CRS presents as a broad-band measure because of its various scales, it is best used as an ADHD assessment tool. Conners (1997) has stated, "The main use of the Conners' Rating Scales, Revised, will be for the assessment of ADHD. However, the CRS–R can have a much broader scope, as they also contain subscales for the assessment of family problems, emotional problems, anger control problems, and anxiety problems" (p. 5). This reasoning likely stems from the lack of discriminant validity evidence for the six-factor scales, as well as more evidence supporting a three-factor

Just the Facts: Conners' Rating System, Revised

Ages:	3 to 17
Purpose:	Assessment of ADHD and, to a lesser extent, general emotional and behavioral problems
Strengths:	Compatible with the *DSM-IV* Extensive norms
Limitations:	Despite scales that measure broad band behaviors, primarily a narrow band tool for assessment of ADHD
Time to Administer:	Short form: 15 minutes (27 or 28 items) Long form: 30 to 45 minutes (59 or 80 items)
Time to Score:	10 to 15 minutes by computer 20 to 30 minutes by hand

scale structure than a six-factor (Hess, 2001). Additionally, the manual reports little evidence on discriminant validity for the subscales that are not related to ADHD (e.g., predicting differences on the Anxiety-Shy scale) and instead, primarily reports discriminant validity evidence for predicting groups with ADHD from groups with "emotional problems" and a nonclinical group. Although previous manuals of the CRS have reported such information, the CRS-R manual does not (Hess, 2001; Knoff, 2001). This lack of reporting limits the use of the CRS-R beyond assessing ADHD.

Cultural Validity Issues in Using Behavior Rating Scales

Having reviewed three popular behavior rating scale systems, we now turn our focus to certain cultural validity and sensitivity issues to consider when evaluating and using such measures. First, issues related to sample size and norms are discussed, followed by an examination of group differences and interpretative issues.

Normative and Standardization Issues

One of the ongoing debates regarding culturally appropriate uses of standardized norm-referenced instruments is in regard to the desirable or minimal proportion of representation of various ethnic/racial groups within the general norm group. The current most common practice is for instrument developers to compare group representation with that of the general U.S. population (assuming the instrument is developed in the United States), based on the most current data available from the Census Bureau, and to try to match the standardization sample of their assessments to these general U.S. figures. In reality, this practice, although laudable and viewed as best practice, does not necessarily show a priori cultural validity of an instrument. In fact, some experts have criticized the practice because minority groups still comprise a minority within the norm sample against which their scores are to be compared.

For illustration purposes, based on the 2000 census, slightly less than 1% of the population in the United States is Native American. Using the standard practice of instrument development, representation of Native Americans in about 1% of the norm sample should satisfy the notion of normative equivalency. However, 1% is still a very small proportion, even when it represents the general percentage of a specific subgroup within a general group. For this example, assuming there is a total norming sample of 1,000 for a specific measure, only 10 Native American youths would be required in the standardization group to make the Native American sample proportional to the actual percentage in the U.S. population. Such a simplistic application of proportionality raises many questions. For example, if our 10 Native American youths in the norming sample are all members of the Yakima tribe in the Pacific Northwest, should we assume that Native American youth have been sampled, or is there concern regarding generalizing the statistical representation to other subgroups, such as the Ojibwa tribe in the Northern Midwest? Along this same line of reasoning, it has been proposed that small representation, even if it is in proportion to the percentage of the group within the total population, might be presumed to result in test bias (e.g., Harrington, 1988). There are also other vexing issues to consider: Does it matter if the Native American youth in the standardization sample are highly acculturated into the general U.S. population, or if they are primarily acculturated within their respective tribal group? There are no easy answers to these issues, and it is important to consider that having a specific ethnic/racial group represented proportionally within a test norming sample does not guarantee that the test will be valid for that group, just as having it underrepresented does not necessarily mean that the test will not be valid for that group.

The current accepted practices for group representation in norming samples can be neither vindicated nor vilified in the absence of more compelling evidence. However, an interesting study by Fan, Wilson, and Kapes (1996) provide some interesting clues on this issue. Fan et al. (1996) used varying proportions (0%, 5%, 10%, 30%, and 60%) of differing ethnic groups (European American, African American, Hispanic, Asian American) in a tightly controlled standardization experiment on a cognitive assessment measure and found that there was no systematic bias against any of the groups when they were in the not represented or under represented conditions. Fan and colleagues referred to the notion of proportional representation or overrepresentation of racial-ethnic minority groups as a best practice as a "standardization fallacy." This study did not target specifically assessment of social-emotional behavior, and a replication using this performance domain would be useful. It is one of the few tightly controlled studies, however, to address the issue of representation of specific racial/ethnic groups within standardization groups. Based on the results of this study, it seems that the most important aspects of developing assessment instruments that have wide cultural applicability and validity are the actual content development procedures (to eliminate biasing items) and the use of good sampling methods for construction of the norm group. Other instrument development procedures also may be useful for showing appropriateness with differing racial/ethnic groups, such as conducting specific comparisons with subsamples of various racial/ethnic groups regarding such characteristics as mean score equivalency, internal consistency properties, and factor structure.

Group Differences

Because of the fairly consistent findings with regard to race/ethnicity and gender in cognitive assessment (i.e., cognitive assessment instruments have been shown to yield consistent mean score differences between specific racial/ethnic groups, and also to be susceptible to assessment bias when used with some individuals from racial/ethnic groups; Reynolds & Kaiser, 1990), it might seem logical to make the same set of assumptions for research-and-development efforts with behavior rating scales. Yet group differences in behavior rating scale and other social-emotional assessment data may follow quite a different pattern than with cognitive assessment instruments, and some of the generalizations based on cognitive assessment findings may be misleading. This section discusses group differences as it pertains to gender and to racial/ethnic group.

Gender The issue of gender and behavior rating scale data provides a good example of how group differences should not necessarily be construed as evidence of bias, or as evidence of differential prediction patterns. Numerous behavioral and emotional disorders are known to exist at substantially different levels across gender lines. For example, according to the *Diagnostic and Statistical Manual of Mental Disorders* (*DSM-IV*; American Psychiatric Association, 1994) and various epidemiological studies, the prevalence rate of ADHD and conduct disorder is significantly higher for males than for females, and the prevalence rates for depression and eating disorders are much higher among females than males, particularly after the onset of adolescence. Therefore, behavior rating scales, unlike cognitive assessments, should be expected to yield significantly different mean scores for samples of males and females, particularly when these scales include constructs that are known to have differing ratios across gender lines. In fact, demonstration of such group differences would be one type of evidence for the construct validity of the measure. Evidence of these types of differences can be found in such rating scale measures as the Conners' Rating Scales, Revised (CRS; Conners, 1997), and the Social Skills Rating System (SSRS; Gresham & Elliot, 1990), as the size of the group differences between gender range from one half to one standard deviation (SD) for the CRS and from one third to one half for the SSRS.

Race/Ethnicity Unlike the area of cognitive assessment, where there has been substantial research, best selling books and, at times, bitter controversy regarding racial-ethnic efforts and issues, the area of social-emotional and behavioral assessment has experienced relatively little activity. Because there is a limited theoretical basis upon which to build a priori predictions regarding racial-ethnic differences in rating scale scores, and because this area generally lacks the controversial and politically charged implications manifest in the cognitive assessment arena, researchers and instruments developers have had little reason to explore such differences. However, the yield of what little work there has been in this area indicates that race-ethnicity probably plays a minor role in terms of group differences and differential prediction with child behavior rating scales. Based on previous examinations (see Merrell, 2007; Merrell & Gimpel, 1998), the covarying influence of socioeconomic status may account for much or even most of the small but statistically significant racial-ethnic group differences that are found. In other words, if a large nationwide dataset containing behavior rating scale scores of children and youths were carefully analyzed, some small but meaningful effects for race and ethnicity might be found. But, if socioeconomic status (such as family income and/or parents' education levels) were used as a covariate in the analysis, or if cases were matched by race-ethnicity and socioeconomic status using a randomized block design, then it is very likely that any score differences between groups would be negligible.

Despite the apparently limited influence of race-ethnicity in behavior rating scales, there are a few interesting (and sometimes conflicting) pieces of evidence that are worth examining. First, it is possible that an individual's race-ethnicity may influence the way that they value particular child behaviors, if not actually influencing their objective ratings of behavior. For example, a study by O'Reilly, Tokuno, and Ebata (1986) found significant differences in the way that European American and Asian American mothers ranked the relative importance of eight social skills. Second, research conducted by Lethermon and colleagues (Lethermon et al., 1984; Lethermon, Williamson, Moody, & Wozniak, 1986) found that child behavior ratings may be influenced by the similarity or difference in ethnicity between the rater and the subject of the rating. Presumably, such similarity-difference effects might also be extended to the construct of gender. Although this research area does not appear to have been carried out by any other researchers, the findings by Lethermon and colleagues are interesting because they indicated that raters were more likely to positively evaluate the social behavior of children who were similar to them in terms of race-ethnicity, yet the most socially valid ratings appear to be obtained by rater-rate pairs who were *dissimilar* in race-ethnicity. This line of research raises some interesting questions regarding the effect of race-ethnicity on child behavior ratings provided by teachers in school settings, but there is simply not enough evidence to speculate any further at this point.

Of the child behavior rating scales currently in widespread use in public schools, some have been carefully analyzed to study the possibility of racial-ethnic effects in their normative samples. The results of such investigations generally support the notion that race-ethnicity exert only a minor influence on scores. For example, an early investigation in the development of the ASEBA system (Achenbach & Edelbrock, 1981) analyzed parent ratings of child behavior in a sample of 2,600 children, half of whom were Caucasian, and half of whom were African American. Using CBCL scores in the analysis, minimal differences were found in problem behavior and social competence when race was used as an independent variable, and these group differences tended to diminish further when socioeconomic status was added as a covariate. Additionally, Merrell found low correlations between the race-ethnicity of the child and parents and scores on the School Social Behavior Scales (Merrell, 2002) and the Preschool and Kindergarten Behavior Scales (Merrell, 1994). Finally, the CRS-R manual includes evidence examining the effects of race-ethnicity on the various scales. In general, the results of a series of analysis of covariance (ANCOVA) using race-ethnicity as the independent variable and age level as a covariate resulted in no significant effects in most instances. If it did, follow-up comparisons did not result in significant differences between groups or there were not consistent patterns to the differences found. In addition, the effect sizes between the groups with significant differences resulted in effect sizes of less than .30. As seen from the studies aforementioned, race-ethnicity appears to play a minor role (if any) in affecting the results of behavior rating scales.

Interpretive Issues   A final and critical cultural issue to consider when using behavior ratings scales lies within interpreting the specific scores and the range they fall in. As with any significant score on a rating scale (i.e., a score in the clinical range), scores must be understood within the context of the youth's immediate environment, in conjunction with other assessment data, and in relation to the person completing the rating form and his or her relationship with the youth. However, the interpreter must take extra caution to ensure that the significant score is also understood within the proper context of the youth's cultural and ethnic background, as described by the ecological model proposed by Brofenbrenner (1979). That is, a score should be viewed less as existing solely within the child, and instead, be considered within the context of the youth's environment (see Miranda, 2002). This way of thinking involves having knowledge of the common behavioral and emotional issues that the youth's culture may present or expect to see in order to avoid assuming a significant score means too little (i.e., false negative) or too much (i.e., false positive). To further complicate matters, the common cultural behaviors seen in the youth's culture may or may not be reflective of the youth's own personal emotional, social, and behavioral repertoire; thus, one cannot assume that a significant score that matches the expected or common behaviors of the youth's culture are not a cause for concern (or vice versa). Essentially, interpreters must ask two questions when interpreting scores on behavior rating scales: Is this behavior expected, given the youth's cultural background, and is this behavior expected, given the youth's own personal behaviors and issues? The end result is a complex process of interpreting and understanding assessment data within both the youth's larger cultural context and the smaller personal and family system. The process of being cultural proficient is an ongoing process (see Sue & Sue, 2003) and the issue is made no easier when using behavior rating scales that are standardized largely on the majority population with populations from varying backgrounds.

Rhodes, Ochoa, and Ortiz (2005) raised another important issue when considering the norm sample of behavior rating scales. Assuming that a measure has an appropriate representation of a minority group, the issue of acculturation (the process by which the views and behaviors of one group change as a result of contact with another group; Miranda, 2002) may still prevent valid conclusions from being drawn from the scores. That is to say, although a group may be represented within a sample for a given measure, the extent to which the person being rated has a similar or different *experiential background* affects the extent to which his or her group is represented more so than skin color or race does. For example, an African American youth who is more acculturated than another African American may affect the interpretation of their respective scores more so than the fact that their racial group is represented in the norm sample. Rhodes and colleagues argued that acculturation differences are more important to consider when evaluating test scores than whether or not the youth's race is represented in the norm sample, but unfortunately, tests do not systematically control for acculturation differences at this point in time. To deal with this issue, it is important to gather information on the youth's acculturation status and stress using various assessment methods (see Rhodes et al., 2005, p. 128).

Undoubtedly, the issue of interpreting scores from groups with varying backgrounds is a complex issue and an ongoing process of understanding one's own biases and beliefs against the informant's and youth's (Sue & Sue, 2003). Best practices insist on using an ecological framework in understanding the result of an assessment tool, ensuring the cultural background of the youth is represented in the sample, and using extensive assessment of acculturation and environmental factors to ensure the scores are interpreted accurately and within the right context (Miranda, 2002; Rhodes et al., 2005; Sue & Sue, 2003).

Current Controversies in Using Behavior Rating Scales

Although the use of behavior rating scales is generally not very controversial at this point in time—at least in comparison to the late 1970s to mid-1980s when many of the seminal developments occurred—certain issues still remain and are important to understanding the use and application of behavior rating scales. This section focuses on two general topics that might be considered controversies or challenges to some extent: the issue of rating scales as indirect measures and the psychometric properties of rating scales.

The Criticism of "Indirect Measurement"

During the seminal period of innovation and development of child behavior rating scales—the 1970s and 1980s—this assessment method was viewed with considerable suspicion by many clinicians and researchers who had a strong behavioral orientation. Perhaps the greatest criticism or controversy from this group was the indirect nature of behavior rating scales. A point that was well founded in this regard is that almost all behavior rating scales are retrospective in nature, given that they require the examiner or informant to evaluate a child's behavioral or emotional functioning based on a specific prior time period, for instance the previous 3 months, or the previous 6 weeks. Thus, behavior rating scales that utilize this typical rating procedure tend to rely on the somewhat subjective judgments of raters, as well as their memory of past events. For this reason, it is correct to consider rating scales indirect measures of behavior, in contrast to direct observation of child behavior, which is a uniquely direct method that requires little retrospection, subjectivity, or memory. It is also true that behavior rating scales and direct observational data tend to have relatively low correlations, often in the .20s, and at times not statistically significant.

That said, the past 2 decades of research on behavior rating scale assessment have helped to dispel some of the concerns from the behavioral camp, and in turn, some recent research on behavioral observation methods has highlighted the limitations of this method (e.g., Hintz, 2005; Hintz &

Mathews, 2004). It is interesting to note that behavior rating scale data tends to predict important future behavioral outcomes better than direct observations of behavior. For example, a unique study by Walker, Stieber, Ramsey, and O'Neil (1993) examined long term predictive validity of various behavior assessment methods (teacher's social skill ratings, direct observations of students in two settings, and school discipline contacts) of high risk boys in grade 5, to determine which method of assessment best predict later arrest rates during the teenage years. Teachers' ratings of student social skills, using a standardized social behavior rating scale, proved to be the best predictor, accounting for nearly 60% of the explained variance in the correlational and regression procedures.

Current best practice among behaviorally-oriented clinicians is to use both methods—behavior rating scales and direct behavioral observations—in tandem. Such an assessment design allows the assessor to use the strengths of both methods in evaluating the behavior of a child or adolescent. In the case of rating scales, the strength is the ability to predict important future outcomes, compare the child's ratings to a standardization sample, and consider their behavior over a period of time. In the case of direct observation, the strength is the molecular level of analysis that direct observation may provide, which may allow for precise examination of behavior-environment relationships, as well as detection of possible functions of the behavior in question.

Psychometric Aspects of Behavior Rating Scales

Rating Format

One of the most basic measurement variables that may affect the technical or psychometric properties of a rating scale is the actual rating format of the scale and how it is constructed. The two rating formats that appear to be the most common for child behavior rating scales are 3-point and 5-point scales. Each numerical value in the rating format is keyed or anchored to a descriptor (for example, 0 = never, 1 = sometimes, 2 frequently). As a general rule, more accurate ratings are obtained when there is a concrete definition for each possible level. In other words, descriptors such as sometimes and frequently may be more effective if the rating scale provides examples for these categories. Although 3-point and 5-point rating formats appear to be the most widely used in construction of child behavior ratings scales, there has actually been very little discussion of how many rating points or levels are appropriate. Worthen, Borg, and White (1993) suggested that a common error in scale construction is the use of too many levels. The assumption here is that a higher level of inference is needed in making ratings when more possible rating points are involved, which increases the difficulty in reliably discriminating among the various rating levels. In general, a good heuristic is for scale developers to use the fewest rating levels needed to make an appropriate rating discrimination, and to avoid scales that require an excessive amount of inference in making discriminations among rating points.

It is also important to ensure that rating levels and anchor points of a measure are meaningful and easy to understand. Although most behavior rating scales use rating points that are anchored to broad descriptive statements (for example, sometimes and often), an alternative rating format, which we (Merrell, 2007) have referred to as a frequency of behavior format has emerged, and is proving to be increasingly popular. One behavior rating scale that utilizes this frequency of behavior rating format is the ADHD Symptoms Rating Scale (Holland, Gimpel, & Merrell, 2001), a 56-item rating scale based on *DSM-IV* characteristics of ADHD in children and adolescents. The rating format used in the ADHD-SRS requires raters to estimate a fairly precise time element in which the specific problem behavior occurs, such as "occurs from one to several times an hour," "occurs from one to several times a day," or "occurs from one to several times a week." Our preliminary analysis of this rating format indicated that it was equally reliable in comparison to the standard rating format, but teacher raters preferred using it. Future research and developments with respect to rating formats may shed additional light on the best uses of alternative formats.

Time Element

Another characteristic that may impact the psychometric properties of rating scales is the time element to be considered in making the rating. According to Worthen and colleagues (1993), there is a tendency for recent events and behavior to be given disproportionate weight when a rater completes a rating scale. This idea is based on the notion that it is easier to remember behavioral, social, and emotional characteristics during the previous 2-week period than during the previous 2-month period. Rating scales differ as to the time period on which the ratings are supposed to be based. The most common time periods that child behavior rating scales appear to be based on range from about 1 month to about 6 months, with some indicating no time period at all. A related measurement issue raised by Worthen and colleagues is that it is easier for raters to remember unusual behavior than ordinary behavior. Typical, uneventful behaviors may be assigned less proportional weight during the rating than novel, unusual, or highly distinctive behaviors.

Directions for Use

A final technical aspect to consider regarding rating scales includes their directions for use. Some scales provide highly detailed instructions for completing the ratings, such as which persons should use the rating scale, the time period involved, and how to approach and interpret the items. Other scales may provide a minimum of directions or clarifications. It is recommended that users of behavior rating scales select instruments that provide clear and tangible directions for conducting the rating and decision rules for interpreting blurred distinctions (Gronlund & Linn, 1999). In sum, the characteristics of rating scale technology that make behavior rating scales appealing also may negatively affect the consistency and utility of the measure. As with any type of measurement and evaluation system, consumers of behavior rating scales are advised to evaluate a potential instrument based on the important technical characteristics.

Method of Subscale Construction

In addition to the three areas of psychometric concern that have been discussed thus far regarding challenges in developing and using behavior rating scales, some other issues have emerged in recent years. One such issue is the development of subscale structures within rating scales. It is typical for most rating scales, particularly those with 30 or more items, to have several narrow-band scales or subscales. In many cases these narrow-band scales are clinically informative, given that they are comprised of a small number of items that have similar content or that relate to a specific area of concern, such as ADHD, depression, or aggressive behavior. It is important to recognize that there are no general standards regarding subscale development and construction, which sometimes leads to disagreements between test developers and test reviewers or test users. It has become increasingly common practice for behavior rating scale test developers to create subscales through the use of factor analytic and structural modeling statistical procedures. Although such efforts are often laudable, there are sometimes disagreements regarding the use and interpretation of these techniques. It is also important to consider that such advanced multivariate statistical techniques, although they are increasingly common, should not be considered a defacto standard for test creation. In fact, scales and subscales have been developed a variety of ways and using a variety of procedures, ranging from rational-theoretical approaches to content validation panels, to advanced statistical analysis (Merrell, 2007). What may be more important than the method used to develop scales and create subscale configurations is how well the particular scales perform. In other words, the reliability and validity of the scales and subscales—including their internal consistency, concurrent and predictive validity, classification power, sensitivity to group differences, and so forth—is probably a more important consideration than the method used to develop the scales. Test reviewers and potential test users are advised to be cautious about rushing to a quick judgment about particular behavior rating scales they are considering simply because of the use or lack of use of advanced statistical procedures in developing subscale structures. Rather, it is better

Cautions

- Behavior rating scales should be selected carefully, according to the specific clinical assessment questions that are presented.
- Behavior rating scales are best used with other assessment methods as part of a multimethod, multisetting, multisource assessment design.
- Best practice is to obtain behavior rating scale data from more than one source, and across more than one setting, in order to reduce error variance.
- Selection of behavior rating scales should involve an analysis of social-cultural validity and psychometric characteristics of the instrument.

practice to examine all of the evidence regarding the scales and subscales before reaching a conclusion about the quality of the scales. Frankly, how well a particular subscale structure holds up under reliability and validity analyses is usually more important than esoteric issues such as whether a three factor solution is better than a five factor solution.

Chapter Summary

This chapter has provided a detailed introduction to the use of behavior rating scales in child and adolescent assessment. Behavior rating scales have grown extensively in their use and technical advances over the past couple of decades. Although they measure perceptions of behavior, they are advantageous because of their strong psychometric properties, ease of administration and scoring, and ability to measure behaviors that may not be easily or frequently observed. In addition, behavior rating scales offer the ability to assess various sources and settings, and can be used for various purposes, including screening, progress monitoring, intervention planning, and research. For assessment purposes, the limitations and error variance of their use can be reduced by adhering to the *multimethod, multisource, multisetting assessment* method.

To summarize the major points discussed in the chapter, the following list of key issues is presented:

- Behavior rating scales provide summary judgments regarding a child's behavioral characteristics.
- Behavior rating scales meet the criteria of objective measures.
- Rating scales are algebraic rather than additive.
- Behavior rating scales are less expensive, provide data on low-frequency behavior, and provide information on children who cannot readily report such information.
- *Bias of response* and *error variance* can threaten the validity and reliability of behavior scales.

- By using the multimethod, multisource, multisetting assessment, the error associated with rating scales can be reduced.
- The BASC-2 provides a wide range of information on a child's general functioning, but may be too lengthy to be used for routine progress monitoring.
- The ASEBA provides information on a child's social, emotional, and behavioral characteristics, and is in many ways considered the gold standard for child behavior rating scales, but it perhaps best used for assessing child psychopathology.
- The CRS-R is aligned with *DSM-IV* criteria for ADHD and is best used as an ADHD assessment tool.
- One cannot assume that because a population is represented within a norming sample at a proportion similar to general census figures that it is necessarily valid for use across specific racial and ethnic subgroups. The social-cultural validity of item and scale construction procedures may be a more important issue in this regard than the proportional representation of specific groups.
- Gender differences may not be indicative of test bias within rating scales. In some cases (e.g., ADHD, depression, eating disorders, conduct disorders), evidence of significant gender differences in test scores may actually bolster the validity of the scales.
- Race/ethnicity proportions of norming samples appears to have limited effect on rating scale scores, especially when they are covaried with socioeconomic status.
- Scores should be interpreted within an ecological framework to avoid false positives and/or false negatives. Such practice is especially important with individuals of lower socioeconomic status and who are members of racial/ethnic minority groups.
- Factors such as the format rating, time element, directions for use, and method of scale construction are technical issues that may affect the psychometrics of behavior rating scales.

In sum, child behavior rating scales offer a unique perspective and set of strengths within the broader realm of personality and behavior assessment. When used as part of a comprehensive and multimodal assessment design, behavior rating scales may add to the validity and clinical utility of the overall assessment. Significant advances in behavior rating scale technology during the past 2 decades have greatly enhanced their stature and acceptability among clinicians and researchers. Future efforts to refine child behavior rating scales and to answer some of the remaining questions about this assessment method will be of value as the field of behavioral, social, and emotional assessment moves forward.

Key Points to Remember

- Multimethod, multisource, multisetting assessment helps reduce error variance associated with behavior rating scales.
- Behavior rating scales are one piece of a comprehensive, best practices assessment methodology.
- ASEBA is useful for assessing child psychopathology.
- BASC-2 assesses wide variety of emotional and behavioral problems, and provides information on social and academic functioning.
- CRS-R is primarily good for assessment of ADHD.
- Race-ethnicity appears to have little effect on scores of behavior ratings scales.

Important References

Achenbach (2001a; 2001b)	ASEBA test manuals
Conners (1997)	CRS-R test manual
Merrell (2007)	Comprehensive text on social and emotional assessment of children and adolescents
Reynolds & Kamphaus (2004)	BASC-2 test manual
Rhodes, Ochoa, & Ortiz (2005)	Information on assessing multicultural populations

Note

1. Portions of this chapter have been adapted and modified with permission of the publisher, from: Merrell, K. W. (2007). *Behavioral, social, and emotional assessment of children and adolescents* (3rd ed.). London: Taylor & Francis.

References

Achenbach, T. M. (2001a). *Child Behavior Checklist for ages 6–18*. Burlington, VT: Research Center for Children, Youth, and Families.

Achenbach, T. M. (2001b). *Teachers Report Form for ages 6–18*. Burlington, VT: Research Center for Children, Youth, and Families.

Achenbach, T. M., & Edelbrock, C. S. (1981). Behavioral problems and competencies reported by parents of normal and disturbed children aged four through sixteen. *Monographs for the Society for Research in Child Development, 46*(1 Serial, No. 88).

Achenbach, T. M., McConaughy, S. H., & Howell, C. T. (1987). Child/adolescent behavioral and emotional problems: Implications of cross-informant correlations for situational specificity. *Psychological Bulletin, 101*, 213–232.

American Psychiatric Association. (1994). *Diagnostic and statistical manual for mental disorders* (4th ed.) (*DSM-IV*). Washington, DC: Author.

Bracken, B. A., & Keith, L. K. (2004). *Clinical Assessment of Behavior*. Lutz, FL: Psychological Assessment Resources.

Brofenbrenner, U. (1979). *The ecology of human development: Experiment by nature and design*. Cambridge, MA: Harvard University Press.

Christenson, S. L. (1990). Review of the child behavior checklist. In J. J. Kramer & J. C. Conoley (Eds.), *The Supplement to the Tenth Mental Measurements Yearbook* (pp. 40–41). Lincoln, NE: Buros Institute of Mental Measurements.

Conners, C. K. (1969). A teacher rating scale for use in drug studies with children. *American Journal of Psychiatry, 126,* 884–888.

Conners, C. K. (1997). *Conners' rating scales*(Rev. ed). North Tonowanda, NY: Multi-Health Systems.

Conners, C. K., & Werry, J. S. (1979). Pharmacotherapy. In H. C. Quay & J. S. Werry (Eds.) *Psychopathological disorders of childhood* (2nd ed.). New York: Wiley.

Dedrick, R. F. (1997). Testing the structure of the child behavior checklist/4-18 using confirmatory factor analysis. *Educational and Psychological Measurement, 57,* 306–313.

deGroot, A., Koot, H. M., & Verhulst, F. C. (1996). Cross-cultural generalizability of the youth self-report and teacher's report form cross informant syndromes. *Journal of Abnormal Child Psychology, 24,* 648–671.

Doll, B., & Elliott, S. N. (1994). Representativeness of observed preschool social behaviors: How many data are enough? *Journal of Early Intervention, 18,* 227–238.

Drotar, D., Stein, R. K., & Perrin, E. C. (1995). Methodological issues in using the child behavior checklist and its related instruments in clinical child psychology research. *Journal of Clinical Child Psychology, 24,* 184–192.

Elliott, S. M., & Busse, R. T. (1990). Review of the child behavior checklist. In J. J. Kramer & J. C. Conoley (Eds.), *The Supplement to the Tenth Mental Measurements Yearbook* (pp. 41–45). Lincoln, NE: Buros Institute of Mental Measurements.

Elliott, S. M., Busse, R. T., & Gresham, F. M. (1993). Behavior rating scales: Issues of use and development. *School Psychology Review, 22,* 313–321.

Fan, X., Wilson, V. T., & Kapes, J. T. (1996). Ethnic group representation in test construction samples and test bias: The standardization fallacy revisited. *Educational and Psychological Measurement, 56,* 365–381.

Flanagan, R. (1995). A review of the Behavioral Assessment System for Children (BASC): Assessment consistent with the requirements of the Individuals with Disabilities Act (IDEA). *Journal of School Psychology, 33,* 1–14.

Gresham, F. M., & Elliot, S. N. (1990). *Social skills rating system.* Circle Pines, MN: American Guidance Service.

Gronlund, N. E., & Linn, R. L. (1999). *Measurement and evaluation in teaching* (8th ed.). New York: Prentice-Hall.

Harrington, G. M. (1988). Two forms of minority group test bias as psychometric artifacts with animal models (Rattus norvegicus). *Journal of Comparative Psychology, 102,* 400–407.

Hess, A. K. (2001). Review of the Conners' rating scales. In B. S. Blake & J. C. Impara (Eds.), *The Fourtheeth Mental Measurements Yearbook* (pp. 332–334). Lincoln, NE: Buros Institute of Mental Measurements.

Hintze, J. M. (2005). Psychometrics of direct observation. *School Psychology Review, 34,* 507–519.

Hintze, J. M., & Matthews, W. J. (2004). The generalizability of systematic direct observations across time and setting: A preliminary investigation of the psychometrics of behavioral observation. *School Psychology Review, 33,* 258–270.

Holland, M. L., Gimpel, G. A., & Merrell, K. W. (2001). *ADHD symptoms rating scale.* Odessa, FL: Psychological Assessment Resources.

Kazdin, A. E. (1979). Situational specificity: The two-edged sword of behavioral assessment. *Behavioral Assessment, 1,* 57–75.

Knoff, H. M. (2001). Review of the Conners' Rating Scales. In B. S. Blake & J. C. Impara (Eds.), *The fourteenth mental measurements yearbook* (pp. 334–337). Lincoln, NE: Buros Institute of Mental Measurements.

Lethermon., V. R., Williamson, D. R., Moody, S. C ., & Wozniak, P. (1986). Racial bias in behavioral assessment of children's social skills. *Journal of Psychopathology and Behavioral Assessment, 8,* 329–337.

Lethermon., V. R., Williamson, D. R., Moody, S. C., Granberry, S. W., Lenauer, K. L., & Bodiford, C. B. (1984). Factors affecting the social validity of a role-play test of children's social skills. *Journal of Behavioral Assessment, 6,* 231-245.

Martin, R. P. (1988). *Assessment of personality and behavior problems.* New York: Guilford.

Martin, R. P. Hooper, S., & Snow, J. (1986). Behavior rating scale approaches to personality assessment in children and adolescents. In. H. Knoff (Ed.), *The assessment of child and adolescent personality* (pp. 309–351). New York: Guildford.

Merenda, P. F. (1996). Review of the BASC: Behavior Assessment System for Children. *Measurement and Evaluation in Counseling and Development, 28,* 229–232.

Merrell, K. W. (1994). *Preschool and Kindergarten behavior scales.* Austin, TX: PRO-ED.

Merrell, K. W. (1999). *Behavioral, social, and emotional assessment of children and adolescents.* Mahwah, NJ: Erlbaum.

Merrell, K. W. (2000a). Informant report: Rating scale measures. In E. S. Shapiro & T. R. Kratochwill (Eds.), *Conducting school-based assessment of child and adolescent behaviors* (pp. 203–234). New York: Guilford.

Merrell, K. W. (2000b). Informant report: Theory and research in using child behavior rating scales in school settings. In E. S. Shapiro & T. R. Kratochwill (Eds.), Behavioral assessment in schools (2nd ed., pp. 233–256). New York: Guilford.

Merrell, K. W. (2002). *School social behavior scales* (2nd ed.). Eugene, OR: Assessment-Intervention Resources.

Merrell, K. W. (2007). *Behavioral, social, and emotional assessment of children and adolescents* (3rd ed.). London: Taylor & Francis.

Merrell, K. W., & Caldarella, P. (2002). *Home and Community Social Behavior Scales.* Eugene, OR: Assessment-Intervention Resources.

Merrell, K. W., & Gimpel, G. A. (1998). *Social skills of children and adolescents: Conceptualization, assessment, treatment.* Mahwah, NJ: Erlbaum.

Miranda, A. H. (2002). Best practices in increasing cross-cultural competence. In A. Thomas & J. Grimes (Eds.), *Best practices in school psychology IV* (pp. 353–362). Bethesda, MD: National Association of School Psychologists (NASP).

Myers, K., & Winters, N. C. (2002). Ten-year review of rating scales. I: Overview of scale functioning, psychometric properties, and selection. *Journal of the American Academy of Child & Adolescent Psychiatry, 41,*114–122.

O'Reilly, J. P., Tokuno, K. A., & Ebata, A. T. (1986). Cultural differences between Americans of Japanese and European ancestry in parental valuing of social competence. *Journal of Comparative Family Studies, 17,* 87–97.

Reynolds, C. R., & Kaiser, S. M. (1990). Bias in assessment of aptitude. In C. R. Reynolds & R. W. Kamphaus (Eds.), *Handbook of psychological and educational assessment of children: Intelligence and achievement* (pp. 611–653). New York: Guildford.

Reynolds, C. R., & Kamphaus, R. W. (2004). *Behavior Assessment System for Children* (2nd ed.). Circle Pines, MN: AGS Publishing.

Rhodes, R. L., Ochoa, S. H., & Ortiz, S. O. (2005). *Assessing culturally and linguistically diverse students.* New York: Guilford.

Sandoval, J., & Echandia, A. (1994). Review of the Behavioral Assessment System for Children. *Journal of School Psychology, 32,* 419–425.

Sue, D. W., & Sue. D. (2003). *Counseling the culturally diverse: Theory and practice.* Danvers, MA: Wiley.

Verhulst, F. C., Koot, H. M., & Van-der-Ende, J. (1994). Differential predictive value of parents' and teachers' reports of children's problem behaviors: A longitudinal study. *Journal of Abnormal Child Psychology, 22,* 531–546.

Walker, H. M., Stieber, S., Ramsey, E., & O'Neill, R. (1993). Fifth-grade school adjustment and later arrest rate: A longitudinal study of middle school antisocial boys. *Child and Family Studies, 2,* 295–315.

Worthen, B. R., Borg, W. R., & White, K R. (1993). *Measurement and evaluation in the schools: A practical guide.* White Plains, NY: Longman.

CHAPTER 8

An Introduction
to Rorschach Assessment[1]

GREGORY J. MEYER
DONALD J. VIGLIONE

Introduction

The Rorschach is a performance-based task or behavioral assessment measure[2] that assesses a broad range of personality, perceptual, and problem-solving characteristics, including thought organization, perceptual accuracy and conventionality, self-image and understanding of others, psychological resources, schemas, and dynamics. The task provides a standard set of inkblot stimuli, and is administered and coded according to standardized guidelines. In many respects, the task is quite simple. It requires clients to identify what a series of richly constructed inkblots look like in response to the query, "What might this be?" Despite its seeming simplicity, the solution to this task is quite complex, as each inkblot provides myriad response possibilities that vary across multiple stimulus dimensions. Solving the problem posed in the query thus invokes a series of perceptual problem-solving operations related to scanning the stimuli, selecting locations for emphasis, comparing potential inkblot images to mental representations of objects, filtering out responses judged less optimal, and articulating those selected for emphasis to the examiner. This process of explaining to another person how one looks at things against a backdrop of multiple competing possibilities provides the foundation for the Rorschach's empirically demonstrated validity. Unlike interview- based measures or self-report inventories, the Rorschach does not require clients to describe what they are like but rather it requires them to provide an in vivo illustration of what they are like by repeatedly providing a sample of behavior in the responses generated to each card. Each response or solution to the task in this overall behavior sample is coded across a number of dimensions and the codes are then summarized into scores by aggregating the codes across all responses. By relying on an actual sample of behavior collected under standardized conditions, the Rorschach is able to provide information about personality that may reside outside of the client's immediate or conscious awareness. Accessing information obtained from observing a client's personality in action can be a considerable and unique asset for clinicians engaged in the idiographic challenge of trying to understand a person in her or his full complexity.

The Rorschach is taught in about 80% of United States doctoral clinical psychology programs (Childs & Eyde, 2002; Hilsenroth & Handler, 1995; Mihura & Weinle, 2002). Internship training directors expect incoming students to have good working knowledge of the Rorschach (Clemence & Handler, 2001), and it ranks third in importance for them after the Wechsler Adult Intelligence Scale (WAIS-III; Wechsler, 1997) and the Minnesota Multiphasic Personality Inventory (MMPI-2; Butcher, Dahlstrom, Graham, Tellegen, & Kaemmer, 1989). Among doctoral students in training, Mihura and Weinle (2002) found the Rorschach was viewed as most useful for understanding a client's personality. Their survey showed students were more satisfied with it and anticipated using it more in the future when they had more didactic and practical experience with it, more familiarity with its empirical literature, and more positive attitudes toward it in their training program. Among clinical psychologists in practice, the Rorschach is typically the third or fourth most commonly used assessment instrument, following the WAIS and MMPI (Camara, Nathan, & Puente, 2000; Watkins, Campbell, Nieberding, & Hallmark, 1995). The same rank ordering has been found internationally in a survey of psychologists in Spain, Portugal, and Latin American countries (Muniz, Prieto, Almeida, & Bartram, 1999). With respect to its research base, the Rorschach has been the second most investigated personality assessment instrument (following the MMPI), with about 7,000 citations in the literature as of the mid-1990s (Butcher & Rouse, 1996).

Although the Rorschach is frequently taught in graduate programs, valued on internship and in clinical practice, and regularly researched, it also has generated notable controversy throughout much of its history. Why is this? Although we cannot provide a definitive explanation, we provide insight into some of the key research relevant to its use as part of evidence based practice. In the process, we address several critical questions that have been raised over the last decade about the Rorschach. These include: (a) What does the evidence show about the reliability of Rorschach scores, (b) what strengths and limitations are present in the evidence for the construct validity and utility of its scales, (c) does the instrument have a reasonable base of normative data, (d) can it reasonably be applied across cultures, and (e) does the evidence suggest certain modifications should be made to traditional interpretive postulates?

Because it is not possible to learn how to do Rorschach administration, scoring, and interpretation by reading a single book chapter, we assume that readers interested in gaining applied proficiency with the instrument will rely on other resources. As such, even though we provide readers with a general understanding of the Rorschach and how it is administered, scored, and interpreted, our goal in this chapter is to emphasize the psychometric evidence and issues associated with its use.

Theory and Development

The Rorschach consists of inkblot stimuli[3] that were created, artistically refined, and studied by Herman Rorschach from 1917 to 1920. Exner (2003) provides an overview of their development, which we briefly summarize here. The final set of 10 stimuli was first published in 1921 (Rorschach, 1921/1942). Before publication, Rorschach experimented with 40 or more inkblots, many of which appear to be less complex, nuanced, and detailed precursors to the final set. Figure 8.1 is an example of one of these inkblots; it appears to be an early version of what is now the second inkblot. Rorschach developed his task largely as a means to understand and diagnose Bleuler's newly described syndrome of schizophrenia. Rorschach's doctoral dissertation, which did not focus on inkblots, examined hallucinations in schizophrenia and it was directed by Bleuler. In 1917 another of Bleuler's students, Szymon Hens, completed a dissertation that used eight inkblots he created to determine the content-based distinctions observed among 1,000 children, 100 adults, and 100 patients with psychoses. Rorschach was more interested in perceptual processes than content per se and thus pursued a different direction in his own research. Most of Rorschach's research took place with 12 inkblots, though he was forced to give up 2 to secure a publisher. All 10 of the final inkblots appear to have been artistically embellished by Rorschach, who added details, contours, and colors "to ensure that each figure contained numerous distinctive features that could easily be identified as similar to objects stored in the memory traces of the individual" (Exner, 2003, p. 8). Thus, despite common belief to the contrary, the images are not arbitrary, haphazard, or accidental inkblots. Instead, they are purposively altered images that were refined through trial and error experimentation to elicit informative responses. Each inkblot has a white background; five are achromatic (i.e., gray or black) color only, two are in red and achromatic color, and three are in an array of pastel colors without any black. During the initial printing process, gradations in color and shading became accentuated. Although initially dissatisfied,

Figure 8.1 Early inkblot for possible use created by Hermann Rorschach. (Used with permission of the Hermann Rorschach Archives and Museum; the original is in color.)

Rorschach concluded that this unexpected change offered new possibilities for capturing individual differences in perceptual operations.

Rorschach died in 1922, just 7 months after his book was published. Over the next 40 years, different systems of administration, scoring, and interpretation developed. In the early 1970s, Exner (1974, 2003) developed what he called the Rorschach Comprehensive System (CS), which synthesized what he believed were the most reliable and valid elements of the five primary systems in the United States—those developed by Samuel Beck, Marguerite Hertz, Bruno Klopfer, Zygmunt Piotrowski, and David Rapaport. Since that time, the CS has become the dominant approach to administration, scoring, and interpretation in the United States (Hilsenroth & Handler, 1995; Mihura & Weinle, 2002) and it is widely used internationally (e.g., in Argentina, Belgium, Brazil, Denmark, Finland, France, Holland, Japan, Israel, Italy, Norway, Peru, Portugal, Sweden, and Spain; see Butcher, Nezami, & Exner, 1998; Erdberg & Shaffer, 1999).

A wide array of formal variables can be coded on the Rorschach, though clinicians also draw personality inferences based on numerous response features and testing behaviors that are not formally coded (e.g., Aronow, Reznikoff, & Moreland, 1995; Exner & Erdberg, 2005; Fischer, 1994; Peebles-Kleiger, 2002; Weiner, 2003). With respect to coded variables, there are a large number of scales and indexes described in the literature that are not included in the CS, and many of them have accumulated substantial evidence of reliability and validity (see, e.g., Bornstein & Masling, 2005). Not surprisingly, a range of test construction models have influenced the formal coding criteria for these scales, including those in the CS.

Scale development procedures can be considered on a dimension that ranges from purely empirical, in which items are selected based on statistical relationships with a criterion regardless of whether they make conceptual sense, to fully rational, in which items are selected based on logic and a theoretical understanding of the construct to be measured regardless of whether there is statistical evidence to support that belief. Adopting this framework and applying it to the Rorschach, the empirical end of the continuum would be anchored by some of the actuarial indexes found on the CS, such as the Perceptual Thinking Index (PTI) and the Suicide Constellation (S-CON). Although both indexes were influenced to some extent by theory, they were developed primarily by atheoretical empirical findings using discriminant function analyses in a contrasted groups design (Exner, 2003).

Other indexes were developed using a combined rational and empirical approach. For instance, the developers of the CS-based Ego Impairment Index (EII-2; Perry & Viglione, 1991; Viglione, Perry, & Meyer, 2003) initially identified variables that both had empirical research support and theoretically should be related to impaired object relations and ego functioning. These scores were then refined to create the final scale by using factor analysis and regression-based factor scores to differentially weigh the relative contribution of each variable.

A bit further on the continuum toward the rational end are scores that are largely defined by a theoretical model but that are also refined and specified in such a way that they take into account the unique qualities and limitations associated with the Rorschach inkblot stimuli. The CS Good and Poor Human Representation variables (GHR and PHR; Perry & Viglione, 1991; Viglione, Perry, Jansak, Meyer, & Exner, 2003) are good examples. These indexes are founded on object relations theories in which healthy functioning is defined by perceptions of self and others that are complete, accurate, realistic, intact, independent, and generally benevolent or supportive as opposed to partial, distorted, confused, damaged, enmeshed or fused, and generally malevolent or aggressive. From a theoretical perspective, the healthiest object relations are those in which human others are perceived accurately as whole and complete figures that are not embellished with mythic or fictionalized attributes. However, the Rorschach stimuli provide limited opportunities to observe such objects (i.e., there are relatively few places in the ten inkblots where it is conventional to see a complete person). Consequently, the GHR and PHR scoring algorithms take into account instances when it is typical for people to perceive nonhuman or partial human figures in specific inkblot locations.

At the rational end of the empirical versus rational continuum are scales created by theory that do not make special provisions for the stimulus pull of specific Rorschach inkblots. A good example is the Rorschach Oral Dependency scale (ROD; Bornstein, 1996, 1998, 1999; Masling, Rabie, & Blondheim, 1967), which is a well-validated measure of dependency based on response content. The coding criteria are theoretically derived from the psychodynamic construct of orality (Schafer, 1954) and include imagery such as food sources, oral activity, nurturance, passivity, and helplessness. Another example is Blatt's Concept of the Object Scale (COS; Blatt, Brenneis, Schimek, & Glick, 1976). Like the GHR and PHR scores, the COS is based on object relations theory. However, unlike GHR and PHR, the COS coding criteria are derived entirely from theorizing about developmental processes; they do not make allowances for the stimulus pull of the individual inkblots and the extent to which that pull produces typical responses that do not conform to theory. As a result, some of the things that people typically or normatively see on the Rorschach receive less healthy COS scores than do perceptions that are normatively atypical or unusual. For instance, the stimulus features of Cards IV and IX pull for people to see quasi-human or human-like figures (e.g., a monster or a wizard) rather than ordinary people. Even though these responses are so common they are considered "Popular," the COS assigns them a less than optimal score because the latter is reserved for human beings.

There are at least three other models for understanding types of Rorschach scores; those that are founded on (1) simple classification, (2) clinical observation, and (3) behavioral similarity. The first is the least important. These are response features that are coded primarily to exhaust a coding category. Probably the best examples are some of the content codes in the CS. Every response is coded for the content it contains, though not all of the content categories are interpretively valuable. For instance, the CS has separate categories for household objects, science based percepts, botany as distinct from landscape content, and an idiographic category for not otherwise classifiable objects. None of these distinctions factor into standard interpretation.

Clinical observation is a form of empirical keying, in that response features are linked to personality characteristics through clinical experience even if there is no obvious parallel between the response feature and the characteristic that is thought to be indicated by the score. As an example, clinical observation suggested that the perception of moving inanimate objects (an *m* score) is associated with environmental stress, internal tension, agitated cognitive activity, and loss of control, while responses that are prompted by the general shading features in the ink (*Y* scores) are associated with disruptive experiences of anxiety or helplessness. In each example there are nonobvious links between the score and the construct that it is hypothesized to measure. The big difference between scores based on clinical observations and those based on empirical keying is that the former may or may not demonstrate empirical relationships when actually tested. However, both of the example scores (*m* and *Y*) have replicated data supporting their construct validity (e.g., Hartmann, Nørbech, & Grønnerød, 2006; Hartmann, Sunde, Kristensen, & Martinussen, 2003; Hartmann, Wang, Berg, & Sæther, 2003; McCowan, Fink, Galina, & Johnson, 1992; Nygren, 2004; Perry et al., 1995;

Sultan, Jebrane, & Heurtier-Hartemann, 2002). As has been the case for *m* and *Y*, other clinical observation scores that garner empirical support over time also typically develop an experiential explanation or theory that links the observed test behavior to the criterion construct. For instance, in hindsight it is now not too difficult to see how at an experiential level a person who feels considerable stress, tension, and agitation may see an elevated number of nonliving objects in motion (e.g., percepts of objects exploding, erupting, falling, spinning, tipping, or shooting).

Finally, many Rorschach scores are rationally constructed "behavioral representation" scores, in that the response characteristic coded in the testing situation closely parallels the real-life behavior that it is thought to measure (Weiner, 1977). That is, what is coded in the microcosm of the test setting is a representative sample of the behavior or experience that one expects to be manifested in the macrocosm of everyday life (Viglione & Rivera, 2003). For instance, the CS morbid score (MOR) is coded when dysphoric or sad affect is attributed to an object or when an object is described as dead, injured, or damaged in some manner. When responses of this type occur fairly often, they are thought to indicate a sense of gloomy, pessimistic inadequacy. Thus, the behavior coded in the testing situation is thought to be representative of the dysphoric, negative, damaged mental set that the person generally uses to interpret and filter life experiences. Similarly, the CS cooperative movement scores (COP) is coded when two or more objects are described as engaging in a clearly cooperative or positive interaction. Higher COP scores are thought to assess a greater propensity to conceptualize relationships as supportive and enhancing.

Probably the most well-known and best-validated behavioral representation scores on the Rorschach are the indicators of disordered thought and reasoning. In the CS these are called the Cognitive Special Scores and they are coded in a number of instances, including when responses are circumstantial or digressive, when objects have an implausible or impossible relationship (e.g., two chickens lifting weights), and when reasoning is strained or overly concrete. In all these examples, the coded test behavior represents the extra-test characteristic it is thought to measure. Thus, behavioral representation scores require relatively few inferential steps to link what is coded on the test to everyday behavior.

Basic Psychometrics

Reliability

Reliability is the extent to which a construct is assessed consistently. Once assessed consistently, it is necessary to establish that what is being measured is actually what is supposed to be measured (validity) and that the measured information is helpful in some applied manner (utility). We briefly address each issue; more details can be found in Meyer (2004) and Viglione and Meyer (2007).

There are four main types of reliability: internal consistency, split half or alternate forms, test-retest, and interrater. Internal consistency reliability examines item-by-item uniformity in content to determine whether the items of a scale all measure the same thing (Streiner, 2003a, 2003b). Split-half and alternate forms reliability operate at a more global level; they examine consistency in total scores across parallel halves of a test or parallel versions of a full length test. They allow for some item-by-item heterogeneity because they evaluate whether the composite of information on each form of the test produces a consistent and equivalent score. Although there are exceptions (e.g., Bornstein, Hill, Robinson, Calabreses, & Bowers, 1996; Dao & Prevatt, 2006), researchers typically do not investigate split-half and alternate forms reliability with the Rorschach because each Rorschach card and even each location within a card has its own distinct stimulus properties that pull for particular kinds of variables (Exner, 1996). For instance, the cards vary in the extent to which they are unified versus fragmented, shaded, colored, and so on. As a result, each item on the test, whether defined as each response to the test or as the responses to each card on the test, is not equivalent and internal consistency analyses are generally considered inapplicable. The same factors make it impossible to split the inkblots into truly parallel halves or to produce an alternative set of inkblots that have stimulus properties equivalent to the original.

Somewhat different issues affect internal consistency analyses of the CS Constellation Indexes (e.g., Dao & Prevatt, 2006). There are six of these indexes; the Perceptual-Thinking Index (PTI), the Depression Index (DEPI), the Coping Deficit Index (CDI), the Hypervigilance Index (HVI), the Obsessive Style Index (OBS), and the Suicide Constellation (S-CON). These indexes were created as heterogeneous composite measures to maximize validity, not as homogeneous scales of a single construct, which makes internal consistency reliability largely immaterial (Streiner, 2003a). Psychometrically, predictive validity is maximized by combining unique and nonredundant sources of information, so strong validity can occur despite weak internal consistency reliability, even with a short and simple measure.

Test-retest or temporal consistency reliability evaluates the stability of scores over time to repeated administrations of the same instrument. Temporal consistency has been studied fairly often with the Rorschach, and Grønnerød (2003) recently conducted a systematic meta-analysis of this literature. The results show acceptable to good stability for Rorschach scores, including for the CS (also see Meyer & Archer, 2001; Viglione & Hilsenroth, 2001). For the CS and other systems, scores thought to measure more trait-like aspects of personality have produced relatively high retest coefficients, even over extended time periods, while scores thought to reflect state-like emotional process have produced relatively low retest coefficients even over short time intervals. Grønnerød found that across all types of Rorschach scores and over an average retest interval of slightly more than 3 years (38 months), the average reliability was $r = .65$ using data from 26 samples ($N = 904$). Meyer (2004) organized results from all the meta-analyses of test-retest reliability in psychology, psychiatry, and medicine that had been published through 2001. Grønnerød's results compare favorably to the stability of other characteristics included in that review, including self-reported Big Five personality traits ($r = .73$ over 1.6 years); personality disorder diagnoses (kappa = .44 over 7.1 months); disorganized parent-child attachment patterns ($r = .34$ over 2.1 years); and the extent to which the same professionals in medicine, psychology, business, meteorology, and human resources make consistent judgments over time about the same information ($r = .76$ over 2.9 months).

Although these meta-analytic results indicate the stability of Rorschach scores compares favorably to other variables, a recent well-designed French study examining CS stability found lower than anticipated consistency over a 3-month retest period (Sultan, Andronikof, Réveillère, & Lemmel, 2006). A factor that may influence stability is the overall complexity of a person's protocol when tested on both occasions. The two variables that index the overall richness or complexity of a protocol are R, the number of responses, and Lambda (or PureForm%), which indicates the proportion of responses prompted by relatively simple form features rather than other more subtle or complex qualities of the inkblot. In the Sultan et al. (2006) study, stability coefficients for these variables were .75 and .72, respectively. Because these variables are excellent markers of the primary source of variance in Rorschach scores (i.e., the first dimension in factor analysis; see Meyer, Riethmiller, Brooks, Benoit, & Handler, 2000), when they are unstable, most other scores also will be unstable. Indeed, this is what Sultan et al. observed; the median 3-month stability coefficient across 87 ratios, percentages, and derived scores that are emphasized in interpretation was .55. Although lower than expected or desired, this level of stability is similar to that observed with memory tests and job performance measures (Viglione & Meyer, 2007). Perhaps not surprisingly, Sultan et al. found that stability was moderated by R and Lambda; it was higher when people had values that did not change much over time and lower among those with values that did change. Although more research on Rorschach stability is needed and Sultan et al.'s findings should be replicated, their results indicate that generally healthy people who volunteer for a study can provide noticeably different protocols when tested by one reasonably trained examiner and again 3 months later by a different reasonably trained examiner.

The final type of reliability is inter-rater reliability, which assesses the consistency of judgments across raters. For the Rorschach, this type of reliability concerns scoring reliability as well as the reliability of interpretation across clinicians. Rorschach scoring reliability has been studied regularly and there are four meta-analyses summarizing this literature. Two of them were related studies addressing CS reliability (Meyer, 1997; Meyer et al., 2002) and the other two addressed the Rorschach Prognostic Rating Scale and the Rorschach Oral Dependency scale (see Meyer, 2004). The meta-analyses indicate that reasonably trained raters achieve good reliability, with average Pearson or intraclass correlations (ICCs) for summary scores above .85 and average kappa values for scores assigned to each response above .80.[4] Meyer (2004) compared Rorschach interrater reliability data to all other published meta-analyses of interrater reliability in psychology, psychiatry, and medicine, and the data showed it compared favorably to a wide range of other applied judgments. For instance, Rorschach raters agree more than supervisors evaluating the job performance of employees ($r = .57$), surgeons or nurses diagnosing breast abnormalities on a clinical exam (kappa = .52), and physicians evaluating the quality of medical care provided by their peers (kappa = .31). For many Rorschach variables, scoring shows the same degree of reliability as when physicians estimate the size of the spinal canal and spinal cord from MRI, CT, or X-Ray scans ($r = .90$); dentists and dental personnel count decayed, filled, or missing teeth in early childhood (kappa = .79); or when physicians or nurses rate the degree of drug sedation for patients in intensive care ($r = .91$, ICC = .84). These comparisons show that Rorschach coding for trained examiners is typically fairly straightforward and agreement is attainable across raters.

At the same time, there are challenges or difficulties associated with Rorschach scoring. Several studies show how the reliabilities for low base rate variables are erratic (e.g., Acklin, McDowell, & Verschell, 2000; McGrath et al., 2005; Meyer et al., 2002; Viglione & Taylor, 2003). Roughly speaking, low base rate variables occur on average once or less often per record (i.e., in < 5% of responses; e.g., sex, reflections, color projection), so that large samples are needed to accurately estimate their reliability. In addition, there are some more common codes that generally show lower reliability and thus appear to be more challenging to code accurately (e.g., types of shading; the extent to which form is primary, secondary, or absent when coded in conjunction with color or shading responses; differentiating botany, landscape, and nature contents; classifying specific types of cognitive disorganization). Viglione (2002) developed a coding workbook that addresses these issues.

Students learning Rorschach assessment also need to realize that inter-rater reliability is not a fixed property of the score or test instrument. Rather, it is entirely dependent on the training, skill, and conscientiousness of the examiner. Thus, repeated practice and calibration with criterion ratings are essential for good practice.

Another issue is that most reliability research (for the Rorschach and for other instruments) relies on raters who work or train in the same setting. To the extent that local guidelines develop to contend with scoring ambiguity, agreement among those who work or train together may be greater than agreement across different sites or workgroups. As a result, existing reliability data may then give an overly optimistic view of scoring consistency across sites or across clinicians working independently. Another way to say this is that scoring reliability (i.e., agreement among two fallible coders) may be higher than scoring accuracy (i.e., correct coding).

This issue was recently examined for the CS. In a preliminary report of the data, Meyer, Viglione, Erdberg, Exner, and Shaffer (2004) examined 40 randomly selected protocols from Exner's new CS nonpatient reference sample (Exner & Erdberg, 2005) and 40 protocols from Shaffer, Erdberg, and Haroian's (1999) nonpatient sample from Fresno, California. These 80 protocols were then blindly recoded by a third group of advanced graduate students who were trained and supervised by the second author. To determine the degree of cross-site reliability, the original scores were compared to the second set of scores. The data revealed an across site median ICC of .72 for summary scores. Although this would be considered "good" reliability according to established benchmarks, it is lower than the value of .85 or higher that typically has been generated by coders working together in the same setting.

Findings like this suggest there are complexities in the coding process that are not fully clarified in standard CS training materials (Exner, 2001, 2003). As a result, training sites, such as specific graduate programs, may develop guidelines or benchmarks for coding that help resolve these residual complexities. However, these principles may not generalize to other training sites. To minimize these problems, students learning CS scoring should find Viglione's (2002) coding text helpful and should thoroughly practice their scoring relative to the across-site gold standard scores that can be found in the 300 practice responses in Exner's (2001) workbook and in the 25 cases with complete responses in the basic CS texts (Exner, 2003; Exner & Erdberg, 2005).

Beyond agreement in scoring the Rorschach, an important question is the extent to which clinicians show consistency in the way they interpret Rorschach results. Interclinician agreement when interpreting psychological tests (not just the Rorschach) was studied fairly often in the 1950s and 1960s, though it then fell out of favor (Meyer, Mihura, & Smith, 2005). The reliability of Rorschach interpretation in particular has been challenged, with some suggesting that the inferences clinicians generated said more about them than about the client being assessed. To examine agreement on CS interpretations, Meyer et al. (2005) had 55 patient protocols interpreted by three to eight clinicians across four data sets. A total of 20 different clinicians participated in the research. Consistency was assessed across a representative set of 29 personality characteristics (e.g., "This person experiences himself as damaged, flawed, or hurt by life."). Substantial reliability was observed across all the data sets, with aggregated judgments having higher agreement ($M r = .84$) than judgments to individual interpretive statements ($M r = .71$). As Meyer et al. (2005) illustrated, these findings compared favorably to meta-analytic summaries of interrater agreement for other types of applied judgments in psychology, psychiatry, and medicine. For instance, therapists or observers ratings the quality of the therapeutic alliance in psychotherapy produce an average agreement of $r = .78$, while neurologists classifying strokes produce an average agreement of kappa = .51.

At the same time, it was also clear that some clinicians were more reliable than others. For aggregated judgments, the average reliability among the three most consistent judges was $r = .90$ and among the three least consistent judges it was $r = .73$. Thus, the findings indicated that experienced clinicians could reliably interpret CS data; when presented with the same Rorschach data, they drew similar conclusions about patients. However, some clinicians were clearly more consistent than others, which highlights how one needs to conscientiously learn principles of interpretation and then carefully and systematically consider all relevant testing data when conducting an idiographic clinical assessment.

Validity

Construct validity refers to evidence that a test scale is measuring what it is supposed to measure. It is determined by the conglomerate of research findings related to both convergent and discriminant validity. Convergent validity refers to expected associations with criteria that theoretically should be related to the target construct, while discriminant validity refers to an expected lack of association with criteria that theoretically should be independent of the target construct. Evaluating the validity of a complex, multidimensional measure like the Rorschach is challenging because it is difficult to systematically review the full historical pattern of evidence attesting to convergent and discriminant validity for every test score. As such, we focus primarily on results from meta-analytic reviews.

Thousands of studies from around the world have provided evidence for Rorschach validity (e.g., for narrative summaries of specific variables see Bornstein & Masling, 2005; Exner & Erdberg, 2005; Viglione, 1999). Meyer and Archer (2001) summarized the available evidence from Rorschach meta-analyses, including four that examined the global validity of the test and seven that examined the validity of specific scales in relation to particular criteria. The scales included CS and non-CS variables. For comparison, they also summarized the meta-analytic evidence available on the validity of the MMPI and IQ measures. Subsequently, Meyer (2004) compared the validity evidence for these psychological tests to meta-analytic findings for the medical assessments reported in Meyer et al. (2001).

Although the use of different types of research designs and validation tasks makes it challenging to compare findings across meta-analyses, the broad review of evidence indicated three primary conclusions. First, psychological and medical tests have varying degrees of validity, ranging from scores that are essentially unrelated to a particular criterion to scores that are strongly associated with relevant criteria. Second, it was difficult to distinguish between medical tests and psychological tests in terms of their average validity; both types of tests produced a wide range of effect sizes and had similar averages. Third, test validity is conditional and dependent on the criteria used to evaluate the instrument. For a given scale, validity is greater against some criteria and weaker against others.

Within these findings, validity for the Rorschach was much the same as it was for other instruments; effect sizes varied depending on the variables considered but, on average, validity was similar to other instruments. Thus, Meyer and Archer (2001) concluded that the systematically collected data showed the Rorschach produced good validity coefficients that were on par with other tests:

> Across journal outlets, decades of research, aggregation procedures, predictor scales, criterion measures, and types of participants, reasonable hypotheses for the vast array of Rorschach ... scales that have been empirically tested produce convincing evidence for their construct validity. (Meyer & Archer, 2001, p. 491)

Atkinson, Quarrington, Alp, and Cyr (1986) conducted one of the earliest meta-analytic reviews of the Rorschach and found good evidence for its validity. They noted that the test is regularly criticized and challenged despite the evidence attesting to its validity. To understand why, they suggested that "deprecation of the Rorschach is a sociocultural, rather than scientific, phenomenon" (p. 244). Meyer and Archer (2001) reached a similar conclusion about the evidence base and concluded that a dispassionate review of the evidence would not warrant singling out the Rorschach for particular criticism. However, they also noted that the same evidence would not warrant singling out the Rorschach for particular praise. Its broadband validity appears both as good as and also as limited as that for other psychological tests.

Robert Rosenthal, a widely recognized and highly regarded expert in meta-analysis, was commissioned to conduct a comparative analysis of Rorschach and MMPI validity for a Special Issue of the journal *Psychological Assessment*. He and his coworkers (Hiller, Rosenthal, Bornstein, Berry, & Brunell-Neuleib, 1999; Rosenthal, Hiller, Bornstein, Berry, & Brunell-Neuleib, 2001) found that on average the Rorschach and MMPI were equally valid. However, they also identified moderators to validity for each instrument. Moderators are factors that influence the size of the validity coefficients observed across studies. The Rorschach demonstrated greater validity against criteria that they classified as objective, while the MMPI demonstrated greater validity against criteria consisting of other self-report scales or psychiatric diagnoses.[5] The criteria they considered objective encompassed a range of variables that were largely behavioral events, medical conditions, behavioral interactions with the environment, or classifications that required minimal observer judgment, such as dropping out of treatment, history of abuse, number of driving accidents, history of criminal offenses, having a medical disorder, cognitive test performance, performance on a behavioral test of ability to delay gratification, or response to medication. Viglione (1999) conducted a systematic descriptive review of the Rorschach literature and similarly concluded that the Rorschach was validly associated with behavioral events or life outcomes involving person-environment interactions that emerge over time. In general, these findings are consistent with the types of sponta-neous behavioral trends and longitudinally determined life outcomes that McClelland, Koestner, and Weinberger (1989) showed were best predicted by tests measuring implicit characteristics, as opposed to the conscious and deliberately chosen near-term actions that were best predicted by explicit self-report tests (also see Bornstein, 1998).

In the most recent Rorschach meta-analysis, which was not considered in the previous reviews, Grønnerød (2004) systematically summarized the literature examining the extent to which Rorschach variables could measure personality change as a function of psychological treatment. The Rorschach produced a level of validity that was equivalent to alternative instruments based on self-report or clinician ratings. Grønnerød also examined modera-tors to validity and, consistent with expectations from the psychotherapy literature, found that Rorschach scores changed more with longer treatment, suggesting that more therapy produced more healthy change in personality. Grønnerød also noted that effect sizes were smaller when coders clearly did not know whether a protocol was obtained before or after treatment but larger in studies that clearly described scoring reliability procedures and obtained good reliability results using conservative statistics.

Overall, the meta-analytic evidence supports the general validity of the Rorschach. Globally, the test appears to function as well as other assessment instruments. To date, only a few meta-analyses have systematically examined the validity literature for specific scales in relation to particular criteria. The evidence has been positive and supportive for the ROD, the Rorschach Prognostic Rating Scale (RPRS), and the precursor to the PTI, the Schizophrenia Index (SCZI), though it has not been supportive of the CS Depression Index (DEPI) when used as a diagnostic indicator. As is true for other commonly used tests, such as the MMPI-2, Personality Assessment Inventory (PAI; Morey, 1991), Millon Clinical Multiaxial Inventory (MCMI-III; Millon, 1994), or Wechsler scales (e.g., Wechsler, 1997), additional focused meta-analytic reviews that systematically catalog the validity evidence of particular Rorschach variables relative to specific types of criteria will continue to refine and enhance clinical practice.

Utility

In general, the utility of an assessment instrument refers to the practical value of the information it provides relative to its costs. The Rorschach takes time to administer, score, and interpret. To make up for these costs, the Rorschach needs to provide useful information that cannot be obtained from tests, interviews, or observations that are readily available and less time consuming. One way to evaluate this issue in research is through incremental validity analyses (see Hunsley & Meyer, 2003), where the Rorschach and a less time intensive source of information are compared statistically. To demonstrate incremental validity, the Rorschach would need to predict the criterion over and above what could be predicted by the simpler method. Such a finding demonstrates statistically that the Rorschach provides unique information.

Although utility cannot be equated with statistical evidence of incremental validity, the latter is one commonly obtained form of evidence that can attest to utility. Utility also can be demonstrated by predicting important real-world behaviors, life outcomes, and the kind of ecologically valid criteria that are important in the context of applied practice with the test. Research reviews and meta-analyses show that the Rorschach possesses utility in all of these forms, such that Rorschach variables predict clinically relevant behaviors and outcomes and have demonstrated incremental validity over other tests, demographic data, and other types of information (Bornstein & Masling, 2005; Exner & Erdberg, 2005; Hiller et al., 1999; Meyer, 2000a; Meyer & Archer, 2001; Viglione, 1999; Viglione & Hilsenroth, 2001; Weiner, 2001).

We do not have the space to review more than a sampling of utility findings. With respect to incremental validity, recent studies published in the United States and Europe show the Rorschach yields important information that is not attainable through simpler, less time consuming methods. The criteria include predicting future success in Norwegian naval special forces training (Hartmann et al., 2003), future delinquency in Swedish adolescents and adults based on clinician ratings of ego strength from childhood Rorschach protocols (Janson & Stattin, 2003), future psychiatric relapse among previously hospitalized United States children (Stokes et al., 2003), future improvement across a range of interventions in United States adults (Meyer, 2000a; Meyer & Handler, 1997), future benefit from antidepressant medication in adult United States inpatients (Perry & Viglione, 1991), previous glucose stability levels in diabetic French children (Sultan et al., 2002), and future emergency medical transfers and drug overdoses in United States inpatients during a 60-day period after testing (Fowler, Piers, Hilsenroth, Holdwick, & Padawar, 2001). In these studies, the Rorschach demonstrated incremental validity over various alternative data sources, including self-report scales, collateral reports, *DSM* diagnoses, and intelligence tests.

Studies have repeatedly shown that Rorschach and self-report scales have minimal correlations even when they purportedly measure similar constructs (e.g., Bornstein, 2002; Krishnamurthy, Archer, & House, 1996; Meyer & Archer, 2001; Viglione, 1996). Although this lack of association was unexpected, it suggests that the Rorschach should display incremental validity over self-report scales. If both types of measures are related to a criterion but not to each other, each should maintain a unique association to the criterion and thus provide incremental validity over the other. At this point, more research has documented the limited associations between these two data sources than their combined value.

There are exceptions, however. For instance, studies have shown how it is the combined interaction of Rorschach-assessed and self-reported dependency that affords the optimal prediction of certain kinds of dependent behavior (Bornstein, 1998). In addition, the CS scales of psychotic symptoms (i.e., PTI or SCZI) have shown incremental validity over MMPI-2 scales of psychotic symptoms when predicting psychotic disorders (e.g., Dao, Prevatt, & Horne, in press; Meyer, 2000b; Ritsher, 2004). Rubin and Arceneaux (2001) recently illustrated this phenomenon with a case study.

A recent series of studies examining obese patients in Sweden demonstrated the utility of the Rorschach by predicting practical behavioral and life outcome criteria. Rorschach scores predicted the rate of consumption during an experimental meal, atypical acceleration in consumption during that meal, eventual weight loss in an obesity treatment program, and a positive response to weight loss medication (Elfhag, Barkeling, Carlsson, Lindgren, & Rössner, 2004; Elfhag, Barkeling, Carlsson, & Rössner, 2003; Elfhag, Carlsson, & Rössner, 2003; Elfhag, Rössner, Carlsson, & Barkeling, 2003; Elfhag, Rössner, Lingren, Andersson, & Carlsson, 2004).

Two other recent Swedish studies examined the Rorschach in relation to psychotherapy considerations. Bihlar and Carlsson (2001) documented how particular CS scores obtained before treatment predicted whether therapists would have to alter their initial plans for treatment over time, suggesting that the Rorschach scores identified characteristics that were not obvious from interview and history information. Nygren (2004), using a selected set of hypothesized variables, found CS scores (a) differentiated patients who were selected versus not selected for intensive, long-term psychoanalytic therapy, and (b) were associated with clinician ratings of ego strength and capacity to engage in dynamic therapy.

Lundbäck et al. (2006) studied Swedish patients who had recently attempted suicide. They examined cerebrospinal fluid (CSF) concentrations of 5-hydroxyindoleacetic acid (5-HIAA), a serotonin metabolite, because previous research indicated low CSF 5-HIAA was associated with more violent and severe suicide attempts. As expected, the S-CON was negatively correlated with 5-HIAA levels ($r_S = -.39$). Post hoc analyses showed that responses in which shading gives rise to depth or dimensionality (vista) and the extent to which the form of objects perceived is secondary to their color (color dominance index; CF + C > FC) were the strongest individual predictors among the S-CON variables. In this study, 5-HIAA was unrelated to scores on the DEPI ($r_S = -.21$) and the Coping Deficit Index (CDI; $r_S = .26$). These results echo Fowler et al.'s (2001) United States findings, where the S-CON predicted subsequent suicidal behavior but the DEPI and CDI did not. Both sets of results provide evidence for both the convergent and discriminant validity of the S-CON.

As a final example, many studies have examined the ROD as an index of dependency. These have been systematically reviewed and meta-analyzed (Bornstein, 1996, 1999), with results showing that ROD scores validly predict help-seeking behavior, conformity, compliance, suggestibility, and interpersonal yielding in laboratory and clinical settings. Results also show the ROD has discriminant validity by being unrelated or minimally related to scales of alternative constructs like social desirability, IQ, and locus of control.

Our brief summary of recent studies addressing utility is limited in several ways. Although the authors for all of these studies carefully articulated hypothesized associations, some of the samples were small and the findings need to be replicated. There also were negative findings where the results did not support the hypothesized variables. For instance, Elfhag, Rössner et al. (2004) did not find support for the ROD in relation to eating behavior and Nygren (2004) did not find support for several anticipated variables as predictors of who would be selected for intensive psychotherapy (e.g., inanimate movement, distorted or arbitrary form quality, dimensionality based on form).

Nonetheless, based largely on the kinds of findings reviewed in this section, the Board of Trustees of the Society for Personality Assessment (2005) synthesized the available evidence and issued an official statement on the

Quick Reference

- The Rorschach can evaluate personality and problem solving in psychiatric, medical, forensic, and nonclinical settings.
- It is used with children, adolescents, and adults in any language or culture.
- The task is individually administered in a collaborative two-step process that elicits responses with the prompt, "What might this be?", and then clarifies the what, where, and why of each percept.
- Responses are recorded verbatim. The CS requires a minimum of 14; data and cost benefit considerations support prompting for at least two per card but obtaining no more than four.
- Proper administration, scoring, and interpretation require considerable training.
- Computer-assisted scoring is recommended and likely will become increasingly important.

scientific foundation for using the Rorschach in clinical and forensic practice. They concluded "the Rorschach possesses reliability and validity similar to that of other generally accepted personality assessment instruments and its responsible use in personality assessment is appropriate and justified" (p. 219).

Administration and Scoring

The Rorschach is used across a wide range of settings where questions of personality and problem solving are relevant, including inpatient and outpatient psychiatric settings, inpatient and outpatient medical settings, and forensic contexts. It can also be used to assess normal range personality functioning and to assist generally healthy people with goals for professional development or life enhancement. Because reading skills are not required, the Rorschach can be used as readily with children and adolescents as with adults, and as readily with people from the United States as with people from other countries around the world. Indeed, the International Society for the Rorschach boasts 20 member countries and more than 3,000 individual members from the African, Asian, European, North American, and South American continents.[6]

The CS provides guidelines for standardized administration and scoring, as well as reference data for children (in 1-year age increments from 5 to 16), adults (age 19 to 86), and several patient groups (see Exner, 2001, 2003; Exner & Erdberg, 2005). Practitioner surveys indicate that the CS takes about 45 minutes to administer and about 40 minutes to score (Camara et al., 2000).

Administration

The Rorschach is typically administered in the context of other assessment measures and the adequacy of any personality assessment depends on the quality of the collaborative working relationship established between the examiner and client (see Fischer and Finn, chapter 10, this volume). Rorschach testing is not different and should not be attempted "cold" without first establishing decent rapport. Administration requires three tools: the inkblot stimuli, recording utensils (either notepaper with a pen or pencil or a laptop computer), and a location sheet that provides miniature inkblot images for recording where the key features of each response are located. Standardized CS administration takes place with the examiner seated next to the client to minimize visual cues from the examiner and to help him or her see what the client perceives, with the location sheet out of sight, and the inkblots face down on a table. The task is generally introduced as "the inkblot test" and because many people have heard of it the examiner typically asks the client what he or she knows about the test and if it was ever taken before. If the client has questions about the test or why it is being used, the examiner responds in a straightforward manner (e.g., "It's a test that provides some information about personality characteristics." or "No, there are no right or wrong answers.").

The administration itself is a two phase process consisting of the Response and Inquiry phases. In the Response phase, the client is sequentially handed each inkblot in order and at the outset is asked the standardized question, "What might this be?" The examiner numbers each response and records it verbatim, along with all additional commentary by the client. Once the Response phase is complete for all ten cards, the examiner introduces the Inquiry phase by explaining to the client that they will go through the responses a second time to ensure that the examiner sees each response in the same way that the client perceived it. The goal of this stage is not to elicit new information but to gather sufficient information to accurately score each response. The examiner primarily wants to know three things: what is being perceived (i.e., the content), where it is in the inkblot (i.e., the location), and how particular inkblot features contribute to or help determine the response (i.e., the so-called determinants of the response). The Inquiry begins with the examiner explaining that he or she wishes to briefly go through each response again to "see the things you saw and make sure I see them like you do." The examiner elaborates by saying, "I want you to show me where it is in the blot and then tell me what there is there that makes it look like that to you so I can see it just like you did." The somewhat awkwardly worded instructions to "tell me what there is there that makes it look like that" emphasize how the goal is not just to know what objects are seen where but also what aspects of the inkblot contribute to the perception. The examiner initiates the inquiry for each response by reading the verbatim portion from the Response phase and again records verbatim the further elaborations and examiner questions that emerge during the Inquiry phase. As the Inquiry proceeds, the examiner completes the location sheet by roughly outlining the location of each numbered response and identifying its key features in sufficient detail so that another examiner will readily recognize the correct response location.

The first two inquiry goals (content and location, or what and where) are often obvious from the Response phase and may not need further clarification during the Inquiry. If they do, it is typically accomplished easily. The last goal (determinants or how inkblot features contribute to the percept) can be more complex, as clients often use indirect key words or phrases that suggest but do not confirm certain determinant scores. In the CS, determinant scores are related to the perception of movement (coded as human [M], animal [FM], or inanimate [m]), symmetry [reflection images, Fr or rF or paired objects, 2), shading (diffuse [Y] or involving a tactile impression [T]), color (chromatic [C] or achromatic [C']), and depth (based on shading [V] or on form [FD]). Determining whether movement and symmetry are present is typically straightforward and most often these features are coded without the examiner asking any additional questions during Inquiry. However, clients may not so clearly describe whether the shading, color, or depth contributed to their perception.

As such, to obtain the information that will allow for accurate scoring, the examiner must be alert to key words or phrases in the response suggesting these features and then generate a query to clarify the ambiguity. For instance, "a pretty flower" suggests that color may be an important determinant of the response; "trees on the horizon" suggests that depth may be important in forming the response; "it looks like a soft and furry rug" or "it's a wispy rain cloud" suggests that shading features may be important for the response. In each of these examples, the proper coding is uncertain, so the examiner has to formulate a question that will efficiently clarify how to code. What constitutes an effective and efficient question will depend on the context, including the quality of the relationship between the examiner and client and the kinds of Inquiry questions that already have been asked. At times, an efficient question may be quite general (e.g., "I'm not sure I see that like you; can you help?"), though more often the examiner would strive to ask a question that is focused directly on the key word or phrase (e.g., "You said it looks pretty?"; "On the horizon? I'm not sure what makes it look like that."; "What about the inkblot makes it look soft and furry?"), rather than being nonspecific (e.g., "Can you say more?" or "Help me see it like you"), tangential (e.g., "I'm not sure I see the flower" or "Where is the flower?"), or "double-barreled" and referring to multiple response elements (e.g., "Help me see the pretty flower," which would allow the client to address location or form features without necessarily addressing the prettiness that suggested color may be involved).

Standard CS administration requires a client to give at least 14 responses to the 10 inkblot stimuli and, although there are procedures in place to limit excessive responding, there is not a fixed limit to the upper end of the range. CS normative data indicate that an average protocol contain 22 or 23 responses, with 80% in the range from 18 to 27 responses. Because the CS norms are most applicable to protocols with 18 to 27 responses, it is desirable for all protocols to be in this range. However, existing administration guidelines (Exner, 2003) often produce protocols that fall outside of this range in clinical settings. Recent evidence (Dean, Viglione, Perry, & Meyer, in press; Sultan, 2006; Sultan et al., 2006) shows that the number of responses in a protocol moderates the test-retest stability and validity of scores, and that both are maximized when R is in the optimal range. Consequently, we have recommended simplified administration guidelines to maximize the prospect that examiners will obtain records of an optimal length (see Dean et al., in press). Specifically, this R-optimized administration uses a "prompt for two, pull after four" guideline. To ensure an adequate minimum, if only a single response is offered to any card, examiners should prompt for a second. To ensure the maximum number of responses is not excessive, examiners would remove any card after four responses. In preliminary work, when the impact of these revised administration guidelines was modeled on normative reference data, the score means were essentially unchanged but their variability decreased, suggesting a potentially better ability to discriminate typical from problematic functioning.

These modified guidelines are consistent with the evidence and also with cost-benefit principles. Short protocols tend to provide insufficient information and they lead to false negative errors of inference (i.e., incorrectly concluding that the client does not possess a characteristic). Lengthy protocols tend to provide unnecessarily redundant information and they lead to false positive errors of inference (i.e., incorrectly concluding that the client does possess a characteristic; one which is often unhealthy or pathological). In addition, both short and long protocols can be time consuming and frustrating for examiners and their clients. Under current CS guidelines examiners must administer the test a second time starting from scratch when less than 14 responses are obtained. This effectively doubles the testing time and often leaves clients confused about whether they should repeat initially offered responses. At the other end of the spectrum, lengthy protocols of 40 or more responses are time consuming to administer and score, and their complexity is often draining or exhausting for both the examiner and client.

Scoring

To score the Rorschach, codes are typically applied to each response and then aggregated across all responses. In the CS the codes assigned to each response form what is known as the Sequence of Scores and the tally of codes across all responses is known as the Structural Summary. The scoring process can be fairly simple for single construct scoring systems, like the ROD, or fairly complex for multidimensional scoring systems, like the CS. However, scoring according to any system requires the same ingredients: a clearly articulated set of scoring guidelines, an understanding of those guidelines by the coder, and the coder's repeated practice of scoring against gold standard example material until proficiency is obtained. For a multidimensional system like the CS, fairly substantial training is required for proficiency. Table 8.1 provides a brief list of the standard CS codes that can be assigned to each response to generate the Sequence of Scores. These scores are then summed across responses and form the basis for about 70 ratios, percentages, and derived scores that are given interpretive emphasis on the Structural Summary. Because of the complexity of this material, we do not provide a detailed description. However, a full guide to interpretation can be found in standard interpretive texts (Exner, 2003; Exner & Erdberg, 2005; Weiner, 2003). These sources make it clear that formal coding is only part of the data that contributes to an interpretation. There are behaviors expressed during the testing, themes associated with response imagery, and perceptual or content based idiosyncrasies that are not captured by the formal scores but that may nonetheless be very important for helping to develop an idiographic and unique understanding of the client (e.g., Peebles-Kleiger, 2002).

The requirements for competent administration and interpretation are similar to the requirements for coding. In order to perform an adequate administration the examiner must first understand scoring in order to formulate suitable Inquiry questions. Like with scoring, developing proficient administration skills requires practice and accurate feedback about errors or problems. The latter can be accomplished most adequately when a thoroughly trained supervisor is physically present to observe and correct the student's practice administrations as they are occurring, though supervisory feedback on videotaped administrations also can be quite helpful. The least optimal training occurs when supervision feedback is only provided on hand written or typed protocols, as many nuances of nonverbal interaction are not captured by this written record and it is not possible for the supervisor to see how adequately the written record captured what actually transpired during the administration.

Table 8.1 A Brief Summary of Rorschach Comprehensive System Scores

Location and space	The client either makes use of the *whole* inkblot (W), one or more of its *commonly perceived detail* (D) locations, or one or more of its *small or rarely used detail* (Dd) locations. The background white *space* (S) can also be incorporated with each location (i.e., WS, DS, or DdS).
Developmental quality	The object(s) perceived either have definite or *ordinary* form demands (o) or they are characteristically formless or *vague* (v). When more than one object is identified they also are designated as either being *synthesized* in a meaningful interaction (o becomes +; v becomes v/+) or not.
Determinants	• *Movement* is scored when an object is perceived as being in motion or in a state of tension and it is designated separately for human activity (M), species appropriate animal activity (FM), or inanimate motion (m). Each type of movement is further designated as *active* (a) or *passive* (p).
	• *Color* scores can be of two types. Use of *chromatic color* is scored when the red or pastel colors are important to a response. Like all the remaining determinants, scores are differentiated by the extent to which form is also an important feature to the response, such that form can be primary and color secondary (FC), color can be primary and form secondary (CF), or form can be nonexistent (C). Use of *achromatic color* (FC', C'F, C') is scored when the white, black, or gray colors are important to a response.
	• *Shading* is scored in three ways. *Diffuse shading* (FY, YF, Y) is scored when the light and dark gradations of ink contribute to a response. *Texture from shading* (FT, TF, T) is scored when the light and dark gradations of ink give rise to a tactile quality, such as soft, furry, wet, or cold. *Vista from shading* (FV, VF, V) is coded when the light and dark gradations of ink give rise to a perception of depth or dimensionality.
	• *Form Dimensional* scores (FD) refer to instances when just the outline or form of an object generates a perception of depth or dimensionality. By definition form dominates this kind of response, so form is never scored as secondary or not present.
	• *Reflections* (Fr, rF) are scored when one side of the inkblot is a reflected or mirror image of the other. Form is considered inherent in such a response, so it is never coded as absent.
	• *Pure Form* (F) responses are assigned when it is only the shape or outline of an object that is salient. It is also a default score; it should be assigned when no other determinants are present and not assigned when other determinants are present.
	• *Blends* are instances when more than one determinant is present in a response; each is separated by a period. For instance, the score M^a.FC.C'F indicates the response contains active human movement, form dominated chromatic color, and form secondary achromatic color.

(continued)

Table 8.1 Continued

Form quality and popular responses	These scores characterize whether it is conventional to see an object in a particular location on a given card. Responses with at least some form are classified as *ordinary* (o; or + if thoroughly described) if they are commonly seen, *unusual* (u) if they are infrequent but consistent with the blot contours, and *minus* (–) if they are arbitrary, distorted, or impose nonexistent lines to define the object. To assign these codes the examiner consults an extensive table derived from more than 200,000 responses from 9,500 protocols. These tables document percepts perceived in W, D, or Dd locations to each card. In addition to the codes noted above, objects that were seen in at least one third of the 9,500 protocols are separately coded as *Popular* (P).
Pairs	A *pair* (2) is coded when the same object is identified on each side of the blot. This is a symmetry based score, like the reflection response.
Contents	Each object perceived is classified into a content based category. • There are four types of human or animal objects that are differentiated on two dimensions: whole versus partial and realistic versus fictional or mythological. The *human* codes are H versus Hd, for realistic whole objects versus realistic partial objects, and (H) versus (Hd), for fictional whole objects versus fictional partial objects. The *animal* codes are A versus Ad and (A) versus (Ad), respectively. In addition, *human experiences* (Hx) are coded when human emotions or sensory experiences are described. • Another class of content addresses body related imagery, including internal *anatomy* (An), *X-ray* or MRI-type images (Xy), *blood* (Bl), and *sexual organs or activity* (Sx). • A number of content codes relate to the physical environment, including *botany* (Bt), *landscape* (Ls), *nature* (Na), *clouds* (Cl), maps and *geography* (Ge), *fire* (Fi), and *explosions* (Ex); or to human creations, including *household* objects (Hh), products of *science* (Sc), *art* objects (Art), or cultural/historical images (Ay for *anthropology*). There is also a category for *food* items (Fd) and for percepts that are unique to the client or not otherwise classifiable (Id for *idiographic*)
Organizational activity	*Organizational Activity*, or Z scores, are coded for their *frequency* (Zf) and for the *degree of synthesis* evident in the response (Z-value or ZSum). The degree of synthesis is determined separately for each blot as a function of whether the response uses the whole inkblot (ZW), describes meaningful relationships between adjacent (ZA) or distant (ZD) objects, or integrates white space (S) with the rest of the blot (ZS).

Cognitive special scores	Six codes index disrupted or illogical thought processes. These include use of mistaken or inappropriate words (DV for *Deviant Verbalization*), circumstantial responses or use of inappropriate phrases (DR for *Deviant Responses*), describing one object with implausible or impossible attributes (INCOM for *Incongruous Combination*), describing two objects in an implausible or impossible relationship (FABCOM for *Fabulized Combination*), seeing two objects superimposed on each other and merged into a single percept (CONTAM for *Contamination*), and showing highly strained or overly concrete reasoning (ALOG for *autistic logic*).
Other special scores	The remaining codes identify a mix of notable features in a response. • Several of the codes are representational scores related to thematically defined images, including *aggressive* interactions (AG), *cooperative* interactions (COP), and *morbid* (MOR) perceptions where objects are broken, damaged, dead, spoiled, or imbued with dysphoric affect. • Other codes quantify instances when percepts are fixed, rigid, or *perseverative* (PSV); deal with symbolic, intellectualized, or *abstract* content (AB); imbue cards with color even though none is present (CP for *color projection*); or justify perceptions based on authority derived from *personal* knowledge (PER). • Two final codes provide an indication of object relations, though they are not independently assessed. Rather the *Good* and *Poor Human Representation* variables (GHR and PHR) summarize other scored information in the protocol, drawing upon determinants, content, form quality, cognitive special scores, and the COP, AG, and MOR special scores.

Interpretation

Not surprisingly, Rorschach interpretation is the most complex or difficult activity, as proficiency requires knowledge and skills in multiple areas. These include:

- an understanding of interpretive postulates associated with the various scores obtained from the test;
- an understanding of the kind of information the Rorschach can and cannot provide (i.e., its locus of effectiveness);
- knowledge of the psychometric research literature on the types of systematic bias that can affect Rorschach scores;
- knowledge of the psychometric research literature on the reliability and validity of the test scores to be interpreted;

- a thorough understanding of personality and psychopathology, particularly of the condition(s) being assessed;
- recognition of the kind of judgment errors that can adversely influence clinical inferences;
- the capacity for disciplined reasoning to rule in and rule out inferences; and
- the ability to integrate Rorschach-based inferences with inferences obtained from other tests, from observed behavior, and from history as reported by the client and other sources of collateral information.

Of course, to adequately perform the last step of integration, the examiner must also have parallel forms of knowledge about the other tests and sources of information that are contributing inferences. That is, for each non-Rorschach data source, the clinician must understand the interpretive postulates associated with the observation, understand the kind of information that the data source can and cannot provide, know what forms of systematic bias influence the data source, and know the reliability and validity evidence for the alternative data source. To become proficient with the idiographic task of correctly interpreting a complex array of personality test results, including Rorschach scores, requires considerable closely supervised clinical experience with a well-trained individual.

Computerization

Although computerized administration has been used in Rorschach research, standard CS test administration does not lend itself to automated, computer-adapted administration or to computer automated scoring. However, computer-*assisted* scoring and interpretation for the CS is quite common, with the two primary software programs being the Rorschach Interpretive Assistance Program (RIAP), which is now in its 5th edition, and ROR-SCAN, which is now in its 6th edition and authored by Philip Caracena. Reviews of each program can be found in Acklin (2000; for the 4th edition of RIAP) and Smith and Hilsenroth (2003; for the 6th edition of ROR-SCAN).

Because the CS Structural Summary tabulates many different scores and then generates numerous other ratios or derived scores, we strongly recommend computer-assisted scoring to minimize the prospect of computational errors. For computer-assisted scoring, the examiner manually assigns codes to each response on the sequence of scores, but allows the computer algorithms to generate the final Structural Summary. Doing so has a number of benefits. First, it allocates the clinician's time and expertise where it is required, which is with judging what codes should be assigned to each response, and it leaves the mundane (but error prone) mathematical operations to a machine that is perfectly suited to these clerical tasks. Second, computer-assisted scoring would allow all users to obtain CS-based variables like the Ego Impairment Index (EII-2; Perry & Viglione, 1991; Viglione, Perry, & Meyer, 2003) that are too complex for hand scoring.

Third, although commercial programs currently do not do so, they can be programmed to generate complex scores that will facilitate clinical interpretation. For instance, programs could provide scores that are adjusted for the overall complexity of the protocol (i.e., first factor variance) or they could provide congruence coefficients that empirically show how well a client's pattern of scores fit with the average scores from a criterion group (e.g., patients diagnosed with schizophrenia or borderline personality disorder). Future computerization also could enable users to maximize information at the level of individual responses or cards. Currently, scores are summarized at the protocol level, aggregating equally across all responses and cards. However, because of card pull, responses that occur to specific cards and location areas may have differential validity that should be taken into account during interpretation.

With these potentials in mind, reliability, validity, and utility can be maximized by more fully harnessing computer resources. At the same time, users should be cautious when considering computer generated interpretative reports. These can certainly be helpful but their ready accessibility can tempt less experienced or proficient clinicians to cut-and-paste material into a final report without sufficiently considering idiographic contextual issues or the nature and limitations of Rorschach-based scores.

Applications and Limitations

As noted above, the Rorschach can be used in a wide range of settings, including inpatient and outpatient psychiatric and medical settings, in forensic contexts, and in nonclinical situations for professional development, personal enhancement, or counseling. With minimal extra-test modifications, it can also be used in the same form with children, adolescents, and adults, regardless of culture, language, or nationality.

Clinicians may choose to use the Rorschach for many different reasons. However, it is often selected precisely because it is an office based procedure that provides a unique source of information—one that differs considerably from the self-reported characteristics that form the basis for the many inventories or structured interviews[7] available for assessing personality (e.g., those described in other chapters of this text).

A number of authors have described important distinctions between self-report scales and Rorschach measures (Meyer, 1997; Meyer & Archer, 2001; Viglione & Rivera, 2003). Self-report measures require clients to determine the extent to which verbal statements, adjectives, or symptoms are charac-

Just the Facts

Ages:	5 or 6 to elderly
Purpose:	To assess personality and problem solving characteristics using a sample of spontaneously generated behavior and imagery collected under standardized conditions.
Strengths:	Provides an in vivo demonstration of personal characteristics, many of which may reside outside of conscious awareness.
Limitations:	Many assessed characteristics are implicit and independent of self-reported characteristics, which make it risky to interpret test scores in isolation.
Time to Administer:	about 45 minutes
Time to Score:	about 40 minutes for the CS

teristic of their personality. Although there is some variability from instrument to instrument, because of how the task is structured, the information obtained from a self-report measure is dependent upon the client's conscious understanding of himself or herself, ability to accurately characterize himself or herself relative to others when determining if a characteristic is or is not self-descriptive, and willingness to convey information in an accurate and forthright manner. Under optimal conditions, self-reported data is particularly adept at addressing and quantifying the presence and severity of specific, consciously recognized preferences, affective states, and symptoms.

In contrast, the Rorschach task requires clients to identify and articulate images in response to a set of complex and novel stimuli. Although subject to its own sources of bias and error, as a sample of actual behavior obtained under standardized conditions, the information obtained from the Rorschach does not depend on the client's consciously represented self-image or ability to accurately evaluate him or herself. Under optimal conditions then, this allows Rorschach data to provide information about problem solving styles and implicit or tacit personal qualities that may reside outside of consciousness, even though these characteristics may regularly guide and motivate behavior or provide the schematic templates that filter and interpret experiences.

One way to understand the distinction between these methods of assessment is to consider them in the context of assessing intelligence. It certainly can be informative to directly ask people how intelligent they are or how they compare to peers in their specific abilities, such as capacity to solve verbal problems, to identify visuospatial relationships, to quickly and easily process information, or to mentally transform and manipulate information in short-term memory stores. However, most people do not have a clear awareness or understanding of their cognitive abilities, are uncertain how they stack up against their peers, and/or are motivated to describe their abilities in an overly positive light (or overly negative light, depending on the circumstances). Consequently, when it is important to have an accurate understanding of someone's actual intelligence, psychologists typically administer a standardized intelligence test that provides a behavioral sample and in vivo demonstration of problem solving, information processing, verbal ability, and so on. Not surprisingly, this performance based information is quite different than self-reported results. Depending on the ability construct and sample considered, research reveals the correlation between self-reported and performance based methods of assessing cognitive ability range from about $r = .00$ to $r = .30$ (Meyer et al., 2001; Paulhus, Lysy, & Yik, 1998).

Returning to personality assessment, self-reported information from a cooperative client can provide critical information about many clinical conditions, personal experiences, and normative characteristics. For example, when assessing depressive suicidality, self-report measures can quantify specific symptoms and warning signs, such as consciously experienced and persistent depressed mood, diminished interest or pleasure in almost all activities, excessive or inappropriate guilt, and deliberate suicidal ideation with intention and means. No matter how many responses are available for consideration, one simply is not able to assess these specific characteristics with the Rorschach. In contrast, however, the Rorschach can measure the extent to which experiences are filtered through a depressively biased schema, whether underlying affect is chaotic or modulated, and the extent to which implicit coping resources are disorganized and unavailable, all of which are personality features associated with variables on the CS S-CON. Although these characteristics are not readily assessed by self-report and although there is no correlation between the S-CON and self-rated depressive symptoms or suicidality (Meyer, 1997; Meyer et al., 2000), as noted above, research has consistently documented that the S-CON predicts self-harm behavior.

The issues are different for clinical conditions in the psychotic spectrum. Here, although self-reports can be useful to understand some specific symptoms (e.g., hearing voices, identifying whether seemingly nonsignificant events feel imbued with personal meaning, beliefs that one is being plotted against by others), many of the most relevant symptoms are based on observable behavior, including the accuracy or conventionality of one's perceptions, faulty and overly personalized or concrete logic, fluid and disorganized thinking, or a difficulty maintaining conceptual distinctions among events, experiences, and images of self and other. The latter are not readily assessed by direct questions or self-reported endorsement of specific characteristics. However, they often can be readily observed in, or distilled from, the in vivo sample of behavior obtained with the Rorschach. As a standardized behavioral task that requires visual processing, problem solving, and verbal expression, the Rorschach is adept at identifying atypical or distorted perceptions and disrupted thought processes.

There are a number of limitations associated with using the Rorschach in applied practice. For instance, it is time intensive to learn proper administration, scoring, and interpretation. This can be a particular limitation in increasingly crowded graduate curricula, where less-than-adequate time may be devoted to teaching students how to conduct idiographic and in-depth personality assessment and students may be inadequately prepared to use the instrument in a competent and useful manner. Another limitation is that even though the CS is the dominant system used in the United States and abroad, the validity evidence for some scales that are not included in the system (e.g., ROD, RPRS, or Mutuality of Autonomy Scale [MOA; Urist, 1977]) has eclipsed the evidence for some scales that are part of the system (e.g., Isolation Index, Obsessive Style Index, active to passive movement ratio, the PSV score).

Several limitations associated with scoring also can be noted. First, some of the CS scoring distinctions are of dubious value (e.g., the distinction between botany, landscape, and nature content categories; the household and science content categories; instances when different form quality codes are assigned to similarly shaped objects), particularly because they make the system more difficult to learn, consume teaching resources and scoring time, and contribute to unreliability.

Second, some CS scoring principles are not optimally refined to assess a targeted construct. For instance, the Isolation Index is thought to assess a sense of isolation or remoteness from others and it is formed by considering the number of responses containing content codes for botany, landscape, nature, clouds, or geography. However, each of these scores can co-occur with content codes for human or human-like objects, which would suggest an interest in others rather than a sense of isolation or remoteness from others. Thus, the overall Isolation Index can be elevated even when every response in a protocol contains perceptions of human characters.

Third, most CS scoring criteria are based on abstract principles that do not offer specific guidance for applying those principles to the inkblot stimuli that are most likely to elicit them. For instance, out of the 10,512 responses that make up the 450 protocols in the current CS normative sample (Exner & Erdberg, 2005), shading generated a sense of texture most often on Card VI (302 responses; 66% of all texture responses), followed by Card IV (102 responses; 22% of all texture responses), and then rarely on the remaining eight cards (all < 13 responses; < 3% of all texture responses). Given this, and assuming this patterning generalizes to other types of samples (which our data indicates it does), it would be desirable to have scoring guidelines that are specifically tailored to the types of responses that are typically found on Cards VI and IV.

It also would be desirable to have specific guidelines for instances when abstract coding criteria are challenging to apply to commonly given responses. For instance, the D1 area on Card VII is very commonly described as a girl or woman's head. Typically, the object is also described as having her hair sticking up in the air and coders would benefit from specific guidelines for when inanimate movement should be coded in this common response (e.g., Viglione, 2002).

Finally, in many instances there is a degree of irreducible uncertainty associated with scoring because of the ambiguity that is inherent in a verbalized response. Much like a reversible figure or Necker cube, even after being adequately inquired, some responses can be interpreted in two notably different and mutually exclusive ways. This allows for reasonably trained people to disagree on what exactly was perceived and described by the client, and thus will lead reasonably trained people to disagree on scoring. At times, coders also can disagree on what is included in a response. For example, clients sometimes change their perception from the Response to the Inquiry phase, or examiners may be unsure when multiple objects are identified if they constitute one combined response or several distinct

Important References

Bornstein and Masling (2005). This text provides an overview of the evidence for seven approaches to scoring the Rorschach that are not part of the CS. Scores that are covered include the ROD for assessing dependency, as well as scales to measure thought disorder, psychological defenses, object relations, psychological boundaries, primary process thinking, and treatment prognosis.

Exner (2003), Viglione (2002), Exner and Erdberg (2005), and Weiner (2003). Together these four resources provide the basic information needed to learn standard CS administration, scoring, and interpretation. Exner also provides an overview of evidence for each CS score, Viglione elaborates on and clarifies basic scoring principles, Exner and Erdberg review relevant research in the context of an interpretive guide that addresses particular referral questions, and Weiner complements the latter by providing an easy to read general interpretive guide.

Meyer (1999b) and Meyer (2001c). These citations reference a special series of eleven articles in the journal *Psychological Assessment*. The authors in the series participated in a critical, structured, sequential, evidence based debate that focused on the strengths and limitations of using the Rorschach for applied purposes. The debate took place over four iterations, with later articles building upon and reacting to those generated earlier. This series gives an overview of all the recent criticisms of the test.

Society for Personality Assessment (2005). Drawing on the recent literature, this document is an official statement by the Board of Trustees of the Society for Personality Assessment concerning the status of the Rorschach in clinical and forensic practice. Their primary conclusion was that the Rorschach produces reliability and validity that is similar to other personality tests, such that its responsible use in applied settings is justified.

responses. Such ambiguities need to be addressed in the future to increase reliability in the test.

Despite these limitations, the Rorschach offers clinicians a rich sample of behavior on which to base carefully considered, disciplined, and synthesized inferences about personality. In the applied arena, the meta-analyses and individual studies reviewed above have shown it can predict important and clinically relevant behaviors, predict subsequent treatment outcome, identify qualities associated with good and poor treatment prognosis, quantify change in personality as a function of treatment, and assist in differential diagnosis, particularly for psychotic disorders.

Research Findings

In earlier sections we described the evidence base for the Rorschach in some detail. We documented how meta-analyses have shown its scores can be reliably assigned, are reasonably stable, and, when evaluated globally, are as valid as those obtained from other personality assessment instruments. We also documented how the Rorschach can validly assess a range of personal characteristics that have meaningful utility for applied clinical practice, including diagnosing psychotic difficulties, planning treatment, and monitoring the outcome of intervention. Here we focus on some of the relatively unique challenges that are associated with documenting the construct validity of its scores and validly interpreting them in clinical practice.

Foundation for Interpretive Postulates

Authors over the years have discussed challenges associated with validating Rorschach-derived scales (e.g., Bornstein, 2001; Meehl, 1959; Meyer, 1996; Weiner, 1977; Widiger & Schilling, 1980). One challenge arises because some scores do not have an obvious or self-evident meaning. In other words, the behavioral or experiential foundation for the response is not completely obvious. Examples of these scores include diffuse shading (Y), use of the white background (S), or the extent to which form features are primary versus secondary in determinants (e.g., FC vs. CF; see Table 8.1 for score descriptions). These are largely the scores we described above as being based on clinical observation. Historically, these response characteristics have been observed and studied in psychiatric settings with disturbed individuals where the base rates of serious symptoms and failures in adaptation are high. As a result, the standard interpretive algorithms (Exner, 2003) may be skewed or biased toward negative and pathological inferences rather than toward the positive or healthy inferences that may be relevant when such responses are present in nonpsychiatric settings.

Unique Assessment Methodology

Another challenge relates to the uniqueness of the method itself. Because of its uniqueness, the correlation between one Rorschach scale and another Rorschach scale is rarely put forward as evidence for validity. For instance, both the MOA (Mutuality of Autonomy Scale) and the HRV (Human Representation Variable) assess the quality of object relations and theoretically should be related to each other. However, researchers have not tried to validate either scale by showing that they are correlated. Although this type of research is rare with the Rorschach, it is a pervasive practice with other assessment methods, where, for example, the correlation between two self-report scales or two performance tasks of cognitive ability are regularly put forward as validity evidence.

Instances when two scales from the same assessment method (e.g., two Rorschach scales or two self-report scales) are correlated with each other are known as monomethod validity coefficients (Campbell & Fiske, 1959) and they are contrasted with the heteromethod validity coefficients obtained when scales from two different assessment methods are correlated (e.g., when a Rorschach scale is correlated with ratings of observed behavior). It has been well-documented for the past half-century that monomethod validity coefficients are substantially larger than heteromethod coefficients. This is because method-specific sources of systematic error inflate the monomethod coefficients (Campbell & Fiske, 1959; Meyer, 2002b).

For instance, consider self-report questionnaires to assess depression. To document convergent validity, depression scales on the MMPI-2 and PAI have been correlated with each other and scales on both instruments have been correlated with the Beck Depression Inventory (BDI; Beck, Steer, & Brown, 1996). Several factors conspire to artificially inflate these correlations, and these factors are forms of systematic error. First, and most importantly, there is an issue of what is known as criterion contamination in these studies. Standard psychometric texts (e.g., Anastasi & Urbina, 1997) define criterion contamination as instances in which knowledge of a predictor variable can potentially influence the criterion variable (e.g., IQ scores are to be validated by teacher ratings of intelligence but teachers see their students' scores before making their ratings). These texts also document how it is essential to avoid this problem in validity research to ensure validity coefficients are not falsely inflated. In the case of two self-report scales, not only can knowledge of what is reported on one scale influence what is reported on the other, but in fact the same person—the respondent—determines the scores that will be present on both the predictor scale and the criterion scale. This circularity where the same person determines the data on all measures is a serious methodological confound. Exacerbating the difficulty, people also strive for consistency when answering similar items on two different inventories. Thus people will strive to give consistent answers regarding sadness, tearfulness, or lack of energy on two different depression scales.

It is also the case that self-ratings on two measures of depression (or any other construct) are artificially equated by virtue of psychological defenses, by genuine limitations in self-knowledge, by an inability to realistically appraise oneself relative to others, and by intentional or unintentional desires to create an overly positive or an overly negative impression. All of these processes artificially inflate convergent correlations because so many methodological confounds are intertwined (see Campbell & Fiske, 1959; McClelland, 1980).

Psychometrically, this kind of monomethod research produces results that are more like estimates of alternate forms reliability than of actual validity (Meyer, 2002b). Because monomethod coefficients are rarely presented as validity evidence for Rorschach scales, a casual or unsophisticated review of the research literature that fails to appreciate these issues can readily but erroneously lead one to believe that self-report scales produce higher validity coefficients than Rorschach scales.

The Rorschach method elicits a sample of problem-solving behavior in the verbal descriptions of what the blots might be, which is then coded by the examiner on a range of structural and thematic dimensions. Although this is a unique method for assessment, the Rorschach is like other assessment procedures in that its method variance is large relative to desired trait variance (e.g., Meyer et al., 2000). For the Rorschach, a primary source of method variance can be seen in the way scores on the test rise and fall in tandem with the number and complexity of the responses that a person gives. This can have a dramatic impact on many final scores, particularly for protocols that fall at either extreme of the simplicity-complexity dimension[8] (Viglione & Meyer, 2007). Validation research is needed to more fully understand this dimension of response complexity and its implications for personality, coping resources, and test-taking defensiveness. In addition, in many situations researchers should control for its impact when attempting to validate specific scales derived from the test.

Implications of Methodology for Interpretation and Research

Given the methodology of Rorschach assessment, there is no aspect of the data collection and scoring process that requires or even suggests that the behaviors coded from the task should quantify consciously represented or consciously experienced personal characteristics. These characteristics may be in consciousness; however, this is not required. Indeed, one of the most pervasive and consistent findings in the literature is that that Rorschach and self-report scales with similar names tend to be minimally correlated (e.g.,

Krishnamurthy et al., 1996; Meyer et al., 2000). Part of this may be due to the fact that the Rorschach task begins with visual perception. Compared to the solely verbal expression and processing required to complete a self-report inventory, the Rorschach response process likely involves somewhat different filters or censoring processes, as well as inadvertent or unself-conscious expressions of personal characteristics. In either case, the Rorschach's methodological uniqueness has implications for both research and clinical interpretation.

With respect to research, validation criteria have to be selected so they are consistent with the type of information the Rorschach can provide. This includes focusing on spontaneously chosen behaviors observed over time. One promising but untried approach is with experience sampling methodology, in which participants record over a period of days or weeks what activities and experiences are occurring at the moment when they are electronically prompted (e.g., McAdams & Constantian, 1983). This kind of methodology should be particularly well suited for some of the representational scores described earlier (e.g., MOR, COP). In addition, Rorschach researchers will need to begin taking fuller advantage of methodological procedures that are used in the social-cognitive literature for validating implicit measures of personality, mood, and attitudes, including experimental procedures that induce particular affective states or prime particular thematic material (see Bornstein, 2001; as well as Balcetis & Dunning, 2006; Long & Toppino, 2004; Payne, Cheng, Govorun, & Stewart, 2005).

Considering Rorschach data from a behavioral representation model adds another dimension to consider when evaluating the Rorschach's locus of effectiveness. When generalizing from test problem-solving behaviors to everyday life, we need to consider functional equivalence (Foster & Cone, 1995), or the extent to which behaviors in the microcosm of the Rorschach environment generalize to particular external environments. More specifically, this perspective should help researchers to conceptualize the discriminative stimuli, antecedents, consequences, and environmental conditions to which we should be able to most assuredly generalize Rorschach behaviors.

With respect to clinical interpretation, the Rorschach's methodological uniqueness has important implications for the extent to which clients are aware of Rorschach assessed characteristics. We bring this issue up in part because there are times when the language used in standard interpretive texts could be misunderstood. For example, an elevated number of diffuse shading responses are typically interpreted as being associated with feelings of helplessness or anxiety. But an elevated number of Y scores does not also imply these feelings are consciously recognized. The client who describes how the shading in the ink was influential in his perception may or may not also say he is anxious or feeling helpless. To confidently draw inferences about the conscious experience of anxiety or helplessness a clinician would have to consider the Rorschach data in light of other sources of information (e.g., self-reported, observer-rated, behavioral observation).

So, even though a Rorschach score may be associated with a conscious experience, that may not be the case, as people fail to recognize their internal states and experiences for various reasons (e.g., because they lack intrapersonal sophistication and insight or because they have defenses that push these threatening feelings from awareness). The notion that clinicians should not infer that a score necessarily implies a conscious and self-reportable experience applies to a long list of constructs often considered in the course of CS interpretation (Exner, 2003), including affective distress, depression, sadness, stress, overloaded coping resources, inability to concentrate, needs for closeness, loneliness, introspectiveness, self-criticism, emotional deprivation, emotional confusion, interest in or discomfort with affective stimuli, oppositionality, hypervigilance, suicidality, passivity, dependence, inflated sense of personal worth, negative self-esteem, bodily concerns, pessimism, interest in others, or the expectation that relationships will be cooperative and/or aggressive. Even though validity data indicate Rorschach variables actively influence perception, behavior, and thought, research also indicates these experiences may not be consistently accessible in consciousness and available to self-report. Recognizing this constraint when interpreting data and writing test reports will help ensure inferences are consistent with the Rorschach's methodology and the evidence about its locus of effectiveness.

The Implications of Card Pull for Summary Scales

With respect to interpretation, we note another caution that can be overlooked when following the standard approach found in textbooks. An average protocol contains about 23 responses. However, each response is given to a specific card and uses one or more specific locations. Each location and card has unique stimulus properties that pull for certain kinds of perceptions, including content categories and determinant scores. Thus, even though summary scores are formed by aggregating codes across all responses, for many scores, only a portion of the responses would be relevant for a particular score (e.g., color responses are impossible to obtain on half the cards). Consequently, a summary score derived from a 23-response Rorschach is not equivalent to the kind of summary score that would be obtained from a 23-item scale on most other personality or cognitive ability tests. Because each Rorschach response is not like a test item that consistently evaluates the same underlying dimension, psychometrically most CS summary scores should be viewed as being derived from relatively brief scales (i.e., fewer than 20 relevant items; at times perhaps just several items), which results in many scores having a truncated distribution where most participants obtain scores of just 0, 1, or 2.

To illustrate this point, we mentioned earlier that the vast majority of texture scores occur to two of the inkblots (in the CS reference sample almost 90% of these scores occur on Cards VI and IV). Because most people generate two responses to each of these cards, for most people there is a reasonable opportunity to observe a texture response just four times in a protocol. Thus, the stimulus features of the inkblots limit the opportunities to observe a score and result in a summary scale with a truncated range (e.g., 97% of the people in the CS reference sample have 0, 1, or 2 texture scores).

Such truncated scales are particularly sensitive to a form of random error that is not captured by scoring reliability coefficients. Rather, this type of error concerns the factors that interfere with the examiner's ability to transcribe and score what the client actually sees and tries to articulate. These factors include the client's choice of particular words to describe the percept, the examiner's attentiveness to key words or phrases, the sophistication of the examiner's inquiry questions and choice of particular inquiry words, the client's speech, which at times may be inaudible or too rapid for an accurate verbatim transcript, the examiner's misperception of what was said, and so on. These factors can negatively impact all Rorschach scores, but relatively speaking their impact will be more pronounced on those with a small range.

As a result, while keeping in mind the overall complexity of a protocol, we encourage clinicians to focus interpretation on global scores that either are assigned to every response and thus aggregate information across all responses (e.g., form quality, organizational activity, cognitive special scores) or incorporate multiple response features (e.g., the EII-2 or HRV, which combine information from determinants, form quality, contents, and special scores), because these tend to be the most reliably measured variables. In addition, clinicians should cautiously and conservatively interpret Rorschach summary scores with truncated distributions. This means that clinicians should mentally impose fairly wide confidence intervals around observed scores on the test. For instance, even though a client may have produced one texture response, there is enough potential random error in the administration, recording, and scoring process that the savvy clinician will keep in mind how the client's "true" score actually may be 0 or 2.

Cross Cultural Considerations

In this section we address both the cross-cultural applications of the test as well as normative issues more generally. As suggested by some of the data reviewed above, the Rorschach appears to be as valid when administered in other countries and with other languages as it is in the United States with English. In addition, considerable research shows that scoring can be done reliably on an international basis, with the scores that are more challenging to reliably code in the United States also being more challenging in other countries (Erdberg, 2005). Three fairly recent studies directly examined cross-cultural issues with the CS (Meyer, 2001a, 2002a; Presley, Smith, Hilsenroth, & Exner, 2001). In addition, Allen and Dana (2004) provided a thorough review of existing evidence, as well as a detailed discussion of methodological issues associated with cross-cultural Rorschach research.

Presley et al. (2001) compared CS data from 44 African Americans (AA) to 44 European Americans (EA) roughly matched on demographic background using the old CS nonpatient reference sample norms. They examined 23 variables they thought might show differences, though found only 3 that differed statistically (the AA group used more white space, had higher SCZI scores, and had fewer COP scores). While preparing this chapter, we examined ethnic differences in the new CS reference sample of 450 adults (Exner & Erdberg, 2005). This sample contains data from 39 AAs and 374 EAs, with the remaining 37 participants having other ethnic heritages. We could not replicate the findings of Presley et al. Although there were small initial differences on the number of responses given by each group (AA $M = 21.4$, $SD = 3.5$; EA $M = 23.8$, $SD = 5.9$), once we controlled for overall protocol complexity, ethnicity was not associated with any of the 82 ratios, percentages, or derived variables on the Structural Summary (i.e., the variables found in the bottom half of the standard CS structural summary page). Across these 82 scores, ethnicity did not produce a point biserial correlation larger than $|.09|$.

Meyer (2002a) compared European Americans to a sample of African Americans and to a combined sample of ethnic minorities that also included Hispanic, Asian, and Native American individuals using a sample of 432 patients referred to a hospital based psychological assessment program. He found no substantive association between ethnicity and 188 Rorschach summary scores, particularly after controlling for Rorschach complexity and demographic factors (gender, education, marital status, and inpatient status). In addition, CS scores had the same factor structure across majority and minority groups and in 17 validation analyses there was no evidence to indicate the test was more valid for one group than the other.[9] These data clearly support using the CS across ethnic groups.

Meyer (2001a) contrasted Exner's (1993) original CS adult normative reference sample to a composite sample of 2,125 protocols taken from nine sets of adult CS reference data that were presented in an international symposium (Erdberg & Shaffer, 1999). Although the composite sample included 125 (5.8%) protocols collected by Shaffer et al. (1999) in the United States, the vast majority came from Argentina, Belgium, Denmark, Finland, Japan, Peru, Portugal, and Spain. Despite diversity in the composite sample due to selection procedures, examiner training, examination context, language, culture, and national boundaries, and despite the fact that the original CS norms had been collected 20–25 years earlier, relatively few differences were found between the two samples. Across 69 composite scores, the average difference was about four tenths of a standard deviation (i.e., equivalent to about 4 T-score points on the MMPI or 6 points on an IQ scale). Also, preliminary analyses using the initial participants in Exner's new normative sample indicated that it differed from the old reference data by about two tenths of a standard deviation, such that the international sample was more similar to the new norms. These data suggested that the CS norms were generally adequate even for international samples. However, there are caveats to this conclusion because, as we discuss next, there are issues associated with the application of the CS norms in the United States as well.

Wood, Nezworski, Garb, and Lilienfeld (2001a, 2001b) criticized the CS normative reference sample for being unrepresentative of the population and for causing healthy people to be considered pathological or impaired. The research that inspired their critique was the study conducted by Shaffer, et al. (1999), who used graduate students to collect a reference sample of 123 nonpatients from the Fresno, California area. For most scores, the values reported by Shaffer et al. were consistent with the CS normative reference group. However, there were also some surprising divergences. Most striking was the lack of complexity in the Shaffer et al. sample. Their participants gave fewer responses and more responses where no determinants were articulated. As a result, their protocols looked more simplistic or constricted relative to the CS reference sample (and relative to a number of other reference samples as well). Building on this research, Wood et al. (2001a) selected 14 scores to examine in a review of the literature. Depending on the score, they compared the CS reference values to values derived from between 8 and 19 comparison samples. They reported small to very large differences, all of which suggested the comparison samples had more difficulties or problems relative to the CS norms.

There were many problems with the samples Wood et al. included in their analyses, which is why Meyer (2001a) contrasted Exner's (2001) old adult normative sample to the composite international sample. As noted above, most scores in the international sample were similar to Exner's values. However, people in the composite international sample used more unusual location areas, incorporated more white space, had less healthy form quality scores, made less use of color, tended to see more partial rather than full human images, and showed a bit more disorganization in thinking.

To more fully understand these differences and to determine whether they may have resulted from changes in the population over time, Exner collected a new adult normative reference group from 1999 to 2006. Although he did not complete data collection before his death, Exner and Erdberg (2005) provide the reference data for 450 new participants. Relative to the old CS norms, the new reference sample also looks less healthy. People in the contemporary norms incorporated more white space into their responses, had less healthy form quality scores, made less use of color, tended to see more partial rather than full human images, and showed a bit more disorganization in thinking.

As such, changes seen within the CS norms over time are very similar to the differences that had been found when comparing the original CS norms to the composite international sample. However, the new CS reference sample does not eliminate differences with the composite international sample. In particular, the current CS norms continue to show less use of unusual detail locations, better form quality, and more color responding than is seen in the reference samples collected by others.

To understand the factors that may account for this, we compared the quality of administration and scoring for protocols in Exner's (Exner & Erdberg, 2005) CS norms relative to Shaffer et al.'s (1999) sample from Fresno, CA (FCA; preliminary findings were reported in Meyer, Viglione, Erdberg, Exner, & Shaffer, 2004). Two sets of results are notable. First, the FCA protocols were less adequately administered and inquired, with more instances when examiners failed to follow up on key words or phrases. This is not surprising given that graduate student examiners collected all the protocols, though it does indicate that some of the seeming simplicity in the FCA records was an artifact of less thorough inquiry. Second, we found that many of the seeming differences between the FCA and CS samples were reduced or eliminated when 40 protocols from each sample were rescored by a third group of examiners. This indicates that the Shaffer et al. records and Exner protocols were coded according to somewhat different site-specific scoring conventions. In general, the new scoring split the difference between the CS and Shaffer et al. samples, making the CS protocols look a bit less healthy than before and making the Shaffer et al. protocols look a bit more healthy than before. There were two exceptions to this general trend. For complexity, the rescored protocols resembled the CS norms more than the FCA scores. In contrast, for form quality the rescored protocols resembled the FCA scores more than the CS norms. The overall findings suggest that site-specific administration and coding practices may contribute in important and previously unappreciated ways to some of the seeming differences across normative approximation samples (also see Lis, Parolin, Calvo, Zennaro, & Meyer, in press).

Although this research has been conducted with adults, the issues appear to be similar with children. For instance, Hamel, Shaffer, and Erdberg (2000) provided reference data on 100 children aged 6 to 12. Although rated as psychologically healthy, a number of their Rorschach scores diverged from the CS reference norms for children; at times dramatically. Many of the differences were similar to those found with adults (e.g., lower form quality values, less color, more use of unusual blot locations, less complexity), though the values Hamel et al. reported tended to be more extreme. At least in part, this appears due to the fact that all protocols were administered and scored by one graduate student who followed atypical procedures for identifying inkblot locations. This in turn led to a very high frequency of unusual detail locations and consequently to lower form quality codes (see Viglione & Meyer, 2007). However, other child and adolescent samples in the United States, France, Italy, Japan, and Portugal (Erdberg, 2005; Erdberg & Shaffer, 1999) suggest clinicians should be cautious about applying the old CS norms for children. The CS normative data for children have not been updated recently like they have for adults.

Based on the available evidence, we recommend that examiners use the new CS sample as their primary benchmark for adults, but adjust for those variables that have consistently looked different in international samples, including form quality, unusual locations, color, texture, and human representations (for specific recommendations see Table 8.2). The Shaffer et al. sample can be viewed as an outer boundary for what might be expected from reasonably functioning people within the limits of current administration, inquiry, and scoring guidelines.

For children, we recommend using the available CS age-based norms along with the adjusted expectations given in Table 8.2 for adults. Although we do not recommend using the Hamel et al. sample as an outer boundary for what could be expected for younger United States children, the data for that sample illustrate how ambiguity or flexibility in current administration and scoring guidelines can result in one obtaining some unhealthy looking data from apparently normal functioning children. Besides Hamel et al. (2000), child and adolescent reference samples have been collected by other examiners in the United States, France, Italy, Japan, and Portugal (Erdberg & Shaffer, 1999; Erdberg, 2005). Although these samples vary in age, they also show unexpected variability in a number of scores, particularly Dd (small or unusual locations), Lambda (proportion of responses determined just by form), and form quality scores. These scores differ notably from sample to sample. It is unclear if these differences reflect genuine cultural differences in personality and/or in childrearing practices or if they are artifacts due to variability in the way the protocols were administered, inquired, or scored. However, the composite of data suggest that the adjustments offered above for adults should be made for children too.

In addition, clinicians working with children should consider developmental trends. Wenar and Curtis (1991) illustrated these trends for Exner's (2001) child reference data across the ages from 5 to 16. Although limited, the available international data suggest similar developmental trends are

Table 8.2 Recommended Adjustments to Adult CS Normative Expectations

Variable	New guidelines based on international samples	Old guidelines based on the current CS reference Sample[a]
Location and form quality		
Dd	3 or 4	1 or 2
X-%	.15–.25	.09–.14
X+%	.45–.60	.65–.70
XA%	.70–.90	.80–.95
WDA%	.80–.90	.85–.95
Avoidant style (Lambda > .99)	2 or 3 of 10 people	1 of 10 people
Human representations		
Pure H	2 or 3	3 or 4
H : Non pure H	H+1 = Non pure H	H > Non pure H
COP	1	2
AG	1 in 2 people	1 per person
GHR to PHR ratio (HRV)	Between 3:2 and 1:1 ratio	2:1 ratio
Color and associated variables		
FC: CF+C	FC = or < CF+C	FC > CF+C +1
WSumC	2.5–3.5	4.5
Afr	.45–.55	.55–.65
Extratensive	1 or 2 of 10 people	3 of 10 people
Ambitent	3 or 4 of 10 people	2 of 10 people
EA	6–8	9
Texture		
T = 0	5 to 7 of 10 people	2 of 10 people
T = 1	2 or 3 of 10 people	6 of 10 people
T ≥ 2	1 or 2 of 10 people	2 of 10 people

Note: [a] Exner & Erdberg, 2005, N = 450

present, including age-based increases in complexity markers like DQ+, Blends, and Zf, as well as increases in M and P. In addition, as children age there is a decrease in WSum6 and to a lesser extent in DQv. Unlike Exner's CS reference samples, however, the alternative reference samples for children generally show that as children get older there is a decrease in Lambda and an increase in healthier form quality scores. The field would benefit from additional carefully designed studies that examine developmental processes as expressed on the Rorschach.

Although the research evidence reviewed in this section supports the validity of the Rorschach across ethnic groups in the United States and across languages and cultures around the world, this does not mean that culture and ethnicity are unimportant when using the Rorschach. To the contrary, it is important for clinicians to recognize the ways in which culture and acculturation influence the development, identity, and personality of any particular individual. It is as important to take these issues into account when interpreting the Rorschach as it is with any other personality test.

Current Controversies

The Rorschach has been controversial almost since its publication. Historically, clinicians have found it useful for their applied work, while academic psychologists have criticized its psychometric foundation and suggested that clinical perceptions of its utility are likely the result of illusory biases. An early and prominent critique by Jensen (1965) gives a flavor of the sharp tone that has characterized some of the criticisms. Jensen asserted that the Rorschach "is a very poor test and has no practical worth for any of the purposes for which it is recommended" (p. 501) and "scientific progress in clinical psychology might well be measured by the speed and thoroughness with which it gets over the Rorschach" (p. 509). Although Exner's (1974, 2003) work with the CS quelled many of these earlier criticisms, over the past decade there has been a renewed and vigorous series of critiques led by James Wood, Howard Garb, and Scott Lilienfeld, including arguments that psychology departments and organizations should discontinue Rorschach training and practice (see e.g., Garb, 1999; Grove, Barden, Garb, & Lilienfeld, 2002; Lilienfeld, Wood, & Garb, 2000). Counterarguments and rejoinders also have been published and at least seven journals have published a special series of articles concerning the Rorschach.[10]

The most thorough of these special series was an 11-article series published in *Psychological Assessment* (Meyer, 1999b; 2001c). Authors participated in a structured, sequential, evidence based debate that focused on the strengths and limitations of using the Rorschach for applied purposes. The debate took place over four iterations, with each containing contributions from authors who tended to be either favorable or critical of the Rorschach's evidence base. At each step, authors read the articles that were prepared in the previous iteration(s) to ensure the debate was focused and cumulative. As noted earlier, Robert Rosenthal was commissioned for this special series to undertake an independent evidence based review of the research literature through a comparative meta-analysis of Rorschach and MMPI-2 validity. In addition, the final summary paper in the series was written by authors with different views on the Rorschach's merits (Meyer & Archer, 2001). They attempted to synthesize what was known, what had been learned, and what issues still needed to be addressed in future research. We strongly encourage any student or psychologist interested in gaining a full appreciation for the evidence and issues associated with the applied use of the Rorschach to read the full series of articles (Dawes, 1999; Garb, Wood, Nezworski, Grove, & Stejskal, 2001; Hiller et al., 1999; Hunsley & Bailey, 1999, 2001; Meyer, 1999a, 2001b; Meyer & Archer, 2001; Rosenthal et al., 2001; Stricker & Gold, 1999; Viglione, 1999; Viglione & Hilsenroth, 2001; Weiner, 2001).

More recently, the Board of Trustees for the Society for Personality Assessment (2005) addressed the debate about the Rorschach. Drawing on the recent literature, their official statement concluded that the Rorschach produces evidence of reliability and validity that is similar to the evidence obtained for other personality tests. Given this, they concluded that its responsible use in applied practice was justified.

Nonetheless, as we indicated in previous sections, there are still unresolved issues associated with the Rorschach's evidence base and applied use. Some of the most important issues concern recently recognized variability in the way the CS can be administered and scored when examiners are trying to follow Exner's (2003) current guidelines, the related need to treat normative reference values more tentatively, the impact of response-complexity on the scores obtained in a structural summary, and the need for more research into the stability of scores over time.

Another issue that we have not previously discussed concerns the evidence base for specific scores. The meta-analytic evidence provides a systematic review for several individual variables in relation to particular criteria (e.g., the ROD and observed dependent behavior; the Prognostic Rating Scale and outcome from treatment), but much of the systematically gathered literature speaks to the global validity of the test, which is obtained by aggregating evidence across a wide range of Rorschach scores and a wide range of criterion variables. It would be most helpful to have systematically organized evidence concerning the construct validity of each score that is considered interpretively important. Accomplishing this is a daunting task that initially requires cataloging the scores and criterion variables that have been examined in every study over time. Subsequently, researchers would have to reliably evaluate the methodological quality of each article so greater weight could be afforded to more sturdy findings. Finally, researchers would have to reliably classify the extent to which every criterion variable provides an appropriate match to the construct thought to be assessed by each Rorschach score so that one could meaningfully examine convergent and discriminant validity. Although conducting this kind of research would be highly desirable, we also note how no cognitive or personality test in use today has this kind of focused meta-analytic evidence attesting to the validity of each of its scales in relation to specific and appropriate criterion variables. We say this not as an excuse or a deterrent, but simply as an observation. Because of the criticisms leveled against the Rorschach having this kind of organized meta-analytic evidence is more urgent for it than for other tests.

Clinical Dilemma

Dr. A is a 30-year-old unmarried Asian man who has been in the United States for 5 years and is employed as a university math professor. Two months before being referred for psychological assessment, he was evaluated psychiatrically for the first time in his life and diagnosed with major depression, for which he was receiving antidepressants by a psychiatrist and weekly cognitive-behavioral psychotherapy by an outpatient psychotherapist. His depression has been present for 2 years, with symptoms of weakness, low energy, sadness, hopelessness, and an inability to concentrate that fluctuated in severity. At the time of assessment, he taught and conducted research for about 40 hours per week and spent almost all of his remaining time in bed. He denied any previous or current hypomanic symptoms, had normal thyroid functions, and reported no other health problems. In his home country, his father had been hospitalized for depression, his brother diagnosed with schizophrenia, and his sister was reported to have "problems" but had not received psychiatric care. His father was physically abusive to his mother, his siblings, and him. Dr. A reported that his father hit him in the face or head on an almost weekly basis while growing up. He is the only one in his family in the United States and he has no history of intimate relationships, though sees several friends for dinner approximately every other week.

Dr. A's outpatient therapist requested the evaluation to assess the severity of Dr. A's depression and to understand his broader personality characteristics. In particular, the therapist wondered about potential paranoid characteristics. Dr. A was primarily interested in whether he had qualities similar to his father or brother and, if so, what he could do to prevent similar conditions from becoming full blown in him. The assessment involved an interview, several self-report inventories (including the MMPI-2, BDI, and a personality disorder questionnaire), and the Rorschach.

Dr. A produced a very complex Rorschach protocol with 42 responses, of which only 8 were determined by straightforward form features (i.e., the percent of pure form responses [Form%] was .19 and the proportion of pure form to non-pure form responses [Lambda] was .24). As a result, his protocol was an outlier relative to the CS norms. The complexity of his record appeared to be a function of his intelligence, his desire to be thorough in the assessment, and also some difficulty stepping back from the task with a consequent propensity to become overly engaged with the stimuli (particularly to the last three brightly colored cards, to which he produced almost half of his responses [20 of 42]). After adjusting for the length and complexity of his protocol, Dr. A exhibited some notable features. First, his thought processes were characterized by implausible and illogical relationships, with the weighted sum of cognitive special scores (see Table 8.1) several standard deviations above what is typically seen in nonpatient or even outpatient samples. Importantly, however, this occurred in the context of perceptions that had typical and conventional form features (XA%, which is the percent of all responses with adequate form quality, was .79 and WDA%, which is the percent of responses to the whole card or to common detail locations with adequate form quality, was .92). In addition, even though he would be considered to have extensive assets for coping with life demands (M = 18, Weighted Color = 14.5, Zf = 33, DQ+ = 22), he saw an unexpectedly large number of inanimate objects in motion (m = 7), suggesting he was experiencing a considerable degree of uncontrollable environmental stress, internal tension, and agitated cognitive activity. Finally, he had a marked propensity to perceive objects engaged in aggressive activity (AG = 8) and to identify percepts where objects were damaged, decaying, or dying (MOR = 10). This combination of scores suggested he had an implicit depressive perceptual filter in which he experienced himself as deficient, vulnerable, and incapable of contending with a dangerous, menacing, and combative environment.

Although this chapter does not provide the actual inkblot images, we include his responses from a number of the cards to give a flavor of the characteristics described above. As a general principle, response verbalizations should be considered after examining the previously presented quantitative data so as to minimize the prospect for erroneous speculations.

At the bottom of the second card, Dr. A saw, "Blood. Yeah, I don't really want to say—it's dirty words—but it looks like an asshole with blood coming out of it . . . spilling over, all over the place." A bit later using the entire card he saw, "the face of a human being . . . looks like its weeping. It may be partly vomiting… The eyes look like they're teary… this is what it's vomiting." To the third card Dr. A saw "two people meeting and bowing to each other, but they're kind of hating each other…this red thing signifies the hatred between the two people." In his next response he saw "two ugly waitresses—actually they look like birds—who are bringing some strange plate or dish… I mean gruesome stuff like snakes, spiders, something like that." On the next card he saw "a gruesome monster… as tall as a tower…it's about to come and crush me out. He looks very angry at me… these look like his hands but also like a weapon and it's very, very dangerous…the whole posture makes me feel like it's angry. I don't see any specific… maybe the only thing that makes me feel that way is the hidden expressions." The final response to this card consisted of "a small animal… which has been killed on a street by a car—flattened out… sometimes you can see small animals dying on the road." On the fifth card he returned to the same themes, seeing "a butterfly which is kind of dying—injured and dying" and "a witch with two horns… trying to approach me and catch me… some massive, dark object." On the ninth card he saw "a knife thrust into a body and blood is coming out as a result," which was followed by the perception of "two monsters... who are maybe shaking hands," and then a new response of "three people... sitting in a row... controlling from behind... the red person controlling the green one and the green one is controlling the yellow one." On the final card, Dr. A saw "an abdomen of organs which are not functioning because of the various poisons. The organs are poisoned, as you see from the colors... weak and not functioning... very bad condition." In another response to the whole inkblot he saw "an island as you see it from the skies. Island where there is a military secret. So it's very secret. And they are hiding the ships and weapons in the very center of the island. So they make use of the very complicated coastline. And they made a lot of traps so that you can't very easily approach the center of the island... traps to capture the enemies." This response was followed by "interior walls of some organ, like stomach or heart... these look like ulcers... this portion looks deteriorated, somehow damaged." Next he saw "a flying monster which is about to attack—attack something with its chisel-like mouth." As his final response to the task, Dr. A saw "two people fighting with weapons... they don't have heads somehow."

Although this is incomplete information, the curious reader could stop here and ponder several questions. To what extent do the scores and the images or themes in his responses suggest that Dr. A is depressed? Dr. A's outpatient therapist was concerned about paranoid characteristics. Do the data suggest that concerns in this regard are warranted? Also, do the results suggest that Dr. A might have other personality characteristics or personality struggles that were not part of the initial referral question but that will be important to consider? Dr. A was concerned about the possibility that he was like his brother who had a schizophrenic disorder. What features of the data would be consistent with a psychotic disturbance? Alternatively, are there features of the data that would contradict a disorder on the psychotic spectrum? These are important questions to address and how they are addressed will have significant consequences for Dr A. Thus, although we focus in this chapter on just the Rorschach data, in actual practice the assessment clinician would need to carefully consider each question while taking into account the full array of available information from testing and from history.

With respect to the Rorschach data, Dr. A's vivid images provide idiographic insight into his particular way of experiencing the qualities suggested by the relatively impersonal quantitative structural summary variables. We learn and come to understand his deep fears, fragile vulnerabilities, and powerful preoccupation with aggression and hostility. As suggested in his last response, identification with aggression is likely to leave him feeling "headless" and out of control. Although generally it is not possible to determine whether clients positively identify with aggressive images or fear them as dangers emanating from the environment, the extensive morbid imagery of damaged, decaying, dying, pierced, and poisoned objects all suggest the latter (as did his denial of anger and aggressiveness on self-report inventories). Depression, at least for some people, can be understood as aggression turned toward the self rather than directed outward at its intended target. Given the pervasiveness of aggressive imagery in his Rorschach protocol, Dr. A's therapist could pursue this hypothesis in her work with him after he stabilized at a more functional level.

Key Points to Remember

- The Rorschach provides a sample of behavior obtained under standardized conditions in response to artistically elaborated visual stimuli in which problem solving operations are elicited by the prompt "What might this be?"
- The term "projective" is not a good label to describe the type of information obtained by the Rorschach (and the term "objective" is not a good label to describe the type of information obtained from self-report inventories).
- Rorschach responses can be reliably scored on a wide number of variables that characterize structural, perceptual, or thematic features of the response.
- The Rorschach Comprehensive System (CS) is the approach to administration and scoring that is most commonly taught, used in clinical practice, and researched. When the CS was developed, it integrated the most reliable and valid features of five previous systems used in the United States.
- At the present time, some scores that fall outside the CS have a larger body of psychometric evidence supporting their use than some scores within the CS.
- Meta-analytic summaries support Rorschach reliability for scoring and the stability of its scores over time.
- Meta-analytic summaries support the general validity of the Rorschach across scales that have been subjected to research. Globally, it is as valid as other personality tests.
- Meta-analytic summaries support the focused validity of the Rorschach for predicting dependent behavior, assessing disordered thinking and psychotic disorders, predicting response to therapy, and quantifying change as a result of therapy. However, the CS Depression Index does not validly identify patients with a diagnosed depressive disorder.
- Recent evidence suggests some of the seeming differences between normative samples collected in the United States and internationally are likely due to unexpected differences in local benchmarks used for administration and scoring.
- The Rorschach is considered a valuable asset in clinical practice because it is an office based procedure that provides a unique method for observing personality characteristics.
- Characteristics assessed by Rorschach scores are not necessarily represented in conscious awareness and they reflect perceptual, schematic, or processing propensities rather than focused, overt, and conscious symptoms. To understand how these propensities are experienced and expressed, Rorschach data needs to be integrated with other sources of information.

Paranoid themes were also evident in Dr. A's responses (e.g., people bowing in respect but internally hating each other, "bird" waitresses serving snakes or spiders, creatures with weapons for appendages, hidden expressions, secretive traps guarding weapons, external control by others). In combination with the disrupted formal thought processes seen on his Rorschach and results from the other tests he completed, Dr. A was considered to be experiencing a severe agitated depressive episode with psychotic features. This was considered a conservative diagnosis because psychological assessment provides a snapshot of current functioning so it was not possible to determine whether a major depressive disorder was co-occurring with an independent and longer standing delusional disorder. However, the latter seemed less likely, given the pervasiveness of his affective turmoil and the fact that the form quality of his perceptions remained healthy and conventional despite such a lengthy and complex protocol. In feedback to Dr. A, his therapist, and his psychiatrist, it was recommended that Dr. A begin antipsychotic medication on at least a trial basis and that therapy be ego-supportive rather than uncovering, with an emphasis on cognitive interventions to evaluate suspicions and correct his propensity to misattribute aggressive intentions onto others in the environment.

Chapter Summary

It is not possible to learn Rorschach administration, scoring, and interpretation from a chapter like this. Consequently, our goal was to provide readers with an overview of the Rorschach as a task that aids in assessing personality. We described the instrument and the approaches that have been used to develop test scores. We then focused on the psychometric evidence for reliability, showing that its scores can be reliably assigned, are reasonably stable over time, and can be reliably interpreted by different clinicians. We also focused on evidence related to its validity and utility, showing that it is a generally valid method of assessment that provides unique and meaningful information for clinical practice. In the process, we pointed out the kinds of information the test generally can and cannot provide and provided psychometrically based guidelines to aid with interpretation. Next, we reviewed current evidence associated with its multicultural and cross-national use and noted a need for tighter guidelines governing administration and scoring to ensure consistency in the data that is collected across sites around the world. Finally, we provided a case vignette that illustrated how a person's perceptions could be meaningfully interpreted in idiographic clinical practice even in the absence of the inkblot stimuli themselves.

Although additional research and refinement are needed on numerous fronts, the systematically gathered data indicate there is solid evidence supporting the Rorschach's basic reliability and validity. Overall, we advocate for an evidence-based, behavioral- representation approach to conceptualizing the test that attempts to focus on concrete and experience near test-based inferences at the expense of more elusive abstract ones. We hope readers will pursue some of the additional readings we have suggested and other studies we have cited. Also, we urge readers to seek out high quality training from qualified supervisors so they can experience the Rorschach's strengths and limitations first hand. Doing so will provide important experiential data about the test's utility that will help when considering the evidence presented here and the recurrent controversy about this unique instrument.

We close with a final caution to keep in mind when considering some of the controversy associated with the Rorschach. Consistent with evidence based principles, we urge readers to attend to the systematically generated evidence and to be wary of partial reviews or selective citations. On average, personality and cognitive tests produce heteromethod validity coefficients that are about equal to a correlation of .30 (Meyer et al., 2001). This means that about half of the research literature will produce validity coefficients that are lower than this and about half will produce coefficients that are higher. Authors who selectively cite the literature or focus on just a subset of individual studies can (inadvertently or intentionally) make the literature seem more or less supportive than is actually warranted.

Notes

1. The authors would like to thank Joni L. Mihura and Aaron D. Upton for their helpful comments and suggestions.
2. Historically, the Rorschach was classified as a "projective" rather than "objective" test. However, these archaic terms are global and misleading descriptors that should be avoided because they do not adequately describe instruments or help our field develop a more advanced and differentiated understanding of personality assessment methods (see Meyer & Kurtz, 2006).
3. There are other inkblot stimuli that have been developed and researched over the years, including a complete system by Holtzman, a series by Behn-Eschenberg that was initially hoped to parallel Rorschach's blots, a short 3-card series by Zulliger, an infrequently researched set by Roemer, and the Somatic Inkblots, which are a set of stimuli that were deliberately created to elicit responses containing somatic content or themes.
4. For ICC or kappa values, findings above .74 are considered excellent, above .59 are considered good, and above .39 are considered fair (Cicchetti, 1994; Shrout & Fliess, 1979).
5. At the same time, data clearly show that Rorschach scales validly identify psychotic diagnoses and validly measure psychotic symptoms (Lilienfeld, Wood, & Garb, 2000; Meyer & Archer, 2001; Perry, Minassian, Cadenhead, & Braff, 2003; Viglione, 1999, Viglione & Hilsenroth, 2001; Wood, Lilienfeld, Garb, & Nezworski, 2000). Unlike most other disorders, which are heavily dependent on the patient's self-reported symptoms, psychotic conditions are often diagnosed based more on the patient's observed behavior than on their specific reported complaints.
6. At present, one or more national Rorschach societies exist in the following countries: Argentina, Brazil, Canada, Cuba, Czech Republic, Finland, France, Israel, Italy, Japan, The Netherlands, Peru, Portugal, South Africa, Spain, Sweden, Switzerland, Turkey, United States, and Venezuela.
7. Fully structured interviews can be differentiated from semistructured interviews. To some degree, semistructured interviews allow a clinician's inferences to influence the final scores

or determinations from the assessment. However, the inferences and determinations remain fundamentally grounded in the client's self-reported characteristics. Fully structured interviews are wholly dependent on this source of information.

8. The Rorschach's first factor is a dimension of complexity. The first factor of a test indicates the primary feature it measures. The Rorschach's first factor typically accounts for about 25% of the total variance in Rorschach scores. For self-report scales like the MMPI-2 or MCMI, the first factor, which is a dimension of willingness versus reluctance to report problematic symptoms, typically accounts for more than 50% of the total variance in scores (see Meyer et al., 2000).

9. There was evidence suggesting that CS psychosis indicators may underpredict pathology in AAs, a finding that also has been observed with MMPI-2 psychosis indicators (Arbisi, Ben-Porath, & McNulty, 2002), though it was not possible to fully evaluate this finding.

10. These journals include *Assessment*; *Clinical Psychology: Science and Practice*; *Journal of Clinical Psychology*; *Journal of Forensic Psychology Practice*; *Journal of Personality Assessment*; *Psychology, Public Policy, and Law*; and *Psychological Assessment*.

References

Acklin, M. W. (2000). Rorschach Interpretive Assistance Program: Version 4 for Windows [Software Review]. *Journal of Personality Assessment, 75*, 519–521.

Acklin, M. W., McDowell, C. J., & Verschell, M. S. (2000). Interobserver agreement, intraobserver reliability, and the Rorschach Comprehensive System. *Journal of Personality Assessment, 74*, 15–47.

Allen, J., & Dana, R. H. (2004). Methodological issues in cross-cultural and multicultural Rorschach research. *Journal of Personality Assessment, 82*, 189–206.

Anastasi, A., & Urbina, S. (1997). *Psychological testing* (7th ed.). New York: Macmillan.

Arbisi, P. A., Ben-Porath, Y. S., & McNulty, J. (2002). A comparison of MMPI–2 validity in African American and Caucasian psychiatric inpatients. *Psychological Assessment, 14*, 3–15.

Aronow, E., Reznikoff, M., & Moreland, K. L. (1995). The Rorschach: Projective technique or psychometric test? *Journal of Personality Assessment, 64*, 213–228.

Atkinson, L., Quarrington, B., Alp, I. E., & Cyr, J. J. (1986). Rorschach validity: An empirical approach to the literature. *Journal of Clinical Psychology, 42*, 360–362.

Balcetis, E., & Dunning, D. (2006). See what you want to see: Motivational influences on visual perception. *Journal of Personality and Social Psychology, 91*, 612–625.

Beck, A. T., Steer, R. A., & Brown, G. K. (1996). *Manual for the Beck Depression Inventory – II*. San Antonio, TX: Psychological Corporation.

Bihlar, B., & Carlsson, A. M. (2001). Planned and actual goals in psychodynamic psychotherapies: Do patients' personality characteristics relate to agreement? *Psychotherapy Research, 11*, 383–400.

Blatt, S. J., Brenneis, C. B., Schimek, J. G., & Glick, M. (1976). Normal development and psychopathological impairment of the concept of the object on the Rorschach. *Journal of Abnormal Psychology, 85*(4), 364–373.

Bornstein, R. F. (1996). Construct validity of the Rorschach Oral Dependency Scale: 1967–1995. *Psychological Assessment, 8*, 200–505.

Bornstein, R. F. (1998). Implicit and self-attributed dependency strivings: Differential relationships to laboratory and field measures of help-seeking. *Journal of Personality and Social Psychology, 75*, 779–787.

Bornstein, R. F. (1999). Criterion validity of objective and projective dependency tests: A meta-analytic assessment of behavioral prediction. *Psychological Assessment, 11*, 48–57.

Bornstein, R. F. (2001). Clinical utility of the Rorschach Inkblot Method: Reframing the debate. *Journal of Personality Assessment, 77*, 39–47.

Bornstein, R. F. (2002). A process dissociation approach to objective-projective test score interrelationships. *Journal of Personality Assessment, 78*, 47–68.

Bornstein, R. F., & Masling, J. M. (Eds.) (2005). *Scoring the Rorschach: Seven validated systems*. Mahwah, NJ: Erlbaum.

Bornstein, R. F., Hill, E. L., Robinson, K. J., Calabreses, C., & Bowers, K. S. (1996). Internal reliability of Rorschach Oral Dependency Scale scores. *Educational and Psychological Measurement*,

56, 130–138.

Butcher, J. N., & Rouse, S. (1996). Clinical personality assessment. *Annual Review of Psychology, 47*, 87–111.

Butcher, J. N., Dahlstrom, W. G., Graham, J. R., Tellegen, A., & Kaemmer, B. (1989). *MMPI-2: Minnesota Multiphasic Personality Inventory-2: Manual for administration and scoring.* Minneapolis: University of Minnesota Press.

Butcher, J. N., Nezami, E., & Exner, J. (1998). Psychological assessment of people in diverse cultures. In S. S. Kazarian & D. R. Evans (Eds.), *Cultural clinical psychology: Theory, research, and practice* (pp. 61–105). New York: Oxford University Press.

Camara, W. J., Nathan, J. S., & Puente, A. E. (2000). Psychological test usage: Implications in professional psychology. *Professional Psychology: Research and Practice, 31*, 141–154.

Campbell, D. T., & Fiske, D. W. (1959). Convergent and discriminant validation by the multitrait-multimethod matrix. *Psychological Bulletin, 56*, 81–105.

Childs, R. A., & Eyde, L. D. (2002). Assessment training in clinical psychology doctoral programs: What should we teach? What do we teach? *Journal of Personality Assessment, 78*, 130–144.

Cicchetti, D. V. (1994). Guidelines, criteria, and rules of thumb for evaluating normed and standardized assessment instruments in psychology. *Psychological Assessment, 6*, 284–290.

Clemence, A. J., & Handler, L. (2001). Psychological assessment on internship: A survey of training directors and their expectations for students. *Journal of Personality Assessment, 76*, 18–47.

Dao, T. K., & Prevatt, F. (2006). A psychometric evaluation of the Rorschach Comprehensive System's Perceptual Thinking Index. *Journal of Personality Assessment, 86*, 180–189.

Dao, T. K., Prevatt, F., & Horne, H. L. (in press). Differentiating psychotic patients from non-psychotic patients with the MMPI-2 and Rorschach. *Journal of Personality Assessment.*

Dawes, R. M. (1999). Two methods for studying the incremental validity of a Rorschach variable. *Psychological Assessment, 11*, 297–302.

Dean, K. L., Viglione, D. J., Perry, W., & Meyer, G. J. (in press). A method to increase Rorschach response productivity while maintaining Comprehensive System validity. *Journal of Personality Assessment.*

Elfhag, K., Barkeling, B., Carlsson, A. M., & Rössner, S. (2003). Microstructure of eating behavior associated with Rorschach characteristics in obesity. *Journal of Personality Assessment, 81*, 40–50.

Elfhag, K., Barkeling, B., Carlsson, A. M., Lindgren, T., & Rössner, S. (2004). Food intake with an antiobesity drug (sibutramine) versus placebo and Rorschach data: A crossover within-subjects study. *Journal of Personality Assessment, 82*, 158–168.

Elfhag, K., Carlsson, A. M. & Rössner, S. (2003). Subgrouping in obesity based on Rorschach personality characteristics. *Scandinavian Journal of Psychology, 44*, 399–407.

Elfhag, K., Rössner, S., Carlsson, A. M., & Barkeling, B. (2003). Sibutramine treatment in obesity: Predictors of weight loss including Rorschach personality data. *Obesity Research, 11*, 1391–1399.

Elfhag, K., Rössner, S., Lindgren, T., Andersson, I., & Carlsson, A. M. (2004). Rorschach personality predictors of weight loss with behavior modification in obesity treatment. *Journal of Personality Assessment, 83*, 293–305.

Erdberg, P. (2005, July). Intercoder Agreement as a Measure of Ambiguity of Coding Guidelines. Paper presented at the XVIII International Congress of the Rorschach and Projective Methods, Barcelona, Spain.

Erdberg, P., & Shaffer, T. W. (1999, July). International symposium on Rorschach nonpatient data: Findings from around the world. Paper presented at the International Congress of Rorschach and Projective Methods, Amsterdam, The Netherlands.

Exner, J. E. (1974). *The Rorschach: A comprehensive system, Vol. 1.* New York: Wiley.

Exner, J. E. (1993). *The Rorschach: A comprehensive system, Vol. 1: Basic foundations* (3rd ed.). New York: Wiley.

Exner, J. E. (1996). Critical bits and the Rorschach response process. *Journal of Personality Assessment, 67*, 464–477.

Exner, J. E. (2003). *The Rorschach: A comprehensive system, Volume 1* (4th ed.). New York: Wiley.

Exner, J. E. (with Colligan, S. C., Hillman, L. B., Metts, A. S., Ritzler, B., Rogers, K. T., Sciara, A., D., & Viglione, D. J.) (2001). *A Rorschach workbook for the Comprehensive System* (5th ed.). Asheville, NC: Rorschach Workshops.

Exner, J. E., & Erdberg, P. (2005). *The Rorschach: A Comprehensive System, Volume 2: Advanced Interpretation* (3rd ed.). Oxford: Wiley.

Exner, J. E., Jr. (2001). *A Rorschach Workbook for the Comprehensive System* (5th ed.). Asheville, NC: Rorschach Workshops.

Fischer, C. T. (1994). Rorschach scoring questions as access to dynamics. *Journal of Personality Assessment, 62,* 515–524.

Foster, S. L., & Cone, J. D. (1995). Validity issues in clinical assessment. *Psychological Assessment, 7,* 248–260.

Fowler, J. C., Piers, C., Hilsenroth, M. J., Holdwick, D. J., & Padawer, J. R. (2001). The Rorschach suicide constellation: Assessing various degrees of lethality. *Journal of Personality Assessment, 76,* 333–351.

Garb, H. N. (1999). Call for a moratorium on the use of the Rorschach Inkblot Test in clinical and forensic settings. *Assessment, 6,* 313–317.

Garb, H. N., Wood, J. M., Nezworski, M. T., Grove, W. M., & Stejskal, W. J. (2001). Towards a resolution of the Rorschach controversy. *Psychological Assessment, 13,* 433–438.

Grønnerød, C. (2003). Temporal stability in the Rorschach method: A meta-analytic review. *Journal of Personality Assessment, 80*(3), 272–293.

Grønnerød, C. (2004). Rorschach assessment of changes following psychotherapy: A meta-analytic review. *Journal of Personality Assessment, 83,* 256–276.

Grove, W. M., Barden, R. C., Garb, H. N., & Lilienfeld, S. O. (2002). Failure of Rorschach-Comprehensive-System-based testimony to be admissible under the Daubert-Joiner-Kumho standard. *Psychology, Public Policy, & Law, 8,* 216–234.

Hamel, M., Shaffer, T. W., & Erdberg, P. (2000). A study of nonpatient preadolescent Rorschach protocols. *Journal of Personality Assessment, 75,* 280–294.

Hartmann, E., Nørbech, P. B., & Grønnerød, C. (2006). Psychopathic and nonpsychopathic violent offenders on the Rorschach: Discriminative features and comparisons with schizophrenic inpatient and university student samples. *Journal of Personality Assessment, 86,* 291–305.

Hartmann, E., Sunde, T., Kristensen, W., & Martinussen, M. (2003). Psychological measures as predictors of military training performance. *Journal of Personality Assessment, 80,* 88–99.

Hartmann, E., Wang, C., Berg, M., & Sæther, L. (2003). Depression and vulnerability as assessed by the Rorschach method. *Journal of Personality Assessment, 81,* 243–256.

Hiller, J. B., Rosenthal, R., Bornstein, R. F., Berry, D. T. R., & Brunell-Neuleib, S. (1999). A comparative meta-analysis of Rorschach and MMPI validity. *Psychological Assessment, 11,* 278–296.

Hilsenroth, M. J., & Handler, L. (1995). A survey of graduate students' experiences, interests, and attitudes about learning the Rorschach. *Journal of Personality Assessment, 64,* 243–257.

Hunsley, J., & Bailey, J. M. (1999). The clinical utility of the Rorschach: Unfulfilled promises and an uncertain future. *Psychological Assessment, 11,* 266–277.

Hunsley, J., & Bailey, J. M. (2001). Wither the Rorschach? An analysis of the evidence. *Psychological Assessment, 13,* 472–485.

Hunsley, J., & Meyer, G. J. (2003). The incremental validity of psychological testing and assessment: Conceptual, methodological, and statistical issues. *Psychological Assessment, 15,* 446–455.

Janson, H., & Stattin, H. (2003). Prediction of adolescent and adult antisociality from childhood Rorschach ratings. *Journal of Personality Assessment, 81,* 51–63.

Jensen, A. R. (1965). Review of the Rorschach Inkblot Test. In O. K. Buros (Ed.), *The sixth mental measurements yearbook* (pp. 501–509). Highland Park, NJ: Gryphon Press.

Krishnamurthy, R., Archer, R. P., & House, J. J. (1996). The MMPI-A and Rorschach: A failure to establish convergent validity. *Assessment, 3,* 179–191.

Lilienfeld, S. O., Wood, J. M., & Garb, H. N. (2000). The scientific status of projective techniques. *Psychological Science in the Public Interest, 1,* 27–66.

Lis, A., Parolin, L., Calvo, V., Zennaro, A., & Meyer, G. J. (in press). The impact of administration and inquiry on Rorschach Comprehensive System protocols in a national reference sample. *Journal of Personality Assessment.*

Long, G. M., & Toppino, T. C. (2004). Enduring interest in perceptual ambiguity: Alternating views of reversible figures. *Psychological Bulletin, 130,* 748–768.

Lundbäck, E., Forslund, K., Rylander, G., Jokinen, J., Nordström, P., Nordström, A.-L., et al. (2006). CSF 5-HIAA and the Rorschach test in patients who have attempted suicide. *Archives of Suicide Research, 10,* 339–345.

Masling, J. M., Rabie, L., & Blondheim, S. H. (1967). Obesity, level of aspiration, and Rorschach and TAT measures of oral dependence. *Journal of Consulting Psychology, 31,* 233–239.

McAdams, D. P., & Constantian, C. A. (1983). Intimacy and affiliation motives in daily living: An experience sampling analysis. *Journal of Personality and Social Psychology, 45,* 851–861.

McClelland, D. C. (1980). Motive dispositions: The merits of operant and respondent measures. In L. Wheeler (Ed.), *Review of personality and social psychology* (Vol. 1, pp. 10–41). Beverly Hills, CA: Sage.

McClelland, D. C., Koestner, R., & Weinberger, J. (1989). How do self-attributed and implicit motives differ? *Psychological Review, 96*, 690–702.

McCown, W., Fink, A. D., Galina, H., & Johnson, J. (1992). Effects of laboratory-induced controllable and uncontrollable stress on Rorschach variables *m* and *Y*. *Journal of Personality Assessment, 59*, 564–573.

McGrath, R. E., Pogge, D. L., Stokes, J. M., Cragnolino, A., Zaccario, M., Hayman, J., Piacentini, T., & Wayland-Smith, D. (2005). Field reliability of comprehensive system scoring in an adolescent inpatient sample. *Assessment, 12*, 199–209.

Meehl, P. E. (1959). Some ruminations on the validation of clinical procedures. *Canadian Journal of Psychology, 13*, 102–128.

Meyer, G. J. (1996). The Rorschach and MMPI: Toward a more scientifically differentiated understanding of cross-method assessment. *Journal of Personality Assessment, 67*, 558–578.

Meyer, G. J. (1997). Assessing reliability: Critical corrections for a critical examination of the Rorschach Comprehensive System. *Psychological Assessment, 9*, 480–489.

Meyer, G. J. (1999a). Introduction to the special series on the utility of the Rorschach for clinical assessment. *Psychological Assessment, 11*, 235–239.

Meyer, G. J. (Ed.). (1999b). Special Section I: The utility of the Rorschach for clinical assessment [Special Section]. *Psychological Assessment, 11*, 235–302.

Meyer, G. J. (2000a). Incremental validity of the Rorschach Prognostic Rating Scale over the MMPI Ego Strength scale and IQ. *Journal of Personality Assessment, 74*, 356–370.

Meyer, G. J. (2000b). On the science of Rorschach research. *Journal of Personality Assessment, 75*(1), 46–81.

Meyer, G. J. (2001a). Evidence to correct misperceptions about Rorschach norms. *Clinical Psychology: Science & Practice, 8*, 389–396.

Meyer, G. J. (2001b). Introduction to the final special section in the special series on the utility of the Rorschach for clinical assessment. *Psychological Assessment, 13*, 419–422.

Meyer, G. J. (Ed.). (2001c). Special Section II: The utility of the Rorschach for clinical assessment [Special Section]. *Psychological Assessment, 13*, 419–502.

Meyer, G. J. (2002a). Exploring possible ethnic differences and bias in the Rorschach Comprehensive System. *Journal of Personality Assessment, 78*, 104–129.

Meyer, G. J. (2002b). Implications of information-gathering methods for a refined taxonomy of psychopathology. In L. E. Beutler & M. Malik (Eds.), *Rethinking the DSM: Psychological perspectives* (pp. 69–105). Washington, DC: American Psychological Association.

Meyer, G. J. (2004). The reliability and validity of the Rorschach and TAT compared to other psychological and medical procedures: An analysis of systematically gathered evidence. In M. Hilsenroth & D. Segal (Eds.), Personality assessment. Vol. 2 in M. Hersen (Ed.-in-Chief), *Comprehensive handbook of psychological assessment* (pp. 315–342). Hoboken, NJ: Wiley.

Meyer, G. J., & Archer, R. P. (2001). The hard science of Rorschach research: What do we know and where do we go? *Psychological Assessment, 13*, 486–502.

Meyer, G. J., & Handler, L. (1997). The ability of the Rorschach to predict subsequent outcome: A meta-analysis of the Rorschach prognostic rating scale. *Journal of Personality Assessment, 69*, 1–38.

Meyer, G. J., & Kurtz, J. E. (2006). Guidelines editorial—Advancing personality assessment terminology: Time to retire "objective" and "projective" as personality test descriptors. *Journal of Personality Assessment, 87*, 1–4.

Meyer, G. J., Finn, S. E., Eyde, L., Kay, G. G., Moreland, K. L., Dies, R. R., et al. (2001). Psychological testing and psychological assessment: A review of evidence and issues. *American Psychologist, 56*, 128–165.

Meyer, G. J., Hilsenroth, M. J., Baxter, D., Exner, J. E., Jr., Fowler, J. C., Piers, C. C., et al. (2002). An examination of interrater reliability for scoring the Rorschach Comprehensive System in eight data sets. *Journal of Personality Assessment, 78*, 219–274.

Meyer, G. J., Riethmiller, R. J., Brooks, R. D., Benoit, W. A., & Handler, L. (2000). A replication of Rorschach and MMPI-2 convergent validity. *Journal of Personality Assessment, 74*(2), 175–215.

Meyer, G. J., Viglione, D. J., Erdberg, P., Exner, J. E., Jr., & Shaffer, T. (2004, March). *CS scoring differences in the Rorschach Workshop and Fresno nonpatient samples.* Paper presented at the annual meeting of the Society for Personality Assessment, Miami, FL, March 11.

Mihura, J. L., & Weinle, C. A. (2002). Rorschach training: Doctoral students' experiences and preferences. *Journal of Personality Assessment, 79,* 39–52.

Millon, T. (1994). *Manual for the MCMI-III.* Minneapolis, MN: National Computer Systems.

Morey, L. C. (1991). *Personality Assessment Inventory: Professional manual.* Odessa, FL: Psychological Assessment Resources.

Muniz, J., Prieto, G., Almeida, L., & Bartram, D. (1999). Test use in Spain, Portugal, and Latin American countries. *European Journal of Psychological Assessment, 15,* 151–157.

Nygren, M. (2004). Rorschach Comprehensive System variables in relation to assessing dynamic capacity and ego strength for psychodynamic psychotherapy. *Journal of Personality Assessment, 83,* 277–292.

Paulhus, D. L., Lysy, D. C., & Yik, M. S. M. (1998). Self-report measures of intelligence: Are they useful as proxy IQ tests? *Journal of Personality, 66,* 525–554.

Payne, B. K., Cheng, C. M., Govorun, O. & Stewart, B. D. (2005). An inkblot for attitudes: Affect misattribution as implicit measurement. *Journal of Personality and Social Psychology, 89,* 277–293.

Peebles-Kleiger, M. J. (2002). Elaboration of some sequence analysis strategies: Examples and guidelines for level of confidence. *Journal of Personality Assessment, 79,* 19–38.

Perry, W., & Viglione, D. J. (1991). The Ego Impairment Index as a predictor of outcome in melancholic depressed patients treated with tricyclic antidepressants. *Journal of Personality Assessment, 56,* 487–501.

Perry, W., Minassian, A., Cadenhead, K., Sprock, J., & Braff, D. (2003). The use of the Ego Impairment Index across the schizophrenia spectrum. *Journal of Personality Assessment.* 80, 50–57.

Perry, W., Sprock, J., Schaible, D., McDougall, A., Minassian, A., Jenkins, M., et al. (1995). Amphetamine on Rorschach measures in normal subjects. *Journal of Personality Assessment, 64,* 456–465.

Presley, G., Smith, C., Hilsenroth, M., & Exner, J. (2001). Clinical utility of the Rorschach with African Americans. *Journal of Personality Assessment, 77*(3), 491–507.

Ritsher, J. B. (2004). Association of Rorschach and MMPI psychosis indicators and schizophrenia spectrum diagnoses in a Russian clinical sample. *Journal of Personality Assessment, 83,* 46–63.

Rorschach, H. (1921/1942). *Psychodiagnostics* (5th ed.). Berne, Switzerland: Verlag Hans Huber. (Original work published 1921).

Rorschach, H. (1969). *Psychodiagnostics: A diagnostic test based on perception* (7th ed.) (P. Lemkau & B. Kronenberg, Trans.). Bern, Switzerland: Hans Huber. (Original work published 1921)

Rosenthal, R., Hiller, J. B., Bornstein, R. F., Berry, D. T. R., & Brunell-Neuleib, S. (2001). Meta-analytic methods, the Rorschach, and the MMPI. *Psychological Assessment, 13,* 449–451.

Rubin, N. J., & Arceneaux, M. (2001). Intractable depression or psychosis. *Acta Psychiatrica Scandinavica, 104,* 402–405.

Schafer, R. (1954). *Psychoanalytic interpretation in Rorschach testing.* New York: Grune & Stratton.

Shaffer, T. W., Erdberg, P., & Haroian, J. (1999). Current nonpatient data for the Rorschach, WAIS-R, and MMPI-2. *Journal of Personality Assessment, 73*(2), 305–316.

Shrout, P.E. & Fliess, J.L. (1979). Intraclass correlations: Uses in assessing rater reliability. *Psychological Bulletin, 86,* 420–425.

Smith, S. R., & Hilsenroth, M. J. (2003). ROR–SCAN 6: Rorschach Scoring for the 21st Century [Software review]. *Journal of Personality Assessment, 80,* 108–110.

Society for Personality Assessment (2005). The status of the Rorschach in clinical and forensic practice: An official statement by the Board of Trustees of the Society for Personality Assessment. *Journal of Personality Assessment, 85,* 219–237.

Stokes, J. M., Pogge, D. L., Powell-Lunder, J., Ward, A. W., Bilginer, L., DeLuca, V. A. (2003). The Rorschach Ego Impairment Index: Prediction of treatment outcome in a child psychiatric population. *Journal of Personality Assessment, 81,* 11–19.

Streiner, D. L. (2003a). Being inconsistent about consistency: When coefficient alpha does and doesn't matter. *Journal of Personality Assessment, 80,* 217–222.

Streiner, D. L. (2003b). Starting at the beginning: An introduction to Coefficient Alpha and internal consistency. *Journal of Personality Assessment, 80,* 99–103.

Stricker, G., & Gold, J. R. (1999). The Rorschach: Toward a nomothetically based, idiographically applicable configurational model. *Psychological Assessment, 11,* 240–250.

Sultan, S. (2006). *Is productivity a moderator of the stability of Rorschach scores?* Manuscript submitted for publication.

Sultan, S., Andronikof, A., Réveillère, C., & Lemmel, G. (2006). A Rorschach stability study in a nonpatient adult sample. *Journal of Personality Assessment, 87*, 113–119.

Sultan, S., Jebrane, A., & Heurtier-Hartemann, A. (2002). Rorschach variables related to blood glucose control in insulin-dependent diabetes patients. *Journal of Personality Assessment, 79*, 122–141.

Urist, J. (1977). The Rorschach test and the assessment of object relations. *Journal of Personality Assessment, 41*, 3–9.

Viglione, D. J. (1999). A review of recent research addressing the utility of the Rorschach. *Psychological Assessment, 11*, 251–265.

Viglione, D. J. (2002). *Rorschach coding solutions: A reference guide for the Comprehensive System.* San Diego, CA: Donald J. Viglione.

Viglione, D. J., & Hilsenroth, M. J. (2001). The Rorschach: Facts, fictions, and future. *Psychological Assessment, 13*(4), 452–471.

Viglione, D. J., & Meyer, G. J. (2007). An overview of Rorschach psychometrics for forensic practice. In C. B. Gacono & F. B. Evans with N. Kaser-Boyd & L. A. Gacono (Eds.), *Handbook of forensic Rorschach psychology* (pp. 21–53). Mahwah, NJ: Erlbaum.

Viglione, D. J., & Rivera, B. (2003). Assessing personality and psychopathology with projective tests. In J. R. Graham & J. A. Naglieri (Eds.), *Comprehensive handbook of psychology: Assessment psychology* (Vol. 10, pp. 531–553). New York: Wiley.

Viglione, D. J., & Taylor, N. (2003). Empirical support for interrater reliability of the Rorschach Comprehensive System coding. *Journal of Clinical Psychology, 59*, 111–121.

Viglione, D. J., Perry, W., & Meyer, G. (2003). Refinements in the Rorschach Ego Impairment Index incorporating the Human Representational Variable. *Journal of Personality Assessment, 81*, 149–156.

Viglione, D. J., Perry, W., Jansak, D., Meyer, G. J., & Exner, J. E., Jr. (2003). Modifying the Rorschach Human Experience Variable to create the Human Representational Variable. *Journal of Personality Assessment, 81*, 64–73.

Viglione, D. J. (1996). Data and issues to consider in reconciling self report and the Rorschach. *Journal of Personality Assessment, 67*, 579–587.

Watkins, C. E., Campbell, V. L., Nieberding, R., & Hallmark, R. (1995). Contemporary practice of psychological assessment by clinical psychologists. *Professional Psychology: Research and Practice, 26*, 54–60.

Wechsler, D. (1997). *WAIS-III manual: Wechsler Adult Intelligence Scale* (3rd ed.). San Antonio, TX: Psychological Corporation.

Weiner, I. B. (1977). Approaches to Rorschach validation. In M. A. Rickers-Ovsiankina (Ed.), *Rorschach psychology* (pp. 575–608). Hungtington, NY: Krieger.

Weiner, I. B. (2001). Advancing the science of psychological assessment: The Rorschach Inkblot Method as exemplar. *Psychological Assessment, 13*, 423–434.

Weiner, I. B. (2003). *Principles of Rorschach interpretation* (2nd ed.). Mahwah, NJ: Erlbaum.

Wenar & Curtis (1991). The validity of the Rorschach for assessing cognitive and affective changes, *Journal of Personality Assessment, 57*, 291–308.

Widiger, T. A., & Schilling, K. M. (1980). Toward a construct validation of the Rorschach. *Journal of Personality Assessment, 44*, 450–459.

Wood, J. M., Lilienfeld, S. O., Garb, H. N., & Nezworski, M. T. (2000). The Rorschach test in clinical diagnosis: A critical review, with a backward look at Garfield (1947). *Journal of Clinical Psychology, 56*, 395–430.

Wood, J. M., Nezworski, M. T., Garb, H. N., & Lilienfeld, S. O. (2001a). The misperception of psychopathology: Problems with norms of the Comprehensive System for the Rorschach. *Clinical Psychology: Science & Practice, 8*(3), 350–373.

Wood, J. M., Nezworski, M. T., Garb, H. N., & Lilienfeld, S. O. (2001b). Problems with the norms of the Comprehensive System for the Rorschach: Methodological and conceptual considerations. *Clinical Psychology: Science & Practice, 8*(3), 397–402.

CHAPTER **9**

TAT and Other Performance-Based Assessment Techniques

STEVEN J. ACKERMAN
J. CHRISTOPHER FOWLER
A. JILL CLEMENCE

Introduction

Similar to other personality assessment techniques, the Thematic Apperception Test (TAT; Murray, 1943), Early Memory Protocol (EM; Adler, 1931),
and Hand Test (HT; Wagner, 1983) are widely used in clinical and research
settings as methods for understanding complex patterns of thoughts, feelings,
and defenses. Moreover, these performance-based measures are sensitive to
revealing information not readily accessed with other assessment methods,
and often provide information about a person's approach to interpersonal
events, underlying psychopathology, and overt behavior. This chapter offers
an evaluation of each of these measures (TAT, EM, HT) with emphasis placed
on describing their clinical application and utility. The information supplied
in this chapter should help you answer the following questions:

1. Are performance-based personality assessment techniques such as the
   TAT, EM, and HT valid measures of psychopathology and individual
   personality functioning?
2. Are there valid rating scales for the TAT, EM, and HT?
3. What are the current clinical applications of the TAT, EM, and HT?

Thematic Apperception Test

The TAT consists of 31 achromatic picture cards that include 11 for adult males and females, seven for adults and adolescents of either gender, one for adult males only, one for adult females only, one for children of either gender, one for male children only, one for female children only, and a blank card for all patients. Each card contains scenes that vary in ambiguity and portray either a solitary individual, individuals in diverse interpersonal situations, or landscapes. For example, in one card (3BM), a huddled human form is on the floor against a couch with its head bowed on its right arm and besides it on the floor is an object that looks like a revolver or a set of keys. Although Murray (1943) originally intended all 31 cards to be administered in a standard order over two sessions, examiners typically use a subset of selected cards (Dana, 1982). To obtain a representative sample of clinical material, at least five cards should be administered in a standard procedure (Westen, 1995); however, the specific number of cards depends on the assessment question, context, and individual demographics.

Several surveys of psychological instrument usage among professional psychologists identify the TAT as one of the most commonly used performance-based personality assessment technique regardless of patient demographics or purpose of evaluation (Archer, Maruish, Imhof, & Piotrowski, 1991; Archer & Newsom, 2000; Camara, Nathan, & Puente, 2000; Cashel, 2002; Rossini & Moretti, 1997). The TAT elicits information not readily accessed with other methods, and various characters developed in a TAT narrative may be seen as a window into the variety of self and object representations that make up an individual's internal world. Therefore, the TAT provides rich data about an individual's capacity for relatedness in many situations such as family, work, or friendship.

Historically, TAT interpretation has been based on clinical intuition and experience,which generates controversy about its reliability and validity. Although there is little adequate reliability and validity data available for the TAT , recent empirical investigations and the development of objective scoring strategies such as the Social Cognition Object Relations Scale (SCORS; Westen, 1995) have lead to more than acceptable levels of psychometrics. Other scoring systems include those that measure an individual's ego defense mechanisms, communication deviance, problem solving, and motives. Many of these scoring methods have been used to aid in making clinical decisions, developing treatment plans, and diagnosis (i.e., Cramer, 1991; Dana, 1959; Ackerman, Hilsenroth, Clemence, & Weatherill, 1999; Westen, 1990, 1991).

Because the SCORS is one of the most widely studied and empirically supported rating system for the TAT, it will be the method focused on in this chapter and described in greater detail in the section on administration and scoring. In general, the reliability and validity of the SCORS to rate TAT narratives has been demonstrated in a number of previous studies investigating the relationship quality of a wide range of psychological conditions including major depression and borderline personality disorder (Ackerman, Clemence, Weatherill, & Hilsenroth, 1999, 2001; Freedenfeld, Ornduff, & Kelsey, 1995; Hibbard, Hilsenroth, Hibbard, & Nash, 1995; Ornduff, Freedenfeld, Kelsey, & Critelli, 1994; Ornduff & Kelsey, 1995; Peters, Hilsenroth, Eudell-Simmons, Blagys, & Handler, 2006; Porcerelli, Hill, & Duaphine, 1995; Stricker & Healey, 1990; Westen, 1990, 1991; Westen et al., 1991; Westen, Lhor, Silk, Gold, & Kerber, 1990; Westen, Ludolph, Block, Wixom, & Wiss, 1990: Westen, Ludolph, Lerner, Ruffins, & Wiss, 1990; Westen, Ludolph, Silk, Kellam, Gold, & Lohr, 1990).

Theory and Development

The first series of TAT cards were put together by H.A. Murray (Morgan & Murray, 1935) at the Harvard Psychological Clinic as a tool for validating his need-press theory of personality. The development of the TAT followed the working assumption that, in response to being asked to create an imaginative scenario about ambiguous stimuli, individuals would shape narratives based on a combination of past and present experiences by including, emphasizing, distorting, or omitting various content related to important themes in their lives. Subsequently, an assessor could make interpretations about the "needs" and "press" of conscious and unconscious personality dynamics.

According to Morgan (1995, 1999, 2002, 2003), many of the TAT cards were taken from everyday magazines, advertisements, or commissioned from artists. Over its evolution, different authors developed various series of TAT cards that retained, deleted, or added cards to the original 31: Series A and Series B (Rappaport, Gill, & Shafer, 1946; White, Sanford, Murray, & Bellak, 1941); Series C (Clark, 1944); and Series D (Murray, 1943). Today, most clinicians and researchers use the Series D cards and an accompanying test manual (Murray, 1943). Morgan (2003) has suggested that the content of the TAT cards did not undergo any additional revisions after 1943 because Murray left his position at the Harvard Clinic to take a government position during World War II. Although the TAT was designed for use with both children and adults, additional versions of the test, such as The Children's Apperception Test (Bellak & Bellak, 1961), have been created for more specific populations and culturally diverse racial groups [e.g., Tell Me a Story (Malgady, Constantino, & Rogler, 1984)].

Murray (1943) believed that narratives were more revealing of projective material and interpretations could be more valid if "most" of the cards used matched the gender of the individual being examined. But this has not been supported by recent research. In one study (Katz, Russ, & Overholser, 1993), authors suggest that the use of a range of cards that depict common intrapersonal and social dilemmas reveals an adequate sampling of data. Another interesting finding that is inconsistent with one of Murray's (1943) early beliefs is that the TAT cards are actually less emotionally ambiguous than originally intended. Alvarado (1994) found that when examined together, an individual's responses from multiple cards are often more similar than different, and reflect a common emotional tone.

Basic Psychometrics

Reliability

Similar to other performance-based personality measures, there are those who endorse the use of the TAT and those who don't. Critics (e.g., Entwisle, 1972; Fineman, 1977; Garb et al., 2002) reject the TAT as a reliable and valid measure of personality assessment. This contention is based on the assumption that the TAT cannot be a valid measure because it has questionable reliability. Supporters of the TAT (e.g., Ackerman, et al., 1999, 2001; Atkinson, 1981; Cramer, 1996, 1999; Hibbard, Mitchell, & Porcerelli, 2003; Westen, et al., 1990, 1991) believe that the low internal consistency is the result of the narrative response style inherent in the TAT, thus making classical test theory inappropriate (Tuberlinckx, De Boeck, & Lens, 2002). Coefficient alpha is also an incompatible measure of reliability for the TAT because of the tendency of different cards to elicit card-specific themes. For example, one card may reveal issues related to achievement and another, issues of intimacy or aggression. Therefore, it is unlikely that the narrative or ratings of narratives using a rating scale would be statistically related. One study that examined this issue (Hibbard et al., 2001) reported grouping the SCORS ratings of TAT narratives into a cognitive factor (Complexity of Representations and Understanding of Social Causality), and an affective factor (Affect Tone, Capacity for Emotional Investment and Moral Standards), which increased the internal consistency to an acceptable level ($\geq .70$) when using at least 10–12 different TAT cards.

A better measure of reliability for the TAT is interrater reliability, preferably using a standardized scoring strategy such as the Cramer Defense Manual (CDM; Cramer, 1987) or the SCORS, on a card-by-card basis (Cramer, 1999). Moreover, the likelihood of achieving acceptable levels of interrater reliability is greatly increased when using a training manual that includes a description of the theoretical background for each scale, detailed scoring criteria, and an ample number of examples. More specifically, studies using SCORS ratings of TAT narratives have reported reliability coefficients of .80 and larger consistently, when used to distinguish adult (Ackerman et al., 1999; Weston, Lohr, et al., 1990) and adolescent (Weston, Ludolph, Lerner, et al., 1990) borderline patients from other psychiatric and normal comparison groups, as well as when differentiating children and adolescents who had been sexually abused from non-abused control samples (Ornduff et al., 1994).

Validity

The validity of the TAT, which is based on the extent that it reveals important and otherwise hidden information about an individual's emotional world, has been questioned. For instance, Garb (1998) states that the incremental validity of the TAT is negatively affected when empirically validated objective scoring strategies are not used in the interpretation of TAT data. As mentioned previously in this chapter, the most promising scoring approach to the TAT is the SCORS.

The convergent validity of the SCORS has been established in studies of normal samples (Barends, Westen, Byers, Leigh, & Silbert, 1990) and samples of patients diagnosed with DSM-IV Axis II personality disorders. Moreover, complexity representations of people, capacity for emotional investment in relationships, affect tone, and understanding of social causality scales of the SCORS have been found to correlate with measures of complexity (Blatt, Wein, Chevron, & Quinan, 1979), ego development (Loevinger, 1976), and social adjustment (Weissman & Bothwell, 1976). Coche and Sillitti (1983) reliably rated TAT stories for the presence or absence of depressive themes and examined how individuals ended their stories. They found significant correlations between both the presence of depressive themes and story endings with the MMPI depressive scale and the Beck Depression Index. Ackerman and his colleagues (2001) extended prior research supporting the convergent validity between the Rorschach Mutuality of Autonomy (MOA) and TAT by comparing SCORS ratings of TAT narratives with the Rorschach. They found that protocols with more benevolent-healthy SCORS ratings also had a greater number of benevolent-healthy MOA ratings, and that more malevolent-negative SCORS ratings were significantly related to a greater number of malevolent-negative MOA ratings. A study by Niec and Russ (2002) provides further support for the validity of the SCORS by reporting a positive relationship between all the SCORS variables and self-report and teacher reports of empathy in a sample of young children. In a recent study, Peters and his colleagues (2006) found additional support for the convergent validity of the SCORS variables as a gauge of psychiatric, social, occupational, and interpersonal functioning.

Administration and Scoring

Administration

The TAT is appropriate for use in a variety of settings with individuals needing only the capacity to see a picture and tell a story. Therefore, it is suitable for children, adolescents, and adults. While all 31 cards were originally intended to be administered over two one-hour sessions, recent modifications to the number of cards selected for presentation has reduced the typical administration to a single one- to two-hour session. Although the TAT can be administered alone, it is more helpful as part of a comprehensive battery of measures. During the administration it is important to provide an environment that includes comfortable seating and a welcoming atmosphere. Originally, instructions given to the individual highlighted that the TAT was a test of creative imagination and fantasy, a form of intelligence (Murray, 1943). Recent alterations to the instructions de-emphasize the role of imagination and intelligence. Instead, test administers simply ask for a story that includes a description of the scene pictured in the card, an explanation of what is happening, what led to what is happening, what the character(s) are thinking and feeling, and its outcome (Rappaport, Gill, & Shafer, 1968).

While no special training is needed to administer the TAT, interpretation requires at least some clinical experience and education. According to Murray (1943), "to be able to discriminate what is unusual the interpreter must have a good deal of experience with this test, must have studied at least 50 or more sets of stories" (p. 10). In the TAT manual, he discusses an interpretive system based on an analysis of content. This system begins with distinguishing the character in the narrative that the individual identifies, and then observing what the character thinks, feels, or does. Interpretations are generated through the observation of frequent themes or situations that the character endures within the narratives, and paying special attention to the outcome.

Scoring

Early scoring systems such as the one described above (Murray, 1943) were believed to be more informal, often relying on clinical inference to draw conclusions. While more recently developed scoring methods continue to utilize clinical inference, in comparison, they are more elaborated, complex, and empirically driven. Examples of existing scoring systems that report their own adequate psychometric properties include those that measure an individual's object relations, ego defense mechanisms, communication deviance, problem solving, and motives. Some of these scoring methods have been used to aid in making clinical decisions, developing treatment plans, and diagnosis (Ackerman et al., 1999, 2001; Cramer, 1991; Dana, 1985; Westen, 1990, 1991). Even with the application of empirically grounded quantitative scoring systems, a disciplined approach to TAT interpretation should include an examination of content themes and character development to reveal underlying conflicts and traits (Dana, 1985).

The most detailed and validated TAT rating system to date is the SCORS. It focuses on the types and quality of social interactions as well as the way in which these experiences are internalized as mental representations. The SCORS was created to assess a variety of personality features from narrative data such as the TAT. One of the unique features of the SCORS is the ability to independently assess various levels of personality functioning at one time. While there are no norms for the SCORS, its reliability and validity to rate TAT narratives has been demonstrated in a number of previous studies investigating the relationship patterns of a wide range of psychological conditions such as major depression and personality disorders (Ackerman et al., 2001; Freedenfeld et al., 1995; Hibbard, et al., 1995; Ornduff et al., 1994; Ornduff & Kelsey, 1995; Peters, et al., 2006; Porcerelli et al., 1995; Stricker & Healey, 1990; Westen, 1990, 1991; Westen et al., 1991; Westen, Lhor, Silk et al., 1990; Westen, Ludolph, Lerner, et al., 1990; Westen, Ludolph, Silk, et al., 1990).

The SCORS is made up of eight variables rated on a 7-point anchored rating scale ranging from 1 (pathological) to 7 (healthy). Each TAT narrative is rated with all eight variables and mean scores are generated for each variable. Lower ratings (e.g., 1 or 2) indicate the presence of more pathological responses and often signify poor, unstable interpersonal relationships, whereas higher ratings (e.g., 6 or 7) indicate healthy responses that represent better quality interpersonal relationships and a richer understanding of relationships in general. The Complexity of Representations variable (Complexity) assesses relational boundaries and the ability to integrate both positive and negative attributes of the self and others, as well as the richness of representations. The Affective Quality of Representations variable (Affect) assesses how significant relationships are described with an emphasis on the expectations from others in relationships. The Emotional Investment in Relationships variable (Relationships) identifies the level of commitment and emotional sharing in relationships. The Emotional Investment in Values and Moral Standards variable (Morals) distinguishes between individuals who "behave in selfish, inconsiderate, or aggressive ways without any sense of remorse or guilt" (Westen, 1995, p. 30), and those who "think about moral questions in a way that combines abstract thought, a willingness to challenge or question convention, and genuine compassion and thoughtfulness in actions" (Westen, 1995, p. 30). The Understanding of Social Causality variable (Causality) identifies the extent to which a person can understand why others do what they do. The Experience and Management of Aggressive Impulses variable (Aggression) assesses an individual's ability to control and appropriately express aggression. The Self-Esteem variable (Esteem) assesses the affective quality of self-representations, and the Identity and Coherence of Self variable (Identity) assesses level of fragmentation and integration (Westen, 1995).

A potential limitation of the SCORS is that some the variables of an earlier version have been found to have moderate to high correlations with one

Quick Reference

Social Cognition and Object Relations Scale (SCORS; Westen, 1995)
The SCORS focuses on the types and quality of social interactions, as well as the way these experiences are internalized as mental representations. It was created to assess a variety of personality features from narrative data such as the TAT. One of the unique features of this scale is its ability to independently assess various levels of personality functioning at one time.

Complexity of Representations of People—assesses relational boundaries and the ability to integrate both positive and negative attributes of the self and others, as well as the richness of representations.
Affective Quality of Representations—assesses how significant relationships are described with an emphasis on the expectations from others in relationships.
Emotional Investment in Relationships—identifies the level of commitment and emotional sharing in relationships.
Emotional Investment in Values and Moral Standards—distinguishes between individuals who lack a sense of guilt about their behavior and those who have the capacity to both question authority and act in thoughtful ways.
Understanding of Social Causality—dentifies the extent to which a person can understand why others do what they do.
Experience and Management of Aggressive Impulses—assesses an individual's ability to control and appropriately express aggression.
Self-Esteem—assesses the affective quality of self-representations
Identity and Coherence of Self Variable—assesses level of fragmentation and integration

another (range = .18 to .81; Hibbard et al., 1995). Despite this limitation, the interrater reliability of the SCORS to rate TAT narratives has been established in a number of previous studies (Ackerman et al., 1999, 2000; Hibbard et al., 1995; Westen, 1991; Westen, Lohr, et al., 1990; Westen, Ludolph, Lerner, et al., 1990; Westen, Ludolph, Silk, et al., 1990).

Computerization

To date, there has been no efforts made to adapt the TAT for computer administration. The nature of TAT scoring and interpretation does not lend itself easily to computer adaptation because the intuition and creativity involved in the task would be lost.

Applications and Research Findings

The TAT has been shown to be an appropriate assessment technique in a variety of clinical and research settings such as inpatient psychiatric hospitals, outpatient clinics, and private clinical practice. One early study (Stix, 1979) even adapted the TAT into a shared task to evaluate and facilitate the diagnoses of couples in marital crises. A more recent study (Johnson, 1994) found support for using the TAT as an instrument to assess hospitalized patients with dementia of the Alzheimer's type (DAT). The author found that compared to non-demented psychiatric inpatients, the DAT patients used significantly fewer words, had more trouble remembering the task instructions, and provided more card description responses. Perhaps the most important finding from this study was the support for using the TAT as a screening tool to help determine a need for neuropsychological assessment.

One of the strengths of the TAT compared to other assessment techniques is its ability to expose both overt and hidden facets of personality. The TAT is also easily adapted to empirical and theoretical conclusions. For example, Bellak and Abrams (1997) described several theoretical guidelines for detecting psychopathology, such as a narcissistic and borderline personality disorders, psychotic process, severe anxiety, and splitting defenses. The authors suggest that a psychotic process can be seen "in the presence of direct sexual and aggressive themes, as well as themes of persecution, magical transformation of characters, and omnipotence" (p. 235); severe anxiety is depicted through "characters in a narrative that engage in sudden and chaotic repetitive actions in the face of danger or threat" (p. 236); and primitive splitting can be seen when characters in a narrative have more than one side to their personalities such as all good or all evil and angels or devils" (pp. 236–237).

As stated earlier, when combined with an empirically-based scoring system such as the SCORS, the TAT has reliably demonstrated the capacity to distinguish dissociative inpatients from a general inpatient sample (Pica, Beere, Lovinger, & Dush, 2001) and adult (Ackerman et al., 1999; Weston, Lohr, Silk, et al., 1990) and adolescent (Weston, Ludolph, Lerner et al., 1990) borderline patients from other psychiatric and normal comparison groups. In addition, it has been effective in differentiating children and adolescents who had been sexually abused from non-abused control samples (Ornduff et al., 1994).

In one of the first empirical investigations using the TAT to study the impact of childhood sexual abuse on object relations, Kaufman, Peck, & Taguri (1954) found that victims depicted maternal figures as malevolent, unfair, and depriving, while paternal figures were described with a wider range including caring, ineffectual, and frightening. More recently, there have been several empirical studies using SCORS ratings of TAT narratives that document the impaired object representations in victims of sexual and physical abuse (Freedenfeld et al., 1995; Ornduff et al., 1994; Ornduff & Kelsey, 1996; Stovall & Craig, 1990; Westen, Kelpser, Ruffins, Silverman, Lifton, & Boekamp, 1991; Westen, Ludolph, Block et al., 1990). These studies underscore the significant differences between the quality of object of relations in abused and non-abused individuals. A summary of these differences includes abused children having more primitive, malevolent, and non-functioning relationships that are described with limited psychological mindedness (Stovall & Craig, 1990; Westen, Ludolph et al., 1990). Moreover, other studies using SCORS ratings of TAT narratives have reported a correlation between abuse and grossly pathological relational functioning, as evidenced by lower levels of emotional investment in relationships and moral standards, less complexity of representations, and limited understanding of basic human relationships (Freedenfeld et al., 1995; Ornduff et al., 1994; Ornduff & Kelsey, 1996).

Westen and his colleagues have also done extensive work examining SCORS ratings of TAT narratives of children, adolescents, and adults diagnosed with Borderline Personality Disorder. In these studies, the authors consistently reported lower ratings on the Affective Quality of Representations (greater malevolence) and Emotional Investment in Relationships (tumultuous or few, if any, relationships) in adolescent and adult borderline patients compared to clinical and non-clinical samples. Ackerman, et al., (1999) found the TAT narratives of a sample of borderline patients were rated significantly lower across all eight SCORS variables compared to the narratives in a sample of narcissistic patients, and significantly lower on the Affect, Morals, Aggression, and Identity variables compared to the narratives in a sample of patients with a Cluster C Personality Disorder. Additionally, in this study the authors reported that the TAT narratives of a sample of antisocial patients were rated significantly lower on the Complexity, Relationships, and Causality variables compared to the narratives of a sample of narcissistic patients.

Earlier studies have suggested that there is a direct relationship between aggressive fantasy in TAT narratives and overt acting out of aggression (Magargee & Cook, 1967). Stone (1956) examined army prisoners who had committed both nonviolent and violent crimes and found that the violent group had significantly more hostile representations in their TAT narratives compared to the nonviolent group.

Purcell (1956) found that a sample of army trainees diagnosed as antisocial had more aggressive themes with direct expression of hostility and punishment from external sources than a sample of non-antisocial trainees. In a more recent study using SCORS ratings, Porcerelli and his colleagues (1995) found that sociopathic and psychotic patients had lower levels of relational compassion and thoughtfulness in their TAT narratives compared to a non-clinical sample. Several studies have also been completed that provided support for both the reliability and construct validity of the TAT as a treatment outcome measure (Ackerman et al., 2000; Cramer, 1999; Kempler & Scott,

Important References

Ackerman, S. J., Clemence, A. J., Weatherill, R., & Hilsenroth, M. J. (1999). Use of the TAT in the assessment of DSM-IV Cluster B personality disorders. *Journal of Personality Assessment, 73*, 442–448.

The authors reported that borderline patients were rated lower than narcissistic patients on all eight SCORS variables. In addition, compared to a group of *DSM-IV* Cluster C personality disorder patients, borderline patients were rated lower on the SCORS variables: affective quality of representations, emotional investment in relationships, moral standards, experience and management of aggressive impulses, and identity and coherence of self. The results indicate that SCORS ratings of TAT narratives can effectively differentiate *DSM-IV* personality disorders.

Fowler, J .F., Ackerman, S. J, Speanburg, S., Bailey, A., Blagys, M., & Conklin, A. C. (2004). Personality and symptom change in treatment-refractory inpatients: Evaluation of the phase model of change using Rorschach, TAT, and DSM-IV Axis V. *Journal of Personality Assessment, 83*(3), 306–322.

The authors reported that SCORS ratings of TAT narratives demonstrated a small to medium effect size change for a sample of treatment-refractory inpatients. More specifically, a medium effect size were found for the cognitive dimensions of the SCORS (complexity of representations and social causality variables) and small effect sizes were found for the more affective-relational dimensions (affective quality of representations, emotional investment in relationships, moral standards, and experience and management of aggressive impulses variables).

Hilsenroth, M. J., Stein, M. S., & Pinsker, J. (2004). *Social Cognition and Object Relations Scale: Global Rating Method (SCORS-G)*. Unpublished manuscript, The Derner Institute of Advanced Psychological Studies, Adelphi University, Garden City, NY.

This is an updated manual that consists of materials that expand on Westen's (1995) original training manual for using the SCORS. It provides a recommended training schedule as well as examples to facilitate the learning of how to rate narrative data.

Westen, D., Lhor, N., Silk, K. R., Gold, L., & Kerber, K. (1990). Object-relations and social cognition in borderlines, major depressives, and normals: A Thematic Apperception Test analysis. *Psychological Assessment, 2*, 355–364.

The authors found that adolescent and adult borderline patients were rated lower on the affective quality or representations (greater malevolence), emotional investment in relationships (tumultuous relationships, if any), and moral standards (behaving in selfish ways without a sense of remorse) SCORS variables compared to non-borderline and normal comparison groups. The results of this study indicate that SCORS ratings of TAT narratives can effectively differentiate adolescent and adult borderline patients from non-borderline and normal comparison groups.

1972). For example, Kempler and Scott (1972) compared ratings of pre and post treatment TAT stories of antisocial adolescents with teacher behavior ratings and community adjustment data. The authors found a significant correlation between TAT outcome ratings and teacher behavior ratings but not with community adjustment data.

A potential limitation of the TAT is that there has been limited support of Murray's (1951) statement that individuals being assessed are unaware of what they project. In fact, in a study of the stimulus properties of the TAT, Murstein and Mathes (1996) reported that pathological stories might simply be reflections of the stimulus properties of the cards rather than actual evidence of pathology. The authors concluded that individuals being assessed with the TAT might be evaluated as more pathological as a result of not taking into account the stimulus property of the task or the context of administration.

Cross-Cultural Considerations

TAT cards for use with specific racial groups have been designed to address a concern about cross-cultural applicability. Although they do not appear to be widely used, one example is the Tell Me a Story (TEMAS; Malgady, Constantino, & Rogler, 1984) technique. The TEMAS is an adaptation of the TAT for use with both ethnic minority and non-minority children and adolescents. It consists of chromatic stimuli depicting characters mainly interacting in urban and family settings. The reliability and validity of the TEMAS for use with Hispanic and African American children and adolescents has been supported by previous research (Malgady, Constantino, & Rogler, 1984). Some researchers have also examined the utility of the TAT for use with ethnic and minority individuals. In an archival study, Monopoli and Alworth (2000) examined the recurrent themes in the TAT data of acculturated and non-acculturated Navajo Veterans. While he found no significant differences between the two groups, several themes emerged as consistent in both groups including economic deprivation, physical suffering, isolation, interpersonal conflicts, and aggression. Hibbard and his colleagues (Hibbard, Tang, Latko, Park, Munn, Bolz, & Somerville, 2000) coded defenses on the TAT for Asian and European American students using the *Defense Mechanism Manual* (*DMM*, Cramer, 1991). The authors reported modest validity, as well as a pattern of over predicting desirable criteria for Asians and undesirable criteria for Caucasians.

The creation of special cards for specific cultural groups is necessary; however, it is insufficient without the examiner having specialized training. Unfortunately, limited knowledge about various cultures has led to negative assessment of certain culture-specific behavior and at times gross misunderstandings of minority individuals. In response to clinical and ethical considerations, most clinical training programs have added a specific training requirement to increase assessor knowledge and cultural competency. In order for students, clinicians, and researchers to be culturally competent they should be aware that interpretation of TAT narratives from culturally different individuals must take into consideration the context of the individual's particular culture as well as the interpersonal nature of the assessment procedure (Dana, 1985).

For individuals from some cultures the expectation to disclose personal information to others, especially information related to problems, may be incongruent with their beliefs. For example, individuals from Asian cultures may respond to the TAT by providing brief, general narratives that limit disclosure of more personal information. It is important at these times to not immediately interpret this type of protocol as guarded, defensive, or lacking self-awareness; instead it may represent a desire to uphold essential cultural values.

Early Memories Protocol

The Early Memories protocol (EM; Adler, 1937) is an implicit, performance-based measure of personality functioning that relies on narrative descriptions of specific childhood events to assess basic self-schemas, interpersonal relationship functioning, affect modulation, and personality pathology. Since its inception, clinicians and researchers developed various systems for gathering and scoring EMs, providing assessors options for assessing psychological functions.

The EM protocol is conducted using a semi-structured interview in which the assessor inquires about specific and global memories from the client's childhood. There is no consensus as to what constitutes early versus later childhood memories, but most authors agree that the central datum for the narrative is a memory for a specific event, rather than a "pattern" or purely iconic (picture memories) memory. Early memories can be recorded verbatim or written by the client, though some evidence suggests that written accounts may be more heavily censored than spontaneous verbal accounts evoked during an interview (Fowler, Hilsenroth, & Handler, 1996a).

Theory and Development

Procedures to elicit early childhood memories work from the basic assumption that early childhood memories are retrospective narrative creations that reveal aspects of psychological functioning rather than objective truths about the person's life. Narratives are analyzed using a variety of content and structural scoring systems to assess psychological distress, object-relations themes, character styles, and behavioral problems. The Early Memories test is based in part on the cognitive theory of reconstructive memory—the central postulate of which is that memory is under the influence of distortion, generated both by external and internal forces. From a psychodynamic perspective, early childhood memories are conceptualized, not so much as a matter of strict historical truth, but rather as modifications that confirm and conform to long-standing ingrained images of self and others (Mayman, 1968). Evidence supporting cognitive, internally determined reconstructions appeared as early as the 1930s with Sir Frederick C. Bartlett's (1932) experiments on schema-based reconstructive memory. These reconstructions and distortions are generated from personal expectations about how the world around us operates, and from personal experience. Modern cognitive researchers

Quick Reference

The Early Memories interview is conducted to generate narratives for specific events and should be recorded verbatim. Pattern and iconic (picture memories) memories are not considered relevant. The client is asked to recall scenes in which specific activities occurred. While there are many probes and prompts to query specific themes, some common probes and their significance are listed below:

- What is your earliest childhood memory?
- The initial probe is considered the least directed probe, reflecting themes of self-definition, emotional themes, coping skills, and interpersonal themes.
- What is your earliest memory of your mother?
- Pulls for themes related to maternal care, dependency, and level of maturity.
- What is your earliest memory of your father?
- Pulls for themes related to paternal authority, independence, and relationship themes.
- What is your earliest memory of your first day of school?
- Pulls for themes related to separation and adaptation to novel situations, as well as peer relationships.
- What is your most vivid memory from childhood?
- Often reveals central themes of self-definition and identity.
- What is your happiest memory from childhood?
- This probe begins a series of emotional probes that pools for specific affective experiences and the context in which a person remembers specific feelings.

generally agree. For example, Barclay and DeCooke (1988) emphasize the constituting effects that early memories play in creating, enhancing, and maintaining self-image and self definition. It seems that both psychoanalytic and cognitive theorists have come to an agreement about early memories (a truly rare phenomenon).

The EM test has undergone minor modifications and additions to keep pace with psychodynamic theory evolution, from Adlerian self-schema approaches, to ego psychology and object-relations theory. The latest development in the EM test is Bruhn's Cognitive-Perceptual Model (Bruhn, 1985, 1990, 1992a, 1992b). Bruhn's basic theorem is built on cognitive and ego-psychology principles, emphasizing the cognitive basis for memory distortion: "According to the cognitive-perceptual method, perception aims for a 'general impression' rather than a detailed picture of the whole, a point made long ago by Bartlett (1923). The basis of *selectivity* in perception is that needs, fears, interests, and major beliefs direct and orchestrate first the perceptual process itself and later the reconstruction of the events which are recalled" (Bruhn, 1985, p. 588).

In addition to outlining a cognitive theory, Bruhn and his colleagues have constructed a systematic procedure for gathering data (Bruhn, 1990), and a

Comprehensive Early Memory Scoring System (CEMSS: Last & Bruhn, 1983; Last & Bruhn, 1985) used in variety of empirical investigations.

Basic Psychometrics

Reliability

The reliability of early childhood memories must be distinguished from the veracity or historical accuracy of memory. The latter issue is deeply divisive and hotly debated and is of great importance in many areas of psychology, but is of peripheral importance here. Because theory holds that EMs are primarily accurate reflections of psychological states and traits, two forms of reliability are critical to the test. The degree to which independent judges can agree on the underlying constructs, or interrater reliability can be assessed with any given scoring manual. The second important form of reliability is the degree to which psychological phenomena embedded in the EMs remains stable over a brief test/retest interval. Interrater reliability for scoring systems ranges from fair to excellent depending on the system and the clarity of the scoring manual.

While early theorists tended to assume temporal stability of EMs, only one published study reports on test/retest reliability (Acklin, Bibb, Boyer, & Jain, 1991). Coefficients for 10-week test/retest stability indicates that self-representation ($r = .48$), representation of others ($r = .69$), and perception of the environment ($r = .41$) are differentially affected by naturally occurring mood states at the time of testing.

Validity

The convergent validity of EMs has been demonstrated in an array of studies of diagnostic groups and personality types, assessing psychological distress, detecting naturally occurring depressive moods, assessing aggressive potential, assessment of the quality of interpersonal relationships, and treatment outcome and risk for relapse. The divergent validity for the EM scoring systems is limited. Fowler (Fowler, Hilsenroth, & Handler, 1996) found that EM scores for dependency were not significantly correlated with measures assessing aggression or general quality of object-relations. Similarly, Fowler (Fowler, Hilsenroth, & Handler, 1998) demonstrated that a measure of imaginative and creative play was not correlated with independent measures of the dependency or general quality of object-relations.

Administration and Scoring

Administration

The EM test is appropriate for use in a variety of settings. While no definitive studies have been conducted on the proper age range for employing the EM test, most research has found that adolescent and adults are the best

Just the Facts

Ages:	Most appropriate for adolescents and adults.
Purpose:	Elicits information about quality of relationships, self-definition, coping patterns, and personality styles.
Strengths:	Quick and easy to administer. Helps build a therapeutic bond and is easily integrated into counseling and psychotherapy.
Limitations:	Lack of normative data and limited consensus about interpretive strategies.
Time to Administer:	Approximately 1hour.
Time to Score:	Approximately 1 hour.

candidates for the test. Several studies (Hedvig, 1965; Monahan, 1983; Weiland & Steisel, 1958) yielded negative findings for classifying children's level of psychopathology, suggesting that the test may not be valid for children under the age of 12. The test is easily administered in a single session as a brief screening instrument or as part of a comprehensive battery. The brevity, simplicity, and face validity of the test give it value as an adjunct to other assessment instruments in a battery, while at the same time making it useful as a screening tool when time is limited.

Administration of the EM test is relatively simple. All memories are queried for specific events rather than pattern memories. Specific queries for earliest memories of mother, father, first day of school, and for particular experiences are the standard probes. Specific probes for themes are numerous (for example, Mayman [1968r] lists 16 probes). Memory narratives should be recorded verbatim, using audio recording and written transcripts. There is no minimum educational requirements when the examiner administers the test, but when individuals are asked to complete a structured take-home EM packet, the educational requirements demand a minimum of writing proficiency. To the best of our knowledge, there are no age restrictions.

Scoring

Scoring of EMs from an idiographic interpretive frame tends to be less formal and structured, often relying on clinical inference and the clinician's preferred theory base. Formal scoring systems generally rely on specific thematic material emergent in the memory narratives. Investigators have preferred to create new scales to assess an ever-expanding array of psychological functions, rather than create a program of research to replicate and build on previous studies (Malinoski, Lynn, & Sivec, 1998). The various systems for gathering and scoring EMs have created an abundance of options for clinicians and researchers. Several systems have been proposed to integrate and standardize administration and scoring (Bruhn's CEMSS being the most comprehensive), but the response from researchers and clinicians has continued to emphasize idiographic interpretation and continued elaboration of new thematic scoring approaches.

Computerization

There has been no effort to adapt the EM test for computer administration. The nature of the EM narrative interview administration, the complex scoring, and interpretation does not lend itself easily to computer adaptation.

Applications and Research Findings

In the realms of psychological assessment and treatment, memory of past events is an inevitable source of psychological data for assessing psychological distress, diagnosis of personality characteristics, treatment planning, and for assessing treatment outcome in the form of changes in personality functioning. Asking a potential patient to tell you childhood memories has obvious face validity and is generally considered to build a strong alliance between examiner and patient. The EM interview can provide a seamless entry into the clinical interview, and is often experienced as an interesting task.

The empirical evidence for EM scoring systems is extensive and extends into areas of counseling psychology that will not be reviewed here. In the fields of clinical psychology and psychodynamic psychotherapy, published results from empirical studies span over 50 years. Early studies demonstrated modest differences between the EM profiles of various diagnostic groups, primarily focusing on differences between schizophrenic patients and other disturbed psychiatric groups (Charry, 1959; Friedman, 1952; Friedman & Schiffman, 1962; Furlan, 1984; Hafner, Corrotto, & Fakouri, 1980; Hafner & Fakouri, 1978; Hafner, Fakouri, Ollendick, & Corrotto, 1979; Pluthick, Platman, & Fieve, 1970). Later studies assessed the degree to which EM profiles could detect the presence of personality traits, such as narcissism (Harder, 1979; Shulman, McCarthy, & Ferguson, 1988). Shulman (Shulman, McCarthy, & Ferguson, 1988) applied DSM-III criteria to score EM narratives in order to assess narcissistic traits in normal subjects. The authors found EM scores to be significantly correlated with a self-report measure of self-absorption and self-admiration, as well as significant prediction of narcissistic traits as determined by a senior clinician who conducted extensive diagnostic interviewers with each participant. Tibbals (1992) examined the EM profiles of 70 male university students with high and low degrees of narcissism on self-report measures. The author found that highly narcissistic subjects produced more early memories reflecting a need for admiration, high levels of grandiosity, and themes of interpersonal exploitation than did other men.

Detecting mood disorders and degree of depression from EM profiles has met with some success. Acklin and colleagues (Acklin, Sauer, Alexander, & Dugoni, 1989) investigated the utility of EMs in predicting naturally occurring depressive moods in college students ($n = 212$), finding that EM variables significantly predicted Beck Depression Inventory scores, correctly classifying approximately 62% of the sample into depressed, mildly depressed, and non-depressed groups. Depressed students produced early memories in which others were perceived as frustrating their needs, perceived themselves as more damaged and threatened, and perceived their environment as unsafe and unpredictable. Several additional studies (Allers, White & Hornbuckle, 1990; Allers, et al, 1992; Fakouri, Hartung, & Hafner, 1985) found similar patterns of negative affect and passivity embedded in EMs of individuals with high BDI scores.

In an impressive series of studies of psychological distress, Shedler (Shedler, Mayman, & Manis, 1993; Cousineau & Shedler, 2006; Karliner, Westrich, Shedler, & Mayman, 1996) demonstrated that individuals who underestimate their level of psychological distress on self report measures, but produce disturbed early memories (thereby engaging in defensive denial of psychological distress) are more prone to excessively high heartrates, and are at higher risk for stress-related illnesses. Defensiveness and self-deception are more easily cloaked on self-report measures, but are not as easy to conceal in EM narratives. This series of studies demonstrated that some individuals underestimate their level of distress, and that such defensive underestimation comes at the cost of heightened coronary reactivity, which is a known risk factor for medical illness.

Several studies have focused on the ability of EMs to inform clinicians of aggressive and delinquent behavior. Hankoff (1987) found incarcerated males to develop EMs with dramatic and unpleasant themes, especially themes of disturbed and aggressive interaction with others. Quinn (1973), by contrast, found no difference among prison recidivists and nonrecidivists, or a difference among criminals who had committed crimes against individuals and those who committed property crimes. Bruhn & Davidow (1983) used EMs to classify delinquent behavior in 32 adolescent males, 15 of whom had been arrested for property crimes. Delinquent males were more likely to recall traumatic personal injuries, failures in attempts at mastery, and were more likely to cast themselves as victims. Tobey & Bruhn (1992) demonstrated criterion validity in the classification of the criminally dangerous. Using a sample of 30 dangerous and 30 nondangerous psychiatric inpatients, the authors accurately classified 73% of the patients into the correct group. In addition to those classified as dangerous, the false-positive rate was low (6%), providing a high degree of utility in clinical and probate settings.

Because of their reconstructive nature, early memories allow patients to express critical life themes and attitudes about interpersonal relationships and object-relations. Acklin, Bibb, Boyer, and Jain (1991) developed the Early Memories Object-Relations Scale (EMORS). The scores from the early memory protocols were found to demonstrate a high level of convergent and criterion validity with a number of self-report measures of attachment style, mood, psychiatric symptoms, and personality. The quality of relationships expressed in early memories was associated with meaningful patterns of maladjustment on the self-report measures.

Ryan & Bell (1984) assessed change in object-relations functioning manifested in the EMs of psychotic inpatients collected at admission, and at nine months into treatment and at six months post discharge. Psychotic patients demonstrated a significant improvement in object-representations at the 6-month follow-up after discharge. Specific changes were noted in the complexity of representations and affect tone, from poorly differentiated, disorganized, and empty, to greater organization, albeit somewhat shallow and narcissistic. A sub-sample of patients was followed to examine object-relations scores in relation to relapse and rehospitalization. Patients with greater disturbance in object-relations reflected in the 6-month follow-up EMs were twice as likely to be re-hospitalized than those that manifested more organized and benevolent object-relations.

Ryan and Cichetti (1985) utilized EMs and other pre-treatment performance-based data to predict the quality of alliance during the first psychotherapy hour. Memories were scored on the Ryan Object-Relations Scale (RORS), serving as the sole pre-treatment measure of object-relations. Approximately 40% of the variance for prediction of the quality of alliance was explained by pre-treatment variables, with EMs being the single best predictor of alliance in the first hour.

Utilization of EMs in assessing psychopathology in children and adolescent populations was considered by some clinicians to yield far less useful information than for adults (see Bruhn, 1981 for the theoretical rationale). Several studies (Hedvig, 1965; Monahan, 1983; Weiland & Steisel, 1958) yielded negative findings for classifying children's level of psychopathology, giving some credence to this position. Since that early phase, a series of studies have demonstrated criterion validity for early memories in classifying various pathological conditions and personality traits of children and adolescents. Lord (1971), for example, showed that the valence of affect in adolescent boys' early memories was associated with TAT measures of identity formation, differentiation of body concept, and representations of activity level in human figure drawings. The EMs did not predict self-report measures of vocational goals or sense of effectiveness in coping with life stresses. Kopp and Der's (1982) assessment of adolescent outpatients demonstrated that

Important References

Bruhn, A.R. (1990). *Earliest memories: Theory and application to clinical practice.* New York: Praeger.
> Bruhn's comprehensive treatment of autobiographical memory takes a modern, cognitive/perceptual framework to expand upon Adler's approach to the analysis of memory. Bruhn's approach emphasizes the importance of EMs as fantasies about the past that reveal concerns about the present and future.

Fowler, C (1995). A pragmatic approach to early childhood memories: Shifting the focus from truth to clinical utility. *Psychotherapy: Theory, practice, research, and training*, 31, 676–686.
> This article expands on Mayman's work while addressing the hotly debated topic of repressed memories of Satanic ritual abuse.

Mayman, M. (1968). Early memories and character structure. *Journal of Projective Techniques and Personality Assessment*, 32, 303–316.
> Mayman's "Presidential Address to the Society for Personality Assessment" is a thorough discourse on memory, inner reality, and the way people express inner conflicts, personality, and strengths through the guise of autobiographical recollections. He spells out theoretical constructs, a detailed method for assessing EMs, and offers clinical examples thereby creating an impressive synthesis. The theory is deeply rooted in psychoanalytic formulations of internalized representations of self and other (known as object-relations theory), and may be viewed by some as too speculative.

levels of activity in early memories differentiated acting-out adolescents from passive and withdrawn ones.

Cross-Cultural Considerations

Various studies employ normal, non-clinical samples, yet there has been no effort to construct a representative normative sample for comparison. Due to the free response nature of the task and the universality of individual memory, the test is assumed to be virtually free of cultural bias. However, it has yet to be determined how cultural and ethnic influences shape the structure and content of memories. While the EM test and procedure has been used throughout North America and Europe, and more recently in Asian and the Middle East, only recently has there been an effort to conduct cross-cultural studies. Two large scale comparisons of Caucasian Europeans and Taiwanese (Wang & Ross, 2005; Wang, 2006) found that Caucasians tend to recall specific events focusing on a central individual, whereas Asians tended to provide memories of general, routine events centering on collective activities and social interactions. These first studies point to the importance of contextualizing an individual's ethnic or cultural background when using assessment techniques.

The Hand Test

The Hand Test (HT; Wagner, 1983) is a performance-based assessment instrument that uses simple stimuli to assess attitudes and action tendencies that are close to the surface of experience and are likely to be exhibited in behavior. The HT has been found to be effective in identifying acting-out behavior in particular, and also used in a variety of clinical contexts as a tool for diagnosis and treatment planning with both children and adults (e.g., Sivec, Waehler, & Panek, 2004; Young & Wagner, 1999; Clemence, 2007). The measure is easy to use and requires little time to both administer and score, making it a good choice as an addition to a standard test battery. The measure consists of 10 cards presented to the examinee one at a time. Nine cards contain achromatic drawings of hands in ambiguous positions and the tenth card is blank. The examinee is asked to describe what the hand might be doing on each of the first nine cards. On the tenth card, the examinee is asked to "imagine a hand and tell what it might be doing." Responses are recorded verbatim, along with the time it takes to provide the first response that can be scored.

Theory and Development

The HT was initially designed as a projective instrument for predicting overt behavior based on the rationale that hands hold much meaning regarding our interactions with the external world, both interpersonally and physically (Sivec et al., 2004). The quantitative scoring categories thus reflect successful actions within these realms (Interpersonal, Environmental) as well as the failure to evoke meaning and/or effect action in general (Maladjustive, Withdrawal). Scoring items were developed using rational methods based on theory (e.g., Bhagavan Das' theory of emotion [Sivec et al., 2004]; Murray and Piotrowski's work with the TAT and the Rorschach [Wagner, 1983]) and empirical validation of the ability of the HT scores to predict acting-out behavior (Bricklin, Piotrowski, & Wagner, 1962).

The HT was originally published in 1962, and had a major revision in 1983. The revised HT manual includes additional normative data, updated research findings, case studies, and typical HT responses for 11 diagnostic groups. A child and adolescent manual supplement was published in 1991 (Wagner, Rasch, & Marsico) and, more recently, a supplement providing norms for patients suffering from different types of brain damage became available (Wagner et al., 2006).

Wagner (1999a, 1999b) has also elaborated additional qualitative variables to aid in interpretation based on theory and years of experience using the instrument. These scoring categories complement previous scoring criteria and are related to response idiosyncrasies, such as noteworthy verbalizations (Fabulations, Mysterious Expressions, Paralogical Expressions), clarifications of the Bizarre response (Hypo, Hyper, Morbid), degrees of reality testing (Integrated, Suppressed, Uncertain Responses), etc.

Basic Psychometrics

Reliability

The HT has shown excellent interrater reliability with scores ranging from 82% (Smith, Blais, Vangala, & Masek, 2005) to 94% (Walter, Hilsenroth, Arsenault, Sloan, & Harvill, 1998) agreement across the 15 quantitative variables. Correlations for individual scoring categories have also demonstrated strong reliability (.85–.97: Moran & Carter, 1991; .85–.97: Hilsenroth, Arsenault, & Sloan, 2005). However, when response frequencies are low, the scoring of individual variables at times falls into the "good" range (e.g., ICC =.62 for Withdrawal: Smith, et al, 2005; $r = .59$ for FEAR: Panek, Skowronski, Wagner, & Wagner, 2006).

Validity

The convergent validity of the HT has been demonstrated in studies of the withdrawal score and mental status in elderly adults (Panek & Hayslip, 1980; Hayslip & Panek, 1982), the Acting Out Score (AOS) and a Rorschach measure of hostility (Martin, Blair, & Brent, 1978), the PATH score with antisocial responses on the PAI (George & Wagner, 1995), the clinical scales of the MMPI-2 (Hilsenroth, Fowler, Sivec, & Waehler, 1994), and ratings of psychopathology (Wagner, Darbes, & Lechowick, 1972).

The divergent validity is supported by findings that the AOS score is uncorrelated with a measure of covert aggression (Holtzman Inkblot Test Hostility Score; Fehr, 1976) suggesting that, as Wagner asserts, the AOS score is likely measuring something more akin to overt aggression. Also, in an investigation of the HT and the MMPI-2, no significant relationship was found between the MMPI-2 validity scales (L, F, and K) and the HT PATH score, even though there were significant correlations with the MMPI-2 clinical scales (Hilsenroth et al., 1994).

Just the Facts	
Ages:	Six and above
Purpose:	Personality assessment
Strengths:	Brief, nonthreatening
Limitations:	Best used to assess behaviors close in time to administration of test
Time to Administer:	Approximately 10 minutes
Time to Score:	Approximately 10 minutes

Administration and Scoring

Administration

The HT is appropriate for use in a variety of settings with individuals age six and above. The HT can easily be administered in a single session as a brief screening instrument or as part of a comprehensive battery. The brevity, simplicity, and incremental validity of the test give it value as an adjunct to other assessment instruments in a battery, while at the same time making it useful as a screening tool when time is limited. Wagner (1999c) provides useful guidelines for using the HT as a screening device, with the caveat that the examiner be very cautious with interpretation using all available information, and taking care not to deviate from standardized administration and scoring.

The administration procedure is typical of what would be expected with most performance-based tasks in that the examiner is encouraged to remain neutral and unobtrusive in the testing situation. For example, on the first card, if the examinee provides only one response, the examiner is instructed to ask, "Anything else?" This is done to inform the examinee that more than one response is acceptable, without the examiner being too directive. There is no limit to the number of responses that may be given to each card, and no further prompts are given after the first card for additional responses. If the examinee is unable to produce a response to a particular card after a 100 second delay, the card is scored as a failure response, and the examiner moves on to the next card. Of course, if a response is given, but it is ambiguous or lacks sufficient detail for scoring, the examiner may ask for clarity or repeat the directions.

Scoring

Scoring is based on 15 quantitative variables (Affection, Dependence, Communication, Exhibition, Direction, Aggression, Acquisition, Active, Passive, Tension, Crippled, Fear, Description, Bizarre, Failure) and 17 qualitative variables (Ambivalent, Automatic Phrase, Cylindrical, Denial, Emotion, Gross, Hiding, Immature, Impotent, Inanimate, Movement, Oral, Perplexity, Sensual, Sexual, Original, Repetition). One quantitative score is assigned to each response, but more than one qualitative score may be given. Qualitative scores essentially serve to add context to and expand upon the quantitative scores by providing information related to cognitive functioning, dynamic conflicts, and expression of drives. There are also several summary scores that are easy to calculate providing information on impulsivity and/or card shock (Average Initial Response Time/High-Low), acting out potential (Acting Out Ratio), interpersonal and environmental attitudes and expectations

Quick Reference

Hand Test Quantitative Scoring

- Affection (AFF): Responses involving a warm, positive interchange or bestowal of pleasure; e.g., "Patting someone on the back."
- Dependence (DEP): Responses expressing a need for help or aid from another; e.g., "Someone pleading for mercy."
- Communication (COM): Responses involving a presentation or exchange of information; e.g., "A child saying how old they are."
- Exhibition (EXH): Responses involving displaying oneself in order to obtain approval or to stress a special noteworthy characteristic of the hand; e.g., "Showing off his muscles."
- Direction (DIR): Responses involving dominating, directing, or influencing the activities of others; e.g., "Giving a command."
- Aggression (AGG): Responses involving the giving of pain, hostility, or aggression; e.g., "Slapping someone."
- Acquisition (ACQ): Responses involving an attempt to acquire an as yet unobtained goal or object; e.g., "Reaching for something on a high shelf."
- Active (ACT): Responses involving an action or attitude designed to constructively manipulate, attain, or alter an object or goal; e.g., "Carrying a suitcase."
- Passive (PAS): Responses involving an attitude of rest and/or relaxation with a deliberate withdrawal of energy from the hand; e.g., "Hand folded in your lap."
- Tension (TEN): Responses in which energy is being exerted, but little or nothing is being accomplished; accompanied by a feeling of tension, anxiety, or malaise; e.g., "Hanging onto the edge of a cliff."
- Crippled (CRIP): Responses involving a sick, crippled, sore, dead, disfigured, injured, or incapacitated hand; e.g., "That hand is bleeding."
- Fear (FEAR): Responses involving the threat of pain, injury, incapacitation, or death; e.g., "Raised up to ward off a blow."
- Description (DES): Examinee does little more than acknowledge the presence of the hand; e.g., "Just a hand."
- Bizarre (BIZ): Responses based on hallucinatory content, delusional thinking, or peculiar, pathological thinking; e.g., "A crocodile creeping along the wall."
- Failure (FAIL): Scored when no response that can be scored is given to a particular card. Reflects the inability of the examinee to respond to the stimuli and may also indicate inappropriate behavioral tendencies manifested under conditions of lowered consciousness.

Summary Scores:

- Interpersonal (INT): Reflects interactions with others and is therefore made up of six quantitative responses AFF, DEP, COM, EXH, DIR, and AGG.
- Environmental (ENV): Represents an examinee's attitude toward the noninterpersonal world and is a combination of ACQ, ACT, and PAS responses.

- Maladjustive (MAL): The combined total of TEN, CRIP, and FEAR responses suggests difficulty in achieving successful interactions, either interpersonal or environmental.
- Withdrawal (WITH): Made up of the total DES, BIZ, and FAIL responses which suggests an inability to establish meaningful and effective life roles.
- Pathology (PATH): Estimates the total amount of psychopathology present as reflected in the individual's test protocol. The PATH score is calculated by adding the MAL score to twice the WITH score or MAL + 2(WITH).
- Acting Out Ratio (AOR): Reflects aggressive behavior tendencies and is determined by comparing the total number of positive interpersonal responses (AFF + COM + DEP) with the total number of negative interpersonal responses (DIR + AGG).
- Average Initial Response Time (AIRT): The average time required for the examinee to provide a response that can be scored to the test stimuli across the 10 cards.

Hand Test Qualitative Scoring:

- Ambivalent (AMB): Responses expressing some hesitation or uncertainty about the action described in the response.
- Automatic Phrase (AUT): Responses involving stereotypic language of the examinee.
- Cylindrical (CYL): Responses in which the hand is manipulating a cylindrical object that is large enough to fill the space between the palm and fingers.
- Denial (DEN): Responses in which the percept is described and then denied.
- Emotion (EMO): Responses charged with emotion.
- Gross (GRO): Responses involving action that is primitive, uncontrolled, or unsocialized.
- Hiding (HID): Responses in which the hand is hiding something.
- Immature (IM): Responses in which the hand is involved with children or animals.
- Impotent (IMP): Responses in which the examinee expresses an inability to respond to the card.
- Inanimate (INA): Responses in which the hand is attributed to an inanimate object such as a statue or a painting.
- Movement (MOV): Responses involving random, purposeless activity.
- Oral (ORA): Responses involving food, liquid, or drugs.
- Perplexity (PER): Responses reflecting the examinee's difficulty responding and sense of puzzlement.
- Sensual (SEN): Responses involving tactual, sensual experiences.
- Sexual (SEX): Responses involving sexual activity.
- Original (O): Responses that are highly unique.
- Repetition (RPT): Perseverative responses.

(Interpersonal, Environmental, Maladjustive, Withdrawal), and the level of psychopathology present (Pathology) in the protocol.

No special training is required beyond that which would be expected for any performance-based test. It is, however, necessary that the trainee be familiar with the standard instructions included in the *Hand Test Manual* (1983) and that the examiner not deviate from the administration procedures outlined therein.

The HT manual provides excellent direction regarding ways to not only interpret the quantitative and qualitative scoring variables of the test, but also to address the more subtle aspects of interpretation, such as word usage, behavior exhibited in the testing situation, etc. One should keep in mind, however, that due to the test's simplicity, some students may overestimate their mastery of the instrument, and as a result, may not derive maximum use of the measure.

Computerization

Due to the brevity and simplicity of administration and scoring, as well as the availability of norms, the HT has potential for computer adaptation. Although it has yet to be developed, computer-aided interpretation could be an asset.

Applications and Research Findings

The HT is nonthreatening and user friendly, making it easily applied within a wide array of clinical settings. The measure has been described as a useful tool for clarifying diagnoses among psychiatric inpatients (Hilsenroth & Handler, 1999) and individuals suspected of having dissociative identity disorder (Young, 1999), as well as for assessing comorbidity among individuals with mental retardation (Panek & Wagner, 1993), to name a few (see Young & Wagner, 1999, for several examples). More recently, Wagner and colleagues (2006) have provided a Brain Injury Score that can be used to identify the presence of brain injury and the level of impairment related to such.

In addition, Clemence (2007) makes a case for using the HT in a medical setting as an aid for consultation and liaison work. Because the HT is brief and can be administered bedside to hospital patients, it is ideal for settings in which discomfort, fatigue, or limited attention capacity are common. Indeed, the HT can be very helpful with such individuals who may struggle to express their emotional needs, given that their medical needs are so dominant. Further evidence for the use of the HT with medical patients is reflected in studies of the ability of the test to differentiate among patients reporting different types of pain (Panek, Skowronski, & Wagner, 2002; Panek, et al., 2006), leading the authors to suggest that the HT may be a useful tool in treatment planning with the medically ill.

The HT has demonstrated usefulness in the assessment of behavioral tendencies of children, adolescents (see Clemence, 2007, for a review), and adults (see Sivec, et al., 2004, for a review), and has been found to differentiate among individuals with a variety of clinical presentations (Wagner, 1983; Hilsenroth & Sivec, 1990; Smith, et al., 2005; Waehler, Rasch, Sivec, & Hilsenroth, 1992; Wagner, et al., 1990). For example, significant support has been found for the HT as a measure of aggressive behavior using the Aggression variable (AGG) and the Acting Out Score (AOS; Miller & Young, 1999; Tariq & Ashfaq, 1993; Campos, 1968; Oswald & Loftus, 1967). More specifically, the AGG and AOS cutoff scores have been found to distinguish aggressive from non-aggressive individuals (Clemence, Hilsenroth, Sivec, & Rasch, 1999; Porecki & Vandergroot, 1978; Selg, 1965), chronic offenders from nonrecidivists (Wetsel, Shapiro, & Wagner, 1967; Bricklin et al., 1962), and assaultive from non-assaultive individuals (Wagner & Hawkins, 1964; Brodsky & Brodsky, 1967).

Research has also found the HT to be an effective measure of psychopathology and a useful tool for discriminating groups demonstrating various levels of social and emotional adjustment. In a review of the HT literature concerning children and adolescents, Sivec & Hilsenroth (1994) identified the PATH variable as a robust indicator of problems among adolescents. Likewise, Clemence, Hilsenroth, Sivec, Rasch, and Waehler (1998) found PATH to be an important screening variable across adolescent patient groups (inpatient, outpatient, and nonpatient). A study of HT scores of adolescents found the PATH score to significantly predict future criminal behavior (Lie & Wagner, 1996; Lie, 1994).

Most recently, Smith et al. (2005) found the PATH, AGG, and WITH scores to differentiate psychiatric outpatients and medically ill pediatric inpatients,

Important References

Sivec, H. J., Waehler, C. A., & Panek, P. E. (2004). "The Hand Test: Assessing Prototypical Attitudes and Action Tendencies." *Comprehensive handbook of psychological assessment, Vol. 2: Personality assessment*. Mark J. Hilsenroth & Daniel L. Segal (Eds.). Hoboken, NJ: Wiley..
The authors provide a general overview of the development of the HT and its clinical and diagnostic utility with children and adolescents.

Wagner, E. E. (1983). *The Hand Test Manual: Revised*. Los Angeles: Western Psychological Services.
The manual provides detailed administration and scoring procedures along with instruction on the interpretation of test variables. Case studies and responses typical of a variety of diagnostic groups are included.

Wagner, E. E., Rasch, M. A., & Marsico, D. S. (1991). *Hand Test Manual Supplement: Interpreting child and adolescent responses*. Los Angeles: Western Psychological Services.
This publication describes the application of the Hand Test to the child and adult population. Normative data on the quantitative and qualitative variables by age group is provided.

with the psychiatric patients scoring significantly higher on each of these variables. Among adults, higher PATH scores have been found in a variety of clinical samples, such as individuals with multiple personality disorder (Young, Wagner, & Finn, 1994), women with eating disorders (Lenihan & Kirk, 1990), and veterans with PTSD (Walter et al., 1998). Although PATH and AOS are more popular research variables, significant findings have also been demonstrated for WITH, MAL, FAIL, BIZ, DES, FEAR, CRIP, ACT, and EXH variables as well (See Sivec et al., 2004, for a review). Panek and colleagues (Panek et al., 2006; Panek et al., 2002) also demonstrated the ability of the HT to differentiate persons with various medical presentations based on underlying personality and coping styles, which could impact the focus of their medical and mental health treatment.

When applied in nonclinical settings, the HT has been found useful for predicting the vocational performance of police officers (Rand & Wagner, 1973), academic performance in medical school (Daubney & Wagner, 1982), and detecting the potential for errant behaviors by employees in management positions (O'Roark, 1999). Furthermore, Lambirth, Dolgin, Rentmeister-Bryant, and Moore (2003) indicate that the HT is a recent addition to the assessment of personality in the area of aviation.

Strengths and Limitations

A clear strength of the HT across settings is that it offers a simple, non-threatening approach to orienting the examinee to the testing situation. The test appears uncomplicated while still providing a great deal of information about the examinee's level of pathology and ability to make use of very simple stimuli. For this reason, problems making sense of ambiguous stimuli that can be easily tied into day to day behavior may denote more serious difficulties with perception and reality testing than do problems managing much more complex stimuli, such as that of the Rorschach. Also, the clear interpersonal pull of the stimuli can be helpful in detecting problems in relating among individuals, such as those with borderline personality disorder (Hilsenroth & Fowler, 1999), or victims of sexual abuse (Rasch, 1999). Another valuable aspect of the test is that it includes scoring for positive interpersonal indicators, like affection, communication, and dependency, all of which denote potential for positive, affiliative behaviors and healthy resources.

When considering a measure as an addition to a standard battery, it is important to discern whether the measure demonstrates incremental validity. That is, does the measure add useful information above and beyond that of the other tests in the battery? Smith and colleagues (2005) attempted to address this question and found that, in a sample of children and adolescents, the HT added significantly to the ability of a common parent rating form (BASC-PRF; Reynolds & Kamphaus, 1992) to differentiate medical inpatients from psychiatric outpatients. What's more, the HT revealed significant differences when the self-report measures were unable to differentiate between the same groups. Such findings demonstrate the ability of the HT to detect subtle but important differences and make a case for the use of the instrument as an addition to a standard battery.

The HT has been criticized for exhibiting limited test-retest reliability (Urbina, 2004), but due to the instrument's emphasis on detecting behavioral tendencies that are close to the surface at the time of testing, it makes sense that test-retest reliabilities would be in the more moderate range given that action tendencies and attitudes likely vary to some degree over time (Sivec et al., 2004). The Hand Test Manual (Wagner, 1983) provides test-retest reliabilities for the quantitative variables, ranging from .51 to .89 over a two-week time frame (Panek & Stoner, 1979); to .52 to .91, with one variable Acquisition as the only variable below .50 (.21) using a 3-week interval (McGiboney & Carter, 1982); and .40 to .83 for all variables except FEAR (.12) across a period of about five weeks (Stoner & Lundquist, 1980).

In general, however, the validity of the HT improves when it is administered close in time to the behavior being predicted. For example, Zozolfi and Cilli (1999) found that hospital staff and case records in a sample of schizophrenic outpatients best-predicted acting-out behavior when behavioral data was obtained 1 month after the administration of the HT (compared to data collected at one-year, two-year, and five-year intervals). It is also important to note that there is little empirical evidence to support the qualitative scores on the HT. Thus, they are best used as an adjunctive tool for hypothesis building regarding personality dynamics, keeping in mind that the interpretations generated from such information is not entirely backed by empirical support. One should use caution when interpreting from the qualitative scores.

Cross-Cultural Considerations

The HT normative sample is made up of 100 individuals, half of whom are college students. The sample is 15% Black and 85% White, reflecting little ethnic diversity within the sample. This suggests that when using the normative data, cultural and ethnic deviations from this sample should be carefully considered. Fortunately, a few studies have been conducted that provide some information related to response styles typical of individuals from diverse backgrounds that can be helpful in increasing validity of interpretation with such groups (Stetson & Wagner, 1980; Oswald & Loftus, 1967; also, see below).

Due to the design of the cards (black and white drawings of hands in ambiguous positions) the stimuli are virtually free of cultural bias. However, it is always important to remember that when using assessment techniques, an individual's ethnic or cultural background should be considered when interpreting the results. For example, Panek (2004) notes that Japanese examinees tend to report a greater number of Dependence responses when compared to a sample of examinees from the United States. He points out that this finding may reflect a greater focus on collectivism in the Japanese culture, in which dependence is viewed as a positive quality reflecting interdependence; while Americans, who tend to be more oriented toward individualism, produce fewer dependence responses, reflecting an orientation toward independence and away from dependency on others. Because Japanese norms are available, it is easy to compare these culturally diverse groups. In general, though, it is up to the examiner to be sensitive to cultural issues when such norms are not available.

Furthermore, Panek, Cohen, Barrett, & Matheson (1998) examined the impact of age on responses to the HT in a Canadian sample and explored the similarities and differences between the response styles of Canadian and examinees from the United States related to age differences. The impact of culture on HT responses was evident, even between two closely related cultures. Thus, even though these differences may be subtle, the HT is apparently capable of detecting them.

The basic stimuli of hands cuts across cultures, making it easily translatable around the world. That is likely the reason why clinicians and researchers from many countries (e.g., Norway, Japan, Italy, Canada, Pakistan, & Romania: Sivec et al., 2004) have become interested in the HT as well. There is at least one translation of the HT for use in other countries (Japan: Yamagami, Yoshikawa, & Sasaki, 2000) that includes normative data on a Japanese sample to support it. In addition, *The Hand Test Practice in Japan* (Yoshikawa, Yamagami, & Sasaki, 2002) describes the HT as a tool for assessing adults with a variety of psychiatric conditions, as well as children exhibiting emotional and behavioral problems.

Current Controversies

The EM and HT have not been subjected to the level of scrutiny and criticism as that of the TAT. The main controversy surrounding the TAT has been questions about its reliability and validity. The reliability and incremental validity of the TAT is greatly reduced when narratives are interpreted only through clinical inference (Garb, 1998). Systematic scoring strategies such as the *Cramer Defense Mechanism Manual* (Cramer, 1991) and Westen's Social Cognition Object Relations Scale (Westen et al., 1995) greatly enhance reliability, and focus the scoring of narratives into a system that makes it possible to assess the validity of the measures, as well as assess the TAT as a method for assessing specific personality constructs. Both of these strategies have established more than adequate reliability and validity coefficients when used to rate TAT narratives. More specifically, the SCORS has demonstrated the capability of being able to detect childhood sexual abuse and severe character pathology (see the Basic Psychometrics and Applications/Research sections of this chapter for more details).

Despite these promising and empirically sound results, critics such as Garb, Wood, Lilienfeld, and Nezworski (2002) continue to argue that the TAT has been minimally supported because there is limited normative data available on scoring strategies like the SCORS to determine the accuracy of ratings, or cutoff scores for various levels of psychopathology (Garb et al., 2002). The authors suggest that TAT is best used as a tool for detecting severe character pathology, and not a useful measure of general pathology. Additional support for not using the TAT as a general assessment tool is that some of the images depicted in the cards have a tendency to evoke specific emotional or aggressive content. Therefore, the presence of depressive and negative emotional content in TAT narratives may be based more on the influence of the stimuli rather than a subjective experience of distress (Romano, Grayston, DeLuca, & Gillis, 1996).

Clinical Case Vignette

This section will discuss examples of verbatim TAT narratives from a middle-aged, single woman of high-average intelligence who lives in the Northeast U.S. She has a long history of treatment refractory major depression and borderline personality disorder. She had made several suicide attempts, including one near-lethal attempt that precipitated hospitalization. In addition, she reported intense loneliness and severe social isolation that left her feeling deeply pessimistic about her life, the utility of treatment, and the future. The TAT was administered at a private psychiatric hospital specializing in long-term psychodynamic treatment, as part of standard assessment battery that also included the Wechsler Adult Intelligence Scale- III (Wechsler, 1997), Human Figure Drawings (Goodenough, 1926), and the Rorschach Inkblot Test (Rorschach, 1951). While only two TAT stories are examined here due to space limitations (Cards 12M and 13MF, administered sequentially), pertinent SCORS ratings, as well as a summary of interpretive comments, are provided to elucidate the clinical utility of the TAT and help answer the following questions:

1. What is the individual's capacity to relate with others in positive and healthy ways?
2. What is the individual's ability to identify and express emotions?

The first card, Card 12M, depicts a young man lying on a couch with his eyes closed, and leaning over him is an elderly man with his hand stretched out above the face of the young man. For this card, frequent themes of religion, emotional disturbance, illness, or hypnotism are often seen. In addition, stories to this card are often interpreted to understand the nature of a therapeutic alliance and predict an individual's response to psychotherapy.

> This is a story about a young man who is lying in bed; he still has his shirt and tie on because I guess he needed to take a nap. The older man is a relative who is kneeling on his bed and feels like stroking him because he's peacefully at sleep.

SCORS Variable	Rating
Complexity of Representations	3
Affective Quality of Representations	3
Emotional Investment in Relationships	2
Emotional Investment in Values and Moral Standards	4
Social Causality	2
Experience and Management of Aggressive Impulses	4
Self-Esteem	4
Identity and Coherence of Self	4

The examinees's story is rated as a 3 on the Complexity of Representations of People variable because it provides relatively simple descriptions of the characters' internal states that are minimally elaborated. It earns a rating 2 on the Emotional Investment in Relationships and Understanding of Social Causality variables because there is only a hint of a relationship between the characters with little understanding of why they are behaving in specific ways.

The second card, Card 13MF, depicts a man standing with his face buried in his arm and behind him is a figure of a woman lying in a bed, bare breasted, with her arm dangling over the side of the bed. For this card, males typically generate story themes about guilt, remorse, death, aggression, and infidelity, while females often construct death and/or illness, remorse, and betrayal themes.

> This is a story about a man and a woman who are involved with one another. She is sleeping and he is up and dressed. The way he's holding his arm over his head shows that he's feeling distressed. He doesn't really want to leave her but he doesn't feel comfortable staying with her either. Shortly he will walk out the door and take a long walk.

SCORS Variable	Rating
Complexity of Representations	3
Affective Quality of Representations	3
Emotional Investment in Relationships	2
Emotional Investment in Values and Moral Standards	4
Social Causality	2
Experience and Management of Aggressive Impulses	4
Self-Esteem	3
Identity and Coherence of Self	2

This story is rated as a 3 on the Complexity of Representations of People variable because it also provides relatively simple descriptions of the characters' internal states that are minimally elaborated. The story earns a rating of 3 on the Affective Quality of Representations variable and a rating of 2 on the Emotional Investment in Relationships variable because the affective tone of the story is negative and the protagonist in the story is selfish and the relationship between the characters is shallow. Similar to the previous story, this one earns a rating of 2 on the Understanding of Social Causality variable because it provides the reader with a limited understanding of why the characters behave the way they do.

This sequence of responses to TAT Cards 12M and 13MF presented above is an example of how, when the stimulus has strong content (card 13MF), the examinee shuts down and can only hint at being "distressed" through an ambivalent, stuck position (i.e., "He doesn't really want to leave her but he doesn't feel comfortable staying with her either."). However, when the stimulus is less provocative and affectively charged, as in card 12M, she can express a slight desire to be in close contact with another person (i.e., the "relative" "feels like stroking" the young man). Taken together, these two stories reveal multiple conflicts around relationships and emotions. Although her desire for relationships is tenuous and distant, she can, if safe, experience a modicum of longing. Generally, however, she relies on the defenses of avoidance and denial in an effort to deaden her emotional life (i.e., when faced with negative emotions, the character simply "walk(s) out the door and takes a long walk" without addressing or resolving their dilemma). Her level of dysphoria appears moderate (Affective quality of representations = 3), but could be underestimated because of her intense efforts to keep affect closed off and out of awareness (Complexity of representations = 3,3).

At best, she can hint at a longing to be closer to others because the closer she gets the more she becomes immobilized by her ambivalence. She can approach and relate with others only under optimal conditions that feel safe enough.

Based on the TAT findings it is very likely that the individual will have a difficult time developing an alliance with a therapist. More importantly, she might feel threatened by a therapist's attempts to get to know her and, in response, prematurely leave treatment. Therefore, the first aim of the treatment would be to define the boundaries of the working relationship in an effort to create a safe space together. This type of effort can often increase the individual's sense of security and trust in the treatment. Given her history of suicide attempts, other goals might include helping her identify alternate ways to express her depressive thoughts and help her to identify her feelings (positive and negative) with the hope of eventually finding a way to express them as well.

Chapter Summary

The empirical data and clinical evidence presented in this chapter support the use of implicit, performance-based personality measures such as the Thematic Apperception Test (TAT; Murray, 1943), Early Memory Protocol (EM; Adler, 1931) and Hand Test (HT; Wagner, 1983). These measures are sensitive to revealing information not readily accessed with other assessment methods, and often provide information about a person's approach to interpersonal events, underlying psychopathology, and overt behavior. Although the EM works best with ideographic and thematic scoring approaches, the TAT and HT have standardized scoring strategies that produce acceptable psychometric properties. Even more impressive has been the capacity for these measures to remain both relatively unchanged and relevant in a changing world of personality assessment. Each is adaptable to a variety of clinical and research settings, as well as with individuals of various ages, cultural backgrounds, and cognitive ability.

- The TAT (Murray, 1943) is a performance-based personality measure, appropriate for use in a variety of settings that utilizes narrative responses to semi-ambiguous stimuli to generate rich data about an individual's capacity for relatedness in many situations such as family, work, or friendship.
- When combined with an empirically-based scoring systems such as the SCORS, the TAT has demonstrated the capacity to distinguish dissociative inpatients from a general inpatient sample (Pica, Beere, Lovinger, & Dush, 2001); and adult (Ackerman et al., 1999; Weston, Lohr, Silk, et al., 1990) and adolescent (Weston, Ludolph, Lerner, et al., 1990) borderline patients from other psychiatric and normal comparison groups; as well as children and adolescents who had been sexually abused from non-abused control samples (Ornduff et al., 1994).

- The EM procedure (Adler, 1937) is an implicit, performance-based measure of personality functioning that relies on narrative descriptions of specific childhood events to assess basic self-schemas, interpersonal relationship functioning, affect modulation, and personality pathology.
- The empirical evidence for EM scoring systems is extensive and has demonstrated modest differences between the EM profiles of schizophrenic patients and other disturbed psychiatric groups (Charry, 1959; Friedman, 1952; Friedman & Schiffman, 1962; Furlan, 1984; Hafner, Corrotto, & Fakouri, 1980; Hafner & Fakouri, 1978; Hafner, Fakouri, Ollendick, & Corrotto, 1979; Pluthick, Platman, & Fieve, 1970); as well as, the degree to which EM profiles could detect the presence of personality traits, such as narcissism (Harder, 1979; Shulman, McCarthy & Ferguson, 1988).
- The HT (Wagner, 1983) is a performance-based assessment instrument that uses simple stimuli to assess attitudes and action tendencies that are close to the surface of experience and are likely to be exhibited in behavior.
- The HT stimuli can be helpful in detecting problems in relating among individuals such as those with borderline personality disorder (Hilsenroth & Fowler, 1999) or victims of sexual abuse (Rasch, 1999); for predicting the vocational performance of police officers (Rand & Wagner, 1973), academic performance in medical school (Daubney & Wagner, 1982), and detecting the potential for errant behaviors by employees in management positions (O'Roark, 1999).

References

Ackerman, S. J., Clemence, A. J., Weatherill, R., & Hilsenroth, M. J. (1999). Use of the TAT in the assessment of DSM-IV Cluster B personality disorders. *Journal of Personality Assessment, 73*, 442–448.

Ackerman, S. J., Clemence, A. J., Weatherill, R., & Hilsenroth, M. J. (2001). Convergent validity of Rorschach and TAT scales of object relations. *Journal of Personality Assessment, 77*, 295–306.

Acklin, M. W., Bibb, J. L., Boyer, P., & Jain, V. (1991). Early memories as expressions of relationship paradigms: A preliminary investigation. *Journal of Personality Assessment, 57*(1), 177–192.

Acklin, M. W., Sauer, A., Alexander, G., & Dugoni, B. (1989). Predicting depression using earliest childhood memories. *Journal of Personality Assessment, 53*(1), 51–59.

Adler, A. (1937). The significance of early recollections. *International Journal of Individual Psychology, 3*, 283–287.

Allers, C. T., White, J., & Hornbuckle, D. (1990). Early recollections: Detecting depression in the elderly. *Individual Psychology, 46*, 61–66.

Allers, C. T., White, J., & Hornbuckle, D. (1992). Early recollections: Detecting depression in college students. *Individual Psychology, 48*, 324–329.

Alvarado, N. (1994). Empirical validity of the Thematic Apperception Test. *Journal of Personality Assessment, 63*(1), 59–79.

Archer, R. P., Maruish, M., Imhof, E. A., & Piotrowski, C. (1991). Psychological test usage with adolescent clients: 1990 survey findings. *Professional Psychology: Research and Practice, 22*(3), 247–252.

Archer, R. P., & Newsom, C. R. (2000). Psychological test usage with adolescent clients: Survey update. *Assessment, 7*(3), 227–235.

Atkinson, J. W. (1981). Studying personality in the context of an advanced motivational psychology. *American Psychologist, 36,* 117–128.

Barclay, C. R., & DeCooke, P. A. (1988). Ordinary everyday memory: Some of the things of which selves are made. In U. Neisser & E. Winograd (Eds.), *Remembering reconsidered: Ecological and traditional approaches to the study of memory* (Vol. 2, pp. 91–125). New York: Cambridge University Press.

Barends, A., Westen, D., Leigh, J., Silbert, D., & Byers, S. (1990). Assessing affect-tone in relationship paradigms from TAT and interview data. *Psychological Assessment: A Journal of Consulting and Clinical Psychology, 2,* 329–332.

Bartlett, F. C. (1932). *Remembering: A study in experimental and social psychology.* New York: Cambridge University Press.

Bellak, L., & Bellak, S. S. (1961). Children's apperception test (C.A.T.) manual (4th ed.), Larchmont, NY: C.P.S.

Bellak, L., & Abrams, D. M. (1997). *The Thematic Apperception Test, the Children's Apperception Test, and the Senior Apperception Test Technique in clinical use* (6th ed.). Boston: Allyn & Bacon.

Blatt, S. J., Wein, S., Chevron, E. S., & Quinlan, D. M. (1979). Parental representations and depression in normal young adults. *Journal of Abnormal Psychology, 78,* 388–397.

Bricklin, B., Piotrowski, Z. A., & Wagner, E. E. (1962). The Hand Test: With special reference to the prediction of overt aggressive behavior. In M. Harrower (Ed.), *American lecture series in psychology.* Springfield, IL: Charles C. Thomas.

Brodsky, S. L, & Brodsky, A. M. (1967). Hand Test indicators of antisocial behavior. *Journal of Projective Techniques and Personality Assessment, 31,* 36–39.

Bruhn, A.R. (1985). Using early memories as a projective technique: The cognitive-perceptual method. *Journal of Personality Assessment, 49,* 587–597.

Bruhn, A.R. (1990). *Earliest memories: Theory and application to clinical practice.* New York: Praeger.

Bruhn, A. R. (1992a). The early memories procedure: A projective test of autobiographical memory, part 2. *Journal of Personality Assessment, 58*(2), 326–346.

Bruhn, A. R. (1992b). The early memories procedure: A projective test of autobiographical memory, part 1. *Journal of Personality Assessment, 58*(1), 1–15.

Bruhn, A. R. & Davidow, S. (1983). Earliest memories and the dynamics of delinquency. *Journal of Personality Assessment, 47,* 467–482.

Camara, W. J., Nathan, J. S., & Peunte, A .E. (2000). Psychological test usage: Implications in professional psychology. *Professional Psychology: Research and Practice, 31*(2), 141–154.

Campos, L. P. (1968). Other projective techniques. In A. I. Rabin (Ed.), *Projective techniques in personality assessment: A modern introduction,* (pp. 461–520). New York: Springer.

Cashel, M. L. (2002). Child and adolescent psychological assessment: Current clinical practices and the impact of managed care. *Professional Psychology: Research and Practice, 33*(5), 446–453.

Charry, J. B. (1959). Childhood and teen-age memories in mentally ill and normal groups. *Dissertation Abstracts International, 20,* 1073.

Clemence, A. J. (2007). Clinical application of the hand test projective instrument with children. In S. R. Smith and L. Handler (Eds.), *The clinical assessment of children and adolescents: A practitioner's guide,* (pp. 223–235). Mahwah, NJ: Erlbaum.

Clemence, A. J., Hilsenroth, M. J., Sivec, H. J., Rasch, M., & Waehler, C. A. (1998). Use of the Hand Test in the classification of psychiatric in-patient adolescents. *Journal of Personality Assessment, 71*(2), 228–241.

Clemence, A. J., Hilsenroth, M. J., Sivec, H. J., & Rasch, M. (1999). The Hand Test AGG and AOS variables: Relationship with teacher rating of aggressiveness. *Journal of Personality Assessment, 73,* 334–344.

Coche, E., & Sillitti, J. A. (1983). The Thematic Apperception Test as an outcome measure in psychotherapy research. *Psychotherapy: Theory, Research and Practice, 20*(1), 41–46.

Cousineau, T. M., & Shedler, J. (2006). Predicting physical health: Implicit mental health measures versus self-report scales. *Journal of Nervous and Mental Disease, 194*(6), 427–432.

Clark, R. M. (1944). A method of administering and evaluation the Thematic Apperception Test in group situations. *Genetic Psychology Monographs, 30,* 3–55.

Cramer, P. (1987). The development of defense mechanisms. *Journal of Personality, 55,* 597–614.

Cramer, P. (1991). *The development of defense mechanisms: Theory, research and assessment*. New York: Springer-Verlag.

Cramer, P. (1996). *Story-telling, narrative and the Thematic Apperception Test*. New York: Guilford.

Cramer, P. (1999). Future directions for the Thematic Apperception Test. *Journal of Personality Assessment, 72*(1), 74–92.

Cramer, P., & Blatt, S. J. (1990). Use of the TAT to measure change in defense mechanisms following intensive psychotherapy. *Journal of Personality Assessment, 54*(1), 236–251.

Dana, R. H. (1959). Proposal for objective scoring of the TAT. *Perceptual and Motor Skills, 10*, 27–43.

Dana, R. H. (1982). *A human science model for personality assessment with projective techniques*. Springfield, IL: Charles C Thomas publisher.

Dana, R. H. (1985). *Thematic Apperception Test* (TAT). In C. S. Newmark (Eds.). *Major psychological assessment instruments*. (pp. 89–134). Boston: Allyn and Bacon.

Daubney, J. F., & Wagner, E. E. (1982). Prediction of success in an accelerated BS/MD medical school program using two projective techniques. *Perceptual and Motor Skills, 1*, 1179–1183.

Entwisle, D. R. (1972). To dispel fantasies about fantasy-based measures of achievement motivation. *Psychological Bulletin, 77*, 377–391.

Fakouri, M. E., Hartung, J. R., & Hafner, J. L. (1985). Early recollections of neurotic depressive patients. *Psychological Reports, 57*, 783–786.

Fehr, L. A. (1976). Construct validation of the Holtzman Inkblot anxiety and hostility scores. *Journal of Personality Assessment, 40*, 483–486.

Fowler, C. (1994). A pragmatic approach to early childhood memories: Shifting the focus from truth to clinical utility. *Psychotherapy: Theory, Practice, Research, and Training, 31*, 676–686.

Fowler, C., Hilsenroth, M. J., & Handler, L (1996a). Two methods of early memories data collection: An empirical comparison of the projective yield. *Assessment, 3*(1), 63–71.

Fowler, C., Hilsenroth, M. J., & Handler, L. (1996b). A multi-method assessment of dependency using the early memory test. *Journal of Personality Assessment, 67*(2) 399–413.

Fowler, C., Hilsenroth, M. J., & Handler, L. (1998). Assessing transitional relatedness with the transitional object early memory probe. *Bulletin of the Menninger Clinic, 62*(4), 455–474.

Freedenfeld, R. N., Ornduff, S. R., & Kelsey, R. M. (1995). Object relations and physical abuse: A TAT analysis. *Journal of Personality Assessment, 64*, 552–568.

Friedman, A. (1952). Early childhood memories of mental patients. *Journal of Child Psychiatry, 2*, 266–269.

Friedman, A., & Schiffman, H. (1962). Early recollections of schizophrenic and depressed patients. *Journal of Individual Psychology, 18*, 57–61.

Furlan, P. M. (1984). "Recollection" on the individual psychotherapy of schizophrenia (7th International Symposium: Psychotherapy of schizophrenia, 1981, Heidelberg, W. Germany). *Psychiatrica Fennica, 15*, 57–61.

Garb, H. N. (1998). Recommendations for training in the use of the Thematic Apperception Test (TAT). *The Forum, 29*, 621–622.

Garb, H. N., Wood, J. M., Lilienfeld, S. O., & Nezworski, M. T. (2002). Effective use of projective techniques in clinical practice: Let the data help with selection and interpretation. *Professional Psychology: Research and Practice, 33*(5), 454–463.

George, J. M., & Wagner, E. E. (1995). Correlations between the Hand Test Pathology score and Personality Assessment Inventory scales for pain clinic patients. *Perceptual and Motor Skills, 80*, 1377–1378.

Goodenough, F. (1926). *Measurement of Intelligence by Drawings*. New York: World Book.

Hafner, J. L., Corrotto, L.V., & Fakouri, M. E. (1980). Early recollections of schizophrenics. *Psychological Reports, 46*, 408–410.

Hafner J. L., & Fakouri, M. E. (1978). Early recollections, present crises and future plans in psychotic patients. *Psychological Reports, 43*, 927–930.

Hafner, J. L., Fakouri, M. E., Ollendick, T. H., & Corrotto, L. V. (1979). First memories of "normal" and of schizophrenic, paranoid type individuals. *Journal of Clinical Psychology, 35*, 731–733.

Hankoff, L. D. (1987). The earliest memories of criminals. *International Journal Offender Therapy and comparative Criminology, 31*, 195–201.

Harder, D. W. (1979). The assessment of ambitious-narcissistic character style with three projective tests: The early memories, TAT, and Rorschach. *Journal of Personality Assessment, 43*(1), 23–32.

Hayslip, B., Jr., & Panek, P. E. (1982). Construct validation of the Hand Test with the aged: Replication and extension. *Journal of Personality Assessment, 46*, 345–349.

Hedvig, E. B. (1965). Children's early recollections as a basis for diagnosis. *Journal of Individual Psychology, 21*, 187–188.

Hibbard, S., Hilsenroth, M. J., Hibbard, J. K., & Nash, M. R. (1995). A validity study of two projective representation measures. *Psychological Assessment, 7*, 336–339.

Hibbard, S., Mitchell, D., & Porcerelli, J. (2001). Internal consistency of the object relations and social cognition scale to the Thematic Apperception Test. *Journal of Personality Assessment, 77*(3), 408–419.

Hibbard, S., Tang, P. C., Latko, R., Park, J. H., Munn, S., Bolz, S., & Somerville, A. (2000). Differential validity of the Defense Mechanism Manual for the TAT between Asian Americans and Whites. *Journal of Personality Assessment, 75*(3), 351–372.

Hilsenroth, M. J., Arsenault, L, & Sloan, P. (2005). Assessment of combat-related stress and physical symptoms of Gulf War veterans: Criterion validity of selected Hand Test variables. *Journal of Personality Assessment, 84*, 155–162.

Hilsenroth, M. J., & Fowler, C. (1999). The Hand Test and borderline personality disorder. In G. R. Young & E. E. Wagner (Eds.), *The Hand Test: Advances in application and research* (pp. 59–83), Malabar, FL: Krieger.

Hilsenroth, M. J., Fowler, C., Sivec, H. J., & Waehler, C. A. (1994). Concurrent and discriminant validity between the Hand Test Pathology score and the MMPI-2. *Assessment, 1*, 111–113.

Hilsenroth, M. J., & Handler, L. (1999). Use of the Hand Test in the differential diagnosis of psychiatric inpatients. In G. R. Young & E. E. Wagner (Eds.), *The Hand Test: Advances in application and eesearch* (pp. 85–101), Malabar, FL: Krieger.

Hilsenroth, M. J., Stein, M. S., & Pinsker, J. (2004). *Social Cognition and Object Relations Scale: Global rating method (SCORS-G).* Unpublished manuscript, The Derner Insitute of Advanced Psychological Studies, Adelphi University, Garden City, NY.

Johnson, J. L. (1994). The Thematic Apperception Test and Alzhiemer's Disease. *Journal of Personality Assessment, 62*(2), 314–319.

Karliner, R., Westrich, E., Shedler, J., & Mayman, M. (1996). The Adelphi early memory index: Bridging the gap between psychodynamic and scientific psychology. In J. Masling & R. Bornstein (Eds.), *Psychoanalytic perspectives on developmental psychology* (pp. 43–67). Washington, DC: American Psychological Association.

Katz, H. E., Russ, S. W., & Overholser, J. C. (1993). Sex differences, sex roles, and projection on the TAT: Matching stimulus to examinee gender. *Journal of Personality Assessment, 60*(1), 186–191.

Kaufman, I., Peck, A., & Taguri, C. (1954). The family constellation and overt incestuous relations between father and daughter. *American Journal of Orthopsychiatry, 24*, 266–279.

Keiser, R. E., & Prather, E. N. (1990). What is the TAT? A review of ten years of research. *Journal of Personality Assessment, 55* (3&4), 800–803.

Kempler, H. L., & Scott. V. (1972). Assessment of therapeutic change in antisocial boys via the TAT. *Psychological Reports, 30*, 905–906.

Kopp, R. R., & Der, D-F. (1982). Level of activity in adolescents' early recollections: A validity study. *Individual Psychology, 38*(3), 213–222.

Krohn, A., & Mayman, M. (1974). Object representations in dreams and projective tests. *Bulletin of the Menninger Clinic, 39*, 445–466.

Lambirth, T. T., Dolgin, D. L., Rentmeister-Bryant, H. K., & Moore, J. L. (2003). Selected personality characteristics of student naval aviators and student naval flight officers. *The International Journal of Aviation Psychology, 13*, 415–427.

Langs, R. J. (1965). First memories and characterological diagnosis. *Journal of Nervous and Mental Disorders, 141*(3), 319–320.

Last, J. M., & Bruhn, A. R. (1983). The psychodiagnostic value of children's earliest memories. *Journal of Personality Assessment, 47*(6), 597–603.

Last, J. M., & Bruhn, A. R. (1985). Distinguishing child diagnostic types with early memories. *Journal of Personality Assessment, 49*(1), 87–192.

Lenihan, G. O., & Kirk, W. G. (1990). Personality characteristics of eating-disordered outpatients as measured by the Hand Test. *Journal of Personality Assessment, 55*, 350–361.

Lie, N. (1994). Offenders tested with projective methods prior to the first offense. *British Journal of Projective Psychology, 39*, 23–24.

Lie, N., & Wagner, E. E. (1996). Prediction of criminal behavior in young Swedish women using a group administration of the Hand Test. *Perceptual and Motor Skills, 82*, 975–978.

Loevinger, L. (1976). *Ego Development*. San Francisco: Jossey-Bass.

Lord, M. M. (1971). Activity and affect in early memories of adolescent boys. *Journal of Personality Assessment, 45*(5), 448–642.

Magargee, E. I., & Cook, P. E. (1967). The relation of TAT and inkblot aggressive content scales with each other and with criteria or overt aggression in juvenile delinquents. *Journal of Projective Techniques and Personality Assessment, 31*, 48–60.

Malgady, R. G., Constantino, G., & Rogler (1984). Development of the Tell Me A Story Test a Thematic Apperception Test for urban Hispanic children. *Journal of Consulting and Clinical Psychology, 52*(6), 886–896.

Malinoski, P., Lynn, S. J., & Sivec, H. (1998). The assessment, validity, and determinants of early memory reports: A critical review. S. J. Lynn & K. M. McConkey (Eds.), *Truth in memory*. (pp. 109–136). New York: Guilford.

Martin, J. D., Blair, G. E., & Brent, D. (1978). The relationship of scores on Elizur's hostility system on the Rorschach to the Acting-Out score on the Hand Test. *Educational and Psychological Measurement, 38*, 587–591.

Mayman, M. (1968). Early memories and character structure. *Journal of Projective Techniques and Personality Assessment, 32*, 303–316.

McGiboney, G. W., & Carter, C. (1982). Test-retest reliability of the Hand Test with acting-out adolescent subjects. *Perceptual and Motor Skills, 55*, 723–726.

Miller, H. A., & Young, G. R. (1999). The Hand Test in correctional settings: Literature review and research potential. In G. R. Young & E. E. Wagner (Eds.), *The Hand Test: Advances in application and research* (pp. 183–190)., Malabar, FL: Krieger.

Monahan, R. T. (1983). Suicidal children's and adolescent's responses to early memories test. *Journal of Personality Assessment, 47*(3), 257–264.

Monopoli, J., & Alworth, L. L. (2000). The use of the Thematic Apperception Test in the study of Native American psychological characteristics: A review and archival study of Navaho men. *Genetics, Social and General Psychology Monographs, 126*(1), 43–78.

Moran, J. J., & Carter, D. E. (1991). Comparisons among children's responses to the Hand Test by grade, race, sex, and social class. *Journal of Clinical Psychology, 47*, 647–664.

Morgan, C. D., & Murray, H. A. (1935). A method for investigating fantasies: The Thematic Apperception Test. *Archives of neurological psychiatry, 34*, 289–306.

Morgan, W. G. (1995). Origin and history of the Thematic Apperception Test images. *Journal of Personality Assessment, 65*, 237–254.

Morgan, W. G. (1999). The 1943 images: Their origin and history. In L. Gieser & M.I. Stein (Eds.), *Evocative images: The Thematic Apperception Test and the art of projection* (pp. 65–83). Washington, DC: American Psychological Association.

Morgan, W. G. (2002). Origin and history of the earliest Thematic Apperception Test pictures. *Journal of Personality Assessment, 79*, 422–445.

Morgan, W. G. (2003). Origin and history of the "Series B" TAT pictures. *Journal of Personality Assessment, 81*(2), 133–148.

Murray, H. A. (1943). *Manual for the Thematic Apperception Test*. Cambridge, MA: Harvard University Press.

Murray, H. A. (1951). Use of the Thematic Apperception Test. *American Journal of Psychiatry, 107*, 577–581.

Murstein, B. I., & Mathes, S. (1996). Projection of projective techniques = pathology: the problem that is not being addressed. *Journal of Personality Assessment, 66*(2), 337–349.

Niec, L. N., & Russ, S. W. (2002). Children's internal representations, empathy, and fantasy play: A validity study of the SCORS-Q. *Psychological Assessment, 14*(3), 331–338.

Ornduff, S. R., Freedenfeld, R. N., Kelsey, R. M., & Critelli, J. W., (1994). Object relations of sexually abused female subjects: A TAT analysis. *Journal of Personality Assessment, 63*, 223–238.

Ornduff, S. R., & Kelsey, R. M. (1996). Object relations of sexually and physically abused female children: A TAT analysis. *Journal of Personality Assessment, 66*, 91–105.

O'Roark, A. M. (1999). Workplace applications: Using the Hand Test in employee screening and development. In G. R. Young & E. E. Wagner (Eds.), *The Hand Test: Advances in application and research* (pp. 25–32), Malabar, FL: Krieger.

Oswald, O., & Loftus, P. T. (1967). A normative and comparative study of the Hand Test with normal and delinquent children. *Journal of Projective Techniques and Personality Assessment, 31*, 62–68.

Panek, P. E. (2004). The importance of cultural/ethnic norms: An example based on American individualism versus Japanese collectivism as reflected in the Hand Test Dependence response. *Journal of Projective Psychology & Mental Health, 11*, 1–3.

Panek, P. E., Cohen, A. J., Barrett, L, & Matheson, A. (1998). An exploratory investigation of age differences on the Hand Test in Atlantic Canada. *Journal of Projective Psychology & Mental Health, 5*, 145–149.

Panek, P. E., & Hayslip, B., Jr. (1980). Construct validation of the Hand Test Withdrawal score on institutionalized older adults. *Perceptual and Motor Skills, 51*, 595–598.

Panek, P. E., Skowronski, J. J., & Wagner, E. E. (2002). Differences on the projective Hand Test among chronic pain patients reporting three different pain experiences. *Journal of Personality Assessment, 79*, 235–242.

Panek, P. E., Skowronski, J. J., Wagner, E. E., & Wagner, C. F. (2006). Interpersonal style and gastrointestinal disorder: An exploratory study. *Journal of Projective Psychology & Mental Health, 13*, 17–24.

Panek, P. E., & Stoner, S. (1979). Test-retest reliability of the Hand Test with normal subjects. *Journal of Personality Assessment, 43*, 135–137.

Panek, P. E., & Wagner, E. E. (1993). Hand Test characteristics of dual diagnosed mentally retarded older adults. *Journal of Personality Assessment, 61*, 324–328.

Peters, E. J., Hilsenroth, M. J., Eudel-Simmons, E. M., Blagys, M. D., & Handler, L. (2006). Reliability and validity of the Social Cognition and Object Relations Scale in clinical use. *Psychotherapy Research, 16*(5): 617–626.

Pica, M., Breere, D., Lovinger, S., & Dush, D. (2001). The responses of dissociative patients on the Thematic Apperception Test. *Journal of Clinical Psychology, 57*(7), 847–864.

Pluthick, R., Platman, S. R., & Fieve, R. R. (1970). Stability of the emotional content of early memories in manic-depressive patients. *British Journal of Medical Psychology, 43*, 177–181.

Porcerelli, J. H., Hill, K. A., & Duaphine, V. B. (1995). Need-gratifying object relations and psychopathology. *Bulletin of the Menninger Clinic, 59*, 99–104.

Porecki, D., & Vandergroot, D. (1978). The Hand Test Acting-Out score as a predictor of acting out in correctional settings. *Offender Rehabilitation, 2*, 269–273.

Purcell, K. (1956). The TAT and antisocial behavior. *Journal of Consulting Psychology, 20*, 449–456.

Quinn, J. R. (1973). Predicitng recidivism and type of crime using early recollections of prison inmates. *Dissertation Abstracts International 35(1-A)*, 197.

Rand, T. M., & Wagner, E. E. (1973). Correlations between Hand Test variables and patrolman performances. *Perceptual and Motor Skills, 37*, 477–478.

Rappaport, D., Gill, M., & Schafer, R. (1946). *Diagnostic psychological testing*, (Vol. 2). Chicago: Year Book.

Rasch, M. (1999). Hand Test response styles of sexually abused girls. In G. R. Young & E. E. Wagner (Eds.), *The Hand Test: Advances in application and eesearch* (pp. 103–115), Malabar, FL: Krieger.

Reynolds, C. R., & Kamphaus, R. W. (1992). *Behavior Assessment System for Children*. Circle Pines, MN: American Guidance Service.

Romano, E., Grayston, A. D., DeLuca, R. V., & Gillis, M. A. (1996). The Thematic Apperception Test as an outcome measure in the treatment of sexual abuse: Preliminary Findings. *Journal of Child and Youth Care, 10*(4), 37–50.

Rorschach, H. (1951). *Psychodiagnostics: A diagnostic test based on perception* (5th ed.). Oxford: Grune & Statton. (Original published 1921)

Rossini, E. D., & Moretti, R. J. (1997). Thematic Apperception Test (TAT) interpretation: Practice recommendations from a survey of clinical psychology doctoral programs accredited by the American Psychological Association. *Professional Psychology: Research and Practice, 28*, 393–398.

Ryan, E. R., & Bell, M. D. (1984). Changes in object relations from psychosis to recovery. *Journal of Abnormal Psychology, 93*(2), 209–219.

Ryan, E. R., & Cicchetti, D. V. (1985). Predicting quality of alliance in the initial psychotherapy interview. *Journal of Nervous and Mental Disease, 173*(12), 717–725.

Selg, H. (1965). Der Hand-Test als indikator for offen aggressives verhalten bei kindern. [The Hand Test as an indicator of overt aggressive tendencies in children.] *Diagnostica, 4,* 153–158.

Shedler, J., Mayman, M., & Manis, M. (1993). The illusion of mental health. *American Psychologist, 48*(11), 1117–1131.

Shulman, D. G., McCarthy, E. C., & Ferguson, G. R. (1988). The projective assessment of narcissism: development, reliability, and validity of the N-P. *Psychoanalytic Psychology, 5*(3), 285–297.

Sivec, H. J., & Hilsenroth, M. J . (1994). The use of the Hand Test with children and adolescents: A review. *School Psychology Review, 23,* 526–545.

Sivec, H. J., Waehler, C. A., & Panek, P. E. (2004). The Hand Test: Assessing prototypical attitudes and action tendencies. In . J. Hilsenroth & D. L. Segal (Eds.), *Comprehensive handbook of psychological assessment, Vol. 2: Personality assessment.* (pp. 405–420). Hoboken, NJ: Wiley.

Smith, S. R., Blais, M. A., Vangala, M., & Masek, B. J. (2005). Exploring the Hand Test with medically ill children and adolescents. *Journal of Personality Assessment, 85,* 80–89.

Stetson, D., & Wagner, E. E. (1980). A note on the use of the Hand Test in cross-cultural research: Comparison of Iranian, Chinese, and American students. *Journal of Personality Assessment, 44,* 603.

Stix, E. M. (1979). The interaction TAT – an auxiliary method in the diagnosis of marital crises. *Psychological Psychotherapy, 27*(3), 248–257.

Stone, M. H. (1956). The TAT aggressive content scale. *Journal of Projective Technique, 20,* 445–455.

Stoner, S. B., & Lundquist, T. (1980). Test-retest reliability of the Hand Test with older adults. *Perceptual and Motor Skills, 50,* 217–218.

Stovall, O., & Craig, R. J. (1990). Mental representations of physically and sexually abused latency-aged females. *Child Abuse & Neglect, 14,* 233–242.

Stricker, G., & Healey, B. (1990). Projective assessment of object relations: A review of the empirical literature. *Psychological Assessment: A Journal of Consulting and Clinical Psychology, 2,* 219–230.

Tariq, P. N., & Ashfaq, S. (1993). A comparison of criminals and noncriminals on Hand Test scores. *British Journal of Projective Psychology, 38,* 107–118.

Tiballs, C. J. (1992). The value of early memories in assessing narcissism. *Dissertation Abstracts International, 52*(8-B).

Tobey, L. H., & Bruhn, A. R. (1992). Early memories and the criminally dangerous. *Journal of Personality Assessment, 59*(1), 137–152.

Tuerlincjx, F., DeBoeck, P., & Lens, W. (2002). Measuring needs with the Thematic Apperception Test: A psychometric study. *Journal of Personality and Social Psychology, 82*(3), 448–461.

Urbina, S. (2004). The Hand Test: Revised. [Electronic version]. *Mental Measurements Yearbook, Yearbook 14.* Accessed August 16, 2007. http://web.ebscohost.com/ehost/detail?vid=9&hid =102&sid=e61094eb-de5d-4cc0-94dd-07c0ec847141%40sessionmgr108

Wagner, E. E. (1983). *The Hand Test Manual: Revised.* Los Angeles: Western Psychological Services.

Wagner, E. E. (1999a). Advances in interpretation: New parenthesized scoring. In G. R. Young & E. E. Wagner (Eds.), *The Hand Test: Advances in application and research* (pp. 3–11), Malabar, FL: Krieger.

Wagner, E. E. (1999b). Levels of reality contact: Fundamental interpretation based on perceptual-motor integrations as manifested in the Hand Test. In G. R. Young & E. E. Wagner (Eds.), *The Hand Test: Advances in application and research* (pp. 13–21), Malabar, FL: Krieger.

Wagner, E. E. (1999c). The Hand Test as a screening technique: Guidelines and examples. In G. R. Young & E. E. Wagner (Eds.), *The Hand Test: Advances in application and research* (pp. 39–57), Malabar, FL: Krieger.

Wagner, E. E., Darbes, A., & Lechowick, T. P. (1972). A validation study of Hand Test Pathology score. *Journal of Personality Assessment, 36,* 62–64.

Wagner, E. E., Frye, D., Panek, P. E., & Adair, H. E., (2006). *The Hand Test Manual Supplement: Assessment of Brain Injury.* Los Angeles:Western Psychological Services.

Wagner, E. E., & Hawkins, R. (1964). Differentiation of assaultive delinquents with the Hand Test. *Journal of Projective Techniques and Personality Assessment, 28,* 363–365.

Wagner, E. E., Rasch, M. A., & Marsico, D. S. (1990). Hand Test characteristics of severely behavior handicapped children. *Journal of Personality Assessment, 54,* 802–806.

Wagner, E. E., Rasch, M. A., & Marsico, D. S. (1991). *Hand Test Manual Supplement: Interpreting child and adolescent responses.* Los Angeles: Western Psychological Services.

Walter, C., Hilsenroth, M. J., Arsenault, L., Sloan, P., & Harvill, L. (1998). Use of the Hand Test in the assessment of combat-related stress. *Journal of Personality Assessment, 70*, 315–323.

Wang, Q. (2006). Earliest recollections of self and others in European Maerican and Taiwanese young adults. *Psychological Science, 17*(8), 708–714.

Wang, Q., & Ross, M. (2005). What we remember and what we tell: The effects of culture and self-priming on memory representations and narratives. *Memory, 13*(6), 594–606.

Wechseler, D. (1997). *WAIS-III administration and scoring manual*. San Antonio, TX: Psychological Corporation.

Weiland, J. H., & Steisel, I. (1958). An analysis of manifest content f the earliest memories of childhood. *Journal of Genetic Psychology, 92*, 1–52.

Weissman, M., & Bothwell, S. (1976). Self-report version of the Social Adjustment Scale. *Archives of General Psychiatry, 33*, 1111–1115.

Westen, D. (1990). Toward a revised theory of borderline object relations: Contributions of empirical research. *International Journal of Psycho-Analysis, 71*, 661–693.

Westen, D. (1991). Clinical Assessment of object relations using the TAT. *Journal of Personality Assessment, 56*, 56–74.

Westen, D. (1995). *Social Cognition and Object Relations Scale: Q-sort for projective stories (SCORS-Q)*. Unpublished manuscript, Cambridge Hospital and Harvard Medical School, Cambridge, MA.

Westen, D., Klepser, J., Ruffins, S.A., Silverman, M., Lifton, N., & Boekamp, J. (1991). Object relations in childhood and adolescence: The development of a working representation. *Journal of Consulting and Clinical Psychology, 59*, 400–409.

Westen, D., Lhor, N., Silk, K. R., Gold, L., & Kerber, K. (1990). Object relations and social cognition in borderlines, major depressives, and normals: A Thematic Apperception Test analysis. *Psychological Assessment, 2*, 355–364.

Westen, D., Ludolph, P., Block, J. B., Wixom, J., & Wiss, C. W. (1990). Developmental history and object relations in psychiatrically disturbed adolescent girls. *American Journal of Psychiatry, 147*, 1061–1068.

Westen, D., Ludolph, P., Lerner, H, Ruffins, S., & Wiss, C.W. (1990). Object relations in borderline adolescents. *Journal of American Academy of Child and Adolescent Psychiatry, 29*, 338–348.

Westen, D., Ludolph, P., Silk, K., Kellam, A., Gold. L., & Lohr, N. (1990). Object relations in borderline adolescents and adults: Developmental differences. *Adolescent Psychiatry, 17*, 360–384.

Wetsel, H., Shapiro, R. J., & Wagner, E. E. (1967). Prediction of recidivism among juvenile delinquents with the Hand Test. *Journal of Projective Techniques and Personality Assessment, 31*, 69–72.

White, R. W., Sanford, R. N., Murray, H. A., & Bellak, L. (1941). *Morgan-Murray Thematic Apperception Test: Manual of directions*, (Mimeograph, HUGFP 97.43.2, Box 5 of 7). Henry A. Murray papers, Harvard University Archives, Cambridge, MA.

Yamagami, E., Yoshikawa, M., & Sasaki, H. (2000). *The Hand Test manual: revised* (Japanese translation). Tokyo: Seishin Shobo.

Yoshikawa, M., Yamagami, E., & Sasaki, H. (2002) *The Hand Test practice in Japan*. Tokyo:Seishin Shobo.

Young, G. R. (1999). Diagnosis of the dissociative identity disorder (DID) with the Hand Test. In G. R. Young & E. E. Wagner (Eds.), *The Hand Test: Advances in application and research* (pp. 33–38). Malabar, FL: Krieger.

Young, G. R., & Wagner, E. E. (1999). *The Hand Test: Advances in application and research* (pp. 59–83). Malabar, FL: Krieger.

Young, G. R., Wagner, E. E., & Finn, R. F. (1994). A comparison of three Rorschach diagnostic systems and use of the Hand Test for detecting multiple personality disorder in outpatients. *Journal of Personality Assessment, 62*, 485–497.

Zozolfi, S., & Cilli, G. (1999). Hand Test Acting-Out and Withdrawal scores and aggressive behavior of DSM-IV chronic schizophrenic outpatients. In G. R. Young & E. E. Wagner (Eds.) *The Hand Test: Advances in application and research*, (pp. 155–164). Malabar, FL: Krieger.

CHAPTER 10

Developing the Life Meaning of Psychological Test Data

Collaborative and Therapeutic Approaches

CONSTANCE T. FISCHER
STEPHEN E. FINN

This chapter follows a different format than the earlier chapters in that it shifts from presenting the major tests through which we gather norm-based information to describing ways in which psychologists can use that data to access clients' actual lives. Traditionally, assessment reports have been test-oriented and technical (presenting test-by-test standing on various constructs and discussing the implications in conceptual terms for other professionals). At the same time our literature has long called for client-oriented rather than test-oriented reports. Similarly, recent versions of the American Psychological Association's Ethical Guidelines and Code of Conduct (APA, 2002) have called on psychologists to present test findings in ways that the client can understand. These calls have been difficult to answer fully because of psychology's historically having identified itself as a natural science. Fortunately, psychology has fully demonstrated its status as a science and is now freer to pursue ways to explore those aspects of being human that lend themselves neither to positivistic philosophy nor to related laboratory methods. Psychology's recent joining with other social science and service disciplines in adopting qualitative research methods is part of our contemporary development, along with adopting the goal of *understanding* in those circumstances when *explaining* is not the most appropriate goal. Over the past 2 decades, several MMPI manuals (e.g., Finn, 1996b; Lewak, Marks, & Nelson,

1990) have included life-world ways to share findings with clients. Our two Rorschach computer interpretation programs, the RIAP (Exner, Weiner, et al., 2005) and the ROR-SCAN (Caracena, 2006) include client reports that present findings in everyday language and in terms of behavior and experience, as do certain reports for several other major psychological tests.

Before this chapter presents ways in which assessors can collaborate directly with clients to explore their actual lives, we want to acknowledge that of course often professionals do want a technical report from the assessor to aid in their development of conceptual understandings. Many questions presented to assessors are readily answerable within our traditional categorical/normative approach. Examples include: Is IQ high enough for a gifted student placement?, Is this person psychotic?, and Is there neurological impairment (and what sort and how severe)? In addition, test data certainly assist psychologists to think conceptually about clients' dynamics and their similarities to persons who carry various diagnoses, whether categorical or dimensional.

Our goal, when we choose to individualize an assessment, is to understand and describe the person in terms of his or her life world. We collaborate directly with the client in order to explore behaviors and experiences to which our test data and clinical impressions have provided access. The resulting understandings are truly individualized; they describe a particular person's ways of going about his or her life, when those ways do and do not work, and what has already been learned about how the client can change course to meet goals and to bypass old hazards. This process in itself is therapeutic in the sense that the client experiences him- or herself as deeply understood and accepted by another person (the assessor), as capable, as having viable options, and as having a new "story" about him- or herself that is more coherent, useful, and compassionate than the previous story.

Philosophical Assumptions of Collaborative and Therapeutic Personality Assessment:

- For test development and categorical research, a hypothetico-deductive and logical positivistic frame is appropriate.
- For individualizing test findings, a life-world orientation is necessary.
- Test data are measures of the way a person goes about life.
- Collaboration with clients and their involved others provides a bridge into lived world instances and contexts of test data.
- The focus is on *understanding* how clients take up and shape situations rather than on *explaining* causes of behavior.

- Through collaborative exploration, clients experience themselves as having options, as being agents.

Procedurally, psychologists who take a life-world approach to assessment ask the client what questions, beyond those of any referring party, he or she would like to explore via the test data. Some psychologists prefer to interview, gather collateral data, and study all test data before meeting with the client to explore "what in the world" their relevance might be. Some psychologists prefer to explore with the client initially after several tests have been scored and studied, and then again after further tests have been scored and studied. Initial discussions typically throw light on tests to be considered later. Typically, a concluding session with the client summarizes the understandings they have reached, any points on which they have agreed to disagree, and any concrete suggestions they have developed. These discussions differ radically from "feedback" sessions in which a psychologist unilaterally presents what he or she has gathered from the test data.

Some psychologists follow Steve Finn's model of Therapeutic Assessment. After studying all his assessment information, he arranges guided experiences (often with test material, such as TAT cards, which the client has not already encountered). During these experiences, the client will come upon, on his or her own, new insights that were suggested to Finn in the test data. He calls these sessions "assessment intervention sessions," for which one goal is to provide deep and memorable experiences for the client—that yield insights way beyond conceptual discussion.

Whatever the logistics, the psychologist shares impressions as such with the client, allowing them to be corrected, affirmed, revised, and expanded. In this process the assessor learns and uses the client's language, collects life examples of test data, and explores with the client the circumstances under which these examples occurred and the circumstances in which they did not occur (when-nots). The client often learns that he or she can transform troublesome circumstances into ones that in the past have allowed constructive action. Reports can be written directly to clients as itemized responses to questions raised, with accompanying suggestions. These reports are intended as reminders for the client of material already discussed. Additional reports for professionals usually spell out the data that grounded assessment explorations; these reports are readable by the clients, who often receive their own copies, at that point recognizing their lives in the more technical report.

Although our practices are based in large part on our clinical experiences and theoretical understandings of psychological assessment and human nature, independent studies support these methods. Hence, before illustrating our particular approaches, we will review some research.

Research on Collaborative Assessment Practices

Interactive vs. "Delivered" Test Interpretations

A fairly large body of research exists—mainly from counseling psychology—that compares different methods of providing assessment feedback to clients. (Cf. Goodyear, 1990, for a review.) Although some controversies remain, multiple studies have shown collaborative/interactive discussions to be superior to those approaches where test findings are unilaterally presented by assessors, with minimal client involvement (e.g., Rogers, 1954; Hanson, Claiborn, & Kerr, 1977; El-Shaieb, 2005). In short, clients rated interactive sessions as deeper, more satisfying, and more influential than those where feedback was "delivered" by the assessor to the client.

Ordering of Information in Feedback Sessions

One study examined Finn's (1996b) assertion that it is important to "tailor" for each client the order in which assessment results are presented in a summary/discussion session. Schroeder, Hahn, Finn, & Swann (1993) found that when individuals were presented first with information that was congruent with their existing self-views, then later with information that was mildly discrepant, they had more positive experiences than did those people who were first given congruent information and then given information that was highly discrepant from how they already thought of themselves. Those in the first group rated their assessment experiences as more positive and more influential, both immediately after feedback and at a 2-week follow-up, than did individuals in the second group.

Oral vs. Written Feedback

To our knowledge, only one study exists that bears directly on the typical practice of collaborative assessors of providing clients with written as well as oral feedback at the end of an assessment. Lance and Krishnamurthy (2003) compared three groups of 21 clients, each assessed with the MMPI-2 and given feedback according to Finn's (1996b) collaborative guidelines. One group received only oral feedback, one only written feedback, and the third both written and oral feedback. In general, the combined feedback condition was superior to the others, with those clients reporting that they learned more about themselves, felt more positively about the assessor, and were more satisfied with the assessment than did clients in the other two groups.

Collaborative vs. Non-Collaborative Assessment Preceeding Psychotherapy

Hilsenroth and his colleagues have conducted an important body of research concerning the differential effects of collaborative vs. non-collaborative psychological assessment just before clients enter psychotherapy (where the assessor subsequently continues the clients' treatment). One of the first studies (Ackerman, Hilsenroth, Baity, & Blagys, 2000) found that clients who received a collaborative assessment were less likely to terminate before their first formal therapy session, compared with those who received a traditional, non-collaborative assessment (13% vs. 33%). In fact, later studies (Hilsenroth, Ackerman, Clemence, Strassle, & Handler, 2002; Hilsenroth, Peters, & Ackerman, 2004; Cromer & Hilsenroth, 2006; Weil & Hilsenroth, 2006) have clarified that collaborative assessment enhances clients' positive alliance to the clinician, and that this alliance is more predictive of clients' alliance to the therapist late in treatment than is the alliance they feel in early therapy sessions. This research underscores the lasting impact that collaborative assessment can have on the client/therapist interaction.

Collaborative Assessment as a Therapeutic Intervention in Itself

Finally, several studies document that collaborative psychological assessment itself can produce therapeutic benefits for clients. Finn and Tonsager (1992) found that—compared to a wait-list control—clients at a university counseling center who took part in a collaborative MMPI-2 assessment showed reduced symptomatology, higher self-esteem, and greater hope about addressing their problems in the future. Newman and Greenway (1997) independently replicated these findings in a sample of Australian counseling center clients, with very similar results. Allen, Montgomery, Tubman, Frazier, & Escovar (2003) found that students receiving individualized, collaborative feedback about the Millon Index of Personality Styles (Millon, Weiss, Millon, & Davis, 1994) showed increased self-esteem and rapport with the assessor, compared with students in a control group that did not receive feedback.

In the next section of this chapter, Connie Fischer provides a variety of examples of discussing tests with clients throughout the assessment. Then Steve Finn provides a detailed case example illustrating both a planned assessment intervention session and how the intervention informed a summary discussion session with a client. Complete recordings of our assessments, however, would show that Finn does some discussion with clients along the way and that Fischer often includes interventional exercises along the way. In the following excerpts, the bracketed T-scores and Rorschach scores and ratios illustrate how these data can be cited for professional readers; where explanations are not provided, familiarity with these kinds of data is not necessary to follow the excerpts. We will close the chapter with a section that addresses questions that often arise in our presentations and workshops. In the meantime, please note that there is no "the way" to take up these practices.

Case Illustrations

Collaborative, Interventional Assessment Across Sessions (Connie Fischer's Approach)

Custody Evaluation: John Russell Mr. Russell and his wife were referred by our Family Court for a custody evaluation. I interviewed each parent alone to gather background information, and again after I had scored the MMPI-2 and 16 PF, separately interacting with the children, and then met with each parent for a discussion of what I planned to say in my report. Along the way I telephoned three persons named by each parent as "collateral" sources of personal familiarity with one or both parents. I also met each parent with his or her current involved other. As is typical for couples who are mandated by the court for custody evaluation, both parents were initially intent on proving that they were wonderful and that the other was unfit. With the parent's permission, I often discuss test patterns in the meeting that includes the involved other. The following excerpt is from a meeting with Mr. Russell and his girlfriend, Grace.

CF: Okay, but if at any time you'd rather not continue talking about your test profiles while Grace is here with us, just let me know. [Both persons nodded at each other and to me]. Alright, this is your profile from the test with all those true-false items. [I hold out the MMPI-2 profile so all three of us can view it.] Most people score between these two lines, as you did for most of the scales. Now this blip [MMPI-2 scale 4 = 67T], as you see, is much higher compared with your own other scales and with other people. I'll bet it will help us to understand a difference in opinion that you and your wife have. Hang in with me while we explore that issue of whether you become angry and whether the kids become frightened of you sometimes. [Mr. Russell stiffens; Grace looks interested.] Yes, this scale's [4] height often reflects that a person frequently feels angry, held back, treated unfairly. [Grace glances at John; he cocks his head.] But look at this other scale [L = 61T]. It can get this high in several ways; one way is typical in these custody evaluations, which is that the person is trying to look good—which shows good sense under the circumstances. [We all nod.] But it also can become this high when a person has very strong moral standards such as yours. When I was reviewing your pattern, this combination reminded me of when you took this test: You filled in each circle with very dark penciling through the whole thing. When I checked on you, you complained that the items weren't relevant to parenting and that you had to get back to your office. You were not a happy camper! [I motion for Mr. Russell to hold his protest for a moment.] But you had agreed to take the test, so you did, without leaving out even a single item. At this point I'm inclined to agree with you that you rarely lose your temper, in part because doing so is against your beliefs. But I think that others sometimes can see that you're restraining yourself from acting in an angry way, and that can be frightening to them. I confess that I felt uncomfortable when I checked in on you.

Mr. R: [voice controlled, but glaring at me] Did you expect me to hit you or something?

CF: No, definitely not. But at that time I would not have been surprised if you had stormed out without finishing the test, although I now know that you, being you, would not have done that.

Mr. R: Of course not. [Grace nods.]

CF: Still, I was a bit confused, not sure what you were going to do or what I should say.

Mr. R: But you're the doctor!

CF: Exactly! So you can imagine that your kids, or even Grace, would sometimes...

Mr. R: [looking a bit softer, more vulnerable] Is this what you [Grace] were trying to tell me last night?

Grace: Yes, honey, exactly. It's what I meant when I said last night that I wish you would say out loud when you're in turmoil [she uses a hand gesture she apparently had used before], and let me know that you'll talk about it later, and that it's not about me—or it is.

Later, when I was summarizing with Mr. Russell by himself all that we had covered, we settled for agreeing to disagree about whether he very often was "in turmoil" when he was with the kids. I told him that I would say in my report that I never found a way to describe that circumstance in a manner that he could agree with, but that I still thought that something like inner protest was happening for him when the kids reported being frightened. I said that I would include in my report that I thought he was now more open to observing himself for signs of being in "turmoil," and that I had suggested that he compare any questionable state with the experience he had of sitting in the room in my suite, being most unhappy with the MMPI-2 but gritting his teeth to live up to his agreement to complete the test. I said that I would suggest that even though he knew he would not be violent in any way, that he ask himself at such times if someone seeing him might sense his tension and be unsure of how he might behave.

Assessment at the Beginning of Therapy: Mr. Ralph Tanner At the end of a psychotherapy intake session in my private practice, I told Mr. Tanner that I was glad he had called me, that his situation was making sense to me, that I'd like to start our next meeting with an experiment that would help me to further understand him, and that I thought we probably could develop some ideas for him through the experiment. I explained that I would show him some pictures (TAT) and ask him to make up stories about the pictures.

CF: [after administration of three cards] See if you can tell a story where there are no bad guys.

Mr. T: I didn't say anybody was bad.

CF: No, actually you didn't. What would you say these people had in common in your stories? [I spread out the three cards, and pointed to the relevant character in each as I read from my notes.] "She's wondering what scheme he's up to" (Card 6GF: woman looking over her shoulder at man); "This one is following her sister, who has left the party and is racing to secretly meet this sister's lover" (Card 9GF: young woman behind tree looking at another young woman running); "He has successfully eluded the crooked FBI agent and is surveying out the window" (Card 14: silhouette of man in window).

Mr. T: People do have to be alert to other peoples' motives!

CF: Yes, your alertness has often helped you.

Mr. T: Damned right!

CF: [nodding] On the other hand if you always assume that people are conniving [Mr. T: "What?"], scheming [Mr. T nods], then friendship and teamwork aren't likely to happen. And you're likely to feel "left out" [Mr. T's complaint via a sentence completion form he filled out at home].

Mr. T: Well, that's life.

CF: Yes, it can happen. But let's continue the experiment. Are you up for it? [Mr. T gestures weakly 'I guess so'] Okay, thanks. On the next picture, how about making up a story where nobody is scheming? On this one that might be difficult, but give it a try [Card 17BM: man climbing rope].

Mr. T: This guy *has* to scheme! He's escaping over a prison wall.

CF: Okay, that story certainly would call for lots of defensive planning. [Mr. T lightly pounds the desk and says "damned right."] Continuing the experiment, imagine a whole different scene.

Mr. T: That's clearly the story! You tell me if you can find a different one.

CF: Okay, how about he's in a gym class and he finally beat his own time in climbing to the top of the rope?

Mr. T: Alright. He's looking down to see if somebody is trying to grab his foot and keep him from claiming his little victory.

CF: Geez! What's wrong with a happy story?! See if you can come up with a happy ending. He's just made his fastest time; maybe say how he feels...

Mr. T: Well, proud, I guess.

CF: Yes! [Mr. T grins a bit triumphantly himself, but then to me looks as though he's about to add a vigilant observation. "No, don't go there!" [Mr. T looks understandably startled; we both laugh.] Please tell me what it's like to stay with this guy's celebration.

Mr. T: [glancing over to read my expression] Not safe; uncomfortable; I don't like this. [He looks at me quizzically.]

CF: As you say, "Damned right." But you bravely tried the experiment, and now we both know that you can imagine positive outcomes and that you can risk trusting, often with rewards. You just trusted me with the experiment, and you trusted yourself. [We're quiet for awhile.] Would you tell me another example of when you trusted both yourself and the other person?

Mr. T: I don't know why, but I've been sort of seeing a picture in my head of when Petey—that's my older brother—used to hold my hand when we crossed the street. [I nod somberly; we're quiet.]

CF: Such a fine memory!

I thanked Mr. T. for trusting me enough to for us to go so far. I said that I imagined that in our therapy work we would explore ways he could "try out" situations instead of automatically being "paranoid" [his word]. My clinical notes indicated: "paranoid organization, but not profoundly fixed."

Before our next meeting he completed the PAI. During our psychotherapy meetings, we both sometimes spoke of Mr. Tanner's "peak score" (PAI Par-H = 71 T) "peaking," and both of us sometimes opined that we should see if there could be "another story."

Typical Steps of a Collaborative/Therapeutic Assessment (Multiple Sessions):

- Obtaining background from the client and any referring party on the issue(s) and agreeing on their respective goals of the assessment
- Acquiring test data and collateral information
- Discussing early data with the client, sometimes leading to client insights and sometimes to exploring alternative actions/reflections the client might pursue on later occasions
- Consulting test manuals, journals, theories, research, etc., in conjunction with personal impressions and background information, to revise current understandings
- Meeting with the client (sometimes jointly with an involved other) to collaboratively explore the psychologist's current impressions in life-world terms:
- Starting with what the client already has said and moving on to areas of which he or she has not been focally aware

- Using the client's language rather than jargon
- Attending to contexts of test behavior and life behavior
- Revising understandings in light of client's input
- Looking into "when-nots" of problematic behavior to find starting points for clients to shift course
- Arranging a closing intervention calculated to allow the client to come to lived insights on his or her own [this step occurs most in Therapeutic Assessment]
- Summarizing with the client (sometimes accompanied by an involved other) what has been learned, and what the client's next steps might be

Self-Referral: Emanuel Baumeister　Mr. Baumeister, age 28, asked if he could be tested for whether he would be likely to profit from psychotherapy. We came to agree that he was vaguely dissatisfied with life but did not want therapy to make him sad or to tell him that something was wrong with him, especially if it was something that could not be fixed. Manny confided that his girlfriend said he should tell me that he is a warm person, but that he is not affectionate or expressive. We later agreed that his request that I call him "Manny" was an instance of his warmth.

During the Rorschach inquiry, I noticed that several times when I expected to score CF (color dominates form, e.g., Card IX: "Oh wow! A flower!" and Card X: "Fireworks. Yes, like on the 4th."), instead I could score only *F* or *m* (form or inanimate movement) in light of the inquiry (Card IX: "Yes, this would be the stem. Here's leaves, and this would be—they're called 'petals,' right?"; Card X: "There's so much going on, moving outward and down, like stuff falling to earth.") The following exchange occurred immediately after the completion of the Rorschach inquiry:

CF:　Manny, I think I just had a glimpse of what Angela sometimes has experienced with you. I would guess that at those times she's attuned to your being emotionally enthused about something, but then you've backed away into a relatively factual position, leaving her confused and disappointed.

Manny:　How did you get that? Somehow it's true.

CF:　I think that an example was "Oh Wow! It's a flower!" [I imitated his enthusiasm], followed by just a factual [I imitated his tone] naming of flower parts. Could you please tell me an example with Angela?

Manny [after some skirting around the issue]: I'm not sure this is an example [CF: Go ahead.], but it seems like last weekend I called her from work and said let's meet at our favorite Thai restaurant, and I'd bring her favorite Pinot Grigio. We were both enthusiastic, but when we met there, I kind of turned away from her beginning to hug me. Angela said I just started talking about a computer problem at work. Our discussion went in predictable directions, exploring when else he had "turned away" from being close to someone and when he had not turned away, and exploring his feeling safer talking about factual matters and work rather than being openly affectionate, especially in public. Then I asked Manny to tell me about the flower again, this time trying to continue and to share his initial delight. He hesitated, saying he now felt vulnerable just as he had during the inquiry.

CF: [thinking about no COP, no H but two (H), and two responses that verged on FT (no cooperative interaction, only fictional humans, and two responses that verged on including texture), along with my having witnessed moments I took to be of uncertain openness as he looked to me but then pulled back] Yes, I think you're right on! And being vulnerable has to do with wanting to connect with Angela—and for that matter with me—differently, but then becoming scared that if you leave your familiar world of logic that [pause] that what?

Somewhat to my surprise, given an MMPI-2 scale 6 (paranoia) of 61T (but also a scale 2–depression—of 64T) and a minimally answered sentence completion form, Manny waded into a description of his fears and anguish. I asked what he thought I would say about his self-referral question; he grinned abashedly and said, "You would tell me that just as I found that I could talk with you, I would find that I could talk with a therapist. [Pause] And I would be relatively safe." I gave him a thumbs-up, and for a couple of moments we both quietly enjoyed the success of our hard work. I offered him the names of several therapists with whom I thought he could work safely and productively. As I saw him to the door with a smile, I challenged him to call Angela and tell her that although he was a bit scared and might be awkward for a moment, that that evening he would tell her his insights from our meeting.

Four years later, Manny contacted me for what turned out to be three follow-up sessions to explore a couple of other topics we had touched on. He reported that after participating in a couple of months of therapy himself, he and Angela had attended half a dozen couples therapy sessions and found them very helpful. They had married, and he was much closer to her and more comfortable in social situations generally.

Example of Assessor Being Corrected: Ms. Marie Pasquale

CF: I wonder if sometimes you've overreacted, with consequences you didn't intend? [e.g., $Zd = -3.5$; FC: CF+ C = 1:2]

Ms. P: Well, I imagine so, but not as an adult. [Long, quiet pause.] Sometimes other people don't like the consequences I intended.

CF: Oh? Could you think of an example to help me understand?

Ms, P: Like yesterday, when the college boys in the apartment next to me started to party, I immediately pounded loudly on the wall. I figured they'd mutter nasty things about me, but it worked. "React fast so things don't get out of hand." I'm quite a bit more restrained when it involves a boss, a policeman, or an old person.

CF: Thanks. That helps!

Excerpt from a Report (Suicidality Evaluation: Mr. Amed)

Summary. Mr. Amed was referred by his physician for assessment of suicidality. I expanded the assessment to consider his judgment, the character of his being depressed, and his life circumstances. Mrs. Amed was a helpful resource via telephone. All sources of data—interview, direct observation, tests [sentence completion, Bender-Gestalt, MMPI-2, Wechsler subtests, Rorschach]—were consistent with the following concluding impressions. At our closing summary session, the Ameds were in agreement with these impressions and helped to refine the suggestions that follow this section of the report.

Concern about self-harm is well-placed. Mr. Amed at first denied being suicidal in that he has not imagined, let alone planned, such a course. He did not like the term "depressed" but eventually agreed that such a term fit his self-descriptions of feeling bogged down, no longer being his usual energetic self, and being preoccupied with the possibility that he might lose his restaurant. His wife's unwavering support and assurances paradoxically have played into his sense that he is not the protector he used to be. At our second session, Mr. Amed and I agreed on the term, "despondent." As he has become ever more despondent, he has not taken actions that are necessary for rescuing his restaurant.

Terminal self-harm is possible in two ways: (a) Not attending to safety, as when he thoughtlessly stepped in front of a bus last week (and was yanked back to the curb by a bystander); (b) bursting into action, as he used to, but now without proper attention to the big picture, for example, perhaps on impulse driving off a cliff on the Caliper Highway.

Suggestions. (1) Mr. Amed has agreed that he will return to his physician to complete medical tests and to discuss medications that might help him to sleep and to get back to his usual more energetic self. I explained that medications can take weeks to be effective, but that just having taken the actions of conferring with his physician and with me most likely would relieve a bit of pressure. We agreed that he is not "mentally ill," but that he is despondent and thereby is at risk for making poor decisions (or for not making any decisions).

(2) He tentatively agreed to allow his older brother to help him evaluate his business situation and to help him to make some hard decisions. Mrs.

Report Options

- Letter to client summarizing discussions (narrative account or bulleted issues/questions with agreed upon findings and suggestions)
- Written or verbal report to another professional with the above material, but including test data of interest to that professional. The client may also receive this report.

The above reports include:

- Everyday language and concrete examples
- Description of discovered contexts of problematic behavior, and the "when-nots" of that behavior
- Itemized concrete suggestions already explored with the client
- Any agreements to disagree
- Any additional suggestions to report-readers (usually already mentioned to
- the client)

Amed pointed out that it is insulting to the older brother to not allow him to help in the same way that Mr. Amed helped his younger brother several years ago. I suggested that Mr. Amed was not demeaned by allowing me (a woman) to consult with him, and that likewise accepting help from his wife in their case is not demeaning, but rather allows her a chance to honor his years of taking responsibility for the entire family.

(3) Mr. Amed declined my suggestion that he contact a psychologist for short-term support as he gets back to his "position of strength." He is considering agreeing to talk with a revered uncle if his wife tells him that she has become worried about his remaining so despondent that his judgment may be questionable.

(4) I promised to mail two copies of this report, with the Summary and Suggestions highlighted, to the Ameds, so both of them could review our ideas and agreements whenever they wished.

Therapeutic Assessment: Assessment Intervention Sessions and Summary Discussion Sessions (Steve Finn's Approach)

Although the following case was hardly typical, involving an involuntarily referred client and a very challenging assessment intervention session, I (Steve Finn) present it because it illustrates well the combined impact of assessment interventions and summary discussion sessions.

Executive Advancement Assessment: William Peters

Background   Mr. Peters was referred for a psychological assessment by the executive vice-president of his nationally known high-tech corporation, who reported that Mr. Peters was being considered for promotion to a very high-level position within the company. His superiors were impressed and satisfied with almost all aspects of Mr. Peters' work but were concerned about one thing: Mr. Peters' supervisees reported that he had a violent temper at times and that he had been emotionally abusive to them recently. Apparently, Mr. Peters had felt embarrassed at a high-level meeting when it became clear that he was unaware of an important piece of information that everyone else in the room knew. His work team said that after the meeting he had confronted them about not giving him the information he needed, insulted them, and threatened to fire them all. Mr. Peters denied these allegations, saying that he did express anger on this and other occasions but that it was within appropriate bounds and was never abusive. The promotions committee was unwilling to recommend Mr. Peters for advancement unless it was determined that his anger was not a problem, or that it was in fact problematic and that Mr. Peters was aware of this and working to remedy it. I agreed to assess Mr. Peters and answer one question for his boss: "Is Mr. Peters' anger at times abusive, and if so, is he willing to acknowledge this and work on it?" The Vice-President agreed that—apart from my answering this one question—all other results from the assessment would be confidential between Mr. Peters and me.

Early assessment sessions and preliminary test results   Mr. Peters impressed me as a suave, intelligent, and dapper man; he came to our first meeting impeccably dressed in an expensive suit and easily discussed the reason for the assessment. He said he was aware of the referral question from his boss and that he was sure I would find out this "was all a misunderstanding." After some discussion, in which he denied that his anger was ever abusive, he was willing to acknowledge that even if it wasn't, other people seemed to be unsettled by it at times. He then posed his own main assessment question, "Why are people so frightened of my anger at times?" I was encouraged by this flexibility in his thinking and was left with the impression of a talented, confident man who thought well of himself and did not suffer fools gladly, but who was respectful and not overly arrogant (at least with me).

Mr. Peters willingly completed the MMPI-2 after our first meeting, and his basic scale profile was completely within normal limits, except for a slight elevation on K ($64T$), Scale 5 ($64T$) and Scale 6 ($64T$). Examination of the Scale 5 and 6 component subscales revealed that Mr. Peters' slight elevation on Scale 5 was accounted for mainly by Mf2 (Hypersensitivity/ Anxiety; $69T$, Martin, 2003) and the one on Scale 6 was accounted for mainly by subscale Pa2, Poignancy ($72T$). These results suggested to me that Mr. Peters was a highly sensitive man but did not wear his feelings on his sleeve, and that he might easily take offense or feel humiliated by others. I also wondered if he struggled with a level of anxiety of which he was unaware.

In our second session I administered the Rorschach, and Mr. Peters clearly found this to be a difficult and trying experience. He seemed unsettled by his inability to know what a "good" answer was, and by the possibility that I might be judging him, frequently commenting that he wondered what I must be thinking of him from his responses. Especially during the Inquiry, he grew rather short with me and several times demeaned the test, commenting at one point that he didn't know how I was going to draw any conclusions from such a "bunch of foolishness." After the administration I pulled my chair around and initiated a discussion of his experience. He admitted to disliking the test and softened slightly when I said that many people find it frustrating. But when I wondered if he might have felt vulnerable to not knowing what his responses revealed, or whether he might have felt "one-down" or "out of control," he denied my interpretations and focused instead on the shortcomings of the test. I even asked him to consider a deeper meaning of his last Rorschach response—"a mask with holes in it"—but he would have none of this.

When I scored the Rorschach, some of my earlier hunches seemed supported by the data. Mr. Peters appeared to be an extremely resourceful, intelligent, and talented man (EA = 27.5. DQ+ = 17) with a certain vulnerability (Fr = 2) that matched aspects of Gabbard's (1989) description of the "hypervigilant narcissist." The Rorschach suggested Mr. Peters was using his considerable psychological strengths and a degree of intellectualization (2AB+Art+Ay = 7) to manage a great deal of underlying painful emotion, including shame (V = 3), depression (DEPI = 5), and anxiety (Sum Y = 5). Although generally this accommodation worked well for him (AdjD = +1), currently he seemed vulnerable to occasional failures of his coping mechanisms (D = 0, m = 4, FC/CF+C = 6/6). I noted his hypervigilant style (HVI positive, Cg = 6) and hypothesized that he wasn't prone to lean on others emotionally when he needed help (GHR/PHR = 6/5; T = 0; Isolate/R = .34). I suspected that Mr. Peters was under considerable stress due to his being considered for the promotion and that he might indeed lose emotional control at times when his self-esteem was threatened. However, I was left puzzled about how to help Mr. Peters grasp these concepts, given that he had been so dismissive of the Rorschach after our last session. Thus, I felt that an assessment intervention was in order.

Assessment intervention   One of the goals of an assessment intervention is to bring clients' problem behaviors into the assessment room so that they can be observed, understood, and possibly solved by the assessor and client working together. Another goal is to help clients discover new things about themselves that the assessor has tentatively gleaned from the standardized testing so that the client comes to "own" these new insights and thereby assimilates them on a deeper level. I had a hypothesis about how to introduce Mr. Peters to his emotional soft spots, and although I was aware of the risk of overwhelming him, I was also emboldened by the fact that he had consider-able psychological strengths and showed a certain flexibility of thought in our first session. I also knew that a great deal was at stake for Mr. Peters in this job promotion, and I wanted to do anything I could (within reason) to help him understand his boss's reservations.

When Mr. Peters arrived for the next session, I told him that we would be doing "a very important test" and that it "could have a lot to do with my report" to his boss. I then proceeded to give him the Block Design subtest of the WAIS-III. I administered in order the first six designs (4-9)—all of which use four blocks. As I expected, he did these effortlessly and quickly, earning full points. I then jumped to the hardest design, which uses nine blocks and has no black guidelines on the design card, but I gave Mr. Peters only seven blocks. He worked on the problem for about a minute, then said, "It can't be done. It takes more blocks." I then lied, "No, this is the crucial part of this test. See what you can do with the blocks you have." Mr. Peters looked upset but kept trying for about a minute, then protested again that he needed more blocks. Once again, I said, "Just keep trying," implying that there was a solution. He appeared to grow more and more frustrated, and after while I pointedly clicked my stopwatch and said, "Well, you didn't get that one." I started clearing the test materials away and the following dialogue ensued:

Mr. P: I tell you, that one was impossible to solve.

SF: Are you so sure?

Mr. P: Damn right I am [angry]. If there's a solution, I want you to show it to me!

SF: I can't do that.

Mr. P: Why not?

SF: Because you're right, you didn't have all the information you needed [putting two more blocks on the table and looking right at Mr. Peters.]

Mr. P: [Red in the face] Why you fucking sadistic asshole!! So was this, this was just about making me feel like an idiot?! You get a hard-on from making other people feel like pieces of shit! Well I don't have to put up with this [stands up and starts to take his coat and leave]—you can just take this evaluation and stick it up your ass!

SF: Wait, please. Mr. Peters. You're right that I misled you. And I know that felt humiliating. But really, I didn't do it to be sadistic or cruel. I wanted you to see something. Please sit down. I'm really sorry to put you through this, but I didn't do it for nothing. [He sits back down and looks at me, fuming.] Now just listen to me for a minute. How would you describe your behavior just a moment ago?

Mr. P: What do you mean? [defensively]

SF: If you had to describe how you just acted, what would you call it?

Mr. P: Justifiably angry!

SF: Of course. And would you say you were abusive?

Mr. P: No, of course not! You deserved it!

SF: I know you felt that. But in a business context, wouldn't it be considered inappropriate to call someone a "fucking asshole" or tell them to stick something "up their ass," even if you were justifiably angry?

Mr. P: I guess so [appearing curious and looking a bit calmer].

SF: You agree? [He nods.] And was this the kind of behavior that your supervisees complained about?

Mr. P: I don't actually remember what I said that day. But I know I was just as angry as I was just a minute ago, so it's possible. So [pause] that would be considered abusive?

SF: I think, if I were your employee, I might say that it was.

We then went on to have a very profitable discussion of anger: what is an appropriate way to express it, how context matters, the vulnerability of employees to a boss's anger, etc. This time, Mr. Peters admitted that some times he "flipped his lid" and lost control of himself when he was angry. He even agreed that this was likely to happen when he felt "shown up" in front of other people. I took a risk and reminded him again of his last Rorschach response, "a mask with holes in it," and this time he agreed that it might be an apt image of how he feels sometimes. He then spontaneously admitted that doing the assessment with me was scary because an important decision possibly hinged on what I said, and he didn't yet know what I thought of him.

We ended the session with an exercise from Systems Centered Therapy (Agazarian, 1997) that I have found useful in addressing shame. I asked Mr. Peters to check and see if he had any fantasies or "mind reads" about what I might be thinking of him after all that had transpired that day. He said he did. I then requested that he ask me a Yes/No question that would check out if his mind read were right. He looked at me directly and asked, "Do you think I'm an ogre?" I said, "No, I do not," and asked him to check inside and see if he believed my response. He said he did but that he had another mind read. "Are you going to tell my boss that I'm unsuitable for this promotion?" I said I was not going to say this, because—first of all—this was not the question that I had been asked. I had been asked to determine whether he was aware of any problems with his anger, and I now believed he was. [He nodded.] Second, I said I thought he could work to address his tendency to "flip his lid" at times, and that this was likely to improve. Mr. Peters said he believed me. We agreed to meet the following week to summarize all the results of the assessment and discuss what his next steps might be.

Preparing for the summary discussion session   Prior to my meeting with Mr. Peters, I spent several hours outlining what I planned to explore with him about his test data. I wanted to start my summary with information that would fit his existing "story" about himself, then proceed to information that might be slightly more challenging, and save for last the information that seemed to conflict most with his previous self-conceptions. (I have written about this strategy and its rationale in other places, cf. Finn, 2007; Finn & Kamphuis, 2006; Finn, 1996b). The following excerpts from my notes show the order I believed would be best:

1) Mr. Peters strengths: Intelligent, successful, generally good social skills, lots of psychological resources, varied coping mechanisms that allow him to handle a great deal of psychological stress. No serious psychopathology (e.g., Axis I conditions).

2) Information suggested by the MMPI-2: sensitivity, concerned about how others view him, anxiety (?).

3) Information that became evident in the assessment intervention session: Can get flooded by emotion and lose control, his judgment and ability to monitor self suffer at such times, hates feeling exposed or shown up, feeling stressed by the questions about his promotion. But when he is supported, he can also regroup quickly, look at himself, and use his ability to analyze and problem-solve.

4) Possibilities suggested by the Rorschach: Managing some underlying painful feelings of which he is only partially aware—shame? depression? anxiety? These leave him sensitive to humiliation and prone to "flipping his lid" when he is in situations where he feels out of control, exposed, insecure. His strengths are so considerable that he can carry on and do well generally, but he doesn't have a lot of "elbow room" for added stresses.

5) Good social skills overall, but doesn't tend to lean on other people for emotional support, which also means he is more prone to stress and emotional flooding.

Of course, I considered all these points to be tentative hypotheses, and I looked forward to reviewing them with Mr. Peters and getting his input.

Summary discussion session (1 week later)   I checked in with Mr. Peters at the beginning of the session, and he said he was excited and curious about the meeting. I inquired how he had been after the last session, and he said he had felt exhausted the rest of the day, but grateful that I had "pushed" him, because he learned things that would help him succeed in his new position.

I commended him for his resilience and his positive attitude and asked if he could put into words what he had learned. He said, "That when I'm really angry, I'm not aware of how I'm acting. I can do things that scare other people, and I've not really seen that before. I want to work on myself so that doesn't happen any more. I hope we'll talk about how I can change all that." I said that his comments implied a good new assessment question, and that we certainly could address that issue. I proposed that before we got to that question, it might be helpful for me to give an overview of his test results. He agreed. I reminded him that psychological tests are imperfect; that he was the "expert" on himself; and that he should feel free to agree, disagree, and "fine tune" what I had come up with from the testing.

I began, as planned, by talking about Mr. Peters' considerable psychological strengths. He beamed as I summarized the information from the first point in my outline, said it all seemed true, and that he was amazed that the tests could tell all those things about him. I said again that tests could only suggest aspects of his personality, and that I was glad that this part of the results seemed accurate. I asked Mr. Peters if he could give me an example from his life of his being able to handle more than other people do. He said that his bosses often gave him the most difficult projects to deal with because they knew that he could "perform well under stress." I asked if this had always been true and he told of being extremely successful and well liked in high school. His senior year in college, he was valedictorian, student body president, captain of the track and field team, and a state champion in debate. I said how impressed I was and that this seemed to fit with the considerable psychological resources that had shown up on his Rorschach (e.g., EA = 27.5).

I then showed Mr. Peters the basic scales from his MMPI-2, explained how to read the profile, and pointed out that he had no scores in the clinical range, which meant to me that he had no serious mental disorder or emotional difficulties, and that his high scores were more about personality than psychopathology. He smiled and nodded. We then went through his three minor elevations, on scales K, 5, and 6. He smiled again when I interpreted K as suggesting he "didn't wear his feelings on his sleeve" and said he had a reputation among his friends and coworkers of "playing his cards close to his chest." We then had the following discussion:

SF: Do you think of yourself as a sensitive person?

Mr.   P: In what way?

SF: Well, these two scores [pointing to Scales 5 and 6] are typical of people who are very attuned to what other people think about them. They want people to like them, they are extremely aware of small things like tone of voice and facial expressions that show what others are feeling, and they usually can't just brush it off when people are mad at them or displeased with them.

Mr. P: Oh, that's me exactly. My ex-wife used to say that I was too thin skinned, but I think my ability to read people has helped me at work a lot.

SF: How?

Mr. P: Well, I can tell what they're thinking even before they say it. I'm not always right, but I am a lot of the time. And I can use that information to help smooth feathers, negotiate, and keep everyone happy.

SF: I bet that's really valuable with your team.

Mr. P: Yep!

SF: So that must have made it even harder for you after the incident where they said you abused them.

Mr. P: It did. And for once, I couldn't figure out how to make them happy.

SF: And would you say that you easily get your feelings hurt?

Mr. P: Hmmm . . . [considering]. Again my ex-wife used to say that I always take things personally. But I'm not sure that's really true.

SF: Well let's keep that in mind as we talk about the rest of the testing.

We talked a bit more about the MMPI-2, and then I said I wanted to talk to him more about his Rorschach. I explained that the Rorschach taps "a different level of personality" than the MMPI-2 and shows things that people are sometimes only partly aware of. I then said I thought the Rorschach helped me understand why Mr. Peters had gotten so angry with me and with his staff.

SF: You see your Rorschach scores suggest that you may be dealing with some painful feelings deep down, but most of the time you're able to ignore these and keep going.

Mr. P: What kinds of painful feelings?

SF: Depression, and anxiety, and shame, to start off with. Perhaps a part of you is confident, but another part of you wonders if you deserve all this success. So when something happens where you feel "shown up," you go into a tailspin, and the angry lashing out is a way to get yourself back in balance.

Mr. P: Like if it's someone else's fault, it doesn't really have to do with me?!

SF: Exactly! Like in our case, if I was a cruel sadist, then you didn't have to feel humiliated for falling for my trick. So the anger temporarily gives you back your self-esteem and feeling of being in control.

Mr. P: And what about that time with my assistants?

SF: I don't know . . . you tell me, but I can guess. Were you blaming yourself deep down for not having asked them for the information you didn't have?

Mr. P: I guess I was. But I didn't see that until right now.

SF: OK.

Mr. P: So I guess I'm not as confident as I think I am.

SF: I think it depends on the situation. The confidence is real, but so are the feelings of shame and anxiety. Could that be true?

Mr. P: Yes. But then what do I do about those feelings when I'm not usually aware of them?

We then went on to talk about the last points in my outline, where I wondered if Mr. Peters tended to rely on his own resources rather than turn to other people for support. I suggested that he wouldn't be so susceptible to "flipping his lid" if he had better supports. He admitted that he tended not to tell others when he was struggling, and he asked me if I thought he could benefit from psychotherapy. I said I thought therapy could help him learn now to manage his emotions better and practice leaning on someone for support. He asked if he could call me for therapy after he thought about all this some more. I told him yes, and that if I wasn't able to see him myself, that I would be glad to hook him up with some excellent colleagues.

Follow-up   Shortly after our summary/discussion session, I telephoned Mr. Peter's boss and told him that Mr. Peters and I had agreed that his anger could sometimes be problematic, that he was fully aware of this, and that he was interested in working on this problem. I also wrote a letter to Mr. Peters summarizing our discussions and what we had learned. He called one month later to tell me that he had received his promotion and had just begun seeing a psychotherapist recommended by a friend. I wished him the best of luck, he thanked me profusely for my work with him, and he said he would let me know how he was doing.

Summary

This chapter has illustrated some ways in which test data can provide access to clients' life worlds, thereby allowing psychological assessment to become most useful to all parties–clients, referring sources, and other helpers. Collaborating with clients helps us to refine and individualize our understandings and to help clients to grasp our discoveries holistically. This process is therapeutic even when that may be a secondary goal. Collaborative, interventional assessment also can be undertaken with therapeutic insight as its goal. Throughout, diagnostic categories, theoretical constructs, and code-types are all regarded as *tools* with which to explore a person's life rather than as final *results*. For us, results are those that the psychologist who has individualized the assessment process can share with other professionals (as well as the client) the ways in which in daily life the person has (and has not) exemplified categories, whether neurological, characterological, psychiatric, or whatever. In addition, we try to identify already available pathways the client may take out of negative ways of coping. The client has participated in the development of understandings and suggestions, owns them, and experiences himself or herself as an agent.

These practices, although grounded in our clinical experience and understanding of human beings, are gradually being shown in controlled research to have positive and long-lasting benefits for clients. Collaborative assessment can itself lead to decreased symptomatic distress, greater hope, and greater self-esteem on the part of clients. Also it can enhance an alliance between therapist and client that impacts subsequent treatment for months afterwards. We are excited about the growing body of research examining collaborative assessment.

Clarifications

As seen in our excerpts, there is no single way to engage in collaborative assessment. The best way to begin is to expand on the ways you have already found yourself exploring in order to discover "what in the world" test patterns might have to do with the client's life. Do look for when (and when-not) the client has experienced and acted in particular ways; contextual rather than deductive thinking is most productive. Deep familiarity with several theories of personality development and with ongoing research is essential, as is detailed knowledge of the circumstances of the persons you serve (e.g., going through custody evaluation, functioning at a retarded level, living with

---

How to Try Out Collaborative Practices

- Take tests yourself and jot down concrete examples, contexts, and when-nots of behavior/experience suggested by your own test patterns.
- Ask a colleague who knows you to provide additional possible examples and when-nots in regard to your test profiles.
- With clients, expand individualized practices in which you already have engaged.
- Gradually try-out other practices, amending, expanding, and inventing to fit your own setting.
- Practice asking clients for life examples of your impressions from test patterns.
- Keep a file of life instances of test patterns.
- Ask clients directly for their participation in understanding their test data; ask for any disagreements, refinements, contrary examples.
- Make use of interactions with clients—share with them assessment relevant events that have happened during the assessment process.
- If your setting requires a particular format, follow that, but experiment with filling it out with life-world exploration and description.
- Ask for feedback from your report-receivers (clients will already have given you their impressions).

neurological constraints, being psychotic, being an Iraq war veteran, being an Asian immigrant). Even when considering medical and environmental factors, the point is to make nonreductive use of all these perspectives; make use of them to explore the client's life world—the ultimate consideration.

Individualized, collaborative assessment can be engaged in with all the populations whom we otherwise assess, with the usual limitations: Folks will be more defensive in forensic situations, where our therapeutic interests often have to be sidelined. We have to change gears to mesh with cognitively limited clients. When multiple parties are involved (e.g., in family assessments), it can be difficult to juggle the different competing agendas. Nonpsychologically minded clients require that we shift out of our usual styles, and so on. As with the example of Mr. Amed, cultural context must be taken into account. But always, to one degree or another, assessors can collaborate, individualize, and encourage clients' sense of agency. If you find yourself in a setting that wants only categorical conclusions, like an IQ score, evidence of neurological impairment, and DSM IV diagnoses (although those rarely require testing), then provide what is asked of you. As you come to know the client population and the persons for whom you are answering referral requests, you can begin to individualize your reports, providing value-added understandings.

Yes, third-party payors do reimburse for collaborative assessment. Both of us conduct collaborative assessments in private practice. In the past, Steve Finn even received referrals from an HMO that asked him to do therapeutic assessment and to bill it as therapy. Most often we can bill sessions as a combination of assessment and therapy (although it's always good to check with your contract providers to make sure they don't consider this to be unethical). Some self-referrals must be paid for by the individuals, as for police academy entrance evaluations. When insurance companies steadfastly refuse to pay, or when insurance is unavailable, many clients are willing to dip into savings, pay over time, or borrow money to purchase a service they anticipate as being individualized and therapeutic.

When psychologists tell us that they are hesitant to intervene or to offer an understanding to a client for fear of being wrong, we reply that it is not wrong to offer an incorrect notion to the client so long as the client understands that your offering is tentative and is meant as a concrete starting point for exploration. Often, an early, mutually agreed upon understanding is disrupted for both parties later in the session, resulting in a reorganization of understandings. Indeed, the process is very much a hermeneutic rather than a deductive one; that is, each clarification leads the assessor, and to some extent the client, to revisit earlier overarching understandings and to reexamine data to see where they now fit. This process is demanding, but it is not fundamentally different from the dynamic process of impression-formation while interviewing a job applicant. We should say, though, that our excerpts here are highlights of the collaborative process; just as in all psychological assessment, there are longish periods of data-gathering and of wondering before insightful moments occur.

We think that our life-world orientation is in many ways commonsensical; but because of our discipline's historically strong identification with the hypothetico-deductive and logical positivist models of natural science, psychology has been slow to differentiate its research model from principles of application and from alternative research methods such as those of qualitative research. However, our times are changing. The public increasingly expects straightforward, down-to-earth communication from its professionals and asks for practical suggestions. Actually, psychologists for many decades have sometimes practiced what we now call collaborative, individualized, and/or therapeutic assessment, albeit not systematically or thoroughly. Many of our colleagues—some for a long while and some more recently—have practiced and taught variations of this approach. Among these colleagues, internationally and nationally, are Judith Armstrong, Ed Aranow, Jennifer Chapman, Ray Craddick, Diane Engelman, Phillip Erdberg, Barton Evans, Marita Frackowiak, Judith Glasser, Tad Gorske, Leonard Handler, Mark Hilensroth, Rick Holigrocki, Jennifer Imming, Jan Kamphuis, Radhika Krishnamurthy, Thomas Lindgren, Helena Lunazzi de Jubany, Hale Martin, Mary McCarthy, Deborah Marcontell Michel, Barbara Mercer, Louis Moffett, Noriko Nakamura, Dorit Noy-Sharav, Rodney Nurse, Carol Overton, Betty Peterson, Wayne Price, Caroline Purves, Dale Rudin, Ruth Sitton, Terry Parsons Smith, Steve Smith, Deborah Tharinger, Shira Tibon, Heikki Toivakka, Mary Tonsager, Ailo Uhinki, Niva Waiswol, Judith Zamorsky, and many, many more.

Below, we present some of our publications, and related works by other authors, that ground, expand, and further illustrate what we have presented in this chapter.

References

Ackerman, S. J., Hilsenroth, M. J., Baity, M. R., & Blagys, M. D. (2000). Interaction of therapeutic process and alliance during psychological assessment. *Journal of Personality Assessment, 75*, 82–109.

Agazarian, Y. M. (1997). *Systems-centered therapy for groups.* New York: Guilford.

Allen, A., Montgomery, M., Tubman, J., Frazier, L., & Escovar, L. (2003). The effects of assessment feedback on rapport-building and self-enhancement processes. *Journal of Mental Health Counseling, 25*, 165–181.

American Psychological Association. (2002). Ethical principles of psychologists and code of conduct. *American Psychologist, 57*, 1060–1073.

Caracena, P. F. (2006). *ROR-SCAN Rorschach interpretive program.* Edmond, OK: Ror-Scan.

Cromer, T. D., & Hilsenroth, M. J. (2006, March). *Personality predictors of patient and therapist alliance during a collaborative feedback session.* Paper presented at the annual meeting of the Society for Personality Assessment, San Diego, CA.

El-Shaieb, M. (2005). The MMPI-2 and client feedback: A quantitative investigation and exploratory analysis of feedback models (Doctoral dissertation, Colorado State University, 2005). *Dissertation Abstracts International, 66,* 2303.

Exner, J. E., Jr., Weiner, I. B., and PAR staff. (2005). *Rorschach Interpretive Assistance Program: Version 5 (RIAP5).* Lutz, FL: PAR.

Finn, S. E. (1996a). Assessment feedback integrating MMPI-2 and Rorschach findings. *Journal of Personality Assessment, 67,* 543–557.

Finn, S. E. (1996b). *Manual for using the MMPI-2 as a therapeutic intervention.* Minneapolis: University of Minnesota Press.

Finn, S. E. (1998). Teaching Therapeutic Assessment in a required graduate course. In L. Handler & M. Hilsenroth (Eds.), *Teaching and learning personality assessment* (pp. 359–373). Mahwah, NJ: Erlbaum.

Finn, S. E. (2003). Therapeutic Assessment of a man with "ADD." *Journal of Personality Assessment, 80,* 115–129.

Finn, S. E. (2005). How psychological assessment taught me compassion and firmness. *Journal of Personality Assessment, 84,* 27–30.

Finn, S. E. (2007). *In our clients' shoes: Theory and techniques of Therapeutic Assessment.* Mahwah, NJ: Erlbaum.

Finn, S. E., & Kamphuis, J. H. (2006). Therapeutic Assessment with the MMPI-2. In J. N. Butcher (Ed.), *MMPI-2: A practitioners guide* (pp. 165–191). Washington, DC: APA Books.

Finn, S. E., & Martin, H. (1997). Therapeutic assessment with the MMPI-2 in managed health care. In J. N. Butcher (Ed.), *Objective psychological assessment in managed health care: A practitioner's guide* (pp. 131–152). New York: Oxford University Press.

Finn, S. E., & Tonsager, S. E. (1992). The therapeutic effects of providing MMPI-2 test feedback to college students awaiting psychotherapy. *Psychological Assessment: A Journal of Consulting and Clinical Psychology, 4,* 278–287.

Finn, S. E., & Tonsager, M. E. (1997). Information-gathering and therapeutic models of assessment: Complementary paradigms. *Psychological Assessment, 9,* 374–385.

Finn, S. E., & Tonsager, M. E. (2002). How Therapeutic Assessment became humanistic. *The Humanistic Psychologist, 30,* 10–22.

Fischer, C. T. (1977). Historical relations of psychology as an object-science and subject-science: Toward psychology as a human-science. *Journal of the History of the Behavioral Sciences, 13,* 369–378.

Fischer, C. T., & Brodsky, S. L. (Eds.). (1978). *Client participation in human services: The Prometheus principle.* New Brunswick, N J: Transaction.

Fischer, C. T. (1980). Phenomenology and psychological assessment: Re-presentational description. *Journal of Phenomenological Psychology, 11,* 79–l05.

Fischer, C. T. (1987). Empowering clients by deconstructing psychological reports. Practice: *The Journal of Politics, Economics, Psychology, Sociology, and Culture, 5,* 134–139.

Fischer, C. T. (1989). A life-centered approach to psychodiagnostics: Attending to the life-world, ambiguity, and possibility. *Person-Centered Review, 4,* 163–170.

Fischer, C. T. (1994). Rorschach scoring questions as access to dynamics. *Journal of Personality Assessment, 62,* 515–525.

Fischer, C. T. (1994). *Individualizing psychological assessment.* Mawah, N J: Erlbaum.(Originally published 1985)

Fischer, C. T. (1998). The Rorschach and the life-world: Exploratory exercises. In L. Handler & M. Hilsenroth (Eds.), *Teaching and learning personality assessment* (pp. 347–358). Hillsdale, NJ: Erlbaum.

Fischer, C. T. (1998). Phenomenological, existential, and humanistic foundations for psychology as a human science. In M. Hersen & A. Bellack (Series Eds.) & C. E. Walker (Vol. Ed.), Comprehensive clinical psychology: *Vol. 1: Foundations* (pp. 449–472). London: Elsevier.

Fischer, C. T. (2000). Collaborative, individualized assessment. *Journal of Personality Assessment, 74,* 2–14.

Fischer, C. T. (2001). Psychological assessment: From objectification back to the life world. In B. D. Slife, R. N. Williams, & S. H. Barlow (Eds.), *Critical issues in psychotherapy: Translating ideas into practice* (pp. 29–44). Thousand Oaks, CA: Sage.

Fischer, C. T. (2001). Collaborative exploration as an approach to personality assessment. In K. J. Schneider, J. F. T. Bugenthal, & J. F. Pierson (Eds.), *The handbook of humanistic psychology:*

Leading edges in theory, research, and practice (pp. 525–538). Thousand Oaks, CA: Sage.

Fischer, C. T. (2002). Guest Ed., Humanistic approaches to psychological assessment, *The Humanistic Psychologist, 30*(1-2), 3–174; (3), 178–236.

Fischer, C. T. (2006a). Bruno Klopfer, phenomenology, and individualized/ collaborative psychological assessment. *Journal of Personality Assessment, 87*, 229–233.

Fischer, C. T. (2006b). Qualitative research an individualized/collaborative psychological assessment: Implications of the similarities for promoting life-world theory and practice. *The Humanistic Psychologist, 34*, 347–356.

Gabbard, G. O. (1989). Two subtypes of narcissistic personality disorder. *Bulletin of the Menninger Clinic, 53*, 527–532.

Goodyear, R. K. (1990). Research on the effects of test interpretation: A review. *The Counseling Psychologist, 18*, 240–257.

Handler, L. (1995). The clinical use of figure drawings. In C. Newmark (Ed.), *Major psychological assessment instruments* (pp. 206–293). Boston: Allyn & Bacon.

Handler, L. (1997). He says, she says, they say: The consensus Rorschach. In J. R. Meloy, M. W. Acklin, C. B. Gacono, J. F. Murray, & C. A. Peterson (Eds.), *Contemporary Rorschach interpretation* (pp. 499–533). Mawah, NJ: Erlbaum.

Handler, L. (1999). The assessment of playfulness: Hermann Rorschach meets D. W. Winnicott. *Journal of Personality Assessment, 72*, 208–217.

Hanson, W. E., Caliborn, C. D., & Kerr, B. (1997). Differential effects of two test-interpretation styles in counseling: A field study. *Journal of Counseling Psychology, 44*, 400–405.

Hilsenroth, M. J., Ackerman, S. J., Clemence, A. J., Strassle, C. G., & Handler, L. (2002). Effects of structured clinical training on patient and therapist perspectives of alliance early in psychotherapy. *Psychotherapy: Theory/Research/Practice/Training, 39*, 309–323.

Hilsenroth, M. J., Peters, E. J., & Ackerman, S. J. (2004). The development of therapeutic alliance during psychology assessment: Patient and therapist perspectives across treatment. *Journal of Personality Assessment, 83*, 331–344.

Lance, B. R., & Krishnamurthy, R. (2003, March.) A comparison of the effectiveness of three modes of MMPI-2 test feedback. Paper presented at the annual meeting of the Society for Personality Assessment, San Francisco, CA.

Lewak, R. W., Marks, P. A., & Nelson, G. E. (1990). *Therapist guide to the MMPI & MMPI-2: Providing feedback and treatment.* Muncie, IN: Accelerated Development.

Martin, E. H. (1993). *Masculinity-Femininity and the Minnesota Multiphasic Personality Inventory-2.* Dissertation, University of Texas at Austin.

Millon, T., Weiss, L., Millon, C., & Davis, R. D. *MIPS: Millon Index of Personality Styles manual.* San Antonio, TX: Psychological Corp.

Newman, M. L., & Greenway, P. (1997). Therapeutic effects of providing MMPI-2 test feedback to clients at a university counseling service. *Psychological Assessment, 9*, 122–131.

Purves, C. (2002). Collaborative assessment with involuntary populations: Foster children and their mothers. *The Humanistic Psychologist, 30*, 164–174.

Rogers, L. B. (1954). A comparison of two kinds of test interpretation interview. *Journal of Counseling Psychology, 1*, 224–231.

Schroeder, D. G., Hahn, E. D., Finn, S. E., & Swann, W. B., Jr. (1993, June). Personality feedback has more impact when mildly discrepant from self views. Paper presented at the fifth annual convention of the American Psychological Society, Chicago, IL.

Tharinger, D. J., Finn, S. E., Wilkinson, A. D., & Schaber, P. M. (2007). Therapeutic Assessment with a child as a family intervention: Clinical protocol and a research case study. *Psychology in the Schools, 44*, 293–309.

Weil, M. P., & Hilsenroth, M. J. (2006, March.) *Patient experience of a collaborative feedback session: The impact on psychotherapy process across treatment.* Paper presented at the annual meeting of the Society for Personality Assessment, San Diego, CA.

CHAPTER 11

Improving the Integrative Process in Psychological Assessment
Data Organization and Report Writing

MARK A. BLAIS

STEVEN R. SMITH

After tests are selected, administered, and scored, the integrative process of personality assessment begins. Through the integrative process, the clinician brings together clinical judgment, theory, and understanding of test scores in an effort to understand the person, their behavior, and his or her phenomenological world. This melding of multiple realms of knowledge makes personality assessment more complex, challenging, and powerful than mere psychometric testing (Handler & Meyer, 1998). The objective of psychological assessment is to answer meaningful questions about real people (usually to predict or explain their behavior). However, real people are complex, dynamic beings capable of a seemingly infinite array of thoughts, feelings, and behaviors. To bring some degree of order to this complexity and allow us to answer specific questions, assessment psychologists measure individuals along known dimensions and traits. This measurement process reduces the complex, real person to their psychometric standing along a few defined variables (such as their degree of extroversion, depression, and verbal intelligence). The integrative process of psychological assessment occurs when we combine our test, thereby "reassembling" the person and writing a comprehensive report that captures (some of) the uniqueness of the individual.

The quality of a personality assessment is determined by the proficiency with which each component in the process is completed. Like the proverbial steel chain, the weakest link in the process sets the upper limit on the overall quality of the assessment. And although psychologists typically receive adequate training in test administration and scoring, few receive systematic training in how to meaningfully organize test data and effectively present their findings in a comprehensive integrated report. The goal of the present chapter is to address these deficiencies by providing a model of personality organization that is sufficient for guiding test integration and report writing.

The Importance of Personality in Personality Assessment

For personality assessment and test interpretation to be maximally effective, the assessment psychologist needs to have a sound understanding of "how personality works" (Mayer, 2005). Understanding the workings of personality, either through the application of theory or a model of personality functioning, enhances the utility of test data by linking them to the components and processes of personality. In the absence of a solid model or theory of personality, it is hard to move your interpretation of the data beyond the information available from a test score. These assessment reports written at this level are often dry, lifeless, and fail to capture the complexities of the patient. Such reports are often organized around specific tests (e.g., "the Rorschach showed" or "on the Personality Assessment Inventory the patient scored"); such reports tell us little about the person assessed.

Sugarman (1991) outlines four reasons that linking test data to a complex personality theory is important in assessment. First, theory serves to *organize* psychological test data. He notes that clinicians must translate the meaning of a test score or finding into the language of their personality theory. Once linked to a theory, the relationships among data obtained from different instruments (e.g., PAI and Rorschach) become more apparent. For example, suppose that a patient's protocol reveals intra-test scatter on the Verbal Subtests of the WAIS-III, depression on the PAI, and idiosyncratic thinking on the Rorschach. Research and clinical experience indicate that all of these test scores relate to important aspects of the patient's thinking. By linking these scores back to a theory of personality, we have organized findings from a number of different instruments within a component of personality. These findings suggest that an inefficient and unusual thought process or style marks this patient's thinking and the content of their thought is dominated by depressive themes and over attention to negative aspects of life.

Second, theory serves to *integrate* test data. Beyond organizing, theory helps clinicians make sense of all pieces of test data, including those data that are seemingly discordant. Research indicates that self-report measures of per-

Key Points to Remember: Purposes of Theory in Personality Assessment (Sugarman, 1991)

Organizes Test Data	Integrates and Reconciles Test Data
Clarifies Gaps in Test Data	Allows for the Prediction of Behavior

sonality such as the MMPI-2, and performance-based measures such as the Rorschach rarely correlate with one another (e.g., Archer & Krishnamurthy, 1997; Krishnamurthy, Archer, & House, 1996; McCrae, 1994; Meyer, 1996). Yet both tests are valid predictors of important non-test behaviors such as the *DSM-IV* (American Psychiatric Association, 2004) personality disorder criteria (Blais, Hilsenroth, Castlebury, Fowler, & Baity, 2001). Therefore, we must have a way to reconcile our data when apparent discrepancies appear within an assessment profile. An adequate theory or model of personality might indicate that self-report data represent explicit personality content, while performance data capture implicit personality processes, thereby bringing order to these findings. Likewise, personality assessment data must be integrated effectively with cognitive and neuropsychological assessment data in many cases. A theory that allows clinicians to articulate the relationship between affect, interpersonal relationships, cognitive styles, learning and memory, and self-concept will provide considerable guidance for integrating these various pieces of test data.

Third, Sugarman (1991) notes that theory allows clinicians to *clarify gaps in the test data*. Because people are complex, even the most comprehensive test battery will sometimes fall short of directly assessing all aspects of a referral question or diagnostic issue. In such a case, theory can be used to "move beyond" test scores and allow the clinician to make educated inferences that may more completely address the specific referral question. We caution that clinicians should be careful when using their particular theoretical lens in this way because biases might distort the test data. Furthermore, we suggest that in cases where this form of extrapolation is employed, clinicians are clear in the report that they have done so. For example, you might write "although test data cannot tell us this directly, it is reasonable to infer that the patient is suffering from..." This point will be clarified further in the section on report writing.

Last, theory allows for the *prediction* of behavior. Although clinical judgment and psychological testing have not been shown to be effective in the prediction of specific behaviors, many general predictive inferences can be reasonably drawn based on personality assessment data. Sugarman (1991) notes that this is particularly relevant when a given situation is likely to stress or give rise to personality dynamics. Therefore, although we may not be able to predict exactly when a client might act aggressive or attempt suicide, we can identify psychological or situational factors that will lead the client to feel angry or hopeless and place them at increased risk for violence or suicide. Similarly, a patient with high levels of dependency and borderline personality traits will likely develop an overly dependent and needy relationship with their therapist, while also causing much conflict and disruption within the therapy relationship. Such predictions require the psychologist to use all available data. Theory-enhanced test data must be integrated with the patient's history and present circumstances to derive a complex understanding of the person that allows us to anticipate (predict) how she or he will think, feel, and behave.

Regrettably, no single and universally accepted theory of personality exists to fulfill these important functions. Clinicians with different theoretical orientations will make somewhat different interpretations of test scores, much like they will make different interpretations with psychotherapy clients regarding the nature of their difficulties. Although all clinicians should have a working knowledge of the tests they use, their psychometric properties, and the research findings related to score interpretation, it is the depth of a clinician's understanding of personality that will give *meaning* to score-based interpretation. Therefore, although test scores may tell us that a client is depressed, introverted, interpersonally outgoing, or grandiose, a clinician is needed to explain *why* this might be, *how* it will be expressed and *what* effect this might have on the patient's relationships, occupational performance, and future.

For this reason, it is important that clinicians continue to refine and broaden their understanding of how personality works. This can be achieved through accumulated clinical experience, coursework, reading personality theory, and learning about neuropsychological functioning. By continuing to advance their knowledge base, psychologists can learn to interpret test data with greater complexity.

A Model of Personality Organization for Personality Assessment

We have argued that a theory of personality is essential for the sophisticated interpretation and presentation of personality assessment data. However, given that there is no unified theory of personality, we offer a trans-theoretical model of personality to help you begin organizing your personality assessment data. Mayer (2005) has identified a number of interrelated "systems" (components and processes) that are central to understanding how personality "works." These are: the nature and quality of thinking, emotional processing, sense-of-self, sense-of-others, and the ability to be aware of the self-in-relation (relationship of the self to the world and others).

By simplifying Mayer's model somewhat, we present four basic personality structures that can be used to organize personality test data. The nature of the complex interactions and relationships among these domains are typical within the domain of personality theory. For the purposes of assessment interpretation and report writing, these personality structures provide a useful organizational heuristic.

a. Nature and quality of thinking: The thinking system is composed of processes that determine the nature, quality, and content of our thoughts, along with those related to information processing style. Thought quality is a combination of both perceptual accuracy (the ability to accurately interpret sensory input) and our associational style (how we use logic, reasoning, and judgment to make meaning out of perceptual input). Information about the nature of thought is also reflected in our thought content (what we think about the most, what occupies our mind). The thinking system also contains the processes that serve attention, concentration, memory, and specific forms of world knowledge.

b. The emotional processing (the emotional system) is comprised of our ability to recognize, process (interpret and integrate), and express our emotions. Emotions can be thought of as the psychological component of our psycho-physiological reaction to information, and whether that information comes from our senses or is internally generated by our thoughts. Emotions vary in their valence (positive or negative), degree of differentiation, intensity, and integration into awareness. Also relevant here is the presence or absence of affective disorders, including major depression, anxiety disorders, or mood instability.

c. The processes and structures in the self-system determine how stable, complex, and realistic our self-image is, as well as our emotional reaction to these qualities (self-esteem). The self-system which produces our *sense of self*. The ultimate goal of the self-system is to produce for each of us a unique and sustaining personal identity. This identity contains our understanding (narrative) of how our life experiences and personal talents have combined to make us the person whom we are now.. Some individuals have very unrealistic senses-of-self, either very positive (as is the case in narcissism) or negative (as is often the case in depression).

d. The quality of an individual's interpersonal relationships are central to the sense of others domain. This relational system contains the structures and processes that determine how we understand and interact with other people. All of us have a typical or habitual manner of dealing with and reacting to other people. This is our interpersonal style. This style is based in part on components of our self-image but mainly reflects how we see others (both individually and as members of social/cultural groups). If we generally see others as trustworthy, open, and helpful, we will relate to them in a different style than if we see others as dangerous, deceitful, and out to take advantage of us.

As Figure 11.1 shows, this model of personality is composed of both *explicit* and *implicit* processes. Research has made it clear that a number of important aspects of personality operate outside of our conscious awareness (Shedler, Mayman, & Manis, 1993). For example, we do not always know why we feel and act in certain ways. Therefore, it is important to remember that some forms of assessment (self-report) assess these domains of personality at the conscious or explicit level, while other forms of assessment (performance-based) might allow for the measurement of unconscious or implicit processes.

Sources of Assessment Data

The data used in psychological assessment arises from multiple sources, each having a different relationship to the person being assessed and the components of their personality. Cattell (1965), Funder (1995), and Mayer (2004) have all proposed systems for classifying the different sources of personality data and understanding the relationship each data sources has to personality. Drawing from these systems, it appears that personality assessment data

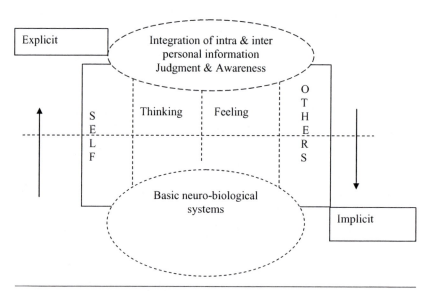

Figure 11.1 A model of personality organization and processes.

can be classified into four sources: life outcome/achievement, observation/ informant, self-report, and process/performance data. Life outcome/accomplishment data reflect the historical record, course, and achievements of the patient's life. This data can be obtained directly from the patient by taking a history or thorough review of historical records (i.e., academic transcripts, medical records, and reports of others). The information obtained through our clinical interview is predominantly life outcome/achievement data. Life outcome/achievement data provide important, but complex molar-level information about the person. The relationship of these data to personality (and specific personality components) is typically indirect and often unclear. Parenthetically, life outcome/accomplishment data are often what we are asked to predict or explain with our assessments (how person X will do at job Y). Such predictions are inherently difficult due to their indirect relationship to personality.

The clinical observations we make during the course of the assessment provide data from the observation/informant source. Information obtained from parents, friends, or significant others are observation/informant-level data. Also included here would be ratings made using behavioral/symptom checklists, including behavior-rating scales, which are the most common form of assessment used with children and adolescents. These data depict the person's current interpersonal and relational functioning, while also containing signs and indicators of other personality components and processes. Although these data originate outside the person, they are more directly related to the components of personality than are life outcome/achievement data.

Data from many of our assessment instruments arise from within the person and represent either self-report or performance data. Self-report data consist of the explicit (conscious) attitudes, opinions, beliefs, and knowledge/ facts that patients report through our instruments. In particular, self-report data show how the patient sees himself and how he wants to be seen by others. Data from the PAI, MCMI-III, and MMPI-2 are examples of self-report data. These data are in the patient's conscious mind available for reporting. The assessment instruments allow this conscious information to be organized into meaningful categories and quantified relative to a known sample.

Performance data reflect implicit cognitive and emotional processes that may be out of the patient's conscious and explicit awareness. They result from the patient's interaction with our assessment instruments such as the Rorschach. A Rorschach response really reflects the patient's attempt to organize a complex visuospatial stimulus. Solving this problem reveals important personality dynamics, processes, and tendencies, in addition to basic neuropsychological processes related to visuospatial organization. Performance data represent implicit (unconscious) processes and tendencies obtained from projective, ability, and intelligence tests. From this perspective, Rorschach data are seen as conceptually more similar to some forms of cognitive and neuropsychological test data, than to self-report personality data (Smith, Bistis, Zahka, & Blais, 2007).

The self-report and performance data that are typically employed in psychological assessment measure broadband psychological traits or dimensions. Broadband psychological traits, like depression or coping adequacy, are heterogeneous and tap many aspects of personality simultaneously. As such, the score from a single measure can inform our understanding of multiple personality systems. Again, using the example of depression, an elevation on a scale measuring depression will provide information regarding emotion, thought, and self-image.

Nuts and Bolts of Report Writing and Test Integration

In a very real sense, the written report *is* the personality assessment. The report is the final and lasting presentation of your expert opinion, effort to address the referral question, and ultimately help the patient. If not presented coherently, the information gained from the assessment is diminished and the client is potentially robbed of an opportunity to receive appropriate treatment or other intervention. With that said, it must be noted that there is no single way to write a psychological testing report. The report that you write will be contingent upon the reason for referral, the intended audience, the setting in which you work, and your communication style, among other factors.

Experiment with different report styles until you find one that works well for you. Modify your writing style as experience teaches you better ways to communicate complex information. The good report you write now will (hopefully) look different from the good report you write in five years. Also, reading reports written by other psychologists can help speed up your learning of what makes a report good and not so good.

What we offer here are some general tips for writing a good psychological report. However, it is important that you continue to work toward refining your writing style and this will be something for which supervisors will provide much guidance. There are also several resources that provide examples of good reports (See Important References). Although there are many strategies for writing good reports, here are a few of the main issues that students face when learning to communicate their findings.

Tip 1: Make it Understandable

Not surprisingly, research suggests that most psychological reports are riddled with jargon and can be difficult for clients, colleagues, and families to understand (Harvey, 1997). For example, Harvey (1997) calculated the

Important References

Braaten, E. B. (2007). The child clinician's report-writing handbook. New York: uilford.
    This new text is a comprehensive manual for child assessment and report-writing. Beyond
    simple report-writing tips, this text suggests components of a test battery that might be
    appropriate for different referral questions.
Kellerman, H., & Burry, A. (1997). Handbook of psychodiagnostic testing: Analysis of personality
    in the psychological report. Boston: Allyn and Bacon.
    This small handbook is a nice overview of personality assessment. The authors guide the
    reader through conceptualizing patient functioning and presenting these in a compre-
    hensive report.
Lichtenberger, E. O., Mather, N., Kaufman, N. L., & Kaufman, A. S. (2004). Essentials of assess-
    ment report writing. New York: Wiley.
    This is a more comprehensive manual for writing reports that include behavioral, per-
    sonality, and cognitive/neuropsychological data. This is a nice introduction, as well as a
    good reference for seasoned clinicians.
Zuckerman, E. L. (2005). Clinician's thesaurus: The guide to conducting interviews and writing
    psychological reports (6th ed.). New York: Guilford.
    A nice companion to the Braaten text noted above, this thesaurus is a great handbook for
    clinical report-writing. This is a good resource for preventing your writing from becoming
    redundant and stale.

reading grade-equivalence for reports written by 22 doctoral-level psychologists and 16 psychologists-in-training. She found that both groups produced reports with a mean readability index at the college level. In another study, Harvey (2006) found that most graduate school textbooks on assessment include example reports that are also written at a collegiate level. Given that most assessment reports will be read by referring professionals who are not psychologists and that clients increasingly read the assessment reports, it is important for psychologists to write reports that are understandable and jargon free. To help accomplish these goals, Harvey (1997) suggests that psychologists keep the following guidelines in mind when writing reports (p. 274):

1. Use short sentences
2. Minimize the number of difficult words
3. Reduce the use of jargon
4. Reduce the use of acronyms
5. Omit passive verbs
6. Increase the use of subheadings

Most major word processing programs are able to calculate grade equivalency scores and we suggest you use them until you get comfortable with the proper voice and style.

As an example, the following paragraph has a grade-equivalency of 12.0 and is sprinkled with psychological jargon:

Testing reflects that Mr. Furlong generally has more psychological resources available for coping with stress than most people his age. He has an intellectualized cognitive style, meaning that he will tend to disavow his affective world. Therefore, when making decisions, he will be likely to be introspective and reflective, but not seek input from significant others in his life. As a result, his worldview is derived from careful cognitive appraisal, rather than emotional reaction.

Conversely, the following paragraph has a readability grade equivalent of 8.3 and conveys the same information:

Results of the tests reflect that Mr. Furlong is more able to cope with the ups and downs of life than most people. He is thoughtful, and has a way of dealing with life that is based on rational judgment. He is not likely to rely on impulses, emotions, or hunches when making decisions. Therefore, he will be drawn to facts in his understanding of the world, rather than feelings.

Tip 2: Say What You Mean

In our experience, it seems that students often have difficulty presenting information accurately and concisely. It seems that either they say too little or they say too much. Some students also feel compelled to use "big words" to make their work sound professional and "official." As we note above with regard to readability, we urge you to avoid the trap of psychological jargon.

This does not imply that you should be insensitive, however. For example, your test results and the patient's history might suggest the presence of a narcissistic personality style, but you would never write in a report that "the patient is a self-centered jerk!" Furthermore, it is too obtuse (and overly simplistic) to *only* say that "this patient has a narcissistic personality disorder." It *is*, however, both clear and accurate to say that "the patient is likely to put their needs, wants, and feelings in front of those of others. She may tend to be unrealistically positive in her self-evaluation."

Related to this, feel free to "talk things out" in the context of a report. If you are presented with a complicated diagnostic picture where things are unclear, you needn't feel compelled to present the "one big answer" that will quickly answer everyone's questions. It is often the case that the pieces do not fit together nicely into one crisp, diagnostic picture. In such cases, discuss the limitations of the data, which pieces fit and which pieces don't. Remember, the goal of personality assessment is to describe a person. Diagnoses and labels are often too confining for the amount of data you will produce in a good personality assessment. Don't lose an opportunity to fully describe a person by focusing on diagnoses or other labels.

Tip 3: Limit the Use of Scale Names and Test Scores

Many written reports get bogged down in scale names and test scores. As a psychologist, your job is to *interpret* test scores, not merely *report* them. Any technician can report test scores, as we have suggested true personality assessment is a far more complicated endeavor. Furthermore, names of some test subscales are not necessarily accurate indicators of what they might measure for a given patient. For example, Scale 5 (Masculine – Feminine) of the MMPI-2 may primarily relate to issues of gender roles, but it may also relate to education, interpersonal expectations, and locus of control. Therefore, we urge you to avoid the excessive reporting of scores or scale names in the body of your report. If a referring provider needs to have a record of those scores, we suggest that you consider putting them in an appendix.

For example, consider the following two brief examples of reports written from PAI data:

> Mr. Baity achieved a test score in the elevated range on Depression ($T = 68$, where the mean is 50, with a standard deviation of 10), Anxiety ($T = 82$), and Schizophrenia ($T = 60$). He also seems to have some difficulties with alcohol use (Alcohol, $T = 84$).

> Mr. Baity appears to be struggling with some significant fears and anxieties that likely leave him quite depressed and down. His worries appear to be significant enough to impact the efficiency of his thinking. He reports a significant use of alcohol that might reflect an attempt to avoid or "medicate" these painful experiences.

You can see that the first example is merely a reporting of test scores and provides little understanding or appreciation of the *relationship* between his observed test scores. The second example provides much more interpretation and even suggests that the patient's anxiety is contributing to his depression

---

Just the Facts: Tips for Writing a Personality Assessment Report

Tip 1: Make it understandable (Harvey, 1997)
- Use short sentences
- Avoid difficult words, jargon, and acronyms
- Omit passive verbs
- Use subheadings

Tip 2: Say what you mean

Tip 3: Limit use of scale names and test scores

Tip 4: Integrate test scores

Tip 5: Know your audience

and cognitive problems. It also provides some rationale as to why he might be having problems with alcohol. The causal relationship between scales in the second example takes a rational leap; the assumption is that anxiety is causing depression and thought problems (and not the other way around). This leap is supported, however, by the magnitude of the test T-scores. We see that (from the first example paragraph) Anxiety is higher than Depression and Schizophrenia. Therefore, our rational leap is not much of a leap at all—it is a small jump based on the data provided by the test scores and our understanding of personality and psychopathology.

Tip 4: Integrate Test Scores

We'll talk more about this below, but it is important that your personality assessment interpretation cut across all forms of data. The different tests should not be presented in laundry-list form as in this example:

> MMPI-2 scores indicate that Mrs. Kim has an outgoing, interpersonal style and adequate access to the full range of her feelings. Although there were some indicators of depression and anxiety, these indicators were not significant enough to suggest a diagnosis or to cause functional impairment. Rorschach scores indicate that she is unlikely to be introspective and that she appears to be depressed. Other Rorschach scores suggest that she may have had some troublesome, interpersonal relationships in the past.

You'll notice that this piecemeal approach is not as rich as it could be. Furthermore, it is quite repetitive and there has been no attempt to make sense of the differing pieces of test data. Your reports should integrate information from all measures and your understanding of personality will help you make sense of these different types of information.

> Mrs. Kim appears to be outgoing, social, and other-oriented. Although her interpersonal skills are adequate, close relationships tend to cause conflict and difficulties for her. She has little ability to reflect on her own motivations, needs or desires (to be psychologically minded) and tends to deal with the world and others on an emotional or affective level. Consciously she is experiencing mild dysphoria and worry, but at a deeper psychological level, she is more sad and unhappy than she can report. Therefore she may be prone to periods of clinical depression.

Tip 5: Know Your Audience

Some personality assessment reports are written for referring psychiatrists and psychologists and it is unlikely that the client will see it. Other reports are intended for the client's eyes and not for other professionals. Last, for those who work with children, it is almost guaranteed that parents will see the report. Because of these different audiences, it is important that you tailor your report accordingly. More technical language is probably appropriate for a report written for a professional, but this should be avoided for client-oriented reports. Also, it is important to realize that once a report leaves your hands you have no control over who reads it or where it ends up ultimately. One of us has found complete copies or large excerpts of his reports on the Internet after they we obtained from the referring clinician as part of unforeseen lawsuits. Therefore, it is important to always assume your reports will be widely read and that you will be called upon at some future time to justify the statements that you made.

There are also times when it is appropriate to summarize test results in a letter to a client or a client's family. This form of feedback and report-writing is practiced by a number of psychologists, including Drs. Fischer and Finn, authors of a chapter in this textbook. When done correctly, a letter to a patient can be a very powerful and informative way to convey test results as well as a general sense of empathy and understanding. We provide examples of all these types of reports in the Appendix of this chapter.

A Psychological Report Template: Integrating Tests and Theory

As we note above, there is no one right way to write a report and all psychologists will have particular styles based on their training, experience, work settings, and client. However, we hope to provide a report template that you can use as a starting point for crafting a good personality test report. In the following sections, we discuss not only the sections and information to be presented in a report, but also the manner in which our model of personality can be presented. Our report template will not be appropriate for all situations and settings, but it should serve as a useful guideline as you set about the test interpretation and report-writing process. As you read and review the following sections, it will be helpful to refer to the example reports in the Appendix.

Heading

At the top of each report, it is important to have basic identifying information for the client including date of birth, age, gender, and date(s) of assessment. Some psychologists choose to include handedness, grade level, referring provider, and ethnicity, among other descriptors. With increasing federal and state guidelines about the transfer of confidential information, we advocate a confidentiality statement as seen in the examples in the Appendix. We have often used some variant of this phrase:

The confidential test results presented in this report are to be used and interpreted only by qualified professionals with the written consent of the client or legal guardian.

Additionally, the heading usually presents a list of tests and procedures that were employed in gathering data. Be sure to include discussions with referring providers as well as records reviews, if appropriate.

Reason for Referral and Background Information

The first paragraph of the report text should present the most relevant, identifying information and the reason for the evaluation. We suggest that this paragraph contains the client's full name, age, ethnicity, handedness (if there is a neuropsychological component to the report), marital status, employment status, and grade level. Most importantly, it is important to present the reason for this particular evaluation. Essentially, in a sentence, it is necessary to state the reason for referral and the particular question(s) that the assessment was designed to answer. Information presented concisely in this paragraph will help the reader quickly identify the client's relevant data and the framework for conducting this assessment. For example:

Barbara O'Reilly is a 43-year-old, single, African American woman who is currently employed by the ABC Manufacturing Corporation of Tampa, Florida. She was referred for a psychological assessment by her psychologist, Dr. Garcia. Dr. Garcia requested further clarification of Ms. O'Reilly's psychiatric diagnosis, as well as her current interpersonal style. Dr. Garcia reports that, despite a lengthy and intensive course of psychotherapy, Ms. O'Reilly has failed to show significant improvement.

The remaining sections of the Background Information section of the report should be consistent with any standards for your setting. For example, in inpatient settings where the personality assessment report will be part of a larger medical record, it is not generally useful to provide a lengthy review of the patient's condition as this is available from other sources. However, for most outpatient settings, this information is crucial in setting the test results and interpretation in a larger context. In Table 11.1, we present the types of information that are generally included in personality assessment results. Feel free to pick and choose among these different domains, depending on your particular case and audience. One way to insure that you obtain all the history and background information needed to write your report is to develop a semi-structured outline to guide your assessment interview.

Behavioral Observations

Most personality assessment reports will have a section on behavioral observations during the assessment. Information included here generally consists

Table 11.1 Domains of Background Information for Personality Assessment Report

Family Constellation	Medical History
Marital history, Current relationships, Children, Siblings, Adoption history, Parents' education / occupations, Abuse history, Social service involvement	Significant illnesses, Last checkup/ vision screening, Head injuries, Hospitalizations, Surgeries, Current medication and dosage, current/ previous diagnoses, Substance abuse (including alcohol)
Psychiatric History	**Educational History**
Current/past psychotherapy, Hospitalizations, Names of treaters, Lengths of treatment, Current/previous medications, dosages, and effects	Grade level, Special education services, Academic accommodations, Typical grades, Learning disability diagnoses, Psychoeducational testing, Disciplinary issues
Developmental History	**Social / Relational History**
Age first word spoken, APGAR scores, Speech delay, Motor delay, Prenatal issues, Toxicity, Prenatal substance abuse, Chromosomal abnormalities, Coordination, Significant injuries	Quality of friendships, Intimacy issues, Sexual functioning, Marital/partnership status and history, History of conflicts, Relational abuse

of a physical description of the client including manner of dress (appropriate versus unusual), physical maturation (for children and adolescents), and interpersonal behavior. Did the client have an unusual or odd manner? How did they deal with frustration during assessment? Were they open in discussing their issues and problems? Were they insightful? What was the rate and intensity of their speech? Did they make eye contact? What was their mood? Did you notice any signs of psychosis or other serious mental illness? Were they on medication at the time of assessment? Most personality assessment reports will have a paragraph or two on behavioral observations, depending on setting. See the Appendix for some examples. Here again, checklists and guidelines are very helpful for obtaining and organizing your behavioral observations.

Test Results and Interpretation

Obviously, the text that outlines the results of the tests and incorporates them into a complex theory of personality is the most important section of the report. In understandable terms, the purpose of this section of the report is to paint a picture of the client's functioning, given the test scores, current living situation, and presenting issues. It is also the time during which you are to answer the referring provider's questions, if appropriate. Given the model of personality presented earlier, we suggest that a personality assessment report have at least five sections: (1) a validity statement, (2) cognitive processing, quality of thinking and coping style, (3) affective processing, (4) intrapersonal functioning, and (5) interpersonal functioning and understanding. We will address each of these below.

At this point, it is important to recognize the subtlety of test integration. All forms of measurement have strengths and weaknesses. Different forms of measurement contribute differentially to the domains of personality described above. For example, what data might you look to in order to understand a patient's thought processes, emotional processing, and self understanding? Not all measures assess these domains equally well, which necessitates the integration of different forms of measurement and information sources. For each of the domains described below, we will highlight particular strengths and weaknesses of different measurement types as they relate to our domains of functioning. This should help you in the interpretation and report-writing process to describe a person in complex and accurate ways.

Validity

It is important to have a few statements regarding the validity of the test data and interpretations. This provides guidance to the reader about how confident they can be in your results. Even if the client's testing does not suggest invalid responding, there are often other reasons that a particular administration may not be valid. For example, if a client is from a racial or ethnic minority or if the language of the test is not their first language, this should be discussed as a potential limitation of the validity of an administration. The question of test validity is not usually an all-or-none proposition. It is more likely that a particular assessment can be more or less valid based on these circumstances. It is up to you to determine the extent to which client motivation, language, setting, and particular presentation might have influenced the robustness of your results.

It must be pointed out that the validity of a test or a test battery conveys important information about a client or patient. We are often tempted to "throw out" a particular test or finding if the validity scales indicate problematic responding. However, consider a client who achieves an elevated PIM (Positive Impression Management) score on the PIY (Personality Assessment Inventory, Morey, 1991). Such an elevation suggests that the individual has attempted to portray themselves in an overly positive light, denying even minor faults (Morey, 1996). We can assume that this style of responding is not only indicative of their approach to the test, but in addition provides substantive information regarding their interpersonal style in general (or at least in the setting where the testing was conducted). Therefore, we might infer that this individual was somewhat anxious about being evaluated negatively by others. They might lack insight or have a narcissistic personality style. The clinical interview will help tease out which of these factors (if any) is at play in a case like this. The point is that, unlike a smudgy X-ray, invalid personality assessment results are invalid for a reason, and that reason is likely related to the personality of the client given the particular assessment situation. Therefore, if supporting evidence suggests that a personality-based interpretation of an invalid profile exists, it is important that this information is included.

Most broadband personality assessment measures (including the MMPI-2, PAI, and MCMI-III) have validity scales designed to address inaccurate or untruthful responding. However, in addition to reviewing the validity of the test data, this section of the report should also inform the reader as to how rich and revealing the assessment data were. This reflects the degree of openness, involvement, and effort the patient put into the assessment process. Although this form of data can be gleaned from validity scales on self-report measures, the quality and quantity of responses to performance-based measurement (including R and *Lambda* from the Rorschach) can also be informative in this regard. Indeed, although some individuals will produce valid test profiles, those test profiles might be lacking in richness, openness, or personal disclosure.

Thinking

Consistent with the model of personality presented above, we believe that it is vital to address the quality and nature of the client's thought processes. Cognitive processes shape the way we see the world, understand ourselves, navigate interpersonal relationships, and cope with stress. Distinction here needs to be made between *thought quality* (processes) and *thought content*. Thought quality encompasses both perceptual accuracy (the ability to accurately encode perceptual information) and the logical (associational) processes used to make sense of the sensory data (reasoning, thinking, and judgment). Thinking that is labored, ineffective, or slow may be perceptually accurate, but might be quite impairing. For example, an individual with a severe anxiety disorder often has thought processes that are ruminative and perseverative, meaning that they will dwell on minute aspects of their environments, get lost in details, and concentrate on unimportant or irrelevant aspects of their environment. This is a disruption in the thought process that is driven by (and contributes to) an affective disturbance.

Data regarding thought processes might be best obtained from performance-based measures such as the Rorschach, as well as other forms of neuropsychological assessment. These forms of measurement directly assess the fluidity of a patient's thought processes. Indeed, the ability to measure ineffective thought is one of the hallmark strengths of the Rorschach (and such indices as the *Perceptual Thinking Index* and *Ego Impairment Index*). TAT stories that are illogical, strained, or devoid of detail can also give clues to ineffective thought. When using self-report measures, data regarding thought processes is often more difficult to glean directly. When using a measure such as the MMPI-2 or PAI, look to indicators that patients experience their thought as confused, obsessive, anxious, or ruminative. Few patients can directly acknowledge that their thought processes are inefficient, but they might acknowledge that they are frequently confused or that they have difficulty concentrating.

As opposed to thought quality, *thought content* refers to the actual material (the idea and images) within one's mind—the content of your thinking. This material can be related to personal goals, needs or desires, or can reflect more pathological features, from overvalued ideas to delusions, hallucinations and paranoid ideation. Obviously, extreme disruptions in thought content are primarily seen in clients with serious mental illnesses or a history of significant neurological impairment. The extent of such disruptions can sometimes be observed at the interview, but this is not always the case. In many, highly structured settings, individuals with thought disorders are often able to function relatively well. However, on unstructured tasks such as the Rorschach or TAT, the extent of these thought content disturbances will be revealed.

As was the case with thought quality, thought content is probably best assessed through performance-based assessment. But self-report measures are often as helpful as performance-based measures when addressing thought content. Most broadband measures will address a patient's experience of hallucinations or delusions. Questions such as "do you hear voices that others do not hear?" are posed on most personality assessment measures. However, many patients with some degree of intact reality testing may not acknowledge these types of experiences, making the clinical interview all the more vital in the assessment of these types of experiences. Again, test data must be integrated with all available sources and the presence of test data does not make a comprehensive clinical interview unnecessary.

In any good personality assessment report, it is important to address issues of both thought quality and thought content Data from neuropsychological assessment can be used to augment the results of personality measures. By combining results from multiple sources of information, you should be able to address the following questions about your client: Are they generally introverted or extroverted? How will they cope with stress? Are they psychotic? Are they "big picture" or "small detail" oriented? What is their thinking like when under stress or affective load? Will they be flexible in their problem solving or are they entrenched in their view of the world? How will others experience their perspective on the world?

Emotional Processing

Closely related to the quality and nature of thought are aspects of a client's affective functioning. Although affect and cognition are intricately intertwined, it is important to explicitly address issues related to the client's emotions. It is often useful to discuss emotional reactions and processes that are normal and those that might indicate psychopathology. We all have relationships with our feelings, and there is a wide variety of these relationships that are "normal." For example, some people are emotionally responsive and expressive—they "wear their feelings on their sleeves." Other people are more emotionally reserved and prefer to interact with the world on a more cognitive level. Neither one of these ways is better or worse, but they make a big difference in terms of how personality is expressed. However, having the ability to blend cognitive and emotional data together (in some ratio) provides a more effective and flexible understanding of the world than relying exclusively on either style alone.

In addition to normative affect, personality assessment should address affect that is disordered or maladaptive. Depression, mania, and anxiety are the most common forms of affect disturbance that we should address in our assessments. Furthermore, as we stated above, some discussion or extrapolation about *why* a client might be experiencing these emotions is an important component of a good assessment. It is also vital to address issues of suicidality in no uncertain terms (in fact, we suggest that if a client appears to be suicidal, this is mentioned as the first point in the test interpretation section of the report).

As was the case with thought processes, we believe that a good personality assessment should allow you to answer several questions about your client's affective functioning. Is the patient currently depressed or anxious? How is their affective disturbance expressed (e.g., if the client is depressed, is he likely to be sad, tearful, angry, ruminative, etc.)? Do they have unusual fears or worries? Do they experience a full range of emotions or are they likely to split their experience into "black and white?" Do they avoid their emotions or deny emotions that might be painful or uncomfortable? What is the relationship between their thoughts and their feelings?

In terms of assessment data that might be the most informative to affective functioning, self-report measures of personality seem to be particularly robust. This is particularly true if there is a positive finding (e.g., a high scale 2 on the MMPI-2). If a patient acknowledges an affective disturbance on a self-report measure, there is little reason to doubt that this is true (unless there is cause for malingering). Performance-based measures with dysphoric or anxious content, a paucity of details, or elevated mood disturbance indices can be important confirmatory data. Furthermore, in addition to explicit

Quick Reference: Domains of a Personality Assessment Report Results Section

Domain	Contributing Test Data	Things to Remember
Validity	Self-report validity scales. Engagement in performance-based techniques.	Tests are invalid for a reason. Note validity concerns in a report.
Thinking	Thought processes: Performance-based measures (especially the Rorschach), neuropsychological test data. Thought content: Interview and self-report measures. Performance-based measures can be good confirming evidence	Affective disturbances have a cognitive counterpart. On self-report measures and interviews, be sensitive to reports of "confusion," "poor concentration," and "distraction."
Emotions	Self-report measures and interview data for conscious awareness of affective disturbance. Performance-based techniques provide data for unconscious experience, perspective, and expectations.	We all have relationships with our affect. Recall that affect influences thoughts and behavior. Attend to cues of suicidality.
Sense of Self	Self-report measures present a patient's conscious self-presentation. Perhaps more informative, regarding self-understanding. Performance-based assessment yields information on internal experience, resources, and self-esteem.	Self-report data cannot differentiate between *who they are* and *who they wish to be.* Differentiate self-esteem from self-understanding
Sense of Others	Behavior ratings of others and behavioral observations of the psychologist will help inform about interpersonal presentation. Self-report data are important here also. For interpersonal expectations, self-report data are vital, along with story-telling techniques and other performance-based measures.	Differentiate interpersonal presentation from interpersonal expectations. Expectations may not be related to the "true" behaviors of others in the patient's life.

experiences of depression and anxiety, we believe that it is possible for patients to experience disrupted mood on an unconscious level (i.e., that they may consciously deny these experiences, but may have a depressive outlook and an underlying feeling of sadness). In these cases, performance-based measures might indicate affective disturbance when self-report measures may not.

Sense of Self

In addition to the relationships with have with others, we have a relationship with ourselves. When assessing a client's self-system, or intrapersonal relationship, it is especially important to consider the strengths and weaknesses used to make interpretations. As we discussed above, self-report measures present a client's conscious/explicit self-presentation where *who they are* might be difficult to distinguish from *who they wish to be*. Beyond the problems of social desirability and impression management, self-reports can be limited by clients who have some difficulty differentiating "truths" about themselves from "wishes." This is not necessarily a problem, however. Like a client's report during psychotherapy, the information from a self-report is an important depiction of how the clients see themselves and this perspective will have important implications for their relationships and their self-esteem.

This is in contrast to information gained from performance-based assessment. This type of assessment might provide a different type of information regarding a client's internal experience, resources, and self-esteem; even if these experiences are not accessible to their conscious awareness. By combining these forms of assessment, we may be able to derive a more complex picture of our client's internal experience of himself or herself.

For the sense of self-portion of the report, it is important to address two broad areas: self-esteem and self-understanding. Simply put, self-esteem relates to how the client feels about him or herself. Self-understanding relates to the complexity, diversity, and integration of the client's self-representation. These two aspects of the self-system are not always interdependent. For example, a client with a simplistic self-understanding might have great self-esteem and another client with a more complex and differentiated self-understanding might have a more nuanced self-esteem. Generally speaking, it is important to address the quality of their self-esteem and the complexity of their self-experience. Comparing and contrasting self-report and performance-based measures will be important in this regard.

Sense of Others

One of the most important purposes of personality is to navigate interpersonal relationships. Therefore, no personality assessment report will be complete without a discussion of a client's interpersonal resources. There are two components to this domain that are important to address. First, what is the client's *interpersonal presentation (style)*? Are they likely to be avoidant, narcissistic, entitled, fearful, without boundaries, aggressive, or shy? In short, personality assessment should be able to predict how a person will interact with others in their environment in most situations.

Self-report measures will be somewhat helpful in describing a patient's interpersonal presentation. To a limited degree, they might be able to acknowledge how they present themselves to others. Particularly for younger patients, behavior rating scales will be informative in interpreting a patient's self-presentation. Vital in this equation are the behavioral observations of the psychologist. The presentation of the patient during the assessment process should give important cues to their presentation in other interpersonal contexts.

The second component of the relational system that should be addressed in a report is their *interpersonal expectations.* Intricately related to interpersonal presentation, a client's expectations about the behavior, motives, and experiences of others are vital to their experience of the world and of themselves. Do they expect others to be malicious and hurtful or helpful and ingratiating? Does the client have a complex understanding of social relationships, or do they see others in only simplistic, behavioral terms? Note that these expectations may not be related to the "true" behaviors of others in the client's current circle of relationships. Most of us have expectations and understandings of others that are rooted in far earlier experiences. For example, if a client is surrounded by helpful and supportive relationships but expects those relationships to be caustic or negative, this will cause substantial difficulty in their lives and will shape their interpersonal behavior.

In terms of assessment data, performance-based, story-telling techniques such as the TAT can be crucial to assessing a patient's expectations of others. When using a rating system such as the SCORS (see chapter 9 in this volume), TAT, Roberts-2, and other story-telling exercises can reflect how patients understand, respect, and conceptualize the activities of others. Given that our experiences of others are often available to our conscious reflection, self-report measures can often provide us this information as well. Last, the inclusion of well-formed human content in performance-based measures, such as the Rorschach, indicate the salience of others in the patient's life.

Summary

The summary section is one of the most important areas of a report. It is here that you will concisely describe the client's functioning across measured domains. We have seen reports where the summary is several pages long, which is hardly a *summary*, but is rather a restatement of the whole report. Unless the case is extremely complicated and there is integration of complex neuropsychological test data, there is no need for a summary to be very long. For most outpatient reports, two to four paragraphs should suffice; for inpatient reports, summaries should be kept to one paragraph. Include a brief restatement of the client's identifying information and reason for referral. The remainder should be a general discussion of the test results and the types of information that led you to your particular conclusions. Again, as we stated above, if cases are complicated or if information is unclear, feel free to "talk this out" a bit. That is, provide supporting or contradictory evidence of your perspective. If it is appropriate to provide a diagnosis, this is the one place to do so.

Finally, a summary often can include a paragraph or a few sentences that describe how the client is likely to respond to treatment. Certainly, this depends upon setting, but if the assessment occurs in context of a treatment, then it will be vital to indicate what type of therapy or combination of services will be most helpful. Likely reactions to therapy will also be important to referring clinicians.

Recommendations

It can be argued that the recommendations are the most important part of the psychological assessment report. The purpose of the evaluation is to describe a person's functioning so that treatment plans can be made and interventions designed. It is important to recall all aspects of a client's functioning when making recommendations. Consider thought processes, affective functioning, and relationships when suggesting *what should be done*. Recommendations can range from the very specific (e.g., Contact Dr. Carlson (telephone number) to schedule an evaluation for medication) to more general (e.g., The client should seek activities that will result in greater interpersonal contact). However, it is the more specific recommendations that are likely to be the most effective for clients in most settings. Also, if there are specific contacts and resources that might be helpful to the client, provide contact numbers, Web addresses, or recommended readings.

Conclusion

In this chapter, we highlighted how one can move from simply reporting test scores to producing an integrated report describing a patient's strengths, conflicts, and unique personality pattern. Developing the skills, experience, and knowledge necessary to become a competent assessment consultant is a challenging but worthy professional goal. The information and tools provided throughout this book and particularly in this chapter can start you on the path to achieving that goal. We encourage you to undertake the journey and commit yourself to becoming a true assessment professional. The process of becoming a competent assessment professional will be arduous, but in the end we believe you will be richly rewarded. We have found that the ability to skillfully use psychological instruments to aid patients who are suffering or guide colleagues who are unsure of some aspect of a case to be profoundly gratifying.

References

Archer, R. P., & Krishnamurthy, R. (1997). MMPI-2 and Rorschach indices related to depression and conduct disorder: An evaluation of the incremental validity hypothesis. *Journal of Personality Assessment, 69,* 517–533.

Blais, M. A., Hilsenroth, M. J., Castlebury, F., Fowler, J. C., & Baity, M. R. (2001). Predicting DSM-IV Cluster B Personality disorder criteria from MMPI-2 and Rorschach data: A test of incremental validity. *Journal of Personality Assessment, 76,* 150–168.

Cattell, R. B., (1965). *The scientific analysis of personality.* Chicago: Aldine.

Funder, D. C. (1995). *The personality puzzle.* New York: Norton.

Handler, L., & Meyer, G. J. (1998). The importance of teaching and learning personality assessment. In L. Handler & M. J. Hilsenroth (Eds.), *Teaching and learning personality assessment.* Mahwah, NJ: Erlbaum.

Harvey, V. S. (1997). Improving readability of psychological reports. *Professional Psychology: Research and Practice, 28,* 271–274.

Harvey, V. S. (2006). Variables affecting the clarity of psychological reports. *Journal of Clinical Psychology, 62,* 5–18.

Krishnamurthy, R., Archer, R. P., & House, J. J. (1996). The MMPI-A and Rorschach: A failure to establish convergent validity. *Assessment, 3,* 179–191.

Mayer J. D. (2004), A Classification system for the data of personality psychology and adjoining fields, *Review of General Psychology, 8,* 208–219.

Mayer J. D. (2005). A tale of two visions: Can a new view of personality help integrate psychology? *American Psychologist, 60,* 294–307.

McCrae, R. R. (1994). The counterpoint of personality assessment: Self-reports and observer ratings. *Assessment, 1,* 159–172.

Meyer, G. J. (1996). The Rorschach and MMPI: Toward a more scientifically differentiated understanding of cross-method assessment. *Journal of Personality Assessment, 67,* 558–578.

Morey, L. C. (1991). *Personality Assessment Inventory: Professional manual.* Odessa, FL: Psychological Assessment Resources, Inc.

Morey, L. C. (1996). *An interpretive guide to the Personality Assessment Inventory.* Odessa, FL: Psychological Assessment Resources, Inc.

Shedler, J., Mayman, M., & Manis, M. (1995). The illusion of mental health. *American Psychologist, 48,* 1117–1131.

Smith, S. R., Bistis, K., Zahka, N. E., & Blais, M. A. (2007). Perceptual-organizational characteristics of the Rorschach task. *The Clinical Neuropsychologist, 21,* 789–799.

Sugarman, A. (1991). Where's the beef? Putting personality back into personality assessment. *Journal of Personality Assessment, 56,* 130–144.

Appendix A

Personality Assessment Report for Outpatient Adolescent

Report of Psychological Evaluation
These test results are confidential and are to be used and interpreted only by qualified professionals with written consent of the patient and/or his legal guardian(s).

NAME:	Robert Zimmerman
DATE OF BIRTH:	04/27/1992
DATE OF EVALUATION:	02/08/2008
AGE:	14 years
PROCEDURES:	Rorschach Inkblot Method
	Personality Inventory for Youth
	Incomplete Sentences
	Thematic Apperception Test
	Brief clinical interview

Background Information

Robert Zimmerman is a 14-year-old European-American male referred for a psychological assessment in order to assess current emotional and personality functioning. Robert has a complicated and extensive psychiatric history including multiple inpatient hospitalizations. A prior assessment with Dr. Longbottom in September 2006 reflected significant concerns about depression and anxiety. The present follow-up testing was requested in order to update this aspect of Robert' functioning.

Robert is a 9th grader from Janesville, Wisconsin. He lives with his two biological parents; his older brother is away at college. His mother reports that beginning in the 3rd grade, Robert began to evidence symptoms of anxiety and somewhat obsessional behavior. He began pharmacological treatment with Dr. Flanders and this was relatively under control for a time. In the 5th grade he experienced a terrifying ordeal, getting caught in a tornado with his grandparents. There was an increase in this anxiety from that point, culminating in his hospitalizations of 2005. Since that time, his mood and anxiety have improved considerably. Dr. Longbottom found evidence of ADD, and he now takes a stimulant to help with attention. He describes his grades as average. He currently takes Luvox, Depakote, Concerta, and Klonopin (PRN).

Robert reports that he has good friends and his interest in, and affinity for, music is exceptional. Always known as a gifted and sensitive child, Robert has excelled in music, playing the saxophone, bass, and piano. He enjoys jazz music especially and stated that he hopes to own a record shop one day.

Behavioral Observations

Robert presented as an extremely likable and interesting young man. He was easily engaged in conversation and little outward signs of anxiety were noted. He stated that his sleep and appetite are fine, but that his concentration is often poor. When asked about his mood, he replied that sometimes he feels down, "but not depressed in a superficial way." He explained that he is a "deep thinker" and that he enjoys reflecting on himself and the "meanings of things." Throughout testing, he was inquisitive, engaging, and creative. Because of his cooperation, the results presented next are deemed to be valid.

Test Results

Robert produced a lengthy but interpretable Rorschach. All validity indices of the PIY were within normal limits suggesting that he struck an appropriate balance between self-disclosure and self-protection. Test results suggest that Robert has above-average psychological resources for dealing with daily stressors. He seems to have a style of thinking and coping that will favor internal reflection rather than external expression. In short, this underscores his notion that he is a "deep thinker," as when faced with challenges, he will retreat inward and rely more on his own hunches, thoughts, and feelings, than those of others. While such a style will make him an independent thinker, others may find his emotional experience to be somewhat inaccessible.

Robert is likely to see the world in a relatively idiosyncratic manner. He may have some thoughts or ideas that others find slightly unusual or unexpected for a youth his age. This is not to suggest that the quality of his thinking is poor; in fact, the opposite is likely more true. It seems that this difference in thinking comes more from a place of creativity than from disrupted thought. However, test results show that he tends to miss some subtleties of his environment, scanning salient details only superficially. Because his style for coping with stress is to retreat inward without checking his perceptions against those of others, this has the potential of leading to some errors in judgment or even erratic behavior when particularly stressed. Furthermore, his coping style is relatively entrenched and pervasive, suggesting that others will have difficulty influencing his thinking, changing his mind, or reassuring him when he feels stressed.

Not unexpectedly, there was evidence of anxiety and depression or a depressed mood. When Robert stated that he does not get depressed in a "superficial way," it is likely that he means that he has a much more cognitive than affective experience of depression. He is likely to have some pessimistic and angry ideas about the world and other people. Test results suggest a ruminative cognitive style that will make him prone to painful self-reflection and righteous indignation. He seems to have an experience of angst in the traditional sense. Yet he does not appear to prone to sadness, hopelessness, or helplessness. There is an energetic and somewhat angry quality to his rumination that likely serves to protect him from the more dysphoric qualities of depression.

Test results suggest that his approach to understanding himself is predictably intellectualized. He tends to be quite introspective, but his views and beliefs about himself are probably quite negative. This is likely part of his depressive style as he seems to believe that he is somehow different, unusual, or defective in some way. Concerns about his body and its functioning were prominent, but not unexpected due to his present hip difficulties. Yet this concern may speak to a feeling of being fragile or vulnerable in a psychological sense. Robert copes with these feelings by adopting a somewhat haughty or self-aggrandizing style. He seems to recognize that he is different in some ways than other kids, and seems to grapple with whether or not this is a good thing. He struggles with his own value, with feelings of anger toward others who he imagines think poorly of him. He feels that he is a man against and apart from the world.

Yet there is some suggestion from testing that Robert is hungry for interpersonal closeness and connection. His distant style seems to protect him from feeling vulnerable or too different from others. He acknowledges that he may not be as socially facile as others his age, but results suggest that he is very interested in others and is likely very attuned to their thoughts and feelings. Others are likely to experience him as interesting and complex, but difficult to know well or intimately.

Overall, it appears as though Robert is struggling with the developmentally-appropriate search for identity and self-definition. Unlike other teenagers, Robert carries a complex history of affective disturbance and psychiatric involvement. It seems that, while he feels better and better about himself and his future, he may still be anxious that his situation will worsen and return to those difficult days. In many ways, those very experiences aged Robert a bit, giving him a sense of perspective that may, in some ways, fuel his pessimistic fire and make him feel further different from others his age. Yet he is redeemed and refueled by music. More than just an interest, it helps him consolidate his identity, giving him a sense of control, expression, purpose, and history. This will continue to be an essential channel for Robert as he continues to explore the world and express the complexity of his experience.

Summary

Robert Zimmerman is a 14-year-old European-American male referred for follow-up psychological testing in order to re-evaluate his emotional functioning. Robert is a delightful and complex young man who has experienced a great deal of upheaval and turmoil in his young life. With the aid of inpatient stabilization as well as medication changes, Robert is performing exceptionally well and is able to give voice to his creative core.

Test results indicate that Robert is psychologically complex, favoring reflective thought and personal judgment over an emotional or interpersonally-dictated coping style. There was no evidence of thought disorder, but his thoughts and ideas may be quite different than those of other teenagers. His thinking style is likely very creative and innovative in nature. In addition, he has a somewhat depressive ruminative style that likely causes him to think pessimistically about the world and others. He seems to care deeply about the world and others, but may have a tendency to dwell on "the bad stuff." To defend his core sense of self from this internal pessimism, Robert seems to adopt a haughty interpersonal style, thinking of and portraying himself as somewhat more informed or capable than others. He is likely to stand apart from others while at the same time wishing to be more connected and intimate.

In sum, Robert is a youngster with a great deal of potential. Music is his guiding force and such a vehicle should serve him exceptionally well. As Robert ages, he will likely continue to grapple with issues of depression and angst, but he seems to have the psychological resources at hand to handle this. Like all teenagers, he must work to form a stable sense of identity and self, at it appears that he has much to work with.

Recommendations

Based on these test results, the following recommendations are made:

1. Although Robert's psychiatric issues are relatively controlled at this point, he may come to revisit their psychological counterparts in coming years. As a bright and verbal youngster, he could make great use of a psychotherapeutic process as he solidifies his sense of self. At the same time, being a psychotherapy patient would run the risk of making him feel even more different or even pathological. Thus it is recommended that his parents and psychiatric treaters continue to listen to Robert for hints that he might feel in need or want of psychotherapy, and make accommodations accordingly.

2. Although it likely does not need to be spelled out, Robert' interest in music is encouraging and unusual. It should be encouraged and supported to whatever degree is feasible.

3. If they have not already done so, Robert' parents may want to explore the possibilities for summer camps for gifted and talented youngsters. Music camps would be particularly appealing.

It was a pleasure to meet this young man. If I can be of further service, please feel free to contact me.

Carl Young, PhD.
Licensed Psychologist

Appendix B

Interpretive Letter to Outpatient Adult

February 13, 2008

Dear Joe:

As I stated in our meeting on Tuesday, the purpose of this letter is to summarize some of the results of my testing. Your doctors have a copy of the "official" report, but because it's largely written in psychobabble, I think that it's more informative to summarize results for patients in this format.

First off, let me say how much I enjoyed meeting you and working with you. You seem like a warm and caring person who is really struggling with important and deep issues. I don't envy you your struggle, but I'm encouraged at the strength and willingness you've shown to examine yourself and to change.

Like I said before, the thing to remember here is that any type of psychological evaluation is like a photograph of your functioning. It's not a movie. What I mean is that these results are a picture of you as you were on January 14th, 2007. Some things may be different already than they were then. In a few years, they'll be even more different. My hope is that you might learn a little something about yourself and that you'll look back on this letter in a few years and marvel at how much you've changed. So on with the results....

Question One: How smart are you?

Pretty smart. Generally speaking, you're brighter (as we define it) than about 70% of folks your age. Your estimated IQ falls at the higher end of the average range. You appear especially facile with verbal, rather than nonverbal reasoning (but your nonverbal reasoning is ok, too). There were no glaring weaknesses and really nothing should prevent you from pursuing any vocation or interests you choose.

Question Two: How's your attention and concentration?

As I said in the meeting, on the big test of attentional difficulties that I gave you (with the Xs on the computer), you did just fine. There were no indicators of inattention. The other test (with the cards) was also fine, but it took you awhile to "get it." It appears as though you got a little overwhelmed by it initially, but then got on board and did just fine. I'll come back to that issue in a little bit, but the general point here is that you don't seem to have

ADHD, or any other signs of attentional difficulties.

Question Three: How do you cope with stress?

I think that this is a weak issue for you. Like we saw with the card test on the computer, it seems like when things are unexpected in your life, you reel from them pretty hard, and pretty quickly. The way you deal with things varies; sometimes you'll get really thoughtful, sometimes you'll be really emotional. While this can make you somewhat flexible, I think that it really contributes to your feeling stressed so much of the time. That is, because you don't seem to have a consistent way of dealing with this, you can quickly get overwhelmed by even little problems. Also, I think that when things are emotionally charged (like relationships), your ability to cope with stress becomes even more haphazard.

Question Four: What's your thinking like?

From the testing, it appears as though you see the world somewhat differently than other folks do. You may be prone to having some ideas or thoughts that other people might find strange or unusual. I wish I could give you an example of what I mean here, but I can't. Maybe you can think of times that you've really felt like people weren't "getting" you or like you weren't on the same page as other people. My guess is that that might have been one of those times; just a time when you were seeing or thinking something that was just a little out of step with others. I think that you also feel as though your thinking isn't so clear or effective. It seems like you feel overwhelmed and confused with some degree of frequency. My guess is that that lack of clarity and confusion has a lot to do with disruptions in your emotional world and the effect of your emotions on your thinking.

Question Five: What's your emotional world like?

I think that this is the most important issue for you, Joe. I think that your experience of yourself and the world is so tied up with depression and anxiety that it's hard to tease them apart. For many people, I like to think about their emotional world as being somewhat distinct from their cognitive world, interpersonal world, and sense of self; I really couldn't do that with you. Depression is such a part of you that it's difficult to tease out what part of that is you, and what part of that is your emotional experience. My thought is that you can't allow yourself to have many emotional experiences other than depression or anxiety. As human beings, we're all a bundle of feelings: sadness, anger, loss, and fear, as well as joy, lust, desire, and bliss. Test results suggest to me that you don't experience much of anything other than depression and sadness.

I asked you on Tuesday if you could conceive of yourself and your world without depression, and you said no. More than anything else, that really struck me and saddened me. I think that part of why your treatment for depression feels like it isn't progressing quickly is because you're not sure who or what else you'd be without it. At least with depression, you're able to define yourself and to identify yourself. Part of your growth from this point forward will be to begin to define who and what you are, and more importantly, who you wish to become. The challenge is for you to begin to imagine a world without depression and anxiety. I know that this will be a long journey for you, because it means losing something very close to who you are. If you can begin to question yourself, to wonder who you really are, I think that depression will begin to lose its luster. But I understand the risk there. Like a ship leaving a port, it may seem as though there's nothing there to guide you or define you. But you might find that your ship will dock elsewhere more habitable. In our first meeting, we talked about your affinity for Shakespeare's works, so you'll understand how this passage relates to this struggle of yours:

> dread … makes us rather bear those ills we have Than fly to others that we know not of *Hamlet*, Act 3, Scene 1

It's hard to change and grow, because change always involves risk, loss, and uncertainty.

Question Six: How do you get along with others?

Testing indicates to me that you feel that you don't really have very good interpersonal skills. I think that you are likely to do pretty well with more superficial contacts, but the idea of closeness is off-putting and frightening to you. I think that you have some difficulty in understanding other people, their motivations, and how they get along. When in the heat of an interpersonal encounter, I think that you'll feel quickly overwhelmed and flustered. The good news here, of course, is that you can have good relationships. Practicing relationships, even superficial ones, can be very helpful and rewarding. And certainly, the relationship you've been able to foster with Dr. ABC is evidence that you can form close and intimate relationships with others.

Question Seven: How do you feel about yourself?

In some ways, I've already covered this question, but I think that it bears repeating. On one hand, it would be easy to say that you don't think very highly of yourself, but this is really only half the picture. I think that you hate the state of your life now and the ubiquity of your depression, but again, I don't think that that's really you. In a sense, you hate depression (who wouldn't?), but you don't really know yourself. I think that you're a relative stranger to yourself, so it's not really fair to say that your self-esteem is low. Depression clouds your experience of yourself so much, that I don't think you can experience much of yourself otherwise.

Question Eight: So what now?

Here are the recommendations I'm putting in the official report:

1. You should continue your important work with Dr. ABC. I think that a good use of your time would be to focus on the details of who you are and who you would like to become. Depression is just one experience, there are others that you're having all the time, probably without your attention.

2. Do things. Be around people. Go to the movies, the bookstore, the library, and the mall. Depression keeps people from having good experiences, thus leading to more intense feelings of loneliness and isolation. Just trying to break the cycle can have a lot of benefit.

3. When it seems that you and someone else aren't on the same page about something, check in with them or someone else to make sure you've got it right or that you're expressing yourself clearly. We all need to check our perceptions from time to time, so don't shy away from checking yours.

So that's it. Again, I really enjoyed meeting you and working with you. If you ever have any questions, feel free to give me a call (whether it be next week or years from now). Good luck, and if I can be of further service, please contact me.

Sincerely,
Carl Young, PhD
Licensed Psychologist

Appendix C

Example Inpatient Personality Assessment Report

Inpatient Psychological Evaluation
Personal and Confidential

Reason for Evaluation: Asked to see this 62-year-old male college professor. He was transferred to Boston-17 status post a drug overdose. The pt reported that his O/D resulted from hopelessness secondary to his inability to obtain relief from chronic knee pain and to adjust to the functional limitations that have resulted from this condition. While he reports being depressed, his perception is that the depression is secondary to his pain and he feels that his mood would rebound if his pain were relieved. This psychological evaluation was requested to assess the depth and nature of his depression, gauge his suicide risk level, and evaluate the quality of his thinking.

Behavioral Observations: Due to his physical condition, the patient was tested at the bedside. However, he was able to sit upright as if he were in a reclining chair. Pt is R handed & had his reading glasses. Again due to limitations of his physical condition, this testing was conducted in two sessions (3/18 and 3/22/08). He was alert, fully oriented, cooperative, and gave a good effort throughout the assessment. He was a little dismissive of the assessment at first, "I grew up with some of the greatest psychologists; these cards, they are like old friends," he said. But with encouragement, he became sufficiently involved in the evaluation to consider his responses a valid sample of his current behavior and level of functioning. The purpose of the testing and limits of confidentiality were reviewed and the patient consented to the evaluation.

Procedures: The patient completed the Personality Assessment Inventory (PAI), the Thematic Apperception Test (TAT) and the Rorschach Inkblot Method.

Validity: All the psychological tests were valid and interpretively useful.

Results: The patient has adequate recourses available for coping with the expected and unexpected ups and downs of life. However, he does not have a well-developed coping style and tends to alternate unpredictably between thinking problems through and employing more action based trial and error problem solving approaches. As a result, his coping abilities are less effective than would be expected. At present, he does not appear to be experiencing notable emotional distress. However, he is prone to experience frequent ruminative and unproductive ideation that intrudes upon his awareness. These ruminative thoughts likely reflect his pre-occupation with health related issues and the profound sense of hopelessness he experiences when his health concerns are activated. His perceptual accuracy is good; he is able to see the world as others do. However, he is somewhat idiosyncratic or in-dividualistic in his perception of events. He does not focus on the common or most obvious features of the world around his rather he seeks out unusual and uncommon aspects of reality to focus upon. His thinking is generally clear, logical, and goal directed. But again, a mild idiosyncratic quality is evident as he too easily slips back and fourth between personal experiences (episodic memory) and the more consensual shared aspects of reality when formulating his understanding of the world. While clearly not psychotic, the combination of these idiosyncratic cognitive processes causes his to make sense of the world in a manner that is not completely accessible to or fully appreciated by others.

His information processing style is complex and ambitious. He has a strong tendency to focus on the big picture when interpreting situations. He strives to find complex relationships within perceptual material. While this information processing style can lead to creative and novel ways of thinking, when engaged in to excess, it becomes inefficient and causes people to miss or disregard simpler more economical explanations for events and experiences. In a similar vein, the patient routinely takes in more information than he can easily organize, comprehend, or act upon. This over incorporative style of information processing can lead people to feel chronically indecisive and to continually desire additional information in order to "completely" understand a situation. However, once a decision has been reached they are reluctant to reconsider or change their minds.

He has the ability to understand and express his emotions. However, he tends to be uncomfortable with emotions and he defensively attempts to avoid emotionally arousing situations. He attempts to control and minimize his feelings through the use of denial and intellectualizing mechanisms. When these defenses are operating effectively, he is able to modulate his feelings and maintain them in the mild to moderately intense range. Presently he is experiencing a moderate degree of depression that takes the form of sadness, apathy, and lack of interest. However, the testing suggests that when his defenses fail his feelings flood over him in an unmodulated and under controlled manner. These episodes of emotional dysregulation have a profound negative impact the quality of his functioning. In these moments he experiences devastating feelings despair and hopelessness. These powerful feelings appear to be associated with events that heighten his sense of interpersonal deprivation or loneliness.

On the surface, this patient's self-image is stable and generally positive although he does have periods of self-doubt or pessimism. He reports having a clear sense of purpose and well-articulated life goals. At a deeper psychological level, it is becoming difficult for him to maintain this positive self-image, as he increasingly sees himself as damaged or dysfunctional. In addition, he is currently struggling to maintain a self-image that prizes self-control, achievement, and self-determination in the presence of increased physical dependency. Previously it appears that he was able to satisfy his dependency needs more indirectly perhaps by defusing them into multiple relationships and role based interactions. At present, his dependency needs are acutely enhanced, both physically and psychologically, and opportunities for indirect satisfaction are insufficient.

The relationships this patient has with others reflect a balance of autonomy and formal friendliness. His need for autonomy makes it difficult for his to fully trust others, and he remains somewhat distant in his relationships. It appears that the more openly dependent he becomes on others the more difficult it is for him to be comfortable and trusting in the relationship. He does better dealing with others in more formal situations.

Impression: Overall the results of this assessment reveal considerable signs of psychological strength and cognitive complexity along with numerous signs that Professor Jackson is suffering from an atypical depression of moderate severity. He is not psychotic and he does not appear chronically preoccupied with suicidal ideation. However, his depression has the potential to escalate rapidly into almost complete despair, hopelessness and devastation. These escalations appear related to his experience of interpersonal loss and deprivation. At these moments the quality of his psychological function is greatly diminished and he is at increased risk for impulsive self-harm. A prominent component of his current difficulty is his effort to maintain a sense of personal autonomy in the presence of dependency needs that, as would be expected, have increased in both frequency and intensity. This is a difficult psychological dilemma for his to solve.

Recommendations:

1. The patient should receive aggressive treatment for his atypical depression.
2. Given that psychological factors play a prominent role in his current emotional difficulties psychotherapy should be an important component of his overall treatment.
3. While his suicide risk level appears to have decreased at present, his emotional reactivity places him at high risk for impulsive self-harm. As such, his risk level should be closely monitored.

Thank you for the opportunity to evaluate this patient. If you have any questions about this report please feel free to contact me.

Carl Young, PhD
Staff Psychologist
Pager # 33324

Author Index

Subject Index

B

Behavior
  description, 3
  prediction, 3
Behavioral assessment, 6–7
Behavior Assessment System for Children,
      Second Edition, 253–258
  administration, 254–255
  applications, 256
  computerization, 255
  development, 255
  limitations, 256
  psychometrics, 255–256
  scoring, 254–255
  standardization, 255
  summary, 258
Behavior rating scales, 247–278
  adolescents
    advantages, 249–250
    bias of response, 250–251
    central tendency effects, 251
    characteristics, 248–252
    cultural validity issues, 266–272
    current controversies, 272–273
    directions for use, 274–275
    error variance, 250–251
    ethnicity, 269–270
    gender, 268–269
    group differences, 268–272
    halo effects, 250–251
    indirect measurement, 272–273
    instrument variance, 251, *251*
    interpretive issues, 270–272
    key points, 276–277, 278
    leniency, 250–251
    multimethod, multisource, multisetting
        assessment, 252
    normative issues, 266–268
    overview of three rating scale systems,
        252–266, *253*
    perceptions of specified behaviors, 248
    problems associated with using, 250–252
    psychometrics, 273–276
    race, 269–270
    rating format, 273–274
    setting variance, 251, *251*
    severity, 250–251
    source variance, 251, *251*
    standardization issues, 266–268
    subscale construction method, 275–276
    temporal variance, 251, *251*
    time element, 274
  children
    advantages, 249–250
    bias of response, 250–251
    central tendency effects, 251
    characteristics, 248–252
    cultural validity issues, 266–272

current controversies, 272–273
    directions for use, 274–275
    error variance, 250–251
    gender, 268–269
    group differences, 268–272
    halo effects, 250–251
    indirect measurement, 272–273
    instrument variance, 251, *251*
    interpretive issues, 270–272
    key points, 276–277, 278
    leniency, 250–251
    multimethod, multisource, multisetting
        assessment, 252
    normative issues, 266–268
    perceptions of specified behaviors, 248
    problems associated with using, 250–252
    psychometrics, 273–276
    race, 269–270
    rating format, 273–274
    setting variance, 251, *251*
    severity, 250–251
    source variance, 251, *251*
    standardization issues, 266–268
    subscale construction method, 275–276
    temporal variance, 251, *251*
    time element, 274
  uses, 247
Bernreuter Personality Inventory, 8
Bias of response, 250–251
Borderline personality disorder, Thematic
      Apperception Test, 367–370
Boundaries, 201–205

C

Central tendency effects, 251
Change, 49–50, *50*
  motivation, 55
Checklist, rating scale, distinguished, 248–249
Children
  Behavior Assessment System for Children,
      Second Edition, 253–258
  behavior rating scales
    advantages, 249–250
    bias of response, 250–251
    central tendency effects, 251
    characteristics, 248–252
    cultural validity issues, 266–272
    current controversies, 272–273
    directions for use, 274–275
    error variance, 250–251
    gender, 268–269
    group differences, 268–272
    halo effects, 250–251
    indirect measurement, 272–273
    instrument variance, 251, *251*
    interpretive issues, 270–272
    key points, 276–277, 278
    leniency, 250–251